ALEXANDRIAN SPHINX

Peter Jeffreys is a Professor of English at Suffolk University in Boston and has written, translated, and edited a number of books about and by Cavafy: *Eastern Questions: Hellenism and Orientalism in the Writings of E. M. Forster and C. P. Cavafy*; *The Forster–Cavafy Letters: Friends at a Slight Angle*; *C. P. Cavafy: Selected Prose Works*; *Reframing Decadence: C. P. Cavafy's Imaginary Portraits*; and *Approaches to Teaching the Works of C. P. Cavafy*. He is a member of the Cavafy Archive Academic Committee at the Onassis Foundation and has served as an exhibition consultant for the Cavafy House in Alexandria and the Cavafy Archive Building in Athens.

Gregory Jusdanis, a Distinguished Arts and Sciences Professor at the Ohio State University, is the author of *The Poetics of Cavafy*, *Belated Modernity and Aesthetic Culture*, *The Necessary Nation*, *Fiction Agonistes*, and *A Tremendous Thing*. He has received fellowships from the Guggenheim Foundation, the National Endowment for the Humanities, the American Council of Learned Societies, the Woodrow Wilson International Center for Scholars, and the Social Sciences and Humanities Research Council of Canada.

Shortlisted for the Anglo-Hellenic Runciman Award 2026

Longlisted for the US National Book Critics Circle Award

Praise for Alexandrian Sphinx

'Deeply researched and engaging . . . [Jeffreys and Jusdanis] brilliantly recreate [Cavafy's] world.' *Guardian*

'Melancholy and majesty . . . [an] extraordinary life story' *New Statesman*

'Restores [Cavafy] to full and vivid life' *New World*

'Peter Jeffreys and Gregory Jusdanis . . . have trawled monographs, memoirs, letters and the Cavafy Archive to bring [the poet] to life, not just in middle age but also as a youth in Liverpool, London and Istanbul . . . A nuanced and original portrait: no hagiography, but warmly empathetic' *Literary Review*

'A painstakingly researched biography of a quiet Alexandrian who left few traces of his life but whose body of poems the world worships and never tires of translating' André Aciman, author of *Out of Egypt* and *Call Me by Your Name*

'Before anyone else, Cavafy spoke for young men with big desires and little money, excluded from society and consumed by love and lust. In his twenties he became ill with debauchery; in his maturity he turned all those wasted nights into the work of a world genius.' Edmund White, author of *The Loves of My Life*

'In the fifty years since a biography of the poet last appeared, Constantine Cavafy has emerged not only as the great Greek poet of the twentieth century but as an essential poet of modernity on the world stage, an exile (in many senses of the word) whose work seamlessly enfolds history, memory, and desire. Gregory Jusdanis and Peter Jeffreys have given us an extraordinary biography, eminently readable and as unconventional, scholarly, and impassioned as its subject.' Mark Doty, author of *My Alexandria*

'An important biography of an indispensable poet – the first to appear in English in nearly fifty years . . . We owe [its authors] a debt for assembling this mosaic of a life and sending us back to the poems where he really resides – at a slight angle to the universe.' *Wall Street Journal*

'[Jeffreys and Jusdanis] have found the perfect 'form' for presenting the complex figure of Cavafy – a relatively solitary and self-determined man who intersected with the events of his time and the people in his life, while still establishing his own sense of time and history in a series of unique poetic reflections.' *New Republic*

'Readers will come away from [*Alexandrian Sphinx*] very much feeling they know the man . . . Jusdanis and Jeffreys have brought him into closer focus than ever before.' *Open Letters Review*

'[The authors'] scholarship is exemplary, but quietly within it beats an unmistakable affection for their subject . . . Extensive and rewarding' *Bay Area Reporter*

ALSO BY PETER JEFFREYS

Approaches to Teaching the Works of C. P. Cavafy
(with Demetres P. Tryphonopoulos)

Reframing Decadence:
C. P. Cavafy's Imaginary Portraits

C. P. Cavafy: Selected Prose Works

The Forster-Cavafy Letters: Friends at a Slight Angle

Eastern Questions: Hellenism and Orientalism in the Writings of E. M. Forster and C. P. Cavafy

ALSO BY GREGORY JUSDANIS

A Tremendous Thing:
Friendship from the "Iliad" to the Internet

Fiction Agonistes: In Defense of Literature

The Necessary Nation

Belated Modernity and Aesthetic Culture:
Inventing National Literature

The Poetics of Cavafy: Textuality, Eroticism, History

ALEXANDRIAN SPHINX

The Hidden Life of Constantine Cavafy

PETER JEFFREYS
AND
GREGORY JUSDANIS

Summit
Books
London · New York · Amsterdam/Antwerp · Sydney/Melbourne · Toronto · New Delhi

Summit Books

First published as *Constantine Cavafy: A New Biography* in the United States by Farrar, Straus and Giroux, 2025
First published in Great Britain by Summit Books, an imprint of Simon & Schuster UK Ltd, 2025
This paperback edition published 2026

1 3 5 7 9 10 8 6 4 2

Simon & Schuster UK Ltd, 7th Floor, 199 Bishopsgate, London EC2M 3TY

Simon & Schuster Australia, Sydney
Simon & Schuster India, New Delhi

www.simonandschuster.co.uk
www.simonandschuster.com.au
www.simonandschuster.co.in

The authorised representative in the EEA is Simon & Schuster Netherlands BV, Herculesplein 96, 3584 AA Utrecht, Netherlands. info@simonandschuster.nl

Grateful acknowledgment is made for permission to reprint the following previously published material: Excerpts from *Cavafy's Levant: Commerce, Culture, and Mimicry in the Early Life of the Poet, by* Peter Jeffreys, *in boundary 2: an international journal of literature and culture* 48, no. 2: 7–39. Copyright 2021, Duke University Press. All rights reserved. Republished by permission of the publisher. www.dukeupress.edu.

Illustration credits for the photo insert appear on pages 533–534.

A CIP catalogue record for this book is available from the British Library

Paperback ISBN: 978-1-3985-5126-8
eBook ISBN: 978-1-3985-5124-4
Audio ISBN: 978-1-3985-5125-1

Designed by Patrice Sheridan

Printed and Bound in the UK using 100% Renewable Electricity at CPI Group (UK) Ltd

FSC www.fsc.org MIX Paper | Supporting responsible forestry FSC® C013604

Dedicated to the memory of
Rika Sengopoulos

CONTENTS

Abbreviations xi
Chronology of Events in C. P. Cavafy's Life xiii
Preface: Writing *Alexandrian Sphinx* xvii

Prologue 3

PART I

THE CAVAFY FAMILY

1. The Family Council: Commerce, Culture, and Letters 17
2. Trauma, Exile, and Loss: The Flight to the Ottoman Capital 43
3. Family Affairs 69

PART II

ALEXANDRIA: THE DREAMSCAPE

4. Constantine's World 111
5. A Tale of Two Cities 143

PART III

FRIENDS

6. Friendship and Intimacy: Cliques or Claques? 179
7. Peri: Aesthete, Artist, and Confidant 207

8. "It Would Have Been You":
Timos Malanos and Alekos Sengopoulos 230

Interlude: Constantine's Reading 249

Part IV

LIVING FOR POETRY

9. Art Above Everything 281
10. The Big Poetic Change 318

Part V

CULTIVATING FAME

11. The Quest for Glory 359
12. Constantine's Literary Radius 381

Epilogue 403

Important People in C. P. Cavafy's Life 419
Notes 429
Works Cited 487
Acknowledgments 501
Index 505

ABBREVIATIONS

L&W: Dimitris Daskalopoulos and Maria Stassinopoulou, *Ο Βίος και το Έργο του Κ. Π. Καβάφη / The Life and Work of C. P. Cavafy* (2002/2013)

PC: Stratis Tsirkas, *Ο Πολιτικός Καβάφης / The Political Cavafy* (1971)

CE: Stratis Tsirkas, *Ο Καβάφης και η Εποχή του / Cavafy and His Era* (1958)

LC: Lena Savidis, *Λεύκωμα Καβάφη, 1863–1910 / The Cavafy Album* (1983)

TPC: Timos Malanos, *Ο Ποιητής Κ. Π. Καβάφης / The Poet C. P. Cavafy* (1957)

GN: Vangelis Karayiannis, *Σημειώσεις από την Γενεαλογία του Καβάφη / Notes from Cavafy's Genealogy* (1983)

DATING OF POEMS

When there are two dates beside a poem title, the first indicates the year of composition, the second the year it appeared in print. A single date indicates the date of composition. An asterisk next to a single date specifies the year the poem appeared in print.

CHRONOLOGY OF EVENTS IN C. P. CAVAFY'S LIFE

1849 Marriage of Peter John Cavafy to Haricleia Photiades in Istanbul.

1855 Arrival of the Cavafy family in Alexandria.

1863 Birth of Constantine Cavafy, April 29.

1864 Constantine's baptism, May 28, in Alexandria.

1870 Father's death.

1872 Facing financial difficulties, Haricleia takes the children and moves to Liverpool.

1874 Family moves to London.

1876 Cavafy & Co is dissolved. Family returns to Liverpool.

1877 Family returns to Alexandria.

1879 Family moves to an apartment on Rue de Ramleh.

1881 Constantine attends the Hermes Lyceum in Alexandria.

1882 June 26, family flees by steamer to Istanbul following the insurrection by Arab Egyptian nationalists. The British bombard Alexandria, causing extensive damage, including to the family house. The family remains in Istanbul, where Constantine deepens his acquaintance with his mother's extended family and is immersed in the Greek culture of the Ottoman capital.

1885 Family returns to Alexandria.

1886 Publication of his first Greek poem, "The Poet and the Muse," in Leipzig.

1889 Death of childhood friend Mikès Ralli at the age of twenty-three. Wedding of his brother Aristides to Marie Vouros.

1891 Death of his brother Peter. Death of his paternal uncle George.

1892 Assumes a position as a clerk in the Office of the Irrigation Service, where he will work for thirty years.

1896 Death of his maternal grandfather, Yiorgos Photiades, in Istanbul.

1897 Travels with John to Paris and London via Marseilles.

1899 Death of his mother.

1900 Death of his brother George.

1901 First trip to Athens, along with his brother Alexander. Meets key writers and intellectuals.

1902 Death of his brother Aristides.

1903 Second trip to Athens. Appearance of influential article on his poetry by the renowned writer Gregorios Xenopoulos.

1904 Moves to an apartment on Rue Rosette with his brother Paul.

1905 Third trip to Athens to visit his ill brother Alexander, who dies of typhoid fever.

1907 Moves with his brother Paul to 10 Rue Lepsius, where he will remain for the rest of his life.

1908 Paul moves permanently to Hyères, southern France.

1911 Constantine considers this as the crucial year, marking a turning point in his poetry.

1915 E. M. Forster arrives in Alexandria as a volunteer for the Red Cross and meets Constantine the following year. Constantine meets Timos Malanos.

1917 Meets Alekos Sengopoulos, his future heir.
1918 Sengopoulos gives his lecture on Constantine either written or heavily edited by the poet himself. Meets the Italian journalist Atanasio Catraro.
1919 Forster publishes an article on Constantine in *The Athenaeum*.
1920 Death of Paul in France.
1921 Poet Tellos Agras gives first lecture on Constantine in Athens.
1922 Forster publishes *Alexandria: A History and a Guide*, which includes a translation of "The God Abandons Antony." Constantine resigns from the Office of the Irrigation Service.
1923 Death of his brother John. Receives a visit from the Greek poet Myrtiotissa.
1924 Marios Vaianos publishes a special issue of the Athenian journal *Nea Techni* on the poet's work.
1926 Awarded the Medal of the Phoenix by the Greek state. Dimitri Mitropoulos composes a musical work, *10 Inventions*, inspired by Constantine's poems.
1927 Meets the novelist Nikos Kazantzakis, who publishes an article on their encounter.
1929 Forster visits Constantine briefly on his way through Alexandria. The Futurist poet F. T. Marinetti visits Constantine.
1930 Meets the future novelist Stratis Tsirkas, who will write two influential books on Constantine's life and poetry.
1931 George Seferis, the future Nobel Prize winner for literature, sends Constantine a signed copy of *Turning Point*, his first collection of poems.
1932 Begins to experience pains in his throat and is diagnosed with cancer of the larynx. Visits Athens for

treatment, where doctors perform a tracheotomy. Greek intelligentsia visit him in the hospital and in his hotel. Kostas and Eleni Ourani organize a recital at their house, where Dimitri Mitropoulos performs his *10 Inventions* inspired by Constantine's poetry. Constantine returns to Alexandria.

1933 His health condition worsens. Unable to speak, he communicates by scribbling notes on pieces of paper. In mid-April, he enters the Greek hospital down the street from his apartment. Continues to work on his last poem, "In the Outskirts of Antioch." Dies on April 29, his seventieth birthday. Rika and Alekos Sengopoulos oversee the funeral. Friends and admirers organize a memorial service a month later.

1935 Rika and Alekos publish the first collected edition of C. P. Cavafy's poetry.

PREFACE: WRITING *ALEXANDRIAN SPHINX*

Although he never stated it to anyone openly, C. P. Cavafy must have wanted someone to write his biography, for he seemed to leave behind much of the material a biographer would need. Anyone looking through his archives[1] will discover not only the predictable material of an ambitious poet—letters, diaries, photographs, drafts of poems, notes about his art, press clippings, reviews, and other memorabilia—but the unexpected as well. A person so preoccupied with great subjects—antiquity, human desire, the effervescence of time, the ethnic and racial mixing of people, the hubris of ancient political figures, homosexuality—also preserved the minutiae of his life with equal assiduousness: train tickets, lists of daily tasks, lists of lists, multiple drafts of letters, instructions on cleaning the house, notes of family debts, wedding invitations, menus, and the like. In many ways, he resembled the scribes in his poems, scribbling in a dusty library in Beirut or Alexandria. In real life, he was a petty civil servant, a clerk with exquisite penmanship whose task was to copy, transcribe, and oversee correspondence. How could an artist who changed the fate of Greek and world poetry, who wrote valiantly about male same-sex desire and predicted our modern globalized world, keep lists about when and how often bread was delivered? Was it because he expected someone to use this material to tell his story?

Indeed, this is one of the paradoxes of the Cavafy phenomenon: one of the most celebrated poets of the twentieth century, the most frequently translated Greek poet into English, has had few biographies. The first, planned by Rika Sengopoulos, one of his literary heirs, never materialized. An early biography was published by his acquaintance Michalis Peridis in 1948, and his contemporaries Timos Malanos and Stratis Tsirkas included much biographical material in their own studies. Dimitris Daskalopoulos and Maria Stassinopoulou published a richly annotated timeline of the poet's life in 2002. But there is no true biography in Greek. And the only one in English, by Robert Liddell, came out in 1974.[2] We can speculate about this absence: the lack of interest in biography as a genre in Greece; the matter of archival accessibility; the predictability and unremarkable nature of the poet's life itself.

Those perusing Cavafy's papers today will confront another irony. The man who saved nearly every letter and note sent to him, who saw himself as the family's recordkeeper and genealogist, would be horrified to learn that most of his own letters have not survived. We do not have, for instance, his side of the rich correspondence he exchanged with his brother John in the early 1880s while he was still in Istanbul waiting to return to Alexandria after the British bombardment of the city in 1882. Nor are there any traces of the numerous letters he sent to his childhood friends and relatively few of those to his brothers or family members.

But there are other silences. There is no tape of his actual voice, even though recordings of Tennyson exist, a poet from a previous generation. Everyone who knew Constantine spoke about his peculiar English accent as they attested to his scintillating conversations. At the same time, much historical material about his family, his friends, and his own life has been lost. We are not even sure which schools Constantine attended in England and Alexandria, and until recently we did not even know the location of Constantine's maternal grandfather's house in Istanbul, the city where he spent two formative years.

There are many reasons for these lacunae. Constantine lived through much social and political instability, which resulted in migration, the physical destruction of property, the disappearance of correspondence and records, and the selling of possessions. The death of his father in 1870 initiated not only the precipitous decline of the family's fortune but also years of volatility that led to the dispersal of many family documents and possessions. In the hope of finding a more stable life in England, his mother either stored or sold their furniture in order to relocate in 1872. The family returned to Alexandria in 1877, only to abandon the city again in 1882 to escape further political turmoil. The Cavafys lost many valuables in this cataclysm, including an oil portrait of the father and many of Constantine's personal papers. Constantine wrote anxiously to his brother John about these missing books and writings upon the latter's return to Alexandria, only to find out that they had perished. It was perhaps this early experience of trauma and destruction that prompted the poet to keep almost every piece of paper that was remotely connected to him.

On the whole, the Cavafy brothers did not have stable lives and thus lacked the physical means to preserve and pass down family correspondence. It was left to Constantine himself, who spent nearly his entire life in his beloved Alexandria and who never traveled outside Egypt after 1905 until he went to Athens for surgery a year before his death, to become the family archivist. The only other letters of Constantine's that we have were those kept by his admirers after he began to gain fame in the early decades of the twentieth century. Of his early life—that is, after the return from Istanbul in 1885—we have his poetry, of course, his prose, his cryptic personal notes, drafts of letters, and diaries. For the years before 1885, we can hear his voice indirectly, mirrored and reconstituted in the responses of his correspondents. This is why we have included so many of these rich letters. Like the speaker in Constantine's poem "In the Month of Hathor," who strains to complete the broken lines of an ancient inscription, the biographer has to imagine the child Constantine playing with his friends in Alexandria, going to church in Liverpool, visiting museums in London, promenading through the streets of Pera in Istanbul, and cruising in the dark alleys of his home city.

At the same time, we have to reckon with the possibility that the archive itself might have been tampered with and that letters were removed. It is possible that Constantine himself extracted items that could have compromised either himself or his family. When he died, he bequeathed his papers to his literary heirs, Alekos and Rika Sengopoulos. Rika was a critic in her own right who did much to promote Constantine's reputation and, with her husband, published the first edition of his poetry in 1935. In her own perusal of his papers, she discovered that the poet had "intervened" in the cache of documents, making "additions and subtractions." Tantalizingly, she says that, being a "parsimonious" person with respect to family secrets, he did not want anyone discovering "undisclosed" aspects of his life, especially his youth. As a result, he removed from the archive material that he wanted to remain "unknown to his future biographers."[3] Of course, it was common knowledge that Constantine, the master self-promoter, managed his own reputation with obsessive finesse until the final weeks of his life. He fed tidbits to those interested in his life, which they used to create the Cavafian "myth" and which, according to Rika, was not always based on reality.

In addition to his own manipulation of his papers, rumors circulated that Rika and Alekos themselves might have cleansed the archive of compromising information, something that heirs and family members often do. Not a single letter, for instance, survives from Alekos to Constantine during Alekos's stay in Benha, Egypt, between 1918 and 1919, though all of the poet's letters to Alekos were preserved. Could Constantine, who saved grocery lists, have destroyed the letters sent to him by Alekos? Or had Alekos removed them? Something similar happened with Constantine's letters to John. Their niece Hariclia Valieri is reported to have thrown away these letters following John's death and according to his specific wishes.[4]

We will never ascertain what happened to these documents. But we are certain that our knowledge of the poet's life has been shaped in large part by the actions and writings of those close to him. After all, they knew him in varying degrees, even though none of these individuals had a full sense of his life before he started to become famous. Rika, who spent a great deal of time with him in the last two decades of his life, makes it clear in the notes she was keeping for her biography that she knew very little about his early life. Having worked with the poet and lived with her husband one floor below his apartment, she was perhaps the best-placed person to create a full picture, but she gave up the project, writing next to nothing about him other than a lecture.

Apart from Rika, Michalis Peridis was granted access to archival material on the basis of which he wrote (in Greek) *The Life and Work of Constantine Cavafy* (1948). Peridis claims that the documents he saw were unorganized, though he believed that Rika had worked on them. In the 1950s, part of the archive came into the hands of Giorgos Papoutsakis, who would later publish the first edition of Cavafy's *Prose* in 1963.[5]

Although we can't determine the exact year that Alekos and his second wife, Kyveli, moved to Athens, we do know that the archive had arrived in the Greek capital by 1961. Following the death of Alekos in 1966, Kyveli sold the papers in 1969, along with certain pieces of furniture, to the critic George Savidis, who had expressed an interest in the archive in 1953 during his trip to Alexandria. Savidis, however, had already photographed the contents of the archive in 1963, an exercise yielding 4,300 pages of microfilm.[6] When first photographing these texts, he had the impression that Constantine had done what he could to facilitate the study of his papers by future critics.[7] Although he urged the "immediate" publication of the archive, a desire he expressed again in 1985, Savidis kept it as his possession with limited access up until his death in 1995, when it passed to his son Manolis, who eventually sold it to the Onassis Foundation in 2012. This archive is now openly available in digitized form through the Onassis Foundation's website.

The vagaries of the history of the archive should warn us against presuming that it allows untainted access to the mind and life of C. P. Cavafy. That the archive offers tangible, visible, and quantifiable material about the poet does not mean it yields a picture of a man waiting to be discovered. Like any archive, it requires that its contents be organized and interpreted. And the Cavafy archive is marked by two conspicuous gaps—the relative absence of material regarding Constantine's erotic life and his views of Muslim Egyptians.

Apart from cryptic comments Constantine wrote mostly in shorthand in the 1890s, the archive reveals little if anything about the sexuality of one of the first major modern poets to write openly about homoerotic desire. There are no letters, no extended comments about his love or his lovers. For a person who defended and celebrated sexual freedom, who never hid his sexual identity from his contemporaries, and who anticipated a more just society for queer people, he left behind few if any extended discussions of his sexuality outside his poetry. Indeed, his case is the opposite of E. M. Forster, who, although his gay novel, *Maurice*, was published posthumously, had written explicit letters about his lover Mohammed el Adl. Rika suggests that the poet himself had removed documents regarding his sexual life. Why would he have done this? Was he fearful still about the situation of homosexuality in Alexandria, or Greece, or Europe more generally? Did he want to keep secret this most personal aspect of his life forever? Or is it possible that Rika herself, or Alekos after their divorce, or Michalis Peridis, Giorgos Papoutsakis, or others who had access to the poet's papers, might have purged material to sanitize the archive and preserve the author's reputation—or their own, or others'? As we shall show, many of the men who wrote about their relations with Constantine made a point of denying any sexual involvement with him.

Whatever their personal motivations, we can say that many of the poet's contemporaries obfuscated the topic of his sexuality. While same-sex relations among men were not uncommon at the time, Constantine was different in naming this activity, in highlighting it as an identity. Constantine lived through crucial decades of the late nineteenth and early twentieth centuries when the "homosexual" arose as a different category of person. The emergence of homosexuality as an alternative way of life meant that heterosexual men who might have engaged in same-sex relations at some point in their lives began to fear being labeled as "homosexual." This anxiety perhaps explains why Constantine's contemporaries often wrote that they had heard of certain incidents or rumors about him but, for reasons of discretion, did not record or allude to them. Consciously or unconsciously, they effectively "unnamed" what the poet was trying to name.

Because of such silences, the physical absence of evidence, the gaps in his records, and our own discomfort with traditional narrations of life stories, in writing this biography we decided not to follow a standard "birth-to-death" chronological direction. The facts of Constantine's life are rather unremarkable and very straightforward. We have chosen, therefore, to start and finish his life story with his death and then tell a circular narrative through various thematic sequences. In other words, we narrate his life by focusing on certain key topics: his family, the city of Alexandria, his friends, his poetry, and his ambitious attempts to promote his work and launch his literary reputation. Each chapter allows us to delve into its wide subject both in terms of breadth and depth. By moving forward, backward, and sideways, we aim to draw a portrait that avoids the evolutionary assumption of life as a linear progression from simplicity to complexity. This thematic approach also enables us to draw attention to the artificiality of biography as a type of writing. Like all genres, it relies on conventions, and the resulting "life" is, to a certain extent, an interplay between real events, dates, documents, and the act of composition. No biography, even the most detailed that span multiple volumes, can be entirely comprehensive and mimetic—that is, equal to the life itself.

Writing a biography nearly a century after the death of the poet has both advantages and disadvantages. The first biographers—Malanos and Peridis—knew the poet personally and drew from their individual encounters in addition to the network of Alexandrian personae who interacted with their subject. Liddell, in turn, had direct contact with many of the poet's contemporaries and took full advantage of the lingering memories held by people who were part of the Alexandrian milieu, availing himself of the surviving oral accounts, rumors, and gossip that shaped the popular Cavafian myth.[8]

Our main motivation in writing this story of a great artist is to provide insight into Constantine's mind, to unearth his fears and anxieties, his inner conflicts, his grand plans and disappointments. Thus, we place as much emphasis on the internal self as on external events—historical dates, births, deaths, travels, moves, publications, readings—the traditional preoccupations of biographies. We focus on key questions in his life in order to draw attention to the main contradictions he confronted: What caused him in middle age to renounce much of what he had written until then? How did the aesthetic preoccupations of his brothers shape his own poetry? What impact did the never-ceasing knock of death have on his life? Did his inability to speak openly about his sexuality or find true intimacy turn him into an advocate for sexual liberty? When did he abandon love for the sake of fame and success? And finally, did his obsession with posterity in his later years cause him to withdraw into his own inner self?

The biography is organized thematically to address and frame these questions. Part one focuses on the Cavafy family, their journeys to England and Istanbul, and the intersection between commerce and culture that shaped the Cavafy brothers. Constantine's shared intellectual and artistic interests with his closest brothers are explored along with the looming presence of the family matriarch, Haricleia. Part two situates the poet in his native city and traces the ways Alexandria served him as the center of his social and poetic world, one that paradoxically proved both restrictive and liberating. Part three considers Constantine's friendships and examines how intimacy waxed and waned in his life. It centers on the closest friends of his youth, middle age, and later life, and reflects on how he both treasured and compromised his friendships. The "Interlude" offers readers a look into his intellectual and reading interests and delineates the various literary influences that shaped his work. Part four scrutinizes his poetic trajectory and evolution from a mediocre poet to the great global writer he willed himself to become.[9] And part five traces his social connections and how he cultivated fame by carefully managing the literary contacts he needed to ensure the rise of his poetic reputation.

The most challenging and perhaps unanswerable question, however, is one about which we can only speculate. How did a man who, until middle age, showed little promise or capacity for greatness, living in a provincial city and writing in a minor language, manage to create poetry that has captured the world? Our biography can answer this only partially because our story ends with his death. After his funeral, a whole new process came into force that turned his individual work into world literature and converted the man into the author—C. P. Cavafy. Our biography, then, is less about Cavafy, the global phenomenon, than about Constantine, the human being.

ALEXANDRIAN SPHINX

PROLOGUE

On April 29, 1933, at around two in the morning—his seventieth birthday—the poet Constantine P. Cavafy died from complications arising from throat cancer. The dates bring an uncanny symmetry to his existence, one fitting for a poet whose craft was steeped in lamenting the transience of life and dramatizing the strange vicissitudes of history. Constantine wrote habitually about death and treated it unsentimentally and forthrightly. His own approaching death following a two-year struggle with an unbeatable malady was another matter altogether. For a solitary poet who surrendered his life to art, like the speaker in "I Brought to Art" (1921), handling his own mortality was beyond artistry. Having spent a lifetime orchestrating the circulation of his poems—printing them on deluxe sheets, disseminating them to a select circle of readers, and deferring the final publication of a definitive volume—Constantine felt he needed many more years to complete his poetic journey. Yet his death marked the beginning of his life as a world-renowned poet. The official publication of his 154 "canonical" poems in 1935 signaled his rise to global fame as "Cavafy," one of the most widely read poets of modernity.

For a lifelong smoker living in a city known for its production of fine Egyptian tobacco, Constantine's existence was seemingly bound by paper—cigarette paper and writing paper. In the final years of his life, he was able to give up cigarettes; his poetry he could not part with, even for a second. Among his final recorded protests was the lament that he still had twenty-five more poems to finish and others that required final touches. The last poem he had printed out was "Days of 1908" (1921?/1932), which focuses on an unemployed working-class youth who escapes his impoverished misery by taking a swim. It includes the frank homoerotic lines for which he was becoming famous: "Your vision / has safeguarded him / as he was when he removed, when he cast off / those undeserving clothes, and that mended underwear. / And stood totally nude; flawlessly beautiful; a wonder."[1] Here on full display was the unabashed celebration of the male body that was one of the hallmarks of Cavafy's mature verse.

The final poem he was working on at the time of his death tilted in another direction—that of history.[2] "On the Outskirts of Antioch" (1932–33) allowed him one last confrontation with his poetic bête noire, the emperor Julian the Apostate, about whom he had already composed numerous poems. In the concluding lines, Julian reacts to the burning of Apollo's temple by Antioch's Christians, highlighting his vexation over the failure to restore and relaunch paganism in a Roman province overrun by Christianity: "Julian erupted and spread the word— / what else could he do—that we the Christians, / had started the fire. Let him blather on. / It hasn't been proven. / Let him blather on. / The most important thing is that he imploded." Some of Constantine's own final frustrations with the fate of his poetry are certainly inscribed in these verses—the acceptance of the inevitable victory of an invincible force and the end of his valiant efforts to control his poetic reputation, the pursuit of which effectively consumed him up to his last days.

Diagnosed with throat cancer in 1932, Constantine left Alexandria in July of that year and traveled to Athens for radiation treatment that included a tracheotomy and the temporary insertion of a metal tube into his throat, procedures that left him physically altered and unable to speak. This struck his close friends, admirers, and even enemies as a cruel fate, for Constantine was known for his conversation and table talk. His theatrical flourishes and affected, almost mannered locutions had become legendary in Alexandria and Athens. Although sadly no recordings of him speaking were ever made, E. M. Forster famously captured the poet's oratorical style:

> . . . he may be prevailed upon to begin a sentence—an immense complicated yet shapely sentence, full of parentheses that never get mixed and of reservations that really do reserve; a sentence that moves with logic to its foreseen end, yet to an end that is always more vivid and thrilling than one foresaw . . . It deals with the tricky behavior of the Emperor Alexius Comnenus in 1096, or with olives, their possibilities and price, or with the fortunes of friends, or George Eliot, or the dialects of the interior of Asia Minor. It is delivered with equal ease in Greek, English, or French. And despite its intellectual richness and human outlook, despite the matured charity of its judgements, one feels that it too stands at a slight angle to the universe: it is the sentence of a poet.[3]

Like his idol Charles Baudelaire, who also lost his ability to speak after suffering a stroke during the last year of his life, Constantine was rendered mute in his final months, reduced to writing down his thoughts in abbreviated form on small slips of paper.

In early April 1933, Constantine was admitted to the Greek Hospital of Alexandria, located just opposite his own address at 10 Rue Lepsius. He would spend his final weeks in a small room with a cot-like bed similar to the one he was accustomed to sleeping on in his own apartment. His recent trip to Greece had affirmed his growing reputation among Greek literary circles, the final reward for a lifetime of cautious publishing and ruthless self-promotion. Indeed, the Greek novelist and essayist Yiorgos Theotokas was surprised during his visit with the poet at the Athens Hotel Cosmopolite in July 1932 to discover how keen Constantine had been to discuss contemporary Greek poetry. Although a "human wreck," the poet still exuded the genteel air of his ancestors. But it was his insistence on talking about current Greek poets that took Theotokas aback. At one point, he leaned toward Theotokas and in a sober and confidential manner, as if relaying a great mystery, whispered very discreetly, "with great seriousness and caution . . . 'they are all romantics, romantics, romantics.'"[4] He, of course, was not given to such bouts of ecstasy and poetic intoxication. In a revealing note written in French sometime around 1930 but published anonymously, Constantine unstintingly described himself as a contemporary poet, disciplined and in control of his craft: "Cavafy, in my opinion, is an ultra-modern poet, a poet of the future generations. In addition to his historical, psychological and philosophical value, the sobriety of his impeccable style which becomes at times laconic, his balanced enthusiasm which is inclined to be intellectually emotional, his perfect sentences which are the result of an aristocratic disposition, and his subtle irony, are factors that will be appreciated even more by future generations who are propelled by the progress of discoveries and the subtleness of their intellectual capacities."[5]

One youthful admirer who surely saw the Alexandrian poet in this "ultra-modern" light and was motivated by his own progressive and extraordinary intellectual capacities was Dimitri

Mitropoulos, the Greek pianist, composer, and conductor who early in his musical career had set ten Cavafy poems to music. A spectacular suite of atonal Schoenbergian "songs" written for piano and a single soprano voice, his *10 Inventions* received its musical premiere in Athens on June 5, 1927.[6] A recital of the entire suite was later given by Mitropoulos in Constantine's honor in 1932 while the poet was convalescing in Athens. The event was hosted by Kostas and Eleni Ouranis, two prominent luminaries of the Athenian literary world,[7] with Mitropoulos himself singing the inventions to his own accompaniment on the piano. The concert surely pleased Constantine, attended as it was by so many Athenian intellectuals.[8] The poet was already familiar with these musical adaptations of his poems—the very first and perhaps the most "modern" of many that would follow.[9] In many ways, he and Mitropoulos were kindred spirits, progressive and subversive both in terms of their artistic avant-gardism and their homosexual orientation. In 1926, Dimitri had written to Constantine asking for French translations[10] of the poems he wished to set to music, offering the following telling comments on their shared modernity:

> Of those 14 songs I will print a series of 10 that I titled Hedonistic Poems!! I don't know what impression this title will make on you but if you don't like it, I simply will not use it! You'll be truly surprised at my boldness in the selection of your songs [poems] but in spite of all the fears I had, the music is so well-matched to their meter and mood that I assure you it appealed to even the most moralistic people. This time the music succeeded in calming the moralistic nerves of some of my audience . . . Rest assured that my music is as modern as is the new tone emitted by your songs [poems]. Mr. Antonis Benakis heard them and can himself convey to you his impression.[11]

Mitropoulos would go on to achieve world renown as the conductor of the Minneapolis Symphony and the New York Philharmonic Orchestra, becoming one of the outstanding musical figures of the twentieth century before his premature death in 1960. His artistic intersection with the poet is telling of the future appeal of Constantine's work; musicians, painters, and poets were beginning to appreciate the poems for their modernity and newness.[12]

Unlike the previous three occasions, when Constantine had traveled to the Greek capital largely for pleasure, the four months he spent in Athens in 1932 (July–October) were bittersweet. Despite the positive initial prognosis he was given by doctors and the respectful homage paid to him by numerous Greek writers, poets, and critics, he sensed that his days were numbered. After he'd written so many poems about young men dying in their prime and old men lamenting the ravages of time, his life was now becoming one with his art. He had perfected his own version of the poetic epitaph, as the touching concluding lines of his poem "In the Month of Hathor" attest: "It seems that Lefkios was deeply loved. / In the Month of Hathor Lefkios went to sleep." A fantasy on death and being both missed and loved, the poem, set in late antiquity in the Egyptian month of Hathor (October–November), features a man who died at the age of twenty-seven. Dates and heightened sentiments remain crucial to this Cavafian funereal formula. For the poet himself, his own circular completion of a life in poetry was confronting him in his final days when he found himself surrounded by a few close friends who did greatly love him, foremost among them Rika and Alekos Sengopoulos. Alekos was the poet's heir and literary executor, and his wife, Rika, served as the editor of the literary magazine *Alexandrini Techni* (Alexandrian Art), a publication Constantine founded and practically directed to advocate for his work. They lived in the apartment below him and were loyal companions and attentive caregivers, in addition to being great appreciators and promoters of his poetry.

By February 1933, his health had declined appreciably. His tireless advocate Giorgos Papoutsakis was one of the few whom the poet wished to see in his final days. In a letter dated February 1, Papoutsakis writes to his fellow Alexandrian Yiorgos Vrisimitzakis in France that in his regular visits he found Constantine "sullen" and unwilling to leave the house. He was disturbed that, while the poet was able to speak with a weak and hoarse voice in the early days after his arrival from Athens, he could now no longer utter a word. "Even eating his meals tires him. He eats slowly and only consumes soft food . . . It's terrible, and I fear that this story will end badly." A month later, he notes that "he is melancholic and sits in his chair holding his head in his hands. He leaves the house only to see his doctor. A nurse comes every evening to change the tracheotomy tube and stays until the next morning. No one else visits his salon."[13]

In early April, Alekos and Rika decided they had no choice but to transfer the poet to the Greek hospital. In these final moments, Rika was exposed to a more humane, vulnerable side of Constantine that neither she nor anyone else had known previously. While gathering a few articles of clothing and some papers for the hospital, she pulled down an old valise. As soon as Constantine laid eyes on the small suitcase, he began to sob: "We tried to calm him during this heartbreaking moment when he was leaving his house forever. He took his small writing pad and scribbled: 'I bought this valise thirty years ago in haste one evening in order to go on a pleasure trip to Cairo. Then I was healthy, young and not unattractive.' "[14] It must not have escaped Rika's notice that Constantine had omitted to say "old and dying," refusing in some respects to become one of the ridiculous people of his poem "The Souls of Old Men" (1898/1901) whose spirits shiver at the thought of dying and dwell so "comico-tragically" in "their old and ragged skins."

During his final days Rika had arranged for Constantine to receive Holy Communion, despite the skepticism of his friends about the possible negative effect of his seeing a priest. When a cleric finally appeared outside the hospital room door hours before he died, the poet allegedly protested but soon gave in when he realized that the priest was accompanied by the Patriarch of Alexandria, Meletios Metaxakis. Constantine could not have known why it was that the patriarch himself was on hand to administer the final sacrament, honored though he certainly was by his presence. He sat up in his chair and received these last rites with humility and compunction. The great poet of the city—the patriarch of letters, as it were—who had celebrated hedonism, defied poetic convention, and transgressed bourgeois boundaries with his homoerotic verse and the open secret of his homosexuality, would likely have scandalized a mere rank-and-file priest. Patriarch Meletios wished to avoid any such religious prudery and took the matter—along with the chalice—into his own hands.[15] A tall and imposing figure, he was a charismatic and flamboyant prelate with a checkered past, a political opportunist aligned with the liberal Venizelist government in Greece,[16] and a progressive ecumenist who advocated the unification of the Orthodox and Anglican churches.[17] His own career was mired in political wrangling, Byzantine intrigue, and a desperate struggle to preserve his episcopal status atop the slippery slope of Greek Orthodox ecclesiastical politics in the post-Ottoman Levant.[18]

Meletios, in turn, knew and appreciated the artistic caliber of the man to whom he was administering the sacrament. There would be no scandal, censure, or excommunication tainting Alexandria's most celebrated poet. Constantine received Communion and the final patriarchal blessing for the remission of his sins calmly, adhering to the dignified protocol expected of the last sons of one of the "first families" of Alexandria's Greek community. According to those present, after accepting the sacrament, Constantine raised his hands dramatically in a posture of hieratic supplication.[19] Witnesses were struck by both the timing and the finality of the gesture. The poet seemed to be at peace following this telling gesticulation. Some say he died with a smile on his face, serene with himself and the poetic legacy he left behind.[20]

All the visitors to the hospital could not help but notice that Constantine, who according to Rika was "distingué" in his dress until his final days, lay in bed, vulnerable in pajamas, the only time anybody must have seen him in a state of undress. Unbuttoned, weak and helpless in his nightclothes, he was without his usual tie or scarf, and his exposed neck revealed a gold chain bearing a small cross. It mystified many of his friends, as did his ambivalent behavior before receiving the sacred rites of the Orthodox Church.

Constantine's supplicatory deathbed gesticulation was not unprecedented; he had been observed on previous occasions making similar dramatic gestures in private while surreptitiously writing verse in his office at the Irrigation Service—an agency administered by the British Ministry of Public Works—silently declaiming his poetic lines like an actor performing before an invisible audience.[21] In the poem "Voices" (1903/1904), he had described remembering the "voices" of his own imagination, where life and art were constantly competing for his attention; now they surely appeared and spoke to him during these precious remaining moments—"sometimes they speak in our dreams; and our mind listens to them in our thoughts." He was, after all, a man who had lived intensely through his imagination.[22]

Constantine's hand movement might have been a prayer. Or perhaps it was the repetition of that private gesture that now signaled a final attempt to communicate with those poetic "voices." It might also have been the last release of creative energy, an exorcising of poetic demons, as it were, in anticipation of death. This was a poet who throughout his life was fascinated by death—even obsessed with it—a fact that led to the rather uncharitable comment by the Greek novelist Yiorgos Theotokas that "Cavafy is the culmination of Greek poetry's preoccupation with death. His work isn't simply the expectation of or invitation to death, it is the final arrival of death itself."[23] This was a cutting statement that riled Constantine perhaps because he felt it was unjust and an unfair rejection of his work. When the end finally arrived, the voices, images, and memories traversing through his mind kept vigil with him as he encountered the reality of death unmediated by art. He was about to join the imaginary company of the dead for whom he created tombs, epitaphs, and stories: the grammarian Lysias; the youths Evrion, Ammonis, Iasis, Ignatios, Lanis, Lefkios, Kleitos, Myris; the historical figures Caesarion, Aristovoulos, and Manuel Komninos. Entombed along with him would be his poetic creations, the images and voices that hovered before him as he slipped away. These voices would soon become world-famous and resonate globally with the official publication of his poems.

Constantine was buried on Saturday, April 29, 1933, following a funeral service at the Saint Savvas patriarchal church in Alexandria, a few steps from his apartment on Rue Lepsius. He was interred at the grand Greek cemetery in the Chatby neighborhood with the other members of his immediate family. Two years following his death, with the first published edition of his 154 canonical poems, a new story begins—another life commences: that of C. P. Cavafy, the global poet. This biography is the life story of that man and that poet.

Part I

THE CAVAFY FAMILY

1

THE FAMILY COUNCIL

Commerce, Culture, and Letters

"BUILDERS" (1891)

Progress is a great structure—each man
lifts his stone: one carries words and intentions, another
acts—and daily it raises its head
higher still. If a storm, or a sudden gust

should come, the good laborers rush in unison
to salvage their lost work.
Lost, because each life is spent
enduring abuse, suffering pain for future generations,

so this generation might know untainted happiness,
and long life, and wealth, and wisdom,
without vulgar toil, or base labor.

But this legendary generation will never come about:
its very perfection will be its ruin
and this fruitless labor will start again.

Returning home from the Penasson printing company one day in September 1892, Constantine Cavafy held the pages of his first printed poem with pride and satisfaction. After publishing it in the Athenian periodical *Attikon Mouseion* (Attic Museum) a year earlier, he now perused the sonnet "Builders" beautifully printed on crisp individual broadsheets.[1] This moment effectively inaugurated what would become a lifelong relationship to the printed page, an obsession with paper that gave rise to the process of distributing his typeset poems as individual broadsheets, pamphlets, bound volumes, clipped batches, or sewn notebooks. He would share and circulate these strategically, carefully building his reputation poem by poem, batch by batch, stone by stone. He relished the fresh feel of the white paper, the distinct smell of ink that marked his arrival as a poet, signaling his unconscious rivalry with his brother John, who also published poems. Years back, John had shared a rather humorous "recipe" for making a poet: "To make a poet, take liberally of shimmering sunshine, strain through a rhyming dictionary, and add equal parts of love-sick adjectives, archaic adverbs, and such other words as you may never have heard of. Set in a warm place, where the whole may be intimately mingled, and garnish with long hair, seedy clothing, and an empty stomach."[2] Now at last they were on a par as artists.

"Builders" is a poem about making something of oneself, which, for Constantine, was above all an artistic endeavor; for his family, however, progress remained largely a socioeconomic pursuit. The sonnet speaks of fleeting success, the looming failure of family fortunes, and the illusion of prosperity, matters that weighed heavily on the Cavafys following the death of their father, Peter John, in 1870, whose financial assets proved inadequate to provide for his widow and seven sons. For the youngest son, age seven when his father died, life took an abrupt turn.

Up until this point, Constantine had been reared in luxury. At the time of his birth, the family resided at the leased Maison Zogheb on Rue Chérif Pasha in Alexandria. Constantine would write years later in his wistful family genealogy: "Peter John Cavafy (my father) lived lavishly; his house employed a French tutor, an English nurse, four or five Greek servants, in addition to an Italian chauffeur and an Egyptian groom. His furniture, his carriages, his silver plate and crystal were all of the rarest quality in comparison to that possessed by the Greeks of that period. His property holdings were small, however, and he left little when he died. But he earned much and spent abundantly, enjoying the social position of a great businessman. He frequented the [Egyptian] royal palace of Ismail Pasha."[3] With the wounded pride that would continue to inform so many family memories, Constantine incorporated what little information existed about these earliest years into his genealogical writings. He grew up hearing and speaking three languages, with English enjoying first rank as the metropolitan language of commerce and culture, vying with Greek as the mother tongue, followed by French. As the youngest child, he was coddled and doted on by his mother, Haricleia. More lasting than the fleeting memories of pampered wealth, however, were those engendered by the family's swift fall from economic stability. Money, or the lack of it, would become a dominant factor not only in the family's interpersonal dynamics—drawing the brothers together in their attempt to carry on the family business—but, more significantly, in the psychological development of the family's two poets. Their swift fall from prosperity produced a reactionary gravitation that pushed the Cavafy brothers toward the arts, allowing them to maintain some semblance of dignity while salvaging their self-worth. If they failed in business, they aimed to succeed in art.

The earliest extant photo of Constantine (1865) was taken in Livorno during a family trip and shows him at the age of two standing on a chair between his brothers John (age four) and Paul (age five). His right hand is placed on Paul's shoulder—he would later in life occupy an intermediary position between the profligate Paul and the puritanical John, who grew to disapprove of his older brother's wayward life. John and Paul are meticulously dressed in matching outfits, which were no doubt carefully chosen by their mother to convey both their social class and British taste. Constantine is wearing a dress, typical for young boys during the Victorian age. The myth that Haricleia dressed him up as a girl to make up for the loss of her child Eleni, who died in infancy, has absolutely no merit; according to Victorian custom, boys weren't "breeched" until the age of four or five. The brothers are decked out in what would have been normal Victorian attire that spoke to their status as the children of a wealthy British merchant. The photo captures a moment of brotherly intimacy in addition to conveying the social position of the Cavafy family. That Constantine is elevated on a chair suggests his eventual coddled position in the family as the youngest boy and hints at the special treatment he will receive from Haricleia. Conversely, his placement on a chair situated between his two smartly dressed siblings may also be seen as necessarily precarious; he will soon be forced to step down from this chair to live a life of economic uncertainty and hardship among six competitive brothers.

The photo effectively encompasses the many factors at play that contributed to the formation of Constantine's character. For the poet, these traits include cultivating an almost aristocratic sophistication, acquiring wealth, and safeguarding the family reputation. These merits would culminate in an obsession with artistic fame, whereby he would ultimately redeem the Cavafy name in Alexandria. Thus, when the Greek treasury minted a commemorative five-euro coin in 2013—the Year of Cavafy—imprinted with the poet's image, the tribute proved fitting in a number of ways. Constantine had a great fondness for coins, having penned many poems that fixate ironically on numismatic commemorations. But there is a nineteenth-century irony at play here as well, one that has much to do with the importance of money and commerce for the Cavafy family and the poet's own emerging sense of his place in the family network. He himself marked the final phase of the family, the end of the Cavafy name (no male heirs) following the depletion of his family's once-significant fortune. In his less high-minded moments, Constantine often extolled the importance of commerce and capital. In a letter to his heir and friend Alekos Sengopoulos (October 17, 1918), he wrote, "Commerce is a great and wonderful thing."[4] To E. M. Forster he once said, "Never forget about the Greeks that we are bankrupt. That is the difference between us and the ancient Greeks and, my dear Forster, between us and yourselves. Pray, my dear Forster, that you—you English with your capacity for adventure—never lose your capital, otherwise you will resemble us, restless, shifty liars."[5] Other recorded comments corroborate these sentiments: "We have commerce in our blood"; "Just as a good businessman advertises his wares in order to sell them, a poet must publicize the goods he is offering."[6] These statements should be seen in the larger context of the Greek diaspora with its commercial "*paroikies*" (settlements) that played a central role in the development of the Greek nation and the evolution of modern Hellenism. To Constantine's mind, the existence of these Greek communities in the urban centers of the Levant was crucial for the survival and advancement of Greek letters as well as commerce. Without them, Greek culture would forfeit its unique cosmopolitan character. And he, an Egyptian

Anglo-Greek with Constantinopolitan roots, was, as he recognized, a product of this milieu.

The Cavafy family was above all else defined by a Victorian mercantile ethos stemming largely from the network of the Anglo-Greek community that operated out of Manchester, Liverpool, and London. The Cavafy and Co. import-export firm was once one of the largest and most successful businesses in the Levant. The story of Greek commercial power and interests overlaps with the history of nineteenth- and twentieth-century Hellenism and the plight of the Greeks of Egypt in particular. The Greek kingdom, eager to expand its borders, embarked on what would become the ideology of the "*Megali Idea*" (Great Idea)—the reconstitution of the Byzantine state with Constantinople as its capital and Asia Minor (western Turkey) as its heartland. This expansionist ideal was high on the agenda of Greek politicians at the turn of the century and deceptively within reach at the conclusion of World War I. The basis of this was less imperial than it was economic, largely inspired by the British model of unimpeded free trade. The chief beneficiaries of course would have been the Greek tradesmen, bankers, and businessmen who stood to amass and solidify their fortunes and secure future investments. Constantine came from this demographic of merchant-wholesalers and was highly attuned to and influenced by the ways this class viewed itself as consisting of cosmopolitan Greeks and "pioneers" in business and culture. His comments on the loss of Smyrna (Izmir) in 1922 following the Greco-Turkish War—the "Asia Minor Catastrophe" as it is referred to by Greeks—illustrate this almost perfectly: "How terrible that we lost Smyrna and Constantinople—they would have been great urban centers where Greek intellectuals could have marketed their work."[7] This statement should be viewed within the context of the idea of economic expansion held by many Greek officials at the time: "Five cities . . . Athens with Piraeus, Constantinople, Smyrna, Thessaloniki, and Alexandria are the axis on which the development of Greece's economic life will depend."[8]

This entrenched economic opportunism reveals the fundamental dynamic of the "*protoklassatoi*" (first-class) caste of Alexandrian Greeks to which Constantine's father belonged. Constantine never really abandoned this way of thinking, as was noted by M. M. Papaioannou in 1955: "Cavafy emerges from the climate of the Greek communities in the Middle East at the moment when they embarked on the road to bankruptcy and dissolution."[9] As Cavafy's early critic Timos Malanos put it, "He was interested in the class to which he belonged, albeit as a fallen member . . . Quite often he would remind others of it himself, wearing rings on his fingers, like an Oriental (family heirlooms), allowing himself to boast about genealogical trees, relatives, grandeur and such. He desperately wished to be seen as a member of his parents' social class."[10]

At the end of his life, Constantine remained fully aware of the paradox of how his carefully constructed poetic reputation emerged from the shored-up ruins of his family's vanished fortunes. This discrepancy is discernible in the final chapter of Athanasios Politis's book *Hellenism and Modern Egypt* (1928/1930)[11]—a thousand-page two-volume work largely focused on the industrial and business achievements of the Greeks in Egypt—which is subtitled "The Intellectual and Artistic Life of the Greeks." It features a lengthy section on Cavafy (the poet allegedly dictated this section of the book to Eftychia Zelitas "word for word," since Politis, newly appointed as consul general in Alexandria, didn't know enough about the poet to write it himself[12]). In justifying and disguising their largely parasitic economic relationship to the land they lived in, the Greeks of Alexandria sought to define themselves as "pioneers of civilization."[13]

Alexandrian Greek merchants defended their economic presence in Egypt by presenting themselves as "enlightened crusaders" despite the fact that their "contribution" was rooted in economic practices that were basically exploitative.[14] And the one agricultural product that made it all possible was the supreme raw material of Egypt: cotton.

The Cavafy family was among the first to invest and trade in Egyptian cotton; their early businesses were founded along with the Cassavetti and Nicolopoulos families, with whom they had set up wholesale emporia as early as 1854.[15] By 1860, Egypt had become the sixth most important supplier of the British market for cotton and cereals.[16] With the outbreak of the American Civil War and the disruption of the cotton trade in the Confederate South, England would undergo a trade crisis that threatened its fiscal stability. The Greeks of Egypt rose to the occasion and were well-positioned to pick up the slack of the cotton supply; within a few years, they managed to fill the void. The result was the amassing of huge fortunes, and the Cavafy family was among the great beneficiaries. Similarly, the Crimean War had brought about an earlier crisis in the grain trade where Greek-Egyptian wholesalers stepped in to offset disruptions to Russian grain exports to Great Britain, with similar lucrative results. In fact, some have argued that the Greeks of Alexandria saved the British Empire from ruin and also positively influenced the outcome of the American Civil War, since the Confederate States were counting on the British to intervene in their favor.[17] In this sense, the Greeks of Alexandria were the ambitious "builders" of Constantine's poem, whose "vain work" would ultimately be ruined by "its very perfection" once economic and political circumstances shifted. The poem subtly interrogates the opportunistic and, in the end, deceptive nature of the progress that these "pioneers" of trade and culture were banking on.

Commerce, finance, and family relations were all part of this complex and fragile equation of community networking. The foundation of the Bank of Egypt by Greek businessmen and the importation of the first ginning machines into Egypt by Greeks—Constantine's father had fifty in his cotton factories[18]—paved the way for quick profits and a high return on the cotton yield. Cotton could be harvested twice a year. In effect, Lord Cromer (1841–1917), the British controller-general in Egypt, had converted the country into a mono-cultivating cash crop colony for the textile mills of Manchester. Of course, extensive and efficient engineering was needed to guarantee the vast irrigation of the land, in projects that called for careful and constant supervision. That Constantine would end up working as a civil servant at the British-controlled Office of the Irrigation Service was an irony he was surely aware of; for at the end of the day, so much depended on water. At the same time, he supplemented the modest income from this position by speculating at the Bourse, where people bought and sold shares in cotton. Cotton would remain part of Constantine's own history right through to the end of his life.

Constantine's complex familial connection to commerce, both on his maternal Photiades side and on his father's, is evident in his meticulous and extensive assemblage of family history: his *Genealogical Gossip* (1883), *Memorandum About the Cavafy Family* (undated), *Prose Notes* (1903), and *Genealogy* (1909–1911).[19] During his stay in the Ottoman capital following the bombardment of Alexandria by the British in 1882, Constantine began honing his intellectual and artistic skills by compiling facts for the eventual composition of a family history. Working in his grandfather's library, he took full advantage of the presence of his relatives when gathering the factual details he needed to draft these wide-ranging genealogical documents. As he discovered while amassing this information, at every turn his paternal and maternal families were linked through trade, commerce, foreign investment, and community building. Constantine created his own version of his family legacies—largely economic but also ecclesiastical, philanthropic, and, on occasion, political. He was conscious later in life, as he continued to edit these records, that, with no male heirs (his brothers Aristides and Alexander both had daughters), the name "Cavafy" would survive only through his poetic achievement. With a lineage linked to Phanariot[20] aristocrats and prelates in the Ottoman Empire, and a spurious Byzantine connection to the imperial house of Ducas,[21] he wished to document his ancestry for posterity.

Constantine's notes on his father betray a certain detachment, not surprising from a son who probably saw little of Peter John Cavafy when young and lost him when he was a boy of seven. His paternal inheritance was truly bittersweet, as his father, despite his erstwhile wealth and lavish lifestyle, left behind a depleted estate. Peter John was born in Ottoman Salonika in 1814 to a Constantinopolitan family with an established foothold in trade; the wider Cavafy family enterprises involved establishing branches of Cavafy and Co. and Cavafy Bros. in nine cities.[22] That he would sire nine children seems most fitting in light of this commercial fact. The family would engrave the following sentimental epitaph on his marble tombstone: "A tender father and beloved husband / whose death was, for his relatives, a much-lamented loss."[23]

An early undated photograph taken in Geneva captures Peter John's austere, intimidating aura. From his distant memories, the poet describes him as a "rather tall man, of a pleasing and distinguished countenance."[24] Peter John's closest associate was his older brother George, who established himself in commerce, settling in Manchester in the 1830s and forging business alliances with the Cassavetti and Ionides families in addition to setting up the Cavafy trading house. In a letter dated February 16, 1850, he urged Peter John to move to Alexandria to oversee the operations of the company branch there.[25] Constantine had a great deal of respect and admiration for his uncle George, whom he would get to know well when living in London after his father's death. He felt his uncle had "a broad education and was the wisest of his contemporary London Greeks."[26] George Cavafy's stoic and Victorian work ethic served as a credo that defined the business stamina of the Cavafy family.

Like many of the Greek merchants who operated out of Britain, Peter John and his brother George would have apprenticed as clerks while setting up their own branches of the family company. Peter John, although a junior partner in the firm Cassavetti, Cavafy and Company, still needed to apprentice with a junior clerk in the 1840s to learn "the routine of the English house." In order to become fluent in English, he enrolled at the Liverpool Mechanics' Institute.[27] Uncle George would have preceded his brother as one of "many Greeks learning English," along with their close friend Alexander Ionides, who had studied at a school run by a Mr. Hine at Brixton.[28] Their cosmopolitan background and international capital gave the first-generation Cavafy brothers a clear advantage over many of their British competitors.[29] Their children would, in turn, become assimilated and prosper as Anglo-Greeks in their adopted land.[30] Although Constantine spent the first nine years of his life in Alexandria, the family possessed a British ethos; they cultivated the hybrid Anglo-Greek identity that defined the commercial and familial network out of which they conducted their business and social lives. He would speak Greek with a distinct English inflection to the end of his life, although some thought this was a deliberate affectation. It may have been to some degree—he could have ironed out the pronunciation had he wished, rather than playing it up as he did for effect—but it was based on the reality of his unmistakable Victorian upbringing and his family's inclination to identify as British.

Peter John's commercial itinerancy would lead him to move his family back and forth among Istanbul, London, Liverpool, and Alexandria, which largely prevented his sons from being enrolled in or attending schools for extended periods. This pattern continued after his death, necessitating the sporadic employment of tutors for Constantine's education. It also fostered a flâneur's sensibility in him whereby various great cities would cast their spell on his impressionable imagination and emerging artistic temperament. Liverpool was one of these cities. The family would reside there intermittently during their extended sojourns in Great Britain. Shortly after marrying in 1849, Peter John relocated to London in 1850 with Haricleia and their firstborn son, George, and lived in Liverpool from 1851 to 1855, in the fashionable downtown core on Bedford Street, where Aristides was born in 1853. When Haricleia later returned to Liverpool as a widow in 1872 with Constantine in tow, she was well-acquainted with what was then the epicenter of British global trade, a metropolis with magnificent modern architecture and bustling promenades. The city's horse-drawn trams, newly constructed train sheds, and rich municipal buildings and shops were indeed impressive. In the shadows of this great commercial hub, however, there lurked a "nether world teeming with desperate individuals fighting for economic survival."[31] Crime, vice, and health considerations surely led the family to choose a location two and a half miles outside the city center. Balmoral Road in Fairfield was adjacent to the recently built 121-acre Newsham

Park, which opened in 1868 and offered a healthy alternative to living in the congested and unsanitary urban core. Constantine notes in his family memorandum that the eight-room house was affordable, the rent not exceeding sixty-five pounds a year.[32] The semidetached, three-story home leased by Haricleia was part of newly built housing that subsidized the construction of the public park. Designed for exercise, leisure, and entertainment, Newsham Park boasted two large lakes for fishing and sailing, grand boulevards, and fountains. It would eventually be the site of the Seamen's Orphanage. The allure of such an organized park for the Cavafy family was great, as it offered Haricleia and her sons opportunities for evening strolls and promenades. The proximity of other Anglo-Greek families in the area (Ralli, Rodocanachi, Sergiades, and Notaras) only increased the neighborhood's appeal.

A photo taken of John, Paul, and Constantine in 1873 captures something of the expectations of success that the city offered them. The brothers are arranged in dandified poses that seem intent on conveying their status as heirs to a great mercantile company. John is even holding a cricket bat. The city's many cultural offerings included concerts at the grand neoclassical Saint George's Hall, exhibits at the Walker Art Gallery, book-borrowing privileges at the Lyceum, which housed the oldest lending library in Europe, and theatrical performances at the various music halls and playhouses. The grand span of the Lime Street Train Station, which had just expanded in 1867, made it the largest iron-and-glass train shed in the world. Liverpool was above all a city devoted to commerce, whose architecture has been described as a "combination of rugged solidity and sublime grandeur."[33] Its merchants opened the world's first commercial enclosed wet docks[34] in 1715. By 1850, raw cotton imports and manufactured cotton goods constituted half of the city's trade.[35]

This commercial power was in part made possible by the city's role in the slave economy: "Liverpool was the European Capital of the Transatlantic Slave Trade 250 years before it became the European Capital of Culture."[36] As Rev. William Bagshaw Stevens observed in 1797, "throughout this large-built-town every brick is cemented to its fellow brick by the blood and sweat of Negros."[37] Even after the abolition of the slave trade in 1807 and slavery in 1833, Liverpool continued to profit from transatlantic slavery for decades. The city's economic influence is powerfully captured in the allegorical depiction of the *Spirit of Liverpool* that was commissioned for the Walker Art Gallery in 1877. Carved by the British sculptor John Warrington Wood, it portrays Liverpool as a Greek goddess wearing a crown and laurel wreath and sitting on a bale of cotton; in her left hand she holds a steamship propeller and in her right a trident, signifying her domination over the sea. At her feet lie a painter's palette, a compass, and a set square, the combination of which are "meant to symbolize that the arts find their support from trade and industry."[38] The statue, carved from white marble, weighs twelve tons, and prior to its being hoisted onto the roof of the Walker Art Gallery, it was on public display at the entrance of the new gallery during the final weeks of July 1877.[39] It serves in many ways as an apt metaphor for the Cavafy family's own composite identity as members of the Anglo-Greek community that was eager to connect to the arts while channeling a classical inheritance, drawing attention to themselves as heirs to Greek antiquity.

The Greek community of Liverpool expressed its commercial stature with the erection of the Church of Saint Nicholas, dedicated to the patron saint of sailors.[40] Although Greek parishes existed in London and Manchester, the Liverpool Greeks were eager to make a statement about their hard-earned mercantile status in the city. The church is an enlarged replica of the Constantinopolitan tenth- or eleventh-century Church of Saint Theodore with four domes and elaborate exterior brickwork, presently the Vefa Kilise Camii Mosque. The structure was completed in 1870 and consecrated in 1871 amid great fanfare. An extraordinary choice for the time and a fine example of Comnenian/Palaiologan Byzantine architecture that one could otherwise see only in the Ottoman capital and in the Balkan provinces, it proclaimed the ethnic and cultural pride of the Greeks of Liverpool as well as their growing prosperity and confidence in their status in their host country.

The construction of the church was almost perfectly timed with the sojourn of Haricleia and her sons in Liverpool. When the Cavafy family returned to the city in 1876 following their stay in London, they leased a three-story terraced house at 45 Huskisson Street, a five-minute walk from the church. The building loomed large in the life of young Constantine, who spent many hours with his mother under its domes during his years in the city. The simple and elegant features of its interior likely planted the seed for his poem "In Church" (1906/1912?) and inspired his lifelong preoccupation with Byzantium:

I love the church—the six-winged processional fans,
the silver liturgical plate, the candlesticks,
the lights, the icons, the pulpit.

When I enter a Greek church,
with its scent of incense,
the liturgical voices and harmonies,
the grand presence of the priests,
arrayed in their resplendent vestments,
and the somber tempo of their gestures—
my mind goes to the great triumphs of our race,
to our glorious Byzantinism.

The double-headed Byzantine eagle over the elaborate entry to the exonarthex, with its banded masonry and elaborate brickwork, proclaims the glorious Byzantine heritage of the poem's last line. The unusually spare and uncluttered features of the church's interior—there are no painted frescoes or mosaics on its walls—are virtually replicated in the streamlined simplicity of the poem. The church contains a basic iconostasis with panel icons with two large candleholders positioned before it and a striking pulpit situated off to the side. The simple and elegant details of its interior stand in stark contrast to its elaborate exterior, which leads one to believe that this building must have been the prototype and inspiration for the poem that in effect deconstructs the experience of worship in a Byzantine church.[41]

The Cavafy family's connection to Liverpool predates Constantine's stay there, as his father had his own civic, social, and commercial relationship with the city.[42] The prevailing notions of masculinity that defined how men behaved and conducted themselves during the Victorian era are of particular interest in this regard. The diaspora Greeks were eager to be accepted socially as well as financially in their host society and patterned their highly assimilated lives on the dominant work ethos of the British. Victorian manliness would become solidly identified with work, and Peter Cavafy's children inherited a Protestant work ethic from their father's generation, along with the prevalent practice of unmarried siblings sacrificing themselves for the good of the family.[43] In this case, the role was played by the unmarried brothers—Paul, John, and Constantine.

Being the youngest child, Constantine managed to be on the receiving end of this family labor distribution, not having to work as hard (or at all) and patterning his life and masculinity not on the Victorian businessman model but on a more retrograde aristocratic mold, fancying himself above the toil-based identity adhered to by most of his older brothers. This paradigm may have become more apparent to him later when living in Istanbul, where leisure would have been the rule for wealthy or privileged Greek youth. To be sure, a certain degree of idleness was necessary for him to read and prepare for his calling as a poet, and it was his family that sustained this somewhat self-indulgent "vocation." The coddling likely began in Istanbul, despite the onus falling on the brothers at large to provide for the family.

Constantine's maternal relations were similarly focused on business, although they remained largely centered in the Ottoman capital. His mother's family, the Photiades, were in trade and were landowners; his grandfather Yiorgos (1800–1896), to whom Constantine would refer affectionately and honorifically as a "*tselembis*" (gentleman), was a diamond merchant who came from a well-connected family securely established in diverse branches of trade. Constantine would get to know him well during his sojourn in Istanbul from 1882 to 1885, where, in the role of the adoring and talented grandson, he began to impress his mother's branch of the family with his literary and intellectual potential—writing poems and essays, translating Shakespeare, and availing himself of the rich intellectual offerings of this epicenter of Hellenism. This intimacy with his mother's relations colors Constantine's portrait of his mother in his genealogical writings, which is extensive and more detailed than that of his father, as would be expected given the great closeness between Haricleia and her youngest son—the "fat one" and "thin one" as they were fond of calling each other. Born in the Yeniköy suburb of Istanbul in 1834, Haricleia married her husband in 1849 at the age of fourteen. She would give birth to nine children, two of whom died in infancy: George (Istanbul, 1850); Peter (London,

1851); Aristides (Liverpool, 1853); Eleni (Alexandria, 1855—died an infant); Alexander (Alexandria, 1856); Paul (Alexandria, 1858—died an infant); Paul (Alexandria, 1860); John (Istanbul, 1861); and Constantine (Alexandria, 1863).

As is often the case in large families, the Cavafy siblings tended to bond in curious ways. The boys were expected to go into the family business, which the eldest brothers did, proving, however, to be less than adept masters of commerce. Eventually the brothers all wound up in either clerical or civic positions in Alexandria and Cairo: Peter served on the Sanitary Council, Aristides became a broker on the stock exchange, Alexander worked for Thomas Cook and Son, Paul found employment with the municipality of Alexandria, and John worked for the R. J. Moss agency.[44] Constantine was late in securing full-time employment, since he was spoiled by his mother, brothers, and extended family—a situation he manipulated to maximize his leisure time, which he devoted to reading and writing.

Based on extant letters, we can get a sense of how close the brothers were after the death of their father in 1870 when the family was more or less thrown back on its own resources, though initially the sons tried to establish new business endeavors in England. The London offices of Cavafy and Co. were located on 31 Threadneedle Street, the prestigious locale in the city's financial hub, close to the Baltic Exchange and the Bank of England. Very little exists to document how Haricleia and her sons passed their time in London, where they resided between 1874 and 1876, and there is no record of whether Constantine ever formally attended school there. Quite possibly he studied at Hellenic College, a grammar school for boys at Kensington Gardens Square.[45] Prior to this, the older brothers George, Peter, and Aristides had been sent to London and France for studies; they are registered in the 1861 London census as scholars in the establishment of William Birch at 19 Saint George's Terrace in South Kensington.[46] No doubt the family had employed tutors at various stages of their stay in Liverpool and London—Aristides must have taken drawing lessons in some venue or even with relatives given his artistic abilities.

In terms of commerce, the Cavafy brothers were expected to follow in their father's entrepreneurial footsteps. After Peter John's death, when the family moved to England in 1872 to improve their financial situation, George and Peter were involved in the family business, which was directed in London by their uncle George (Cavafy and Co. folded shortly thereafter in 1876). Eager as they were to achieve financial success through investment opportunities and commercial alliances, they were well-placed to take advantage of the tightly knit business network of the Anglo-Greeks. They proved, however, to be less successful with their finances and speculations. This is borne out by the fact that in 1877, George was declared bankrupt in the high court, having been sued the prior year for debts exceeding sixteen thousand pounds, which brought financial ruin upon his immediate family.[47]

Constantine's stay in England during the greater part of the 1870s would shape his social, cultural, and literary tastes, a process greatly bolstered by his direct contact with the artwork and artists he encountered there, since his relations were quite active in the art scene. In London, he was exposed through the Anglo-Greek community to the works and lives of numerous Victorian painters. The English Aesthetic movement of the 1870s decisively influenced Victorian cultural tastes as well as Constantine's own future poetry and aesthetic interests. Constantine was uniquely positioned to encounter many artists through his wealthy London relations who were patrons, collectors, collaborators, models, and even artists. The presence of important painters in his extended family history left an unmistakable mark on the impressionable young poet. It also demonstrated the family's business connections and patronage practices along with the important role played by the Anglo-Greeks in promoting and supporting art in England. The Cavafy brothers would have felt compelled to fashion identities based on this cultural dynamic—the fusion of wealth, breeding, and talent. In fact, with the collapse of the family finances, it was erudition and talent that allowed the younger brothers to weather the indignity of their impoverished circumstances. Talent and commerce were thus tightly interwoven in the wider family nexus, and the cultivation of their artistic interests would provide Aristides, Paul, John, and Constantine in particular with something tangible to fall back on as they coped with family misfortune.

In the Anglo-Greek community, the name Ionides is renowned owing to the family having left a significant artistic legacy in its wake. Less known is the fact that the Ionides clan were business partners with the Cavafy family from early on. The poet's grandfather John Cavafy conducted trade with his Phanariot friend Constantine Ipliktzis (later Ionides), importing and exporting goods from England and Istanbul and establishing offices in Manchester and later, through their progeny, in Liverpool and London. The sons of these two entrepreneurs, among whom may be counted Constantine's father, Peter John, his uncle George, and Alexander Constantine Ionides, solidified their business investments by marrying into their own and other mercantile families, most notably the Cassavetti and Ralli clans.[48] These diaspora families eagerly assimilated into the English upper-middle class and were proud to display and showcase their art collections in their opulent estates.[49]

Many painters regularly frequented the Ionides and Cavafy homes.[50] George Cavafy and Alexander C. Ionides began to commission portraits from the then unknown but unmistakably talented George Frederic Watts. The American expatriate James McNeill Whistler was also invited early in his career to paint river pictures for the Anglo-Greeks. Whistler would cultivate his advantageous relations with the Ionides and Cavafy families. George Cavafy made significant purchases from Whistler, as did Alexander Ionides, whose niece Helen Ionides married the painter's brother William in 1877. The opulent Ionides house at Holland Park—a monument to high aestheticism decorated as it was by William Morris, Philip Webb, and Walter Crane—became a meeting place of artists, musicians, and diplomats. Haricleia and her sons partook in the family gatherings and artistic soirees held here. Although Constantine was young, these evenings provided him with the opportunity to encounter some of the most brilliant artists and patrons of the time, a dizzying experience no doubt for one born in what must have seemed, by contrast, a provincial city. This unique dwelling, a baroque hybrid of Japanese, Persian, and neoclassical styles, showcased the burgeoning Ionides art collection. Alexander's son Constantine, also an avid collector and connoisseur, would leave his own art collection to the South Kensington / Victoria and Albert Museum in 1901.[51]

In addition to the wealth and patronage of the Ionides-Cavafy families, there is the equally significant participation of female relatives in the art scene. The cousins Maria Zambaco (née Cassavetti) and Aglaia Coronio (née Ionides), together with their friend Marie Spartali, were collectively known in the Pre-Raphaelite circle as the "Three Graces." Along with Marie's sister Christina, all had modeled at one time or another for Watts, Whistler, Rossetti, and Burne-Jones. Among the paintings they sat for were Burne-Jones's *The Mill* (all three graces), his *Beguiling of Merlin* (Maria Zambaco), and Whistler's *Rose and Silver: The Princess from the Land of Porcelain* (Christina Spartali), which became the centerpiece of the famous "Peacock Room," an interior similar to the Orientalist rooms of the Ionides "Palace of Art" at Holland Park.[52]

In addition to studying painting and sculpture, these Anglo-Greek sophisticates held unconventional relations with the artists for whom they modeled. The most notorious of these was the relationship between Burne-Jones and Maria Zambaco, who had "glorious red hair and almost phosphorescent white skin," in the words of her cousin Luke Ionides.[53] Zambaco was openly known to be Burne-Jones's mistress. Equally impressive is the career of one of the other graces, Marie Spartali Stillman,[54] who, breaking the barriers of ethnicity and gender, became a full-fledged member of the intellectual and artistic circles that radiated around Rossetti and Ford Madox Brown. She had connections with Sara and Thoby Prinsep in the Holland Park social set as well, Sara being the sister of the photographer Julia Margaret Cameron, who would later famously photograph Marie. The Spartali family acquired property on the Isle of Wight and was in the family orbit of Virginia Stephen (later Woolf), Julia Margaret Cameron being the Bloomsbury author's great-aunt. Marie was also a close friend of Harriet "Minnie" Marian Thackeray, Leslie Stephen's first wife and daughter of the famous novelist. And rounding off this extraordinary confluence of artists and authors, it is thought that Marie's stepdaughter Lisa Stillman, an artist and friend of Vanessa Bell's, served as the prototype of the character Lily Briscoe in Woolf's *To the Lighthouse*.[55] How curious that this intellectual network would reconfigure itself decades later when, via E. M. Forster, the path of Virginia and Leonard Woolf would intersect with that of Constantine during their futile attempt to publish an English translation of his poems at the Hogarth Press.

It is here in these Anglo-Greek social circles where the roots of Constantine's entrenched cultural Anglophilia lie. To a large extent, he saw himself as culturally British, as technically he was a British citizen since his father had been granted naturalization as a British subject in 1850. When Haricleia eventually settled in London in 1874 at Queensborough Terrace,[56] she was well-ensconced in the orbit of the Anglo-Greeks who lived clustered nearby in the Bayswater district and beyond. To begin with, Uncle George's home at 26 Pembridge Gardens—an impressive four-story mansion—was a mere ten-minute walk from their residence, as were the various Ionides homes: Alexander and Aglaia both at Holland Park, Constantine at Holland Villas Road, Haricleia Ionides-Dannreuther at Orme Square. These families regularly hosted soirees, dinners, and open houses at their opulent and elegant dwellings. Added to this was Kensington Gardens, with Kensington Palace a mere fifteen-minute jaunt, and the allure of the city's grand museums—the South Kensington Museum located nearby and the British Museum farther afield. There were gallery openings as well, concerts[57] and lectures, along with the obligatory family weddings,[58] baptisms, and funerals that regularly drew these clans together.

How much of this cultural ambience would a precocious adolescent have absorbed? This high saturation of culture by Constantine proved to be decisive in shaping his aesthetic tastes and interests. These factors contributed to what might be called the Cavafian "museum ethos," something that sprouted while the poet lived in Liverpool and London, which were the only places where he would have been exposed to what were essentially Europe's first modern museums in terms of their content, function, and public access.[59] Many Anglo-Greek families took a great interest in the South Kensington (Victoria and Albert)

Museum, living as they did in such close proximity.[60] Given these connections, Constantine's exposure to this space would leave deep impressions, in particular the Cast Courts galleries that replicated masterpieces of world architecture and sculpture. In addition to these galleries, the British Museum also held the young Constantine in thrall, and we know that he viewed the Parthenon marbles up close, an encounter that would later lead him to take up the topic of their return to Greece once he began his official foray into journalism in the early 1890s. The roots of Constantine's fascination for antique artifacts and aesthetic art owe their genesis to these days of his youth spent amid artists, collectors, and patrons.

In 1895, in the middle of the decade that marked his transformation as a poet, Constantine wrote a prose poem that captured his family's complex relation to the arts and its position at the intersection of commerce and culture.[61] Like many poems from this period, the unpublished "Ta Ploia / The Ships" is something of an experiment, opening with lines that invite the reader on a fanciful commercial voyage: "From Imagination to Paper. It is a difficult crossing, a dangerous sea. At first sight the distance appears short, but in fact the journey is a long one, and very damaging for the ships that undertake it."[62] The prose poem then proceeds to note the "delicate nature" of the cargo being transported: "In the markets of the Imagination, the majority of wares and the best items are fashioned out of delicate glass and diaphanous ceramic, and despite all worldly precaution, many break on the journey and many break when they are being unloaded on to land."[63] Perhaps the most intriguing dimension of this piece is how it expresses Constantine's early anxieties about the reception of his own imaginative work—specifically the inability of his contemporary and future readers to appreciate and comprehend him: "There is one other thing that is lamentable, most lamentable. This is when certain great ships pass by, festooned with coral and masts of ebony, with great white and red flags unfurled, ladened with treasures, which never even approach the harbor since either all of their cargo is banned or the harbor is not deep enough to receive them. And they continue on their way. A tail wind fills the sails of silk and the sun illumines the glory of their golden prows, and they sail off gently and majestically, distancing themselves from us and our shallow port forever."[64] This aesthetic rendering of the ships reveals how art trades in beauty the way merchants deal in commercial goods. The speaker is spellbound by the splendor of the ships and their precious cargo, a dynamic that recalls the poet's own family's circumstances as merchants with cultural interests and investments.

How fitting that Constantine would choose this trope of the markets of the imagination and the metaphor of shipping as relevant to his craft, since ships were so central to the Cavafy family business. He concludes the piece with a nod to the classical world, inflecting his meditation with a homoerotic reference to Homeric heroes:

> Fortunately, these ships are quite rare. At most we will see two or three during our lifetime. And we quickly forget them. [. . .] And after a few years pass, if one day—while we sit indolently watching the light of day or listening to the silence—if by chance some inspired verses return to our mind's ear, reminding us that we have heard these melodies before—we do not recognize them at first, and we rack our brains to remember where we once heard them before. After much effort, our old memory awakens and we recall that these strophes were part of the song sung by the sailors—sailors as beautiful as the heroes of *The Iliad*—when the

> great ships were passing us by, those sublime ships that were heading—who knows where.[65]

This clever equation of material goods and imaginative thoughts—the connection between commerce and art—is a dynamic that will remain pivotal to the poet's identity as the son of a prosperous entrepreneur.

2

TRAUMA, EXILE, AND LOSS

The Flight to the Ottoman Capital

The family's return to Alexandria in 1877, after the energy and glamour of the British metropolis, must have come as a terrible shock to the Cavafy brothers. Haricleia and her sons took up residence at an eight-room apartment on Rue Mahmoud Pacha el Falaki and struggled to recover from their steep losses. Constantine attended the Hermes Lyceum and studied with Constantine Papazis, who created a nationalist curriculum promoting a Hellenocentric chauvinism that the poet and his classmates would later rebel against. He became friends with relations of the Anglo-Greek families he knew in England—Mikès Ralli, John Rodocanachi, and Stephen Schilizzi.

The 1882 British bombardment of Alexandria, which forced the Cavafy family to seek refuge in Istanbul, generated a trove of letters and written documents that allows us some invaluable insights into the trauma, loss, and subsequent process of "retrieval" in the poet's imaginative and emotional life.[1] The most important urban influence on him after that of Liverpool and London, and prior to his permanent return to Alexandria, was "the City"—Constantinople/Istanbul, the bustling and alluring epicenter of the Ottoman Empire. The city was technically the place of origin for both the Cavafy and Photiades families, difficult though it was for the destitute Cavafy brothers to feel any real sense of "home" there. It was a rather peculiar homecoming in that Haricleia and her sons were arriving as impoverished refugees. Despite this, the city would offer Constantine the opportunity to apprentice in the Greek language, to engage with the most important currents of Greek intellectual thought, and to explore his sexual orientation.

When conditions in Alexandria became untenable owing to political turmoil,[2] Haricleia and her sons, with no independent source of wealth, made plans to flee to her father's house in Istanbul. But in the last days before the British assault, she was not sure she could even secure the tickets for passage on one of the last vessels to leave the port. "Great confusion is reigning everywhere," her youngest son writes; for just prior to embarking on the journey to Istanbul, Constantine began a "diary" of sorts in English, which he titled rather ambitiously "Constantinopoliad, an Epic." The entries that compose this document—his earliest extant writing[3]—offer us a sample of his young voice and emerging narrative style. These passages reveal the budding intellectual aspirations of a nineteen-year-old cut adrift from the world he knew, while recording the intimacy shared by members of the "family council," as he terms it.

With the bombardment days away, the family could no longer delay their flight from Alexandria. When Paul tried to book passage on the Austrian liner SS *Castore*, he learned that it was "doubtful if there will be any place for us" given the large number of foreigners rushing to leave Alexandria.[4] Their relatives in Istanbul expressed their disquiet. And as a sign of uncertainty to come, Haricleia discovered that her father had leased their grand house in Yeniköy and had rented a smaller house on the Asian side of the Bosporus. Would there be enough space for all of them in this new accommodation?

In Alexandria, all around them Europeans were departing by the thousands with businesses collapsing. Constantine heard that "in Cairo there is not a vehicle to be seen in the streets." In the meantime, Peter, who had initially planned to stay, decided to leave as well because everyone feared a "second massacre of the Christians."[5] The rumor had spread that the Europeans "have poisoned the waters of the town." While Peter "is talking at the head of the table about the incident with his usual verbosity; John & Aristides sit listening to him, the former emitting from time to time a dry remark or two."[6] His mother, Paul, and Alexander withdraw to the balcony, while Constantine writes in his journal. With the world falling apart around him, he could not abandon poetry and would fill his narrative with literary quotations from Shakespeare, Milton, Hesiod, and Addison. Here he anticipates one of his future literary personae: the imaginary poet Phernazis of his poem "Darius" (1917/1920), who was attempting to write an epic in 74 BCE, only to have his plans thwarted by the Roman invasion of his town on the Black Sea. Yet Phernazis just could not give up his plans and "the poetic idea comes and goes tenaciously."

Almost everyone Constantine knew in Alexandria had already abandoned the city, including his closest friends, John Rodocanachi (nineteen years old), who had departed for England with his family well before the unrest, and Mikès Ralli and Stephen Schilizzi (both eighteen years old), whose families sought refuge in Athens. John, writing from England, was relieved to know that Constantine was planning to depart. These friends were concerned for Constantine's safety. When Mikès arrived in Athens in mid-June 1882, he had heard that "Alexandria and

Cairo were all in a blaze" but was pleased to find through the papers that these rumors were false.[7] The actual bombardment took place three weeks later.

Constantine's first entry in his journal sets the general tone of panic over the uncertainty that besets the family:

> 23 JUNE, FRIDAY
> BEFORE STARTING
>
> Hour 3.30 p.m.—John & Polly [Paul] are out. Alexander is at my writing-table scribbling; Aristides sitting on a trunk reading; Mamma in her room packing. We are leaving on Tuesday for Constantinople, & great confusion is reigning everywhere. We have huddled everything we do not stand in absolute need of into a great wardrobe in Alexander's room. Johnny, Alexander, Aristides & I have disposed of our things, consigning our clothes to a portmanteau—of reverend antiquity, it having been in the family according to Mamma's statement, 35 years—& our linen to a tin box. We have secured places in the Austrian S.S. "Castore." But tho' we have secured our places, & packed up our things, it is by no means certain that we are going. Only an hour ago Mamma & Alex. solemnly decided on staying, & were scarcely persuaded to the contrary by Paul's expostulation on the absurdity of the resolution. The reason of the voyage's being unwelcome to us is Impecuniosity. We start with barely more than £100. That is why we look as glum as owls, & we contemplate Constantinople in the same light as who should say:
>
> *"That distant country from whose bourn*
> *No traveller returns." (Cowper)*[8]

Constantine's lifelong fondness for ironic epigraphic flourishes begins to show itself here, although these verses cited from memory are not of course Cowper's but Hamlet's. It is interesting to note that Haricleia initially wished to remain in Alexandria and that their "impecuniosity"—an ostentatiously Latinate word choice for poverty—nearly did them in. The family did not even have the capital to secure the safekeeping of their meager possessions.

The next entry is even more explicit about their dire circumstances and introduces the notion of bad luck and the "jinx" on the Cavafy family:

24 JUNE, SATURDAY

[. . .] Paul of course returned in a great rage, & reproached Alexander bitterly on the subject for having brought about the scarcity of place in the ship, thro' the malevolent influence of a sort of rheumatism of which he complains lately. This view of the case has been adopted by the majority of the Family Council, & I cannot say I am quite insensible to the cogent arguments by which it is supported. "Gioursouzia" (anglicé, ill-luck) has ever been regarded as a powerful factor in the destiny of our house, & no true Cavafy can think, without a shudder, of calling it into question. Alexander—tho' he makes use of the argument against others almost daily—proves quite restive under the charge, refusing to recognise in the boat's being full aught else but the hand of Providence that forbids our departure; but in vain—none listens to him and his voice is lost as

"A voice of shipwreck in a sea of storm!"

[. . .]

Tho' politics are somewhat quieter of late yet there is considerable reason for uneasiness. People are departing by thousands, & shops closing by hundreds. In Cairo there is not a vehicle to be seen in the streets. All the big-wigs are at Alexandria at present,—Raghet Pasha, the new Premier; the Khedive; Derwish Pasha, the Sultan's Commissioner; Arabi Pasha, the Minister for War, & the actual dictator of Egypt;—but their presence is not very re-assuring. Raghet, the Khedive, Derwish are puppets; all the power is vested in Arabi. When he goes out, the Arabs flock by thousands in his path to catch a glimpse of him—like Shakespeare's Romans they pass the whole day in live-long expectation

"To see great Pompey pass the streets of Rome."

We will see how long "great Pompey" will be allowed his sovereignty![9]

The line from Tennyson's play *Queen Mary* should read, "A voice of shipwreck on a shoreless sea," and the Pompey reference is from Shakespeare's play *Julius Caesar.* What strikes the reader is the Anglocentric pose and manifest "stiff upper lip" in moments of extreme duress, as well as the poetic erudition.

When safe passage is finally procured, Constantine's tone shifts from Shakespearean tragedy to Byronic bathos combined with Dickensian parody, with quotes from Byron's "Greek War Song" and a playful reference to Dickens's Silas Wegg in *Our Mutual Friend*:

25 JUNE, SUNDAY

Our tickets taken. On Tuesday morning will be on board the "Castore"; and

"The seven-hilled city seeking
Fight, conquer, till we are free"

i.e. till we are back again. By-the-bye the reader of these notes must by fully satisfied as far as "dropping into poetry" is concerned—a quality in which I admit of no rival except Mr. Silas Wegg.[10]

Once aboard the ship, his mood changes into one of steadfast calm, concluding with sentimental lines from Byron's "Childe Harold's Pilgrimage":

26 JUNE
FIRST DAY ON BOARD THE "CASTORE"

Everything has gone off quietly & well. Trunks sent on board 9 a.m.; ourselves conveyed on board 10.15 a.m.

At present it is 4 o'clock in the afternoon. Mamma is sitting in an easy chair on the deck. I in another in front of her, writing these lines on my knees. Peter & Aristides are talking with the Captain near at hand; & John & Alecko looking out at the ships anchored in the port. Paul is sleeping in the ship's saloon.

The Captain is a tall fellow, with grey whiskers & moustache—a Triestene. He has a curious, familiar way of talking which would seem to savour of impertinence if it were not so natural.

There is nobody else on board except a gaunt-looking Greek gentleman (?) with black mustachios; & a French lady.

Our cabins are horrid—teeming with beetles. Mamma says she won't be able to sleep in them.

Tomorrow, about 5 p.m. the ship will start. I wish

it would start sooner. I wish we were already far from Alexandria:

"My greatest grief is that I leave
No thing that claims a tear."[11]

Constantine's "epic" diary ended abruptly with the family's arrival in Istanbul on July 8, 1882, where they were received "affectionately" by their family, among them his three Plessos cousins, including Tassos, who was "the handsomest of the three."[12] Until July 16, the family resided in a hotel in Therapia, on the European bank of the Bosporus, where prosperous denizens of the city and its diplomatic core had summer residences. Constantine composed a poem in English about their time there titled "Leaving Therapia," which he never published:

Good-bye to Therápia & joys of the hotel—
Good dinners that make you exultingly swell,
Good beds that refresh you from the toil of the day
Fine sights near which you'd wish ever to stay—
To all these good things the time is well nigh
I must bid a Good-Bye!

However Catíkioy's opposite shore
I must hail tho' by far more simple & poor:
But they say what is simple is good at the heart
And where goodness is we may well spare art:
So at humble Catíkioy let us not rail
But bid it All Hail![13]

Having enjoyed the respite provided by Therapia, especially after the horrors of a besieged Alexandria, he and the entire family had reservations about moving across the Bosporus to Cadiköy on the Asian side, where Haricleia's father had rented a house for the summer, having already let his grand residence in Yeniköy to the Persian consul.[14] That the once-proud "landowner" had leased his estate to strangers surely struck the young Constantine as a worrisome sign. His mother had already warned him before their departure that, although Cadiköy was a "respectable and fashionable quarter" of Istanbul, she feared the new house would be "small and not quite fit to receive six persons." She hoped that her husband's sole surviving sister, "Mme. Plesso," who also lived there, could provide hospitality "to two or three of us."[15]

Initially Constantine expressed his pleasure about coming to the great city of his ancestors. In his diary entry before their departure, he hinted at this grandeur, writing, "Northward ho! Northward for the great city in which my ancestors have flourished, powerful and generous . . ."[16] Unlike the view from Therapia or even Yeniköy, which afforded vistas onto the other bank of the Bosporus, from the windows of this rented house Constantine had a commanding view across the water of Istanbul proper with its undulating skyline of minarets and the Galata neighborhood in the distance. At this age, in contrast to his adulthood when he had little interest in natural landscapes, he appreciated one of the world's most extraordinary urban topographies, representing millennia of civilization and set in the spectacular confluence of waters: the Bosporus, the Golden Horn, and the Sea of Marmara.

It was in this rented house and later in his grandfather's villa that Constantine wrote his first lines of poetry, though he could not have been anything but disappointed by the cramped dwelling. At first, Haricleia benefited from the rest this seaside address offered her after the traumatic shuffle from Alexandria. And she was surely relieved to be reunited with her family after an absence of nineteen years. Constantine and his brothers must have been bored by the isolation, especially in comparison to the urban vitality they were accustomed to back home in Alexandria. He soon exhausted the reading material he had brought with him: "I do not read much for the good reason that I have very little to read & husband my books as much as I can."[17] But it was astonishing how much he had read and understood to date. In one paragraph at the end of the "Constantinopoliad," he refers to a study of Greek geography published in 1807 (still included in his surviving library)[18] and has the confidence to judge the book as lacking good style while connecting its author to the ancient geographers Strabo and Pausanias.[19]

The situation improved at the end of the year when the family relocated to his mother's ancestral house in Yeniköy.[20] Moving there and spending time with his maternal family proved influential for the young Constantine, as he was inspired to collect material for the family genealogy that he began drafting in July 1882. He was so fascinated by his family's narrative and his Phanariot-Byzantine roots that he decided to embark on this most arduous project. This is telling of his future interest not only in tracing historical lineages—whether Hellenistic, Roman, or Byzantine—but also in creating historical portraits. His time in Istanbul showed him that this villa represented what was left of the extensive holdings and wealth the Photiades family had accumulated a century earlier. Looking at the grand manor house and its vast gardens, along with those of an aunt next door, he could not help but feel once again how unlucky the family was.

His stay among his relatives reinforced the Phanariot connections the family had to Byzantium, Istanbul, and the Ottoman Empire. Two of the poems from this period, written in the heavy katharevousa (a purist, formal language) typical of Phanariot poetry, take on Ottoman themes. In "The Beyzades to His Beloved"

(1884), a young Ottoman nobleman addresses his lady love.[21] And "Dünya Güzeli" (1884), a figure right out of Ottoman and Greek folklore, concerns a lovely denizen of the harem who is the "most beautiful woman in the world." The poem reflects Constantine's exposure to Greek folklore that dominated Greek letters during this period, which was marked by the search for the uninterrupted continuity of the Greek identity. Composed in the mode of Greek Romantic poetry, these two poems reveal a young poet still enthralled by the intellectual currents of Istanbul. At such a young age, it was understandable that he was searching for a suitable writing style and thus came under the heavy influence of the reigning Phanariot school of Greek poetry.[22]

The Ottoman capital presented Constantine with many challenges but with many opportunities as well. Navigating the city was perhaps the first of these; haphazard living arrangements in different outlying suburbs and neighborhoods of the city, however, soon afforded him cover to come and go as he pleased, hidden from the oppressive eyes of his mother and relatives. Crisscrossing the city as he did and having no regular employment to make demands on his time, he was a free agent and likely used this autonomy to arrange the covert trysts and sexual assignations he reputedly engaged in during these years. Much has been made of this sexual experimentation, but less of the intellectual and historical stimuli of Istanbul, which, with nearly three hundred thousand Greek inhabitants, was the undisputed center of Hellenism both commercially and culturally. Indeed, the last two decades of the nineteenth century marked the period when the Greek population of the city achieved unprecedented levels of affluence, power, and autonomy, taking full advantage of the relaxation of Ottoman oversight and the freedoms accorded them by the various reforms granted decades earlier by the sultan. Perhaps the greatest example of this economic and intellectual ascendancy was the erection of the educational institution unapologetically named "The Great School of the Nation," which opened its doors in 1882 to much fanfare and pomp. The iconic building, a striking neo-Gothic edifice built of red bricks imported from France, looms over the city to this day. With its distinctive domed tower, which houses an observatory, it was designed to make a powerful statement about the commitment of the Greek community to education and post-Enlightenment humanist values. Given the involvement of the Photiades relatives in community and church organizations in the city, the family would have been present at the inaugural festivities (Patriarch Ioakeim conducted the official dedication of the building on September 12, 1882).[23] The building, designed by the Greek architect Pericles Demadis, dominates the Phanar district. A major landmark of the city to this day, it gives the impression of an Anglo-Saxon college, as Alexander Massavetas notes in his book on Istanbul.[24] Constantine would have been too old to enroll in classes here (it was technically a high school). But the excitement and magnitude of the building's dedication, an event occurring just months after his arrival, not only attests to the significant intellectual energy and ambitions of the Greeks during this period but also symbolizes the apogee of Greek cultural accomplishments in the city that proved definitive for his own intellectual formation at this critical juncture. There was no other place that could offer this sort of stimulus—not even Athens, which seemed to many a quaint provincial backwater in comparison. And Alexandria, of course, was in shambles following its bombardment by the British, although it would soon be rebuilt to achieve a cosmopolitan luster on a par with that of Istanbul's "European" enclaves of Galata and Pera.

At this stage in his life, after a peripatetic series of sojourns and exiles (London, Liverpool, Alexandria, and now Istanbul), the nineteen-year-old Constantine was presented with the challenge of living up to his forbears in the city where Greek culture was undergoing a renaissance of sorts. It was an unimaginable opportunity for him to define and refine himself and align his intellectual energies with those of the Greek community around him. As was the pattern of the Cavafy brothers, the safety net proved to be erudition and culture, which served to offset the tragic hand they had been dealt following their father's death, the family's subsequent bankruptcy, and their humiliating return to Alexandria. These years in Istanbul were perhaps the most significant in terms of Constantine's future intellectual orientation and linguistic commitment to the Greek language and Greek letters more broadly. The Ottoman capital served, one could say, as his urban finishing school. Here he had the vast ocean of Greek culture at his fingertips and the freedom to explore it. The availability of dozens of newspapers and journals in the city, owing largely to Ottoman reforms permitting a relatively free press (some one hundred were published by certain estimates[25]), played an important part in his lifelong interest in erudite journalism and prodded him in this direction vocationally. There was also the significant presence of the many Greek literary societies and cultural clubs in Istanbul—some seventy-five according to scholars of the period[26]—the most influential one being the Greek Philological Society of Constantinople, which functioned as a sort of Ministry of Education for the Greeks of the Ottoman Empire.[27] With its imposing neoclassical building in Galata on Topçilar Street, Stavrodromi—the very heart of this Greek-inhabited district—the Society housed a vast library and hosted numerous free lectures for Constantine to attend, giving him access to the cultural debates and intellectual topics of the day. Evidence of this influence is borne out by the subject matter of his early prose writings, musings that emerge from his stay in the city and are heavily inflected by Greek folklore and the debate about the unbroken continuity of Hellenism. With two aunts, Amalia Kalinous and Evoulia Papalambrinoudi, living in the vicinity of the Greek Philological Society, Constantine had plenty of opportunities during his visits to take advantage of its many cultural offerings.

Pera, which means "beyond" in Greek, both literally and symbolically, was the more modern and European district of the city. To get there from Yeniköy one had to take a steamboat ferry to Eminönü and then cross the elegant bridge of Galata, with its prominent lampposts set along the iron railings. Approaching the dock, one observed the Topkapi Palace of the Sultans at the tip of the peninsula, and then the great monument of Hagia Sophia slightly to the left, the Sultan Ahmet Mosque behind a bit, and then a series of other mosques with their towering minarets to the right. A vivid description of the traffic on the Galata Bridge is offered by Edmondo De Amicis, an Italian writer whose popular travel book *Costantinopoli* (1878) captures the aura and ambience of the city, albeit with an Orientalist slant. Standing in Galata at the far end of the bridge, one could see the crowd coming "in great waves, each one of which is of a hundred colors, and every group of persons represents a new type of people . . . Behind a throng of Turkish porters who pass running, and bending under enormous burdens, advances a sedan-chair, inlaid with ivory and mother of pearl, and bearing an Armenian lady; and at either side of it a Bedouin wrapped in a white mantle and a Turk in a muslin turban and sky-blue caftan, beside whom canters a young Greek gentleman followed by his dragoman in embroidered vest."[28] Once in Galata, the chaos of life became intense: "The streets are almost all narrow and tortuous, bordered by taverns, pastry-cook shops, butchers' and barbers' shops . . . A dense and busy crowd throng the streets, constantly opening before carriages, porters, donkeys, and omnibuses."[29]

From here there was the uphill climb on the famous 118 cobbled steps—*ta skalakia*—or the narrow streets through Galata with its dominating tower built by the Genoese in 1348. Once arriving at the tower, it was easier to access Pera,[30] whose population was half foreign. Some eighty thousand Greeks lived there, a demographic similar to Alexandria's with its commercial and cultural diversity.[31] Here there were numerous cafés popular among non-Muslims, many of which were modeled on European establishments, a mixture of literary salons and social clubs that were frequented by intellectuals.[32] A city with distinguished and long traditions in Ottoman, Greek, Sephardic, and Armenian poetry, Istanbul allowed Constantine the opportunity to partake in conversations about literature and meet young men with similar interests that certainly would have been more exciting and diverse than what he had been used to back home. In the late nineteenth century, Istanbul was undergoing a period of literary effervescence. This was made possible thanks to the Tanzimat reform movement (1839–76), which attempted to modernize Ottoman society, politics, and culture. Greeks, Armenians, and Jews were instrumental in translating works of European literature into Ottoman Turkish and thereby introducing readers to the novel and the theater.[33] At this time, the Muslim and non-Muslim communities were much less separate politically and geographically. When Constantine arrived in Istanbul in 1882, he entered into a cosmopolitan literary culture blossoming in cafés, newspapers, literary societies, and publishing houses where communities of different languages shared "the same literary experiences."[34]

Yet despite Pera's European outlook, it had maintained its Ottoman character. "In the midst of Turkish houses, rise European palaces; behind the minaret stands the bell-tower; above the terrace, the dome; beside the dome, the battlement wall."[35] Although Ottoman leaders had hoped to undertake the same urban renewal that planners had introduced in Vienna along the Ringstrasse in the 1860s or in Rome in the 1880s, the empire, nearly bankrupt, could not afford such reconstructions. Hence, Istanbul never achieved the regular urban façade of these cities or the cosmopolitan aesthetic that postbombardment Alexandria itself would eventually acquire. Although neighborhoods were largely ethnically organized, built around mosques, churches, and synagogues, there was no profound "barrier" separating Europeans and Muslims as in Alexandria, a city divided into two sections. The capital of two great civilizations, the city had amassed swaths of different ethnic and religious groups, all living side by side, as dictated by the millet system of the Ottoman Empire.

The streets were narrow, of irregular width, and very crowded. Around the Golden Horn, the houses were "all of wood, painted in different colors, their upper stories projecting over the lower; and the windows protected in front by a sort of grated gallery, and closed by small wooden lattices, giving to the street a singular aspect of mystery and gloom" as described by De Amicis.[36] Pera, the cultural, business, and entertainment hub of the city—a place "proudly cosmopolitan"[37]—featured many structures built in the Classical Revival style in imitation of Paris. Neoclassical façades stood next to Ottoman-style edifices, making for a truly hybrid architectural aesthetic.

The European crowd here was different from that traversing the bridge of Galata: "Almost all wear stove-pipe hats and the ladies are crowned with plumed and flowery French bonnets. There are exquisites from Greece, from Italy, and France; merchants of high pretensions, attachés of the different legations, officers of foreign ships of war, ambassadorial coaches, and equivocal figures of every country." De Amicis's Orientalist description captures something of the stereotyped auras of the city's diverse population: "The Turk is motionless, and all his lineaments repose in a kind of quiet without thought, like that of a ruminating animal . . . The Greek on the contrary, is very mobile, and reveals in a thousand changing expressions of life and eye everything that is passing through his mind; he tosses his head with the movement of a spirited horse . . . his whole person betrays vanity and ambition."[38] Promenading past its monumental embassies, with their long, tended gardens guarded by tall iron gates, visitors stood before the elegant shops stocked with household articles, others selling European fabrics, and stores full of Parisian accessories for women.

Standing in grand opposition to Pera and Galata was Ottoman Stamboul, the old city, where the ruined relics of Byzantium beckoned. The ironies of history's master narratives about the rise and fall of empires were in full evidence here for Constantine to ponder and behold as he meandered through the city in search of its diminished Byzantine past and his family history. As the poet John Ash put it, "In Istanbul, it is hard to escape a recurring sense of loss: no civilization fought harder than the Byzantine to preserve the past for future generations, yet so much that was great in its own art and architecture has vanished."[39] Constantine felt this, as did many Greeks.[40] The city's famous land and sea walls, for one, were a thing of wonder, having protected Constantinople for over a thousand years. In various states of miraculous preservation and sublime ruin, replete with Greek inscriptions and enclosing Byzantine palaces, churches, monasteries, and even prisons, they were tragically demolished to accommodate the city's modern railway. Indeed, the Byzantine walls stand as a powerful metaphor for the city's past. Byron was so moved by them that he declared: "I never beheld a work of nature or art which yielded an impression like the prospect on each side from the Seven Towers to the end of the Golden Horn."[41] There were plenty of grand structures besides the imposing churches of Hagia Sophia, Saint Irene, and Saints Sergius and Bacchus, or the massive Aqueduct of Valens, for Constantine to visit and experience. In fact, there were roughly a dozen Byzantine religious and imperial monuments scattered throughout Stamboul. He had reason to frequent the old city given that the members of the Cavafy and Photiades family were connected to the church of Saint Constantine[42] located in the Samatya (Psomathia) section of the old city.[43] When attending church here to celebrate his name day on May 21, he could ponder the nearby Byzantine monastic church of the Stoudion, one of the empire's most revered institutions, where Theodore the Studite led his successful defense of religious images in the ninth century. The Stoudion was still standing in the 1880s, functioning as a mosque, as were the majority of these surviving Byzantine monuments.

These monuments were mostly from the Comnenian and Palaiologan periods (1081–1453), which is precisely the span of Byzantine history Constantine would focus on when he eventually wrote his poems on Byzantine themes. Indelible impressions were surely made by the more imposing of these buildings.[44] He had occasion to see the original edifice of the Church of Saint Theodore of Tyron / Vefa Kilise Camii, on which the Church of Saint Nicholas in Liverpool was based, adding a direct connection to his life back in England, where the world of Gothic Revival intersected with his latest exile to a city where he was to experience his own Byzantine reawakening. For a young man who was discovering his family's genealogy in this city, how poignant it must have felt to link these two churches and to conjoin the fate of his family with the span of Greek history, something that would become the hallmark of his poetry. Here amid all these transformed buildings, the trauma of cultural displacement was staring him full in the face as he wandered through the remains of a vanquished civilization. This sentiment of unjust misfortune will resurface and be distilled alchemically into one of his most poignant poems—"Of Colored Glass" (1925*)—which recounts late Byzantine decline:

One detail greatly moves me
from the Blachernai Palace coronation of John Kantakouzinos
and Irene Adronikou Asan.
Since they had only a few precious stones
(such was the poverty of our wretched state)
they wore fakes. An array of glass pieces,
red, green, or blue. For me there's nothing
humbling or undignified
in these little bits of colored glass. On the contrary,
they seem like a sorrowful protest
against the unjust fate of those two being crowned.
They're the symbols of what was befitting them,
what was above all right for them to have
at their coronation, a Lord John Kantakouzinos,
a Lady Irene Andronikou Asan.

Istanbul was unique in another important way in terms of its urban landscape: its late-antique and Byzantine monuments were physically present for Constantine to observe, rather than having to be evoked, as was the case in Alexandria, where virtually nothing survived from the Hellenistic past. Istanbul did not lend itself to metaphorical interpretations, at least not the ones Constantine would later develop in Alexandria. Its material culture, as manifested in its numerous monuments, allowed him to revisit history in ways different from the speculative search for the vanished Ptolemaic glories of Alexandria. Upon returning to the city of his birth, he would be forced to seek the past in imaginary underground tombs and in the veiled spaces of his apartment.

Culture, religion, and Hellenism were not the only attractions that Istanbul held for Constantine; the city's many hamams would have offered him opportunities for sexual adventures. Unfortunately, we have no direct evidence of his having visited any of these establishments. We have only one reference to his early sexuality in a series of interviews given by Rika Sengopoulos, who claimed that he had his first sexual encounters while residing in this city, without providing any more details.[45] It is very possible that a young man in his early twenties, unburdened by his family's prying eyes, would have diffidently ventured into these highly accessible places where sensuality and pleasure beckoned. Throughout the Ottoman Empire, the hamam served as a place where men could seek and find illicit erotic expression. At least during the early period of the empire, men could pay for male prostitutes, usually adolescent "unbearded" boys—a practice that was widely prevalent and perhaps even institutionally acceptable.[46] In later years, the hamams acquired a reputation for providing an eroticized, ambiguous space where men could meet in dark corners or special rooms.[47] The most famous hamam on the peninsula was the Cemberlitas Hamami; built in 1583, it remains one of the largest bathhouses in the city and one of the most frequently visited.[48] Although homosexual activities were denounced in Islamic moral and legal literature, "in practice very little was done to curb or inhibit them, provided they were done away from the public eye."[49] As long as male-to-male sex was confined to bathhouses or other private spaces (that is to say, not labeled publicly as "homosexual"), it was practiced freely.

Constantine never referred to sexual experiences in his correspondence with the friends who had returned to Alexandria after the British bombardment. He must have described enthusiastically his sojourns through Istanbul, so much so that Mikès Ralli wrote to him back in January 1885, complaining: "I cannot understand your strange infatuation in adoring C/ple as you do; very picturesque it may be, it may be beautiful to wander forth towards evening and take a walk by the silent Bosporus tinged by the setting sun; from Pera you may command a wide view to recall to your mind the doings of our brave and mighty ancestors" (letter dated January 11, 1885).[50] But Mikès wondered what else his friend could have been doing for two years, what other amusements he might have had. Constantine engaged in intellectually stimulating exchanges with his brother John and with Mikès, often seeking bibliographic information from them. He longed for his books and papers, all burned in Alexandria. Mikès asks, "What kind of books have you at your disposal now?" Acknowledging that the few books he took with him "must have been read by you over and over again," he asks if there are any "circulating libraries in Constantinople" (January 1, 1884).[51] "I suppose you will not take it on yourself to declare Con/ple a more civilized town than Alexandria," Mikès writes. Then he assures him that "we have something better to offer you than dry and dusty walks" (January 1, 1884).[52] Yet it was these dusty walks that solidified another aspect of Constantine's urban personality and fostered his assimilation of a great city's allure, with Istanbul now vying with London, Liverpool, and Alexandria for the budding poet's creative allegiance.

Although none of the many letters Constantine wrote from Istanbul to his friends or to his brother John survive, he began experimenting with prose and poetry during this period, making a commitment to writing in the Greek language when he surely could have embarked on a literary career in either English or French. The unpublished narrative "A Night Out in Kalinderi," composed in 1885 during his final year in the city and completed upon his return to Alexandria in 1886, records his intimate and intense engagement with Istanbul and its environs. This text, along with the poems "Nichori" and "Leaving Therapia," are the only documents we have about his actual stay in Istanbul. In a letter to his friend Pericles Anastasiades written sometime in 1896, Constantine identified "A Night Out in Kalinderi" as an "old article" and explained that he tried to experiment with the language, using a blend of the spoken tongue and formal written language.[53] The narrator of "A Night Out in Kalinderi," speaking in the first person, tells us that "Kalinderi" refers to the coast between Neochorion (Nichori in Greek, Yeniköy in Turkish) and Therapia, where the family stayed upon its arrival in Istanbul. Wanting to get some fresh air, the narrator takes a walk along the seaside road in the direction of a café. It being Saturday night, people around him are rushing about in preparation for Sunday: "The night was magical" and the full moon cast its silver glow upon the waters of the Bosporus while on the Asian side opposite him, the small white houses and minarets are all aglow. His soul was lifted up by the beauty of the landscape, and as he enters the café, he overhears conversations of the patrons before finding solitude in "the best part of the café" under the large branches of a tree. Taking two chairs for himself, he orders some coffee, "coffee that you can only find in the City," and spends two enchanting hours "marveling at the beautiful view which nature had unfolded" before him. The speaker is left speechless by the town, its location along the Bosporus, and its natural beauty. Lost in thought, he considers himself fortunate to be there and concludes that no matter how overcome one was with worry, one only needed to stroll in the outskirts of the "City" and amble along the coast to find some relief. "The Spirit of Byzantine Nature whispers to you 'God provides.'"[54]

"A Night Out in Kalinderi" is a hybrid text in many ways: a fictionalized version of a real night spent in a suburb of Istanbul; an attempt at Orientalism; a flâneur narrative in the tradition of Edgar Allan Poe's "The Man of the Crowd"; a foray into Greek folklore; and lastly, a melancholic meditation on mortality. This combination of themes and narrative modes barely holds together, but the overall result is a pastiche that captures the various intellectual currents pulling at Constantine as he returned to his life in Alexandria. Orientalist touches include the minarets on the Asian side of the Bosporus that seem like "a charming stage set of a magical theatre," the hookahs, the worry beads, and the coffeehouse with its idling habitués and aura of Greco-Ottoman languor. There is an added critique here of Western classical music, which is also deliberate: "The frigid music of the salon piano" that "agitates the nerves," clearly an attempt to establish parity for the Greek folk lament with which the piece climaxes. The narrator strikes a cosmopolitan/Eurocentric pose: the leisurely nonchalance of the self-possessed dandy who tosses off astute critical insights, particularly the mythological gloss he offers on the joyful waves of the Bosporus and the soothing quality of Byzantine nature. He refers to the myth of Europa in connection with the etymology of the Bosporus—indicating how influenced he was by the scholarly methods of the Philological Society and its publications, which abound in these sorts of erudite glosses. Eclipsing this reverie is the sudden eruption of melancholia. In this experimental work, we get a vivid and singular sense of how Constantine must have felt in Istanbul and what he processed from his experience in the city. At the very least, the story expresses the enthusiasm of a young man for the metropolitan landscape, its buildings, and its history. Unlike his mature poetry, where natural beauty is completely absent, here it seems to provide solace and transcendence.

Constantine expressed similar sentiments in the poem "Nichori" (1885), written either in Istanbul or after his return to Alexandria. Although he never published it, he preserved it, later clipping a note on the page with the following comments in English: "Not for publication; But may remain here," and then he added "as autobiographical." Although we don't know when he drafted the note, it seems likely that he did so during the period of "emendation" starting in the mid-nineties when he began to rethink his poetic achievements. Written in demotic without the katharevousa elements typical of other compositions from his twenties, it has an *abab* rhyming pattern, with the last word always being "Nichori." Like "A Night Out in Kalinderi," the poem extols the charms of Nichori but uses unoriginal language and metaphors to express the delight of the speaker:

Stranger, when you see a village where nature rejoices,
and by every plane tree a girl is hiding
beautiful as a rose—stop there, stranger,
for you have arrived at Nichori.

Subsequent lines praise the beauty of the town's walnut trees, cool springs, scents, green fields, the church of the Virgin Koumariotissa, and the Quay of Gregory. But Constantine would never return either to the place itself or to nature per se as a poetic topic. At the same time, he must have valued the poem for the memories it evoked of the village where his mother was born and where his family found refuge after their flight from Alexandria. And though his mother would complain about the family's economic difficulties at Nichori, Constantine at least found his stay there productive.

Constantine used this period to compose and revise his first works of criticism in anticipation of a possible career in journalism. He did not, however, have the confidence to publish these pieces. In his first attempt at literary criticism (written in English)—"What I Remember of My Essay on Christopulus"—he rewrites from memory a lost essay he had already drafted but left behind in Alexandria. It deals with the poet Athanasios Christopoulos (1772–1847), who wrote lyrical "anacreontic"[55] poems in demotic Greek. That Constantine composed his first prose essay on this poet shows his eagerness to engage with the current debate on language in philological publications and in the literary societies of Istanbul. This took on a heightened importance now that he was living in a place where people held inflexible and even fanatical opinions on the language issue (purist versus demotic). As an aspiring poet and intellectual, he had to decide—and quickly—in which mode he would write his verses and essays. This would indeed become a lifelong stylistic struggle with these two modes of modern Greek, one that he would ultimately solve by synthesizing both registers into his own poetic idiom.

Byzantine lore continued to inspire Constantine poetically. The historic imperial sites of "the City" came back to haunt him later in life when he composed his unfinished poem "From *The Secret History*" (1923), which presents a rather gothic episode from one of the most notorious Byzantine chronicles, Prokopios's *The Secret History*:

Quite often Justinian's look
induced horror and repulsion in his servants.
They suspected something that they never dared reveal;

by chance one night they ascertained
he was a demon from Hell,
slipping out of his bedchamber very late and circulating
headless in the palace halls.

A sixth-century historian, Prokopios recorded the achievements of the Byzantine emperor Justinian, who ruled the Eastern Roman Empire from 527 to 565. In this particular poem, Constantine, with his penchant for unconventional angles, focuses not on the emperor's vaunted imperial buildings, legal codifications, or military victories. He selects instead a scandalous anecdote from Prokopios, which in itself offers a haunted and slanderous exposé of palace intrigue and oppression. Constantine treats this incident with the utmost simplicity and directness, allowing its phantasmagorical content to come through without qualifying comment. As such, he presents a coded critique of the "great Justinian" from the pen of an accomplished court historian that speaks for itself and stands as legitimate palace gossip. This seemingly transparent poem reveals the ghostly presence of Byzantium in Constantine's poetry—its monuments, imperial rulers, and history—and his lifelong fixation on his family roots along the shores of the Bosporus.

3

FAMILY AFFAIRS

While in Istanbul, Constantine maintained regular communication with his brother John, who returned to Alexandria with Peter in August 1882 right after the bombardment. The closeness of Constantine and John in these early years is borne out by a cache of John's letters (Constantine's side of the correspondence has not survived). From these rich documents, written in English, it is clear that the brothers shared a genuine bond and possessed none of the Victorian aloofness later attributed to them by their niece Hariclia Valieri, who claimed that John had an extremely cold and puritanical disposition and that the brothers in general had few friends.[1] On the contrary, John's missives to Constantine are solicitous and affectionate, playful and defiant, despite being written during dire circumstances and amid the family's financial ruin. The following selected excerpts from these letters allow the brothers' intimacy to speak for itself. In a letter dated August 7, 1882,[2] John writes:

> My dear Constantine,
>
> I have just time to scribble these few lines in accordance with my promise to you before leaving. From my letter

to mother you will see that I am unable to execute your request given in your "Park and Grounds and royal residence and demesne in Cadikeuy." I sincerely feel for your loss. You cannot imagine what a sad sight the old house was to me when I saw it for the first time!—

But you must take courage and start afresh—you have a good memory, and the restoring of [an] old manuscript will be, comparatively speaking, an easy task to you. By next opportunity I will write you a lengthy letter; in the meanwhile pray send me a line when you have time.

With love to all
Your affectionate brother and fellow-sufferer
John

P.S. The papers I left in the office are safe—

The loss of personal possessions and the destruction of the family dwelling are acutely felt.

That his siblings were already sensitive to their youngest brother's precocious erudition may be seen in the tender tone of John's letter dated August 12, 1882,[3] where the lost papers are lamented over:

My dear Constantine,

I wrote yesterday to mother and aunt Ευβουλία [Evoulia], and as I have half an hour to spare, I will while it away in the pleasant labour of writing to my dear brother and Mentor . . . I trust you are all well and that you my dear Costi are slowly acclimatizing yourself to the loss of your papers—It is no use crying

> over spilt milk, and you must try and make up for lost time.

Frequently signing his letters "Johannisberg," John takes the leading role as a father figure here. We may infer from the shared tone that Constantine's letters were equally intimate and effusive in detail. In a letter dated September 17, 1882,[4] John notes his brother's interest in compiling a family tree and forecasts his brother's fame:

> Your genealogical notes are always interesting, and the genealogical tree, will be gladly received and duly appreciated by an unworthy descendant of the Imperial House of Ducas, which however will, in days to be, rise to greater eminence and renown through the labouring genius of Constantinus.
>
> I say this in earnest—for I feel confident that the day will come, when you will reap great advantages from the lore you have amassed, and use it to your benefit and fame.

In this same letter, we get a glimpse of the lessons of hardship the brothers were learning while they were waiting for the British to settle the indemnity claims that kept the family hanging on by a thread for years:

> How do I spend my Sundays? Much the same as other week-days. This for instance is a Sunday. I turned out of bed at six (since I left Constantinople I have become an early bird) and sat down at my little table to read the Weekly Times. At seven I began dressing and left the house at eight for church, where I remained till

about nine and whence I proceeded to the Office. Work till about noon, when I got your letters, read them and went to show them to Peter at the Intendance. Thence together we went to have something to eat, and returned home to lie down for an hour or so. The weather is exceedingly hot. As I write Mrs. Jones' hall-clock strikes 2, and although I am arrayed in [an] airy dress i.e. drawers and flannel-singlet the sweat comes gushing through every pore. When I finish this letter I intend to take a nap till three, then dress and sit down to work at a poem I have in hand, then go out for a stroll and then return to my room again to read and think, to think of you mostly, of you whose voice is ever ringing in my ears, and to wonder what the future has in store for us. God knows the day may be far distant yet when I shall see you again:—and so I creep to bed, and the fingers of the clock move round, and time goes on, and everything repeats itself.

David Copperfield and Martin Chuzzlewit are yours, most decidedly yours, and I only wish I had the means to supply you with more books. Poor boy, you must feel the want of books sorely, as I do myself.

Mamma's postscript to your letter is veracity itself.

I scarcely need assure you that I fully appreciate your communications and carefully preserve them.

The literary nature of these exchanges is striking (an extension of Constantine's tone and tenor in his "Epic"), with John behaving as the actual mentor in matters of language and taste.

Notes of uncertainty and ruin are alleviated by literary allusions to the novels of Dickens. He manages to show an endearing deference to the unmistakable talents of his younger brother, who has succumbed to a "literary depression," as we learn in this letter dated October 30, 1882:[5]

> My dear Constantine, I am unable to describe with what pleasure I take up my pen to write to you. I like to be perfectly quiet with your last letter at my left-hand-side, to write down "winged words" and bid them speed with what haste they may to reach you. When I get up on a Tuesday morning I say to myself, "this is my mail-day, I must write to the wise Constantinus", and so, during the whole day, I look forward to the still hours of night with intense enjoyment.
>
> [. . .]
>
> I am sorry to see your late literary depression, but no matter what happens I am confident that you will one day succeed, and succeed brilliantly.
>
> [. . .]
>
> Somehow or other little bits of dirt clog my pen every now and then, and create something like an oasis of ink—
>
> However it is time I should end and trouble you no longer to decipher these irregular characters.
>
> I love you dearly and am always
>
> Your faithful
>
> *Johannisberg*

Poems are shared, verses are exchanged, and recent books are both recommended and commented on:

[ALEXANDRIA] 20 NOVEMBER 1882
10 PM

My dear Constantinus,

I have just returned from a heavy day's work, and though somewhat fatigued, willingly sit down to answer your nice letter of the 12th which I received yesterday. I am glad you like the proem of my "Arabesque": it was written in a happy moment. I cannot, however, adopt your amendment of the last line, for I wish it to be clearly understood that the prologue is, virtually, an epilogue, and composed after the entire execution of the poem. Here is another extract.

[. . .]

Your extracts from our grandfather's notebook have much amused and interested me. The style is indeed quaint and strongly smacks of Biblical diction.

Έρως αλγοφόρος [Eros Algophoros[6]]—will do nicely—Thanks to thee, omniscient brother. Your quotation from Victor Hugo, I am well acquainted with, and so are you if I mistake not. I remember seeing it in the Misérables, where it is given as an epitome of the frame of mind of Marius after a vain search in the Luxembourg for Cosette.

The great master! When will there appear such another genius?

[. . .]

My fancy borrows the winged sandals of Hermes,—skims the waves, and, lighting at thy side, bids thee be of good cheer for the sake

Of your loving
Johannisberg[7]

Despite the grueling routine of having to earn a meager wage, John manages to show a rather resilient and defiant attitude, never compromising his aristocratic expectations for what might have been his due as the son of a wealthy merchant and a man of leisure, an attitude of entitlement that Constantine imbibed from his older siblings and would retain throughout his life. A stalwart Victorian work ethic is on full display in a letter dated November 27, 1882:[8]

> My dear Constantine,
>
> [. . .]
>
> You ask from me to send you "Periplus" and "Streams"[9] etc. I shall comply with your request next mail—Copying is dreary work, and I have very little time to myself. Were it not that I always expect to get on with Mr. Moss, I should really feel annoyed at the way I am overworked in the Office—Kneen has—so to speak—handed me over the entire correspondence of the firm; and this, besides my other work, is, on mail days especially, enough to drive one mad. Do not think I complain, for I hold as my first tenet that work—true, loyal work—whether written or active, is the one, true guide to peace of mind, and preservation from evil;—but unfortunately I am of those who, if it were possible to avert the necessity of work,—would sit moping and dreaming from early dawn to darkening night.—

The mild resentment of the new generation of Greek entrepreneurs is offset by discussions about Thackeray, Sand, and Dickens:

[ALEXANDRIA] 23 JANUARY 1883

My dear Constantine,

[. . .]

"Copy-book" is not the equivalent for the Greek "τετράδιον" [tetradion]. I would rather use "note-book" or "scribbling-book".

Thanks for your recommendation of Sand's Lelia. I am now reading Thackeray's Adventures of Philip, lent to me by Ambrose and which I believe you are acquainted with. I like it very much and begin to find out that Thackeray's style of writing is superior to Dickens! Better late than never. There is a sort of dry irony pervading the whole work which is very pleasant and alleviates the sorrow attached to the tragical phases of life therein described. The Shabby Genteel Story is also very amusing.[10]

The strain of living hand to mouth and feeling pressured to send money to Haricleia and the brothers in Istanbul were trying at times, despite John's fervent aim "to please and amuse my wise little Mentor,—to claim a brotherhood with his extensive knowledge and acute observation, is the only wish of his affectionate John" (February 13, 1883).[11] Constantine's letters to John must have contained many pleas for money and surely described their desperate plight in Istanbul. At the same time, they must have been equally indulgent and prolific in terms of their literary flourishes and lavish detail, since John notes on June 5, 1883:[12] "Your epistolary style is reaching the very climax of perfection." John appears to have been the self-sacrificing son and brother, spending precious money on his brother's reading needs.

Constantine's demands, apparently, betrayed a certain degree of insensitivity:

[ALEXANDRIA] 14 AUGUST 1883

My dear Constantine,

[. . .]

I note your postscript to mother's letter about subscribing to the Gentleman's Magazine. This I am doing: but, my dear little brother, do you think that I have not done so before because of any bad will? You perhaps forget that I keep myself on as little as I possibly can, and that some times 'tis hard work to continue and make the two ends meet.

You perhaps forget that the clothing I possess is very meagre; that it naturally wears out, and must either be replaced or repaired; that when you are sadly in want of some article of dress, you have to cut and economise, thus leaving but little to live upon.

Far be it from me to complain. There is nothing I dislike more than entering into such details about myself: and I should certainly never refer to them were it not to shew why I did not at once accede to your demand, and that it was not on account of disregard or oversight, but from the mere, actual want of means wherewith to do so.—

I enclose for your perusal Shelley's "Ode to the West Wind", the rare beauty of which I am sure you will appreciate. Haply you are already acquainted with it.—As regards my own efforts, they are, I am afraid, of a desultory nature, and this is much enhanced by the limited leisure I am able to claim.

Peter and Aristides join with me in tendering you their love—

Believe me ever, my dear Constantine,
Your affectionate brother[13]

This letter casts a long shadow forward to the eventual cooling of the two brothers' relations in the final years of John's life, initially over John's refusal to support Constantine's attempt to marry his friend and heir Alekos Sengopoulos to their niece Eleni (Alexander's daughter). Following John's death, Constantine would discover, much to his dismay, that he was left only a meager sum in his brother's will.[14]

In his letter of July 15, 1884,[15] John strikes a note of overt despair that must have resonated heavily with his brothers and mother, as they were all at the end of their "profitless and sorrowful" tether:

My dear Constantine,

I write to you in the quiet and solitude of my room at an hour far advanced in the night. I have been reading hard at my favourite mathematics, but even these now have lost the charm they had for me once. I feel sad, very sad, and everything appears to me profitless and sorrowful. I feel sad, I say, and mostly so when I think of the future, not for me individually but for those that are dear to me—Can it be possible that there is no joy, no ease in the world, or is it that we alone of all beings are debarred from a sense thereof? There is an evil influence in night, that somehow disappears with the rays of the sun, but tonight I feel more than ever dejected, tho' the beautiful Egyptian skies above me sparkle with a thousand stars. Looking at them a short while ago, I could not help thinking how strange a mockery it seems, that the myriad spheres above us, seemingly so tranquil, should watch over a world so rent with care and internecine strife.

The clouds of poetic dejection (John's Baudelairean attempt to channel the "poète maudit") do lift somewhat in the ensuing letter. Here he reestablishes his usual stoic tone, replete with the literary references and the poetic dalliance shared between the brothers where matters of style trump matters of depravation:

[ALEXANDRIA] 12TH AUGUST 1884

My dear Constantine,

Your greatly valued and endearing letter of the 1st only reached me yesterday, and has still further served to prove to me (if another proof were needed) the kindliness of your good heart, and the nobleness and rectitude of your sentiments. In all things I admire you, and the generosity of your character influences me,—as is always everywhere the case,—to higher and to better thoughts. In all sincerity I look to you as a wise Mentor, for you are wiser and more learned, than is generally the share of others to be at your age: and I am sadly impatient for that happy moment that will bring us two together. "Arcades ambo",—but in its better sense. And now 'tis an intense satisfaction to me to perceive in how masterly a fashion you wield the pen. Your English, as far as my poor knowledge admits of judging, is well-nigh faultless, and, above all things that which is most to be admired, you have style—"Le style c'est l'homme" says Voltaire, and your letters speak of your individuality thro' every line.[16]

Once arrangements for the indemnities are finalized (see chapter five for a full account of the British bombardment of Alexandria and the matter of the indemnities), we see the hope that reemerges and a sense of unity as the family reconstitutes itself—with a hint of fraying nerves as John laments his fallen state:

ALEXANDRIA 23RD AUGUST 1885
SUNDAY.

My dear Constantine,

Aristides has just received mother's letter of the 18th instant and I answer thereto in the name of all three. The Indemnities are now in course of payment, by order of nationalities, and there is little doubt we shall be paid next week, thus enabling us to send you the £140 by the mail of the 2nd September.

[. . .]

As far as the monthly remittance is concerned, I regret I shall be unable to send you at the end of this month the usual £10: I require this sum to furnish myself with many necessaries; such as shirts, flannels, drawers, socks, a suit of clothes, boots, a hat etc. Peter is in a like state of nudity, and he will keep this month what he usually sends you, to purchase an outfit. It is impossible to make clothing last for ever, nor is it decent to go about one's business "en guenilles". It appears strange to us how this has never crossed your minds; for surely you cannot think that £10 a month are sufficient for board and lodging and the replenishing of an empty wardrobe, and I will not do you the injustice to believe that you wish us to walk the streets like beggars.

These are truths,—unpleasant if you will,—but none the less truths, which must be told and met.

Give our sincere love to mother, Alexander and Paul,

and believe me dear Constantine,

Yours affectionately[17]

And in the final surviving letter from this period, we find a tone of remorse and an apology to the beleaguered mother for money-related misunderstandings:

[ALEXANDRIA] SUNDAY 6 SEPTEMBER 1885

My dear Constantine,

I received this morning mother's letter of the 31st August. I have gone thro' it carefully, and it has caused me much pain to detect, between the lines, an undercurrent of reproof.

[. . .]

I am well aware that you are much worse off than I am: none feels it more than I do: but how could I have acted in these three years otherwise than I have done? I shall look upon the £10 as so much money borrowed from the family, and I shall refund them as soon as possible.

I am sorely grieved that I should have unwittingly

offended our good mother, and I request you my dear Constantine, to tender her the sincere apologies of a son and a gentleman.

Due note is taken of mother's wishes about pillows and the furniture in general. I trust the £140 will have reached you safely.—

Mr. Moss is still here.

I am
Yours affectionately
John.[18]

P.S. Poor Pegasus has lost his wings and is now an eminently prosaic beast!

John's early letters chronicle a crucial juncture when the family was struggling to adapt to new economic, social, and intellectual circumstances. His mentoring pose as elder counsel to a younger brother included many facets: an emotional sentimentality, a stoic resilience, a determined resistance, and ultimately the desire to see the family reunited, which he managed to broker with the final processing of the indemnity remuneration. He counsels Constantine in matters of French and Greek translation, proper English pronunciation, British politics, poetic sentiment and craft, and family protocol. Among other things we learn that John published two poems in the British paper *Public Opinion*—"By the Rivers of Babylon" (1884) and "The Poetry of Song" (1885); and that Aristides took out a loan from the Schilizzi family to make ends meet. Constantine, we discover, suffered from a hernia, chilblains, and strained vision. Yet it was poetry and literature that kept these letters buoyant and allowed the brothers to transcend their otherwise miserable debt-ridden lives; they clung desperately to the remnants of their British culture, their erudition, tastes, and talents.

John's status as the senior family poet would not last for long. He brought out a self-published volume of his early poems between 1893 and 1896 titled *Early Verses by John C. Cavafy*, which manifests the brothers' artistic solidarity. A surviving copy of this book in the Benaki Museum archive includes supplementary handwritten material—additional poems by John himself and translations by John of two of Constantine's poems: a handwritten translated version of "Ode and Elegy of the Streets" and "My Walls"—a broadsheet incorporated into the back cover that serves as a highly ironic and telling addendum.[19] This was one of the first poems Constantine arranged to have printed and clearly John was proud of it. Yet it winds up inserted in the back of his own volume of printed poems, a gesture that signals brotherly approbation but also hints at sibling rivalry. John, it should be noted, was his brother's first translator—as will be discussed more thoroughly in chapter nine—and rendered sixty-three of his poems into English, although he failed to publish any of them. Here John effectively anthologizes his brother, enclosing him between the covers of his own volume, an act that may be viewed as supportive but also self-serving. The final verses of the poem offer an ironic self-referential comment on this curious document: "And yet I never heard the noise, the cry / of builders at their work;—when were they there?— / Out of the world they shut me unaware." Family bonds, such as they were, remained challenging for the youngest member of the "family council," who doubtless benefited from coddling but, at the same time, clearly suffered under the weight of fraternal patterns of authority.

Much like the fictional persona of the early unpublished harem poem "Dünya Güzeli" (1884)—Turkish for "the most beautiful woman in the world"—Haricleia Cavafy, after living a pampered life as the wife of a wealthy commercial merchant, had to adjust to the painful isolation of a widow. From early photos she seems to have possessed a pleasant but unremarkable appearance, though her beauty was overpraised by her adoring sons. She was the eldest of eight children (seven daughters and a son) and, judging from her surviving letters, possessed a fluent command of formal Greek—the solid bourgeois literacy common among young women of her class during this period.[20] By all accounts she was a doting mother, but vain and unhappy. She suffered a fatal stroke on her way to a photographer's studio to sit for her portrait, the culmination of what appear to have been recurring episodes of ministrokes and brain hemorrhages that would intensify later in life.[21] The regard the Cavafy brothers felt for her was reciprocated in kind by a woman who, although wretched thanks to her fallen social status, found some solace in expressing and showing her love for her children. Her surviving letters to her sons—all written in Greek—vividly convey both her maternal instincts and her tendencies to domineer and exaggerate.

Haricleia's character traits come through in a letter dated July 17, 1890,[22] to Constantine, who is away in Cairo for a few days. She expresses her dependence on her youngest son: "Yet, Thin One, without my baby I cannot live and I don't know what I'll do if ever you take a trip to Constantinople." "The Fat One," as he affectionately called her—not perhaps without a tinge of malice—was not above complaining about her reduced circumstances, as we discover in a later letter to Constantine dated December 9, 1896:[23] "Without money, my darling, life is not worth living, because one is denied all these wonderful things." In her letters written to John and Constantine during their 1897 trip to France and England, she becomes the stereotypical worrying mother. Wishing them a good stay, she makes playful use of the word "enjoy" by hybridizing it into a Greek verb—"να το enjoyεστε" (do enjoy)—and closes by asking, "My Johnny, kiss the thin one and he you" (letter dated May 8, 1897).[24] On May 21 she writes, "Your letters from Marseilles gave us great pleasure and entertained us, as Paul received the letter you wrote to him, my Costaki [Constantine], and we sent them to Alekos [Alexander] who says he will read them day and night until he knows them by heart."[25] One week later (May 28, 1897)[26] she writes to them in Paris: "If only Paris were inexpensive, how good the World would be! I'm happy that you're taking it all in; see what a bright thing the Bois [de Boulogne] is? . . . Costaki, when you go to the zoo, don't go too close to your friends the animals because sometimes they become aggressive. Make sure you eat well and a lot of Beef so you gain weight, my dear children, if only I were with you, my heart yearns more for England!! For me it seems like Home sweet Home."[27]

Constantine lived with his mother until her passing in 1899, an event that marked a major transition in his life; for only at the age of thirty-six was he finally free from her prying presence. Her death left him liberated but bereft. The detailed notes he kept chronicling her final years and ailing last days confirm the compassionate but sentimental postmortem comments he records in his 1903 Genealogical Prose Notes,[28] a manifestation of his Victorian obsession with documenting death, grief, and mourning.[29] Constantine fondly recalls that in her glory days, his mother was something of a social butterfly: "Alexandrian society soon recognized in Haricleia Cavafy the most beautiful woman of Alexandria"; during her visits to the Viceroy Said Pasha's "Europeanized court," she was "distinguished by the Viceroy who very often offered her his arm." After the family returned from England to Alexandria in 1877, "her life was by no means happy. None of her sons had success in life or became wealthy." Although "brave in adversity and dignified," she suffered from rapidly failing health and a very "trying twitching of the face" and, from 1889, "recurrences of attacks" that made her lose her powers of memory for hours on end.[30] The only change of pace she had from her life's monotony was spending "a few days at Cairo with her son Constantine towards the end of 1893."[31]

During the final years of her life, Haricleia lived with four of her sons—Alexander, Paul, John, and Constantine—all of whom were "eligible" bachelors.[32] Alexander eventually married Thelxiope Theodorou in 1901 and settled in Athens. The other three would remain single. One must give some credence to the opinion of the novelist and future Cavafy scholar Stratis Tsirkas that Paul, John, and Constantine remained bachelors largely because there were no suitable women from the old class of "first families" left for their mother to fix them up with.[33] For the homosexual brothers Paul and Constantine, the demands of a domineering and cloying mother surely allowed them to sidestep the living lie of married life. But the domestic situation in which these four men lived with their mother was far from harmonious. There were festering resentments and tensions, judging from Constantine's journal notes. The brothers felt the burden of having to accompany their mother socially to various places in Alexandria, as the following entry from his notes recording their visit to the San Stefano Casino vividly betrays:

> One Sunday, maybe in the month of November, she went to San Stefano with Paul. I was with Micky Ralli[34] and we stood conversing. Micky Ralli behaved very cordially towards her. Then we left her. The poor thing didn't complain; but it was terrible for her to know she

> was dependent on Paul and if Paul grew tired of her, there was no option for her. And he, in the end, put on a pouting face, showing her he was weary of being with her. Whenever I withdrew from her or avoided going out with her, the poor soul would give me a pained look. She never dared say anything, because she knew that her expectations were "anormales [not normal]." But her whole life was anormale, and either we adjusted to her anormalité, or she would die.[35]

Paul, it appears, could be quite uncharitable, resenting this "anormale" dependency more than did his other siblings, as it no doubt impinged on his social life: "She criticized Paul," Constantine writes, "for tiring of her, for showing it, as when he abandoned her at the Sporting Club and ran away from her, and when he speaks to her in the carriage and shows her how much she's aged."[36] On another occasion, Paul behaves with borderline cruelty:

> 2 February—Thursday—[. . .] During the afternoon—at tea I believe [. . .]—she put on a hat and asked Paul his opinion. Paul, who was sitting opposite me, told her it was ugly. She was annoyed. When Paul left, the poor thing stood up—she seemed quite agitated that day—before the mirror that hung above the long couch she looked in the glass and asked me if it really was ugly. I told her it was lovely. [. . .] And she added, "What can I do—I made it myself."[37]

Alexander could also be impatient and abrasive, especially in regard to the family's living arrangements, wishing to move to more comfortable quarters despite his mother's objections, which, in the end, overruled his. Haricleia suffered greatly during these protracted exchanges regarding the family's prospective move.

There were more tender occasions, of course, and we learn that Haricleia and her youngest son enjoyed domestic moments and even had compatible reading tastes:

> In the evening stories were told and she enjoyed them very much. She was very interested and when one story finished, she often took two cookies and put jam between them and ate them and she called them her "pastizzeria." Of late she had been crazy about pastries, but she never bought any in order to save money, to put aside money in order to leave it to me. Fat One! One evening, I relayed to her the story of Mary Stuart. I was reading [James] Froude's History [of England] at the time. Thus sometimes we'd stay up until 10:30 p.m.[38]

One evening, Constantine read to her from Honoré de Balzac's novella *Le Bal de Sceaux* (*The Ball at Sceaux*) about a young woman, Émilie de Fontaine, who refuses to marry any of her young suitors because they are not aristocrats, including the cloth merchant Maximilien, whom she meets at the village of Sceaux:

> On Sunday 15 January . . . The Fat One returned early, according to her custom and after she undressed and sat in her armchair near the long couch, I narrated to her the stories of Balzac. The story of "[Le] Bal de Sceaux"[39] and of **** who loved a woman. She became enthusiastic, the Fat One. "How well you narrate" she said. And she said that it had been years since she passed such a pleasant evening.[40]

Of all her sons, Constantine was closest to her. He often stayed awake at night during her bouts of illness, "worrying about her death." He would tiptoe to her door to make sure she was still breathing despite John's protestations not to disturb her.[41] He showed this same concern during Paul's trip to London in 1898. While the brothers were descending to the Alexandrian quay to send Paul off, Constantine's thoughts ran back to their mother crying at home alone. So he decided to return home and check on her. Although his brothers tried to dissuade him from going back, he took a cab, despite the added expense, and stayed with her for about fifteen minutes. After reassuring himself that she was fine, he rejoined his brothers to bid Paul farewell.[42]

At the same time, he felt remorse for not being sufficiently considerate toward Haricleia, such as not always reading Paul's letters to her from abroad when she was not able to read them by herself. He also felt ashamed for not accompanying her more often on excursions out of the house, something that gave her pleasure: "My guilt of conscience is horrible . . . I avoided taking her out. It seemed ridiculous for us to be together. I, like a child, a man 34 years old, with my mother."[43] Constantine is his most honest and most confessional in these pages. It pained him that Haricleia could not go on trips for financial reasons, and even more so to find out that she was in fact saving money for him. Indeed, she continued to support him financially until her death.

Not surprisingly, money remained a flash point, in particular the question of the meager inheritance Haricleia would leave her boys:

> 31 December she gave me the regular New Year's gift. 3 lira the poor thing. Once she gave me 2, the last years she made them 3. The poor thing. She gave them to me in such a fine manner. I had given her some perfume as

> usual. What a sacred thing the maternal instinct is, though. She was the most frugal woman—made that way by her circumstances, afraid she'd be left on the streets. And despite this, with what ease she gave me the 3 lira. Three lira for her was a great sum. It's true that she knew me to be very good with money and that she expected the sum to remain unspent. But in the end she didn't have full assurance of this because I hid the amount of my finances from her.[44]

Yet Constantine never hesitated to ask for financial assistance: "I needed furniture, some dinners I hinted—I was young."[45] When he made these "hints," she reacted bitterly, saying that only he of her sons wanted her to spend money. Despite her protestation, however, she decided to leave almost all her possessions to him:

> And if she did die! Her will was entirely made out to me—she wouldn't be persuaded by anything I could have done. Because those diamonds she left to the others she hadn't meant to leave them. It was after a day when Paul's demeanor made her think that maybe he wouldn't honor the will, when she decided to leave him things so as to propitiate him. And then, in the name of fairness, she left things to the others, rewriting her will.[46]

In Haricleia's final months, she was increasingly afraid to remain alone and evidently knew that her days were numbered: "She said she would wait for Paul to return [from Europe] before she died."[47] During one of her episodes of delirium, she began speaking in broken Italian: "She had gotten up from her bed and with a terrifying plea she said 'Tsayette il bianco,'"[48] apparently requesting them to light a candle. Constantine felt pangs of guilt over his conflicted emotions, denying to himself that he ever wished her dead, perhaps anticipating the effects of her carefully articulated comment to her family: "Costis will be the only one who will cry for me when I die."[49]

Haricleia died on February 4, 1899. On the morning of her death, she suffered a stroke, and when Constantine came home at 1:00 p.m., he found her unconscious. She was given an impressive funeral, the details of which were duly recorded by her youngest son. This list of funereal expenses, her photos, letters, a recipe book, and a journal recording her social visits constitute the material archive that Constantine would save and safeguard in her memory.

In his Genealogical Prose Notes, Constantine records some direct thoughts about his older siblings, the few familial feelings he ever expressed on this subject.[50] George and Peter—the two eldest—remained remote presences in his life. They were responsible for the mismanagement and ruin of the family's business prospects. About George he notes somewhat sympathetically that "during his youth he was led astray by the temptations of London and engaged in unhappy speculating which proved his ruin and contributed to the speedy liquidation of the firm."[51] Peter, who was "kindhearted," shares the blame for engaging in faulty speculation in bonds and sugar, and is pitied for having to work later in Alexandria for a paltry wage, feeling this "acute humiliation" with much bitterness.[52] Of Aristides he offers a more detailed portrait: "Aristides was of middling size. He became early bald. He was handsome, at least he was much loved by women of the demi-monde. He was kindly and obliging, and very active . . . He was a very good father to his little girl."[53] Aristides was the one brother who made an advantageous marriage; his wife, Marie Vouros, came from a wealthy family: her mother, a Rodocanachi, was connected to the London Greek community. It appears that the marriage was one of social and economic convenience, as is borne out by an episode that rocked and nearly disgraced the Cavafy family. In August 1889, a debt-ridden Aristides left his wife and decamped to Marseilles and then Lyon, taking with him a sum of eighty pounds and writing to his brother-in-law Dimitris for an additional ninety pounds after confessing to having lost his wife's dowry. His excuse for these financial and behavioral improprieties was a nervous breakdown allegedly brought on by the stress of speculating for cotton shares on the Bourse. The real reason, based on interviews with Aristides's daughter Hariclia Valieri, appears to have been sexual in nature, with Marie refusing to consummate the marriage owing to shyness, fear, or sexual incompatibility.[54] In any event, in addition to causing emotional grief to both families, Aristides was in violation of the law. The letters exchanged between the brothers betray how dire the situation was.

Curiously, it was Constantine who was charged with the task of writing to Aristides and urging him to return to his wife. On September 23, 1889, in consultation with his brothers, he drafts an encouraging letter gently urging his brother to become once again the "first Aristides" and assuring him that all would be forgiven when he came home.[55] The siblings even edit the explanatory letter to Marie that Aristides had sent them, returning it to him with suggested excisions and directing him to rewrite it with less emphasis on health matters. The family is clearly concerned about the legal ramifications of what John bluntly terms a "misleading and premeditated" act, one that would "ruin the family" (letter dated September 6, 1889).[56] Under British law, John notes, "divorce, criminal prosecution, and arrest for absconding and abandoning his wife" await him if he refuses to return. Aristides delayed his return, asking for money to be sent to France, prompting Constantine to write with ire that his behavior was incomprehensible and telling him to sell his personal possessions if necessary; the family was too broke to bail him out any further (letter dated October 14, 1889).[57] After hydrotherapy sessions ("traitement hydrothérapique"), Aristides eventually came home to his wife in January 1890, legal charges were dropped, and peace was restored.

Notwithstanding this familial contretemps, Constantine enjoyed an artistic relationship with Aristides, similar to the one he shared with John. This is demonstrated in Aristides's *Album de Dessins* (Drawing Album). Aristides was clearly supportive of his younger brother's talents, as is evident from the presence of four early Cavafy poems in this book, which Aristides illustrated most lavishly and attentively: "Dünya Güzeli," "When, My Friends, I Was in Love," "The Blooms of May" (later renamed "The Elegy of the Flowers"), and "Vain, Vain Love." The illustrations of the poem "Vain, Vain Love," an adaptation of a Scottish ballad, "Auld Robin Gray" by Lady Anne Barnard, are noteworthy in that they narrate the rather sentimental subject matter of the poem—the thwarted passion of two star-crossed lovers. The album also contains two poems by John as well as the printed broadsheet of John's translation of "My Walls." Here we have a similar instance of brotherly intertextuality, as it were—fraternal bonding through art. Like John's album of verses, Aristides's book is a unique volume, and a fine edition in its own right. It is literally an example of what historians of the book term "the art of the book," covered as it is with expensive leather, embossed with gilt lettering, and executed on high-quality paper. Although it is a personal scrapbook, it falls into the category of a deluxe edition, even approximating an illuminated manuscript, in which Constantine's poems are given a pictorial treatment that anticipates the lavish first edition of the poems produced by Rika and Alekos Sengopoulos in 1935, which are accompanied by the decorative calligraphic illustrations of Takis Kalmouchos. Aristides's album reveals his remarkable versatility as a draftsman, including as it does clever caricatures, one of a conductor and one of an office clerk. Both John's edition of his *Early Verses* and Aristides's *Album de Dessins* demonstrate the artistic solidarity of the Cavafy brothers. There was clearly much artistic talent in the family. Unlike their many contemporaries, who thrived in the world of commerce, these young men did not easily fit this mold. In giving expression to their aesthetic talents, they showed perhaps that their minds and hearts were not devoted to trading in cotton and grain, the business that had brought their father to Alexandria.

Paul Cavafy held a similar view of himself as a talented sibling, although in many ways he came to be seen as the black sheep of the family. His letters are another rich batch of documents that allow us a glimpse into the emotional and artistic dynamics of the family. Paul was reputedly homosexual,[58] a bon vivant who enjoyed the high life but sadly ended his days as an exiled reprobate. From his extant papers kept by Constantine (the brothers lived together for many years following Haricleia's death) and Paul's own scrapbook, we see that he led a full social life in Alexandria. He was fond of traveling and departed Alexandria abruptly in 1908, most likely fleeing creditors and scandal. He apparently planned to take an early retirement the following year from his position with the Alexandrian municipality—his official title was "Chief Inspector of the Scavenging and Plantations Departments." Back in 1898, we find him traveling in England, allegedly on business and to visit family. His letters are as warm and effusive as John's and betray a nostalgia for the dandified life that had slipped away from him. In this sense, he sets the mold for his younger brother who, once Haricleia dies, will follow in these hedonistic footsteps, although with less recklessness. In a letter dated July 4–6, 1898, and written in Greek to both Haricleia and Constantine, Paul brings up the curious topic of his bad name: "I received, dear Kosti, the two words you wrote me. I'm very sorry about your glasses. I assure you it wasn't my fault. I gave him your sample and he looked at them in front of me and then found four others. If they don't suit you send them back . . . You didn't send me the *Reforme*,[59] my Kosti—why not? Is it because they are writing nasty things about me—and you don't want that I should make bad blood? Don't worry."[60]

In a subsequent section of this letter dated July 6, 1898, Paul recounts his experiences at the Henley Regatta: "The weather here is bright and my health is bright as well. How I think about you mother in the heat. I donned my smart gray suit, my straw hat, and I'm going to take the train to Henley to see what I assume will be another wonderful sight—the Henley Regatta is one of the events of the season . . . I assure you I enjoy [εντζοῦρω/enjoyiro] London more than even an Englishman could." Here we should note the conversion of the English verb "enjoy" into a Greek verb, as we saw previously with Haricleia—what John will call their hybrid "baragouin" or gibberish.[61] The reiterated trope of savoring family letters is articulated by Paul as well: "Dear Mother, what joy your writing brings to me, with what relish I read your letters two and three times" (July 7–8, 1898);[62] "Kostaki's letter gives me such joy—that writing style of his—what a bright boy he is and how I love him" (August 26, 1898).[63] Paul's letters reveal none of his caddish behavior toward his mother that Constantine recorded in his diary. He was certainly beloved of Haricleia, and being removed from her cloying domesticity allowed him to perform the role of the doting son. This may be seen in the intimate fashion advice he gives her in a letter dated July 7, 1898:[64]

> I see what you write me about your *commis[s]iones*—I regret to tell you, mother, that I went everywhere and looked, and they only had new things . . . Why do you write so despondently about your toilettes[?] You should see the finery the women here deck themselves out in—and you, what do your toilettes have, they are always fine, and I'm sure that if you were here you would make an incredible impression—because, although they dress expensively [here], only nature can bestow that sort of elegance.—And why shouldn't you hold a white parasol? . . . White parasols are for ladies, not girls . . . It pains me to see you write this way. When I return, I'll have to give you some life and brighten you up. You have no idea, mother, how much I love you, last night I dreamt of you again.

Their nasty exchange over the ugly hat and the numerous social vexations seems to be in the past and have been conveniently forgotten.[65]

When read against the letters that Paul sends later in life while living in France, abroad once again but this time in semi-disgraced exile, we get a fuller sense of how these early vulnerabilities and repressed fears of failure would return to haunt the family.[66] Given that Paul and Constantine were housemates prior to Paul's permanent relocation to France, we can assume that they shared a certain intimacy, including knowledge of their sexual preferences.[67] Upon leaving Alexandria, Paul eventually took up residency in the resort town of Hyères on the French Riviera, barely subsisting on his modest pension. He corresponded regularly with John and Constantine, and his letters are truly extraordinary as chronicles of a dissolute life of poverty and despair. A few choice excerpts give a sense of the person whose plight is best described in the opening line of Constantine's poem "Days of 1896" (1925/1927): "He was completely degraded." Owing to bureaucratic complications over receiving his meager pension payments, Paul was without money or means of subsistence. In letters written in Greek from late 1908 to early 1909, he sought help from his brothers. He reminded them of their closeness—"We are only three—and three with one heart and if one errs, the others can't abandon him—because three are one."[68] He begged them to send money, as he was ill, "absolutely starving,"[69] and shamefully admitted to being an "object of consternation and disgust" for his brothers,[70] repeatedly imploring them to save him. He feared insanity and debtors' prison, and compared himself to the "wandering Jew."[71] Upon receiving money from his brothers, he spent it in Paris, where, after what appears to be a bout of reckless touring, he found himself destitute once again, starving, and begging on the streets for charity.[72]

Eventually his pension payments came through and he managed to rebound by taking a position as a private secretary to a retired, frail, and nearly blind eighty-six-year-old British officer. General William de Horsey, despite his physical handicaps, proved to be a godsend for Paul not only owing to the salary and room and board he provided—Paul lived at his bastide manor house in the adjacent coastal town of Almanarre—but also for his social connections: "He's an old aristocrat—related to the exclusive British families, from the era of our father—who knew . . . Théophile Gautier, Bulwer Lytton . . . his conversation is delightful. He has travelled all over the world, been invited to all the royal courts, and knows the Prince of Wales."[73]

Like his younger brothers John and Constantine, Paul viewed himself as a littérateur, harboring thwarted ambitions of becoming a playwright.[74] In Hyères, he supplemented his income by writing for local newspapers, showing his flair for language and talent for hobnobbing. In an engaging society column composed for *The Riviera News* (the "Journal of Anglo-Saxon Society in the Riviera"), dated December 18, 1910, and titled "Letters to Jack," we get a sense of his voice and style. Signed "Prince Paul,"[75] the letter is an urban narrative addressed to an imaginary old man. The column begins by refusing to conform to the expected high-society reporting on the "who's who" of the resort town's social elite:

> I can give you no thrilling account of the movements out here of: Royal or Serene Highnesses; Exiled Crown Heads; Distinguished Exotics; Poets seeking inspirations in woods and orange groves; Dramatists studying problems of humanity at the Gambling Tables; Millionaires ignorant of the amount of their wealth throwing away gold and notes in such absurd fashion as to make one positively sick; Members of Aristocracy and old Nobility with rather a spirit of economy; Parliamentary Swells; Men and Women of the Day; Actors and Actresses of universal repute and mature years; Professional Beauties firmly resolved to remain so, if only for the benefit and admiration of subscribers to the illustrated papers which produce at regular periods artistic "get ups" of their enduring "never say die" beauty; People notorious in Divorce or Bankruptcy Courts; Sweet smiling naughty-looking, carmine-lipped, crayon-eyed, tight-robed, huge-hatted, ex-

> pensive personalities of the Half World, renowned as a rule for ropes of pearls, blue or pink diamonds, and other such wonderful and unique jewel possessions which they simply adore to exhibit on every possible occasion and encourage crime; and all the rest of lesser magnitude perhaps but not less personal importance; some being inventors of:—tooth washes, tie clips, baby food, invalid couches, so on and so on; others having defied nature by transforming the obese into lean and the lean into plump, covering heads as bald as ivory balls with Samsonian locks, so on and so on.[76]

Prince Paul goes on to note and praise French charitable institutions, the "crèche" day-care nurseries that look after the children of the working class, the soup kitchens that feed the poor, the town's quaint door knockers, the lovely weather, and the friendliness of the shopkeepers. His eye for detail led him to publish a guidebook of the town in 1913 and to be approached by local businessmen to start his own newspaper—a project that never came to fruition.[77]

Paul's artful letters to his brothers are punctuated with affectation, a conflicted snobbery, a vanity-laden self-pity, open self-reproach, and nostalgia for his family. He is conscious of aging, suffers from hair loss, and is plagued by fistulas. One interesting detail buried within these documents is his request for his multivolume diary that chronicles thirty years of his life and that Constantine dutifully sent him in 1914. Recorded in these personal books (now lost) are passages from letters Constantine had written during the sojourn in Istanbul—presumably copies of the entries of the "Constantinopoliad." Paul expresses his rediscovery of these in language that echoes the fraternal pride of shared family talent: "What subtle wit, what style, what knowledge—and you were only 16 years old."[78] (Constantine was actually nineteen at the time.) Paul goes on to note his brother's superiority to the intellectuals he's met in France and laments that Constantine remains unappreciated in Egypt. Curiously missing from these exchanges with Paul is any mention of his brother's poetry, which leads one to wonder if perhaps Paul was deliberately minimizing the growing fame of his younger brother or perhaps remained truly oblivious to it. At one point, he confides to John that Constantine had ceased to write to him and fears that he has displeased Costi, asking, "Involuntarily, have I, perhaps, written something which could have vexed him?"[79] The ostensible cause of this breakdown in communication was likely Paul's relentless requests for money, chronic complaining, and excessive need for emotional support; quite conceivably it also could have been his self-absorbed inability to inquire into his brother's literary pursuits, especially when Constantine himself was fixated on orchestrating his own literary fame.

Paul corresponded with John and Constantine up through the final days of his life; he died in 1920. The brothers shared a collective awareness that age and death were taking their toll on the family. Three final extant letters from John to Constantine (one written in 1908 and two in 1920) reveal a less playful and more somber tone that qualifies the intimacy of the brothers. The first letter, dated July 12, 1908,[80] begins in Greek but includes English, concluding with a curious postscript comment (mostly in Greek) on how Greek, their "supposed language," when combined with English, lapses into baragouin: "P.S. Adding to all our tribulations, my Kosti—is that terrible 'baragouin,' our supposed language. I don't know it. To you only do I attempt to write in it. The letters wear me out and drive me to despair, and the silly accents, etc., and so much other silliness."

In later years, John gives in to a sort of dark depression, and a heavy Victorian tone pervades, manifesting itself as self-grieving—the return of the repressed anxieties of earlier years and the repetition of pride for his brother's own accomplishments:

HELOUAN 24.1.'20,
Σάββατο, 9 μμ. [Saturday, 9 P.M.]

Αγαπητέ μου Κωστή, [My dear Costi,]

[. . .]

Όσο για την υγεία μου, τι να πω; αισθάνομαι [As far as my health is concerned, what can I say? I feel] miserable both physically and morally. "A man's soul is sometime wont to bring him tidings",—and my soul announces that my life is over and finished, and what appalls me is the meagre result I have to show for the many years I have lived. . . . But don't let me sadden you: you are my brother, and that is no small thing, for I am proud of you and of your work, and I do my best to make the value of that work known among my small circle of English-speaking acquaintances.[81]

And in a subsequent letter, John comforts Constantine for Paul's sorry demise at Hyères, which clearly constitutes a blight on the family honor:

[HELOUAN] 6/2/20

My dear Costi

My telegram of this afternoon will, I am sorry to think, have horribly upset you. The news of poor Paul's death

> has been a severe shock for me and I am feeling it very acutely. The more so because I fear that I have not done for him all that I might to help him in his days of penury and suffering. I send you the telegram itself of the British consul at Hyères which did not come into my possession until about two o'clock this afternoon. [. . .] The urgent thing that appears to me to be incumbent on you and me to do is to make the best decent arrangements we can in respect of burial ground and tombstone: [. . .] Bear up, my dear Costi, there are only the two of us left now.
>
> Ever yours affectionately
>
> *John*[82]

Constantine held John in the very highest regard, as expressed in the entry he recorded in English about him in the Genealogical Prose Notes: "Of great integrity, presented the rare combination of great acquaintance in business and great acquaintance in letters. A man deserving of a much higher position than the one to which he was limited by adverse circumstances and the ungratefulness and meanness by which his toil were repaid by those who profited by it. Certainly the finest character that the writer has met with in the family's record. Most disinterested, most straightforward, most manly, most enlightened."[83] There are many shared traits here, and to a large degree, these comments could well be applied to the poet himself, so deeply were the brothers affected by "adverse circumstances" and suffered from the "ungratefulness and meanness" that besot them as fallen members of Alexandria's commercial elite. These sentiments, coming from a member of the "family council,"[84] betray the poignant and profound sense of loss and sorrow connecting the brothers.

After John's death in 1923, Constantine would be the last surviving member of the family. He hoarded his memories, partly out of grief, partly because they stimulated his artistic process and induced poetic reverie. One of the most commented-on aspects of the poet's rooms was the way they seemed to be repositories of his family heirlooms and memorabilia. His friend Atanasio Catraro remembers a framed photograph of Haricleia on the wall, balanced by a framed plaster engraving of the Empress Theodora,[85] a pairing that makes perfect sense when one considers how female abjection features in his poems of Byzantine empresses and imperial women. This attests to the image of the abject mother that he carried within. Another account mentions that Constantine had a pair of his mother's red velvet plumed slippers, which he supposedly caressed when in need of poetic inspiration.[86] However one wishes to interpret these physical details, there is no denying the lingering presence of his mother and brothers, the collective "family council" that haunted his memories and inspired his poems. In his final decade, Constantine concentrated his energy on managing his reputation, in effect assuring himself that through him, his family's name would live on. In the process, he engaged directly with each of his brothers: he became the family poet, thus succeeding John; his refined pictorial poetics excelled Aristides's painterly eye; and he outpaced Paul the flâneur by taking up their shared urban and erotic interests, alchemically converting them into verse. This is a complex web of fraternal sympathies, to say the least. Perhaps like the anxious voice in that early poem "Builders," Constantine feared that his own "progress" might ruin the loss, suffering, and pain of those who came before him. He walked a perilous line, fearful that his poetic toil might be undone by its very perfection. The "approbation" of his brothers—to use one of his favorite words—spurred him on to build the "great structure" of his poetic canon—his 154 stones, as it were—even though he lived in constant dread that some whirlwind of criticism or a sudden torrent of competition from a rival poet might bring it all crashing down.

Although Constantine managed to promote and perfect his artistic reputation, he was not able to prevent his family from falling into destitution, as is borne out in a letter written by his niece Hariclia Valieri (Aristides's daughter) to a distant relative in Alexandria in January 1972.[87] This document closes out the narrative of the family's fallen fortunes. Much like her uncle Paul,[88] Hariclia found herself broke in the final decades of her life, seeking the charity of her relations. She was one of three persons named in the poet's 1923 will—the other two were Alexander's daughter Eleni Coletti and Alekos Sengopoulos, who was appointed chief heir and became his literary executor. Although her inheritance was a mere two hundred Egyptian pounds, Hariclia was beloved of Constantine and a favorite niece. Her marriage to Geronymo-Georgio Valieri, a member of an aristocratic Greco-Venetian family, delighted her uncle, who relished a connection to a noble clan—she in fact held the title of contessa. Along with jewelry, Hariclia inherited a considerable fortune both from her mother's Vouros relatives and from her uncle John Cavafy, with whom she and her mother lived during the final years of his life.[89] She used her inheritance to travel widely and in high style from 1923 to 1947 but wound up living in poverty during her last fifteen years in the run-down hotel ironically named Megali Vrettania (Grande Bretagne) on the island of Mytilene:[90]

MYTILENE, GREECE
13 JANUARY 1972

Dear Sir,

I've long hesitated to write you despite having learned that you were part of the Vouros family, of which I am the last descendant of the Alexandria branch, and whose cousins owned a large home on Place de la Constitution.

Before continuing this letter that will undoubtedly surprise you, I must tell you that my mother was Maria Vouros, daughter of George Vouros and Julia Rodocanachi, and my father was Aristides Cavafy, brother of Constantine Cavafy, and that I am also the last remaining descendant of this family.

I must now reveal the exceptional circumstances that, I think, justify the reason why I am writing to you, though you do not know me. My purpose is to beseech you to use your influence with the Department of Public Works so that, given these exceptional circumstances, I can be granted a pension that would allow me to live. A few years ago in Athens, at 72 years of age and with a weakened heart, I had to undergo a serious operation.

Having lost my entire fortune, I continued to work as a French and English tutor to make ends meet. But at this point in time, I am now 75 years old, my heart condition is worsening, and my physical strength is waning—I don't know where else to get support or help. I've sold my jewelry and all of my family heirlooms and no longer have close family to whom I can turn.

If I hadn't reached this absolute state of debility, and weren't truly at the end of my rope, please know that I would not have allowed myself to disturb you. I must also beg forgiveness to have written to you in French, but having always lived abroad, my knowledge of my native language is not extensive enough to write to you in it.

I don't need to tell you that if you can help and intervene judiciously on my behalf, I would be infinitely grateful. You have my sincere best wishes,

Hariclia Valieri[91]

This poignant letter is the last document ever written by a member of the immediate Cavafy clan. Although the Cavafys experienced decline right after the death of Peter John, they were still able to live well and maintain their social connections to Alexandria's bankers and cotton barons. And Constantine himself managed to keep many family heirlooms as mementos of their once-illustrious past. Yet here was his niece having to sell his mother's jewels to survive. Perhaps Constantine foresaw his niece's humiliating act in the poem "Of Colored Glass" (1925*), which deals with the wedding ceremony of John Kantakouzinos, the Byzantine emperor who, because of the poverty of the empire, had no crown jewels during the coronation ceremony and had to use glass baubles instead. "For me," the speaker says, "there's nothing / humbling or undignified / in these little bits of colored glass." Rather they represent a "sorrowful protest" against "unjust fate."

Hariclia would live another eleven years and retain a positive outlook, despite her circumstances. In an interview given on February 8, 1983 (she died a month later on March 5), she made the following rather remarkable confession about living a rich and fulfilling life full of travel and cosmopolitan delight:[92] "All these rich memories accompany me from then to today—here to these dire straits—and for me they constitute true happiness."

Part II

ALEXANDRIA: THE DREAMSCAPE

4

CONSTANTINE'S WORLD

"BY THE HOUSE" (1917/1919)

Strolling yesterday through a neighborhood
on the outskirts of town, I paused by the house
I had frequented when I was very young;
where Eros with his extraordinary power
had taken hold of my body.

And yesterday,
as I passed by the old street,
the shops, sidewalks, the stones,
the walls, balconies, and windows
suddenly turned lovely under the enchantment
of Eros;
all ugliness vanished.

And as I stood and studied the door,
standing and hesitating by the house
my whole body radiated
all the sensual feeling buried in me.

The city Constantine wrote about was a territory of infinite expansion experienced through dreams, recollections, and aesthetic re-creations, very much like the poem cited above. Constantine's real Alexandria, however, was limited to the radius of the fifteen-minute walk from his apartment to his office. Everything he needed could be easily reached on foot. It would have taken him ten to fifteen minutes to arrive at the Office of the Irrigation Service, his place of employment from 1892 until 1922. From Rue Lepsius, he would turn right onto Salah Mostafa and then left on Al Lewaa Abd Fatah Al Hadari to reach the grand building on the Corniche—what is now the Metropole Hotel.[1] The offices were located on the upper floors, above the Grand Trianon patisserie and restaurant, which still exists today. Upon reaching this building, he could have taken the splendid, circular staircase with its ornate iron railings, or used the small elevator. Because he often arrived late, Constantine preferred to climb the stairs and thus avoid seeing his coworkers or supervisors in the elevator. His servant would even come to the office for instructions on what to cook or to show him a chicken purchased for dinner.[2]

His colleague Ibrahim el Kayar said that, to arrive on time at the office, Constantine on occasion took a carriage despite the short distance from his house. Although he was supposed to start at 8:00 a.m. and stay till 1:30 p.m., he often appeared at 9:30. And he instructed his assistants to make alibis: "If the Englishman comes before me and asks where Mr. Cavafy is, you'll say he was here, and has just gone down about something urgent. If he asks after ten minutes, subtract them from the half hour and say Mr. Cavafy will be back in twenty minutes."[3] For this reason, perhaps because his supervisor was not pleased with his work, one day he chastised him: "Mr. Cavafy, you are not giving satisfaction," to which the poet replied, perhaps with irony,

"I shall try to give you satisfaction."[4] Yet in his annual reports after 1910, he received high grades and was praised as a "useful clerk," "trusting," "intelligent and very responsible but a trifle overdeliberate"; one time, his superintendent reported that he continued "to give full satisfaction." Every year the superintendent recommended an increase in his pay for his excellent work. On one rare occasion (March 8, 1897), Constantine himself sought a raise, pointing to the "satisfactory work" he had been performing.[5]

He finished work at 1:30 p.m. and came home without major responsibilities or cares but with the rest of the day at his disposal. It was a dreary and limited job for one with such a brilliant mind. "Friday, and Saturday, Sunday, Monday, / are all the same. I live—without hope" he wrote in an early but later repudiated poem "Vulnerant Omnes, Ultima Necat" (1893). The poem curiously anticipated his daily routine, but Constantine himself never complained of its monotony. The freedom to think and write made the tedium bearable. At the start of his career, he seems to have derived some pleasure from his position and was genuinely interested in the approbation of his superiors. He recopied in his own hand and kept in his files the recommendation by the inspector general of the Office of the Irrigation Service that he be hired permanently at the salary of seven pounds a month. "Mr. Cavafy, Greek by descent but an English subject[,] is of a highly respectable Alexandrian family. [. . .] I have since found him so useful, showing so much intelligence and working so diligently that I do not know how the work in the office could be done without him" (December 11, 1890).[6] When offered a better job in the offices of the Choremi-Benaki Company (an import-export firm), he declined because he wanted to avoid being scrutinized by the Choremi and Benaki families.[7] He preferred his anonymous position at the Office of the Irrigation

Service, feeling freer as a petty civil servant within the British bureaucracy than as an employee of Greek merchants. It was perhaps on the way from work that E. M. Forster ran into him one afternoon, as Constantine ambled along in his straw hat. "His arms are extended, possibly. 'Oh, Cavafy . . . !' Yes, it is Mr. Cavafy, and he is going either from his flat to the office, or from his office to the flat. If the former, he vanishes when seen, with a slight gesture of despair."[8] He was eager to talk to people in the shops or to those he ran into along the way.

From late 1907 until his death, Constantine lived in a working-class neighborhood, steps away from the Church of Saint Savvas, which was built in 1687 on the site of an ancient sanctuary (circa 615 CE), and the Greek hospital, which was erected in 1880 on the ruins of a Hellenistic palace.[9] He moved here with Paul from a flat they had been sharing at 17 Rue Rosette since 1904. His second-floor apartment was located at 10 Rue Lepsius, named after Karl Richard Lepsius (1810–84), a German Egyptologist. That he lived on a street bearing the name of a man who studied ancient Egypt was an irony lost neither on him nor on his visitors. His house quickly became a gathering place for local poets, intellectuals, and journalists and eventually a pilgrimage site for all lovers of poetry visiting Egypt. It now serves as a museum and the street has been renamed "Cavafy St."[10]

Constantine was not at all bothered by the incongruity of his residence, an apartment full of antiques located in a seedy district abutting brothels. Passing a few prostitutes in his neighborhood, he once said to a friend, "Egotistical beings, these women, thinking they are the only ones capable of bestowing pleasure."[11] One evening as he and his friend Gaston Zananiri were leaving his apartment at the moment when the prostitutes would begin to appear, the poet said: "Up here is the spirit; down there is the flesh."[12] When he went on his customary walks and would encounter someone, he often commented that his neighborhood had everything residents required—a brothel on the ground floor of his building, where they sinned; a hospital opposite, where they died; and a church around the corner, where they were buried.[13]

Yet the apartment on Rue Lepsius was a far cry from the former grandeur of the family residence on Rue Chérif Pasha, or even the more modest dwellings at Rue Tewfik Pasha and Boulevard de Ramleh. When Constantine's father, Peter John, landed in Alexandria in 1855 with his wife and their first three children (George, Peter, and Aristides), the Greek population numbered only a few thousand. It seems that his father was unhappy about coming to Alexandria, preferring to move to London instead. But Peter John's brother George wrote to him in Istanbul from London on February 16, 1850, arguing that it was financially prudent for the family firm that Peter John direct the office in Alexandria. George was reassured to discover that his brother's "reluctance" to make the move to Alexandria had to do with reasons of health.[14] When they arrived in the city, they leased a house on prominent Mohammed Ali Square. Despite his initial misgivings about the move, Peter John quickly rose up the social ladder of Greek Alexandria and was elected vice president of the Greek community in 1857.[15] Five years later, he moved his family to a grander house, the Okelle Zogheb on Rue Chérif, the elegant street for cotton merchants that even at the end of the century was still characterized as "the brightest of all the European streets in Alexandria."[16] Constantine was born in this house in 1863 and remembered this period wistfully as a time when the family lived a charmed life, with servants, fancy coaches, and scented gardens.

Despite the financial calamity he experienced in Alexandria and the consequent loss of his former social position, Constantine came to love his city and chose to live here even though he could have moved to Athens or other European capitals. He went out to bars and cafés, visited people's houses, attended social events, and enjoyed his daily jaunts through the streets. The protagonist of Constantine's short story "In Broad Daylight" gives a sense of him ambling through Alexandria's neighborhoods: he takes a carriage to the Zizinia Theatre[17] and lives in a house on Rue Chérif Pasha, as Constantine himself had, which contains three "well-furnished rooms" and his own servant and "the services of my landlady." One August afternoon when "the sun was brutally hot," he "strolled leisurely down Rue Chérif Pasha to avoid perspiring. The street was deserted, as it usually was deserted at this time of day."[18]

After the introduction of cars in 1903, Constantine found his movements around town less pleasant; his favorite streets swarmed with automobiles, carts, carriages, and bicycles. At peak hours, the main corridors of Rue Rosette (later Fuad and now Hurriya) and Shari' Al-Sab' Banat (Rue des Soeurs—the center of Arab-Egyptian commercial activity) were noisy and crowded, with traffic accidents, caused by car or cart, not uncommon.[19] Alexander A. Boddy (1854–1930), an English chaplain who made his way through Alexandria on his bicycle in 1899, complained about the clamor and found the streets "full of unearthly noises." Vendors of fruit and drink shouted, as did drivers and pedestrians: "O gentleman look out! O daughter, look out! Look at your feet!" Boddy found the streets perilous to a cyclist: "The middle of the narrow street is crowded," he wrote, with carriages passing by "furiously" or crawling. People "walk in shoals" in the middle of the street, taking up the space left by these carriages. "The turbaned *arabági* [carriage driver], in his eagerness to catch a fare, often wheels round unexpectedly and causes an accident."[20] These streets, usually unpaved, were filled with dirt.[21] Not much had changed sixteen years later when Martin S. Briggs

(1882–1977), who would distinguish himself as an architectural historian with a specialty in Baroque architecture, wrote about the city in *Through Egypt in War-Time*, an account of his march through the country in 1916. Moving into the "Oriental" part of the city, he noted that "there is hardly a single picturesque feature to relieve the dismal squalor of the Rue des Soeurs . . . Half the frontage is occupied by shabby little restaurants . . . In this quarter one may find everything that is least attractive in the cosmopolitan life of a great seaport, without any of the mystery or glamour of the East."[22]

Rue Rosette was the long, grand avenue of Alexandria, lined with imposing edifices, villas, offices, hotels, and shops. European residents admired it for its elegance, seeing it as focal to their lives. In ancient times it was known as the Canopic Way, the main east-west thoroughfare of the city.[23] Constantine promenaded along this street to get to the Mohammed Ali Club, where he often went for a meal or simply to meet friends for a drink. On New Year's Eve 1895, he had dinner there, starting with fish and ending with dessert, and he actually kept the menu with his signature on it.[24] This was the avenue that exemplified the famed cosmopolitanism of Alexandria.

On Boulevard Ramleh stood the tiny bookshop Friends of the Book. Divided into two parts by a long bench, it was a place where patrons stood on either side of the bench, talking or leafing through books or magazines. Constantine came here often, seeking out the owner for the latest book or news about literary happenings in Greece.[25] The poem "In an Old Book" (1922*) has the speaker leafing through the pages of a volume, which is "more than a hundred years old," only to discover a forgotten and unsigned watercolor of a young man.

Nearby on 39 Rue Fouad was Pastroudis, one of the most popular restaurant-cafés in the city. Not far from Constantine's house, it stood next to the Cinema Amir, and its façade featured striking Ionic columns that emphasized the explicit connection the owner, Yiorgos Pastroudis, wanted to make with classical antiquity. Constantine came here frequently for its famous chocolates, pastries, and sorbets; he also would have drinks at its striking marble bar and, if the weather permitted, enjoy his coffee in the outside sitting area along the sidewalk. From under the café's blue awning, he had a clear view of Alexandria's imposing railway station.[26]

Shari' Al-Sab', perpendicular to Rue Rosette, was the main street for Arab-Egyptian commercial activity. Unlike Rue Rosette, its structures were largely wooden. It was more densely populated and inhabited by recent arrivals and by people with little means. To Europeans, the street seemed a vulgar avenue, associated with poverty, prostitution, and violence. While its population may have been a mixture of races and ethnicities, it was never celebrated as cosmopolitan the way the European neighborhoods were. Loaded donkeys, carts, horse-drawn carriages, bicycles, as well as some automobiles (after 1900) made their way along the street. People complained about the incessant noise and the whistles of police officers trying to direct traffic. Death and injury by cart were not unusual.[27]

Constantine frequented the grand Mohammed Ali Square (now Midan el Tahrir), which was laid out in 1830 and was dominated by the equestrian statue of Mohammed Ali, who ruled Egypt between 1805 and 1848 and who tried to modernize the country. It was here that many of the rebels of the 1882 uprisings had been hanged. Most of the square and its buildings, except the statue of Mohammed Ali and the Church of Saint Mark (1855), were destroyed during the bombardment. On either side of this statue, city planners laid out parks filled with tall trees where pedestrians could escape the heat in the summer months.

Near this square stood the Bourse, or cotton exchange, with its arcades and clock where Constantine worked as a young man. He was so proud to have received a temporary admission card to the Bourse as a journalist for the daily paper *Telegraphos / The Telegraph* on February 18, 1886, within one year of his return from Istanbul, that he kept the "Carte D'Entrée Provisoire" in his possession all his life.[28] The Bourse served as the heart of the city, much as the library had done in ancient Alexandria.[29] Near the Bourse were the Mixed Law Courts, which oversaw legal cases between Egyptians and Europeans. Here he would be approached by the many shoeshiners as well as vendors of the *Egyptian Gazette.* Sitting on a stool, Constantine would face the Church of Saint Mark and read through the newspaper while getting a shoeshine. Afterward he could relax on one of the benches under the trees, break his cigarette in half, light it, and then gaze at the crowd.

Nearby he would take a tram along Al-Sab' to Pompey's Pillar for a whiff of antiquity. To the left of the Bourse, he promenaded along the Rue Chérif Pasha, where the grand house of his birth stood before its destruction in 1882. After its reconstruction, the street regained its magnificent character, becoming in E. M. Forster's words "a smart little street bristling with flag staffs."[30] Most of the shops were owned by Greeks, Austrians, French, Jews, Armenians, or Italians. At night "when the electric light shows up the colored fabrics in Chalon's windows, or the wonderful toy bazaars, one might dream one was in some Continental boulevard."[31] Many decades later, Martin S. Briggs similarly celebrated the European character of the city. Having disembarked in Alexandria with the other British troops, he noted that "the eastern half of Alexandria is not Oriental at all . . . The streets are labelled with French names while on the pavement one seems to meet far more English and French and

Italians and Greeks than Egyptians . . . In the Rue Chérif Pacha at Alexandria one might imagine oneself in the Via Roma at Genoa or in the Toledo of Naples."[32]

When Constantine ambled in front of these shops, he could reminisce about all the great funeral corteges, including that of his father, that had passed along this street. Certainly he recalled that of George Averoff on August 3, 1899, who died six months after his own mother. Further back in memory would have been the funeral for his friend Stephen Schilizzi, which began at 9:30 a.m. on April 9, 1886, at the house of the deceased, commenced at the Cathedral of the Annunciation, and then ended at the Greek cemetery at Chatby, where a friend, Anthony Theodore Rallis, gave the eulogy.[33]

He frequented the Ramleh Station to take the tram to the leafy suburb along the seacoast, with its famous San Stefano Casino. The first tram in Alexandria had been introduced three years before his birth in 1860, signifying to his parents the modern potential of the city. Indeed, they could boast that Egypt had one of the best train and tram networks outside Western Europe and North America, certainly better than Greece at the time. He often rode to Ramleh as a young man to visit his friend Mikès Ralli or the casino. He would swim there as well, and it was a place he commemorated in many erotic poems. To many Alexandrians like himself, taking this train, being "borne along the coast, through the cool breezes, with the blue sea nearly always in view" was a delight.[34] And then there were the brilliant villas of the suburb, with their magnificent arches, their white colonnades, red roof tiles, and balconies with cascading bougainvillea. He often came here to play tennis in his younger days.

During one of his regular workdays, after stepping out of the Office of the Irrigation Service, he visited one of his favorite cafés, the Athineos. Decorated in art nouveau and art deco style, it was originally housed on the first floor beneath his offices.[35] Its owner, Constantine Jean Athineos, stood behind the cash register with his long mustache, linen suit, and bow tie. Upon entering the establishment, Constantine could peek into the cabinet with pastries and bottles of liquor. On the other side stood the cabinet with the fine chocolates. And between them was the door leading to the sitting area that featured tall mirrors, white columns, and palm plants.[36] In the early evenings of summer, flower sellers would assemble and hold up fragrant bouquets to passersby.[37] From there it was a few steps to Sa'ad Zaghloul Square, named after the Egyptian nationalist who began his campaign for independence in 1918. Standing in the small park under the palm trees swaying with the powerful wind, like his fellow Alexandrians, Constantine could enjoy the vista across the bay to Fort Qaitbay built on the site of the ancient Pharos lighthouse. On the square stood the famous entertainment club aptly named Belle Vue, which he frequented as a young man. On each side and for many miles he could behold the marvelous Corniche or New Quay, which was built in 1905 and afforded one of the most beautiful seaside promenades in the Mediterranean. Adorned by grand buildings, banks, offices, cafés, and consulates, this seaside promenade was popular with Alexandrians seeking the views and the fresh sea air.[38] For Europeans, it represented the openness and cosmopolitanism of the city, its harbor enabling commercial trade across the Mediterranean. They could not help but feel the historical vibrations of the square, for on this actual spot, Cleopatra had built a huge temple, the Caesareum, in honor of Mark Antony.

Constantine rarely walked along the Corniche in later life, preferring the contained intimacy of the inner city. Despite working his whole life by the sea, as an adult he was not moved by the beauty of nature.[39] Indeed, the sea appears only once in his work as the direct subject and then only as an absence. Despite his effort, the speaker of "Morning Sea" (1915*) can't really enjoy the water before him. Try as he may, he isn't able to appreciate the view or move beyond his desires and dreams:

Let me stand here. And let me observe nature for a while.
The luminous blue and amber shores
of the morning sea and cloudless sky;
all beautiful and full of light.

Let me stand here. And let me fool myself that I am seeing them
(I did see them for a moment when I first arrived);
and not my fantasies again,
my reveries, visions of pleasure.

While he personally no longer found pleasure in the waterfront, in his poems the sea served as a place of erotic freedom from social constraints. The speaker of "Days of 1908" (1921/1932) seeks solace, beauty, and diversion on the beach. An unemployed, working-class youth, he earns some money by playing backgammon in "common coffeehouses," perhaps like the Billiards Palace, which the poet himself frequented. But sometimes to escape the hopelessness of his routine, the young man went to the seashore. There he would cast aside the one suit he could afford, of faded "cinnamon-color" cloth. No longer weighed down by the "unworthy clothes and stitched underwear," he appeared "totally nude, faultlessly beautiful, a wonder," standing in his "nakedness," bathed by the morning sun.

Later in his life, Constantine preferred to stay in his apartment with its promises of aesthetic refuge. His resistance to abandon himself to the pull of the ocean in his old age stands in contrast to the summer he spent in Athens with his brother Alexander from mid-June to the end of July 1901. This was a trip both brothers made in grand style, traveling first-class and staying in luxurious hotels. They often took a hotel in the beach town of Phaleron, where they swam daily. "Swaims [swarms] of people on the beach," Constantine writes in his entry for July 15: "Very few people yesterday on the plage [beach]." At thirty-eight, then, he was able to enjoy activities like swimming, promenading by the Corniche, dining with his brother and acquaintances in cafés along the seashore.[40] But by the time he composed "Morning Sea" fourteen years later, he seems to have lost any attraction to this most important feature of his city, at least as a poetic subject. "Morning Sea" thus best captured his feelings about the natural world, namely that he could perceive it only if it was filtered by his dreams, desires, and remembrances. He was an urban poet delighting in his jaunt along the sidewalk, crossing the street to meet a friend in the Billiards Palace, going to the Rialto Cinema, charmed by a handsome youth in a storefront window who might be arranging rows of shirts. Perhaps one moment such as this inspired the poem "He Was Asking About the Quality" (1930*), in which a young man returning from work spots such an attractive assistant in the shop. Incapable of resisting him, he enters the store on the pretext of inquiring about the quality of the goods for sale when his real intent was "for their hands to touch over the handkerchiefs," for their faces to draw near, for the bodies to consummate "a momentary brush" against each other. "Quickly and furtively, so that the store owner / who stood in the back would not take notice."

On his way home from his office, following the Boulevard Ramleh, which was one of his favorite avenues, he frequented the famous restaurant and bar Ioannidis, where he could overhear men discussing the latest price of cotton in Liverpool. From there he passed by a Greek fruit vendor where shoppers would make their latest purchases before lunch. And as he made his way past the Italian barbershop, he would come to the corner of Rue Nebi Danyal, where, in front of the shop of the upholsterer, a Muslim-Egyptian farmer stood holding a basket of watercress. And in a melodious voice, so familiar to pedestrians in the late afternoon, he would shout out, "Aal cresson, aal cresson, cresson salade, cresson salade."[41]

Farther along there were three important bookshops, one owned by the Greek brothers Chrysanthou, the French establishment Papyrus, and the international store run by Spyros Grivas, who made sure no one left his business empty-handed.[42] Just opposite stood the patisserie Petit Trianon, in the garden of which he often met his friend the editor Nikos Zelitas (1888–1938)—who was also known by his pen name, Stephanos Pargas—the painter Yiannis Kephalinos,[43] and other intellectuals. In a distance of five hundred meters that separated the Gran and Petit Trianon cafés, many Alexandrians would stroll along the sidewalks or stop in a bar in the hopes of meeting an acquaintance. This stretch constituted for many Europeans the intellectual and artistic heart of the city.[44]

Constantine lived fully in this urban setting. Even in his declining years, he shuffled about on the sidewalks of Alexandria, slightly hunched, ready to converse with anybody on the street. Like visitors at his home, people on the street confessed to not being able to avoid his austere but penetrating eyes.[45] He would often talk to himself and drop into cafés, offices, banks, and shops in order to exchange greetings. Before returning home in the afternoon, sometimes he stopped at Halley's Comet, a general store and bar where he would read the shop's newspaper. He would linger by the door with his arms outstretched, holding the paper in front of him. But just as often, without notice, he would turn, using the newspaper as a shield, to avoid talking to an irksome or annoying customer.[46]

On Rue Missala (now Safiya Zaghloul) stood the Billiards Palace, a bar with sixteen snooker tables and four French billiard tables where Constantine regularly met with Sotiris Liatsis, the director of the newspaper *Tachydromos*, and smoked a water pipe.[47] Pausing there on the way home from work, when the house cat approached him, he petted it, referring to it as the "literary cat." In the evenings, the poet ambled into these bars, especially the Café Al Salam and Billiards Palace, where, holding a glass of raki (an anise-flavored alcoholic drink), he'd try to open a conversation with simple, uneducated young men.[48] He would praise them and seek out their company.[49] One day, a friend who found him in a working-class bar expressed his surprise; the poet brazenly proclaimed that "the truth comes out of the mouths of young men and drunks." Another friend, Gaston Zananiri, who sometimes accompanied him on these visits, heard him defend these young men, arguing that dire circumstances drove them into a life of ill repute.[50]

Timos Malanos claims that Constantine continued to go to the Café Al Salam even as late as 1930 to pick up young men. Citing a letter from an anonymous intellectual who frequented Al Salam in those years, he provides rare details about the poet's erotic life. Apparently, Constantine would often pass by in the evening looking for a certain individual, asking, "Do you know if a young man named Totos is here?" When he got a negative response, he would say, "Thank you," and leave. His inquiries about Totos were so regular that they became the topic of amusement in the café. According to Malanos's informant, Constantine got to know Totos, a mechanic and chauffeur, and his acquaintances, Spiros S. and Yiorgos K., an accountant, around 1929 and saw them for about three years. He first came upon Spiros and Yiorgos in the dark garden of Al Salam, which they frequented along with other "street-urchins." They introduced him to Totos with the understanding that he would be available; Constantine would take them home and offer them money. And "when asked by me, they smiled revealingly and then they denied that they . . . ,[51] with a cold and listless 'no' and only friendship." At other times when the informant saw them, they would show him the money Constantine had given them, again declining to say the reason and smiling "conventionally." When the informant returned to the matter years later, they seemed embarrassed to discuss the indiscretions of their youth. "They respect me very much for they are illiterate and immoral, and I am their superior." This firsthand account reveals not only that Constantine enjoyed the company of working-class young men, talking and sharing a drink with them in his later years, but that he also paid them for sex even late in his life.[52] For reasons of discretion, Malanos refuses to identify his source, who, in turn, declines to provide the last names of the young men. In their anonymity they paradoxically acquire a certain reality, for they resemble the young men populating the poems: nameless shadows in the dark alleys of Alexandria.

By the late 1920s, Constantine was an elderly man pursuing much younger men. The topic of age had preoccupied him since 1894, when he wrote the first draft of "An Old Man," a poem he published three years later. An elderly man sits in a café, "bent over a table" with a newspaper before him. In his "miserable old age," he considers how little he enjoyed life and recalls that he had been young "just yesterday," when caution and foresight fooled him into believing that "tomorrow, you will have time." In 1903, Constantine wrote a series of comments on this poem that illuminate presciently his later jaunts into the Café Al Salam: "The Poem 'Γέρος' [Geros/Old Man] quickly settled. These positions are merely kept as records. December 1903."[53] Switching into Greek, he reflected further on the limits of old age, saying that the old man can no longer express "erotic words to young men."[54] The fragility and shortcomings of old age prevent him from mixing with them and he knows that he is out of place. But then he seemed unhappy with the sense of resignation of these lines and added an enigmatic postscript: "And even at 40 he seems handsome and well-preserved and appears 10 years younger just like me, and presents himself as a young man. And at this age, his discourse is brilliant."[55] Was he thinking of himself at this moment, for he had turned forty when he wrote this note? We know that he feared losing his looks and that in middle age he began dyeing his hair and wearing a scarf to hide his sagging neck. At forty he believed he looked ten years younger. Did he have similar thoughts in his late sixties? The elderly man cruising in the Café Al Salam did not recognize the bounds of his own age, as described in the poem. He certainly resisted the fatalism of its concluding lines: "But with so much thinking and remembering / the old man becomes dizzy. And he dozes off / bent over the table in the café."

It was not far from the Billiards Palace to Rue Debbane, where Nikos Zelitas, along with his wife, Eftychia, ran Constantine's favorite bookstore, Grammata. In a few years, the store had quickly turned into a small cultural center, sponsoring lectures and exhibitions, with almost all of Alexandria's artists, poets, and intellectuals passing by regularly.[56] It offered "atmosphere, company, and conversation" to anyone who entered.[57] Zelitas himself sat in his office interminably writing to the point that customers often wondered what he wrote. But he always dropped his pen when a patron popped in and thus no one felt ignored. Constantine came here twice or even three times a day to chat with the couple or pick up gossip. "Nothing escapes us, Niko," he would say. "Whatever happens on earth, even on Mars, either you, Niko, or I, will learn of it."[58] Often, he brought packages of his poems for Zelitas to mail to admirers in Greece or other European countries, since the latter functioned in effect as his literary agent, sending out poems to readers abroad. Once, Constantine arrived at the couple's house around 10:30 at night, delivered a poem, and said, "I have brought it now, Niko, so that I can calmly go to sleep." On another night, he knocked at the door, saying, "Take it, Niko, since it's burning my hands."[59] If he did not find the Zelitases in the shop or at home, he left his visiting card, informing them that he would be at his apartment that afternoon. These visiting cards act as an archaeological trove of his daily life. On August 13, 1928, for instance, Constantine asked Mr. Zelitas, "Please send to Stavrinos these three translations." Another note requested that copies be mailed to the distinguished writer Alkis Thrylos at the designated address.[60] He was particularly fond of Mrs. Zelitas, whom he, like other Alexandrians, found to be a warm person. Many of these cards were left for her: "Dear Mrs. Zelitas," says one, "I will certainly be home at 7. Please phone Mrs. Voltou. With friendship, C. P. Cavafy. Saturday afternoon." Another: "Are you free to visit me between 2:30 and 6:15?"

Before opening the bookstore in 1923, Nikos and Eftychia also produced the most important literary magazine in Alexandria, *Ta Grammata* (Letters; 1911–21). Constantine was particularly grateful to the couple for having published a poem of his, "Things That Are Finished," in the very first issue of 1911; and he sent them material over the next two years up until April 1913, when in light of the controversy over a scurrilous, anti-Cavafy tract by Roberto Kambos (pseudonym for the poet Petros Magnis), *Ta Grammata* printed an anonymous letter, characterizing Constantine as a minor poet.[61] But he resumed his relationship with Nikos four years later, even after *Ta Grammata* published a critical article by Michalis Peridis in 1915.[62]

Near the Grammata bookstore stood the Greek Orthodox Cathedral of the Annunciation, the place where Constantine was baptized. Built as a neo-Gothic structure and consecrated in 1856, the church departed from the traditional Byzantine style, perhaps indicating the Westernizing and cosmopolitan tastes of Alexandria's elites, and thus stood in marked contrast to the late Byzantine style of the Church of Saint Nicholas in Liverpool, which Constantine attended in his youth. E. M. Forster found the structure in "bad taste," an unexceptional building that he devoted only four lines to in his *Guide.*[63] Though it was not as grand, Constantine preferred the Church of Saint Savvas just around the corner from his apartment whenever he attended services, perhaps because of its historic associations with the city's past. This was the seat of the Greek Orthodox Patriarch of Alexandria, the spiritual leader of the Orthodox Christians of Egypt (and later of all Africa). Constantine often visited the library in the offices of the Patriarchate at Saint Savvas to consult books for his poems.[64] A church was built on the exact site in 615 CE over the ruins of a Temple of Apollo, though the current structure dates from 1687.[65] There were eight ancient columns in the nave and a fresco of the Virgin Mary and Child in the apse, built directly over an early Christian church.

Like many Greeks, Constantine considered himself an Orthodox Christian without feeling the need to attend church regularly. He was moved by the ritual of the liturgy, the incense, the candlelight, and the mysticism. During his first trip to Greece in 1901, he made a point of visiting the capital's many churches, including the main cathedral ("Having just returned from the Metropolitan Church where Alexander and I heard mass," he noted in his journal on June 23.)[66] Two days later, the brothers visited the eleventh-century church of the Panagia Kapnikarea in the Plaka neighborhood, along with the Church of Saint Irene, "an ancient church with a Byzantine look about it."[67] His ongoing interest in church architecture is surely a continuation of the habits and patterns of his youth, where, as previously discussed, during his years abroad in Liverpool, London, and Istanbul, he witnessed how church buildings functioned as the heart and soul of the Greek communities.

Throughout his life, he enjoyed the services of Holy Week, as he told a young admirer, Memas Kolaitis,[68] while they were walking from the Grammata bookstore toward the Billiards Palace one Good Friday. At one point, Constantine suggested that they stand by the Greek hospital to witness the religious street procession of the Epitaphios, the funeral bier that replicates Christ's sepulcher in Jerusalem. As the Epitaphios passed in front of them, Constantine did not cross himself as was customary, simply whispering, "Maki, my friend, the Orthodox Church has long lost its spirituality, but the tradition is nearly two thousand years old."[69] Five years later, he himself would lie dying around the time of Holy Week. Unable to attend service or even speak after his throat surgery, he scribbled a note to a friend, asking him to attend the Good Friday service and pray for his health. In the course of this exchange, he lost himself deep in thought, a solitary candle casting shadows on his face. A few minutes later, he came to and crossed himself.[70] In his final days, he seems to have embraced his religion, agreeing, as noted in the prologue, to receive Holy Communion. He was, however, Orthodox more in the cultural than in the religious sense of the word.

Nevertheless, the observation of religious ritual and presence of ancient churches near his house enabled him to feel rooted to the past. These links to antiquity, however elusive, were crucial to him because, for all his attempts to convey the history of the city, Constantine could not find much direct evidence of the classical heritage, since so little of it had survived. In fact, in his lifetime there were few public monuments that recalled Alexandria's gloried past. He could take the tram to Pompey's Pillar, a red granite column erected in 297 CE to the Emperor Diocletian and one of the largest monolithic structures in antiquity, which Forster found "an imposing but ungraceful object."[71] A further ten-minute walk would bring him to the Catacombs of Kom el Shoqafa, a series of tombs dating from the second to the fourth centuries CE, which were discovered in 1900 and were "unique both for their plan and for their decorations."[72] For Constantine, they offered a fascinating blend of Greek and Egyptian elements and also visually represented the transition from paganism to Christianity, which he converted into a major trope in his poetry. They were, however, among the few visible and material reminders of the ancient past extant during his lifetime. The physical absence of classical antiquity compelled him to evoke the past in his mind. As Michael Haag notes, "Unlike Rome or Athens with their monuments extant, Alexandria is all intimation: here (some spot) is where Alexander lay entombed; here Cleopatra and Antony loved; here the Library, the Serapeum, and so on—and there is almost nothing physically there."[73] To be sure, Constantine first experienced antiquity on a grand scale during his trip to Greece in 1901, when he and Alexander went up to the Acropolis within two days of their arrival in Piraeus: "Saw the Parthenon, the Erechtheum, the Propylaea, the view of Athens from the Acropolis, the Museum of the Acropolis. Sublime, sublime!" he wrote in his journal on June 20, 1901.[74] In the morning, the brothers walked to the Archaeological Museum with Constantine noting the "particularly beautiful" bust of Antinous.[75] He was surprised and pleased to be invited by a descendant of Heinrich Schliemann (1822–90)—the famous excavator of Troy and Mycenae—into their private residence on Panepistimiou Avenue (presently the site of the Numismatic Museum): "I could only see that part of the antiquities that is placed in the vitrines of the smoking-room. They are very rare and beautiful . . . The Maison Schliemann is a remarkable residence. The frescoes, the mosaics, the furniture are marvelous."[76]

But the delight and eagerness of viewing grand monuments wore off as Constantine aged. And he was not at all bothered by the absence of visible antiquity at home. On the contrary, this material dearth helped him develop his own peculiar and spectral understanding of the classical heritage, another instance in his life when necessity obliged him to rethink himself and his society. Rather than pining for magnificent temples and masterpieces of sculpture, he welcomed the ghosts of Hellenistic Alexandria at home.[77] His house on Rue Lepsius, after all, was built over the center of the once-ancient city. And in an early article (1892) on the recently established "Greco-Roman Museum," he thanked the Alexandrian citizens for their munificence but begged them to support archaeological excavations: "The ground upon which we live undoubtedly conceals many relics and remains from ancient Alexandria."[78] It is these remains that he tried to evoke in his many poems. Yet this museum, about a ten-minute walk from his house on Rue Lepsius, offered glimpses of ancient daily life without overpowering him with the artwork of famous artists.[79] It could not boast vases by Exekias or Euphronius or sculptures by Praxiteles, as did museums in Athens, Berlin, Paris, London, and Rome. While visitors found its Doric façade impressive, with the word "Mouseion" engraved in Greek across the architrave, its exhibits mostly told the story of ancient, especially Hellenistic Alexandria, a historical period that did not excite either historians or poets as much as the classical period. Forster, who devoted many pages to the collection in his guidebook, found the works "not of the first order," but if used correctly, the visitor would find that "a scrap of the past has come alive."[80] This is precisely what Constantine strove to achieve in his poetry—to conjure up antiquity for contemporary readers and for those reading in the future—bits of parchment, broken inscriptions, and shards of pottery that he found in the dust of his home city.[81]

Although the bookstore run by the Zelitas couple functioned as a literary focal point of the city, Constantine's apartment served as a gathering place for locals and a site of pilgrimage for foreign visitors. He was home to receive guests every afternoon and evening, often greeting them at the door.[82] As he gained more fame, his very house on Rue Lepsius acquired its reputation as a place of whimsy, illusion, and aesthetic promise. To be sure, when visitors passed through the door, they entered a space with few compensations for comfort or modernity. (Constantine, in fact, refused to install electricity in his flat or a radio and telephone.) The shadows in the corners, the flickering light of the candles, the fading fabric on the curtains, and the heaviness of the furniture gave them an impression of a domain that was sui generis. They could not help but feel that they had crossed a boundary from the actual world below to the aesthetic realm above. Nothing announced this transition from the everyday to the imagined more than the passageway visitors entered upon opening the door.

Inevitably visitors described their entry into the apartment almost as an aesthetic initiation, as if, like characters of his poems, they too were being admitted into the universe of art. For they knew that Constantine often portrayed in his poems young men crossing the barrier between reality and the imagination. In "Passing" (1914/1917), for instance, a young man abandons himself into dissolute living, "as is right for our art," thereby becoming worthy of entering "the Lofty World of Poetry." In "Thus I Gazed" (1911/1917), the speaker delights in "lines of the body, red lips, sensual limbs, / locks as if borrowed from Greek statues." In the darkness of the room, the speaker of "So That They Come" (1920*) says that "only one candle is enough" for him to "conjure up visions," to indulge in reverie, and invoke the "Shades of Love." Musing in his room, the poet of "I Brought to Art" (1921) brings "half-seen faces or lines of imperfect loves" to "Art," begging poetry to "create Forms of Beauty" out of the raw materials of life. More often than not, however, the speakers of the poems ask poetry to preserve the beauty of youth and stave off the wrinkles and pain of old age. The aged aesthete of "According to the Recipes of Ancient Helleno-Syrian Magicians" (1931*) wonders if the sorcerers of antiquity could concoct a magic serum that might bring back the days of his twenty-third year. Over his entire poetic career, Constantine sought to fashion an idealized world devoid of pain, of age's sagging flesh and depleted forms, and removed from the dust and sordidness of the neighborhood around him. He created in his apartment a physical representation of this poetic realm, a space impervious to the chaos of the city outside, thus luring in his many visitors with promises of aesthetic transcendence.

When the Athenian poet Myrtiotissa (Theoni Drakopoulou, 1885–1968) stepped into the apartment hall in October 1923, she needed some time to adjust to the darkness of the room after the brightness of the Mediterranean sun outside. Straining in the shadows, she could make out Constantine's "enigmatic eyes" and his dark, bushy eyebrows. She too felt that the whole visit had an air of unreality, enhanced later by the whiskey that Constantine had his (black, Arab) servant[83] offer. The Athenian poet Kostas Ouranis had an impression of impending illusion and possibility upon entering the flat in 1932. "A black servant opened the door and I found myself in an apartment sunk in shadows. The passage was a corridor of shadow and the servant himself, who led me, glided like a ghost. The little, muted light that emerged from a neighboring room that lay a bit further made the shadow still more mysterious."[84] This dimness prepared visitors for their initiation into the Cavafian world, leading them into what the Athenian poet and critic Aristos Kampanis described as a "phantasmagorical setting."[85] The young Kampanis certainly sensed that he had been admitted to a magical realm. Over the years, he came to believe that Constantine had created this eccentric atmosphere to lure visitors into his poetry.[86] Atanasio Catraro, the scion of a distinguished family in Trieste who worked in the cotton business and later became a journalist, was, like Kampanis, overwhelmed by this strangeness when he arrived with Alekos Sengopoulos one afternoon in 1918. When Constantine's servant[87] Ali opened the door, Catraro caught a glimpse of the gloomy, long hall, stacked with furniture and collectibles. Finding the hallway oppressive and "melancholic," he rested his eyes on the huge and austere bookcases.[88] The glass "windows" on the upper and lower panels of these cases lessened the feel of Victorian cheerlessness. Vases on top of them almost reached the ceiling. A smaller case stood to the right with two large vases on the top shelf.

These bookcases housed a crucial part of Constantine's poetic and psychic world. Although he borrowed material from other libraries, he drew on his own books for his personal edification and for his poetry: ancient Greek, Byzantine, and Latin texts, historical studies, European literature, Modern Greek literature, dictionaries, and lexica, which, according to Gaston Zananiri, were not organized in any particular order.[89] A number of these texts included his annotations and marginalia. He even had a book by the Indian poet Rabindranath Tagore, who had visited Alexandria in 1926, though there is no evidence that Constantine actually met him. By the 1920s, as he became more famous, he began to receive signed copies from Greek authors, many of which remained unread. The poetry of Kostas Karyotakis (1896–1928) is inscribed with a personal note but its pages remained uncut.[90] Constantine was not a bibliophile who accumulated books for their beauty or antique value, but he prized his collection and often imagined himself as a historian rather than a poet. It is not surprising that it was the bookcases that people first encountered upon entering the flat. Although he had nowhere else to place them, Constantine must have been pleased to have his guests confront these imposing pieces and the learning they contained.

Constantine used his library constantly. Zananiri described how he would suddenly get up from the salon, withdraw to the hall to consult a book, and return with the volume in question.[91] He spent many hours here when he was alone, bringing a candle even during the day to search for a particular volume. But he lost little time in locating it, since he was familiar with the order of books. He sat at the far end of the hall next to a window and underneath an oil lamp where he had a comfortable armchair and a little table with "just enough space for an ashtray for the ashes of his cigarettes and a glass of whisky," or some raki.[92]

It was perhaps in this corner that he wrote but never finished the poem "It Had to Be the Alcohol" in 1919. "It had to be the alcohol that I drank last night," the speaker says. "It had to be what made me sleepy and tired all day."[93] Confused, he wonders why he suddenly loses sight of a wooden column in front of him with its ancient head on its pedestal, the red armchair, and the small settee, while his mind goes to Marseilles, which he had visited as a young man. This flashback somehow refreshes him, and his soul, "pressured by the weight of the years," finds relief in memories of a "corrupted young man who was never ashamed of anything." Then comes the sad realization that "the house is closed. No one will come tonight. It's past twelve."[94]

Standing in the large central hall from which the apartment's eight rooms radiated, visitors would count a number of doors in various directions, each leading to separate rooms. On the way to the salon, they got a glimpse of the bedroom, a bare space that housed a narrow bed with four posters decked with mosquito netting; by the window stood a desk covered with papers and a wicker chair and next to it a rusty tripod, where on hot summer evenings Constantine, working late into the night, would dip a cloth into the water to cool his face.[95] There was also a religious icon in front of which he had a vigil lamp that he lit frequently.[96] It was the only unadorned and plain room. Its very austerity allowed visitors to appreciate the very high ceilings of the entire apartment, which they might not otherwise have sensed because the walls were cluttered and obscured by bookcases, tall furniture, paintings, tapestries, and oil lamps.

Continuing down the hall, visitors made their way to a small, formal salon where the poet received important guests and where he arranged his best furniture: upholstered pieces with carved wood, small tables inlaid with mother-of-pearl, silk cushions embroidered with flowers and birds, and marble side tables. Abutting this salon was a room with a small balcony opening onto the street outside. Constantine would shuffle out in the late afternoon to catch a bit a commotion below after the siesta. One night, he stood there along with Gaston Zananiri, looking down at the garden of the Greek hospital while the bells of Saint Savvas rang next door, and whispered: "Look, I have everything around my house: the hospital, the church."[97] It was this balcony that Constantine had in mind when composing "In the Evening" (1916/1917). Overwhelmed by the sense of old age and the passing of time, the speaker says: "With melancholy I went out to the balcony— / I went out to change my thoughts at least / by catching a brief glimpse of my beloved city, / a slight movement in the street and the shops."

Next to the formal salon was a large living room with a divan and two small armchairs, the walls covered with paintings of flowers and mirrors. Constantine received most guests in this less stately space, sitting in one armchair while asking a visitor to take the one opposite him. A small table seemed crammed between them. A black desk stood to the side along with folding chairs and green velvet armchairs.[98] The chairs were covered in costly fabric trimmed with gold braid, giving the impression of lost prosperity. The fabric on the chairs was faded and fraying; the wooden frames looked dingy and discolored, ready to fall apart. Overall, the apartment gave one the impression of a bazaar.[99] Constantine took great pride in the fact that, not being nouveau riche, he had inherited all his possessions, probably from the opulent house his family once occupied on Rue Chérif.[100]

To I. A. Sareyiannis, the place seemed like a furniture store. Finding himself there one morning in 1929 to pick up poems on the way to Paris, he had time to examine the rooms in bright sunlight. He was amazed at all the "whimsical things," old but "nothing extraordinary or really beautiful."[101] The style of the apartment seemed to belong to an earlier Victorian aesthetic, a quality that surprised those who marveled at the poet's experimental and sometimes controversial poetry.[102] Despite his progressive literary taste, he did not care for modern décor, preferring faded elegance to contemporary efficiency. In fact, he seemed to delight in the tattered genteel atmosphere of his flat.[103] When asked why he never installed electricity, he dissembled, saying that he had moved sixteen to eighteen years earlier with a friend without any intention of staying. But when the friend moved out, he thought of leaving but ended up staying and then it was "too late" to wire the apartment for electricity.[104] He never really cared for the directness of electric lights, favoring instead the evocative glow of candles, which he had everywhere and which he used to control conversation. Many visitors noticed how he adjusted the light in order to see and not be seen, asking them to reveal themselves while showing little of himself. Preferring to hide in shadows, he placed his guests on the divan to his right near the candles.

Timos Malanos remembers encountering the poet in an armchair of his salon for the first time, with a "hieratic expression," playing with his *komboloi* (worry beads). Candles on a nearby table melted in front of a large mirror, casting the only light in the room and suggesting to Malanos an air of sanctification. Two other armchairs formed a circle.[105] Constantine had a Rembrandtesque preoccupation with light, both natural and artificial, a quality that comes through in many poems. The speaker of "In the Evening" (1916/1917) holds a letter, "reading it over and over again" until darkness filled the room. Light also features in "Caesarion" (1914/1918), where the speaker, hard at work reading volumes of Hellenistic inscriptions late into the night, deliberately lets the lamp die out the moment he feels the ghost of the Caesarion, Cleopatra's son, appearing in his room. And in "Candles" (1893/1899), the passing of time is represented by a row of "burned-out candles." Shunning the discouraging sight of cold, melted wax, the speaker keeps his eye on the bright flames lying ahead: "I don't want to look back lest I see and shudder / at how quickly the darkened line lengthens, / how quickly the burned-out candles multiply."

Like a stage director or photographer, Constantine would get up and adjust the shutters of the windows, draw or open the curtains, modulate the light of the acetylene lamps, and blow out or add more candles. If a visitor asked indiscreet questions, he would extinguish a candle and continue to do so until the interrogation stopped. At the same time, if a guest proved to be charming or very good-looking, he would get up and light more candles.[106] His fixation on the quality of the light and the overall atmosphere of the sitting room was yet another manifestation of his obsessive personality. Everything had to be properly planned and set for his visitors, whom he tried to impress as much by his poems as by the mood of his apartment. He could rarely abandon himself to the pleasure of the moment without thinking about how to dazzle others with his brilliance and command of ancient history.

Constantine spoke in a slow, almost declarative tone, with an idiosyncratic pronunciation, inflected by the slight English accent he had developed during his formative years in Liverpool and London. This peculiar enunciation always accentuated his sense of being foreign at home and sounded "strange to the ear of an Athenian."[107] Kostas Ouranis was struck by the poet's almost adolescent voice, a cross between the intonation of a "youth that was and the man that was to become."[108] He was also taken aback by Constantine's face. Rather than a human visage, it appeared to him like a "lithograph that had descended from its frame." The poet's lined, almost geological countenance seemed immobile while at the same time possessing something "sharp" about it. It was not the face of an old person who still seemed youthful but "of a young man who had become old." He confirmed what Malanos had always felt, namely that the poet was born an old man.[109] This is, of course, how Constantine portrayed himself, saying to the critic Georgios Lechonitis that he was a poet "of old age." Not inspired by the present, he needed time to pass so that he could remember what had happened in the past.[110]

Listening to his phrases, observing his face, and sensing the decaying atmosphere of the room, Ouranis wondered whether he had just arrived at someone's salon or was encountering a literary creation. Was he in modern-day Alexandria or in Ottoman Istanbul? With his round spectacles and his old-fashioned collar, Constantine appeared to him bookish and studious—a scholar from the Enlightenment such as Adamantios Korais. To Malanos, he gave the impression of a Byzantine monk but with dyed hair. He had an "unusual color and a fatty sheen in his sunken face."[111] Nikos Kazantzakis, the novelist, however, during his brief visit in February 1927, described the poet as a "Cardinal in fifteenth-century Florence, privy councilor to the Pope, special envoy to the palace of the Doge in Venice." He sat before Constantine in the formal salon with his knees touching the table between them, which was "filled with glasses of whiskey and *masticha* [a liqueur made from the resin of the mastic tree] from Chios." As they spoke, Kazantzakis tried to "make out his countenance in the dim light," to discern "his beautiful black eyes" that sparkled from the light of the candles. The poet's voice seemed "sly, coquettish, painted, embellished." And at one moment, anxious that Kazantzakis was observing him in silence, Constantine added, "Aren't you drinking at all! It's from Chios. I swear! Why have you become so quiet?"[112]

No one left the apartment unaffected. So overwhelmed was Myrtiotissa by her encounter with the poet that upon exiting the flat and returning to the grit and clamor of Alexandria, she began to doubt whether she had actually spoken to him. When her companion Nikos Zelitas asked for her impressions, she responded by questioning whether she had indeed beheld the poet, experiencing in the apartment a cognitive dissonance. "I'm not sure that I actually saw and heard that man," she said, and then added: "Are you sure we can see him again?" As soon as she set foot in Rue Lepsius, however, the artistic illusion of the apartment dissipated: "The noise of the city appeared even more unbearable and the shouting of the *arapides* seemed apotropaic." But as she made her way to the hotel, she sensed the "poet's form" with his large eyes pursuing her.[113]

This is how Constantine looks out at the viewer in the now-iconic photograph portrait of 1929, which was taken by the Racine Studio of Alexandria for the volume on Alexandria by Athanasios Politis. He wears a striped, dark three-piece suit, a white shirt, a silk tie, a handkerchief in his breast pocket, and he rests his left arm on the sofa, revealing a costly cuff link. Behind him hangs an antique, slightly tattered, late-nineteenth-century Chinese tapestry from the Qing Dynasty that had been brought from China by his aunt Sevaste.[114] The tapestry, along with his silk tie, starched shirt, and finely tailored suit, convey the aura of nineteenth-century aestheticism rather than revolutionary modernism. At the age of sixty-six, comfortably resting on his accomplishments, Constantine wanted to project a cosmopolitan image of a dapper man about to go to the theater or an elegant dinner party. Yet he also expressed a quiet resistance to the world, a person not open to emotional interaction with others apart from posing for the photographer, a man who could no longer be influenced at all. His gaze was nonconciliatory, his eyes penetrating but inscrutable.

5

A TALE OF TWO CITIES

We don't know how often Constantine actually visited the archaeological zone surrounding Pompey's Pillar. To get there, he would have had to enter what to him would have been a forbidding and somewhat threatening neighborhood. From the tram he would have seen fewer and fewer Europeans on the streets and more Muslim Egyptians. If he wanted to go beyond the pillar to the catacombs, he'd have had to make his way on a narrow dirt road past men dressed in gallabias drinking tea and smoking water pipes. Vegetable and fruit sellers would be beckoning with good deals, their carts standing by open water pools left by the night's rain. In this neighborhood, the city would have appeared to him much poorer and he would have heard only Arabic. In other words, the visit to these catacombs would have compelled him to confront the paradoxes of life in his city.

Constantine knew very little Arabic.[1] We have a record of his rudimentary knowledge in the journal he kept during his mother's illness. On January 28, 1899, when he returned from an afternoon of errands, his mother remarked how "flavorless" the house was without him. And when she said the very same thing to the "wretched" Ahmed, he responded in Arabic, which

Constantine transliterated in Greek.[2] But he could not carry out a conversation in this language. We have no evidence that he had any Muslim friends or that any of his lovers were Arab Egyptians. Nor can we say with any certainty what his attitude was toward the Muslim Egyptian residents of the city. His coworker Ibrahim el Kayar remembered that while Constantine was charming and effusive with his British colleagues, he was "laconic with us about anything outside our work." He was "taciturn. He showed great reserve, above all to us his Egyptian colleagues, and usually had no conversation with us, perhaps out of disdain."[3] Most likely, he never even visited the house of an Egyptian, as Alexandria was segregated along class, racial, and religious lines.

In order to grasp Constantine's relationship to Alexandria's Arabs, it is useful to consider how Greeks of his class regarded their place in this largely Muslim society.[4] In her memoirs about her childhood in Alexandria, Penelope Delta, the future fiction writer and the sister of Antonis Benaki, who owned a large villa on Rue Rosette that Constantine often visited, learned enough Arabic to speak with the servants.[5] Only her younger sister Argini acquired the language with any fluency. The Benaki children, like other upper-middle-class offspring, grew up with little knowledge of the local language. As a result, the young Penelope, who often spoke French at home, was astonished that during her trip to Paris, she was able to comprehend for the first time in her life conversations of people strolling on the sidewalk.[6] Not surprisingly, she felt more at home in Paris than in her native city.

At the same time, many upper-class Greeks, like the city's other Europeans, were multilingual. Constantine and his brothers were fluent in English and proficient in French. The children of the elites spoke English or French. In many cases, they knew these languages better than Greek.[7] Penelope, for her part, hated texts written in purist Greek, finding them dull in comparison to her English and French novels. As a child, she often wondered why she had to learn written Greek at all. Her French teacher, Mademoiselle Dufay, never encouraged her to read Greek.[8]

Europeans congregated largely among themselves and stratified nationally with the English dominating the ethnic hierarchy, followed by the Italians, Greeks, French, and other minorities. The famed cosmopolitanism of Alexandria was limited to Europeans of the middle and upper classes. Few if any took any interest in Islamic culture. An exception was Penelope's brother, Antonis, who began to purchase Islamic art to add to his treasures in Greek antiquities. In 1925, along with his cousin Alexandre Benaki, the historian Christophoros A. Nomikos, and M. S. Lagonikos, he organized the first ever exhibition of Islamic art in Alexandria, featuring work they owned.[9] When Antonis Benaki moved to Athens in 1927, he brought his vast collection with him, eventually exhibiting the various works in the extraordinary neoclassical villa his father had built in the vicinity of the royal palace, which he converted into the Benaki Museum three years later.

The interest of these men in art from the Islamic world was rather uncommon. On the whole, Greeks and other wealthy Europeans kept a social and cultural distance from native Egyptians.[10] Many expressed open racial hostility toward the fellahin (peasants, laborers), often referring to them as "*arapides*" (blacks).[11] Penelope narrates an example of this prejudice involving her uncle Stamatis. Coming out from a store, he was about to put on his hat when a gust of wind blew it on the ground. A "little black man" rushed to pick up the hat and give it to its owner. But instead of expressing gratitude, Stamatis shrank back lest the Arab touch him, and then he let the Good Samaritan keep his hat.[12] "We 'whites' had the greatest contempt for the fellahin. We considered them almost like beasts," Penelope writes. She remembers her father striking their gardener for "being insolent," who then had to kiss his hand and jacket. Incredibly she believed that the Arabs had to accept all the humiliations in order to gain self-confidence and rise against the Europeans.[13]

Egyptian Greeks[14] like Penelope and Constantine drew a mental barrier between Europeans and the bulk of the Egyptian population, which they considered a separate race, as can be seen in the following episode from Constantine's life. The poet was in a café with his friend Makis Antaios, a member of the Grammata group of writers and editors and an ardent supporter of his poetry, when at a nearby table he saw two English sailors in each other's arms, kissing. At that point, he motioned to Makis to stay because "things would become interesting." Later in the evening, after the departure of the English sailors and seeing only "*arapades*"[15] around them, Constantine grew uneasy. When Makis asked him if "*arapades*" could become "*attrayants*" (attractive), he responded, "It should not happen, Antaio, it should not happen." And then "disgusted" from the "nonsense" around him, misquoting his famous poem ("I have looked so much"), he added: "I thus observed ugliness and am disgusted by its sight."[16] Without further context, we don't know the age of the Arab men, what they were doing, or whether they were Copts or Muslims. Constantine's reaction to the Arab men, however, does not foreclose the possibility that he may have had Arab lovers, especially in his youth.

When Greeks referred to fellahin as "*arapades*," they actually brought together five separate groups into one category: city dwellers, fellahin, nomads, inhabitants of Nubia, and protected minorities such as the Copts.[17] They did not see or care to understand the subtle differences among the indigenous population of Egyptians.[18] Although they were collectively unified by their ethnicity and religion, they were stratified by class.[19] On the top tier were the wealthy cotton exporters and factory owners, like the Benaki family. The majority of the population, however, worked as retailers and white-collar workers.[20] Greeks of all classes were very much attached to their own community and rarely married non-Greeks even if the latter were Orthodox Christians.[21] This sense of ethnic introversion is best expressed by a letter Penelope Delta received from the Greek politician Ion Dragoumis, who arrived in Alexandria in 1905 to serve as Greek vice-consul.[22] Like many Greek dignitaries, he was welcomed by the Benaki family.[23] "I like the atmosphere of your house because it does not exhibit anything Levantine or cosmopolitan," he wrote.[24]

While Dragoumis was graciously received at the Benaki residence, this was not the case for non-Greeks. Penelope described her community as being "splendid, rich, closed to foreigners who tried nevertheless to gain access."[25] A very limited number of these "foreigners" did manage to gain entry, among them consul generals, directors of banks and large department stores, a few Jewish visitors, and even fewer Syrians "whom we contemptuously called Levantines."[26] She remembers how generously the community gave to its own, having established schools, hospitals, and churches. For this reason, she could not imagine the existence of other, nonaffluent Greeks. All Greeks seemed prosperous, she writes, with "money flowing in the streets."[27] They lived in a world unto itself. At times they came out of their enclaves to sponsor collective celebrations, such as the annual Lenten carnival that represented the highlight of the social calendar, especially in the latter decades of the nineteenth century. Under the direction and sponsorship of the Synadino and Zervoudaki families, a parade of costumed celebrants formed around Mohammed Ali Square, which then proceeded past Rue Chérif, down Rue Rosette, until it reached the city hall. Contemporaries spoke of thousands of merrymakers, elaborate and ostentatious floats, and lavish uniforms that together cost more than thirty thousand Egyptian pounds.[28]

We can get a glimpse of the charmed life led by elite Greeks by looking at the social activities of Constantine's brother Paul. A member of the Sporting Club,[29] he regularly took part in athletic events there, in addition to attending society weddings, literary readings, dinners, theater, recitals, the Queen's Jubilee receptions at the British consulate, and Fourteenth of July celebrations at the French consulate. Paul's social calendar from the 1880s was full. In those days, members of the Cavafy family still counted as part of the elect Greek circle and were invited to the most exclusive weddings. Just in 1889 alone, the year Aristides was married, Haricleia and her sons attended at least eight weddings in the most illustrious Alexandrian houses, including those of the Benakis (for their daughter Alexandra), the Menasces (for their daughter Celine), and the Apostolidis (for their son Constantine).[30]

Constantine, for his part, took comfort that up to the 1890s the Cavafys could still lay claim to the cachet of Alexandrian gentility. Indeed, during the trip to Athens in 1901, he and Alexander behaved as if they still occupied the same top rank as the other first-class passengers on the steamship *El Kahira*. Constantine often ran into old acquaintances on board and talked to them with the self-assurance of a person who felt himself their equal. On the second day on board, for instance, he came upon Mr. Helmi, "a tobacco merchant of Cairo. Rather pompous. But he bowed to me today, though not introduced, and seems desirous of making my acquaintance."[31] While waiting for the quarantine period on Delos, he spoke with Mme. Roucho about "the old times when we were neighbors in the Okella Spanopoulos in 1886, 15 years ago!"[32]

In the 1880s and '90s, the Cavafys could still count on the

prestige of the name and their residual status as well-connected Anglo-Greeks to compensate for their social decline. But with each decade, this dissembling must have been more and more difficult. In Athens that summer, despite keeping up appearances, Constantine felt removed from the illustrious circles of his day. On July 16, having come down to the sea at Phaleron, he and Alexander dined with four distinguished men: "All these were young men 'de la haute'; consequently conversation was of society and its doings, of that Greek 'upper ten thousand' which has many different 'groupements' (Athens, Alexandria, Constantinople, London, Marseilles, etc.) but is so closely bound together by marriage and social ties that all the important events and the leading names of one 'groupement' are thoroughly known to the other."[33] The shame of his family's gradual financial disintegration and the fear of being excluded from upper-class social circles help explain why Constantine dreaded scandal and avoided ostentatious displays of homosexuality. He did not want to end up a social pariah like Oscar Wilde. Constantine's niece Eleni Coletti believed that her father and uncle felt insecure and embarrassed over their social decline. "In Alexandria," she claimed, "anyone who loses his fortunes drops down socially," adding that her uncle suffered from the "complex" of a fallen aristocrat.[34]

The affluence of the Greek community was exemplified by George Averoff, who, after his death in 1899, left a fortune twice as large as that of the richest textile baron in Manchester. As the dynamic president of the Greek *koinotita* (community) since 1885, he helped endow schools and cultural institutions both in Alexandria and in Greece, where, among other projects, he provided funding for the first modern Olympics held in Athens in 1896.[35] His funeral on August 3, 1899, was a public event for European Alexandrians. The city came to a standstill for the cortege, which stretched seven kilometers from the city center to Ramleh.

At its head rode the police, followed by consular guards, then students from Greek schools, representatives of the city guilds, the governor, members of the city council, the Patriarch, religious dignitaries of all confessions, and then ordinary Alexandrians.[36] Every Greek in Alexandria would have wanted to see and, in turn, be seen at this moment of great spectacle and pride for the community. The Greeks attending Averoff's funeral had many reasons to boast about their accomplishments. In a couple of decades, they had created their own separate society with cafés and newspapers and numerous institutions—schools, hospitals, orphanages, a cathedral, and many other churches. Their schools, according to Athanasios Politis, were the envy of the city's other European communities.[37] Surprisingly for such a mercantile group of people but crucially for Constantine, Greeks had also developed a lively literary culture, of which he would emerge as its foremost representative.

The Greek population in Egypt continued to grow until well into the 1930s. In 1897, there were 38,208 Greeks; in 1907, 62,794; in 1917, 56,731; and in 1927, 99,794. In Alexandria itself, the Greeks were the dominant foreign group, with a population of 25,393 in 1917. By 1937, four years after the poet's death, the Greeks numbered 37,000 and boasted four primary schools for boys and four for girls and two high schools for boys and two for girls.[38] When Alexander A. Boddy visited the city in 1899, he found the Greeks so numerous that Alexandria felt to him like a suburb of Athens, with many omnibuses bearing Greek letters and numerous shops with Greek names.[39] Eight years later, the overall population of the city stood at 332,246, of which 24,602 were Greeks, 15,916 Italians, 8,190 British, and 4,304 French.[40]

There is no doubt that the middle- and upper-class Greeks of Egypt flourished during Constantine's lifetime. They and other Europeans owed their prosperity to treaties known as the Capitulations, which exempted these foreign nationals from local laws and taxation. Originally signed by the Ottoman Empire with Venice and France in 1535, they were extended after 1855 to citizens of other European powers (including Greece), with which the sultan enjoyed diplomatic and commercial relations. These treaties granted extraterritorial rights to Christians, freeing them from legal and tax obligations to the state, until they were abolished in stages between 1922 and 1937.[41] For instance, they guaranteed that trials of European criminals were conducted in the consular offices of the respective countries rather than in Egyptian courts. Moreover, Europeans, but not Egyptians, were allowed to carry guns and knives, often licensed by their own consulates. And the consulates themselves preserved the right to station ships in the harbor in case they were needed for emergencies. In a sense, these treaties had the indirect effect of distancing the Europeans from Muslim and Coptic Egyptians and encouraging them to see themselves as part of their own separate communities.[42] This meant that the Greeks of Egypt did not need Ottoman passports, since their legal status existed outside the Ottoman state. Rather than seeking formal ties with the Egyptian administration, they felt closer to Greece judicially and politically.

In addition to the legal and political barriers, cultural walls divided Greeks from Muslim Egyptians. For the Greeks, along with other foreigner residents of Egypt, considered themselves part of the Levant, a constellation of urban centers stretching from Thessaloniki to Istanbul, Smyrna, Beirut, and reaching Alexandria.[43] Since they identified their cultural and economic interests with this greater diaspora, Egyptian Greeks were strong supporters of free trade and looked toward Athens, Istanbul, Marseilles, Paris, and London, rather than Cairo or Upper Egypt, as places to visit and emulate. And they depended on Greek consuls, and increasingly on Britain, to protect their commercial enterprises and way of life.[44]

Their political loyalties to the Greek kingdom, their cultural attachments to the Greek community of Egypt, and their international economic outlook blinded the Greeks to the Egyptian nationalism spreading at the end of the nineteenth century, one fed by peasants and intellectuals who resented the extraterritorial privileges of the Europeans, Britain's oppressive policies, and the fear of being left behind by the changes of modernization. Enjoying their social, economic, and political benefits, the Greeks, like other Europeans, did not sufficiently understand that their entitlements were a source of anger for Egyptians. The Greeks, in other words, were not sufficiently sensitive to their own fragile status in a society that was becoming increasingly more nationalistic.[45] Countless poor Egyptians lived in simple mud huts and dressed in rags. And their children were often thin and diseased, and had swollen stomachs. More often than not, the foreigners who visited the few ancient ruins had to pass by and witness their dire situation.[46] But like the Europeans who had settled in Alexandria before them, the Greeks learned to ignore the predicament of ordinary Egyptians. It's as if foreigners and Egyptians were living in two separate cities. In reality, however, the luxury and sensuality of the Corniche was geographically not far removed from either the slums or the middle-class residential districts of Egyptians. After all, Alexandria was primarily a Muslim city.

Economic and political resentments, festering for decades, exploded openly in the third quarter of the nineteenth century as the Egyptian state faced bankruptcy. The expansion of the economy, which had brought the Europeans to Egypt, was in part made possible by taxation of the peasants. At the same time, the state borrowed heavily to bankroll building projects, irrigation systems, and military expeditions into Sudan. For instance, Khedive Ismail (1830–95) financed through debt the building of the museum in Cairo, the National Library, and the Opera House, which commissioned Verdi to compose *Aida* in 1871. But with the end of the American Civil War, as noted earlier, cotton prices plummeted by 25 percent along with state revenues. As a result, the public deficit in 1879 stood at ninety-three million Egyptian pounds, an amount Egypt could never pay back, forcing the government to divert huge financial resources to service it.[47]

Khedive Ismail had no choice but to declare bankruptcy and accept French and British control of his government in 1876, six years after the death of Peter John Cavafy and one year prior to the return of Haricleia and her sons from England. This foreign intervention reinforced the greatest dilemma Egyptian leaders faced since Mohammed Ali: how best to use Western technological know-how and money in order to win independence. The surrender of the Egyptian economy to British and French experts exacerbated the national sense of humiliation while increasing the number of foreigners employed by the Egyptian government. In 1882, for instance, one thousand Europeans worked in the administration, constituting only 2 percent of the workforce but drawing nearly 16 percent of the payroll.[48] At this time, thousands of Egyptian young men, trained in the new schools, were competing directly for jobs with children of the Europeans, such as the Cavafy sons.[49]

Egyptian military officers also grew increasingly resentful that their advancement was blocked by the continuing presence of Turks in the upper echelons of the Egyptian army. Their complaints coincided with the frustration among the general fellahin.

Members of both classes became receptive to the calls of an assertive nationalism and to the slogan of "Egypt for Egyptians." Ahmed Bey Arabi (1841–1911), as a son of peasants and also one of the disaffected colonels, came to represent the growing dissatisfaction over European control of Egypt.[50] He mobilized a formidable movement that challenged the authority of the new Khedive Tawfiq, who had assumed his position on June 25, 1879, after the Ottoman Sublime Porte forced the resignation of his father, Ismail. Arabi accused Tawfiq of succumbing to European political pressure, instigated rallies around the country, and organized a huge demonstration in Alexandria in September 1881. Ordinary Egyptians hailed him as their savior from their own corrupt rulers and the influence of the Europeans, believing that the departure of the Europeans would relieve them of their huge debts.[51]

For their part, European residents of Egypt began to fear for their lives and foreign powers worried about their financial and political interests. The situation became very tense and unpredictable when on June 11, 1882, a riot broke out in Alexandria following a fracas between an Egyptian and a Maltese. Mistaking this as a political protest, Greeks and Maltese began to fire at the brawlers below them from their windows and balconies. As news spread about this attack, Muslim Egyptians, armed with wooden sticks, assaulted Europeans throughout the city.[52] A mob raged in the streets with some shouting "Death to Christians." Despite efforts by Arabi to contain the mayhem, the country descended into chaos, leading to the deaths of 250 Egyptians and 50 Europeans.[53] In the ensuing days, panic spread around the city, compelling foreigner residents to abandon Alexandria out of fear of an insurrection both against them and the khedive. The port filled with European vessels taking away their nationals. By June 17, 1882, close to twenty thousand had fled.[54] Meanwhile,

French and British warships had docked in the harbor to end the uprisings and protect foreign residents and property. An attack on the city was imminent. The situation for the Cavafy family was precarious, as Constantine wrote at the time, and the family luckily escaped on June 26.

The British wanted to bring Alexandria under control by firing immediately into the city. The French, however, reluctant to undertake such severe measures, drew up their anchors and sailed away. Left alone, the British warships began to bombard Alexandria on July 10, 1882, destroying parts of the waterfront and city center. This act of violence had the desired result of forcing the rebellious Arabi to cease his insurrection. With Khedive Tawfiq publicly supporting the British actions, the Ottoman state declared Arabi a rebel, sentencing him to death. Facing the opposition of the Egyptian government and the overwhelming firepower of the Anglo-Indian army, Arabi surrendered on September 15, 1882. His death sentence was commuted, however, and he was allowed to seek exile to Ceylon.[55] Writing about the end of this "mock" trial to Constantine, John expressed his dismay that a man who instigated so many crimes was allowed to go "scot-free." He characterized the commutation of his death sentence a "height of folly, not to say, cruelty" (December 4, 1882).[56]

The Arabi revolt had come to an end with Britain firmly in control of Egypt, and with Khedive Tawfiq as legal ruler of the state. Arabi had underestimated British determination to protect both the European residents and the British interests: access to the Suez Canal and the repayment of Egyptian government debt.[57] (Arabi remained a hero in the Egyptian imagination until 1952, when Gamal Abdel Nasser presented himself as a modern Arabi to launch his own revolution against foreign rule.) The hegemony that Britain gained over Egypt, however, emboldened Greeks like the Cavafy brothers along with other Europeans to believe that Britain would guarantee their protection well into the future. To be sure, having exercised authority over Egypt, with an occupying army of five thousand and about five hundred officials, Britain secured Alexandria as an outpost of Europe and Greece in Egypt.[58] For its part, the British government understood the crucial role played by Greek merchants as intermediaries between their colonial rule and the Egyptian population. Thus, authorities strained to pacify the situation in order to enable the quick repatriation of the foreign residents. Among those returning expatriates were the three Cavafy brothers, Peter, Aristides, and John, in August 1882.

Haricleia and Constantine remained in Istanbul until 1885. As discussed in chapter three, their financial state had deteriorated and they began to rely on monthly remittances from the three brothers in Alexandria. In addition to their economic miseries, they had no house to return to. When the British bombarded Alexandria, they destroyed a significant part of the city center, including the grand residence on Rue Chérif that Peter John Cavafy had rented in 1860. The Okelle Debbane on Rue Machmoud Pacha el Falaki, to which Haricleia moved after the family's return from Britain in 1877, also sustained damage.[59] The residence on 32 Boulevard Ramleh, where the family moved in 1879, was only partially damaged and they were able to save many of their possessions.[60]

In his letter to Constantine of August 7, 1882, John wrote, "You cannot imagine what a sad sight the old house was to me when I saw it for the first time." He complained about hordes of flies and excessive heat. Almost a month later, he asked Constantine to remind their mother that the application for an indemnity for the damages to their house "must be in Peter's name in conformity with the contract." The issue of this dispensation had become a daily obsession of the family, since the uprooting of Haricleia and the remaining sons depended on it. John, therefore, often provided updates regarding this matter, referring specifically to two public commissions named in Britain to consider the issue.[61] Obviously, the brothers in Egypt were responding to the anxious inquiries from family members still in Istanbul. Although few of these letters survive, we have one sent by Alexander on June 4, 1883, while he was visiting his aunt Amalia Kallinous in Pera, to his mother in Yeniköy. Although Alexander's intent was to let his mother know that Paul was not seriously ill, he also informed her of news from Aristides in Alexandria that "we will receive the money. Patience."[62]

John openly revealed his pro-British sentiments to Constantine and his letters no doubt reflected the relief of the entire Greek community at the arrival of the British forces. He was satisfied that the sultan had declared "Arabi and his followers rebels" and hoped this move would allay the "fanaticism" of the troops (August 12, 1882).[63] Not surprisingly, given his realization that Britain guaranteed Greek interests in Egypt, he expressed support for the British policy of "annexation" of Egypt. "The war is now over," he wrote, and then described the "disarmament" of the rebels at various locations.[64]

The issue of the compensation for the foreign residents of Alexandria who suffered damages by the riots and bombardment continued to preoccupy British policymakers. Eventually they forced Khedive Tawfiq to apportion four million Egyptian pounds in compensation to these individuals, an action that added to the public debt and the sense of national shame.[65] Overall, nine thousand indemnities were paid to those foreigners who could claim damaged property.[66] In effect, Egyptians paid for the damage caused by the British to their own city. Almost all of John's letters made some reference to this issue. In May 1885, he alluded to rumors regarding the positive resolution of this matter. "Heaven will it so? And thus allow me to embrace you all in ease as I do now in imagination" (May 2, 1885).[67] On August 23, he wrote with much relief that they were about to receive their payment of £17,500.[68] He sent his mother £140 for their transportation and noted that the brothers were looking to rent a house on the Boulevard de Ramleh and were shopping for furniture. With great anticipation, Haricleia, Alexander, Paul, and Constantine returned in October 1885. They must have been able to salvage some of the old furniture from the house on Boulevard Ramleh because Constantine claimed to have inherited pieces in his possession. The family was still able to afford at least two servants.[69] But Haricleia still harbored delusions of grandeur and liked the idea of naming the whole building where their apartment was located "Okella Cavafy."

A question that preoccupied Constantine's contemporaries concerned his own understanding of the political upheavals he experienced in his youth and witnessed as an adult. How did he define his own place in Egypt? Did he possess a national identity? Upon his return from Istanbul in 1885, it appears he refused or neglected to apply for a British passport (he would have been covered up until this point under the official naturalization document issued to Haricleia in 1877 that listed himself, Peter, and John) and acquired or "returned" to his Greek citizenship that year.[70] As noted, he saw himself more as an Egyptian Greek (*Egyptiotis*) rather than as a Greek citizen. This latter point must have been reinforced during his visits to Greece in 1901, 1903, and 1905, when the locals would have highlighted his "Egyptian" identity, as indeed happened during his 1905 trip to Athens to visit his ill brother Alexander. The attending physician said that he "cared [for?] another Egyptian at the Evangelismos [hospital] from typhoid fever."[71]

At the same time, Constantine came to identify Great Britain as a protector and guarantor of his economic interests and personal security in Alexandria. To be sure, he knew that his father's original fortune was created through the export of cotton to Britain. His years in England and Anglo-Greek identity surely complicated his view of the British Empire. And the modest life he enjoyed in Alexandria as a civil servant depended on British hegemony in Egypt. But this did not make him a mindless supporter of British imperialism. Malanos did hear him criticize British policies on numerous occasions.[72] As a son of parents who hailed from the Greek community of Istanbul, he shared a common historical and cultural legacy with Egyptian Arabs in the Ottoman Empire and a history of common exploitation.[73] Moreover, being a poet, a homosexual, and an observer of the power of empires in antiquity, he sometimes identified with the plight of Egyptian peasants struggling against British injustice. And in his many poems on the ancient Mediterranean, he brought attention to ethnic and racial mixing. In "Return from Greece" (1914), the unnamed speaker addresses his companion, Hermippus, on their voyage back home from Greece, saying that Greece is no longer the center of their world. "We too are Hellenes," he asserts, but with "Asian affections and emotions."

Although he did not publicly express any political sympathies for Egyptian nationalism or rail against British imperialism, he occasionally treated these subjects in some of his unpublished poems. In 1908, one year after he moved to Rue Lepsius and the year Paul left for France, he composed what was for him an atypical poem, "June 27, 1906, 2:00 p.m.," which he never published. Although its subject—a young man of seventeen and an object of the speaker's erotic gaze—did not depart from the poet's usual thematic repertoire, the boy's ethnicity and religion did. For the first and only time, he explicitly depicted a Muslim youth and wrote an unambiguously political poem, jotting down the young man's name in pencil on the lower part of the page: Yousef Housein Selím.[74] Of course, the young men whom he evoked in his poems set in modern Alexandria may conceivably have been Arabs. But they were not identified as such; the poet emphasized their idealized youth and beauty rather than ethnicity or race. In contrast, the young man of this poem had a Muslim name. Departing further from his usual practice, Constantine composed the poem in the manner of a ritual lament, a mode of poetic expression going back to Homer's *Iliad*, specifically Andromache's dirge for the dead Hector and Achilles's lamentation for his friend Patroclus.[75]

The poem refers to the public executions of four Egyptian peasants accused by the British authorities of involvement in the notorious Denshawai Affair, a watershed in the rise of Egyptian nationalism and the general effort to gain independence from Britain. In June 1906, a group of British officers arrived at the Delta village of Denshawai to shoot pigeons, an act angering the villagers who had kept their own birds nearby. A fire erupted and the villagers, thinking that the foreigners had been the cause, attacked the officers with wooden clubs. Terrified by the ensuing violence, the officers shot at the crowd, killing a local woman. The villagers for their part were so agitated by this murder that they counterattacked, causing the officers to flee. As they ran back to the camp, one of them died of sunstroke. When a villager tried to help the fallen officer, the British comrades, thinking he had killed their compatriot, beat the Egyptian to death. The British officials, meanwhile, feeling that this was a premeditated attack, tried the fifty-two villagers in a special court, which condemned four to death by hanging and others to be flogged publicly.

This brutal act, widely covered in the press, provoked general anger in Egypt and even among some circles in Britain. Many condemned the collective punishments and even Lord Cromer, the ccontroller general of Egypt, who was in Britain during the event, found the measures excessively severe and resigned after the public outcry. These civic punishments seemed to have permanently inflamed the Egyptian population against the British occupation. For the first time since the Arabi rebellion, countless Egyptians became politically aware of their dependent status and turned to protests and violence.[76] This was especially true of the fellahin population, still heavily impoverished.[77] There was a growing sense among Egyptians that economic dependence on foreigners contributed to a national weakness that permitted Britain's unchallenged brutality in Denshawai.

Constantine too was outraged by the injustices meted out in the village. Although he rarely referred to actual events in his mature poems, in this instance, he sided with the victims of empire. He showed his solidarity with the Egyptians by adopting the voice of Selím's mother. The poem is narrated in the third person but clearly its sympathies lie with the Muslims of the village:

When the Christians brought out for hanging
the innocent, seventeen-year-old boy,
his mother, near the scaffold,
crawled on the earth, beating herself
under the ferocious, midday sun,
sometimes she howled and bayed like a wild wolf
and sometimes, the martyr, exhausted, she wailed—
"I only had you for seventeen years, my child."
And when they led him up the scaffold
and hooked the rope to throttle him,
the innocent boy of seventeen years

who dangled pitifully in the empty space,
in the seizures of his dark anguish
his adolescent body, handsomely formed,
his mother, the martyr, was rolling in the dust.
but she no longer bewailed his years;
"Only seventeen days," she wailed,
"You were my treasure for only seventeen days, my child."

The first line refers to Christian violence, as if we are looking at the world from the villagers' position. And when the authorities haul the young man to the scaffold, the speaker seems momentarily taken by the beautifully apportioned adolescent body, much as the Greek warriors were entranced by Hector's naked corpse in the *Iliad* and the sailors mesmerized by the dangling body of Billy Budd in Melville's novella. But his attention quickly turns to the mother who reels on the dusty ground below, wailing that she had had her son for only seventeen years/days. Thus, although for one moment the speaker allows himself to identify erotically with the beautiful victim, his eyes never swerve from the horrors Selím's mother has to witness; and he cites words from her lamentations and shows her crawling on the earth.

Missing here is the Cavafian historical detachment of the later poems and the chilling irony usually directed at historical figures, such as that found in "Aristobulos," a poem written in 1916 and published two years later, about the eponymous prince of Judea. At the instigation of his mother and his sister, and in order to prevent the prince's possible succession to the throne, Kind Herod I ordered his drowning, even though Aristobulos was the brother of one of his wives, Mariamme, and had been recently appointed by Herod himself as high priest. Predictably, Constantine has the palace "in tears" and King Herod, the arch hypocrite, "inconsolably laments" at the "accidental drowning."

Alexandra, Aristobulos's mother and Herod's mother-in-law, publicly weeps. But when she withdraws to her chambers, she curses the "criminal king" for his betrayal and castigates herself for not catching on to palace intrigues and thus allowing her plans for succession to be thwarted. As a member of the royal household, she has to bear "their lies," not being able to rush out and inform the people of her son's murder. In "Aristobulos," Constantine coolly analyzes the duplicities and power struggles in Judea with the disinterested attitude of a historian.

In "June 27, 1906, 2:00 p.m.," however, the speaker can't separate himself from the pain and horror of the public execution, the mother's wailing, and the son's frail body hanging from the scaffold. The poem stands as a unique document in the Cavafian corpus and a testament to his outrage at the injustices committed by the British against the fellahin. The two-year gap between the event itself (1906) and the date of composition (1908) shows how preoccupied Constantine was with the subject. In the meantime, he may have gotten to know the Arabic poems that had been composed about Denshawai, considering his own text as a contribution to this tradition.[78]

Ultimately, he chose not to publish "June 27, 1906, 2:00 p.m.," as was the case with countless other poems. We have no way of knowing the reasons for this decision. Perhaps this text was a formal experiment in the ritual lament that had not succeeded in his eyes. Given his perfectionism, he may have found it weak, if not sentimental. At the same time, he rarely wrote about contemporaneous events. After all, he preferred distant historical periods to the barbarism of British colonialism and the suffering of his contemporaries. This was his aesthetic stance toward the world and toward the grief and anguish of others. It was also a personal preference to avoid the messiness of life's toil, the path he usually took in his private relationships. Quite conceivably, being a British civil servant, he might have feared retribution from his superiors. He had the example of Mahmud Tahir Haqqi, who, having written a novel about Denshawai, was repeatedly harassed by the authorities until he resigned from his position in the civil service.[79]

But Constantine continued to follow the repercussions of this affair, having gathered a stack of newspaper cuttings regarding a similar political debacle four years later: the murder trial of Ibrahim al-Wardani, who was indicted and confessed to the murder of the Egyptian prime minister Butrus Pasha Ghali. During his trial, al-Wardani accused Ghali, a Copt, of being more British than the British but above all for having acted as one of the two Egyptian judges who oversaw the Denshawai case. Constantine then added a lengthy note in Greek in which he wrote that "the Egyptian people showed sympathy for Wardani, pitying the individual—at least a greater part of them—rather than approving the act."[80] He then went on to record that after the execution "of the unfortunate young man," demonstrations took place all over Egypt: "Poems were written in praise; students of various higher studies wore black ties in mourning; people gathered around his grave, giving emotional speeches; and friendly hands brought beautiful flowers."[81] Constantine was so taken by these events that he saved the issues of the Alexandrian newspaper *La Réforme*, which described the progress of the Wardani case, from his arrest to the trial and eventual execution. On May 12, 1910, the newspaper chose to highlight a long letter from Emmanuel Benaki on the cotton commission rather than on Wardani. But two days later, the trial was the lead story with the headline "Wardani Condemned to Death." And on June 28, the newspaper headlined his execution. It cited his final words as "Je crois en Dieu de qui vient la liberté" (I believe in God from whom comes freedom).[82]

This long preoccupation with the Denshawai Affair shows that Constantine was neither a mindless mouthpiece of his ethnic group nor a passive admirer of British imperialism. He clearly sided here with the exploited peasants of Egypt. As an intellectual, poet, historian, and homosexual, he gained insights into the racial mixture of history from his study of ancient Alexandria and thus could step back and judge these acts of injustice. In the latter part of his life, he wrote a few articles that indicate his more nuanced understanding of Greeks in Egypt and the relationship between Greek and Egyptian intellectuals and writers. In an unpublished piece (1929) on the endeavors of the literary magazine *Lanterne Sourde*[83]—newly established to promote Arab-Egyptian writing in Europe—he characterized the goal of the periodical as quite valuable. While he recognized the significance of this specific focus, he himself wished to bring attention to other writers who were "racially non-Egyptian," such as "Greeks and Syrians," who were "nevertheless children of Egypt, because here they grew up, lived, and many were born."[84] The Greeks of Egypt, he continued, inevitably produced works "of this environment." Being familiar with the "Egyptian way of life" and "Egyptian way of thinking," as well as coming into contact with "Arabic-speaking colleagues," these writers were in the position to offer "beautiful ideas" and "initiatives."

In another article published a year later in Alexandria, he encouraged Arabic-speaking Greeks of Egypt "to introduce contemporary Arabic literature of Egypt to the Greek reading public."[85] It seems that he was aware of these texts, since in a letter, dated May 9, 1928, to Stavros Stavrinos, the editor of the *Semaine Égyptienne* (an important literary journal founded in 1926 and in print until 1951), he referred to the special issue the journal was planning on the Egyptian writer Ahmed Rassin. He wrote that whenever he sees "an article by Ahmed Rassin in the *Semaine Égyptienne*, I rush to read it, knowing that it would be charming and interesting." While acknowledging that he could only read Rassin's work in French, he was certain that a talented author would write just as brilliantly in Arabic.[86] And in a conversation recorded by Eftychia Zelitas on February 2, 1928, he praised a celebration taking place in Cairo for three Egyptian poets. He did refer, however, to the much smaller market for Greek books in Egypt: Greek poets having three million potential readers, while Egyptian writers had twenty-four million. Although he was invited to participate in this event, he declined, probably because he had ceased traveling outside Alexandria by this time. He did send a letter of appreciation, which was read during the proceedings.[87]

His interest in Arabic poetry and his intense scrutiny of the Denshawai Affair demonstrate that, at the very least, Constantine remained equivocal with respect to the British Empire. When in 1914 Alexandria was brimming with British soldiers, he kept his distance, never expressing his support nor striving to get to know any British regulars or officers apart, of course, from E. M. Forster.[88] No military figure is known to have ascended the stairs to his flat on Rue Lepsius.[89] He never marched with the crowd, abandoning himself to the excitement of the moment, but remained an Anglophile, devoted to progress.[90]

He followed with intense interest the Balkan Wars (1912–13) and Greece's entry into World War I, and read attentively about the country's victories. And he was disturbed by what the Greeks call the Asia Minor Catastrophe, which led to the destruction of Smyrna in August of 1922 and the forcible exchange of population between Greece and Turkey in 1923. Following an aborted march by Greek armed forces into Anatolia, Turkish troops under the command of Kemal Atatürk pushed back, routing the Greeks. Atrocities were committed by both sides. Thousands died, with many Greeks jumping into the sea from the quay of Smyrna to save themselves. In order to prevent any further conflict between the two countries, the foreign powers imposed a mandatory exchange of populations under the Treaty of Lausanne by which 1.3 million Christians (ethnic Greeks) had to abandon Turkey and about three hundred thousand Muslims (ethnic Turks) had to leave their homes in Greece for Turkey.

Needless to say, these were trying times for the Greeks of Egypt. Yet Constantine never directly mentioned this cataclysm in his correspondence with friends. But in September 1922, when Polys Modinos visited him in his apartment, he found Constantine slouched in his chair, silent and nearly morose. Then, as noted earlier, the poet whispered to him: "What a horrible thing is happening to us. We are losing Smyrna, we are losing Ionia, we are losing the gods." And then not able to continue, he began to sob, tears sliding down his furrowed face.[91] Modinos could not understand why Constantine equated the expatriation of Greeks from Smyrna with the departure of the pagan gods. Constantine was clearly moved by the expulsion of Greeks from territory where they had lived for millennia. Yet the reference to Ionia and the exodus of the ancient deities indicates that for him the loss of Asia Minor was tragic in terms of both its human and cultural toll. In an early poem, "Ionic" (printed in 1895, rewritten in 1905, and published in June 1911), he mourns the flight of the gods from Ionia. That we smashed their statues, he writes, that we drove them from their temples does not mean that the gods have died. "O land of Ionia, they love you still, / their souls still remember you." And in the sunrise of an August morning, "an ethereal adolescent form . . . makes its way across the hills." In this poem, the gods of Ionia still hover over the landscape, perhaps because Greeks continue to live there, their memory evoked however indistinctly. But after 1922, Constantine says that these pagan ghosts have withdrawn forever.

Try as they may, later commentators, such as the poet George

Seferis, sought to unearth references to the Asia Minor Catastrophe in Constantine's poems, such as "On Behalf of Those Who Fought in the Achaean League." Written in 1922 about a struggle in 146 BCE by Greeks against Roman forces, it speaks about men who "fought and died nobly," not fearing those who conquered everyone before them. If this poem contains any reference to the events of 1922, it is indirect. Constantine was not a poet of contemporary politics. He wrote about battles in antiquity, wars between empires, and the stratagems of emperors trying to stay in power. But like Jane Austen, who lived during the tumultuous times of the French Revolution without writing about them, he chose not to turn World War I, the Egyptian struggle for independence, or the Asia Minor Catastrophe into poetic subjects. He never ceased repeating that "current events did not really interest" him, at least as subject matter for his poems.[92] As he confessed to Timos Malanos, although he followed with much anxiety news about the Balkan Wars in 1912 and 1913, often stepping out of the house in the evening to get the latest news from the front, he never wrote a single poem about these events. "I am not a patriotic poet," he added.[93]

He was, of course, criticized for not writing about the cataclysmic events in Greece during his time. Malanos unkindly says that, while the whole city was preoccupied with World War I, Constantine was investigating the proper vestments that Caesarion, the son of Cleopatra, would have worn.[94] Moreover, in the spring of 1897, Malanos adds, when "all of Greece and, with it, Greek Alexandria" were following the atrocities on Crete during the war of independence against the Ottoman Empire, Constantine seemed untouched, worried more about an upcoming trip to London and Paris with John.[95] While Malanos's comments may be overstated, it is true that Constantine did not refer to the violence on Crete in any of his personal notes that have survived.

Nor did he volunteer to join the war effort as other young Greek men from Egypt did in 1897.[96] Michalis Peridis, who met Constantine around the end of 1914, writes that, although the poet was not ideologically driven, he did follow political developments in Greece and often kept cuttings from newspapers in his desk. He left behind a stack of articles relating to the Balkan Wars of 1912–13.[97]

It is safe to conclude that Constantine was interested in Greek politics and followed events in Greece from his safe harbor of Alexandria. He was a liberal humanist, more sexually than politically progressive, fervently believing in individual autonomy.[98] He did say to Malanos in 1924 how "horrible it is for someone not to be able to use his body as he likes."[99] Unlike Penelope Delta, obsessed with the Balkan Wars and besotted with the nationalist Ion Dragoumis, or her father, Emmanuel Benaki, who moved to Athens to enter politics, Constantine kept his sense of national identity complex, playful, and hard to define. He expressed this vagueness by saying mischievously that he was not "Greek" but "Hellenic" and certainly not one "who imitates Greeks."[100] Rika Sengopoulos, who knew Constantine better than most people around him, called him a "true Greek of Egypt."[101]

An important question, however, is whether he truly understood political developments in Egypt. Did he comprehend the implications for Greeks of the slogan "Egypt for Egyptians"? To be sure, 1922 marked a sharp ideological divide between Greeks of Egypt and their Muslim neighbors. While Greeks were mourning the loss of life in Asia Minor, some Egyptian political parties sent messages of congratulations to Turkish nationalists.[102] That very year, Muslim Egyptians also celebrated their freedom from British rule.[103] Decades earlier, they had begun to express their widespread dissatisfaction with British imperialism.[104] For some time, intellectuals had been accusing the British government of keeping the country in a state of ignorance to justify the occupation.[105] They spoke openly of "Egyptianism," a national identity spanning from Pharaonic times to the present.[106] Needless to say, this nationalism did not include foreign communities, such as the Greeks, because Egyptians saw the Europeans as part of an exploitative system.[107] It is not surprising then that the Muslim Brotherhood was founded by Hassan al-Banna in 1928 to rescue Muslim youth from the corruption of European dominance.[108] At the heart of his protest was the conviction that Egyptians had little control over their country.[109]

At the age of sixty-five, Constantine was probably not aware of the Muslim Brotherhood. Nor did he fully appreciate the inner logic of Egyptian nationalism or understand that he and his Greek community were not part of its narrative for the future of Egypt. We can compare his disinterested attitude toward Egyptian nationalism and the plight of the peasants to the astute judgments of another Greek writer, Nikos Kazantzakis, who traveled through Egypt in 1927 and, as noted, visited Constantine in Alexandria. Of course, Kazantzakis was an outsider and could observe political developments in Egypt from a fresh perspective. A Marxist and world traveler, he realized that Egypt, along with the colonized nations of Africa and Asia, were ready to overthrow the "colonial structure."[110] Kazantzakis met intellectuals in Cairo who discussed with him the nationalist turmoil in their country. In his conversations, he concluded that Egypt, like many other nations of the continent, was ready for a nationalist revolution.[111] Constantine, however, did not seem to be aware that Muslim Egyptians, gaining the confidence to run their own affairs, no longer needed foreigners. He was blindsided by the emerging nationalist currents, like most of the city's Europeans.

In 1928, the year of the founding of the Muslim Brotherhood, Constantine was enjoying the spread of his popularity in Egypt, Greece, and Europe. Laudatory articles were appearing in Egyptian and Greek magazines by leading critics[112] along with condemnations and even a parody of his work by Malanos in May. In April, a favorable article appeared in Paris. He printed a number of poems while republishing others. In February, as previously noted, the editors of *Lanterne Sourde* invited him to give a talk on Egyptian poetry in Cairo, while in May, he was asked to write an article in Cairo's *La Semaine Égyptienne*. And in September, *The Criterion* of London published two poems translated by George Valassopoulo, and Karl Dieterich issued in Leipzig his anthology of modern Greek poetry, *Neugriechische Lyriker*, which included twelve poems by Constantine. In November, the Parisian *Libre* printed a translation of "You Didn't Understand," while in Greece another parody of his poetry appeared. A month later, the "Amis de l'Art" of Alexandria organized a poetry reading of various Francophone poets of the city where two Cavafy poems were read. At year's end, he counted the publication of nine poems. By all measures, it was for him an annus mirabilis, one that saw encomia and satires, articles and translations, all indicating the poet's ever-spreading fame. At an age when he was slowing down socially, even refusing to travel to Cairo to give the talk to the *Lanterne Sourde*, he did not seem to pay extraordinary attention to political developments in Egypt.

At the same time, he seems to have forgotten the deeper lessons of the 1882 Arabi rebellion, his family's flight to Istanbul, the British bombing of Alexandria, and the consequent destruction of his house and personal possessions. His commanding knowledge of historical change and the power struggles in antiquity did not provide him with insights into the social transformations taking place around him. Or perhaps his allusive, nonreferential writing, where the city was transformed into sensations, streets remained indistinct and names half-remembered, prevented him from detecting the tremors of history outside of his apartment. It is quite possible that his modernist poetics got in the way of his capacity to grasp the anti-colonial struggle. The man who dreamed of becoming a historian did not always draw the necessary lessons from his favorite métier.

Ultimately Constantine was most happy, free, and true to himself in the Alexandria of his creation. He tried realism in verses he later renounced and in others he never printed, poems like "Sham-el-Nessim," which appeared in 1892 but which he later rejected. Written in a mixture of demotic and katharevousa and with varying patterns of rhymes, it deals with the annual Egyptian springtime festival and refers specifically to the Alexandrian neighborhoods Khabari, Mex, Muharram Bey, Mahmoudiya, and Ramleh that are filled with celebrants. Similarly, the short story "In Broad Daylight," which he wrote around 1895/96, is also set in contemporary Alexandria.

Of course, Constantine was literal in his journals. His descriptions of Athens during his first trip in 1901 were very thorough and exact. As we have seen, he wrote about the places he visited, the archaeological sites, the streets, names of hotels, squares, and cafés. The names and the people are obviously real. But in his mature poetry, he was reluctant to write about modern Alexandria, the place on the map. Unlike Joyce's Dublin, Constantine's city floats in his poems less as a real community with traffic signs, markets, cafés, dirt, gutters, than as an idealized, anonymous realm where not even the young men have names. The poem titled "In the Street," for instance, does not identify the street at all, nor the "attractive" young man who saunters by. He is twenty-five years old but looks twenty, "pale" with "brown eyes" who yet has something "artistic in his dress" as he makes his way down the street, "hypnotized by the unlawful" pleasure he had just experienced. We do not know whether the café of "At the Entrance of the Café" (1904?/1915) is the Billiards Palace or the Café Al Salam or just an imaginary place. In the same way, the idol who appears at the café door, sculptured beautifully by Eros, does not resemble anyone specifically. The men in general, in their dreamy, distant beauty, are always anonymous; not a single one in modern Alexandria bears a name: no Mohammed, no Petros, no Henry.

Even the privation is not real—"Naked feet, unheard of in your verses," the English poet D. J. Enright quips in his poem "To Cavafy, of Alexandria."[113] Poverty exists insofar as it forces young men to wear tattered clothes or enter a life of ill repute. In "One Night," the speaker remembers the poor and sordid room above a suspect tavern where from the window he could glimpse the narrow and dirty alley and hear the voices of workers playing cards. But on this vulgar, ordinary bed, he felt "the body of love." And years later, writing about this experience in his "solitary house," he becomes "intoxicated again." Similarly, in "Below the House," a man enters a distant neighborhood and comes to a house where, in his youth, he made love. As he stands outside it many years later, that memory of pleasure "beautifies" the entire neighborhood. "Nothing ugly remained there." Were these two houses real or a creation of Constantine's imagination? We do know that when he returned from Istanbul, Mohammed Ali Square had been converted into a "bazaar of love" and there were many male brothels he could visit.[114] In his thirties, he frequented one at the corner of El Attarine and Selím Gobtan and pointed it out to his friend Vasilis Athanasopoulos when they had passed by it in 1917.[115] If either of these poems do refer to this establishment, they contain no signposts for us. Similarly, in the unfinished poem "News in the Paper" (1918), the speaker is caught up with events of a salacious murder while taking the tram. Disturbed by the moralizing tone of the article regarding "corrupted morals," he mourns to himself, for he remembers the time he spent with the victim the year previously in a place that was "half hotel, half brothel." Again, Constantine does not locate it, nor name the newspaper, nor tell us which tramline the speaker takes.[116] Sareyannis says that he "did not wish his poems to be tied to a specific reality and he tried by every possible manner to obscure the apparent manner of their birth."[117] His refusal to describe the actual Alexandria stemmed from an aesthetic stance rather than from a lack of talent, as some contemporaries had claimed. He understood that the source of his work's emotional energy lay in evocations, dreams, allusions, and feelings rather than in realist descriptions. "For me," he said once to Eftychia Zelitas, "unmediated impression does not lead to work. The impression must first wear out, to turn false on its own through time, rather than for me to falsify it."[118] He expressed as much in his poem "Understanding" (1915/1917), where the speaker confesses that "in the dissolute life of my youth, the designs of my poetry took shape, the territory of my art took form."

Constantine's poetic Alexandria was a place and, at the same time, a no-place, a utopia in the literal sense, a fusion of suggestions, glances, half-glimpsed faces, and incoherent gestures unburdened by the distractions of car horns, street smells, or the hum of the crowd. He captured his city in poems like "In the Evening" (1916/1917), where the speaker, weighed down by memories from his youthful past, steps out onto the balcony, to clear his head and catch a glimpse of the city he loves, "a little movement in the streets and in the shops." To a certain extent, Alexandria existed as an abstraction in his poetry, a blank canvas that he could "shape more freely in his mind," as he said of the prince Caesarion, the forgotten figure of Hellenistic history. This is why he chose to stay there his entire life. As he wrote on

April 28, 1907, "I have grown accustomed to Alexandria, and even if I were rich, most likely I would remain here. [. . .] Because it is like a homeland, because it is connected to my life's memories."[119] In its insubstantiality, his Alexandria often threatened to dissolve into thin air, to depart, as he put it in the sublime "The God Abandons Antony"—"say goodbye to Alexandria that is retreating" (1910/1911). But he lured it back with allusions and incantations. He needed his Alexandria near him after all. He craved a home that was oblique and silent, one that neither imprisoned him with its significance nor constricted him with its denotation.

Part III

FRIENDS

6

FRIENDSHIP AND INTIMACY

Cliques or Claques?

"A COMPANY OF FOUR" (1930?)

[. . .]
Beautifully dressed, as befits
such handsome boys; and theatre, and bars,
and their car, and an occasional trip—
they lack for nothing.

[. . .]
They all share their money
so they can dress well and spend,
to make their lives elegant as becomes
such handsome boys to help their friends
and later, as is their way, to forget what they spent.[1]

Sometime in the year 1930, feeling his age, bereft of siblings, and lacking intimate relationships, Constantine gave vent to a wistful nostalgia by writing what would remain an unfinished poem; "A Company of Four" may be read as an expression of the poet's emotional and artistic frame of mind during the final years of his life. Enjoying growing fame and not yet afflicted with the throat cancer that would ultimately kill him, he confronted his own senescence while manifesting his growing poetic audacity with a formula that reads as a kind of ironic lament much like the rejuvenating recipe of the speaker of his poem "Following the Recipe of Ancient Greco-Syrian Magicians" (1931*), who seeks a magic potion to bring back his youth along with his twenty-two-year-old lover. "A Company of Four" not only conjures up visions of Constantine's youthful friends, but also foregrounds the number four, the tally of his earliest cluster of mates (Mikès Ralli, Stephen Schilizzi, and John Rodocanachi, along with Constantine himself). The poem speaks powerfully to the patterns of his friendships and their varying degrees of intimacy, prompting the question: Did Constantine maintain any genuine friendships or cultivate close relationships outside his family nucleus?

Friendships do more than simply define and complete individuals in the conventional sense of allowing us to be judged based on the "company we keep." Friends provide glimpses into the more obscure recesses of a person's character and often function as another self. Private though he was, Constantine had indeed forged a number of close friendships during his life. These relationships fall quite nicely into the three categories outlined by Aristotle:[2] pleasure-friendships, virtue-friendships, and advantage-friendships.[3]

Fortunately, we have some rich documentation of the intensity and scope of the poet's relationships, largely in the form of letters. Without question, emotional intimacy proved to be a great challenge for Constantine, who opted in his mature years to sacrifice personal relations on the altar of his growing fame.

He is on record as having made the following pronouncement on the subject to his erstwhile friend and later arch-critic and antagonist Timos Malanos: "I don't recognize friendship or enmity except as they relate to my work."[4] How did he come to this extreme position where intimacy all but gives way to opportunism and fame? And at what cost to his happiness and emotional and intellectual well-being?

The most significant relationships outside Constantine's family about which we can speak with some degree of assurance were formed with a small cluster of people—friends from his early adolescent and young-adult years like Mikès Ralli, Stephen Schilizzi, and John Rodocanachi. In Aristotle's taxonomy of "*philia*" (friendship), these would be called "pleasure" friends, and it is clear from his interactions with them that they enjoyed each other's youthful company immensely. Later in life, Constantine would bond more deeply with two other significant personalities—Pericles Anastasiades and Alekos Sengopoulos, who might be categorized as "virtue" friends in that they shared the poet's values and tastes in addition to providing him with tangible and enduring support. More problematic and complex, however, is his relationship with Timos Malanos, who may well have been a virtue friend but in the end proved to be an "advantage" friend who became an enemy, rendering Constantine's words to him regarding friendship a self-fulfilling prophecy.

In his adolescent and young adult years, Constantine was aligned with a group of men who would later call themselves the "clique": Mikès Ralli, Stephen Schilizzi, and John Rodocanachi. He met them after returning to Alexandria from England in 1877, when the Cavafy family eventually took up residence on the Rue Ramleh. Constantine would congregate in the garden of this dwelling with this new set of friends who happened to be blood relations with the Anglo-Greeks with whom the Cavafys were intimately affiliated. The boys were also connected as fellow students in the Hermes Lyceum, a school run by Constantine Papazis, which the poet attended briefly between the years 1881 and 1882. These three youths were members of families who hailed from the island of Chios and had established extensive and powerful mercantile and banking dynasties in the Levant, Russia, and Western Europe. Two of them died early: Stephen in 1886 and Mikès in 1889. But there is a wider dimension to these relationships that speaks to Constantine's own fascination with history and its ironic dynamics.

In January 1822, some months after the outbreak of the Greek uprising against the Ottoman Turks, the Ottoman sultan summoned the three most prominent Greek men on Chios to the Sublime Porte in response to revolutionary activity on the island. These three men were charged with treason, imprisoned, and eventually hanged. Thodoris Ralli, Michalis Schilizzi, and Pandelis Rodocanachi were prosperous merchants from an island that enjoyed a unique status as a veritable paradise where a combination of imperial favor, botanical fecundity, and native industriousness created a place that bore little resemblance to the majority of Greek islands in the Mediterranean. The execution of these three Chians was a prelude to what would follow in May 1822—the near-wholesale massacre of the Greek population of Chios when some thirty thousand people were slaughtered. Survivors eagerly sought refuge with expatriates in London and Liverpool, creating a large Chian diaspora. It is no coincidence that Constantine's best friends would be descendants of these prominent clans. These young men would be educated in both English and Greek in preparation for their internships as clerks in a Greek-owned company, and groomed for apprenticeship and advancement in commerce, trade, and banking.

The Ralli family established itself in England as early as 1815, setting up headquarters in London and gradually expanding its operation to five continents, becoming one of the largest merchant trading companies in the world.[5] The various branches of the firm partnered with other major families from Chios, including the Schilizzi clan. In the 1850s, the Ralli firm employed four thousand clerks and fifteen thousand workmen; together with the Rodocanachi family, who ran the most important mercantile family operation in the Black Sea, these two Greek firms had the largest organization and capital of any merchants operating in London.[6] Given this level of spectacular wealth, Constantine felt his family's fall from affluence and social displacement acutely. The letters exchanged between him and his friends during their collective flight from Alexandria in 1882 capture in both tone and content a linguistic and stylistic connection with the metropolitan center of empire, bearing witness as they do to an unmistakable cultural "mimicry."[7] Since Constantine's responses to these letters do not survive, we have to imagine the dialogue that ensued. But given his own cultural fluency, it is not a stretch to say that he was at least their equal in terms of the British tone and tenor of these exchanges (Stephen Schilizzi even claims that Constantine might well be "styled a Londoner" given his years spent in the British capital).[8]

The correspondence of this foursome gives us a rare glimpse into the intimate social and emotional life Constantine experienced with them. The letters show how highly invested these young men were in keeping alive the intense filial connections that were so abruptly uprooted.[9] Informing each letter is the assumption that these boys shared a special bond, hence their self-conscious designation "the clique." Socially there was little else in Constantine's life that provided him with the emotional buoyancy he surely derived from his friends' dispatches.

One may as well begin with Mikès's letters to Constantine, which offer a captivating look into the world of the clique and Constantine's rather peculiar and calculated detachment from it. He received most of these letters while in Istanbul, where, as noted, he remained highly secretive about his own sexual exploits, unlike his friends who flaunted them and had no qualms about detailing their dissolute lifestyles. Mikès is a fascinating figure in the life of the poet—in many ways another self in Aristotle's sense of the ideal friend. He shows the extent to which so many of the Alexandrian Greeks, following the example of the Anglo-Greeks for whom they worked in various capacities, were thoroughly—even absurdly—anglicized. Mikès, for instance, repeatedly calls his father "the governor" when he's not telling his interlocutor to "hang it all."[10] They were, to a certain extent, "mimic men" whose willing assimilation into English manners required them to cultivate and even perform a Victorian version of masculinity.[11] These boys were also, of course, being groomed to run a commercial empire within a political empire: the Ralli firm, which spanned from New Orleans to Calcutta.

The portrait of Mikès that emerges is that of a self-possessed, profligate, and ambitious youth who is preparing to climb the social ladder held out to him by his family. He also appears to have had an affinity for literature and culture that was expected of this cosmopolitan class of Victorian merchants. Corresponding with Mikès was surely one of the high points of Constantine's early adult life. Mikès's first letters were sent from Athens in 1882, where the Ralli family[12] had taken temporary refuge. Mikès trains his keen eye on the Greeks in Athens and Syros—the Aegean island that served as a hub for the commercial elite and the postmassacre Chian diaspora. He meets a distant relation, "a certain Negroponte," describing him as "a thorough degenerate Greek, as Papazis[13] would call him," but "to me the best and jolliest fellow alive." He "hardly knows a word of Greek," having studied in England, and "looks down with the greatest contempt on everything belonging to Greece" (June 17, 1882).[14] Likewise, Mikès betrays a condescending attitude toward Greek nationals by ridiculing the students at the University of Athens, where "all the idlers and good-for-nothings resort" (September 19, 1882).[15] His bias against bookish pseudo-intellectuals is a self-validating prejudice likely shared by Constantine, who would never have the chance to study at university. Stephen Schilizzi makes similar comments in his letter from the island of Tinos when he exposes the healing scams being run by the priests of the shrine of the Virgin.[16] Constantine would not visit Greece until 1901, when he makes an effort to correct this sneering attitude, chronicling his appreciation of the country and its sites in a diary and reversing, as it were, the shared negative opinion of the clique.

Once back in Alexandria in October 1882, Mikès comments on the ruined state of the city but wastes no time indulging in newly discovered vices of drinking, smoking, and gambling. He writes with rather reckless abandon to his friend in the Ottoman capital: "Did you ever play cards? You can't imagine how exciting and how sublime it is to stake all you have on red or black; if you win you treat your friends; if you lose more than you can pay, a thing which occurs very often to me, you sell a batch of old books, pay your debts and gamble away the remainder" (February 28, 1883).[17]

Money was not in short supply for the Ralli family, but Mikès nonetheless was not given much of an allowance, as the Chian merchants refrained from spoiling or indulging their offspring. The letters reveal that Mikès and Constantine shared many interests: for one, they both enjoyed the "trashy old novels" that Mikès sold to pay for his drinking, gambling, and "coquettes" (his code word for prostitutes). He taunts Constantine by reminding him that he too liked these hawked novels: "Yes, my dear fellow, on your return you will miss The Channings and your old friend Roland York, as well as pretty Barbara in East Lynne,[18] with whom you had fallen so violently in love. All your old friends have been removed from the places they filled so long . . . for as I throw my eyes on the rows you once occupied and see your ranks daily diminished, I feel now and then a sort of sorrow, but that sorrow is as often drowned with a glass of beer, handed to me by a pretty barmaid."[19] Here Mikès inaugurates what will later become the Cavafian trope of the young man who intended to read but wound up bored with his books and seduced by other hedonistic enticements, as we see in the poem "He Came to Read."

With the characteristic impertinence that informs so much of what these young men say and do, Mikès undermines the Delphic maxim "know thyself" by vaunting the high virtues of card-playing: "The best possible amusement is winning at cards; next to that is losing; and next to losing (i.e. when you have nothing to lose) is looking at others playing. I remember not where I came across this remark but it is far more true than the γνῶθι σαυτόν ["*gnothi safton* / know thyself"] of pedantic old Greece" (February 28, 1883). Mikès shares a few more tidbits in this letter: his finances are ever "topsy-turvey"; and he quotes fellow clique member John Rodocanachi's opinion that Liverpool is "the best place in the world for young men." This claim is borne out by the dissolute lifestyle John and Mikès take up there a few years down the road—one that Constantine himself could surely relate to, having witnessed something similar in the social patterns of his older brothers while the family lived in the city.

Early on, the friends show a shared flair for details that they feel will both delight and shock, as in the following debunking of their teacher: "That stuck-up pig-headed pedant [Papazis] has reopened his school opposite the Greek Hospital. I go there likewise for three hours a day, during which time he gives lessons in Thucydides and Homer, and twice a week he gives lectures on Optics, as a treat" (January 22–24, 1883).[20] Mikès is very conscious of the precious nature of these letters and the value of receiving them in a timely manner—a very British fixation Constantine will mirror and maintain in his correspondence. Constantine relied on his friends for textual citations, as he did on his brother John, a penchant for consulting sources that will become legendary later in life:

> I have just received your letter, and luckily found out with the greatest ease the passages relating to Barrère's [*sic*] and Robespierre's love of animals. I took copies of them and will do so with the greatest pleasure, for any other extracts you should desire, provided I can get hold of the book required. As for that poem of Tennyson's, which you wished me to copy,[21] I stated to you in my last letter the reasons for my not being able to copy. The wife of the esteemed editor of the Egyptian Gazette has done me the favor to borrow the book of me and has been so kind as not to return it. You are not very explicit about the publication. When and where do you intend publishing it? I sincerely hope it will meet with success, which is by no means improbable as the theme is very interesting, and must offer much matter of consideration to such a well-read fellow as you. (January 1, 1884)[22]

Mikès and Constantine were both troubled by vision problems ("sorry to hear that your eyes are in such a bad state . . . I have become very short sighted of late"—February 11, 1884).[23] And lest Constantine miss out on the hijinks of the clique, he is kept informed on Mikès's attendance of the French operettas at the Zizinia Theatre in Alexandria, where the boys make a habit of flirting with the opera singers (March 18, 1884).[24] Shakespeare is discussed—"The lines to which you refer are sung by Ariel" (April 14, 1884)[25]—as are the more mundane concerns of the Ralli family's new postbombardment living and drinking arrangements:

> I went to see yesterday the new houses that [they] are building up at Rosetta Gate . . . We are going to remove to them on our return from Ramle[h], that is to say about the end of October. When I go there I am going to spend a lot in making my room neat and I am going to smuggle in drinks, jams, biscuits and cigars (I scarcely ever smoke cigarettes now). I hope you will be there by that time for though I know you will not like to partake of brandy and cigars you may like the ginger biscuits and raspberry jam. (May 5, 1884)[26]

This tender note is often struck in other letters: "I hope you will soon be here; I begin to miss you sadly" (June 2, 1884);[27] and two years later, when corresponding from Liverpool, Mikès writes, "The only thing I look forward in being back in Egypt is seeing you" (August 5, 1886).[28] No doubt the feelings were mutual, with such sentimental expressions creating a desire in Constantine to return from exile. He shared a degree of emotional intimacy that disappeared in his later life. Without Constantine's responses, we can only surmise how he felt at the receipt of Mikès's letters that documented his daily excursions. For while

Mikès spent lavishly on amusements, Constantine and his family lived in penury along the shores of the Bosporus, waiting anxiously for the next remittance of cash from his older brothers in Alexandria.

Mikès breeds canaries and pigeons and is something of a huntsman: "Pray do not speak lightly of fishing or shooting. You are entirely ignorant of their pleasures" (July 26, 1884).[29] At the same time, he has an intellectual and sensitive side. On many occasions, he shares his reading interests, which include the writers Carlyle, Macaulay, Shakespeare, Disraeli, Scott, Goldsmith, Lord Lytton, Dickens, and Thackeray (January 31, 1885).[30] In October 1884, he subscribes to *The Athenaeum*, wishing to keep up with new books appearing in England. Neither young man could possibly imagine that several decades later Constantine's poems would appear in this periodical, embedded in E. M. Forster's articles on Alexandria.[31]

During Mikès's 1886 sojourn in England, he takes full advantage of the cultural opportunities available in that country. His visit to London is filled with cultural highlights.[32] In Liverpool, there was plenty of carousing and profligacy as well:[33] "It is queer how all the clique is given to betting. They never win by it and except on the rarest of occasions and then all the money goes in suppers with champagne and in paying bills" (June 20, 1886).[34] He brags rather shamelessly that "my spending propensities have greatly developed since I came to England" (July 27, 1886), a predicament that indicates how vulnerable these young men were to the imperial culture that ironically allowed their families to amass huge fortunes but which kept them desperately short of cash amid so many urban temptations. Given this constant boasting about his spending habits, one wonders how sensitive Mikès was to Constantine's dire financial situation before and after the family's return from Istanbul. Or perhaps Constantine never fully admitted to his friends the depth of the family's penury out of pride or discretion.

Nevertheless, these excerpts reveal the charming and attractive dimensions of Mikès's personality and an intimacy between him and Constantine. Mikès's attentiveness to his friend and solicitous affection display a tenderness not uncommon in Victorian male friendships. One also senses the probability of a romantic attraction here, at least on the part of Constantine, who will deeply mourn Mikès's early death from typhoid at the age of twenty-three. His death cuts short a relationship rooted in socializing and pleasure-seeking but one that might certainly have developed into something deeper and more intellectual. During Mikès's illness, Constantine keeps a detailed account of his visits, as he will later do while attending to his ailing mother and dying brother Alexander. The diary reveals how deeply attached he was to Mikès, "my beloved and only true friend."[35]

Beginning on September 15, 1889, and ending September 29, Constantine's diary reveals his growing worry over Mikès's health. After describing a few pleasant outings with Mikès and other friends, he writes that he met Mikès at the stock exchange on Tuesday, September 15, and remarked how bad he looked. He urged his friend to take care of himself: "Who would have known that this would be the last time he saw both the Stock Exchange and Alexandria."[36] The next day, not knowing about the severity of his condition, Constantine wrote Mikès a few lines, telling him that he would be at the casino in Ramleh. Constantine took the tram to the Ralli residence, where he witnessed his friend's fever and attempted to persuade him to change doctors. During a visit on Wednesday, he tried to bolster Mikès's spirits by telling him that he had surely exhausted himself during his recent trip to France, where he overindulged in amusements and hunting. He just needed rest—but "neither he nor I really believed this."[37]

On Thursday, while visiting the casino with his mother and friends, Constantine learned that Mikès had only a couple of hours left to live. So he rushed to Mikès's house, "not knowing whether we would find him alive."[38] This proved to be a false alarm. Mikès's condition fluctuated during the following week, but on September 27, hearing that his friend was fading away, Constantine begged the doctor to take the next train to the Ralli house, asking to be kept informed. Not having received a call by ten in the evening, he went to the doctor himself and, not finding him in, walked to the train station to await the doctor's return. When he appeared, the doctor looked shaken, telling Constantine in English, "He is in a very, very bad state—typhoid state,"[39] offering little hope. "That night I did not sleep." Despite a brief improvement in his condition, Mikès died on October 1. His death brought to a close the first intimate friendship of the poet's life and left a traumatic void.

The diary reveals Constantine as a loving friend. His letters to Stephen Schilizzi document an equally intimate but less intense relationship. Like Mikès, Stephen hailed from an illustrious Chian family, one that transcended commerce, however, with an imperial pedigree dating back to the Byzantine court historian John Skylitzes, who lived during the second half of the eleventh century.[40] This pedigree must have intrigued Constantine in his later years when he became a great enthusiast of Byzantine historians who, he argued, wrote history dramatically but were undervalued in the West.[41] The Schilizzi connections[42] would move in an equally eminent political direction in the twentieth century; in 1921, Helena Schilizzi, Stephen's cousin, married Eleftherios Venizelos, who served as prime minister of Greece and was one of the most significant Greek politicians of the early twentieth century—another example of the affluence and far-reaching sway of the diaspora Chians. Helena emerged as one of the major donors in London who established the Koraes Chair of Greek Letters at King's College London, whose first occupant, Arnold Toynbee, created great controversy with his critical view of the conduct of the Greek army during the Greco-Turkish war of 1919–22. This imbroglio would have significant repercussions on Constantine's withholding of permission for the promised English translation that E. M. Forster wished to bring out with the Hogarth Press, owing to the problematic involvement of Toynbee in the translation project.[43]

Stephen's letters are far more verbose than Mikès's and, consequently, less charming. Nevertheless, they demonstrate many of the foursome's shared preoccupations and mutual vices, especially the common condescension felt toward mainland Greeks and parvenu merchants—the Zervoudaki family of Alexandria in particular receives relentless ridicule. The overriding tone here is one of self-conscious Britishness and strident cosmopolitanism. In a letter dated October 30–31, 1883, when the Schilizzi family rides out a cholera outbreak by traveling to Glasgow, Liverpool, Edinburgh, London, and Paris, Stephen recounts his travels with an aplomb that must have sparked some envy from its recipient in Istanbul. The letter confirms that British culture remained an aspired-to ideal for them and shows a remarkable sensitivity and love of the English capital and countryside. Visiting all the main sites, attending theater every evening, venturing farther afield to the environs of London, and taking in exhibits on fisheries and machinery—all these activities attest to the connection between commerce and culture that was so central to this network of families.[44] The letter includes what must have been a hurtful allusion to homosexuality—their friend Leoni Scanavi is mocked for carousing with working-class "donkey" boys[45] who ridicule him: "He has been accused and is suspected to do a very dirty business with them." Mikès made a similar reference in a letter dated June 18, 1886,[46] where he derided an Alexandrian clerk with a crush on John Rodocanachi, whom he dubbed "John's barber" for his common appearance.

A curious scrape nearly occurs in Alexandria when Aristides Cavafy asked Stephen to read one of Constantine's letters, which apparently alluded to something that should have remained private. This prompted Stephen to urge the future adoption of "cryptography," with the final pages of his letter containing the coded alphabet to be used in future correspondences (April 10, 1882).[47] This very likely may have been the impetus for Constantine to develop the cryptic shorthand he employed throughout his life when composing drafts of letters, diary entries, and personal notes—a variation of the standard shorthand required of all the Anglo-Greek clerks. In a later letter, Constantine is chided for his secrecy ("you write us nothing about your private life"—May 24, 1883).[48] These tensions develop into a full-blown argument, with Stephen taking umbrage at a phrase used by Constantine, who dismissively derides him by refusing to be "foolish enough to be angry with a fellow" (no date, 1884).[49] Here Constantine displays a nonchalance and an unflappable self-restraint—no doubt a reaction to the unsubtle probing by Stephen into his private life. This epistolary spat was likely his way of creating a deflection and establishing some emotional autonomy. It reads like the sentimental musings of a character in a Victorian novel and serves as an example of how many young men of the period had recourse to popular fiction to explore and express (or camouflage) their emotions and sentiments, as we saw with Mikès.[50]

In contrast to the letters of Mikès and Stephen, those of John Rodocanachi strike a more relaxed, urbane tone, which is not surprising, since he had been sent to study early on in England at the Uppingham School in Rutland, East Midlands. His irreverent letter dated June 5, 1882,[51] pokes fun at the flight of the

Greeks from Alexandria "with an umbrella in one hand" (a dig at their British pretensions no doubt) and being chased by barbarians (he anticipates the thematic quandary of Cavafy's future poem "Waiting for the Barbarians" while exhibiting a racist view of Egyptians, which we explored in chapter five). John's derision is furthered by the immediate mention of his own mock-serious preoccupations: breeding canaries and dealing with a predatory cat. In a later letter dated December 16, 1884,[52] John gives us an account of his carousing life in Liverpool, documenting his alleged penury: having to eat his walking stick down to the silver nob, a telling detail in the somewhat precarious lives of these semipampered boys. John's mother's curious comment about her son's lifestyle in the letter—"You are like poets, you spend your time and money on love-making at the beginning of every month, and at the end you lunch on air"—is indicative of the fine line these boys trod between carousing and apprenticing in the Ralli firm. We even get a quote from one of Constantine's letters where he calls John a "sly dog" (December 16, 1884) as well as a hint that he was sharing his early scribblings from Constantinople. In a letter dated March 9 [no year],[53] John comments that Constantine's letters read like "Penny Dreadfuls"—certainly an allusion to his early folklore-inflected essays on lycanthropy, the occult, and ethnography.[54]

Making good on his claim that Liverpool is the best place in the world for young men, John gives a detailed account of his amorous exploits and participation in theatrical performances. We see from his letterhead that he works for the Ralli firm in Liverpool, clerking no doubt but otherwise quite content to live a life fully devoted to pleasure. We learn that he has contracted the clap,[55] owns two Saint Bernards named (with Orientalist abandon) Pasha and Hanoum,[56] and plays the "gay deceiver" with an English woman whom he has no interest in marrying, despite her father's demand that he declare his intentions.[57] He does declare them to Constantine: "Nothing I enjoy more than flirting—it is the greatest ambition of my life." One marvels at how fully John exemplifies the Wildean dandy! He offers his friend solicited fashion advice on clothes, replete with diagrams: collars should be worn with their sharp corners turned down, sailor's knots are "in" for ties, tight trousers are "not only no more worn here but are considered awfully caddish."[58] Constantine surely delighted in receiving these letters, as they provided him with a distraction from his own precarious existence in Istanbul and realigned him emotionally and culturally with the world of commerce, art, and leisured pleasure that the Anglo-Greeks had secured for themselves.

Doubtless there is a lot more that can be said about these intimacies, evolving as they do when Constantine was fashioning his own identity and working through many intellectual, sexual, and emotional challenges. What we have in the landscape conjured by these letters is a world of pubs, sex, and gambling: in short, youthful self-indulgence with all its vulnerable arrogance and enviable luster. And here emerges one of the predominant character formulas of Constantine's late poetry: the portrait of the talented and sensitive young man with vast potential who dangerously throws it all away for pleasure, wasting away prematurely or dying young. Granted that this is later imbued with a pronounced homoeroticism, especially in the mature poems. But its essence and source may be found here in the lives of these three close friends who bond through pleasure. Although two of these friends died early, Constantine returned to the lives they described in their letters as subjects of his latter homoerotic verse. We encounter versions of these friends in poems like "I Went" (1905/1913), a simple lyric that focuses on drinking:

I didn't hold back. I gave in completely. I went.
I gave in to the pleasures, some real,
some fashioned in my mind.
I went into the moonlit night
and I drank of strong wines,
just like the brave partakers of pleasure.

In "He Came to Read" (1924), we find a powerful parallel to Mikès's aforenoted disavowal of books and preference for carousing:

He came to read. Two or three
books lie open: historians and poets.
But after ten minutes of reading,
he has given them up. He's half-asleep
on the sofa. He's completely devoted to books—
but he's twenty-three years old and truly handsome;
and this very afternoon eros
entered his perfect flesh, his lips.
The erotic passion passed
into his flesh where all his beauty lies;
without any foolish shame about what kind of pleasure . . .

In "A Young Man, Versed in Literature, in His Twenty-Fourth Year" [1928*], we are presented with a youth in his prime who is undone by his sexual addictions:

[. . .]
Full of torment, he debases himself.
That he's unemployed just makes it worse.
Painfully he borrows a little money (at times
almost begging for it) and manages somehow to survive.

He kisses those treasured lips, finding pleasure
in that exquisite body—which he now senses only
submits reluctantly.
And then he drinks and smokes; he drinks and smokes;
dragging himself endlessly through the cafés,
lethargically dragging his fading beauty.
[. . .]

Another poem that fits into this category of hedonistic carousing is "Two Young Men, Twenty-Three to Twenty-Four Years Old" (1927*)—Mikès was twenty-three when he died. Although it has a homoerotic twist, the poem replicates the licentious behavior of the members of the clique with their obsessive gambling, drinking, and pleasure-seeking:

He had been in the café since half past ten,
waiting for him to appear at any moment.
At midnight he was still waiting.
At half past one, the café
had nearly emptied.
He grew tired of mechanically reading newspapers.
Of his three meager shillings
only one remained: during the long wait,
he had spent the rest on coffee and cognac.
He had finished all his cigarettes.
All the waiting had exhausted him. Alone
for so many hours, he had become
preoccupied by troubling thoughts
about his depraved life.

But when he saw his friend enter—all at once
his fatigue, lethargy, and troubles vanished.

His friend astonished him with the news
that he had won sixty pounds in a card game.

Their beautiful faces, their exquisite youth,
the sensitive love that brought them together
were all refreshed, revived, and reinvigorated
by the sixty pounds from the card game.
[. . .]

Good looks, exquisite youthfulness, with "sensitive love" added to the equation—it's not hard to envision how the lifestyles of "the clique" set the foundations for poems such as these that beckon to be read as unacknowledged tributes to these close friends.

The topics related to dissolute youth that Constantine extracted from the memories of his friends also find direct expression in his curious short story "In Broad Daylight" (1895/96?)—unpublished but among the lengthiest prose texts he composed. The narrative's density and length owe much to the abundance of autobiographical detail distilled in it. The story was brought to world attention in 1983 when the American poet James Merrill translated it into English for a special edition of the periodical *Grand Street* dedicated to Cavafy.[59] Constantine's experiment in writing a gothic story captures something essential about the interactions of the expanded "clique" in the 1890s and offers invaluable personal insights into his thoughts on various topics: money, old age, the occult, and the consequences of repressing one's emotions.

"In Broad Daylight" is written largely in the manner of Edgar

Allan Poe, whose impact may be traced to Constantine's direct reading of the American writer as well as through his protracted engagement with Baudelaire.[60] It centers on a coterie of three friends who gamble and socialize, much like the members of the clique in the 1890s, when the story takes place.[61] "In Broad Daylight" opens with three young men "sitting one evening after dinner in the Casino of San Stefano in Ramleh . . . We were discussing various things, and since none of us counts himself among the very rich, our conversation naturally turned toward financial matters, the independence that money brings, and the pleasures it supplies."[62] The casino at Ramleh was the clique's regular gathering place (as evidenced by a dinner menu dated September 1895). It was a popular venue for socializing and carousing in Alexandria.[63] The tale's protagonist, Alexander A., prefaces his account with the following claim: "If I wanted to be rich, at this moment I would be a multi-millionaire—but I didn't dare."[64] The unnamed narrator then proceeds to relay Alexander's strange experience as follows: One August evening, after a routine day of socializing, Alexander turns in for the night and dreams he is visited by a stranger, "a man of medium height and around forty years of age entered my room. He was wearing fairly worn out black clothes and a straw hat. On his left hand he wore a ring set with a very large emerald . . . He had a black beard streaked with many white hairs, and there was something strange about his eyes, a look at once sarcastic and sad."[65] The man makes Alexander an offer:

> "I know that you're poor. I have come to tell you about a way to get rich. Near Pompey's Pillar I know a place where a great treasure lies buried. From this treasure I desire nothing—I will only take the little iron box which will be found lying at the bottom. All the rest is yours to keep."

"And what does this great treasure consist of?" I asked.

"Of gold coins," he said, "but above all, precious stones. There are ten or twelve golden chests filled with diamonds, pearls, and I think," as though trying to remember, "sapphires."[66]

Alexander is instructed to meet the stranger the next day between midday and four in the afternoon at a café near a blacksmith's shop. Upon awakening, he dismisses the dream and goes about his business, which includes an afternoon excursion to the countryside and an evening playing cards. His nocturnal slumber is interrupted once again by a second arrival of the specter, sending him into a state of abject terror. After chiding him for not appearing, the specter repeats his directive to meet on the following day, which Alexander manages to ignore once again, as his day already involves attending a wedding, meeting a landlord, and consulting with his lawyer. By a strange coincidence, that afternoon he finds himself unwittingly in the very place of the arranged rendezvous: "Horror! There he was, sitting at the small café. My initial reaction was a sort of dizziness, and I thought that I might faint. I leaned against a merchant's stall and looked at him again. The same black clothes, the same straw hat, the same facial features, the same gaze. And he, unblinking, was staring at me with a fixed gaze."[67] Alexander flees, but in an attempt to prove he had been hallucinating, he instructs his driver to return to the café where, sure enough, the phantom is still sitting:

> He responded to my gaze in kind, with one as penetrating as my own, and with an expression full of anxiety regarding the decision I would make. It seemed as though he were reading my mind, that he had discerned my thoughts in my dream and, in order to dispel any doubt I had about his identity, he

turned his left hand towards me and quite clearly showed me (I was afraid the driver had noticed) the emerald ring that had made such an impression on me in my first dream."[68]

Alexander rushes to the San Stefano Casino, where he arrives in a most dreadful state: "I entered the main hall of the Casino and panicked when I saw myself in the mirror. I was as pale as a cadaver. Fortunately, the hall was empty. I collapsed on to a couch and began planning my next move."[69] Ultimately, he seeks the help of his friend G. V., who happens to be schooled in matters of the occult: "I staggered into G. V.'s room—all these details I remember only vaguely and haphazardly. The only thing I recall clearly is that once I found myself next to him, I began crying hysterically and shaking all over, as I narrated my horrifying experience to him."[70] The narrative concludes with G. V. assuring Alexander that the specter will not bother him again. Alexander then lapses into a "brain fever" that lasts one month, after which he takes a short trip to an Aegean island where he completes his convalescence.

This story provides a rich opportunity to explore the creative, emotional, and social factors at play in Constantine's life at the time he wrote it. Alexander A. possesses many of Constantine's traits and may be seen as a thinly veiled self-portrait.[71] He attends a wedding that was more a burden than a joy—Constantine, enduring mounting pressure from Haricleia to make a lucrative marriage, frequently attended such weddings. Like the clique with their shared Anglophile hauteur, the members of the story's coterie view themselves as superior to their peers. As Alexander boasts: "If I were in any other company—particularly among supposedly 'progressive people'—I would not explain myself, since they would laugh at me. But we find ourselves a bit above the alleged 'progressives.' That is to say, our perfect intellectual development has made us simple again, but simple without being ignorant. We have come full circle."[72]

On a psychological level, the story betrays some of Constantine's deep fears and anxieties. Money problems and the fantasy of making a quick fortune loom large here. The events of the story date back ten years to 1885—the year the Cavafy family returned to Alexandria in dire straits. Constantine was then faced with finding employment and making career choices as the family fretted over money. In 1892, he had accepted a job with the Office of the Irrigation Service, effectively locking himself into a secure position that, while low paying, was undemanding enough to allow him the flexibility to write poetry. "In Broad Daylight" reads like a wish fulfillment story where an occult encounter will magically solve money problems once and for all.

The early deaths of Mikès and Stephen affected Constantine deeply and contributed to a lifelong preoccupation with the topics of loss and mourning. We see this in numerous funereal poems. In "Tomb of Evrion" (1912/1914), we have a grave and an encomium to a young man who died in the prime of his life and beauty:

In this elaborate tomb
carved out of syenite stone,
and covered with violets and lilies,
the handsome Evrion is buried.
An Alexandrian youth of twenty-five.
On his father's side, descended from an old Macedonian
family;

and on his mother's, from a line of magistrates.
He was a student of the philosophy of Aristocleitos
and the rhetoric of Paros. In Thebes he studied
the sacred scriptures. And composed
a history of the Arsinoite prefecture. It will survive.
But we have lost what is most dear—his image,
which was like an Apollonian dream.

Constantine's earliest grave poems include one largely overlooked elegy[73] that was composed in 1886 and titled "To Stephen Schilizzi," where he writes nostalgically about his deceased friend: "as young men we discovered life's first pleasures all together." There is a line in the final stanza that deserves attention, containing as it does a remarkable image, as is often the case in the early unpublished work: "Your gravestone will be, for us, a thin, diaphanous veil." The poem continues with the following lines: "and though you're lost to your friends' eyes, their souls / and memories and hearts will always see you / and keep you, Stephen, their inseparable friend."[74] Constantine turns his friend's gravestone into a veil through which to peer into his soul. Over time, he would develop a nuanced funereal aesthetic, composing close to twelve funerary poems. So it is fair to ask where Constantine had acquired such a sophisticated perspective on death. One likely material source is the Greek Necropolis of London's West Norwood Cemetery, where the names of the members of the clique find themselves inscribed on monument after monument. This confluence of metropolitan ideas, images, and influence both resonates and intersects with the clique's Anglophilia and the Anglo-Greek community's desire for cultural validation. One of the "Magnificent Seven" large private London cemeteries established in the nineteenth century, West Norwood opened in 1837, and by 1842, members of the Anglo-Greek community purchased a lease to a plot there, establishing the Greek Orthodox "Necropolis." Their initial intention was practical, but in time they transformed this space into an elite repository for lives that exemplified their commercial as well as cultural achievements. It became a means of memorializing their legacy, their deft straddling of commerce and culture, and of marking the social ascent they had managed in so short a time span. The monuments and graves they would build there constitute the jewel in the crown of West Norwood, despite their current state of neglect. Although the Necropolis is comparable to other remarkable nineteenth-century Greek cemeteries established in the great urban centers where Greeks flourished, West Norwood is unique in being located at the very center of imperial power. Many of these graves, even in their deteriorating state, remain exceptional in terms of the quality of their design, having been commissioned from leading British architects of the day.[75] They are yet another manifestation of the high-minded agenda of these families to preserve and exhibit their wealth, status, and accomplishments, even in death.[76] As such, they convey materially the emotional and social ties that bound Constantine and his three friends, defined as they were by this privileged way of thinking. Losing Stephen and Mikès at such a young age added an additional layer of trauma to the series of losses Constantine sustained during the first three decades of his life, one that surely inaugurated his lifelong obsession with the *tombeau*, or tomb poem.[77]

Although Constantine's immediate family would be buried in Alexandria, Uncle George and his family were interred in West Norwood. Haricleia and her sons certainly attended burials[78] there during various points of their London and Liverpool years, services that would have been conducted in the mortuary chapel of Saint Stephen[79] built by Stephen Ralli to commemorate the death of his eldest son, Augustus, who died of rheumatic fever in 1872 while at Eton (Mikès would die of typhoid fever nearly two decades later). The Necropolis at West Norwood stands as another grouping of the names Ralli, Schilizzi, and Rodocanachi in a setting where loss is mediated aesthetically through material objects—tombs and mausolea—physical artifacts and works of art in their own right that offer consolation for traumatic loss. The intersection here of mortality, power, and taste speaks to the complex identities of the founders who lie buried in this elite enclosure—and their progeny, who were expected to visit and venerate their memories. Constantine would eventually write a poem about graveyards titled "In the Cemetery" (unpublished, 1893), the opening stanza of which eloquently defines his attitude toward the topic: "When memory directs your footsteps / to the cemetery, / with reverence prostrate yourself / before the sacred mystery of our dark future."

The clique was highly conscious of their privileged status as heirs to commercial empires and were eager to forge meaningful emotional connections with young men who were their equals. The pleasures of youth and the temptations of wealth were ever before them. Yet Constantine stands at a slight distance from this group; having lost his commercial patrimony, he begins charting a different course for himself as an intellectual and a man of letters, opting, like Alexander A., not to become rich. This was a risky plan, as he had limited career prospects and no financial support from anyone in his family. Perhaps he was hoping for assistance from his wealthy uncle in London, who, for reasons that remain obscure, left his brother's widow and her sons nothing when he died in 1891.[80] The camaraderie shared by the clique deeply shaped Constantine's personality, but he was closeted in a way that placed limits on his willingness to be fully honest and sincere in their company. This fortunately would change with the newest member to join the clique, Pericles Anastasiades, with whom he soon established a deeper and more open relationship and, consequently, a more meaningful and enduring connection.

7

PERI

Aesthete, Artist, and Confidant

Constantine's friendship with Pericles Anastasiades dates to his early adulthood, a time when he was becoming more aware of the subtle dynamics of personal relations and certainly more conscious of what he hoped he might extract from them. This relationship is among the more consequential and significant of all his connections. In a study on friendship, Alexander Nehamas observes that we are profoundly defined by our friends and the tastes we share with them. Parsing Aristotle's category of the virtuous friendship,[1] he notes that our friends make us hope for the good things we would not have thought of wishing for without them: "Friendship is a mechanism of individuality because we become who we are in great part because of the friends we have . . . Friendship comes closer to transmuting the self than any alchemist ever came to transmuting his metals."[2] With Pericles Anastasiades, we have perhaps Constantine's closest relationship outside his family, one grounded in a shared aesthetic view of life. Pericles, or Peri as he was affectionally called, held much in common with Constantine in terms of his socioeconomic background and cultural interests. His family belonged to the "protoclassatoi" or upper-crust founders of the Greek community in Alexandria. The son of Aristidēs Anastasiades, who was a director of the Bourse,[3] Peri was seven years younger than Constantine, had studied in England, and was, like the other members of the expanded clique, an Anglophile through and through. He and Constantine met sometime after the latter's return to Alexandria in 1885,[4] and Pericles would fill the void left by Mikès in 1889. A bon viveur whose interests included fencing and painting, Peri worked as a cotton broker; he had a substantial library from which Constantine regularly borrowed, and the two exchanged opinions and ideas on society, art, and literature. Their friendship was founded on cultural as well as social bonds, as is evident from two surviving letters from Constantine to Peri dated circa 1896:

> Dear Peri,
>
> I return you[r] D'Annunzio poems. I'll send my translation later on. I've not yet quite finished the process of squeezing and amputating my verses made of many-syllabled words. I have five or six operations more to perform if poetical surgery should be set about with caution. It won't do, shedding "ichor" [divine blood] too abundantly.
>
> In the meantime, I send you an English translation by John.
>
> Yours,
> *Constantine F. C.*[5]

A subsequent letter that survives in draft form contains an extensive exchange that offers a rare discussion of three shared poems:

Dear Pericles,

[. . .]

"Candles" is one of the best things I ever wrote.

"In the Same City" is from one point of view perfect. The versification and chiefly the rhymes are faultless. Out of the 7 rhymes on which this poem is built, 3 are identical in sound and 1 has the accent on the antepenultimate. But I have "παρακάμει"'d it,[6] and somehow got cramped by the exigencies of the meter; and I am afraid I haven't put in the second stanza as much as should have gone into it. I am not sure that I have drawn in the 2nd, 3rd and 4th lines of the second stanza an adequately powerful image of ennui—as my purpose was. It may be however that by trying to do more I should have overdone the effect and strained the sentiment, both fatal accidents in art. There is a class of poems whose role is "suggestif." My poem comes under that head. To a sympathetic reader—sympathetic by culture—who will think over the poems for a minute or two[,] my lines[,] I am convinced[,] will suggest an image of the deep, the endless "desesperance" [despair] which they contain "yet cannot all reveal."

"Artificial Flowers" is a flight to the lovely realm of Fantasy and Extravagance. One turn of expression, in the 5th line, is, I think, good—"their ephemeral flesh." "Flowers' flesh" doesn't sound commonplace.[7]

Noteworthy in these letters is a shift toward a more aesthetic and even decadent cultural orientation, as evinced by the mention of D'Annunzio's poetry,[8] the emphasis on ennui (decadent boredom à la Baudelaire), the inclusion of French expressions, and, of course, the very notion of artificial flowers. Peri will keep Constantine connected to Paris by virtue of his extensive sojourns in the city, although Constantine will quickly outpace Peri as a more adroit connoisseur of French culture via his focused and sustained engagement with French poets and writers, which intensifies around 1891, when Baudelaire becomes one of his poetic preoccupations.[9] Indeed, Peri will remain a mere dilettante by comparison. Constantine surely valued the aesthetic tastes and refined persona of Peri, who served as an invaluable source of support during the years leading up to Constantine's emergence as a bona fide poet. That he could share such sentiments about his poetry and articulate his struggles as an artist with Peri also chronicles his own growing confidence in his talents; it bears out the notion that we value and love our friends because we love "what we ourselves will become because of our relationship with them."[10] The friendship with Peri was complex but remained founded on this harmonious dynamic of shared interests. Peri functioned as the person with whom he could express intimate views and who provided artistic feedback, offering a context in which Constantine could fashion himself a poet and an intellectual, becoming, in effect, the exceptional person Peri wished him to become.

The intimate nature of their relationship is preserved in numerous letters that reveal an endearing side of Constantine seldom seen. Unlike his exchanges with his brothers and early friends, where so few of his own letters survive, quite a number of his letters to Peri exist (largely in draft form),[11] offering us a more balanced and complete sense of their shared bonds. These letters are at once tender and solicitous, open and sensitive, expressive and revealing. Constantine admired and surely envied Peri to a certain degree, since Peri led the comfortable life of leisure that would have been his own had his family fortunes not collapsed.

Pericles's financial independence allowed him to spend extended periods of time in Paris and London;[12] he lived for pleasure as a dandy and flâneur whose cultural affectations and aesthetic pretenses come through vibrantly in the numerous letters he sends from Paris. Their friendship was imbued with bravado and buoyancy, as may be seen in a letter from Paris dated May 23, 1898:[13]

> My dear Costy,
>
> Your delightful pages afford me great, great pleasure, and I assure you when anything thrills me, my first thought is "I wish Cavafy were there also."
>
> How varied my life is, from the picture gallery, to the theaters, from the Boulevard to that unique Bois—everything is new, interesting, beautiful—[. . .]
>
> I very often go to the Louvre to converse with the immortals they always have something new to say—[. . .]

In a letter written one month later, Peri articulates the hedonistic bond that the two shared: "My thirst for pleasure is as keen as ever and I slake it at all the fountains of joy" (June 22, 1898). What strikes readers of Peri's correspondence is his affectionate tone, as is evident in the following opening excerpts from various letters:

> I miss you very, very much, and am very glad that I will soon welcome you back, even friendship is selfish [. . .] (June 20, 1897)

> Many thanks for your friendly lines. Why are you not with me? My joy would be doubled were you here to

> share all my artistic and intellectual sensations. [. . .] (May 6, 1898)[14]

> You know what pleasure a letter from you is to me, you are ever present in spirit, your friendship is a thing I cherish and I am jealous of—[. . .] (September 7 [no year])

> I read your deeply felt letter and it warmed my heart, believe me. Your friendship is one of the things I value most in life. What a pity we are not together in this beautiful city, so full of charm, the green tall trees which are arrayed along those unique boulevards, the shops, the motley crowd compose the picture we never tire looking at. [. . .] (May 12, 1900)

Constantine was equally affectionate in turn and displays an emotional side rarely expressed in his middle to late years. In undated drafts of letters preserved by the poet, he writes:

> My dear Peri,
>
> It is certainly not necessary to tell you of the great void which your departure has left. It has been a takeaway of so much! But I am glad that you are in that adorable town. I hope you are getting a lot of amusement . . . and it is always good to tread on the dear ground of Paris, to stroll about its lovely streets.[15]

In another letter (an undated draft), we have a rather remarkable confession: "Though you are only a few days away I find that I have to tell you that I already miss you awfully. After so many years of friendship we have become very necessary to each other."[16] Unfortunately, the two never managed to fulfill their mutual wish to be together in the French capital. During Constantine's journey to Paris and London in May/June of 1897, Peri remained in Alexandria, giving Constantine the rare chance to play the dandy and share his own urban impressions.

While in Paris, Constantine and his brother John stayed at the Saint Petersburg Hotel and took in the city's sights and sounds. If the printed material Constantine preserved in the file marked "programmes and other papers from my stay in Paris in 1897"[17] is an accurate indication of his and John's activities in the French and British capitals, then the sheer number of performances they attended and places they visited is altogether staggering. It surely reflects how ravenous the brothers were for European culture. In Paris, they managed to attend plays, concerts, vaudeville performances, and popular entertainment in the following venues: the Olympia Concert Hall, the Casino de Paris, the Nouveau Cirque, the Théâtre du Vaudeville, the Odéon Théâtre de l'Europe, the Moulin Rouge, the Théâtre du Palais-Royal, the Comédie-Française, and the Théâtre National de l'Opéra. These included performances of *Faust*, *Oedipus Rex*, *Tartuffe*, and *Mithridate*.[18]

In addition to visiting the Salon des Champs Élysées to view the annual exhibit there and venturing farther afield to Versailles and Le Trianon, they also took in more popular sites, including the Musée Grévin (wax museum), the Grand Guignol (horror shows), and the Grands Magasins Dufayael (department store). Receipts indicate that they attended horse races (Bois de Boulogne), rented bicycles, frequented music halls, and dined out regularly. They even worked in a visit to the Libraire Arnaud. Among the more unique events they attended was the Montmartre "Vachalcade"—the Fête de la Vache Enragée—that parodied the traditional Fête du Boeuf Gras associated with the Mardi Gras festivities. This was a bohemian procession with floats that sought to raise money for impoverished artists. Chief among these floats was one that represented a "maddened cow." Included in the "programmes" the brothers collected are two fliers for this event, along with a full program replete with the list of floats.[19] They acquired a similarly curious memento while traveling to Paris via Marseilles, where they collected a card from a brothel—Maison Unique—run by Mme Aline. Although there is no way of knowing whether either of the brothers actually visited this establishment (highly unlikely given the puritanical orientation of John and the homosexuality of Constantine), the card includes the following rather humorous instruction: "Notice: Beware of drivers who for their private interest take travellers to second rate house and to their detriment. It is necessary to call attention to such tricks. Be careful to read 'ALINE' on the out side Lanterne and only house closed." As he often did on his trips, Constantine collected odd keepsakes, and this one proved irresistible with its muddled English and brazen directives.

In London, the brothers arrived just in time for Queen Victoria's Diamond Jubilee on June 22. Here, as in Paris, they took full advantage of the cultural moment. The theatrical venues they visited included the Saint James's Theatre, the Royal Lyceum Theatre, the Strand Theatre, and the Empire Theatre, where they saw plays by Arthur W. Pinero (*The Princess and the Butterfly: or, the Fantastics*), Herman Merivale (*The Queen's Proctor*—adapted by Victorien Sardou), and Victorien Sardou and Emile Moreau (*Madame Sans-Gêne*). In addition, they visited the British Museum and toured the Royal Academy of Arts as well as the Victorian Era Exhibition at Earl's Court.

In charming passages from drafts of his Paris letters to Peri,

Constantine reveals his deep-seated interest in painting and the Old Masters:

> It would be stupid of me to say anything about the beauty of Paris, every superlative ought to be made to serve the squares, the boulevards, the streets, the shops. The cafes are simply wonderful. I am going about the place and seeing it as much as I can, but it requires 15 months not 15 days to be properly seen. [. . .]
>
> How are you, my dear boy? What a pity, what a thousand pities you are not here, we'd amuse ourselves together. [. . .]
>
> I paid a long visit to the Luxembourg gallery. I saw wonderful pictures. I got drunk with artistic emotion. One picture chiefly made a great impression on me. It has captured the Virgin and has underneath a sonnet composed by the painter, in which he says that he has seen the Virgin in a dream and it is a faithful [***] as he saw her he placed the image on his canvas; he has the finest gauze to dress her in, has melted the most precious gold to adorn her and has searched to find the fairest lilacs to place at her feet. And the picture bears out the sonnet fully. The Virgin is neither a holy matron, of Greek hagiographers and modern painters or the goddess of catholic idolatry. She is a young girl of eighteen, say, or twenty, very simple, very human, and very [beautiful?]. It is quite a new departure; a realistic perspective; yet new in its treatment.

The tone of voice here is something absolutely unique in the extant correspondence of the poet outside of his family exchanges; enamored of France, he shares his love of Paris, being intoxicated by artistic ardor, and the desire to be with his friend, grounding the latter emotion firmly on cultural and aesthetic foundations.

Notable as well is the focus on art and the direct commentary on an unidentified painting of the Virgin, painterly details that allow poet and painter to bond and that show Constantine's lifelong interest in the fine arts. Although these recorded details only hint at the depth and scope of other such in-person exchanges, they signal a deep and abiding relationship. Peri was the one friend Constantine could turn to for artistic stimulus and validation. We often discover fascinating details that the poet had not shared or documented. For instance, in a comment filed in with the drafts of his letters from Paris, he offers the following opinion on Renaissance artists: "Titian is great. I like him better than Raphael. The 'Gioconda' of Leonardo da Vinci is very beautiful but it is not for the uninitiated. Correggio and Veronese I admired too—but Titian is great." Such exchanges point to a history of many such mutual discussions between the two art aficionados on paintings and schools of art. (This is the only extant opinion of Constantine's taste as far as the Old Masters are concerned.)

These letter drafts also record a rather slighting comment about the painter Theodore Rallis, a distant cousin of Mikès's who was part of the Anglo-Greek Ralli network and had achieved remarkable success and European notoriety as an artist.[20] Constantine quips to Peri that Rallis's paintings are "no big deal" ("not *megalo pragma*"), betraying what must have been a shared envy over the painter's international fame. (Rallis exhibited at the Paris Salon of 1897, which Constantine and John visited.) Art and poetry will intersect seven years later when Rallis paints *The Sea Depths* (1904), inspired, as the painter acknowledges, by the poem "Prayer" (1896/1898).[21] Doubtless Constantine kept his reservations about Rallis to himself and Peri. Neither did he leave any written comments on Peri's paintings, which, in contrast to Rallis's internationally acclaimed canvases, were featured in some minor shows in Cairo that were written up in the Cavafian venue *Alexandrini Techni* between the years 1928 and 1931 (three of these notices are by Rika Sengopoulos). From these brief write-ups it appears that Peri's works included portraits, Orientalist subjects, Egyptian landscapes/seascapes,[22] and scenes from urban life. He even left us a sketch of the poet.[23]

Recent inquiries have led to the discovery of some remarkable sketches by Pericles[24] that confirm another facet of his bond with Constantine, namely a shared interest in the male figure. Indeed, Peri's sketches of young men on the beach call to mind the poem "Days of 1908" (1921?/1932), where the subject strips off his suit for a swim. Other sketches from this series also include Egyptian fellahin and, although inextricably Orientalist, do link painter and poet in a shared interest in the lives and customs of Egyptian youth (as explored in chapter five).

Constantine eagerly shared much with Peri, culminating in a passion for pictorial artwork, which was very central to his poetics. From his letters we see that he was clearly striving to achieve a certain connoisseurship in this dalliance with Peri, who, although a gifted artist, remained more of a poseur in terms of his intellectual and cultural achievements. Nevertheless, he continued to provide Constantine with an important and precious connection to French cosmopolitan culture—its galleries, theater, music, and cafés:

> My dear Costy,
>
> I have missed a mail, Paris is guilty of it. You know how the sights and pleasures of this charming capital make time flie [*sic*]—Your keen critique of Zola's[25] last novel has interested me very much—I was very pleased

to meet your brother Paul on the boulevard the day before he left for London, we had a long chat—[. . .] (June 22, 1898)

In Paris, Peri meets up with the Cavafy brothers Paul (June 22, 1898) and John (June 4, 1899). His letter describing his encounter with John eloquently captures the seductive allure that French culture held for these men:

My dear Costy,

I have read with great pleasure your letters of 4.17 and 25 [. . .] I have neglected you.

During John's stay in Paris, I met him often, we had long strolls and chats together, we walked through the Salon, visited Saint Sulpice; he stood me a splendid lunch at Peter's [. . .], a swell restaurant—we have arranged to meet in London. We were very much upset by the news about the plague. I am glad to see it is not serious, one good will come of it, they will clean the town, and be very severe with those dirty pilgrims.

My life here is very gay, I find hardly time to breathe, and have reduced my hours of sleep to the minimum. I turn in between 2 and 3 in the morning and am always out again by 10. A constant visitor of the Louvre now and then I go through the Luxembourg and stroll in that beautiful garden, occasionally I throw in a critical eye at the Salon, but always swear by the old Masters.

6th. Last night Sarah Bernhardt in "Hamlet" was grand, the translation in prose is a very faithful and clever one. The staging was very artistic. [. . .]

We have had a spell of stifling heat—Levon and I

generally drive to the Bois, and on our return take our aperitif at the Café Napolitain.

We are off to London next week. I must close my letter, as we are going to the races.

Levon sends his love.

Believe me
Yours
Peri

Perhaps the inclusion of meeting John Cavafy in this letter was meant to serve as a proxy for what Peri wished he could share with Constantine—a "very gay" life. Peri's intimate companion Levon is frequently mentioned in these exchanges and although he remains an obscure figure in the clique's circle, he may in fact have been more than a friend and perhaps even Peri's lover. From extant letters he appears to have been connected with the theater scene in Paris—Constantine even read one of his plays.[26]

Rather than seeing these letters as flaunting Peri's opportunities and economic ease, we should read them as ways by which he shared his experiences with his friend, visits and trips that he no doubt embellished further when the two would meet back in Alexandria and engage in many deep conversations about travel and art. This same thirst for high culture is preserved in other letters as well:

SUNDAY, PARIS 14TH MAY 99
CAFÉ NAPOLITAIN 10AM

[. . .]

During my stay in Vienna, Buda Pest and Munich, I revelled in the art treasures I saw in the picture galleries. The old masters are very great. I am an enthusiastic admirer of Rembrandt, Van Dyck, Rubens, modern art, barring landscape, is not à la hauteur.

PARIS 7TH SEPTEMBER[27]

My dear Costy,

[. . .]

I arrived here last week, after a pleasant stay in Munich where I divided my time between sight seeing and Wagner's operas. The music impressed me greatly. But the business letters I got here upset me [. . .] the market had gone against my clients, I was also on the wrong side, but I ought not to have left and am repenting and feeling miserable—I am going to make the best of it by leading a quiet life, give my nerves a rest till I get back to that Pandemonium, the Bourse. I have booked my berth by the Austrian leaving Trieste on the 8th October.

Paris would be more agreeable were there less Alexandrians knocking about.—very few theaters are open so we spend our evenings in music halls and sup at Maxim's as a rule—

Mimi has just arrived from America, very enthusiastic about it; and has a lot to say. I am following the Macedonian crisis, how do you think that the Greeks will profit by this revolution? I do hope if the war comes off, that the Turks will lick the Bulgarians.

When will you be back?

Your very sincere friend,

Peri

Posing at the Café Napolitain was one thing—mastering French letters, quite another. Constantine ultimately surpassed Peri as an intellectual just as he did his brother in poetry; yet he was indebted to both for their desire to see him explore his literary interests and ultimately remain focused on culture and art to become a great poet (notable is the relative absence of commercial matters in Peri's letters, a deliberate choice to forgo the mundane and foreground the intellectual and cultural). His friendship with Peri bears witness to his maturation from a pretentious Anglophile to a cosmopolitan devotee of French culture, as reflected in a private note Constantine penned in October 1905:

> For me, that which makes English literature cold—besides some deficiencies of the English language—is—how shall I say it—the conservatism, the difficulty—or the unwillingness—to stray from the established, and the fear of offending morality, the pseudo-morality, since this is what we should call a morality that feigns naiveté.
>
> During these past ten years, how many French books—both good and bad—have been written that examine and bravely consider the new phase of eros. It is not new; it is just that for centuries it has been ignored, under the assumption that it was insanity (science says that it isn't) or a crime (logic says that it isn't). No English book that I know of [mentions it]. Why? Because they are afraid of confronting prejudice. Nevertheless, this erotic tendency also exists among the English, as it exists—and existed—among all of the nations, to a limited extent, of course.[28]

Constantine recorded here his evolving thoughts regarding homosexuality—"the new phase of eros"—which had been preoccupying him for years. He expressed his frustration that British authors had not been as daring as French writers in their treatment of this theme.[29] Perhaps his correspondence with Peri prompted these comments. That Peri could traverse Paris with his companion Levon and enjoy the pleasures of the city encouraged Constantine to make comparisons not only between Paris and London but also between Alexandria and Paris. At this time, Constantine was himself quite smitten with the Greek poet Alexander Mavroudis, whom he had met during his 1903 trip to Greece. Evidently he writes these notes out of a sense of sexual as well as cultural frustration. Constantine returned to this topic in his later days, as we shall show, when the Greek poet Napoleon Lapathiotis visited him in his hotel room in Athens before Constantine's surgery. During their conversation, Constantine expressed envy at Napoleon's freedom to live openly as a homosexual in Athens while he himself felt constrained in Alexandria.

Peri plays an important part in facilitating the relationship between Constantine and E. M. Forster, a critical encounter that will propel the poet's fame beyond the Greek-speaking world. During the war, Peri worked at the Press Censorship Department with Robert (Robin) Furness, a classicist who was an acquaintance of Forster. Furness was a translator of the Alexandrian poet Callimachus, whose elegiacal epigrams, "sexy and unapologetic about their homosexual lust," had been roundly dismissed by the dons of Cambridge as decadent.[30] Through Furness, Forster met Pericles, whom he "tutored" in English for four pounds a month, an act described as a "disguised form of patronage,"[31] since Peri's English was near perfect. Forster was serving out the war as a searcher in the Wounded and Missing Department of the Red Cross, a role he excelled in, as his interest in wounded soldiers (like that of Walt Whitman during the

American Civil War) allowed him to understand the unique homosocial bonds that men in the trenches felt for each other.[32] He was elected to the Mohammed Ali Club, where, at a dinner on March 7, 1916, he met Constantine, inaugurating a connection that would endure until the end of the poet's life. In addition to the two well-known books and numerous essays that Forster would write about Alexandria, he drafted a clever sketch about Peri and Constantine. "Pericles in Paradise" is a variation of the medieval allegory of the ladder of divine ascent,[33] except that Forster's ironic modernist take involves a staircase on which people are ascending and descending without any real moral direction. Artists who navigate these stairs appear not to know which way a true artist should proceed. Cavafy, as it turns out, descends:

> PERICLES [Laughing]: Hullo! Why are you going the wrong way?
>
> CAVAFFY: A regrettable tendency, my dear Perry, a regrettable tendency.
>
> PERICLES: But surely the show's upstairs. You ought to go up with Sir Bartle[34] and me, not down.
>
> CAVAFFY: Follow the Baronet, my dear Perry, follow the Baronet. Perhaps regrettably, perhaps not regrettably, I descend, I descend, [He does so.][35]

The parodic skit was perhaps Forster's attempt to offer a veiled comment on the fluctuating artistic standing of his friend during this crucial juncture when his poetic reputation was certainly on the rise, but he was often harassed by moralistic/homophobic assaults on his respectability, leading him in an uncertain and even perilous direction in terms of launching his career and establishing himself as an artist.[36]

Perhaps Forster was inspired to write this sketch owing to his own sexual awakening during these years, having just met Mohammed el Adl, a seventeen-year-old Egyptian tram conductor with whom he formed a deep emotional and sexual bond. He was in his late thirties when he entered into this, his first sexual relationship. Whether he and Constantine ever discussed Forster's homosexual novel *Maurice* is a matter of conjecture. But given the poet's bold poetic proclamation of same-sex love and homoerotic desire, it is somewhat inconceivable that Constantine would have remained ignorant of Forster's relations with Mohammed, well-informed as he was in matters of local gossip and rumor. It is interesting how differently they approached their lives and sexuality. While Constantine openly addressed homoerotic love in his poetry but rarely touched it in his correspondence, Forster was the opposite: he wrote explicitly about his erotic exploits in his letters, though he suppressed the homoerotic in his work (*Maurice* was published posthumously).

We do have from Forster the now-iconic portrait of the poet "standing absolutely motionless at a slight angle to the universe," along with the following account of novelist and poet connecting via Forster's reading knowledge of classical Greek:

> The occasion is over thirty years ago now, in his flat, 10 Rue Lepsius, Alexandria; . . . We have been introduced by an English friend, our meetings are rather dim, and Cavafy is now saying with his usual gentleness, "You could never understand my poetry, my dear Forster, never." A poem is produced—"The God abandons Antony"—and I detect some coincidences between its Greek and public school Greek. Cavafy is amazed. "Oh, but this is good, my dear Forster, this is very good indeed" and he raises his hand, takes over, and leads me through.[37]

Forster did more to promote Constantine's poetry in England than the poet could have imagined. Their exchanged letters offer much insight into how the poet responded to enthusiasts of his work who were eager to befriend him—his "claques," as it were. Forster possessed a unique and rather dynamic sense of friendship—connecting with people loomed large in his world ("only connect" is the famous epigraph to *Howards End*). Personal loyalties outranked political or religious considerations. He practiced a code of friendship that has been linked to the Bloomsbury Group, based as it was on G. E. Moore's philosophical writings (his *Principia Ethica* in particular), ideas the novelist imbibed from his early days as a member of the Cambridge Apostles.[38] Writers and artists associated with the Bloomsbury Group prided themselves on valuing the pleasures of human intercourse and enjoying beautiful objects. So it's quite telling that in one of his earliest letters to Constantine (dated July 1, 1917), Forster immediately opens on a frank note:

> Dear Cavaffy [*sic*],
>
> Valassopoulo was over this afternoon and told me that since I saw you something occurred that has made you very unhappy; that you believed the artist must be depraved; and that you were willing he should tell the above to your friends.[39]

The term in question here—"depravity"—also serves as a code word for homosexuality and should be taken in tandem with another comment Constantine made in one of his private notes: "I do not know if perversion gives strength. Sometimes I think so. But it is certainly the source of grandeur."[40] The Greek word "diastrophe" (perversion/depravity/inversion) resonates with cultural decadence and the "perverse" stance of so many writers coming out of this tradition with which Constantine was strongly aligned. We don't know what specifically made Constantine "unhappy." Was Forster referring to a particular incident? A love affair? A discussion? For both poet and novelist, there was much at stake in espousing or disavowing this notion of depravity. Forster as a humanist was less than sympathetic with fin de siècle attitudes and surely sought the opportunity to engage in subsequent conversations with the poet on this fraught subject. There were in fact numerous topics on which the two remained out of sync; these range from the lofty received views of classical Hellenism and British imperialism to the practical need to bring out an English translation of Cavafy poems. Forster's well-intentioned campaign to present his friend's verse to the English-speaking world included marshaling the efforts of T. S. Eliot, Virginia and Leonard Woolf, and T. E. Lawrence, among others. But in the end, Constantine demurred, not quite trusting his British enthusiasts with the project. Peri even weighed in at one point (letter dated July 17, 1925),[41] beckoning Constantine from London to "write to Forster immediately" and grant permission for publication. The project never materialized during the poet's lifetime, to Forster's chagrin.

There were many unrecorded conversations between Forster and Constantine, and the poet was acutely aware of the advantages of his acquaintanceship with the novelist. Constantine was not as trusting as he might have been. Forster knew this, writing after Constantine's death that "it is natural that his [letters] should be the more reserved. He was not as anxious to know me as I him."[42] Yet curiously, in a letter written after Forster made a return trip to Alexandria in 1929, Constantine conveys to him, in perhaps the most intimate of all their exchanges, the value of their literary friendship:

Alexandria
10 Rue Lepsius

15 OCTOBER, 1929

My dear Forster,

Your letter of the 26th September from on board gave me great pleasure.

Your stay here was too short, and I am glad to read you contemplate coming to Alexandria again. The hours we were able to spend together were too few: our friendship required more. At least, during these few hours I had the opportunity to express to you fully my admiration for that beautiful book "A Passage to India", to explain the reasons for my admiration. They have become, ever since 1924, companions of mine:—Mrs Moore, Fielding, Aziz, Adela, Heaslop, the Nawab Bahadur, McBryde. [. . .]

I am delighted at your intention to place in the "Nation" one of the translations of my poems; and I am glad it is easy for you to communicate with [T. S.] Eliot. [. . .]

Ever yours,
C. P. Cavafy[43]

Peri's role in this protracted interaction with Forster regarding the publication of the translations remained that of the tried-and-true supporter who only wanted the best for his friend. He saw Constantine's potential as a great poet and did much to promote him, even loaning him money to take his first trip to Greece in 1901, an occasion that would prove crucial for forging connections with the Athenian literary establishment. Constantine inscribed a dedication in Greek to Peri on the cover of the 1912 poetic collection he gave him: "To my Friend Pericles Anastasiades." The friendship cooled, however, in the early 1900s[44] and the money loaned for the Athens trip was never repaid. In the end, a troubling alienation eventually beset Constantine's relationship with Peri—as also happened with his brother John—two of the most important people in his life. The debt he owed to each became a strange sort of disinheritance. John died in 1923, bequeathing the bulk of his estate to his niece Hariclia and to his mistress, with only a small portion (one thousand Egyptian pounds) left to Constantine, which profoundly upset him. Yet he perversely mirrored this behavior by failing to repay the loan from Peri for his travels to Greece. When Constantine settled his unexpectedly large estate, leaving most of it to Alekos Sengopoulos, Peri, who had fallen upon hard times, reputedly commented: "It looks like Cavafy bequeathed money that wasn't his."[45] These sad finales conjure up the enigmatic and prophetic lines from Constantine's poem "My Walls": "But walls were built and heedless I stood by!" (in John's own 1896 English rendition of the line).[46]

Constantine, it turns out, proved to be the agent of his own alienation and the builder of his own walls. His odd sense of entitled indebtedness led to the breakdown of the dynamics of friendship. In the end, friendship for Constantine became a matter of convenience, reserved for those who served his literary career—friends of his work, as he put it quite plainly to Malanos. Constantine emerged as the great poet of the family and the clique's intellectual aesthete, the person both John and Peri wished him to be. His intimacy with the two people closest to him surely helped him attain his potential: "We become who we are in great part because of the friends we have," as Nehamas writes.[47] Sadly, however, it seems that Constantine failed to fully acknowledge this dynamic or value the role of siblings and friends as important validators of his persona and promoters of his poetry. This failure ultimately overshadowed these relationships and tragically undercut the intimacies preserved in the epistolary amber of these rich and varied exchanges. In the final decades of his life, the poet was intensely preoccupied by two relationships that would prove more challenging to his struggle with intimacy, casting it into sharper relief.

8

"IT WOULD HAVE BEEN YOU"

Timos Malanos and Alekos Sengopoulos

In the winter of 1953, two decades after Constantine's death, Timos Malanos encountered Alekos Sengopoulos on the street in Alexandria. Their resulting conversation speaks to the highly complicated dynamics that defined the poet's relations with these two central figures in his later life. Malanos records the following entry in his diary:

> 12 FEBRUARY, BETWEEN 8 AND 9:30 IN THE EVENING
>
> Returning home, tonight I met the old favorite of the poet in the street [Sengopoulos]. And while we normally greet each other with a formal "hello," today he stops me, extends his hand, and not having anything to do, perhaps, accompanies me to the door of my home. It's quite chilly out and since our conversation about Cavafy seemed to be unending, I suggest he come inside if he wished. He accepts. But in my office, the discussion about the person of Cavafy that began in the street

> becomes animated and suddenly takes a dramatic turn: "You know," he says to me, agitated "that Cavafy loved you and that if it hadn't been me, in my place it would have been you?" and before he finishes his sentence and I ask him what he means, he breaks out in sobs![1]

Given how radically different Constantine's relation was with each of these men, it seems strange that, according to Malanos's account, either might have served as the poet's chosen favorite and, by implication, been entrusted with his literary estate. The fact that Constantine could possibly have considered Malanos for such an important role illustrates how narrow and precarious his emotional life had become in the final two decades of his life. It also raises the question: Why did he favor Sengopoulos and leave him his estate and literary archive? The contrast between these two confidants could not have been greater. Constantine simultaneously cultivated and manipulated these friendships but with quite different objectives. That the two men were born a year apart (Malanos in 1897 and Sengopoulos in 1898) and had been students in the same classroom in 1907—the Tositsas School in Alexandria—is no coincidence; they were destined, it seems, to follow a path leading to Alexandria's great poet, one becoming the legal executor of his estate, the other the self-appointed arbitrator of his poetic legacy. They managed to reach these ends from divergent routes but were both enabled in various ways by the man they sought to serve.

Constantine was confronted with two very promising opportunities for companionship and mentorship in the persons of Timos and Alekos.[2] How should he have approached these two young men, both barely twenty when he first met them, and both eager to win his attention and patronage? He was certainly faced with a choice between two radically different characters with whom he was keen to forge emotional and perhaps even erotic relations. Timos Malanos was the sort of ideal young admirer Constantine would have been thrilled to count among his acolytes in his later years: attractive, ambitious, erudite, talented, and energetic. But he was also unruly—a self-possessed intellectual who was determined to make his own mark in the literary community of Alexandria. As it turned out, Malanos was not looking for the kind of paternalistic mentorship Constantine was offering, since he was anything but malleable. Yet like many young men who approached the "teacher"[3] (*daskalos*), he began his career by imitating him. According to his published memoirs, his first significant encounter with the poet emerged from the founding of a literary journal, *Propylaia*, that Malanos had set up in 1916. Timos had written a poem for it—the highly Cavafian "The Macedonian Alexander"—and managed to solicit two poems from Constantine as well—"When They Come Alive" and "Walls."[4] Ironically, Rika Agallianou, Alekos's future wife, was also involved with the short-lived journal, contributing a poem under her nom de plume, Rodope. *Propylaia* foundered after only two issues, but the more significant ramification from the whole ordeal was the charged exchange with Constantine when Malanos showed him "The Macedonian Alexander":

> He read it, then going through it line by line he kept saying, "This is Cavafian; this is not Cavafian; this parenthesis is Cavafian; this word is not Cavafian." Naturally what was not Cavafian he changed into Cavafian. The end result was a version *à la manière de* . . . But he himself did not see (or perhaps he did not want to see) that in this way we had a parody. His main interest was in the pupil (any pupil) who would follow his footsteps . . . I was 20 years old at the time, and, on that evening, when these suggestions were made, I stayed late

> in his home. We were alone. And then I sensed something. I sensed that his soul, concentrated all in his glance, in the touch of his hands, was about to hazard a movement in my direction like that of a carnivorous plant.[5]

It soon became evident to Constantine that Malanos was one of those friends about whom one should be very cautious—the flatterer and imitator who quickly becomes the foe.[6] The words of Oscar Wilde's fictional mouthpiece in *Dorian Gray*, Lord Henry Wotton, come to mind here: "I choose my friends for their good looks, my acquaintances for their good characters, and my enemies for their good intellects."[7] In the case of Malanos, the good-looking friend would soon become the clever enemy; many saw his book on the poet (published just three months after Constantine's death) as pure libel. Malanos, however, viewed the matter quite differently. He denied ever being an enemy, insisting that he was not necessarily bothered by the flattery that the poet's adulators served up and that Constantine himself cultivated; he was morally troubled by Constantine's approach as a mentor—the manner by which he would take up young admirers and convert them to his cult, creating a generation of fanatic epigones whom he manipulated into waging his poetic battles. Malanos sought to expose this very dynamic that would occur in the regular evening salons held at Rue Lepsius. The irony here is that Malanos, despite his hostility and blatant homophobia,[8] offered great critical insights into the corpus of Constantine's poetry, notwithstanding his penchant to overpsychoanalyze the poet himself (Memas Kolaitis aptly called him a "psychographer"[9]). Constantine must have been perversely flattered by the contradictory impulses driving Malanos, who confessed his wish to become the poet's Eckermann but wound up instead more like his Freud. The teacher soon realized how dangerous his disciple could be and consequently sought someone who would be more submissive and less threatening. He made a deliberate choice—with a yes to Alekos and a no to Timos, apropos of his Dantean poem "Che Fece . . . Il Gran Rifiuto" (1899/1901), a text that sheds much light on the poet's inner struggle with such momentous decisions:

For some the day arrives
when they have to decide between
the great Yes and the great No.
It's obvious who has the Yes ready within himself,
and saying it,

he moves ahead with honor and conviction.
He who refuses does not repent. If asked again,
he'd still say no. But that no—the right no—
cripples him for all his life.

The poem refers to the choice made by Pope Celestine to abdicate the papal throne, an act that, according to Rae Dalven's reading, Constantine interprets as one of humility and high scruple rather than as a sign of "cowardice," the word significantly suppressed from the poem's titular quotation[10] (the full line reads, "che fece per viltate il gran rifiuto / who made through cowardice the great refusal"[11]). Is this preference for Alekos over Timos a similar moment of suppressed timidity on the poet's part—an instance of his inability to face a more challenging and demanding intimacy? In an unpublished comment on the poem, Constantine views the act of refusal as a conscientious decision: "Though the Refuser knows that his refusal was right, still this refusal weighs down upon him during his whole life—it is made to weigh down by the suspicions, and the tales, and the [reproaches?], and the misconceptions of the many."[12] By denying Timos, he made a strategic decision he had to live with, one that would weigh him down in complicated ways and have long-term ramifications for his reputation. By choosing Alekos, moreover, he forfeited any semblance of intellectual rigor and plausibility, something he truly valued in Malanos, though he could not tame or control it. Thus, to rephrase what Alekos confessed to Timos in 1953, since it couldn't have been Malanos, it had to be Sengopoulos. In the end it would be Rika, Alekos's wife, who assumed the full duties of literary heir.

Why it well might have been Malanos may be better understood by reading Timos's own rather fanciful account of his early days with Constantine, where he describes the unique chemistry that existed between the two men:

> During the first years of our acquaintanceship, I saw him very often. I would go to his house two or three times a week. Most often we were alone. We would talk for hours. Or rather I would ask questions and he would speak. I somewhat resembled Wagner, the student of Faustus. With the difference being that my Faustus never felt the need to have recourse to his Mephistopheles in order to be rid of me. Like Wagner, I was eager to learn. But I had none of the hesitations of the innocent. The road that I would take—"an eager youth"—"fanatic for letters," as he writes in his poem—I had already chosen on my own.
>
> I never grew weary of his talk. On the contrary, it always gave me pleasure and, more often than not—at unforgettable moments—transported me afar. Thus I lived, thanks to him, the final night of Antony, as though I were his contemporary. I found myself in Alexandria during the dramatic hours of Cleopatra. I saw the endangered Caesarion. These, I must

> say, were the most enchanting moments that his conversation gave me. Because, usually, his conversations had as their theme the friends and enemies of his work. But even then he was never tiresome. He had spirit. But during these moments he ceased being the magician with the magic wand and became the teacher who prepared the apostles of his fame.[13]

It is telling that Malanos would frame his relationship in a Faustian context. In Goethe's narrative, Wagner dabbles in the magical dark arts by borrowing Faustus's spell book, much the same way Malanos appropriates Cavafy's poetic book—initially as a sycophantic disciple but later as a diabolical critic whose fixation on his subject will spin out of control. The greater irony here is that, at the end of the play, Wagner is made one of Faust's inheritors, amassing great wealth; Malanos, by contrast, is effectively disinherited. In Malanos's mischievous parallel—the opportunistic proximity to an infamous persona and the subsequent boasting and abuse (Wagner shows off to clowns; Malanos pontificates before the Greek intelligentsia)—fact and fiction overlap in significant ways.

Malanos managed to antagonize Constantine quite early on in their "love-hate" relationship during the course of which he was variously in and out of favor. In 1917, Timos wrote a harsh piece criticizing the poet's use of the word "routine" that set off a response by the group of young writers called the "Apuani"[14] who came to the poet's defense. Malanos struck back and so did Constantine via an article signed by Sengopoulos but actually written by the poet himself. This rift, which Kolaitis termed a cat-and-mouse game,[15] went on for years, inaugurating a fraught and dysfunctional relationship that pivoted upon mutual accusations of libel and imitation. An undated letter from Malanos captures the acute intensity of the rancor:

> Mr. Cavafy,
>
> I learned from friends of mine that the term which I used for free verse is your own and therefore, even in that, I am imitating you.
>
> This shows you to be very low in relation to me, especially after the related business of the versification that was once disseminated, that you had taught me.
>
> For this reason either you must ask for an apology in writing—in other words take those frivolous words back, or else you will be punished with a comparative chronography.
>
> I think you have insulted me enough.[16]

How revealing that the word "frivolous" (*elafrous*) is used here by Malanos, echoing the banished anguish of the "Byzantine Nobleman in Exile Composing Verses" (1921): "Let the frivolous call me frivolous." Yet there were other moments when Timos could show his support, most notably when he took a punch for the poet at the brawl that broke out during Socrates Lagoudakis's lecture in which Constantine was denounced as a pervert (see chapter twelve). Still, the poet was determined to stave off his erstwhile adulator, intent though Malanos was to penetrate the inner recesses of the poet's mind and soul. This stance prompted an ever-frustrated Malanos to profess that the poet's defense "was that of the Sphinx: silence."[17]

Relations broke off irreparably in 1926 when Constantine entrusted the editorship of the newly founded periodical *Alexandrine Techni* to A. G. Simeonidis and then to Rika Sengopoulos, deliberately slighting Malanos. The feud that ensued illustrates something of the acrimony that infected the relationship. Malanos attacked Rika as an "eighth-rate litterateuse"[18] and, in response, *Alexandrini Techni* fired back, labeling Malanos a "ninth-rate poet" and a "tenth-rate critic" (there can be no doubt as to who wrote these barbed comments). Malanos, it appears, was so obsessed with the matter of imitation that it still infected his relations with the poet as late as 1926. In a terse letter dated August 9, 1926,[19] Timos writes:

> To the Esteemed Mr. Cavafy,
>
> I learned that you attribute to me some action beneath my character—you attribute to me, as I've been told, the source (*patrotita*) of Evangelou's article in *Isis*.[20]
>
> To your slander I have one answer and my answer is this:
>
> Do you think, Mr. Cavafy, that I would ever reach the point when I would imitate your own methods of seeking adulation?
>
> Respectfully,
> *T. Malanos*

When asked to comment years later on the nature of Malanos's relationship with Constantine and the disclaimer repeatedly made by Timos that he was not the poet's enemy, Rika offered the following insightful explanation: "I'm not sure we should characterize Malanos's stance as hatred for the poet. I would say that he battered and battered, here and there, because he saw that the fortress called Cavafy's poetry could neither be besieged nor would fall."[21] The relationship ended poorly, with Constantine habitually crossing the road to avoid meeting Malanos; according to Kolaitis, "from February 1926 to the day of Cavafy's death in 1933, Mr. Timos Malanos never saw Cavafy even for a single minute."[22] This "gran rifiuto" was certainly a sustained effort on Constantine's part; navigating such an excruciating course with an obsessed critic must have been sheer agony. The spurned Malanos would take his ultimate revenge, having the last word in his book-length study and in the numerous ensuing publications he authored up to the very end of his life.[23] He would continue to write compulsively on the poet until his death in 1984, effectively inaugurating Cavafy studies in the twentieth century, albeit on a highly disparaging and, for many, libelous note.

Malanos was quite adept at framing his own specific gripes against Constantine, rehearsing them repeatedly throughout much of his writing; yet despite them, he maintained a peculiar allegiance and disavowed an overt notion of hatred or malice, protesting perhaps too much to be taken at his word. ("I have never written a hostile article against the work of Cavafy. The only thing I've written are some articles opposing his politics as a teacher.")[24] His infamous book, *The Poet C. P. Cavafy*, is structured in such a way, however, as to render these strategic disclaimers quite disingenuous. For starters, the section headings themselves read like danger signs alerting an unsuspecting traveler to the poet's character flaws and weaknesses. Readers are guided through a litany of faults, among which are the following: Cavafy's egocentrism, cowardice, vanity, inconsistencies, psychoses, prosiness, and fear of time. Beneath these Malanos spins a web of related snares regarding the poet's false modesty, pretentiousness, eccentricities, ambition, narcissism, stinginess, erotic mysticism, obsession with revision, lack of originality, parasitic imagination, frigidity, and repetitiveness, all of which are unduly complicated—and indeed caused by—his inverted sexuality. Cavafy was "born old" and "reminds one of a Byzantine monastic figure"; is "a puppet animated by the strings of his own intellect"; "a craftsman, not a poet"; "like a woman, he wished to be protected by others" and thus resorted to extreme modes of manipulation to ensure this; was "obsessed with posterity"; "wrote poetry like a historian rather than writing history like a poet"; he "had only enough poetic inspiration to write epigrams."[25] Crowning Malanos's most damning comments is the following: "In general, his verse is frigid. Maybe because it is not poetry that sings, that palpitates with pathos, but rather poetry that thinks."[26]

One of the more eloquent and effective rebuttals of Malanos came from R. M. Dawkins, professor of medieval and modern Greek at Oxford, who was introduced to Cavafy's work by William Plomer via E. M. Forster.[27] Dawkins's 1934 review of Malanos's biocritical study eviscerates the critic with a comment that the poet himself might well have made had he lived to see the book issued: "Mr. Malanos, the reviewer feels, shows here and in many other places that he hardly knows what it is that makes a poem: it is a matter for astonishment that with such a poor equipment of poetic sensibility he ever set out to write this book at all. With Cavafy's poetry he is certainly entirely out of sympathy."[28] Malanos, to his credit, was among the first to place Cavafy fully within the context of French and British literature, reading him as a global artist and liberating him to some extent from reductive parallels with contemporary Greek poets. He was also responsible for the most frank and direct discussion of the poet's sexuality to date, albeit one fraught with homophobic distortions and misreadings.

Alekos Sengopoulos, by contrast, was a more passive and conventional personality, with no real ambition beyond enjoying himself in the cafés and bars of the city. He had little to no literary talent nor any notable intellectual interests. In the words of

Dimitris Garoufalias (to whom he was related through marriage), he had a high school education and was thoroughly unremarkable.[29] Yet Constantine had a soft spot for him that defied any ready explanation.[30] There are some revealing details about the intensity of Constantine's feelings for Alekos in a trove of some seventy-two letters written by the poet between 1918 and 1919 while Sengopoulos was clerking in Benha, Egypt. It appears that Constantine initially had high hopes for the youth whose intellectual capacities he tried to elevate, mentoring him to become the worthy companion of a great poet. Prior to his departure, Alekos had already been initiated into the Cavafian mysteries, with the poet grooming him to be his most proficient and articulate reader. This came to a head in a rather melodramatic event—a public lecture that, despite its significance in terms of proclaiming Constantine's unrepentant homoerotic hedonism, nearly devolved into a "dangerous farce" as Malanos described it.[31] Indeed, the "rejected one" narrated the episode with his signature schadenfreude in his memoirs. Constantine arranged to have Alekos deliver a talk on his poetry on February 23, 1918, at the Ptolemy Club in Alexandria. The lecture, Malanos avers,[32] was written largely by Constantine himself with Alekos functioning as his mouthpiece—an arrangement to which Malanos would never have acquiesced but one that surely piqued his jealousy. The event was nearly sabotaged by three schemers—Yiorgos Vrisimitzakis,[33] Stamos Zervos, and Sakellaris Yiannakakis—who enticed Alekos into imbibing a few drinks and then proceeded to waylay him in a horse-drawn carriage in an effort to make him miss the lecture altogether. Realizing their scheme, Alekos escaped the hansom and rushed to the venue, late, semi-inebriated, and out of breath. He proceeded to deliver the scripted "pseudo-lecture" in this rather discombobulated state, practically shouting the poems in his agitation and creating more of a spectacle than an impression. The audience was not pleased either by the frank treatment of the featured poems' erotic content or by the intellectual tenor of the talk. Malanos notes with relish the abrupt departure of a certain Madame Tsimbouki along with other displeased attendees, diminishing an already sparse crowd.[34] "Alexandrian Greeks," he quips, "were largely not interested in literature and even less inclined to receive such intrepid ideas."[35] The evening turned out to be a flop in terms of the public's receptivity but a watershed in regard to poetic honesty.

It's hard to know what Constantine would have thought as an observer of this self-orchestrated fiasco. It was a calculated risk that proved groundbreaking, marking as it did a critical moment in the poet's "coming out," as Dimitris Papanikolaou argues in his treatment of Cavafy's homosexuality.[36] The lecture featured an analysis[37] of four poems—"Thinking Dangerously"(1911), "I Went" (1905/1913), "Long Ago" (1914), and "Return" (1909/1912). The first of these set the general tone for the talk:

So said Myrtias (a Syrian student
in Alexandria during the reign of
Emperor Constans and Emperor Constantius,
partly pagan, partly acting like a Christian):
"Strengthened by thought and contemplation,
I won't fear my passions like a coward.
I'll surrender my body to pleasures,
to dreamlike delights,
to daring, erotic desires,
to the lustful urging of my blood fearlessly,
because whenever I wish—
and I'll have the determination, strengthened
as I'll be by theory and research—
I'll be able to recover my spirit again
at crucial moments, ascetic as before."

"Thinking Dangerously" effectively distills the essence of Constantine the person into Cavafy the poet, foregrounding as it does the fantasy of youth's power and allure, and the illusory solace of age's ability to revisit and relive the moment aesthetically. The choice of this "dangerous" poem offers a subtle comment on the erotic logistics of the lecture itself—selecting a favored youth to deliver the risqué message of the poem, which, from the analytical commentary of the lecture, may be glossed as follows: Artists, unlike those in other professions, require a protracted apprenticeship in sensual indulgence that ideally spans the entire duration of one's youth. A sensitive, aesthetic youth, therefore, must indulge in the quickened sense of life.[38] Perhaps in some ironic way, Alekos's topsy-turvy delivery was appropriate after all, as he seemed to embody youth's intoxicated excess even while articulating the measured control of maturity through a lecture written by an elder poet strengthened by "theory and research." The talk ended with Alekos noting that Constantine was a fierce worshipper of youth and pleasure: "So allow me to conclude my talk by saying that Cavafy often detaches himself; he rejoices sincerely and warmly in the life of youth in others; and he likes to see his cherished wine of pleasure dispensed and imbibed by all."[39] It was rather daring for Constantine to have Alekos deliver such a provocative lecture about his most adventurous poems in 1918 to listeners who, albeit tolerant, must have found both the material and the tone strange and reckless.

Months after the lecture, Alekos departed for Benha (some eighty-nine miles from Alexandria), occasioning the only written documentation of the sentimental and emotional relationship he shared with the poet. Among the most telling particulars of the letters, which are written in Greek, are the following: Constantine urges Alekos to improve his English; to learn the business of trading in cotton; to keep up his French (lest it get rusty);

to improve his spelling; to watch his health (the Spanish flu is raging);[40] to abstain from playing cards; to cut down on his smoking; to wear a coat and avoid drafts; to get involved with the theater when he returns to Alexandria;[41] and to meet people and cultivate relationships. This slew of exhortations betrays an almost parental interest in the future of a son (Constantine's language recalls Haricleia's henpecking tone in her letters to her boys). The fact that Constantine mentions visiting Alekos's family adds another layer of complexity to this peculiar courtship, striking contemporary readers as overbearing and controlling.

Like a father, Constantine wanted to find out every detail about Alekos's life in Benha: "I sensed how deeply sad you were during the moments of your departure" (October 13, 1918);[42] "I think about you a lot. Please take care of your health" (October 14, 1918);[43] "I can't tell you how much your letter pleased me. In every line I recognize my wonderful Alekos" (October 17, 1918). He was saddened that Alekos found the place dull but at least he was learning something about the cotton trade (October 17, 1918).[44] "Tell me what you do at night; and the time you go to bed" (October 19, 1918). Interestingly, Constantine said that he was taking care of his health, now that he was alone "and if I become ill, I have no one to worry about me" (October 19, 1918).[45] He "trembled" with fear about Alekos's health: "Is the food you eat good? Is the water good?" Was his room fresh and airy, he wondered? (November 2, 1918).[46] He urged him repeatedly to write, for his "absence is deeply felt" (November 6, 1918). And, as his brother John had done for him decades earlier, Constantine corrected Alekos's spelling mistakes in Greek (November 6, 1918).[47] "Your letter of the 12th—your beautiful letter—shows my Alekos to be very melancholy. I hope he is feeling a little better now" (November 15, 1918).[48]

Augmenting these counsels is the rather incongruous literary content of the letters, which must be taken in the context of Constantine's ambitious plans for his protégé. We quickly discover that he was determined to mold Alekos, to force him to share his cultural interests, something he must have known would be a losing endeavor. This appears to have been a central component of their early bond, but since they lacked any semblance of intellectual parity, the friendship was doomed to remain lopsided both socially and artistically. Constantine shares the subject matter of his recent reading with Alekos in a way that seems almost deluded in terms of expecting the receptivity of a keenly interested interlocutor on the level of a Timos, Mikès, or Peri. Constantine drops names Alekos has likely never heard of: Suetonius, Palladas (author of epigrams in *The Greek Anthology*), Theocritus, Aeschylus, D'Annunzio, Anatole France, Giacomo Leopardi, Jules Lemaître, and Robert Browning. He repeatedly asks Alekos what he's reading: "If you begin reading, tell which book you've taken in hand" (October 19, 1918).[49] A curious detail regarding a poem by Theocritus animates a letter dated October 27, 1918:[50]

> The day before last, Valassopoulo came by, and we spoke about Greek studies in England . . . Valassopoulo told me about a wonderful edition of Aeschylus' Agamemnon by [Walter] Headlam. Headlam—a very important teacher—died a few years ago at the age of 41. A great loss for Greek letters. I have read a perfect translation of one of Theocritus's poems—a beautiful poem by Theocritus, where the tragic yearning of a ruined love is described. Regarding "Agamemnon" I believe I spoke to you on a previous occasion about a masterful translation of him by Browning, the Great English poet of the last century. In this translation, he

> has managed the very difficult task of preserving the tone of the work, its poetic atmosphere.—

Whether a twenty-year-old apprenticing in a provincial town would find a letter about such matters of interest (or catch the coded erotic subtext of Theocritus) is highly doubtful. Constantine shows a willful blindness in his determination to make Alekos into a literary figure (or lackey), continuing the vexed project he had launched earlier that year by writing the lecture, playing as a ventriloquist would with a toy puppet.

The sentiment of painful separation and anticipated reunion comes through frequently: "As far as my feelings for you are concerned, my Alekos, be sure of my commitment" (January 27, 1919);[51] "I can't describe how much I miss you" (November 15, 1918).[52] Constantine goes as far as to promise to speak to Antonis Benaki and try to get him a job once he returns to Alexandria. His affection for Alekos was surely complex, leading him even into the realm of arranging an advantageous marriage: he went as far as to proffer his own niece Eleni (Alexander's daughter), which caused a rift with his brother John, who strongly opposed the idea.[53] When Alekos eventually married Rika, witnesses reported that Constantine wept uncontrollably (this was allegedly relayed directly to Malanos by Peri). This marriage, paradoxically, was the best thing that could have happened to the poet, as in Rika he found what was lacking in Alekos: a serious devotee and refined intellectual who would safeguard his legacy. And, of course, it was Rika who took care of him at the end, attending to the details of his surgery, convalescence, and funeral.

Not surprisingly, we have the most detailed account of the relationship between Constantine and Alekos from Malanos, who, with hawklike concentration, picked up on all the weaknesses of the bond. That Alekos would refer to Constantine as "gero mou" (my old man) and "my father" struck Malanos as ludicrous and the height of disrespect by inferring (deliberately) that he was the poet's illegitimate son. After Constantine's death, Malanos would pursue Sengopoulos with the same fury he did the poet, openly savaging the heir's negligence of Cavafy's legacy: the careless dispersal of the poet's library, the delaying of the English translation by John Mavrogordato, and the profiting off the first edition of the poems.[54] Alekos and Rika divorced in 1939, whereupon Rika was effectively removed from the picture.[55] In typical Malanos fashion, we learn that later in life Alekos took on Constantine's mannerisms, even in the peculiar imitative way he parted his hair.[56]

Whether there was an actual sexual component to the relationship between the poet and his literary executor and heir remains a matter of speculation. Malanos adamantly maintained that there was, calling Alekos Constantine's "gigolo." It is true that the elder poet behaved rather like a "sugar daddy," writing out his will ten years before he died and leaving Alekos virtually everything, and in the final years of his life, Alekos and Rika were at his side, giving rise to the idea that Alekos was actually his nurse.[57] It is quite possible that Alekos was all these things: an early lover, a confidant, a friend, and a caregiver at the end. In the only surviving letter from Alekos to Constantine, written from Athens on July 3, 1928,[58] we have a curious mirroring of the poet's earlier letters to him:

> My Old Man,
>
> We received all your letters [. . .] I am very pleased old man that you write me that you are well [. . .] the only thing missing here is that you are so far away from me . . . how pleased would I be if you were here with me

> my old man . . . but fortunately the whole world here is talking about you. [. . .] We totally trashed Malanos, Boufides[59] speaks with the greatest disdain for Malanos. Old man, take care of your health, and I beg you to go to bed early now that we are not there and to eat well . . .
>
> With many, many kisses
> *Alekos*

Malanos is on record as saying that Constantine had no close friends, being too selfish and self-absorbed.[60] Malanos's own harsh, self-righteous idea of friendship, on the other hand, proved him to be equally demanding and uncompromising: "I wish for friends who accept me for what I am and as I am. With my rough edges. And not those who wish me smooth, like a round shiny pebble."[61] Perhaps it was this strident hardness that ultimately turned the poet off. Constantine confessed as much in a private commentary recorded in 1910: "How horrible these new philosophical ideas of hardness, of the rightful superiority of the mighty." He preferred a different type: "Not hardness; but Mercy, Sorrow, Forgiveness, Kindness (these, of course, with discretion and without excess) are both Power and Wisdom."[62] The "Übermensch" Malanos gave way to the "underdog" Sengopoulos. In the end, Alekos would remain the chosen one. Voiceless and totally dependent in his final months, Constantine lived and died content with the decision he had made—the "Great Yes." This is evident from a telling and stark note he scrawled on one of the small sheets of paper he would use to communicate his wishes: "Whatever my Alekos says."[63]

INTERLUDE

Constantine's Reading

The reader in the poem "He Came to Read" is "completely devoted to books— / but he's twenty-three years old, and truly handsome; and this very afternoon eros / entered his perfect flesh, his lips." As dedicated to pleasure as he is to reading, this imaginary reader offers a portrait akin to that of Constantine the artist as a young man. As we've seen, Constantine was largely an autodidact. Possessing a bibliophile's passion for reading, he approached books with a scholarly attentiveness and heightened philological regard for their content. He was a stickler for relevant details, textual accuracy, and the citational potential of what he read. From his surviving library we have a good idea of the writers he valued and studied, and from his correspondence, prose writings, and poems, we can construct a list of authors who influenced his thinking and with whom he entered into intellectual and artistic dialogue.[1]

Constantine's surviving books range from a precious and covetable 1556 Latin translation of Aristotle—*De Republica, qui Politicorum dicuntur*, which appears to have belonged at one time to Queen Mary I Tudor[2]—to the popular detective novel *M. Gallet décédé / The Late Monsieur Gallet*[3] (1931) by the Belgian writer Georges Simenon. As veritable bookends of his library, these two texts literally speak volumes about his eclectic reading habits and ability to view classical sources from a contemporary perspective, giving them the Cavafian twist that would define his unique appropriation of antiquity, history, and sensuality. Indeed, he possessed an almost alchemical ability to make dry and arcane topics seem as interesting and gripping as the details of a detective story.

His earliest reading list was documented by the poet himself in his unfinished "Constantinopoliad, an Epic," where he mentions the seven books he took aboard the SS *Castore* when the family sought refuge in Istanbul in 1882. Five of these were British: David Hume's *History of England*, James McKenzie's *The History of Scotland*, Thomas Milner's *The History of England*, Robert Louis Stevenson's *Familiar Studies in Men and Books*, and Sir Walter Scott's *The Antiquary*. They speak to Constantine's Anglophilic orientation and early interest in history and antiquity. The other two were French historical studies—Hippolyte Taine's *Essai sur Tite Live* and Pierre Alexis Pierron's *Histoire de la littérature romaine*.[4] In terms of modern Greek literature, Constantine was aware of the prevalent literary trends of nineteenth-century authors through his protracted reading of the major Greek writers of that period. He knew the first national poets Dionysios Solomos (1798–1857) and Andreas Kalvos (1792–1869), both of whom, coming from the Ionian islands, were heavily indebted to Italian literature. These two national literary titans left little direct influence on Constantine, however, although later he included excerpts from Solomos's verse in the entries he compiled for his commonplace book. A more direct line of inspiration came from the so-called Old Athenian or

Phanariot School, which was heavily Romantic and dominated by the poets Alexander Soutsos, his brother Panayiotis Soutsos, and Alexandros Rizos Rangavis. To this group may be added Athanasios Christopoulos, about whom we have Constantine's direct thoughts from a lost and "re-remembered" essay.[5] Hailing from Phanariot families himself, Constantine identified on some level with these poets—we should bear in mind that Alexander Soutsos visited Peter John Cavafy in Alexandria in 1862 and wrote an epigraph for the Cavafy family tombstone.[6] The learned tradition of the Phanariots loomed large when Constantine was perfecting his command of the Greek language while living in the Ottoman capital. In fact, Timos Malanos argued that Constantine spoke Greek the way Rangavis had written it, and further maintained that his poetry was equally influenced by the Phanariot's erudite style and mannered language.[7] This of course was part of Malanos's larger negative critique of his erstwhile mentor's artificiality and preference for intellect and craft over emotion and inspiration.

Constantine was aware of the two tensions in contemporary Greek writing. On the one hand there was the New Athenian School that rebelled against the excessive Romanticism of the midcentury and gravitated in the direction of the French Parnassians.[8] On the other was the overwhelming presence in the New Athenian School of folklore (*laographia*) and the growing attraction of realism in prose writing, the "Scylla and Charybdis" of late-nineteenth-century Greek letters, as it were. This polarity seemed like a contradiction: "On the one hand writers, translators and critics looked outside Greece to Europe, and particularly to France, and presented what they found there to the Greek reading public; on the other, interest began to be directed with a new intensity and sense of purpose towards identifying, defining, and describing those areas of Greek life which were still uncontaminated by European influence."[9] Constantine's earliest compositions show that he was cognizant of both of these currents, which he navigated by veering more in the direction of the cosmopolitan writers who appealed to him as an aesthete and a diasporic Greek rather than as a Greek national. His contemporaries—the generation of 1880—would have included Nikos Kambas (1857–1932), Kostis Palamas (1859–1943), Yiorgos Drosinis (1859–1951), Lorenzos Mavilis (1860–1912), Ioannis Polemis (1862–1925), Miltiadis Malakasis (1869–1943), and Ioannis Gryparis (1870–1942).[10] As was true in the case of so many of his connections, Constantine stood "at a slight angle" to these poets in that he was not working directly out of a particular Greek tradition. Whereas many Greek writers were either imitating, rejecting, or transforming European literary influences,[11] Constantine emerged more overtly out of British aestheticism (as explored in chapter one), French Parnassianism, and transnational decadence. He effectively sidestepped the dominant folkloric and ethnocentric preoccupations of Greek writers, only to return to them (and folklore in particular) in more subtle ways later in his career. He would interpret Greek poetic trends the way Greek poets interpreted European literary trends, gradually distancing himself from the residual Romanticism[12] and ethnocentric lyricism that found their culmination in the work of Kostis Palamas. Constantine's notorious dismissal of Greek poets as hopelessly Romantic—"They are romantics, romantics, romantics!"[13]—was rooted in his desire to distinguish himself from any "school" of Greek writing, something he managed to achieve with remarkable success. For this very reason, most discussions of Cavafy in histories of Greek literature place him in his own category and avoid aligning him with the major Greek literary schools and movements.

Constantine was much more connected with what would

come to be defined as decadent aestheticism, especially in his early years. In this sense, he kept company with the international group of decadent writers who, as Matthew Potolsky aptly notes, "move within a recognizable network of canonical books, pervasive influences, recycled stories, erudite commentaries, and shared tastes."[14] This nexus defines him less strictly in terms of schools of influence and more fittingly in relation to his own personal literary connoisseurship and highly idiosyncratic reading choices that constitute his unique intellectual pedigree.

How did Constantine's literary tastes evolve? We have what could be called an early inventory of writers and poets he was reading during his years in Istanbul from the letters he exchanged with John, where the two brothers shared reading material and thoughts on poetry and translation. John's interests at the time overlapped closely with those of his brother, and their letters include the discussion of the following writers: Horace, Shakespeare, Cowper, Dickens, Thackeray, Longus, Aristotle, Plato, Byron, Balzac, Goethe, Tennyson, Bossuet, Herodotus, Hugo, Swinburne, Browning, Sand, Felix Arvers, Mary Kingsley, Irving, Shelley, Bulwer-Lytton, Ossian, Alexandros Rizos Rangavis, Joseph Addison, and Max O'Rell.[15] Shakespeare looms particularly large in these exchanges, since, at the time, Constantine was translating *Much Ado About Nothing*, a project he didn't complete, though some passages of this venture survive.[16] He preserved a section he translated from Act III, Scene ii, of the play and the song "Sigh no more, ladies, sigh no more." He went on to write three articles dealing with Shakespeare, one of which, "Shakespeare on Life," contains translated excerpts from *Measure for Measure*.[17] He also composed an early long poem, "King Claudius" (1899),[18] that reimagines *Hamlet* from the perspective of a wronged Claudius: "that most sorrowful history, / that unfortunate King, / killed by his nephew / for some imaginary suspicions."

The first of these, "Professor Blackie on the Modern Greek Language" (1891), is essentially an appreciative review of John Stuart Blackie's essay "Shakespeare and Modern Greek" that appeared in the British periodical *The Nineteenth Century* in 1891. Constantine's initial exposure to Blackie, however, came years earlier when, in a letter dated March 8, 1883, his brother John makes mention of him: "I have also got hold of a book called *Self-Culture* and written by Prof. Blackie of Edinburgh. It is a marvel of cleverness and in a clear, tho' concise, way sets forth a string of rules whereby a student should guide himself in the attainment of physical and moral privileges."[19] John Stuart Blackie was a professor of modern Greek and a Scottish linguist whose book—the full title of which reads *Self-Culture: Intellectual, Physical and Moral: A Vade Mecum for Young Men and Students* (1879)—is divided into three chapters, each of which addresses one of the three themes laid out in the subtitle.[20] In it he makes a number of points that evidently resonated with John, who, even at the young age of nineteen, was already predisposed to concur with what he found expounded in Blackie's moral exordium. We don't know if Constantine ever read this book, and it is highly unlikely that he would have shared John's more conservative views on conduct befitting young men. But the seed for a future engagement with Blackie was planted and would eventually sprout, with its philological offshoot branching in the direction of translation. Blackie's article, in addition to praising Iakovos Polylas's (1826–98) Greek translations of Shakespeare, expressed a number of positive views on the continuity of the Greek language and defended modern Greek against the charges of it being a "barbarous corruption" of the ancient language. Regarding the existence of dual purist and demotic registers, Constantine excerpts the following from Blackie's text: "It is quite possible for the most highly cultivated language to have in familiar use for certain spheres of expression a double type of speech, as the Athenians had when they used the Doric familiarity in the choral odes, or as the Scotch may do when they use the musical language of Burns as the most appropriate form of English for lyrical utterance."[21] This philological validation from the Scottish professor earned Constantine's gratitude: "The entire article exhibits a fervent sympathy for our nation and our literature."[22]

The article "Shakespeare on Life," also published in 1891, opens with a reflection on how to receive ideas and includes a critique of didacticism that is very much indebted to Edgar Allan Poe:[23] "I esteem the observations of great men more than I do their conclusions."[24] Notwithstanding the genius of these great men, he does not have "much confidence in the absolute worth" of their conclusions: "By this I do not mean that I require authors to remain entirely indecisive. This would be extreme. I only wish to say that I do not care for excessive dogmatism." He then offers the example of Shakespeare as an author "who tells us much without imposing upon us anything in particular" and illustrates this with passages from *Measure for Measure* regarding vanity and the value of life.[25] A similar appreciation is offered in the third article, "Traces of Greek Thought in Shakespeare" (1893), a reappraisal of James Russell Lowell's essay "Shakespeare Once More" (*Among My Books*, 1891) where Constantine notes the following for his Greek readers: "Lowell concludes that Shakespeare was not as uninformed by Greek learning as has been previously assumed; indeed, it does not seem improbable if some Latin or Greek edition of the Greek tragedians passed through the dramatist's hands . . ."[26] Constantine closes his essay with some rather speculative thoughts that attempt to align the two tragic traditions: "Although Shakespeare lived and flourished outside the world of Greek literature, yet it remains quite possible that voices and sounds emanating from within it reached his ear during his long poetic career."[27]

These uneven and rather tentative forays into Shakespearean criticism reveal an ambitious young man who was eager to engage with high culture if uncertain about quite how to achieve it.[28] The brothers' shared reading interests reflect a Victorian appreciation of popular British writers, but in Constantine's case, these literary pursuits would gradually veer in a more aesthetic direction and overlap quite closely with the British poets whose writings were favored by the aesthetic pre-Raphaelite circle associated with the Anglo-Greek community in London, as discussed in chapter one. The influence of this circle on Constantine's tastes is evident from his choice of subject matter in his prose writings and early attempts at journalism. These include, in addition to Shakespeare, essays on Keats, Tennyson, Browning, the Elgin Marbles, and marginal notes on Ruskin.[29] During the last two decades of the nineteenth century, he was also an avid reader of British periodicals, namely *The Gentlemen's Magazine*, *The Temple Bar*, *The Fortnightly Review*, and *The Nineteenth Century*. It's quite possible that he wrote his early English essays with the ambitious intention of publishing them in one of these journalistic venues.

The long essay on Keats, titled "Lamia" (1893), focuses on the eponymous poem about this beautiful vampiric creature. Here Constantine tries his hand yet again at translation, and the essay contains extensive passages of Keats's verse. It opens on the familiar note of aligning British and Greek texts[30] followed by a lengthy synopsis of the poem interspersed with translated passages and commentary. Constantine's point here is to compare the Greek original with Keats's reworking of the narrative: "Without question, the beauty of the verse, the inimitable grace of the narrative voice belong unequivocally to Keats, but to the ingenious Greek belong the very idea and fantasy behind the work."[31] After including a passage from Philostratus's *The Life of Apollonius* for readers to savor, he then offers some linguistic observations on the Greek text, wrapping up the essay with the following critical appraisal: "Keats distances himself somewhat from the mythological tradition of the Lamia. This certainly was his right. Poets fashion their own perceptions upon which they then build; they are entitled to delight in the reworking of material with full freedom. I cannot question Keats's right; I simply observe that, had Lamia's character been a bit less virtuous, the poem would have been more expressive and created a deeper impression."[32] The distinctive beauty of the Lamia of the ancients, he laments, "like Milton's Satan—a beauty which may be put on or off at will—remains only as a memory."[33]

Subsequent unpublished essays on Tennyson and Browning proceed in a similar appreciative and comparative vein. Both were written in 1894 and bear witness to his need to assess what he surely considered to be the most significant literary voices of his day.[34] "The Last Days of Odysseus" once again features a comparison between Greek and British traditions and offers a triangulated reading of Homer, Dante, and Tennyson along with a critique of the post-Homeric twist to the story where Odysseus leaves Ithaca for yet another voyage:

> To the English poet less credit is due since he found the raw material of the idea already developed [by Dante]. But he reworked it like a skilled artist. Tennyson's Odysseus is more likable than Dante's. According to Tennyson, he is more human; according to Dante, he is more heroic. Dante has Odysseus depart only because he cannot master the urge to acquire worldly experience . . . Tennyson conveys the additional notion of "incompris" [being misunderstood], the disgust

> induced by a life on his remote island and the obligation to live with his inferiors who do not understand him, "A savage race / That Hoard, and sleep, and feed, and know not me."[35]

Both Dante and Tennyson receive equal praise for their respective renditions. The ambiguity of Tennyson's lines "cast a spell on the spirit, and presents a picture of Odysseus' ship proceeding towards the great Western seas with golden horizons and unknown isles"; Dante's imagination "has fashioned an image not unworthy of the 'sovrano poeta' [sovereign poet]."[36] The essay pays homage to two influential postclassical treatments of the Odyssean theme and points forward, as we shall show, to Constantine's own distillation of this material in what will become one of his most successful poems: "Ithaca" (1910/1911).

The untitled Browning essay presents a similar triangulation of a medieval French ballad involving King Francis, a lion, and a glove, a story respectively treated by Schiller ("Der Handschuh / The Glove" [1797]), Leigh Hunt ("The Glove and the Lions" [1836]), and Browning ("The Glove" [1845]). After offering a synopsis of the shared analogue, Constantine proceeds to analyze the relative merits of each rendition, with Browning receiving the lion's share of praise: "As far as images and verses go, Browning's poem is a true masterpiece. Word for word, nearly all of the lines are trochaic, and the handling of the rhyme scheme presents various and great challenges in terms of English prosody; the description of the lion is a poetic photograph."[37] These comments come nearly a decade after those expressed by John in a letter dated March 16, 1883: "Browning has come out with a fresh volume of poems entitled Jocoseria and written in his usual unintelligible vein: there are however some very good verses in it, and, when you get to think that the author is an old man of 70, you are astonished to find the same vigour of thought that has justly raised the fine work 'Pauline' to an eminence on the British

Parnassus."[38] Clearly the brothers shared a critical admiration for the master of the dramatic monologue, a poetic device that Constantine would adapt so adroitly to his own poetic ends.

In addition to his essays, Constantine's marginalia and written annotations provide invaluable insights into his engagement with other writers. As was the case with Poe's famous marginalia, with which Constantine would have been familiar given that his volumes of Poe show signs of careful reading,[39] Constantine would both write in the margins of his books and on slips of paper inserted into them, marking the corresponding passage with an "x." Those he composed on the Victorian sage John Ruskin are somewhat challenging to process given their expansive range and often dismissive tone, but they remain nonetheless revealing in terms of the poet's aesthetic and moral stance vis-à-vis one of the reigning intellects of the nineteenth century. These reading notes—nineteen in number—annotate *Selections from the Writing of John Ruskin* (volume 1), published by George Allen in 1893, and date somewhere between 1893 and 1896.[40] Constantine records his thoughts on selections from the volume that contained numbered extracts from Ruskin's early writings covering the years 1843–60.[41] The comments are written in Greek and are largely hostile, reflecting an overall disagreement with Ruskin's moral stance on art and disapproval of his didactic ethical tone in general. There are a few instances, however, when the aesthetic ideas of the onetime advocate of "art for art's sake" receive backhanded praise. Ruskin's commentary on beauty—"Remember that the most beautiful things in the world are the most useless; peacocks and lilies, for instance"—is met with the following rejoinder: "This phrase is not at all in agreement with the spirit of the Ethical and Didactic precepts in the middle of which it appears. This does not conflict with it being the dogma of Art."[42]

Among the many comments that irked Constantine is Ruskin's critique of the vulgarity of "keeping up appearances," which Ruskin dismisses as being "a mere selfish struggle of the vain with the vain." To this Constantine retorts: "What is important for our happiness is not how others judge us but how we think they judge us. In our fancy, not in reality, consist the basis of our life."[43] In a similar vein, Constantine offers a most scathing response to the overtly ethical judgment of Ruskin on the moral focus of the painter "who represents brutalities and vices for delight in them, and not for rebuke of them" and who, as a result, receives "no rank at all, or rather of a negative rank, holding a certain order in the abyss." To this Constantine replies: "Precisely the first characteristic of the artist is disregarded—calm of spirit and complete pardon in the face of things which rouse the indignation and rebukes of the vulgar. The true artist writes in serenity of soul. 'N'as tu pas fouillant en les recoins de ton âme / Un beau vice à tirer comme un sabre au soleil?'[44] The true artist does not have, like the hero of a myth, to choose between virtue and vice; both will serve him and he will love both equally."[45] The lines cited here are from Verlaine's poem *Sagesse* and align Constantine with the decadent *poètes maudits* who took a radically different approach to the content of poetry and art, favoring amorality and artifice.

Constantine's surviving library contained more French language books than either English or Greek—363 out of a total of 964.[46] Looming large on this reading list are the Parnassian poets who exerted a marked impact on his early poems. This school was noted for its "tightly constructed and more impersonal lyricism"[47] and approached the poetic form as something that should be meticulously crafted rather than romantically inspired. These poets include Gautier, Leconte de Lisle, Banville, Sully Prudhomme, and Hérédia.[48] The Belgian poet Georges Rodenbach directly inspired the unpublished poems "The House of the

Soul" (1894), "La Jeunesse Blanche" (1895), and most likely the rejected "Vulnerant Omnes, Ultima Necat" (1893), which is set in Bruges. In terms of French novelists, Constantine was well-read in Georges Ohnet, Balzac, Anatole France, Hugo, and Zola. Perhaps his most significant French influence, however, was Baudelaire, whose famous sonnet "Correspondances" Constantine translated in 1891. "Correspondence According to Baudelaire" contains a Greek rendition of the French original embedded in his own opening and closing stanzas that offer poetic comments on the "synesthetic" poem that so profoundly influenced world literature. Constantine frames the poem as follows:

Aromas inspire me like music,
rhythm, beautiful words,
and I rejoice whenever Baudelaire
in harmonious verse interprets
what the bewildered soul if only vaguely
feels and imagines aridly.

[Translation of "Correspondances"]
Don't believe only what you see.

The look of poets is sharper.

For them, nature is a familiar garden.

Others stumble on
a troubling road in a dark paradise.
And the only light which, like an ephemeral spark
occasionally illuminates their way
at night, is a fleeting sense
of a random magnetic presence—

a brief nostalgia, a momentary thrill,
a dream of the hour of sunrise, a joy
with no cause, flowing suddenly
into the heart and fleeing suddenly.

The speaker of the poem delights in the sensual challenge that Baudelaire's synesthetic reading of nature offers, but he also shudders owing to the brevity of the fleeting epiphany and the realization that beauty alone can alleviate the ennui suffered by a world-weary poet. The poem offers a classic statement on the role of the poet as a seer who possesses second sight.[49] More extensive thoughts on Baudelaire are expressed in a self-comment written in 1907:

> This evening I was reading about Baudelaire. And the author of the book I was reading was like a shocked *épaté* with the *Fleurs du Mal.* It's been some time since I re-read the *Fleurs du Mal.* From what I remember, it isn't that shocking. And it seems to me that Baudelaire was enclosed in a very limited range of sensuality. Suddenly last night; or on the previous Wednesday; and on many other occasions, I lived and acted and fantasized, and silently devised pleasures even stranger.[50]

It appears that Baudelaire served Constantine as an influence to be mastered and surpassed, something he aspired to through his poetic pursuit of "even stranger pleasures" and his adaptation of the flâneur persona.

Paul Verlaine surfaces once again in one of Constantine's marginal comments on Edward Gibbon's *Decline and Fall of the Roman Empire,* which were recorded in English between 1896 and 1899. As Glen Bowersock argues, "Cavafy reads Gibbon with a critical eye, corrects his facts, finds fault at times with his methods, but overall admires the historical vision."[51] He approaches him at once as a historian, a philologist, and an artist.[52] A few choice passages will serve to illustrate this most significant intellectual exchange. Constantine comments on Gibbon's account of the behavior of Priscus Attalus, who reigned between 409–410 and 414–15 CE and was named emperor of the West by the Goths. The incident involved Attalus's humiliating predicament when he was appointed to lead the chorus of the Hymeneal wedding song for Adolphus and Placidia. Constantine writes: "The subject for a beautiful sonnet, a sonnet full of sadness. Such as Verlaine would write—'Je suis l'empire à la fin de la décadence.' Lost in the Gothic tumult and utterly bewildered, a melancholy emperor playing on the flute. An absurd emperor bustled in the crowd. Much applauded and much laughed at. And perhaps at times singing a touching song—some reminiscence of Ionia, and of the days when the gods were not yet dead."[53]

Two more historical moments from Gibbon catch Constantine's eye and are related, not surprisingly, to poetic renditions of history. One is the story of Sultan Mahmoud the Gaznevide,[54] who avenges an unhappy subject that, as Gibbon notes, complains of the "insolence of a Turkish soldier who had driven him from his house and bed." The detail is annotated as follows: "This tale is the subject of 'Mahmoud[,]' a beautiful poem of Leigh Hunt. The poet acknowledges his indebtedness to Gibbon."[55] The other lesser-known figure that captures Constantine's attention is the Albanian George Castriot Scanderbeg (1405–68), whose revolt against the Ottoman Turks and "sustained resistance against his former masters," while making him "a hero in the eyes of Christians, is seen in a far less sympathetic light by Gibbon."[56] Commenting on an anecdote where, according to Gibbon, Scanderbeg, "with the dagger at his [the scribe's (Reis Effendi's)] breast, exhorted the firman or patent for the Government of Albania;

and the murder of the guiltless scribe and his train prevented the consequences of an immediate discovery," Constantine writes: "But this is not the only version of the story. According to another tradition, just as reliable, Scanderbeg tried to save the scribe and offered him recompense and honours. But the scribe refused to follow him, & Scanderbeg was lost if he let the Turk return and reveal to [Sultan] Amurath what had passed. Perhaps Longfellow has grasped the position better."[57] This interest in Ottoman history is indicative of Constantine's sensitivity to the so-called "Eastern Question" and the demise of the Ottoman Empire in general. It is a noteworthy coincidence in this regard that, at the juncture of Queensborough Terrace in London—the street where the Cavafy family lived while residing in the city and where a plaque honoring the poet exists—a bronze statue was erected honoring Scanderbeg. The inscription on the statue reads "Invincible Albanian National Hero, Defender of Western Civilization." One can only imagine the ironic smile such a tribute would have elicited from the poet had he lived to see these mutual commemorative honors emblazoned on the streets of London.

The subject of Greek prosody also appears in Gibbon's volumes, namely the reception and assessment of "political verse," the fifteen-syllable line that defined so much of medieval and modern Greek poetry. In response to Gibbon's critique of Byzantine poets ("They confuse all measure of feet and syllables in the impotent strains which have received the name of political or city verses"), Constantine replies: "It is evident that Gibbon knew nothing of the matter. In the 'political' verse no confusion of feet & syllables is possible, owing to the meter's absolute simplicity . . . But the 'Political' verse and modern Greek prosody are not to blame, if Gibbon was ignorant."[58]

The ideological challenger of Gibbon and an equally important source of intellectual material for Constantine was the

Greek historian Constantine Paparrigopoulos (1815–91), who effectively rehabilitated Byzantium for modern Greeks and thus helped establish the historical continuity of ancient, medieval, and modern Greek culture.[59] Constantine was well-read in Paparrigopoulos and owned four volumes of his multivolume *History of the Greek Nation* (1876). The Greek historian's efforts to redeem Byzantine culture from its dismissal at the hands of Enlightenment scholars who viewed it as decadent and corrupt proved foundational for many of the poems Constantine would write on Byzantine topics. The Greek historian's writings likely animated his ambitious essay "The Byzantine Poets" (1892), which is largely a review of Karl Krumbacher's *The History of Byzantine Literature*.[60] Relying heavily on the article "La Littérature Byzantine" by the Greek writer Dimitrios Vikelas (1835–1908) that appeared in the *Revue des Deux Mondes* in March 1892, Constantine's essay offers a synoptic overview of Byzantine poets discussed by Krumbacher and Vikelas and concludes with the following sweeping panegyric on the "beauties and delicacies" of Byzantine literature: "A beneficent fate has endowed the Greek race with the divine gift of poetry. The vast and garlanded realm of verse is like our spiritual homeland. We Greeks are obliged to study our poetry attentively—the poetry of every period of our ethnic life. For in this poetry we will find the genius of our race, and all its tenderness, along with the most precious beating of Hellenism's very heart."[61]

This adulation of Byzantine poets extended to Byzantine historians as well, who Constantine felt were undervalued and wrote history "dramatically." The Byzantine writers who populated his reading list include Prokopios, Michael Psellos, Nikitas Choniatis, John Kantakuzinos, Nikephoros Gregoras, Theodore Prodromos, and Anna Komnene. His familiarity with the church fathers, saints, and hymnographers was also considerable, and he was a regular visitor to the Patriarchal Library of Alexandria in addition to possessing various synaxaria that contained accounts of the lives of the saints of the Orthodox Church.

Historians both ancient and contemporary feature prominently in Constantine's library.[62] These include the ancient authors Herodotus, Thucydides, Plutarch, Xenophon, and Flavius Josephus. He consulted French and British historians regularly, among them Auguste Bouché-Leclercq, Charles Diehl, George Grote, George Finlay, J. P. Mahaffy, Thomas Carlyle, J. B. Bury, Theodor Mommsen, D. C. Hesseling, and Edwyn Robert Bevan. History and classics overlap in many of Constantine's sources, as in the case of the lives and works of the sophists of the Second Sophistic: Philostratus, Eunapius, Callistratus, and Himerius. An essay focusing on these authors and one that brings together so many of Constantine's intellectual interests is "A Few Pages on the Sophists" (unpublished, 1893– 1897), where he praises these overlooked literary figures: "They greatly resembled today's artists in their love for the external beauty of works of art. The idea expressed might have been great; or it might not have made many demands. Its outward rhetorical expression however had to be perfect. They became intoxicated by the sculpting of phrases and the music of words."[63] Related to this sophistic panegeric is the essay "Greek Scholars in Roman Houses" (1896), where Constantine pays tribute to one of his beloved writers—the Hellenized Syrian satirist Lucian of Samosata (born 120 CE). The essay is basically a retelling of Lucian's text "On Salaried Posts on Great Houses" where Constantine indulges in one of his favorite themes: the Hellenization of Rome and the Roman exploitation of Hellenism. He begins by praising Lucian's narrative on "how witty and above all, how characteristically it reflects the period's manners."[64] He then offers a detailed synopsis that highlights Lucian's central focus: the abusive treatment of Greek tutors by their Roman patrons. The tutor "quickly discovers that in a Roman household his individual status as a man matters little and that he is a marionette to be used at the whim of his master who has employed him for anything but his scholarly worth. He cares nothing for Plato and philosophy, or for Demosthenes and rhetoric." The master uses the tutor to convey status, to "make people think him a devoted student of Greek learning." The pay is poor, the tutor's days are "awful and wretched," and, in the end, he is eventually dismissed and replaced by a younger man: "Now no one will have him, owing to his age, and also because of the charges brought against him by the household as a pretext for dismissal."[65] The essay concludes with praise of the "lively descriptions and the feisty style of this great Greek artist [Lucian]."[66]

We know that Constantine spent a lifetime exploring and probing primary sources of ancient poetry and myth; identifying these sources, however, remains a vexed endeavor, as they exceeded the surviving books of his library, those mentioned in his personal letters, and other archival material.[67] We can say with certainty that he had editions of *The Greek Anthology* and *The Palatine Anthology* readily at hand, as well as a number of dictionaries of classical history, Greek and Roman myth, and classical literature.[68] And he no doubt relied on these for his knowledge of the classical, Hellenistic, Roman, and late-antique authors who were relevant to his work and with whom he also engaged directly, namely Homer, Meleager, Callimachus,[69] Theocritus, Euripides, and Aeschylus. We have a few notable instances where, in preserved self-comments, he illustrates the great pains he took with accuracy in matters of classical sources. One concerns the poem "Of Dimitrios Sotir (162–150 BC)" (1915/1919), which centers on the sad fate of Dimitrios Selefkidis, grandson of Antiochos III the Great, ruler of the Seleucid Empire who, at one point in his precarious reign, was held hostage in Rome[70] and ultimately died in battle in Syria defending his throne from the usurper Alexander Valas. The poem anticipates this fatal end by beginning with the line "Every one of his expectations turned out wrong" and explores the frustration of Dimitrios while in captivity: "If only he could find a way to reach the East, / to succeed in escaping Italy— / then all the strength he has / in his soul, all that ardor / he would pass on to the people." The poem crescendos with the admission of cultural defeat and the demise of the Hellenistic dynasties, one of Constantine's favored themes: "Now despair and grief. / The young men in Rome were right. / It was impossible for the dynasties / that evolved from the Macedonian Conquest to survive." Yet he is resolved to go down fighting: "No matter: he tried, / fighting as hard as he could. / And in his dark disappointment, / there's only one thing he thinks about / with pride: that, even in his failure, / he exhibits the same indomitable bravery to the world."

In order to capture the psychological truth of the poem, one that depends on Dimitrios's future courage on the battlefield, Constantine consults three historical sources for the accuracy of Dimitrios's final demise:

> The historian Bevan says—in his account of the battle—that he fell heavily wounded, not surrendering, dying in a manner worthy of the generation of fighters from whom he descended. Josephus says that he fought bravely. But he suffered so many wounds that he couldn't survive and collapsed. [William] Smith says that "he is said to have displayed the utmost personal valour, but was ultimately defeated, & slain." I deduce that, dismayed by his plans, he at least hoped to show his dignity and his lineage during his defeat. I write about a situation before the battle, with the decision taken based on

Josephus and Smith, and considering the opinion of Bevan
that his end was worthy of his lineage.[71]

The final lines of the poem offer a sad gloss on the life of this most intriguing figure of Greco-Roman history: "The rest—they were dreams and futile efforts. / This Syria—it almost no longer seems like his homeland, / it is the country of Heraklides and Valas."

While Constantine was actively engaged with classical texts, his treatment of Greek folklore was more tentative and its overall impact on his writing somewhat convoluted. That he couldn't ignore it is a fact; to be sure, he became something of a reluctant connoisseur of demotic songs, folk poetry, and the various Greek poetic traditions that drew heavily from this dominant discourse. Yet he refused to submit to the ideological sway of "laographia" (folklore) with its strident proclamation of the folk-based continuity of Greek culture and promotion of the "monuments of the word,"[72] aware that, if he composed verse in that mode, his writing would remain confined to Greek anthologies. That his earliest prose writings were heavily influenced by folklore is not surprising, however, given that his teacher Constantine Papazis was a student of Nikolaos Politis, the most prominent Greek folklorist. Politis, it should be noted, was a student of Karl Krumbacher—a connection that lends Constantine's prose writings an additional symmetry in terms of their lines of influence. The titles and topics of these early essays speak for themselves: "The Romaic Folk-Lore of Enchanted Animals" (1884–86), "Coral from a Mythological Perspective" (1886), "Lycanthropy" (1882–84), "Fragment on Beliefs Concerning the Soul" (1884), and "Masks" (1884?). There are also some early poems that overlap with Greek folklore and Greek demotic songs: "The Beyzades to His Beloved" (1882?), "Dünya Güzeli"[73] (1883), and "Vain, Vain Love" (1886).[74]

Constantine published two substantial book reviews on the subject of folklore, one on a foundational text by Nikolaos Politis titled (in translation) *Sections from the Songs of the Greek People* (1914) that appeared in the Alexandrian journal *Nea Zoï* in 1914. The other reviewed a book titled (in translation) *Carpathian Demotic Songs* (1913) by M. G. Michaelidou and was published in 1917 in the Alexandrian journal *Grammata*. The Politis review opens with an overview of the 310-page anthology[75] and then focuses on one or two texts from the various sections, offering a few comments on each. Constantine begins with the famous song about Hagia Sophia that introduces Politis's volume, an example of the laments on the fall of Constantinople (1453) to the Ottoman Turks. In addition to commenting on lyrics that he finds exceptionally moving or uniquely poetic, he informs his reader that his favorite specimen of folk song is the "*moirologi*" (lament), commenting that he wished this section included more examples: "Out of all of our demotic poetry, the laments attract me the most. I get caught up in their emotion, and their exaggerated mourning is precisely what my soul desires; this type of grief in the face of death is what I want."[76]

In 1921, Constantine attempted his own poem on the fall of Constantinople. "It Was Seized" is a difficult title to translate, as the original "Πάρθεν/Parthen" is the past tense of the Greek verb "to take" rendered in the archaic form used by the Pontian Greeks (those who settled around the Black Sea) in their unique dialect. (Constantine documented his own Pontian family roots in his genealogy.[77]) The writing of this poem in 1921[78] falls within the doomed period of the Asia Minor Campaign when the Greek armies were occupying Ottoman lands as part of the postwar arrangement that ultimately culminated in the "catastrophe"

1. From left to right: Paul, Constantine, and John in Livorno, Italy (1865)

2. Peter John Cavafy

3. From left to right: John, Paul, and Constantine (1873)

4. Greek Orthodox Church of Saint Nicholas, Liverpool

5. John Cavafy (right) with his cousin Dimitrios Zalichi in Istanbul (*c.* 1902)

6. Haricleia Photiades Cavafy

7. Aristides Cavafy

8. Aristides's sketch of a conductor

9. Paul Cavafy

10. The staircase and elevator of the Metropole Hotel today, former location of the Office of the Irrigation Service

11. Constantine's apartment at Rue Lepsius

12. The hall

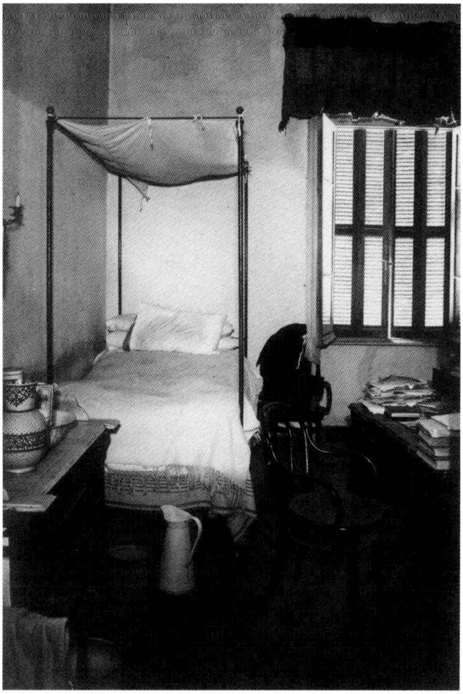

13. The bedroom

14. The salon

15. Photograph of Constantine as a young man

16. Photograph of Constantine by Kyriakos Pagonis (1932)

17. Photograph of Constantine by Racine Studio

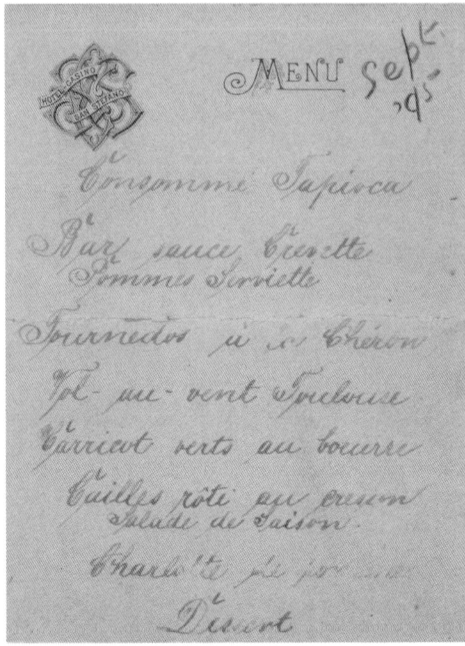
HOTEL CASINO SAN STEFANO

MENU Sept. '95

Consommé Tapioca

Bar sauce Crevette
Pommes Serviette

Tournedos à la Chéron

Vol-au-vent Toulouse

Haricots verts au beurre

Cailles rôti au cresson
Salade de Saison

Dessert

18. The menu from a night out at the San Stefano Casino

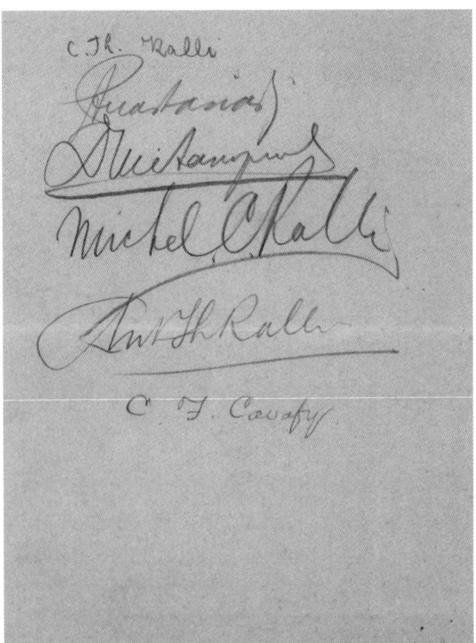
C. Th. Ralli

Michel C. Ralli

Ant. Th. Ralli

C. F. Cavafy

19. The signed back of the menu

20. Pericles Anastasiades

21. Timos Malanos

22–25 Sketches of Alexandrians by Pericles Anastasiades

26. Alekos Sengopoulos

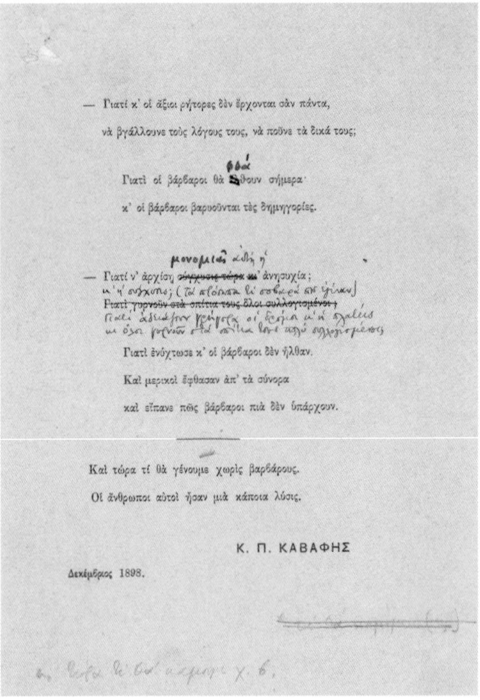

— Γιατί κ' οἱ ἄξιοι ρήτορες δὲν ἔρχονται σὰν πάντα,
νὰ βγάλλουνε τοὺς λόγους τους, νὰ ποῦνε τὰ δικά τους;

Γιατὶ οἱ βάρβαροι θὰ ἔλθουν σήμερα·
κ' οἱ βάρβαροι βαρυοῦνται τὲς δημηγορίες.

— Γιατὶ ν' ἀρχίσῃ ... ἀνησυχία;
Γιατὶ γυρνοῦν στὰ σπίτια τους ὅλοι συλλογισμένοι;

Γιατὶ ἐνύχτωσε κ' οἱ βάρβαροι δὲν ἦλθαν.
Καὶ μερικοὶ ἔφθασαν ἀπ' τὰ σύνορα
καὶ εἶπανε πῶς βάρβαροι πιὰ δὲν ὑπάρχουν.

Καὶ τώρα τί θὰ γένουμε χωρὶς βαρβάρους.
Οἱ ἄνθρωποι αὐτοὶ ἦσαν μιὰ κάποια λύσις.

Κ. Π. ΚΑΒΑΦΗΣ

Δεκέμβριος 1898.

27. Corrections to the printed version of "Waiting for the Barbarians"

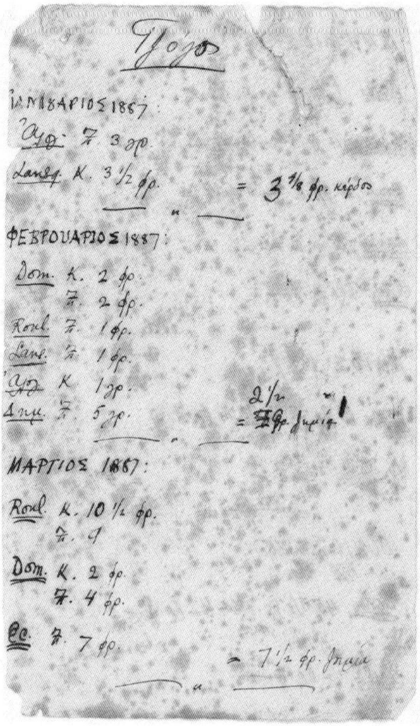

ΙΑΝΟΥΑΡΙΟΣ 1887:

ΦΕΒΡΟΥΑΡΙΟΣ 1887:

ΜΑΡΤΙΟΣ 1887:

28. List of wins and losses Constantine kept per game and per month from January to March 1887

29. Constantine arriving at the wedding of Constantine M. Salvagos, which took place at the Cathedral of the Annunciation on February 27, 1927

30. From left to right: Rika Sengopoulos, the Greek poet Angelos Sikelianos, Alekos Sengopoulos, and an unidentified fourth person at the Second Delphic Festival in Delphi, Greece (1930)

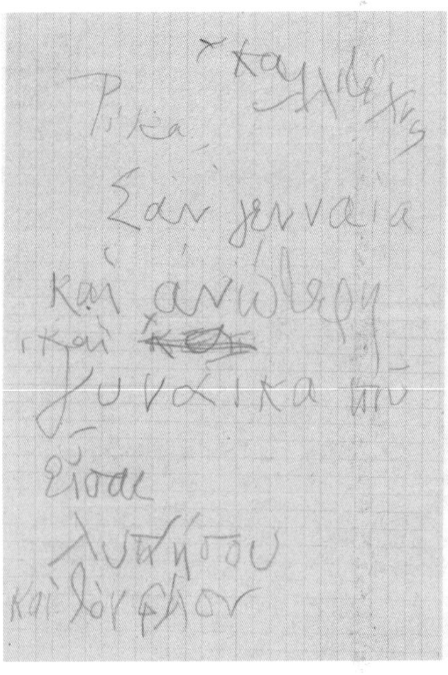
Ρίκα
Σαν γενναία
και ανώτερη
γυναίκα που
είσαι
λυπήσου
και τον φίλον

31. Handwritten note to Rika Sengopoulos: "Rika, like the brave and better woman and artist that you are, pity your friend"

of 1922. The Greeks of the Black Sea region (Pontos) were ultimately uprooted in the ensuing exchange of populations and ethnic cleansing of 1922, as the poem anticipates in an uncanny way.[79]

The poem opens with what is clearly a remembrance of the past act of reviewing books on Greek folklore: "I have spent these days reading folk songs / about the deeds of the klephts[80] and their battles, / agreeable matters, our own, Greek." The poem then shifts its focus to two renditions of the lament for the fall of "The City," the first being the standard "classic" lament that he had singled out in his review of Politis;[81] the second is the more "moving" Pontian song "of Trebizond[82] with its strange dialect / and with the sorrow of those far-away Greeks / who perhaps believed deep down we'd still be saved." The original Pontian poem contains a curious line that is subsumed within the poem and quoted in its original Pontian dialect: "But alas, an ominous bird, 'from Constantinople came' / and on its tiny wing is an inscribed paper." The folkloric analogue includes a gory detail Constantine leaves out: one wing has the written paper attached to it as included in the poem while the other is dipped in blood. The paper can only be read by a youth, the widow's son Johnny, who "takes the paper, / and he reads it and laments. / 'Now he reads, then he weeps, now his heart races. / Alas for us, woe for us, Romania [Greece] was taken.' " Perhaps Constantine preferred this version of the lament because it featured a youth who was able to receive and respond to the tragic news as opposed to the jaded archbishops who could not ("or wished not to") do so. The image of a bird as the carrier of the message, in addition to being an example of the familiar motif of birds as omens in ancient Greek mythology,[83] conjures up the ancient Egyptian, Persian, Greek, Roman, and Ottoman traditions of homing pigeons, a cross-cultural practice that would have appealed to the poet's taste for such hybridized practices. The poem is a rare example of Constantine's direct engagement with folklore and although it was never published, its highly finished state indicates that he took great pains with its overall composition and execution.[84]

A more direct connection to folklore—and its importance for young readers—dates back to 1919, when Constantine, after being approached by members of the Greek Educational Association to assist in creating a student anthology of demotic songs, began to compile a list of suitable texts. Ultimately, this list served as the basis for the final selection adopted by the organization.[85] He also wrote an introduction to the volume that was not included in the final anthology but contains some interesting views on the matter of folk songs and their importance for Greek students. "We would like today's youth to have a somewhat developed artistic sensibility. We want them during the final years of their studies at school and upon graduation to read our authors. Poetry usually attracts young people. And here, our demotic songs—as relates to our language, as noted—show them the first Greek rhythm." He argues that the line of "political" folk verse, "with its beautiful iamb, with its fifteen syllables that sometimes move quickly and lightly and other times heavily and slowly," will prepare students for reading other types of Greek poetry. Moreover, in "demotic songs they will discover some old customs and examples of the character of our race," which, he notes with a twinge of regret, is rapidly becoming more and more European.[86]

The extent of Constantine's interest in folklore is documented in the citation and rhyme dictionaries he compiled, which are replete with examples of demotic folk songs along with quotations from numerous Greek poets and authors who were invested in them.[87] Here the related subjects of the folkloric idiom and poetic diction overlap. When viewed in tandem with the contents of his library, we can see which Greek literary figures Constantine favored.[88] On Alexandros Papadiamantis and Aristotle Valaoritis, Constantine composed brief Greek "opinion" commentaries that are noteworthy. About Papadiamantis, the master of the Greek short story, he writes glowingly that "from the works of his that I have read, his descriptive powers impressed me. It seems to me that he is brilliantly adept with the three facets of description: what should be discussed, what should be omitted, and what is worthy of attention."[89] The poet Valaoritis receives a more nuanced appraisal as a lesser poet than Solomos: "During his era, Valaoritis was not an overlooked poet. He was admired and he inspired the youth—perhaps his patriotic subject matter contributed to this. After his death, his fame decreased somewhat, but he remains one of our greatest poets. His work was very much influenced by the romanticism of his era; this was to his disadvantage, because his poetic personae—Kyra Phrosini, Omer Vryonis, Ali Pasha, Mouchtar—are personalities that don't lend themselves to a romantic treatment."[90] The poetic personae mentioned here are real-life personalities, all of whom were connected to events related to the Greek struggle against Ottoman rule and the events of the Greek Revolution of 1821.

No doubt when writing this aborted introduction in 1924–25, Constantine had a distinct memory of an essay that appeared years earlier in *The Nineteenth Century* titled "The Poet of the Klephts: Aristoteles Valaoritis." This was published in July 1891, along with Blackie's article "Shakespeare and Modern Greek" (December 1891) and the essay by Frederick Harrison on the "Elgin" Marbles, both of which elicited responses from Constantine.[91] The Valaoritis essay was written by James Rennell Rodd[92] and contains copious translations of passages of poems on Omer Vryonis, Ali Pasha, Kyra Phrosini, and Athanasios Diakos, all of whom are similarly singled out in Constantine's text. Rodd's article brought a marginal literary tradition focusing on the Greek Revolution to the attention of the British readership and it undoubtedly would have made an impression on the young Constantine. It opens with an acknowledgment of the klephts, "those unnamed rhapsodists who embodied the martial deeds and heroic spirit of her mountaineers throughout their long and desperate struggle for independence in those terse and graphic snatches of song, handed down from mouth to mouth among the people." Rodd proceeds by building up an appreciative context for his introduction of Valaoritis to the British reading public:

> But it is just this spirit of those nameless singers, this enthusiasm for their country's struggle, wedded to an unusual gift of the highest poetical expression, which entitles Aristoteles Valaoritis above all others to the distinctive position of the national poet of Greece. His published work, which is but small in volume, deals almost exclusively with the story of Suli and the stirring incidents of the insurrection; and the freedom of the mountains, the living sense of a grand and rugged nature, the spirit of liberty and defiance, breathe through every line of his poems.[93]

This extraordinary tribute to "the national poet of Greece" stands as a reminder of what Constantine might have aspired to become in 1891 but chose not to pursue. His retrospective view of Valaoritis is generous, as it bestowed upon the poet his deserved laurels; but this was not a poet Constantine ever wished to imitate. In fact, there is a subtle note of pity in the closing lines of this introduction that, despite their gracious assessment of another poet's talents, betray the subtle condescension that such ethnocentric endeavors elicited in him: "Valaoritis's theory regarding the poetic language was the same as that of Solomos. But his language showed a curiosity that Solomos lacked. With much effort he sought and amassed folk expressions that were not in circulation during his era, rare demotic words."[94]

Much of Constantine's interest in demotic vernacular and the Greek language debate centers around how writers used katharevousa and/or demotic and the manner in which they navigated between the two linguistic registers. Illuminating in this regard is his unpublished essay on Emmanuel Roidis (1836–1904), best known for his novel *Pope Joan* (1866), one of the few nineteenth-century Greek novels to have enjoyed a wide European readership.[95] Constantine wrote an unfinished review for Roidis's philological study of the language question *Ta Eidola / The Idols* (1893) sometime between 1893 and 1897. Roidis, although a "veteran stylist in katharevousa," as Roderick Beaton notes, "surprisingly supported the cause of the spoken language."[96] Like Constantine, he wished to find a compromise between the two opposed extremes in the language question. A few extracts from Constantine's essay illustrate the overlap between the poet's and the novelist's sympathetic view of the purist idiom. Commenting on the chapter titled "The Alleged Deficiency [of Katharevousa]," Constantine states that he does not disagree with Roidis regarding the exaggerated claims made against the purist idiom: "On the contrary, I agree with most of what is asserted in the book. I accept the fact of katharevousa's unnatural, forced, and nonsensical qualities, as it is understood and unfortunately written by most. And I agree with the idea that its inclination towards the archaic should be reined in; that its deformities in terms of the profuse introduction of words and popular forms be corrected; that its shortcomings be offset and that life be given to its moribund splendors."[97]

Constantine is on record for making what should have been

a straightforward and definitive statement regarding katharevousa. In his published essay "The Poetry of Mr. Stratigis" (1893), he confessed in print that "I will not hide that I am a friend of katharevousa, but I believe that when it is used with such grace and perfection even its harshest critics may be [positively] influenced."[98] For decades this sentence was taken at face value until it was scrutinized for the typographical error it allegedly contains and its meaning reversed by an editorial insertion. It was George Savidis in fact who cast doubt on the accuracy of the statement, writing that most likely the sentence should read "*not* a friend of katharevousa," an emendation that was adopted in the 2003 edition of Cavafy's *Prose* edited by Michalis Pieris.[99] The ambiguity here is telling in relation to the larger question of Constantine's complex position in the language debate. Indeed, he made a gradual journey toward using a less formal katharevousa in his prose and a more demotic idiom in his verse.[100] But he never relinquished the linguistic reins in terms of what he felt ultimately intensified the power of the language or gave his phrases the poetic inflection or the beauty he desired. His statement to his cousin Marika Tsalikis on the matter is quite illuminating:

> Some—myself included—hesitate to sacrifice katharevousa in its entirety, and do not agree to condemn all the linguistic work of an entire century (and more than a century) . . . We who are now returning to the demotic language are pilgrims, devoted and passionate pilgrims who are entering into a temple and will remove, of course, all of the gaudy decorations and the superfluous dressing that spoil it, but without violence and without prejudice, so that we do not risk overlooking and discarding in the heap—

> like fools—a certain golden oil-vase or a chest of bright mother of pearl.[101]

The poetic images he uses here recall the aesthetic props found in many of his poems and prose poems and serve to soften the polemic tone that defined much of the language debate.

Beyond the world of art and poetry, Constantine possessed an assortment of twenty-five books that his first biographer, Michalis Peridis, classified as "unmentionable," the bulk of which did not enter in the surviving library.[102] Much of this was risqué fin-de-siècle French literature that overlapped with his broader interest in literary decadence.[103] A number of these texts, however, were more explicit in their sexual content. In his study of Constantine's sexuality, Dimitris Papanikolaou identifies the following books that effectively constitute a veritable queer reading list: Henri d'Agris, *Sodome* (1888), Robert Scheffer, *Le Prince Narcisse* (1897), Jean Rhodes, *Adolescents: Moeurs collégiennes* (1904), Jules Hoche, *Moeurs d'exception: Le vice mortel* (1904), Henry Gauthier-Villars (Willy et Ménalkas), *L'Ersatz d'amour* (1923), Alphonse Daudet, *Sapho. Moeurs parisiennes* (1884), and Armand Dubarry, *Les Déséquilibrés de l'amour. Les flagellants* (1898).[104] In general, these texts deal with alternative sexual practices and explore the desire for "pleasures even stranger" that Constantine had expressed in his note on Baudelaire.

We conclude this intellectual interlude on the poet's reading interests with a comment by Timos Malanos, who repeatedly stated that his onetime mentor had ceased to read anything new or process any recent ideas after 1900.[105] The point Malanos wished to make was that the Cavafian corpus had become hermetically sealed and was impermeable to any new ideas or cultural stimuli. While there is some truth to this in terms of literary influences, Constantine continued to read up until his final days. But this debate does not detract from the more important fact that his poetry continually foregrounds the act of reading itself.[106] As such, his own reading interests remain a fascinating point of entry into his mind, imagination, and creative life.

Part IV

LIVING FOR POETRY

9

ART ABOVE EVERYTHING

"VOICES" (1903/1904)

Idealized, beloved voices
of those who have died or are
lost to us like the dead.

Sometimes they speak in our dreams;
and our mind hears them in our thoughts.

And with their echo for an instant
echoes of the first poetry in our lives come back
like music that fades into the distant night.

No one who knew Constantine as a young man in the 1880s and 1890s would have expected him to turn into a world poet. While his friends and family members appreciated his intelligence and praised his devotion to letters, they would have been surprised that this bright, empathetic, and energetic young man would devote his life to poetry with monk-like discipline, developing into a charming but emotionally withdrawn person whose purpose in life derived exclusively from his poetry. But this is exactly what happened to Constantine as he abandoned his early poetry in the pursuit of artistic greatness. Poetry would become his life and he would live for poetry.

Constantine transformed himself into an artist twice, first in his twenties and then again in middle age. During this second period, Constantine became the poet we know as Cavafy. He remained a bit defensive about his relatively late poetic maturation. He resented, for instance, that Michalis Peridis said in 1915 that Constantine at fifty-two had nothing more to say and that his life's work had been completed. "Many wrote after their forties," Constantine said in response: "The great Anatole France wrote his colossal work after turning forty-five. And many others."[1]

Constantine's early poems, those he repudiated in middle age, revealed little promise of future greatness. While poets like Arthur Rimbaud and George Seferis distinguished themselves with their first collections, Constantine's initial publications struck few as innovative. They showed little sign of his Promethean ambition or his looming struggle against contemporary poets and the titans of the past. Moreover, these early texts were derivative, reflecting the tastes and aesthetic properties of the Greek poetry he was reading in his youth, as explained in the previous chapter. Eventually he came to see this poetry as cold and rhetorical, heavy in katharevousa and laden with tropes of romantic love, nature's beauty, and the Greek nation, subjects he would come to abhor in his middle age. It took Constantine a few decades to free himself from the weight of this tradition, even though there survived, in both his poetry and his speech, traces of the purist language.

We don't know exactly when he began writing his first poems. But in a note written in 1906, he disparaged "the wretched trash" he had written between the ages of nineteen and twenty-two.[2] So it is safe to assume that he embarked upon his first ventures into literature while he was in Istanbul. In his letters to John from this city, Constantine demonstrated an acute interest in words, their meaning and place in a sentence. He had begun compiling a dictionary in 1881 precociously at the age of sixteen, which ended with the entry "Alexander." To his horror, it was one of the items destroyed in the bombardment of 1882. He referred anxiously in his letters to John about his papers back home, only to receive the reply that all was lost. "It is one of the talents of great stylists," Constantine wrote much later in 1902, "to make obsolete words cease from appearing obsolete through the way in which they introduce them in their writing."[3] He might have been thinking here of his aborted lexicographical project.

Contemporaries often reported his near fixation on matters of diction, punctuation, and even spacing in his verses. For instance, when he and a group of young men were discussing a nineteenth-century English poet, Constantine began a meandering passage through the "labyrinth of metrical subtleties." At one point, one of the visitors intervened: "Certainly, maître, all of these are details," to which Constantine responded vehemently, "What else is art but details."[4] As he said in his poem "Of Colored Glass," "I am much moved by a detail." The editor, critic, and friend Giorgos Papoutsakis claimed that, although Constantine had crafted his own innovative poetry, he never abandoned his "devotion to the choice of words."[5] Indeed, Papoutsakis remembers him saying around 1931 that the "majority of Greek poets have not given sufficient attention in their work to the issue of lexical exactness [*kyriolexia*]."[6] To achieve this expressive precision, Constantine carefully worked on poems, polishing each and every word sometimes for close to fifteen years before sending them to the printers. He began "Orophernis," for instance, in 1904 and kept working on it until 1916.

Despite the exhilarating exposure to Greek poetry, journalism, and critical thinking he encountered in the Greek community of Istanbul, Constantine was not happy to be away from his own books and manuscripts and expressed uncertainties about his own talents. For this reason, John, trying to encourage him, lauded his brother's well-written letter, adding that he would "very soon outlimit my knowledge of the [English] language" (January 16, 1883).[7] This was a very generous comment given his own ambitions for fame, especially in writing an experimental poem in the manner of the French Symbolist poet Stéphane Mallarmé (1842–98) totaling four thousand lines. John's literary talents were evident in his letters, some of which he even composed in verse: "I'll answer yours of twenty-nine / October, not in prose but 'worse.' / The Muse directs ecstatic verse, / The thoughts are hers,—the rhymes are mine" (November 7, 1882).[8]

Of course, John too suffered from insecurity, stemming perhaps from the comparisons he made between himself and Constantine: "I lack your versatility of genius and the power to give interest to a mere nothing" (January 16, 1883).[9] In the following letter, John expressed doubts about his own "poetical talents (for such you will have them), they are, I am sorry to say, of the 'touch-and-go' nature. No man is the same under all circumstances; and least your humble servant, who is subject, in the highest degree, to outward objects and the inclemency of the winds" (January 23, 1883).[10] He would later confess that he was not able to write at all: "My poetical vein is at present desultory and spasmodical [*sic*]: I have not much leisure time" (June 5, 1883).[11] By characterizing his efforts to write poetry as "desultory" and "spasmodic," was John implying that his poetic career was coming to an end? Whatever his feelings at the time, the publication in Alexandria of his *Early Verses* made no stir. Sadly, this was the only book he published and eventually he stopped seeing himself as a poet. Around 1890–91, he printed a few poems like "Pygmalion Meditateth" as loose sheets, which he later published in *Rivista Quindicinale.*[12] But that was it. Toward the end of his life, John cast himself largely as a flop. But he remained proud of Constantine and how hard he worked to make his name known among his small circle of friends and acquaintances.[13] Outwardly there seems to have existed no overt competition between them, given that they were nearly two years apart and each possessed grand artistic ambitions. But one wonders if John ever begrudged his brother's surpassing him as a poet.[14]

John's failure could not but have stood to Constantine as a fate he had to avoid. If we look at a couple of John's verses, we can see how derivative they are in versification and subject matter, resembling Constantine's early poems that he eventually disowned. The first stanza of "Pygmalion Meditateth" begins with the following lines: "My poem! It shall be a paradigm, / In marble cadence, of the beautiful, / And therefore true,—perfect in every limb." And it ends with the lines "And so I rise; My poem shall express / The beautiful in marble cadences."[15] Unfortunately for John, these poems did not "rise" at all. In their meter, diction, and themes, they were thoroughly Victorian. No wonder they found no audience, no critics, and no appeal, a silence Constantine could not have failed to notice. He could see that John's work was old-fashioned and unexceptional. It was not, in other words, the type of poetry that could change the "minds of millions," as he hoped to do himself.

In addition to thinking about how to escape John's imitative poetry and scholasticism, Constantine had to consider his own future. What was he going to do when he and his mother returned from Istanbul? During his stay in the Ottoman capital, he thought about a career in political journalism. We surmise this from a letter (November 22, 1883) his godmother and paternal cousin, Amalia Pitaridou-Papou, wrote from Athens in response to his own, which does not survive and which probably sought advice about his career plans. She cautioned him that "success in politics requires studies in law . . . and neither is journalism appropriate for you." Young men nowadays, she continued, went increasingly into banking or business and she encouraged him to pursue this line of work.[16] It appears also that Constantine expressed his desire to write poetry, for she continued, "From your letter I understand that you have an inclination for poetry and I am sure that Constantinople with its beautiful nature can inspire you." This well-meaning but innocuous piece of advice demonstrates that his family did not really understand poetry at all beyond these rudimentary parameters.

When Constantine arrived home in October 1885 at the age of twenty-two, he had few prospects for work and for many years held no firm job, a situation that forced him to rely on his mother for financial support and one that could hardly continue given the family's ever-dire financial circumstances. Yet he was not destined for professional life, certainly not in the cotton business that attracted talented young Greeks. Like many men in their twenties, he was in search of gainful employment without however possessing a particular purpose. One possibility was to engage in journalism, as he had told his aunt. Publicly at least he thought of himself as a journalist, having written, as noted earlier, his first piece (1882) on the poet Athanasios Christopoulos the year the British fleet bombarded Alexandria. So with all the other brothers gainfully employed, Constantine began to work at the Bourse in 1886 as a journalist for the newspaper *Telegraphos*.

As stimulating as it must have been to breathe in the competitive air of the exchange, he never saw himself as a financial reporter. Thus, he returned to his real love—literary and cultural criticism. As shown in the previous chapter, he wrote many critical essays both in katharevousa and in English, most of which remained unpublished. A few dealt with political issues, such as the Cyprus question and the return of the Parthenon marbles. While he demonstrated some talent as a book reviewer, translator, and cultural critic, he abandoned the idea of becoming a professional journalist by 1897. Yet for most of the 1890s, he did not present himself exclusively and publicly as a poet either, even though it was a very productive decade for him poetically.

Increasingly he was turning his energy toward poetry, and he was thrilled when his first poem, "Bacchic," appeared in the Leipzig periodical *Hesperus* in 1886. This was no doubt a great accomplishment for a young man of twenty-three living in provincial Alexandria. Yet his first little triumph, inspired by the Phanariot poet Athanasios Christopoulos (1772–1847),[17] gave little impression of the demoticist revolution taking place in Greek poetry at the time, namely that poets were turning to the vernacular as their medium of expression. He went on to publish a series of poems in katharevousa, with titles like "The Poet and the Muse" (1886), "Builders"[18] (1891), and "Voice from the Sea" (1898).

At this time, he also embarked on many other intellectual ventures. In 1891, as a carryover from his aborted dictionary project, he began work on a *lexicon*—a dictionary of citations. Although it did not seem like a long-term venture then, it would develop into one over time. As he wrote in a draft introduction to this work many years later, he had been using a very good Greek dictionary (without identifying it), which had many more demotic entries than others he had consulted. (He would refer to at least thirteen dictionaries when compiling his catalogue of citations.) But this book had many shortcomings. For this reason, he thought it would be useful to supplement it with his own entries. Thus, during his readings, whenever he encountered a "beautiful or expressive word," demotic mostly but also in purist and ancient registers, he would record it along with the citation and then place the piece of paper in the appropriate page of the dictionary. After a number of years, these entries began to slip out of the volume, so he decided to record them in a notebook "for my own personal use or for the use—if they wanted—of my friends." Not burdensome at all, this work seemed rather "pleasurable."[19] But he collected these words primarily because they were useful to him "as an author," by which he meant a poet. In other words, he pursued this project as a personal resource rather than as a linguistic venture to be published in the form of a book. Some of the words he selected seemed predictable and many were gleaned from his reading of Greek poetry and folk songs. Others showed his linguistic curiosity. Thus, we have entries for the word "vampire," and for the Greek aperitif "ouzo" with its two variants (tsipouro and zibib).[20]

When he ended the project around 1917—that is, nearly thirty years later—he had assembled some 561 entries that collectively constituted a book. Even though he never published it, he showed himself an accomplished lexicographer with a zeal for both the Greek language and an exactitude for expression. Not trained as a linguist, he certainly could have become one, as he could similarly have developed his penchant for history by turning into a historian. This intellectual prowess and range were a mark of his genius and illustrate that, without any university education, he possessed a scholarly knowledge of the Greek language and of Greek history that impressed professional linguists and historians alike.

About two years after he started his dictionary of citations, he developed another useful tool for his poetic craft, a *Rimario* (rhyming dictionary). Written on paper from the Office of the

Irrigation Service and following the example of other poets in the nineteenth century, he compiled lists of rhymes that he culled from various dictionaries. In 1897/98, he began a second catalogue of rhymes he himself gathered from the poets he read. He relied on these two catalogues when composing his poems, and it is possible to identify eighteen of these rhymes in his poems.[21] They were less useful to him after 1900, however, when his poetry relied less on rhyme.

Constantine's primary focus, if not fanatical preoccupation, from 1890 on was poetry. While his family and friends did not see the results of his creative labor in published poems, he recorded the titles of 131 new poems in his catalogue between August 1891 and December 1898. Between January 1899 and December 1903, he listed thirty-two, of which nine were previous drafts.[22]

In the following year, his records indicate twenty-seven compositions, the only one of which that survived being the famous "Candles," published in 1899. Dealing with old age, it is an unlikely topic for a man of thirty. The speaker stares at a row of candles representing his life and is distressed at the sight of the long row of snuffed-out wicks: "I don't want to look at them; their sight saddens me, / I am saddened also to remember their previous light. / I look ahead at my lit candles."[23] Constantine was so pleased with this poem that he wrote about it to Pericles Anastasiades,[24] saying that this was "one of the best things" he had ever written. He repeated his sense of pride to John, who at that time was rendering it into English, characterizing it as "good" and easy "for translation." This three-page draft of a note, composed sometime between 1897 and 1899, reveals how sophisticated his aesthetic theory had become by then. Although the poem appeared to him slightly allegorical, Constantine continued, it was actually "dramatic" and thus different from "Walls" and "The Windows," poems that were "clearly allegorical."[25]

What is striking about the text, however, is not only the maturity of his poetics but also his own self-confidence as a poet. He was no longer beholden to John for advice and guidance and, in fact, reversed the power dynamic of their relationship. In contrast to their correspondence in the early 1880s about John's poetry, in which the older brother seemed to be in command, here the situation was the opposite. In the 1880s, John appeared destined for poetic glory and Constantine's deferential posture tacitly accepted this outcome. By the end of the decade, however, Constantine had overtaken his brother as the artist of the family. From now on attention would fall on his poetic creations, an increasing focus that brought with it greater public recognition but also distance from those dear to him.

Did Constantine have this in mind when he composed the unpublished poem "The Bank of the Future" in 1897?

To shore up my uncertain life
I'll ask for little credit
from the Bank of the Future.

I doubt it has great resources.
And I've begun to fear that in the first crisis
it will suddenly stop paying.

Was he thinking that his poetic vocation required that he be self-reliant? Rika Sengopoulos believed this, pointing out that, apart from occasional support from his brothers and some friends, his early efforts at writing poetry were entirely solitary. In the notes she was keeping for her biography, Rika observed, "Cavafy developed without any context . . . The only real warmth he found at the start of his poetic career was in his family." She claimed that the family encouraged Constantine in his poetic ventures and hoped that he would find financial independence so as to devote himself fully to his craft.[26] But we don't know what his mother or siblings thought of his poems, apart from John's very strong moral boost and his willingness to translate some of them.[27] What is apparent, however, is that in his late thirties, Constantine was becoming isolated from those around him. Of course, testimonials from acquaintances as well as his journals reveal a sociable, outgoing man, who dined with friends, had coffee with visitors, went to the theater, and visited people at home to have hot chocolate or cognac late into the night. But he was increasingly preoccupied with his own poetic and intellectual distinction from others around him. What seemed crucial from now on, as he wrote that very same year in the poem "Addition" (1897), was not to languish in the horde, not to stand "in that great addition (their addition that I hate)." The speaker rejoices at not being another figure in an expansive mediocrity of fools: "In this great mass / I did not count myself. And this joy is enough for me." Both "Addition" and "The Bank of the Future" point to Constantine's growing acceptance of the idea that poetry brings about the segregation of the artist from the world around him.

A number of personal notes from the time bear this out, revealing anguish either about his sexuality or about his insecurity over his poetic talents. Notes from 1897, for instance, express distress and revulsion at undefined acts he was performing.[28] It appears Constantine feared that his "perversion" (*diastrophe*), despite it being a source of poetic inspiration, would harm his health. Specifically, he worried that if he didn't stop his dissolute life, he would not be able to take the trip with John in May 1897 to Paris and London: "I sinned again. I have no hope unless I stop" (March 16, 1897). He seemed to recover after the sojourn in Europe but in August he felt "ugly." "What agony." "I gave in again. Horror, horror." "I am lost."[29] In another note, he expressed aching self-doubt about his poetry: "In the end, what shall I do? I am, aesthetically speaking, wasting myself."[30] Another is a cry for help: "I am undergoing a torture. I got up and am writing now. What should I do and what will happen? What should I do? . . . Help. I am lost" (1905).[31] Late at night, away from his family and friends, he expressed the depth of his inner torment. These moments of emotional panic reveal a stricken, isolated man. While he might have enjoyed champagne in the San Stefano Casino with his friends and his family in these years, he did not have a single soul in whom to confide his personal agony.

In 1905, he gave voice to these disturbing thoughts in the poem "He Swears," which he published ten years later. The speaker declares that he wants to start "a better life" but when night comes "with its own compromises and its own possibilities," he surrenders to his body's yearnings and returns lost "to the same fateful pleasure." The house suggested in this poem apparently stood at the corner of El Attaríne and Selím Cobdan, a working-class district of Alexandria.[32]

The period in which Constantine wrote these comments of inner turmoil coincided with his attempt to carve out a path for his own poetry. Many of the poems from the early 1890s were still quite derivative. Had he continued to write in this vein, he would be unknown by the rest of the world today, sharing the fate of Greek writers he once admired, such as Athanasios Christopoulos, Alexandros and Panayiotis Soutsos, and Alexandros Rizos Rangavis, and, of course, John. But something happened to Constantine that caused him in the late 1890s to rethink his poetry and his place in Greek literature. Interestingly, in 1902 he wrote no poems.[33] At the same time, he was undergoing a fierce reexamination of his work during which he renounced many of the poems he had published at that point. This must have been for him, as for any writer, a painful act, savage in its self-criticism. That he took a knife to his previous work demonstrates, however, the colossal scope of his ambition.

By 1911, he had repudiated a large number of poems, leaving only some with a note in English clipped on each page, "not for publication but may remain here." Not only did he modify his style and develop a new perception of history and of Hellenism; he also came to a different understanding of selfhood. Indeed, in addition to reflecting on his sexuality and on his own place in Egypt, he fashioned a modern conception of personhood, which he saw as flexible rather than fixed. More important, by having men talk about their sexual and ethnic selves in his poems, he showed that identity was self-aware, an object of our own reflection and making. Many of his poems are actually devoted to poetry talking about itself. In "Their Beginning" (1916?/1921), for instance, two young men, having just given in to "illegal pleasure," venture out onto the street, trying to conceal the type of bed they had just slept on. "Except," the coda says, "tomorrow, the day after, or in many years will be written / the strong lines which had found their beginning here." Similarly, in "To Remain" (1918/1919), the speaker describes two young men who are incapable of caution, locked in an embrace with their shirts unbuttoned. The poem ends with a vision of this episode crossing twenty-six years "to remain in this poetry."

Many of these poems refer not only to themselves as literary art but also to the homosexual as a new type of personhood.[34] Specifically, Constantine dared to speak about the "new phase of love," which meant not only writing about homosexuality but also seeing it as a malleable entity. The sexual self was not something fixed forever but changing with the time, like all human creations. He experimented with how to write about sexuality in a manner that reflected the rethinking of homoerotic desire taking place in Europe.[35] Having developed revolutionary vocabularies and poetic form to depict subjectivity by the first decade of the twentieth century, Constantine gradually gained the confidence to instill his new understanding of the human self in his poems.

Crucial in the development of his poetics and reputation was his trip to Athens in 1901, a place he described in a letter as a "Mecca."[36] Unlike the personal notes from the period, which expressed anguish, the journal he kept shows a cheerful and hopeful Constantine describing his experiences in Athens with adolescent-like fervor. "Piraeus itself a very nice little place. We drove to Athens—a 3/4 of an hour's drive. Beautiful scenery. The violet hills in the distance are enchanting. At the Hotel d'Angleterre they made us a very good reception. We have first rate rooms."[37] Rather than being a confessional text, it is, as he admitted in his first entry of June 13, a "diary of occurrences, not of impressions and ideas." He did wonder whether it would become soul-searching, since "it is in the nature of diaries to turn out quite the opposite of what is expected or intended."[38] At the end, however, he opted for description of places, meetings, outings, walks, dinners, and days of indisposition, which forced him to stay in the hotel. While he made no allusions to his sexual life at all, he often referred to attractive men. Having reached Athens, which he characterized as "a very, very pretty town—quite European," he recorded that "the officers' uniforms I liked very much; and the officers and soldiers look all they should be."[39] He found a young acquaintance, Nicola Giannopoulo, "a handsome young man"; one afternoon by a kiosk, he spotted many people, including "several officers," and one day, disappointed with a performance of Puccini's *La Bohème*, he and Alexander left the theater after the third act at 12:00 a.m. and sought refreshments in a café. Below this café, they found "a whorish place . . . a small room with smaller rooms adjoining where people play cards."[40]

Athens made a lasting impression on Constantine. As he said in a letter to his cousin Marigo Cavafy, "he decided to like it" and kept his word, "admiring with all the fervor—which is their due—the classical statues and columns." He was not bothered by the "banality of the imitation—French 'quartiers' for there too I thought of historical evolution and instead of banality I saw the interesting signs of an enduring people's new tendency."[41] Apart from the Plaka, the mazelike district at the foot of the Acropolis that preserved its medieval character, the center of Athens aspired to the broad avenues and grand buildings of Munich. The Ottoman town of ten thousand inhabitants that became the Greek capital in 1833 had grown to 125,000 by their visit. And it was planned as a European city, with broad, tree-lined avenues, which were lit at night and which met at right angles, even if other streets remained uneven and unpaved.[42] When Constantine promenaded along Stadiou Street, he was awestruck by the fashionable stores and smartly dressed shoppers. On Panepistimiou Street, which paralleled Stadiou, he marveled at the three graceful buildings—the University, Academy, and Library—each in its own way expressing Athens's antiquity but also modernity through its neoclassical order. Making his way toward the Royal Palace, he passed in front of the elegant mansion built by Heinrich Schliemann, the excavator of Troy and Mycenae. Finally, in Syntagma Square, the epicenter of the city, he stopped at stylish cafés from where he could admire the palace, which dominated the area. But he described his outings without any flair.[43]

His diary shows a man constantly engaged with other people. He hardly spent a day alone in his room, except when he was unwell. Otherwise, he took walks with Alexander or with acquaintances, met friends in cafés, had dinners, attended lectures and theatrical performances. He often returned late to the hotel. Typical is the entry for July 22. He spent the morning tidying up his room and then went to the dining room, where he met a friend.

In the afternoon, he and Alexander took the train to Kiphissia to see the grand villas. After coffee near the station, they returned to Athens, caught another train to Phalerum (Phaleron), and had dinner with a friend. Constantine went to bed at twelve.[44] He felt he could enjoy his stay in Athens because his financial situation was finally secure, so much so that he and his brother traveled in first class and stayed in luxurious hotels.[45]

More important, his stay in the Greek capital enabled him to meet leading intellectuals, editors, and artists who helped him gain self-confidence in his poetry. Although Alexandria had an impressive literary atmosphere for its size and location, its cultural life was limited in comparison. Its Greek population could not support the theaters, literary magazines,[46] university, newspapers, and lectures that Athens could. And the praise he had received in Alexandria after the publications of poems such as "Inkwell" (1894) and "Sweet Voices" (1894) did not seem nearly as satisfying as the validation he found among Athenian intellectuals.[47] For instance, when he was about to visit the Historical and Ethnological Museum, his companion Georgios Tsokopoulos introduced him to the "superintendent" of the museum, the poet Ioannis Polemis: "He looks a serious man, a little pompous. About 60. Said he knew my name."[48] The fact that Polemis recognized his name showed Constantine that people were reading his poetry outside Alexandria. Even though he did not make much of this conversation, it demonstrated to him that he was gradually acquiring a reputation abroad. For this reason, he returned to the museum again to see Polemis, who was talking with the painter Georgios Jacovides: "They were both very polite. I stayed one hour—literary conversation, of course."[49]

Most notable was his visit to the offices of the *Panathenaia* journal, where he dropped off a poem and, crucially for his career, met Grigorios Xenopoulos (1867–1951), the influential critic and novelist: "I saw the editor Cimon Michaelides with reference to a poem of mine which, I think, he will publish. Mr. Xenopoulos, the 'conteur' [story-teller], was there. I was introduced. A very nice man. He said he admired my poems and I said I admired his 'contes.'"[50] On July 21, Constantine visited Xenopoulos in his private residence on Patision Avenue: "He received me in the most cordial manner, praised me [*sic*] poetry, and gave me a copy of his last work. I stayed over an hour. Xenopoulos speaks well and seems a sincere and good man."[51] In Xenopoulos he found his most influential advocate in Athens to whom he sent many poems upon his return home.

In the summer of 1901, Constantine could not have imagined how decisive his acquaintance with Xenopoulos would become for his future career. Two years later, Xenopoulos published an enthusiastic review of Constantine's poetry in *Panathenaia*, the first systematic presentation of his work in Athens. He described the poet's dark complexion, black mustache, round-rimmed glasses, light English accent, and "pleasant disposition," which at first sight "does not reveal many things." In his portrait, he tried to capture the contradiction many Alexandrians saw in Constantine between the charming exterior and the inscrutable interior, between "his lively, if not, grandiloquent speech" and his profound poetry. Those who experienced his polite manners and ceremonious style, Xenopoulos wrote, could not possibly grasp the real Cavafy. Someone "would have to get to know Cavafy very well to be persuaded that this was the same man who had written those beautiful poems." Such a person would come to understand that this "Alexandrian merchant[52] with his strange manner is full of wisdom and insight" and that his eyes reveal "a man of deep thought and artistic genius."[53] To prove his case, Xenopoulos analyzed eight of Constantine's poems ("Prayer," "Thermopylae," "Interruption," "Candles," "Walls," "The Windows," "Che Fece . . . Il Gran Rifiuto," and "The First Step"), ending with a discussion of "The First Step." In this poem, a young poet, Evmenis, voices his doubt about his own talents and wonders whether he could count himself as a citizen of the "City of Ideas." Unlike Evmenis, Xenopoulos concluded, Cavafy certainly deserves to be a denizen of such a city and should not fear its legislators. So confident was Xenopoulos of his judgment that he offered his article to the legislators—that is, critics—of Athens, so that they might accept the poet into their republic.

To be called brilliant by a leading Athenian intellectual in a prominent publication must have seemed like a heavenly gift to the relatively obscure poet who was thirsting for fame. Xenopoulos's laudatory essay affirmed to the Greek public Constantine's "broad thought" and "artistic genius," which, in those years, the poet confessed only to himself. At the very least, it must have demonstrated to Constantine that his writing had appeal beyond progressive readers in Alexandria, as suggested in a note he had jotted down privately: "The reader to whose life the poem fits, admits, and feels the poem: which is proven by Xenopoulos' liking ('Walls,' 'Candles,') and Pap.'s ('Candles') and Georgios Tsokopoulos' ('Sweet Voices')."[54] The conversations he had with Xenopoulos and other intellectuals at the time reinforced the new direction he was taking. He was gradually realizing that the flowery, formal language and the Romantic themes of his youthful poems (and John's as well) represented an older, now-exhausted tradition.

Constantine revealed his new self-possession in his decision to revise "Sweet Voices," which he had originally published in 1894 and later renounced. But instead of forgetting it entirely, as he had done with the other rejected poems, he transformed it. The new version, "Voices," which he published in *Panathenaia* in 1904, represents a significant milestone in his career.[55] He explained how he reworked it in an undated comment. Composed in the shorthand he regularly employed for personal notes, it shows how preoccupied he was with one particular line of the new version: "And with their echo for a second return echoes." He wonders if "for a second" is not "too short a time." Then he adds that he should consider "that the brain works very fast: this consideration is in favour of, or in extenuation of, the plural "ήχοι" ['echoes']."[56] Interestingly, he adds another line: "When the poem is definitively fixed, get some velocograph copies of it made & put it on the list & in the file of poems available for distribution." Even though he published this new version, he worried that "Sweet Voices" was still in circulation. In fact, he referred to this concern in a draft letter he wrote, probably in 1904, to his cousin Marika Tsalikis, a frequent recipient of his poems. He wondered if she still had a copy of "Sweet Voices," which he had sent her three years earlier. Then he asked her to "destroy" the one she owned, and he included in his letter the new version, "Voices." We don't know if she complied with his request.[57]

He sought to make the existence of "Sweet Voices" null and void because the two versions could not be more different from each other. Without the antiquated style of its earlier incarnation, "Voices" speaks in demotic and flows lightly and hauntingly. And it announces the arrival of a new poetics: the voices of our beloved who have died bring with them "echoes of the first poetry in our lives." Although written only ten years later, this poem comes from and points to another epoch. In the span of this decade, Constantine had the fortitude and frankness to conclude that neither "Sweet Voices" nor its author had a future. He realized that this old poem had been written by a man who wanted to attach himself to a tradition that no longer spoke to a modern audience. "Voices," however, was directed to readers of Constantine's own time who were yearning for new insights into the self and wished to have them delivered in demotic. To achieve the distinction now, Constantine had to write in the manner of

"Voices" and of "Waiting for the Barbarians," which he composed in 1898 and printed in 1904. As a mark of his growing self-confidence, he printed sometime between December 1904 and February 1905 one hundred copies of his first bound edition, containing fourteen poems. He must have felt that 1904 arrived like an annus mirabilis in terms of both his growing productivity and his own self-understanding as a poet.

Another indication of his poetic turn is his decision in 1896 to adopt a new signature: Κ. Π. Καβάφης / C. P. Cavafy. That is to say, he sealed this transitional stage by changing his middle initial from "F" to "P," which stood for his father's first name, Petros.[58] Though seemingly straightforward and perhaps trivial, this substitution came to symbolize his renaissance. It is as if he wanted to create another persona—to match the new understanding of identity he had created—radically different from the young man who had published the now-disowned poems. When years later he was asked about this substitution by Timos Malanos, Constantine claimed that C.F.C. was a distant cousin with whom he no longer had contact. And only later did he admit that 'F' referred to his mother's maiden name.[59] This ruse was part of the way Constantine played the role of being Cavafy the poet. But it also expressed his desire to alter himself in middle age: he was no longer an author of dreary Athenian Romanticism nor one caught in the clichés of Greek nationalism; and he was certainly not writing in his brother's shadow. He was rather the modern Alexandrian about to transform Greek poetry. And perhaps to announce to himself and the world that he was jettisoning his previous self, in the middle of 1904, he and Paul moved into a new apartment on 17 Rue Rosette, one that was haunted neither by family ghosts nor by the oppressive style of Athenian Romantic verse.

Constantine understood the period of "self-scrutiny" as a

turning point in his life, and he identified the year 1911 as a divide in poetic creation. According to I. A. Sareyiannis, Constantine felt that he had become "Cavafy" the poet only after 1911.[60] And in the catalogue to his pamphlet of poems from 1907 to 1915, Constantine wrote the phrase "before 1911," thereby stressing the significance he had personally assigned to this date.[61] Indeed, this very year, in which he published two very important poems, "Ithaca" and "The God Abandons Antony," constitutes a watershed moment in his poetic output and self-understanding.[62]

The poetry he began to write after his forties bears little resemblance to that of his twenties. Although 1911 has come to symbolize a decisive moment in his poetic career, the transformation it heralded was twenty years in the making. It seems, then, that the 1890s represented a time of experimentation and intense productivity. Constantine himself publicly recognized the significance of this period in the profile about his work he had submitted to Athanasios Politis, the Greek consul to Alexandria, for his influential study of the Greeks of Egypt. The profile of the poet in this book states that Constantine started publishing poetry in 1896–97 and represents the years 1896–1911 as a period of transition. It refers to about fifteen texts printed before this date, which the poet had disowned subsequently, in a way asserting that his "poetic career began" around this time.[63]

But in this long interlude of experimentation, the year 1903 is no less significant. In addition to traveling to Athens again, meeting Xenopoulos for a second time,[64] Constantine wrote an essay in English, posthumously mistitled "Ars Poetica," in which he explained his thoughts and feelings during his period of reevaluation.[65] Along with "Emendatory Work" on individual poems, he had to undertake a fuller philosophical scrutiny of his poems. "Flagrant inconsistencies, illogical possibilities, ridiculous exaggerations" had to be corrected, and when this was not possible, the poems should be "sacrificed." He promised to retain only lines that he could use later on. But he cautioned against turning this effort into a "fanatical" crusade,[66] even though this is what it turned out to be.

In another cryptic remark, he revealed again this ruthlessness. "By my postponing, & repostponing to publish, what a gain I have had!" he writes on October 1, 1906, then lists the poems he had written, "of trash (at the age of 24, 25, 26, & 27 / & 28 /) of Byzantine poems," referring to "speaking rot," and a poem with the "stupid voices of Wife, Parents, Child etc.) / & many others which would disgrace me now. What a gain! And all those poems written between 19 and 22. What wretched trash!"[67] Often, he attached the phrase "not for publication but may remain here" in English to poems he did not reject outright, perhaps with the intention of revising them in the future. Constantine likely never discussed this period of reinvention with anyone.[68] In this way, he wanted to give the impression that he had always been Cavafy, the old man sauntering through the streets of Alexandria. And this is the impression visitors had of him in the last decades of his life—that he had always been a mature poet.

Crucially, he saw 1903 also as a time of sexual and poetic emancipation. To be sure, in the following year he composed two erotic poems ("September [of] 1903" and December [of] 1903"), which dealt with his Athenian trip of that year and which he never published. "No poems," he wrote, "were sincerer than the '2 Days of poems', written during and immediately after the gr. cr. of lib. [great crisis of liberation][69] succeeding on my departure from Athens. Now, say that in time Ale. Mav. comes to be indifferent to me, like Sul. (I was very much in love with him before my departure for Athens), or Bra . . ."[70] By "crisis of liberation," Constantine meant both his gradual acceptance of his homosexuality and its inclusion as a topic in his art and, just as important, his aesthetic reinvention. In other words, he developed a new poetics with which to write about his sexuality. As he gradually gained confidence to address his "type of love," he kept sealed the "wretched trash" and the second-rate poet who had composed them. That it took tremendous courage to speak openly about gay love should not mitigate the self-possession he showed in rejecting much of his previous work.

Since Constantine never explained how these poems would bring him shame, we can only conjecture as to why he renounced them. Possibly he was embarrassed by the sentimentality of this early verse, its Romanticism, scholasticism, and unabashed lyricism, as he was distressed by his reliance on metaphors of romantic love and katharevousa diction. In his post-1911 poems, he seems to have abandoned many of these tendencies, apart from sentimentality.

We see this in the poem "The Afternoon Sun" (1918/1919), one of Constantine's masterpieces. On the one hand, the poem offers a brilliant reflection on memory—as the speaker enters a room, he begins to recall a forgotten affair, including the fine detail of the afternoon sun falling on the bed:

This room, how well I know it.
Now it and the one next to it are rented out
as offices. The entire house
has become commercial space
for brokers, businessmen, and companies.

Ah, this room, how familiar it is.

Here near the door the sofa stood,
and in front of it a Turkish rug;

nearby the shelf with two yellow vases.
To the right—no, opposite, a wardrobe with a mirror.
In the middle was the table where he wrote;
and three large wicker chairs.
Next to the window stood the bed
where we often made love.

These poor things must still be somewhere.

Yes, next to the window stood the bed;
the afternoon sun covered half of it.

On the other hand, Constantine seems to undermine the poem's power by adding a coda: "Four o'clock in the afternoon, we parted / for one week only . . . Alas, / the week became forever." Similarly, "Beautiful, White Flowers That Matched So Well" (1929) provides a classic Cavafian portrait of homoerotic attachment. In sparse verse, each line broken in the middle by a caesura, he describes a young man taken advantage of by a lover who demands a suit and silken handkerchiefs. But the lover died, and "they buried him at ten in the morning." When the speaker returns to the café that they frequented, he feels a "knife in his heart," hardly an original image. It seems odd that an artist who was known to write only a few poems a year and who kept working on them, shaping them, revising, and recasting, should preserve lines such as these. Unless, of course, he was not at all bothered by this apparent sentimentality and that the subject matter—homoerotic love—permitted or necessitated it.

During the last decade of the nineteenth and first decade of the twentieth centuries, Constantine was developing a poetry that was unique in Greek and world literature. We can characterize these Cavafian poetics in the following way: rather than using either demotic or the purist language, he invented his own idiosyncratic mixture of both registers, while he often cited words from earlier Greek writing in his poems. Thus, a poem could contain elements of this long linguistic tradition: classical, late-antique, Byzantine Greek. At the same time, he began to experiment with form, as many other modernist poets, such as T. S. Eliot, were doing at the time. Like Eliot, he remained a conservative modernist, never adopting radical techniques. Nevertheless, it was this deliberate flouting of poetic conventions that made his poetry feel strange and unpoetic, even to his early followers in Alexandria.

Of course, Constantine was not writing prose. He frequently made use of iambic meter, true here to his Greek and English poetic inheritance. But quite often his poems did not follow any particular metrical rules. His stanzas were of unequal length. While some were written in couplets and others in quatrains, most were irregular. What infuriated his contemporary readers was his violation of traditional metrics. For Constantine often broke a grammatical unit with a caesura or with an enjambment, which split a phrase between one line and another.[71] Some poems were divided vertically rather than into stanzas, forcing a reader to jump over a break to reach the next word.

In comparison to his contemporaries, like the intensely lyrical Angelos Sikelianos, Constantine did not always use rhyme. Only slightly over half of his poems rhyme.[72] But here again, rhyme could be used for ironical rather than for purely poetic purposes.[73] Most grievous for Greek readers, however, was his general avoidance of the adjective. Indeed, he told Glafkos Alithersis that "the adjective debilitates speech," that it was a "form of weakness."[74] He thus refrained from flowery and metaphorical verse. But these early readers probably did not appreciate how much attention Constantine paid to sound and the arrangement of words. He fully exploited the inflected nature of Greek, where the placing of particular words in the sentence matters less than in English. In reality, his Greek is, as Daniel Mendelsohn notes, "deeply, hauntingly rhythmical, sensually assonant when not rhyming."[75]

That his poetry was less "poetic" and lacking the qualities of proper verse (chiefly rhyme, rhythm, and elevated diction) were persistent criticisms that plagued Constantine throughout his life. Since the prevailing tone of so many of his poems was sensual, their prosodic features often received less linguistic attention than they deserved. The poet himself may have been more complicit in establishing this precedent than he realized, as illustrated in a comment he recorded in 1911. The entry begins with the metrical scansion of lines from a song he overhears sung by two attractive men (—UU—UU—U/—UU—UU—U/—U—U UU—U) and then proceeds to register the following reflection:

> This, more or less, was what it was. This is how I noted it the day before yesterday, on a cigarette box from which I am copying it here.
>
> The vulnerability of art.
>
> When I wrote this—the scansion of the song sung by two passing youths—I thought that I was really doing something. I did nothing. The sound was nothing special, as I now see; but the voices were beautiful and attractive. And as they drew me to the window, the sound and voices became even more beautiful, because the two young men—twenty-two or twenty-three years old—were visions of beauty.
>
> What bodies, what hair, faces and lips! They stopped briefly and then left; and I, the artist, thought

> I was doing something important by collecting and preserving an echo. And truly, with the meter nothing is preserved. Because the poetry I now find to be a small thing and rather worthless. The only poetry that passed before my eyes the other day and reached my ear was the beauty of the two boys. (October 17, 1911)[76]

This is a telling tension that he would struggle with throughout his poetic career, eventually mastering the arousal of the moment and balancing it with an equal mastery of diction, meter, and rhyme.

As early as 1891, Constantine expressed his appreciation for traditional prosody. In an article titled "A Few Words Regarding Versification"—a review of Panagiotis Gritsanis's[77] book "Versification," he singled out mixed meter in particular, offering the following critical comments:

> When a poet has a cultivated musical sense, this type of [mixed meter] verse may be employed most harmoniously . . . In conclusion, I recommend wholeheartedly that those who apply themselves to writing verse should read Gritsanis's "Versification." Not that this Versification or any other has the ability to create a poet, but because the study of prosody perfects the poet. Versification is the grammar of poetry, and every poet must learn it well. The imagination, sublimity, great ideas, in a word divine inspiration, are gifts emanating directly from nature, a secret only known to her that she hides, so that she doesn't have to compete with it. "Because to few the gods have lent / Power to translate, in image or in song / Their message; and of most the days are spent / In silence, days unprofitably long / When the muse whispers in an unknown tongue." (*Telegraphos* 5, October 17, 1891)[78]

The final unidentified poetic lines of this Romanticizing theoretical passage (where nature, the font of inspiration, jealously withholds its virtues from poetry) are from John's poem "Pygmalion Meditateth," which Constantine probably cited as a tribute, although readers were free to believe that the verses were his own (another example of the brothers' unspoken poetic rivalry).

His early interest in prosody is shown by the other essays he wrote on traditional poets, including a review of "The Poetry of Mr. Stratigis"[79] (1893). This is a rather meandering appreciation of a relatively minor Greek poet's very diverse output with a particular appreciation for Stratigis's facility with rhyme and use of the stressed "proparaxytonos" (the antepenultimate syllable), a poetic device Constantine would soon master and employ himself. He also wrote an unpublished technical piece on "The Meeting of Syllables in Prosody" (1902) that shows his familiarity with this prosodic element in Greek and European poetry.

Constantine confronted the rampant criticism of his own metrics and rhyme head-on later in his career when he shadow-wrote the pages on him published in Athanasios Politis's book *Hellenism and Modern Egypt*. In it we find the following illuminating and honest assessment of his own craft as he wished it to be understood and evaluated:

> But what Cavafy is greatly criticized over is his versification. The reader of his poetry discovers that the verse of Cavafy is free verse; this is true for roughly 50 percent of it. It is free verse or, so to speak, "freed verse." Nevertheless, this verse adheres to rules, in particular the iambic rhythm, according to which one unstressed syllable or lightly stressed syllable is followed by an accented syllable.
>
> When one encounters four or five unstressed syllables, they adhere to an iambic meter that predominates and has already manifested itself.

> These are the rules of rhythm that Cavafy follows. One could object that this technique might become at times monotonous; but the poet avoids this by means of his punctuation, which supplies variety to the verse, transforming the iambic meter into trochaic. On occasion, the poet employs verses in which the sounds of the words are stretched out so that they create a mimetic harmony; but such verses are few in number.
>
> Finally, in terms of the criticism that the verse of Cavafy often lacks end rhyme, we must not forget, as the poet himself observes, that Cavafy is a Greek poet and that end rhymes were never a necessary element in Greek prosody.[80]

Despite spelling things out so clearly, Constantine continued to be attacked for precisely the poetic principles he attempted to define here. It would take decades, however, for a full appreciation of his own innovative versification to emerge.

The poetic subtlety of his rhyme, rhythm, meter, and punctuation (so much of which is lost in translation) remains more complex than his early readers were willing to acknowledge. Recent critics have focused on the highly sophisticated and creative techniques he employed, noting the "coexistence of both obsessive care and deliberate disregard for strict form."[81] Taking his cue from Politis, Peter Mackridge observes that "with the exception of five early poems that appear in the *Apokyrigmena* [Repudiated] and the *Anekdota* [Unpublished], four of which were composed in trochees and one partially in anapests and amphibrachs,[82] all his poems—numbering 256—are written entirely in iambic lines, but iambic lines whose rhythm is sometimes so eccentric as to disguise their metrical structure."[83] Monotony is thus avoided "through the use of synizesis, elision and hiatus and a certain amount of syncopation—the metrically conscious reader is constantly caught on the wrong foot!—, but also through enjambment accompanied by punctuation within the line."[84] Constantine also used the split-line as a signature stanzaic feature in some eighteen poems.[85]

Constantine's rhyme is as elaborate and inventive as his meter. Sound patterning, for instance, "occurs in two forms: rhyme (including assonance and internal rhyme) and patterns of recurring vowels and consonants within the line." Fifty-five poems are wholly in rhyme yet these rhyme patterns are "of a great variety . . . Many other poems are partly in rhyme and the rhymes are distributed with great ingenuity," as his early translator Rae Dalven notes.[86] Conventional end-of-line rhyme, internal rhyme, and elaborate and loose rhyme schemes are all employed with the aim of surprising the reader and subverting conventional expectations. Along with a highly strategic use of punctuation and a deliberately restrained vocabulary,[87] all these carefully devised prosodic devices tally into the signature Cavafy style, one admired, imitated, parodied, and ultimately celebrated as both original and unprecedented in modern Greek poetry.

As he violated poetic conventions and naturalistic imagery, Constantine deliberately avoided the broad topics expected of a major Greek poet, such as the fall of Constantinople or social justice. Rather than evoking the public space of national identity or class struggle, he spoke of closed rooms, fleeting encounters between men, veiled desires, guilt, and pleasure. Instead of writing about the ascent of the Greek nation as the fulfillment of its millenarian destiny, he favored inglorious epochs of Greek history, such as the period of late antiquity, which was rejected in his time as decadent. And when he referred to the Byzantine Empire, he focused on its decline and impoverishment. Finally, he conceived of Alexandria as a focal trope, the city that enabled him to bridge the present and the past, and to connect the self with Greek history.

It would be simplistic to claim that all of this happened self-consciously and methodically by 1911 and that Constantine had come to such a self-understanding in a process free of doubt and disappointment. Nor was it a result of a simple choice. In actuality, the period of poetic rethinking was prolonged and contradictory, involving conscious as well as unconscious acts. The many deaths in his family as well as his own social fall also played a role in his transformation as a poet. Constantine pointed to this complexity in conversations with Philippos Dragoumis, the brother of the renowned Greek intellectual, diplomat, and nationalist Ion Dragoumis.[88] Philippos, the future lawyer and politician, met Constantine on his arrival in Alexandria in the spring of 1916 as vice-consul of Greece, describing the poet as a man with "yellowish-green complexion, shaven, Jewish face, with intense dark eyes."[89] He remarked that Constantine never smiled or laughed and spoke with an English accent. In the course of their conversations about Alexandria and the future of Hellenism in Egypt, Constantine made a few insightful revelations about himself, saying that "after the loss of a brother he loved deeply he withdrew from public life." Now "he lives isolated, like an ascetic, and recalls the past."[90]

The brother was probably Alexander, who died of typhoid fever in Athens on August 21, 1905, at the age of forty-nine. Upon hearing of Alexander's illness, Constantine traveled to Athens on August 11 with the hope of finding him still alive. And he wrote about this experience about a month after the death, mostly in Greek but with a few pages in English. Unlike the diary he had written six years earlier about his mother's passing, this reveals very little about his emotional state or his relationship to Alexander. It narrates only practical details such as visits with the doctors, discussions of possible treatments, and Constantine's dilemma between keeping his brother in a hotel in old Phalerum and moving him to a hospital. This question preoccupied him: "It is only yesterday 8 [?] September, I heard from Vernadachi [?] and ascertained from the map of Greece, that carriages make a shorter cut. It is 4 kilometers from carriages, I think, about 2½ English miles. It can be done in ½ hour an hour. While I don't think that from old Phalerum carriages are always available [9.9.05]." Later in the same page, he returned to this question: "Alexander said either on Sunday (13th Aug.) night, or on Monday morning that he was content to go to hospital 'to relax' [in Greek]—meaning, the bustle of the women. Such were his words, I think. They kill me with kindness, he said on Saturday the 12th."[91]

Why did he go into a hyperrational mode? It is as if by maintaining a catalogue of facts, he wanted to keep his grief under control.[92] By recording his thoughts, but not his feelings, he might have wanted the distance of time to process this tragic event. But we have to ask whether he, at the age of forty-two, had been drained of the possibility of emotion, or even of expressing it privately, as he seems to have implied to Philippos. Had all the prior sorrow traumatized him to the point that he sought to protect himself by avoiding inner turmoil? And did he seek refuge in his poetry from the ongoing presence of death in his life, turning his art into a compensatory realm from life's pain? So it is fitting to consider the possible link between his bereavement and his transformation as a poet.

His losses were heavy. By middle age, Constantine had experienced two decades of continual mourning. As noted earlier, his friend Stephen Schilizzi died in 1886 at nineteen, to be followed by Mikès Ralli three years later. His brother Peter died in 1891,[93] his maternal grandfather in 1896, his mother in 1899, his brother George in 1900, Aristides in 1902, and finally Alexander in 1905.[94] In "From Nine O'clock" (1917/1918), Constantine speaks of a man exactly like himself who faces the desolation in his life. It is past midnight and he has been sitting in his room, remembering tragic events: "family bereavements, separations, / feelings of my dear ones, feelings / of the dead so little cherished." Although we can't quite determine the impact of these deaths on him personally, we do know that this decade of misfortune coincided both with his first period of poetic creativity in the 1890s and with his search for a new style. At this time, he abandoned many of the entertainments of his youth, gave up on tennis, and stopped his lavish expenditures on clothes.[95] Sorrow and creativity went hand in hand. But did death force Constantine to become a recluse? How reclusive was he?

This is what he claimed to the Greek poet Myrtiotissa in 1923. She brought with her compliments and adoring comments about his work from leading Athenian poets and intellectuals, which Constantine appreciated hearing.[96] Cognizant of his reputation as a grumpy loner, Myrtiotissa climbed the steps to his apartment with trepidation. After meeting the poet in his dimly lit sitting room, however, she found him lively and the conversation "captivating." She remarked that he was like an exotic creature, nourished by another atmosphere. In the course of the conversation, Constantine told her, "I live locked up in my house alone with my books," without explaining why as he had done to Philippos.[97] It was true, of course, that he lived alone, and by the time he met Myrtiotissa, he probably had given up on the dream of finding a companion, if he ever had desired one. And he certainly had changed from the free, cheerful, vivacious young man he once was. But while he might have buried his inner emotional self, he never became a social recluse. Contemporary observers often portrayed a charming man, eager to engage others in conversation, and one who sought invitations to dinners and weddings until the end of his life. We get an early portrait from F. Printezis, the editor of the Athenian journal *I Physis*, who was visiting Alexandria in October 1894 and who met Constantine, a subscriber to the journal. He describes him as a "perfect gentleman" with an English disposition and upbringing. He enjoyed his host's company and spent the last two days of his visit with him. And on the moment of his departure, Constantine "held my hand tightly" and expressed his wish to see Printezis again.[98]

Contrary to what he told Myrtiotissa and Philippos, Constantine was not a loner. The trove of menus, wedding invitations, and visiting cards he left behind from the 1890s and 1910s suggest a man who enjoyed many social occasions. Typical is a menu from the New Year's Eve dinner party of 1896 that lists the twelve elegant courses along with his place card, "Monsieur Cavafy." This year marked a significant milestone. Whereas his maternal grandfather died in January, in April Constantine published in the journal *Kosmos* "Ode and Elegy of the Streets," his final poem as C. F. Cavafy.[99] Externally, however, his life had not changed. In September, he attended a posh dinner in the casino with many courses. In another party, they drank expensive Piper-Heidsieck champagne. The next year, he took a two-month trip with John to Marseilles, Paris, and London, where, as discussed earlier, they stayed in fine hotels and enjoyed many cultural offerings.

Of course, this does not mean that he was free from internal conflict during this decade. In 1925, he composed an important erotic poem with the title "Days of 1896," about a young man of thirty who had "debased himself" through his "forbidden" sexual pleasures and lost his money and reputation. Obviously, this young man is a far cry from the thirty-three-year-old Constantine enjoying foie gras, Roquefort, and fine champagne that New Year's Eve with his friends.[100] "Days of 1896" points to an internal sexual struggle taking place within Constantine. Another poem, "Confusion," written in March 1896 but never published, deals with this tension between external and internal life:

My soul in the middle of the night
is confused and numb. Outside,
  its life goes on beside itself.

And it waits for the unlikely dawn.
And I await, wasting away, and bored,
  I, too, within it, or with it.

The many personal notes from these years reveal the inner conflicts, fears, and frustrations expressed in this awkward poem. However, Constantine kept this anguish to himself. After middle age, it appears that he closed off from the outside world the man who suffered because of his sexuality, the person who lost so many friends, and the brother who had experienced the death of his siblings. Not even Rika, it turned out, had any inkling of this inner turbulence.

While bereavement and loss of his social standing might have moved Constantine to look for personal salvation in art, they did not turn him into an insular person. Obsessive concern for his work did not mean social isolation. Having a gregarious fondness for people, he met friends daily at the Billiards Palace and on his way there, he would stop and chat with shop owners, exchanging views about daily events.[101] Even in his final days, he loved to meander through the narrow streets of his neighborhood and along Rue Fouad. After his operation for throat cancer in the Red Cross Hospital, he went briefly to Kifisia, a suburb of Athens, to convalesce, but then decided to continue his recovery in a hotel in Omonia Square in the center of the city. But one evening with about twenty admirers in his room, he complained that he needed a breath of fresh air and excused himself before his guests. One of the visitors—Sareyiannis—stepped out and followed him into the swarm of people as he went up and down the streets. Promenading briskly, Constantine had his head tilted slightly to the right with his hands holding both sides of his vest. "As he moved forward, he seemed to enjoy the dusts and scents of the city," while the first lights began to appear, exactly as he had done in Alexandria, like a "friend of the throng."[102] Ever the flâneur, he began to resemble in this moment the old man in Poe's "The Man of the Crowd."

In cafés and at home, his reputation for erudite banter had become legendary. He would frequently engage in verbal battles that others sought out as entertainment.[103] His house was often peopled by visitors, especially in the afternoon and evening. One night, Sareyiannis counted one Jewish guest, two Greeks, one Syrian, and one Belgian, all speaking French.[104] In the correspondence that Constantine maintained with Alekos Sengopoulos between October 1918 and March 1919, he reported on the people he saw at home or at the Athenaios café, the Billiards Palace, or the Grammata Bookshop. "Yesterday I went out for a while to the Athenaios with Polys Modinos" (January 11, 1919).[105] Two days later, he dined at the household of Antonis Benaki with Victor Sinanos, a "man with knowledge and good taste who lived and lives in high society. He narrated for us many interesting anecdotes about old Alexandria" (January 13, 1919).[106] On January 18, he was at "the tea of Mrs. Voltou. Philipidis and Iordanidis were there. We had a wonderful time. The topics of conversation—literary."[107]

He must have enjoyed these elegant weddings and receptions; otherwise, he would not have sought them out and then boasted about them. After all, he was not conducting research for his poetry in the way that William Faulkner was during his chats with the townspeople of Oxford, Mississippi, or Henry James in the mansions of London. They were both collecting stories and turns of phrase, cadences, and grammatical structures for their novels. Constantine's dinners with cotton barons and bankers never ended up as subject matter for his art. He attended them because they gave him pleasure and confirmed his belonging to the elite society of Greek Alexandria.[108] This was part of his contradictory character. One of the most iconoclastic Greek poets spent his free time in the grand houses of Alexandria.

10

THE BIG POETIC CHANGE

Constantine strove to depict himself as an isolated poet, a visionary who was able to offer novel conceptions of reality. Those around him accepted this image. Myrtiotissa, for one, certainly did, writing that Constantine's principal triumph was his ability to "put his stamp on everything . . . His poetic craft is so much his own, so Cavafian, that it's impossible for someone to copy him . . . To write like Cavafy, you must be Cavafy."[1] His greatest accomplishment, she continued, was to "escape from routine," to liberate himself from social conventions, and, "armed with an enormous willpower," to compose original poetry.[2]

What Myrtiotissa and other Greek visitors could not appreciate, however, was that Constantine also freed himself from Greek nationalism by choosing to stay in a city that they all found rather dull and provincial. His capacity to "put his stamp" on reality, in other words, was made possible by his connection to this city. As Constantine himself said to his cousin Marigo Cavafy, during his first visit to Athens, he "prayed for the third advent of our race." But he was not "activated by patriotism. I simply let myself be guided—as I like to do at times—by Sentiment and Illusion" (February 24, 1902).[3] What he meant was that his filtering and reshaping of reality could take place only in Alexandria. He was like an animal or a plant that was adapted for a certain environment. When a city has an "intense character," he told Philippos Dragoumis, who complained of Alexandria's insipidness, it imposes its character upon people, limiting their freedom. "Truly, I feel here much more a master of myself."[4]

In his youth, however, Alexandria "oppressed" him. "What a nuisance, what a burden a small city is—what a lack of freedom."[5] He wondered if London would have been preferable for a "man like me—one so different," believing that a major European center would afford a gay man more autonomy. Yet he did not abandon his city in search of erotic freedom. Although London or Paris might have offered the anonymity for affairs with other men, his hometown promised something more consequential: aesthetic independence. He was first and foremost an artist. Alexandria's blandness and its implicit past served as the blank page for his creativity, maximizing his scope to imagine. This is perhaps another important insight he arrived at during the period of self-questioning and reinvention. On the solitary night of July 5, 1903, Constantine reflected on his duty to truth as an artist: "Doesn't art always lie?" he asked. "Or rather, isn't it when art lies the most that it creates the most?"[6] It is not essential, he concluded, to have lived in the countryside in order to write about it. Sincerity to nature, the nation, religion, or race did not motivate his creativity.[7] Self-conscious artistry or artfulness, he believed, turns life's raw material into something worth remembering and prizing.

Constantine concluded in middle age that art primarily invents and its aptitude for fiction differentiates it from other human activities. His poetry did not express the "real" self but rather re-created the self through its formal devices. This realization suited him well. He was not a very confessional person, after all, even in his journals. In his poetry, he strove neither for naked revelation nor a transparent representation of the world. Ancient Alexandria entered his work only after passing through the sieve of his memories, desires, feelings, and fantasies. Moreover, by tracing a connection between modern and Hellenistic Alexandria, he escaped the European adulation of classical Athens and ideological debates about Greekness in contemporary Athens. In this respect, the absence of a material past in Alexandria was a godsend. He was thus free to recall its residents and conjure up new ones, turning the Hellenistic period into his own.

Constantine began to be fascinated by the Hellenistic and late-antique periods in the 1880s. An early instance of this preoccupation was a marginal note he wrote in 1890 to Edward Gibbon's *Decline and Fall of the Roman Empire* (1776), specifically his discussion of Saint Simeon the Stylite (395–451), a Syrian ascetic who lived thirty-seven years on a platform surmounted on a column. Constantine seemed attracted less to this relatively unknown figure as a curiosity in and of himself than to how he had been portrayed by poets. Thus, he quickly turned his attention to Tennyson's "St Simeon Stylites" (1842), the only modern treatment of this saint he could find.[8] "Though it contains some well-made verses," Constantine wrote in a one-page note in 1890, it "fails in tone." Ultimately, he rejected Tennyson's poem, finding his rendition of the Orthodox saint "vulgar" and deficient because it took the form of a monologue. He conceded, however, that "it was a very difficult task—a task reserved, perhaps, for some mighty king of art—to find fitting language for so great a saint, so wonderful a man."[9] Could he have been thinking of himself as such a "mighty king of art"? Did this young man with no university education have at the age of thirty the self-possession to take on Tennyson and other eminent Victorian figures like John Ruskin? He was certainly searching for alternative historical periods to mine beyond Homeric Greece and fifth-century Athens. But was he entertaining the notion of writing a poem about Simeon to get out from under the shadow cast by Tennyson? If he toyed with such ideas, he kept them dormant until 1917, when, almost thirty years later, he composed his own "Simeon." And he seems to have solved what he thought was the "defect" in Tennyson's original by changing the perspective from that of Simeon to that of an unknown rhetorician, who, after witnessing Simeon's staggering feat, comes to question the value of poetry. He has the speaker witness the Christian faithful praying at the foot of Simeon's pillar. As a pagan beholding Christian piety, he begins to tremble. Confronting absolute belief, he wonders about the capacity of art to compete with the conviction of these zealots. Could poetry, an apparently impractical pastime, hold its own against the absolute devotion of this saint?

Yes, of course, I know his new poems;
all of Beirut is talking about them.
But I'll study them some other day,
since I'm completely distracted now.

He certainly knows more Greek than Libanius.
But more than Meleager? I doubt it.

Oh, Mebes. Who cares about Libanius! Or books!
Or all these trivialities! . . . Mebes, I found myself yesterday—
just by chance—beneath Simeon's column.

I sneaked in among the Christians
who were praying, kneeling, and worshiping silently;
but, not being a Christian,
I didn't have their inner calm—

I was shaking all over, aching;
I trembled with agitation and distress.

Don't smile; just imagine it, thirty-five years—
winter, summer, night, and day, thirty-five years
he was living and bearing witness on top of a column.

Even before we were born—I'm twenty-nine,
I think you're younger—
imagine, before we were born,
Simeon climbed up on his pillar
and since then has stood there, before God.

I'm just not in the mood today for work—
However, Mebes, it's better to concede
that whatever the other sophists say,
I accept that Lamon
is Syria's finest poet.

Constantine distanced himself from Tennyson's original by turning his "Simeon" into a self-reflexive poem that addressed the conflict between the practical and the impractical, religion and literary criticism, and ethics and aesthetics—themes that would preoccupy him throughout his career. In other words, rather than focusing on the actual Saint Simeon Stylites, he reflected on the capacity of artists to compete for attention with great historical figures. In so doing, he transformed his poem into a philosophical meditation on the eternal conflict between art and action. Yet, having achieved a measure of originality over Tennyson's text, he decided for reasons hard to grasp against the poem's publication.

He continued his interests in history's marginal individuals, composing in March 1896 "Julian in the Mysteries" about Julian (330–63), the last pagan emperor of Rome. Although he never published it, he kept it along with five other poems, now lost, under the heading "The Beginnings of Christianity." From 1896 until his death, Constantine would write seven other poems on this fascinating and polarizing figure. Significantly, the last poem he ever wrote, "On the Outskirts of Antioch" (1932), was also about this emperor. Although he had completed it in his final days, he died before sending it to the printers.

Julian came to represent the poet's fascination with forgotten epochs and unconventional individuals, and his search for a place and time that would allow him to make his mark. Polys Modinos believed[10] that his mentor discovered in the Hellenistic period exactly the same independence he found in contemporary Alexandria. Constantine was attracted by the "freedom of the spirit and the want of discipline" of that epoch. In the absence of a religion and a state, people were able to "think more freely." "Laws like those that could condemn a Socrates don't exist in this period." The moral relativism abundant in Hellenistic Alexandria suited his spirit. "Each person was free to create for himself the ethics he desired."[11] Modinos suggests that Constantine was preoccupied with the conditions and the possibility of creative freedom since at least the 1890s. As Constantine wrote in a note on Gibbon's *Decline and Fall of the Roman Empire*, "any interference of the state in the literary or scientific pursuits of the people is tyrannical in its origins, in its essence, and in its effects."[12]

For this reason, as Constantine confessed to Malanos, he preferred the Hellenistic to the Byzantine period, even though the latter stood closer to him chronologically.[13] In fact, he said that he could hardly get himself to place his characters in a Byzantine setting, finding it too constraining, even though he did in fact compose many poems with Byzantine themes: "The Hellenistic period is more amoral, more free, and allows me to move my characters as I see fit."[14] In order to write convincingly about this age, he immersed himself in it. "I feel free in this period. I have made it my own," he said to Sareyiannis.[15] His original angle to Hellenistic history amazed his listeners, including an English scholar who had read his poems in translation. During a conversation, Constantine dazzled him and the other guests so much that one of them presciently said that "in the future we won't have to read about the Hellenistic period. Cavafy's poems are enough."[16] This was an astonishingly prophetic statement on the way the poet came to elevate the significance of the Hellenistic age and the period of late antiquity decades before scholars had.[17]

Of course, his fascination with postclassical Greece did not appear ex nihilo. In the works of the Victorian painters, such as Edward Burne-Jones and George Frederic Watts, and decadent writers like Walter Pater, Oscar Wilde, Charles Baudelaire, and Paul Verlaine, he found the themes of the fall of Rome and the rise of Christianity. He also met people who shared his predilection for uncelebrated epochs. Robin Furness,[18] as noted earlier, a British scholar and friend of E. M. Forster who worked in Alexandria's Egyptian civil service, had published translations of Hellenistic poetry. But nobody before Constantine had built Hellenistic Alexandria into a tower from which to examine civilizational decline, social marginalization, homosexuality, male beauty, and diasporic identities.

To his contemporaries this decision seemed less evident or productive than reckless and incomprehensible. Initially only his key supporters understood how he was shifting the focus away from the glories of fifth-century Athens. "He even looks back upon a different Greece," Forster wrote in *Pharos and Pharillon*

(1923): "Athens and Sparta, so drubbed into us at school, are to him two quarrelsome little slave states, ephemeral beside the Hellenistic Kingdoms that followed them . . . He reacts against the tyranny of Classicism—Pericles and Aspasia and Themistocles and all those bores. Alexandria, his birthplace, came into being just when Public School Greece decayed; . . . his literary ancestor—if he has one—is Callimachus."[19] Rather than simply mining the past for sources, Constantine converted Hellenistic Alexandria into a hallmark, a metaphor of his own quest for originality.[20] This was a momentous step in his becoming a great poet. For he understood a century before Harold Bloom's theory of influence that poets struggle with their precursors to distinguish themselves by fashioning new perspectives on life and history. Constantine spent about two decades thinking about his own unique contribution to world poetry. And he demonstrated the results of all this effort by writing the exquisite "Caesarion":

Partly to verify a certain date
partly to while away the hour
last night I picked up and paged through
a volume of Ptolemaic inscriptions.
The fulsome praise and adulation are
identical for everyone. All are brilliant
illustrious, mighty, beneficent.
All their endeavors Solomonic.
And the women in the family,
all the Berenices and Cleopatras are miraculous too.

When I had verified the period
I would have put the book aside had a
scant and insignificant reference to King Caesarion
not immediately caught my attention . . .

Ah, yes, there you were with your vague
allure. Since history has devoted
so little ink to you,
I could picture you more freely in my mind.
I made you beautiful and sensual.
My skills lend your face an
ethereal, enticing appeal.
And I imagined you so fully,
that late last night when my lamp
was about to go out—I let it burn out on purpose—
I felt you entered my room,
it seemed you stood before me; just the way
you would have been
in conquered Alexandria,
pale and exhausted, transcendent in your sorrow,
hoping that they would have mercy on you,
the cruel ones whispering,
"Too many Caesars."

He began "Caesarion" in 1914 under the title "Of Ptolemy Caesar," and worked on it for four years before publishing it. That on the eve of World War I he turned to Caesarion (47–30 BCE), the last Ptolemy and the son of Cleopatra and Julius Caesar who was put to death by Augustus, seemed self-indulgent to his contemporaries because it demonstrated, in their eyes, Constantine's insensitivity to contemporary events. But Constantine shocked them even further by making the poem focus on an erotic attraction and poetic creation, linking homoeroticism and artistic inspiration. Written in the first person, it depicts a modern poet who, bored by the adulatory descriptions of the great, Ptolemaic rulers, allows his mind to focus on young Caesarion. The poet resembles Constantine himself perusing through volumes of inscriptions in the hall of his apartment.

The scene enacted in "Caesarion" illustrates the copious research that went into his poems. Daily he pored over dictionaries to make sure he had the right word. We see this in comments he recorded on the poem "The Glory of the Ptolemies," particularly his obsessive concern over the adverb "τελείως/teleios" (completely), including references to how this word was used by French authors of the seventeenth century. After much thought, he concluded on May 20, 1911: "I think 'Teleios' as expounded by me in French, as shown in the French meaning marked xx is quite satisfactory, and the poem can stand as it is, and be given out for publication as it is."[21] He also consulted historical texts to verify facts, as we see in a note regarding "The Retinue of Dionysus," where the imaginary sculptor, Damon, is working on a frieze depicting the entourage of Dionysus in Parian marble. Uncertain as to whether Damon could have found Parian marble in Italy, Constantine was relieved after much investigation to discover explicit proof of the export of this type of marble to Rome in a French dictionary on antiquity. He also consulted the English lexicon by Liddell and Scott regarding the word "στιλπνός/stilpnos" (glittering/glistening) in connection with the aesthetic effect of marble.[22]

Similarly, he devoted three pages of notes about the death of the Persian king Darius while he worked on "The Naval Battle," a poem he wrote in 1899 but never published. He referred to Aeschylus's tragedy *The Persians*, which was staged in Athens in 472 BCE, about the defeat of Xerxes (Darius's son) by the Athenian fleet at the Bay of Salamis in 480 BCE. Having undertaken new reading as to where Darius died and was buried, Constantine now felt the need to correct a line and changed "We came now to our Ecbatana" to "Now we shall return to our Ecbatana."[23] And he also had Xerxes make his lamentation on the way back from Salamis rather than in Susa as Aeschylus had done: "Between Aeschylus & Herodotus, I chose the latter. The poem is thus historically accurate." He had misgivings about including the city Persepolis, since neither Aeschylus nor Herodotus alluded to it. But he retained it, as the city was mentioned by the ancient historians Ctesias and Plutarch[24] and in a modern biographical dictionary of antiquities.[25] Yet for all his worry about making sure the poem was "historically accurate," he concluded that "The Naval Battle" was not worthy of publication.[26]

This very act of going through catalogues was an almost daily ritual for Constantine. During his entire career, he kept a careful inventory of his poems, their various revisions, emendations, and corrections, and lists of their recipients in Egypt and Europe. He also maintained lists of all kinds—of clothes, of his mother's jewelry, of kitchen articles such as pots and pans, and of household tasks.[27] Between 1908 and 1914, he enumerated the contents of his house. He saved recipes and instructions on how to cook various foods, writing that "cutlets must be beaten."[28] From 1887 until 1893, he worked on a register of games he enjoyed playing, such as dominoes, roulette, chess, heads or tails, tombola, and bridge, along with a record of wins and losses.[29] And he hoarded everything—old bills, receipts from hotels, and various mementos such as printed menus. He preserved all the letters he received and often drafts of letters he sent to friends, family members, and acquaintances. Moreover, he stockpiled not only important documents, such as annual letters of appointment in the Office of the Irrigation Service, his baptismal and birth certificates, his residence permits issued annually by the Greek General Consul of Alexandria, but also insignificant possessions such as his entry card to the Club Athénien and train tickets from his first trip to Athens in 1901, the receipt from the Grand Hotel Phaleron from that year, and from the Grand Hotel Splendid of Athens from July 29 of 1903.[30] Like a young student on his first trip abroad, he endowed every admission ticket and receipt with major significance.

He even made lists of lists: "2.11.11. Lists of things I req. to take with me for a 2 day excursion . . ." Another list: "List of things I require to take with me for a comfortable [?] 10 days stay in Cairo during next May 14.4.07."[31] After the death of his mother, he also had to manage the household affairs, as attested by the two-page summary he wrote of the domestic tasks. Here is a synopsis: Ahmed does the dishes while Hasan shines the silver. The clock is wound in the direction of the wall. You put two spoons of tea in the black teapot. Ahmed puts three and it becomes heavy. The house is cleaned thoroughly twice a year, once in the spring and the second time in the winter. An assistant comes to scrub the floor, beat the rugs and clean the windows. The baker comes at 6:30 or 7:00 in the morning and leaves a round loaf. For the evening, we get a straight loaf and, if necessary, an additional one. Ahmed knows the various shops in the neighborhood.[32]

He kept detailed catalogues of his monthly expenses—for instance, from March 1 to December 31, 1899, noting the cost of various household articles and their repair.[33] He was quite aware of the money he was spending for restaurants, cafés, groceries, and the servants' salaries. In an undated list, he enumerated the monthly outflow for "restaurant and coffee-house expenses," "bread, milk, washing of clothes, rent," "candles and petroleum," "food for servants," "kitchen requirements."[34] This tendency to maintain careful records about his finances was a lifelong trait, lasting well into adulthood. Even in 1932, he maintained a detailed record of his monthly cash flow.

And he was fully in control of his overall financial situation, asking his banks to sell shares he had inherited or simply making inquiries. He kept copies of his correspondence with his banks. It seems that he sent his last letter to his bank in March 1933, a month before his death. We have a note about shares his mother purchased between 1890 and 1893: "Bills belonging to the shares bought by my mother and which have come to my possession."[35] And with great pride he received on May 21, 1924, a money order from London "on behalf of the Nation Limited" in the amount of three guineas, probably for the publication of his translated poems. But perhaps nothing expresses both his pecuniary character and his penchant for recordkeeping better than a note he had written about a loan he had made to John: "£ St. 250 lent to J. C. Cavafy at 8% per annum, to be repaid me on May 1905 [stroked out], 1910 [stroked out], 1912. Its receipt is in my bedroom [written perhaps later in different ink]. Repaid by J. C. Cavafy in middle of 1917 [written in different ink]."[36] A declaration he wrote and had Paul sign on March 3, 1905, affirmed that furniture they shared in the apartment of Rue Rosette did in fact belong to Constantine.[37]

Sometime around 1901, he jotted down a curious and cryptic kind of list.[38] Rather than the dry itemization of kitchen utensils, card games, or tasks, it records in his customary shorthand a series of anxieties about middle age that find expression in other personal notes and in poems such as "Candles" and "An Old Man." Each line opens with the word "krima" ("what a pity"). In one line, he regrets that his "hair has turned gray" and that he "can't enjoy his youth." In another, he mourns the decline of his vision and weakening of his heart. Many lines bemoan activities he can no longer participate in, such as playing tennis and enjoying time with friends. There is also an obscure reference to a "horrible anguish" possibly of a sexual nature. One line seems to regret his own rejection of his earlier work: "What a pity that I destroy my artistic creation." These comments, ranging from the regret of a lost trip to more pressing preoccupations about artistic invention and sexuality, approximate a prose poem and show how his penchant for catalogues infiltrated his poetry.

So Constantine, the man who made personal lists and consulted historical catalogues daily, very much resembles the speaker in "Caesarion" who finds himself perusing the long register of Hellenistic rulers. In writing "Caesarion," Constantine showed how he could give life to people from antiquity and have them appear in his candlelit apartment. He often told visitors that "one-hundred and twenty-five voices inside were telling him that he could write history."[39] But he never listened to them, preferring to have the past enter his poems because he thought ultimately poetry was superior to history. In "Caesarion," the poet/speaker rescues a prince from the graveyard of amnesia and, in so doing, contrasts the indifference of historiography with the compassion of art. At the same time, the poem showcases the innovative theory of poetry Constantine had been developing: using the detachment of the historical gaze as a way of speaking of the self, shortening the distance between past and present through the emotion of empathy, and employing antiquity to reflect on the self and the self to reflect on antiquity. By focusing on Caesarion's story, he demonstrated that as a modern poet, he was attracted to sidelined, forgotten individuals rather than celebrated kings. At the same time, he gave unabashed voice to homoerotic desire, allowing the speaker to identify with the young prince, almost embracing him.

"Caesarion" dramatizes Constantine's mature phase, the outcome of almost three decades of creative experimentation and questioning. But what made his poetic transformation possible was his outsize ambition to reinvent himself as a poet of major significance. We see early evidence of these aspirations in an essay, "The Last Days of Odysseus" (1894), in which, as noted earlier, he examined the long tradition of the Odyssean theme in

Western literature, from Homer, through Dante, and finally in Tennyson's "Ulysses." This text, which he never published, gives us a glimpse into his fertile and unsettled mind at the time. He recognized, of course, the impossible challenge poets faced to say anything new about Homer's hero: "Furthering the sentence from the place where Homer decided to end by placing a period is a difficult and risky thing for another poet to undertake."[40] How could a modern poet, he wondered, dare to set Odysseus on another voyage after Homer brought him home to Ithaca? Was he sufficiently talented himself to contribute something original to this tradition?

But, as Constantine asserted, it was in "difficult and risky tasks that great artists achieve success."[41] He felt he was such an artist, a "mighty king of art," as he wrote in the note on Tennyson's "St Simeon Stylites," an equal at least to Tennyson. How else but from sheer hubris could he attempt to compose a poem, "Second Odyssey," in 1894, at the age of thirty-one, after having written about the number of luminaries who had interpreted Odysseus? Below the poem's title, he inscribed Dante's *Inferno*, Canto XXVI, and Tennyson's "Ulysses" as his sources of inspiration. Dante was the first poet to return to the Odyssean theme in Canto XXVI of the *Inferno*, in which he and Virgil meet Ulysses (the Roman name for Odysseus). Indebted to Dante, Tennyson took up the Homeric challenge five hundred years later with his unsettled hero, who was discontented leading his life "by this still hearth, among these barren crags." Eager "to sail beyond the sunset" and indifferent to the fate of his wife and son, he pushed away "to strive, to seek, to find, and not to yield." In his "Second Odyssey," Constantine languished in the shadow of literary giants, his Odysseus impatient with his "small Ithaca" and "bored" by Penelope's loyalty and Telemachus's love. Despite his ambition, he added little new to Tennyson's poem. Stylistically he still made use of katharevousa vocabulary and verb forms, indicating that he had still not learned how to distance himself from the purist tradition. "Second Odyssey" offered few promises of future greatness other than the poet's spirited desire to challenge Tennyson.

In the essay "The Last Days of Odysseus," Constantine argued that for a poet to achieve greatness he had to differentiate his voice from that of his precursors.[42] For this reason, he gave less due to Tennyson because he found his raw material in Dante without departing significantly from it, even though "he reworked it like a skilled artist."[43] He must have concluded that, with "Second Odyssey," he too had not traveled beyond Dante and Tennyson. So it is not surprising that he worked on the poem for many years until he transformed it completely into the sublime "Ithaca" in 1910. Symbolically enough, he published it a year later, the date he set for himself as representing his poetic rebirth. Unlike "Caesarion," which announced the Hellenistic epoch as a source of inspiration, "Ithaca" remained captive to the deification of Homer:

As you set out for Ithaca
pray that the way be long,
full of exploration, full of learning.
The Laistrygonians, the Cyclopes,
furious Poseidon, don't fear them.
You won't encounter them along the way
if you keep your mind on higher things,
if a fine essence moves your spirit and body.
The Laistrygonians, the Cyclopes,
furious Poseidon, you won't encounter them
if you don't harbor them inside your soul,
if your soul doesn't conjure them before you.

Pray that the voyage be long.
May you have many summer mornings
when with such delight, such joy
you arrive at unexplored ports.
Pause at Phoenician trading posts
and acquire fine merchandise:
mother-of-pearl, coral, amber, ebony,
heady fragrances of every kind,
as many heady fragrances as you can.
Visit many Egyptian cities;
learn from their scholars and learn even more.

Keep Ithaca always in your mind.
To arrive there is your destination.
But don't hasten your journey in the least.
It's best that it take many years;
so you are old when you land on the island,
rich with what you've found along the way,
not expecting Ithaca to give you wealth.

Ithaca offered you the magnificent journey.
Without her you would not have set out.
She has nothing else to give you now.

And if you find her poor, Ithaca has not deceived you.
As wise as you've become, with such experience
you will have grasped what Ithacas like these mean.

Although it broke no new ground in its subject matter, "Ithaca" distanced itself stylistically from its predecessors. Written in second person, it addresses Odysseus at the start of his voyage home from Troy, in contrast to Dante and Tennyson, who had him depart Ithaca after his return. At the same time, it liberates itself from the linguistic conventions of contemporary Greek writing by adopting a more versatile language, not fully demotic, but without the artificial and stodgy forms of katharevousa. In the fifteen years between "Second Odyssey" and "Ithaca," Constantine reinvented himself from an ambitious but derivative writer into a pioneering poet. In this process, he came to understand that to achieve renown, a latecomer like himself was not powerless. In fact, he had the advantage of uttering the last word, of restructuring the thoughts of his forerunners, of rearranging their sentences, and of changing the meaning of their words. He must have come to this insight in the late 1890s, for in 1900 he wrote a diabolically clever poem, the unpublished and little-known "The Enemies," in which he developed his thinking on what greatness means in literature. An illustrious writer's foes, the speaker says, lurk in the future, wielding weapons with which they change his writing. That which he had presented as beautiful and poetic, his enemies will portray as dry and old-fashioned, just as he had overthrown the aesthetic criteria of his predecessors:

Three sophists came to greet the Consul
who had them sit near him.
He spoke to them amiably and, joking, later told them: "Fame provokes envy.
Your rivals keep writing. You have enemies."
One of the three answered with solemn words:

"Our current foes will do us no harm.
Later our enemies, the new sophists, will come,
when we in our old age lie wretched
and some of us will have gone to Hades. The words

we speak now and our works will appear strange (and
ridiculous perhaps) since the enemies will change
sophistics, style, and fashions. Just as they and I
remade past things,
what we portrayed as beautiful and proper
the enemies will render foolish and useless,
repeating the same things differently (without much effort).
Just as we once expressed old words in a new way."

Constantine discovered in his late thirties that a poet achieves distinction by revising the values, criteria, and tastes of his precursors in order to make space for his own achievements. He had written about this topic some years earlier in the unpublished essay "The Musings of an Aging Artist" (1894–1900?), where an eighty-year-old eminent writer worries that, amid the official adulation, he finds "indifference" among young readers: "Their school is not his school, and their style is not his style. They think and, above all, write differently." The artist, however, feels that he can't switch to their mode of writing. But then he realizes that, even if he could, he would soon be passed over. This is how it had started with him: "He was one of some fifty youths who formed a new school, who wrote with a different style, who changed the minds of millions who used to honor a few predecessors and certain older artists." And then he comes to the realization that every author begins "to appear strange and ridiculous" once he reaches forty or fifty. He concludes that current readers reject him, just as he criticized his own predecessors with "critical judgment" that was "corrupted by contemporary circumstances or even fads."[44]

In the last decade of the nineteenth and first decade of the twentieth centuries, Constantine had been asking if he could hold his own against his great predecessors. Eventually, he concluded that he could. But to enter the canon of literature, he had to open new doors onto myth and history, introduce a new style, create novel approaches to his sexuality, and rebel against both the katharevousa poets of his own past and the demotic poetry of Palamas. After twenty years of reflection and experimentation, he grasped his own capacity for distinction, a realization that was both terrifying and exhilarating.

Crucially, in 1897, he printed a four-page booklet containing "Walls" along with John's translation of the poem in English.[45] "Walls" was the quintessential Cavafian reflection on inner space, on a speaker who finds himself closed off from the outside world. This eight-line poem would become one of his most famous, expressing to millions of readers the hopelessness and claustrophobia of modern life. Given its despairing tone, it is hard to believe that its author was the unripe young man in his early thirties.

Without consideration, without pity, without remorse
they built high, thick walls around me.

And now I sit here in despair.
Thinking of nothing else, this fate eats away at me

because I had so much to do outside.
Oh, why didn't I pay attention, when they were building the walls?

Yet, I didn't hear any sound or noise from the builders.
Imperceptibly they closed me off from the world outside.

Constantine must have understood that "Walls" captured a particular atmosphere, a view of reality that appealed to readers eager for something new in Greek poetry. It conveyed an urban form of isolation that paradoxically seemed refreshing in comparison to the bucolic or national themes of other poets. His conviction about his own originality was reinforced four years later when, in his influential article, Xenopoulos identified "Walls" as the poem that struck him the most. He found himself repeating it silently, hearing in its haunting verses an echo of modern life. Contrary to inaccessible poems by other authors who amazed him initially only to disappoint him later, "Walls," Xenopoulos wrote, continued to defy his analysis, holding him "prisoner" with its masterful language and depth of human perception.[46] At last, a preeminent critic outside Alexandria had recognized Constantine's extraordinary genius. A year later, Constantine printed his first collection of poems, which he sent to Xenopoulos. After two decades of mourning and of obscurity but also of intense creativity and experimentation, his time had come.

Yet however much he could triumph in his ever-growing renown, he felt some ambivalence about it. For he began to worry that he was trading his artistic and personal integrity for fame. Indeed, he wrote a short vignette in 1905 about a young poet who had visited Constantine's apartment on 17 Rue Rosette. Marveling at the grand furniture and fine appointments of his host's flat, the visitor complained about his own poverty. Taken aback by this implied criticism of his own comfortable life, Constantine replied that he had paid dearly for his "small luxuries." In order to acquire them, he confessed, he had to become a public servant—"how ridiculous"—and thus betray his art while his guest, though poor, remained a "true" artist. How many times, he lamented, a particular image came to him at work, a turn of a phrase that he was compelled to push aside. But when he arrived home, he tried to recall it in vain. It was as if "Art" had protested to him that "she" was not a "servant" but the "greatest Lady in the world," whom he deceived for his middle-class security.[47]

As a poet, Constantine faced the classic dilemma: Did his duty to art supersede his need to earn a living? Two years after recording these comments, he turned again to the tug-of-war he felt between artistic freedom and subsistence. Referring to articles in the journal *Panathenaia* on the reading habits of the Greeks, he lamented the sorry state of literature in his day, especially the lack of economic support for authors. But poverty would be preferable, he noted, to betraying the value of artistic freedom. An author, he argued, who worries about future sales would become influenced by the tastes of the public: "No matter how sincere and assured he might be, there will occur . . . moments when he, perceiving what the public thinks, what it likes and what it buys, will make some small sacrifices—will express this piece differently, and will omit that piece. And there is nothing more disastrous for Art (just by thinking about it I am horrified) than phrasing this piece differently or omitting that piece."[48]

On the whole, Constantine remained faithful throughout his life to his aesthetic beliefs. He made compromises, given his precarious financial situation, and thus worked all his life as a civil servant. But he rarely changed lines of his poems to please anybody other than himself. At the same time, however, he feared that by middle age he had compromised the sexual freedom of his youth. In a note from 1905, he grumbled that the "wretched laws of society . . . have diminished my work. They have inhibited my expressiveness."[49] This issue continued to trouble him all his life, as we can see in a conversation he had, twenty-five years later, and months before his death. In October 1932, the poet Napoleon Lapathiotis (1888–1944) and the Cavafy enthusiast Marios Vaianos (1905–75) came to visit him in his Athenian hotel just before he underwent cancer treatment. During the course of their exchange, it became clear that Napoleon was very open about his homosexuality, in contrast to Constantine, who rarely addressed it in public. Envious that Napoleon had chosen to live in a manner true to his own convictions, Constantine said: "I am very jealous, Napoleon, of your freedom, of the life you lead . . . It is as if you have your ideal Republic where you live and invite others for your company." And then he stopped. Napoleon, not wishing to impose on a sick man, responded, "But whoever wants to do something, Mr. Cavafy, can do something," adding that he tried to conduct the life he wanted and found in "Communism" the only "understanding." Whoever followed communism was free, he said. Ignoring the political reference, Constantine responded that such a life was impossible in Alexandria: "People there are very conservative. One surveils the other, through windows and through keyholes. Because of a few poems, they characterize me as unlawful and stigmatized." He added that he could not have led Napoleon's life in Alexandria, even though he wrote "daring poems which shocked but which people like and recite . . . without understanding their meaning and depth."[50]

This must have been a painful admission to make at the end of his life. First, as Sareyiannis commented, "while he concerned himself with sexual matters in his poetry, in his daily life he was almost prudish. It seems that he never made a self-revelation to anyone, apart from the generalities about the various stages of his life."[51] More important, that Constantine had acquiesced to Alexandrian morality undermined the image he had projected of himself in his early writing as someone who violated society's mores. He claimed, for instance, that between the years 1886 and 1891, he had lived such a dissolute nocturnal life that he became ill from "debauchery."[52] Sexual rebellion, he suggested in 1902, or what provocatively he called "depravity," was a source of poetic inspiration. It was important, he once said to Glafkos Alithersis, for the artist to breach moral norms.[53] He often told his friends that a poet, unlike politicians, businessmen, and scholars, must live his youth contrarily. The latter, however, "needing a clear mind," no longer required wild, nightly pleasures and thus gave up their debauchery to pursue practical life. But the artist found his inspiration in dissolute living and, therefore, should not control his excesses in the name of morality. When he himself tried to become "a better human being," he ran the risk of turning into an inferior artist. As a poet, Constantine confessed in a diary note of 1902, he was incapable of becoming successful in a "practical career," something that would have forced him to renounce his "hankering" for poetry. His "weakness" lay in his "inability to renounce literature."[54] Of course, he was practical in the detailed lists he kept all his life and had complete control of his finances. His position in the Office of the Irrigation Service was for him a way of earning a living so that he could further his true vocation—poetry.[55] His job as a scribe ensured his poetic independence. Not very onerous, it allowed him to return home and work on his poetry and receive guests with energy and determination. Despite enjoying a comfortable life, he forfeited the easy luxuries promised him by more lucrative employment.[56]

Constantine identified two ideas running through his poetry—artists need personal liberty to work creatively, and they must demolish social conventions in order to guarantee this artistic autonomy. The speaker of the unpublished "Invigorating" (1903?), for instance, declares that whoever wants to be initiated into knowledge must first free himself from respect and obedience. Not fearing the destructive act, he knows that "half the house must be wrecked." Poetic freedom, knowledge, and virtue all arise out of the rubble of social constraints. Yet however much he believed that art required moral corruption and perversion, Constantine's personal conduct from middle age on seems to have been far removed from the militancy and decadence featured in his poetry. Perhaps he felt that he had fulfilled these directives for dissolute living during his youth. As an adult, he led the life of the "practical" people he so despised in these early notes, ever careful not to provoke moral censure and always seeking the "approbation" of his social superiors, exactly as he confessed to Napoleon and Vaianos. Indeed, he often struck people not only as a gossip-avoiding bourgeois but also as obsequious and conventional. One evening, when an (unidentified) man entered his apartment, Constantine jumped up and almost embraced him, saying how grateful he was that he had come: "You saved me dear and I am so grateful to you for coming here." He was always eager for chatter about the families whose genealogical trees and social status he knew intimately. He would often name-drop: "Tomorrow I am invited by Antonis Benaki." "Timo [Malanos], try this mastiha. It's from Chios, sent to me by [Penelope] Delta." When Malanos saw him at the Benaki residence, Constantine was beaming.[57] And he was thrilled to have gotten an invitation to the wedding of the son of Mikes Salvagos in 1926.[58] In the letters he sent Alekos in Benha, he made sure to mention the times he was dining at the Benaki mansion, which was, after all, only minutes from his flat. Mr. and Mrs. Benaki "show me great friendship."[59] Like the protagonist of his short story "In Broad Daylight," who constantly felt the need to demonstrate his acceptance by the city's social elite—"I went to the wedding where all the best society of the city was in attendance"[60]—Constantine feared social rejection all his life.

Understandably he wanted to avoid scandal given how precarious his social position was as a homosexual in Alexandria.

He could never forget that at any moment he could be rejected as a pariah, especially with the trial of Oscar Wilde and the author's imprisonment and social ostracism seared in his memory.[61] Despite the much-vaunted cosmopolitanism of Alexandria, it could not tolerate open and ostentatious homosexuality. Sareyannis described Alexandria as "narrow-minded." Moreover, the dominant social class had embraced a restrictive Victorian morality especially before 1914: "Cavafy would have risked being shut out from the houses of his own people, he ran the risk of being excommunicated, of not being greeted, he ran the risk—I have in mind certain incidents—of being exiled from the city he loved."[62] Malanos often heard malicious gossip about Constantine's sexuality even among the literary and liberal circles of the city. One day, Malanos was approached by a "cultivated" man who said, "He [John] was a gentleman but that other one . . ." Malanos did not complete the sentence, but one assumes his interlocutor must have used a crude expression about Constantine.[63] For this reason, even in his later years, with his poetic reputation secure, he followed a double strategy of publishing scandalously frank erotic verses while maintaining discretion about his own life.[64]

He said as much in another personal note (June 20, 1910), that "my erotic life *does* get declared—obscure only to the ignorant. Were it declared more extensively, it might not prove sufficient artistic ground to hold me, to sustain me." He came to believe that this tension between openly acknowledging homosexuality in his poetry and censoring himself in life actually inspired and "sustained" his creativity. In this, he went about it "like the ancients," who wrote history, philosophy, and drama through "desire."[65] He preferred, after all, to sift life through his work. "Artistic impressions sometimes go unused for long periods; they produce other thoughts, are reshaped by fresh influences."[66] Constantine believed that he could heighten art's intensity by concealing his passions.

For all sorts of practical and aesthetic reasons, he said little about his sexuality. As noted, he referred obliquely to an infatuation with Alex Mavroudis in Athens in 1903 that gave rise to a number of poems. In the sexually fluid situation of the Mediterranean, where men were less constrained by the rigid divisions between homosexuality and heterosexuality, it is quite possible that he could have had intimate relations with Mavroudis or other friends, or with bisexual men who eventually married. He wrote the poem "In Despair" (1923) about such a possibility. The speaker laments having been abandoned by his lover and having to seek his lips in the lips of others. But the second stanza explains that the man wanted to "save" himself from a stigmatized life and possibly marry:

> *He lost him completely, as if he had never been.*
> *Because—as he said—he wanted to be saved*
> *from that inverted, that unhealthy pleasure;*
> *from that inverted, that shameful pleasure.*
> *There was still a chance—he said—to save himself.*

Constantine even wrote a cryptic note about this poem, perhaps around 1923, referring more generally to the experience described in the poem. He spoke of the "half homosexual," the man who ended up going with women in order to gain social acceptance. The jilted lover then falls into "desperation," not only because he has been abandoned by his partner but also because his love has been declared "shameful." How hard it is, "when, as it often happens, the lover says that he now needs a woman. Or when he is a timid boy who has a penchant for women; or when he sees that he is possessed completely by that other [pleasure] which he has to hide anxiously from the world as something shameful. And this is why he calls it 'shameful' in his exasperation."[67]

In "Days of 1896" a man of thirty has ruined himself because of his "erotic tendency" that was "innate." But it was not his fault at all. His "prudish" society with its "silly" judgments was to blame. Constantine composed the poem in 1925 and published it two years later. In his sixties, he could write with dispassionate psychological insight about experiences that would have been painful when he was younger and more vulnerable to life's disappointments and to the possible punishments meted out by a rigid morality.

The evolution of his erotic poems makes this clear. At the beginning of his career, he was unsure how much sexual content he could reveal. At first, he resolved this dilemma by composing sensual rather than erotic lines. Poems with titles such as "Longings" (1904) alluded unthreateningly to "unfulfilled desires" rather than to men touching each other. At other times, he referred to "illegal" pleasure as a code for same-sex relations. In three poems written between 1913 and 1917, he used three words, whose base was "nomos" (law) but with three different prefixes to indicate lawbreaking. "In the Street" (1913/1916) speaks of "lawless pleasure"; in "The Window of the Tobacco Store" (1907/1917), he writes about "illegal desire"; and "Passing" celebrates "outlawed sexual intoxication." In time, as he began to point to concrete individuals, he camouflaged their gender by exploiting the characteristic of the Greek verb not to require personal pronouns. Only after 1922 did he explicitly define the figures as men. "In an Old Book" (1922*) refers to a watercolor the speaker finds in an antique volume. Although unsigned, the picture bears a title "Depiction of Love." But looking at the representation of the young man, the speaker thinks that a more fitting title would be "Depiction of love of daring aesthetes" because the artist did not wish to portray a youth "intended" for those who "love decently," but rather for those who appreciate "abnormal attractions." In his own experimentation with ekphrasis, the genre of poetry that describes visual works of art, Constantine brazenly celebrates male beauty and refers to the "anomalous" or "abnormal" individual, his ironic reference to a love that violates the rules. And in subsequent poems, such as "Two Young Men, Twenty-Three to Twenty-Four Years Old" (1927*), the veiled homoerotic themes of texts such as "I Went" (1905/1913), "Body Remember" (1916/1918), and "To Remain" (1918/1919) give way to unapologetically sexual relations between men. No one can underestimate his courage in speaking so openly about men loving men, especially when we compare his attitude with the reticence of his contemporaries like Wilfred Owen (1893–1918). Although Owen was much younger and lived for a time in more cosmopolitan cities like London, he eschewed any direct or even indirect references to homosexuality in his verse. His reluctance to write about gay eros or to address it in hushed references in his correspondence only shows how remarkably daring Constantine was.

Ultimately, despite all his efforts, he did not feel completely free to express his sexuality, as he acknowledged to Napoleon. He gave voice to the tension he felt all his life between his desire to reveal and his need to hide in "Hidden" (1908), which he never published but which, since its posthumous publication in 1968, has become of one his most popular and most revealing compositions:[68]

They shouldn't try to find out who I was
from what I did or what I said.
An obstacle kept on altering

my actions and my way of life.
An obstacle kept on blocking me
when I was about to speak.
Only from my most obscure actions
and my most shrouded writings
will they understand me.
But maybe it isn't worth the trouble
so much bother to get to know me.
In the future—in a more perfect society—
someone made like me
will certainly appear and live more freely.

It's hard not to think of this poem autobiographically, written by a man in 1908 still struggling to express his sexual self through his verses. The poem ends optimistically with a reference to the future in a more open society. Although known as a poet of the inner space, of gloomy poems like "Walls" and "The City," here Constantine speaks prophetically about the decades to come. Like Forster's *Maurice*, written in 1913–14 but posthumously published in 1971, it imagines hopefully a society where gay men would not have to cloak their thoughts and their actions.

No one knew if Constantine was a happy person. He certainly derived joy from his poems. This was his principal preoccupation after his forties, the point when he resolved to live for and write great work. A year before composing "Hidden," he recorded a note in which he expressed his resentment at not being sufficiently recognized and admired: "How unjust it is for me to be such a genius and neither to be known everywhere nor get rewarded."[69] As he gradually acquired a greater reputation, however, Constantine could no longer keep private his feelings about his self-worth and openly boasted of his outsize talents. When a group of students once asked him who he thought Greece's best poet was, he answered, "You mean after me . . ."[70] Atanasio Catraro averred that Constantine never wavered from seeing himself as a pathbreaking artist in a league with the most illustrious poets. He not only endeavored to silence his critics with his success but also sought "rare subject matter" and "scandalous verses" with which to distance his work from that of traditional Greek poets. He strove to be both a Greek and a global poet;[71] and he often bragged that not one of his poems resembled another, each one constituting its own world.[72]

Constantine put most of his psychic energy into his future goal at the expense of human relationships. Through his interactions with the poet, Sareyiannis came to believe that Constantine lived for his poetry; he "devoted all his life to Art" and "considered every detail when it concerned his work or the fate of his work."[73] In fact, if someone had suggested that his work would not survive, he felt that he would die of dejection.[74] One solitary night in 1903, Constantine gave voice to his fear of dying unknown, unable to secure his place in the pantheon of world writers: "Yesterday I vaguely considered, it crossed my thoughts, the possibility of literary failure, & I felt suddenly as if all charm would have left my life, I felt an acute pang at the very idea. I at once imagined my having the enjoyment of love—as I understand & want it—& even this seemed—& very clearly seemed—as if it would not have been sufficient to console me of the great deception."[75] That he now set love and poetry as opposites indicates that from that point the major objective in his life was to reach the pinnacle in the "Stepladder of Poetry." This juxtaposition of affection and art only confirmed what those around him were claiming, namely that he valued his triumph in poetry more than the touch of intimacy. In the past, as he suggested in this note, human relations could compensate for life's setbacks; he rationalized disappointment by reminding himself of his affection for other people. But love no longer sufficed.

This explains why people found him charming and erudite, but cold, guarded, and inscrutable. Although he greeted people on the streets or in a shop with a "Hello, friend," in reality he had few close friends.[76] To appreciate the profound change Constantine had undergone in his capacity to form and maintain ties of affinity, we could look again at his anxious thoughts and preoccupations in the journal he kept during Mikès Ralli's illness in 1889. This journal shows Constantine's profound capacity for emotional warmth in his youth. It is the same picture of tenderness that emerges in the epistolary exchange he had with John a couple of years earlier during his stay in Istanbul. John wrote on March 8, 1883: "In one of your letters you say you feel my absence: this is fully reciprocated by me. It is now over 7 months that I have been separated from you, and yet I think 'tis years when I look back at the time elapsed."[77] From John's responses it is possible to grasp how kindhearted Constantine was and how close he felt to his older brother to whom he wrote almost weekly. The loyal friend and the trusting brother was also an affectionate son, as is manifestly clear in the journal Constantine kept during the final months of his mother's illness and eventual death in 1899. Throughout her tribulations, he acted as the loyal, empathic, if not always selfless, caregiver. But the person who experienced these feelings of love and remorse, of tenderness and guilt, somehow faded away in the coming decades. Or, if he maintained such feelings, he kept them well-hidden. We have little evidence of this considerate and compassionate man in any later text of his or in the testimony of any other person, except for a note he scribbled down for Rika in his final hours.[78] On the contrary, we have much documentation of his selfishness, inwardness, and fanatical pursuit of his own interests. The individual who wrote the journals about departed loved ones seems largely to have disappeared along with the rejected poems. It is as if after 1911 we have not only a distinct poetry but also a different person.

In one respect, Constantine transferred his capacity for grief into his writing, as so many of his poems have funerary themes and show individuals in deep sorrow for the loss of their friends or family members. In other words, the traumas of loss and grief that marked his early years matured into a mastery of the elegiacal. In "The Month of Hathor" (1917), a modern speaker examines before him an ancient inscription, attempting to decipher its meaning among the disfigured letters. After some effort, he makes out that the deceased's name was Lefkios, that he died at the age of twenty-seven, and that he was adored by his family. Indeed, the speaker puzzles out words like "our tears," "pain," and our "sorrow":

With difficulty I read on the ancient stone.
"Ky[ri]e Jesus Christ." I detect a "So[u]l.
"In the mo[nth] of Hathor" "Lefkio[s] went to [sleep]."
The reference to his age "He spent his years,"
the Kappa Zeta shows that Lefkios went to sleep as a young man.
In the following damaged section I see "Hi[m] . . . Alexandrian."
The next three lines are quite defaced;
But I discern a few words— "our t[e]ars," "pain,"
Then again "tears," and to [u]s his [f]riends sorrow.
It seems that Lefkios was deeply loved.
In the month of Hathor Lefkios went to sleep.

Even though separated by two thousand years from Lefkios—an expanse of time typographically rendered in the poem by the caesura dividing each line—the speaker is able to establish an empathic link between himself and the deceased. And in "Myris: Alexandria of 340 AD" (1929*), Constantine published one of his most powerful poems. Written in the form of a dramatic monologue, it follows the speaker, a pagan, who arrives at the house of his recently departed friend, Myris, a Christian: "I stood and cried in a corner of the corridor," he says. Fearful of entering the room where the Christian Myris is laid out among his relatives, the speaker recalls moments of happiness he shared with his mate: reciting Greek verse, drinking with friends, and going on outings. In stanzas of varying length, which alternate between describing the speaker's internal state and what he sees in the Christian house, he comes to question his friendship. In the course of the funeral, however, where he stands as a distant observer, he recalls a number of episodes that should have indicated to him that religion separated them in ways neither young man understood. And now, incapable of even touching Myris's body, he wonders if they were always "strangers" to each other. He then rushes out of their "horrible house" before the Christian zeal of the relatives could seize even the memory of Myris.

His many funerary poems attest that Constantine was capable of writing lines of intense pathos and of portraying individuals weighed down by unbearable tragedy. But he seems to have lost this capacity in his own life—to understand other people, to stand in their shoes, so to speak. The Constantine of middle age and beyond little resembled the kindhearted young man. It is not without justification that many contemporaries found him "cynical" and "cold."[79] Of course, most people change with age. It was to be expected that in retirement, Constantine would focus exclusively on his work, even engaging in fewer social outings. But fear of failure was a motivating factor in his life, as we have seen in the private notes he occasionally jotted down. Significantly, he addressed this topic in his poetry, specifically in "The City," one of his most famous poems, which he wrote in 1894 at the age of thirty-one but published in 1910, sixteen years later.

You said, "I'll travel to another land, another sea.
I need to find another city better than this one.
Whatever I do here is doomed.
And my heart, as if lifeless, lies entombed.
How long will my mind disintegrate here?
Wherever I turn, whatever I look at
I see the dark ruins of my life,
where I have spent so many years, wrecking and ruining them."

You won't find new countries or other oceans.
This city will pursue you. You will roam
the same streets. You'll grow old in the same neighborhoods,
turn gray in the same houses.

You will always end up in this city. Don't hope for another—
there is no ship for you, no way out.
Having squandered your life here
in this narrow corner, you've wasted it everywhere.

Readers of "The City" often wonder how a young man could have conceived such a despondent work about closure and collapse. The speaker of the first stanza expresses the desire to change location and leave behind the debris of his life. But a more sober second-person voice forecloses the possibility of transformation, uttering perhaps the bleakest lines in the Cavafian oeuvre.[80]

In the same year, 1894, Constantine drafted a poem with a similar theme, titled "Whoever Has Failed," which he kept, like many others, with a note clipped on the sheet in English: "Not for publication but may remain here." "Whoever has failed, whoever drops down low / how difficult it is to learn poverty's / new language and new ways." The poem then goes on to describe the indignities of a proud person who had to demean himself, to "speak humbly," to bend his once "lofty head." He picks up cruel words that cut into him: "You pretend that you don't hear them / that you are simple and don't understand." This unpublished poem is not a far-fetched description of the family's financial situation and forced peregrinations after the death of his father in 1870. At the age of forty, weighed down with memories of penury, facing the humiliation of working as a civil servant, unmarried and without any relations of intimacy, his only deliverance seemed to be his art. Without any other guardian angel in his life, he could not contemplate any reversals to his grand plans. Quite simply, art became for him compensatory, making up for all of life's disappointments and deficiencies.

Not surprisingly, he turned this view of poetry as redemption into a dominant poetic theme, best expressed in "I Brought to Art" (1921). The poem shows how Constantine saw art as a mediator in life between an imperfect present and a more blissful past. Lost in reverie, the speaker recollects "half-seen" faces and lines of incomplete and unfulfilled relationships. But he carries these "uncertain memories" to "Art," asking "her" to create "Forms of Beauty," to perfect life by stitching together impressions of the past, making up for the loveless present. In this and many other poems, poetry works as a healer, soothing the pain of existence, alleviating anxieties about the passing of youth and the loss of love. A restorative proxy, poetry supersedes human weakness and motivations:

I sit and daydream.   Longings and sensations
I brought to art—   things half-seen,

faces or lines;   uncertain memories
of frustrated loves.   Let me surrender to it.
Art knows how to fashion   Forms of Beauty;
almost imperceptibly   perfecting life,
combining impressions,   combining days.

In the eighteen years between the publication of this poem and the earlier private notes of anguish that the world had not recognized his talents and of fear that he would turn into a failure like his brother, Constantine had deified art as deliverer and rescuer. This elevation of art explains in part the complaints made by his friends that his obsession with his work came at the cost of his personal relationships.[81] He had, after all, very little else.

After the "period of emendation," Constantine seems either to have given up on the possibility of love or sacrificed it in his mission to create great literature. In the high-stakes game of poetic glory, he risked it all. Charming, open to conversation, and eager to perform, while emotionally he seemed to many like an empty shell. For this reason, people came to believe that Cavafy the poet had no existence outside his writing, his life being "his best poem"[82] or that he had "turned his life into art."[83] It would be more accurate to say that he did not distinguish between existence and art. Rika understood this as well and made an insightful observation. As a young man facing the pressures of life, Constantine turned to pleasure for redemption: "Later, when his work was established and he found his own way, he discovered salvation in art." He came to terms with his personal tragedy by bringing into art the "few happy moments of his life."[84]

Many people close to him in Alexandria or those who had visited him from afar saw in Constantine that rare being—a genius pursuing aesthetic perfection no matter what the personal cost. Few pitied him for this. And he certainly did not feel sorry for himself. It is quite possible that he understood his situation as an advantage, realizing that it was impossible to adore one particular individual while striving for kudos. In his zealous pursuit of *arete* and *kleos* (excellence and fame), he believed that love of one person and love of greatness were incompatible.

Part V

CULTIVATING FAME

11

THE QUEST FOR GLORY

"OF THE SHOP" (1912/1913)

He wrapped them with care and skill
in precious green silk.

Roses from rubies, lilies from pearls,
violets from amethysts; the way he determines,

desires, and perceives them as beautiful. Not what he saw
and observed in nature. He will store them in the safe,

creations of his daring, expert work.
When a patron enters the shop

he offers to sell other things—wonderful ornaments—
bracelets, chains, necklaces, and rings.

Constantine did not become a global poet by following the defeatist principles of his imaginary artist in "Of the Shop." This unnamed craftsman prefers to keep his most prized creations in his safe, which he labels "daring" because he fashions them in his mind rather than copying them from nature. Instead of selling what he truly values, he says ironically that he offers customers "wonderful ornaments," "bracelets, chains, necklaces, and rings" and unoriginal things. Indifferent to praise and other monetary rewards, he, rather than his buyers, defines what qualifies as art.[1]

Constantine often saw himself as the artist he portrayed in this poem, as someone withdrawn from life. Speaking through A. G. Simeonidis, the coeditor of *Alexandrini Techni*, Constantine said that he "did not impose himself" on others to become "the greatest poet in Greece." Distributing his poems for free while declining offers by British presses to produce a translation of his poems, he struggled all his life to maintain his independence. Not "a professional poet," Constantine was a genuine artist like Dante or Goethe, a man who loved his work.[2] In other words, he projected a picture of himself as an idealistic poet, unconcerned with the publishing world and the views of others. And he drew the same portrait of himself eighteen years earlier to Pavlos Petridis, a doctor who gave the first ever lecture on the poet in Alexandria. It was only Constantine's "excessive modesty," Petridis observed, that impeded his wider recognition.[3]

In the course of his life, people attached many epithets to Constantine but rarely that of humility. On the contrary, he did everything possible to push his reputation, first in his city and then in Greece and Europe. Although he identified himself as a poet on his last passport, as he himself admitted, it was impossible to earn a living through poetry. While he may have portrayed himself as a "genuine artist" and while he may have wished to behave like the artisan in "Of the Shop"—that is, as a pathbreaking poet not beholden to public tastes—in real life he thirsted for recognition, while denying that he was treating poetry like a commercial transaction.[4] In his actions, he behaved like the professional poet he belittled, one completely given to the promotion of his poems. And he withheld in his study only those texts he considered unfinished or inferior.

In his drive for fame, he resembled the poet in "He Is the One," which he wrote in 1898 but did not publish until 1909. In this poem, an anonymous poet in the ancient Syrian capital of Antioch toils away on his final canto, having completed eighty-three already. He is exhausted with "so much writing, so much lyricism" that he feels weighted down by even "small things." Only one thought delivers him from his "despair," a "brilliant" line from the ancient writer Lucian of Samosata (120–180 CE), the satirical author who traveled throughout the eastern Mediterranean and who wrote "with wit and biting condemnation" about the "pretensions" of contemporary intellectuals.[5] Apparently in his dream, the figure of Culture appeared to the young but impoverished Lucian, promising that one day he would become illustrious and that everyone would point to him with the phrase "he is the one." Like this imaginary poet, Constantine yearned to be identified in the crowd as "the one," the celebrated author Cavafy. These two poems, "Of the Shop" and "He Is the One," capture the contradictory way Constantine saw himself as a creative person. While he peopled his verses with isolated artists who were contemptuous of readers' tastes, in practice he seduced young men to become fanatical disciples for his work. Whereas he portrayed himself as a misunderstood poet, composing lines alone in his apartment, he advanced his poetry in Alexandria like a PR spokesman.

No episode better illustrates this conflict between his professed dedication to ideal beauty and the aggressive manner by which he pushed his work on others than his forceful confrontation with an influential Athenian editor and critic while receiving cancer treatment in Athens in the summer of 1932. Visitors who flocked to the Hotel Cosmopolite to meet the great poet described a man understandably dejected and frightened about the coming operation. Yet despite his dire circumstances, Constantine made sure he saw Giorgos Katsimbalis, the "colossus" of Henry Miller's *The Colossus of Maroussi*, who had published that very year the first bibliography on Cavafy in the periodical *Kyklos*. In five and a half single-spaced pages, this work attested to the wide reach of the poet's work one year before his death. In addition to collecting material by Greek writers, Katsimbalis enumerated articles by foreign authors in English, French, Italian, and German. He also listed translations of poems in the same languages. Amid all the intellectuals and poets who had come to see him in the hotel, Constantine pulled Katsimbalis over and quizzed him on various matters of his bibliography to make sure that Katsimbalis did in fact know how extensive this critical commentary was. Once satisfied, he said: "Make sure, Katsimbalis, to provide a title [to your bibliography] to suggest that there exist many other citations about Cavafy which your work does not include, such as, for instance 'From Cavafy's Bibliography' or 'Selections from Cavafy's Bibliography.' For God's sake, don't write that it is complete lest you run the risk of exposing yourself and be accused of ignoring all the other works written about Cavafy."[6] Katsimbalis was taken aback by Constantine's insistent manner and his presumption that he would publish something incomplete.

Constantine's behavior that day may have been overly assertive, especially in light of his serious illness, but it was not exceptional. Aristos Kampanis remembers being pulled over after a talk he had given on the poet, who complained that the lecture was "unworthy of him" and to suggest that, before publishing it, he should change it. "For your benefit and not for mine." From this experience Kampanis came to understand that Constantine "propagandized day and night for his reputation."[7] Having seen Constantine coax, plead, and cajole others into reading and advancing his poetry, Kampanis seemed crestfallen and concluded, "He loved his glory."

Although Constantine never hesitated to intervene directly on his own behalf, he preferred to work by proxy. When Athanasios Politis wanted material on Cavafy for his second volume on the Greeks of Egypt, he sought, as noted earlier, the assistance of Nikos and Eftychia Zelitas. Finding this an ideal opportunity to advance his work in such an influential book, Constantine himself dictated the text to Eftychia. Not surprisingly, he painted a sketch of himself as a highly original poet who had attained "a prominent position in modern Greek literature."[8] Perhaps the most striking sentence in the entire section is: "Whether one loves the poetry or not, that which remains undeniable, as all his critics aver, is that this poetry is entirely original and that nothing like it exists anywhere else in the world."[9] Politis's book then ended up affirming Constantine's view of his own poetry "as so original—as distinct from other poetic productions in Greece or abroad—that it constitutes a distinguished body of work."[10]

To bolster this reputation and address the ever-increasing number of attacks his work was provoking, Constantine established, as noted, *Alexandrini Techni* in December 1926.[11] Although the journal printed poetry and essays by and about other poets and authors, it served as a pro-Cavafy platform, showcasing his poems and articles about his work. The anonymous "Notes" section at the end of each issue hosted laudatory reviews of and lectures on Cavafy. It also featured rejoinders to hostile articles, such as, for instance, the response to a negative article in the journal *Pnoï* in which the anonymous author in *Alexandrini Techni* said that "the importance of the Cavafian oeuvre—not only in Greece but also in Europe—is that it introduces into the world of poetry new poetic form, a new poetic sensibility, and new poetic possibilities."[12] If Constantine had not been the author of this and similar pieces, then he probably directed them. His voice and hand were the instruments behind the unsigned views.[13]

From the shadows of his apartment, Constantine fed the lines to his supporters, rather like a ventriloquist. And by the last two decades of his life, his efforts had paid off. Never celebrated as a national poet,[14] he had become instead a celebrity in his home city. Alexandrians knew him and heard of him, even if they had not necessarily read his poetry. He made his presence felt, often spreading rumors about himself to spark the interest of others. As a result, people recognized him on the streets or wished to meet him. "How is it possible for Alexandria to have such a great man and for us not to know him?" they would say. Ordinary people would ask Yiorgos Vrisimitzakis[15] how they could meet the poet. One afternoon, sitting with Constantine and a friend in a café, Vrisimitzakis addressed himself in the vocative to the poet, "Mr. Cavafy." At that point the waiter, his eyes beaming, asked if he was indeed about to serve the real Cavafy. When Vrisimitzakis nodded in the affirmative, the waiter stood stationary, in awe of the great man before him.[16]

Atanasio Catraro had heard much about the poet before he finally met him at his home through the intervention of Sengopoulos. When eventually he found himself standing in the poet's salon, staring at the "creased and dry face," which bore a set of round spectacles, Catraro sensed immediately that this man was hiding within himself a "serene mystery."[17] Catraro realized that Constantine wanted people to comment on his strangeness and to peel off layers of costume and mask.[18] Malanos felt he was witnessing something theatrical the first day he met him.[19] And every time he visited the apartment, Malanos waited for Constantine to appear as an "actor" to stage the ensuing conversation. This theatricality is what struck Glafkos Alithersis upon meeting Constantine in 1919. He quickly fell under the poet's spell, only to turn against him because of his constant self-promotion.[20] Konstantinos Ftyaras, who took weekly lessons in history from Constantine in the late 1920s, describes how he and other boys would identify the figure of the poet from a distance as a "strange being," whispering his name in wonder. Ftyaras remembered his large, protruding, "chameleon-like" eyes and his sacerdotal expression that provoked ambivalence and wonder in those around him. He seemed to his schoolmates an imposing person, full of gravitas. Yet one day, he appeared for the lesson uncharacteristically in his long johns.[21] Ftyaras couldn't understand how the imperious poet, so consummate in his dress otherwise, could emerge in his parlor in such an undignified manner. But this paradox was part of the Cavafy mystique.[22]

Constantine played to the public curiosity about him. In the office, his fellow "English" employees found him captivating. Ibrahim el Kayar remembers that Constantine "must have fascinated them, for they often called him into their offices, and got him to talk about historical matters. The English were delighted with him." And Constantine himself was "talkative and agreeable with the English."[23] And he was especially charming at home, since he expected much of learned Alexandria and Greece to come to his house.[24] In addition to being a gracious host, he tried to flatter his visitors with his uncanny capacity to pinpoint their vanity. For instance, when he met the young Sareyiannis in 1915, Constantine praised his parents and ancestors. And after Sareyiannis published essays on two historical poems, he began to refer to the young author's alleged expertise in the Hellenistic period. One day, when he mentioned the historian Plutarch in Sareyiannis's presence, he added: "But why do I need to say anything about this. Yiannis here knows these things better than me. Yianni, you should be saying these things. Am I not right here, Yianni?"[25] This seemed disingenuous to those around them because Constantine knew Plutarch by heart. Others, however, did not succumb to his compliments. One day, when he remarked to the young poet Nikos Santorinios, "What lovely eyes you have, Niko," Santorinios replied with annoyance, "What beauty do you find in them, Mr. Cavafy, when one of them is cross-eyed. I don't like flattery."[26]

His discourse cascaded in front of his listeners with humor, irony, sophistication, and historical references. Those who heard him read his own poetry attest to being transported into his imaginative universe. On the evening of her visit, Constantine invited Myrtiotissa to read one of his poems. Having selected "Gray," she recited it and then, with some hesitation, asked him to read the very poem himself. "How much sorrow and melancholy reverberated through his shallow voice, when he said, 'The gray eyes will have turned ugly—if he's still alive; that beautiful face will have spoiled.' And that invocation 'Dear memory, guard them as they were,' like a sob. What a pity we didn't have the means to record him. We would have a Cavafy completely alive."[27]

Sareyiannis believed that his oral performances were as captivating as his poetry. He describes the magical spell Constantine's words cast upon him, his hours spent with the poet being the most enriching experience in his life. "Each time he changed perspective, referred to another opinion, or opened one of his unending parentheses, he changed voice and mimetic tone, as if suddenly another person were speaking."[28] Malanos, always a harsh and unforgiving critic, hailed Constantine's conversational skills as "enchanting" and "seductive." He would open "ten parentheses, one after another, only to close them after a while one after the other, like a miracle-worker of words."[29]

Upon meeting Constantine in the offices of *Grammata* in 1926, the young Memas Kolaitis was taken by the poet's "labyrinthine thinking," which for the "attentive listener, had the flow of a passage from an ancient Greek text, where a long sentence never needs an asterisk referring to a footnote for an interpretive aside." And he could never forget Constantine's voice, "soft and suggestive as a liturgical chant then sharp and clear-cut as staccato bursts."[30] Sareyiannis regrets not having written down his conversations with the poet. And he mourns that Constantine did not have his own Eckermann to record his thoughts. If we had these conversations, he writes, they would be lauded as being on a par with his poetry.[31]

Constantine's emphasis on performance came at a cost, however. Rarely interested in the opinions of others, he tended to intimidate his listeners and dominate the discussion. At a dinner hosted by an Alexandrian doctor, Constantine found himself with a distinguished professor of history. But wanting to flaunt his own knowledge of the ancient world, he turned the whole conversation into a monologue on various Hellenistic dynasties. As if this had not been enough, he sought to silence the professor with a single question: "In the second century BC . . . do you remember, Professor, Armenia's southern borders?" The man could not; nor did he admit his ignorance. So, he sat there wordless, another victim of Constantine's penchant to brandish his erudition and to subdue his listeners with his superior grasp of historical facts. Sakellaris Yiannakakis, a well-known autodidact, similarly discovered this when one day at the bookstore Grammata, he was pontificating on the economy as the most important agent of historical change. Provoked by such a simplistic approach to history, Constantine asked if other factors contributed to social transformation. When the man said no, Constantine then asked, "And how then could you explain that in AD 600 half the population of Egypt withdrew into the monasteries, an important fact, and, don't interrupt me (no one was interrupting him); and it was not only the poor who went but people from all social classes."[32] Yiannakakis and those around him stood in silence, perhaps out of fear or embarrassment. No one could challenge Constantine's grasp of Hellenistic history, not even experts.[33] At the same time, he re-created historical periods for his listeners, allowing them to experience "the agonies and the problems of these epochs."[34] Constantine's capacity to breathe life into ancient figures is what the young Ftyaras remembered from his tutorials with the poet.[35]

As discussed in chapter two, Constantine developed an intense interest in Greek history in his twenties, if not earlier. And he revealed his confidence in himself as a historian in the notes he wrote on Edward Gibbon that show the still-untried young man correcting the giant of Roman historiography.[36] Eventually he turned his extensive knowledge of the ancient past into one of the hallmarks of his poetry. In poem after poem, Constantine delighted in showing the foibles of kings, the vanity of poets, and the inability of people to see how the world around had changed. Yet his contemporaries noted a paradox in Constantine's painterly capacity to create historical portraits. The man who could analyze the motivations of ancient figures seemed indifferent to the internal lives of his acquaintances. Sareyiannis believed that Constantine was not a "psychologist"—that is, he rarely concerned himself with the hopes, anxieties, and motivations of other people. Intensely preoccupied with the "analysis of his own self," he was rarely able to transcend the limitations of his own ego. People were for him like "heavy and difficult volumes" at the edges of his bookcase.[37] Even Rika, who was devoted to him perhaps more than any other individual, believed that his chief fault lay in "wanting everyone's focus turned towards him." As the youngest child in the family and his mother's favorite, he demanded attention.[38] Malanos was less charitable. "In each new acquaintance," he wrote, "he foresees admiration and the furtherance of his work. He expects complete dedication from others without reciprocity."[39] Anyone approaching him for sympathy would have found in his face an "inhospitable desert." He recognized nobody beyond himself and loved no one, especially after middle age.[40]

So, if he had so little curiosity in others, contemporaries wondered, how had he managed to persuade young men to become fanatical followers? For some, the answer lay in the way he grasped the mutually advantageous interaction between a charismatic figure and his enthusiasts, with the star giving of himself and the fan desiring to communicate with fame. Like attractive personalities in politics, entertainment, or business, Constantine sought out potential admirers by making himself as captivating as his poetry and then demanding tacitly that they pay attention to him. Most important, he persuaded these young men to believe that their lives were enriched by knowing him and talking to him. He then enticed them to publicize his work by offering copies of his poems.

Of course, other writers in history had assembled a group of partisans or partaken in a mutually supportive community, like the Bloomsbury authors in post–World War II London or the intellectuals of the Weimar Republic in interwar Germany. Constantine, however, created something different: a band of true believers who had taken on as their life's ambition not only to defend his work but also to evangelize it. For this reason, he never aspired to forge a school of little "Cavafys," epigones who would write in his mode, though many mimicked or parodied his work. Not wanting fellow poets as competitors, he preferred to create critics and readers.[41] Glafkos Alithersis, who had fallen under the poet's spell upon his arrival from Cyprus, understood early on that Constantine's genius lay in getting others to spread the message.[42] Constantine had come to understand that greatness signified the capacity of one individual to fashion a new reality and then to convince others to embrace and to transmit it further.[43]

Even though his time with Constantine was quite limited to three or four encounters, the novelist and critic Stratis Tsirkas soon realized that his life had changed.[44] Having discovered Constantine's revolutionary poetry and novel conceptualization of history at the age of nineteen, he immediately felt the calling. He later referred to his "good fortune" in getting to know the poet, and came to believe how unhappy or invalid his life would have felt without this mission.[45] After Constantine's death, Tsirkas devoted himself to explicating his work, turning into one of the most influential of Cavafy's subsequent interpreters, with two major volumes and many articles on the poet. By the time Constantine met Tsirkas in 1930, the poet had perfected his strategies of binding young men in a net of attraction and persuasion. He made them feel, as Tsirkas himself confessed, blessed to have engaged themselves with his poetry.[46]

At the same time, of course, he enjoyed their company tremendously, as we see in his interaction with Napoleon Lapathiotis, who had come to Alexandria in 1917 at the age of twenty-nine, as second lieutenant, in the company of his father, the general and defense minister Leonidas Lapathiotis.[47] In his autobiography, Napoleon writes how Constantine sought him out and then showered him with attention in his apartment, lighting his finely made "damask lamps" and serving his special cognac in his prized red glasses. He showed the same enthusiasm when Napoleon and Marios Vaianos paid him a visit in his Athens hotel room during the fall of 1932, days before his surgery. Clearly animated by their appearance at his door, Constantine exclaimed to Napoleon how "you were constantly in my mind and I conjured you alive, just like that time, whenever I came upon a poem of yours."[48] He then took a seat at the foot of the bed and beckoned to Napoleon to come next to him, looking Napoleon straight in the eyes, "as if erotically." Gradually he placed "his left hand on his shoulders and with his right hand stroked his two thighs tenderly and playfully, constantly and with warmth." Feeling awkward, Vaianos withdrew onto the balcony. Upon his return, he found them both staring at the eyes of the other "in unbroken exultation." And then, as if to break the spell, Constantine reminded his guest of the pleasant time they had spent together in Alexandria.: "It was very lovely, when you came. Young, very young . . . But now you are the same, Dorian Gray—and even more young."[49] In the narration of the story, Vaianos implied that the relationship between Napoleon and Constantine was sensual and flirtatious. But it was also bound by Napoleon's love of Constantine's poetry, which he praised and promoted.[50]

Christopher Scaife (1900–88), the English poet and scholar, who met Constantine through E. M. Forster in 1929, sent gushing and effusive letters.[51] On March 31, 1930, he wrote, "I can't tell you how much I am looking forward to meeting you again—for to me, when I think of you, it seems only a day since the delightful period of our intimacy. If there is any strangeness or stiffness, I warn you, it will be on your responsibility, for I am, as I was, with much love. Your enthusiast, Christopher."[52] He addressed Constantine as "Revered and Beloved Greek" and "Dearest and most-revered Poet." In one letter (September 29, 1930), he expressed his determination to translate some of Constantine's poetry, and indeed, the two entered into a translating collaboration, what Scaife playfully termed "a séance of dictation" (December 19, 1930). His letter of February 22, 1932, bears testimony to their shared "polishing" of the poem "The Hall

Mirror": "The repetition of 'things & faces' I warrant by the repetition 'seen & seen', which is in my rough draught, & is of great value for the creation of weight at the end."[53]

While he opened up himself in his letters, Scaife was crushed to discover, like many others before him, how little Constantine revealed of himself. He complained: "Will you, therefore, spare me a few of your treasured letters to reassure me as to your existence and, I hope, good health?" (October 16, 1930). A similar disappointment was felt by Sareyiannis, who had also come to understand that Constantine rarely spoke about his personal life, except for "generalities about different stages of his life."[54] Kostas Ouranis came from Athens seeking insights into the poet's genius. During their entire conversation, however, Constantine was charming but guarded, preventing Ouranis from unearthing anything of his "mysterious psychic world." He thus departed Alexandria "without getting to know the Cavafy I sought." When Ouranis visited the poet in his hospital room in Athens a year later, he expected to find a vulnerable man but left without penetrating his "deep soul."[55]

All these enthusiasts eventually came to realize that in the last two decades of his life Constantine was interested in neither self-revelation nor emotional intimacy. He was animated by their presence and may have felt a sexual pull toward them. Flattered by the attention they were receiving from such a famous poet, they did not always appreciate that he saw them as potential envoys of his work. While they may have been disappointed to step out of his apartment without gaining access to his soul, they carried with them something more prized—his poetic collections.

Such was the case of the actor and future director Alexis Minotis, who arrived in Alexandria around 1926[56] with a theatrical troupe from the National Theatre of Athens to stage *Macbeth* in the Alhambra Theatre.[57] Startled to see Constantine at the door, Minotis, who was in his midtwenties, found himself awkwardly "revealing my pleasure and honor in meeting such an important and famous poet."[58] But he succumbed to Constantine's flattery: "I am told, Minotis, you love poetry." And he accepted the poet's invitation to his apartment to be observed "under the lights of my candles."[59] Finding himself in Constantine's parlor, he sat silently until the poet asked him to recite his favorite Cavafy poem, "as an actor of the verse and the word." When Minotis finished declaiming "The God Abandons Antony," he was stunned when his host asked, "When are you coming out, Minotis? It's time for you to come out as a poet." After this initial shock, Minotis took this question as a "compliment," even though he knew that Constantine had seen no evidence of his poetic talents. "He was a perfect gentleman," Minotis concluded, "a charming friend." As he descended the steps from the apartment, he felt "enchanted by the charm of his spirit, deeply flattered . . . by the deference he showed me without any self-interest or hidden motives."[60] In his hands, however, he bore Constantine's collection (syllogi) of the 1907–1915 poems, with the inscription "To my artist friend, A. Minotis." He would later receive more copies of collections that he was expected to disseminate.[61]

These young men often felt that their host tried to impress them excessively. Antonis Komis arrived with much apprehension at Constantine's apartment, having been initially repulsed by the poet's fractured, almost geological countenance.[62] But as soon as he sat down, Constantine began to speak about his work, showing his visitor poems, drafts, and notes. As he listened to him, Komis picked up some anxiety in his voice, having the distinct impression that his host was trying to dazzle him. Acting as if Komis had been skeptical of his work, Constantine brought out his notebooks, explaining how difficult writing poetry was and how long it took to compose a poem. He wanted to demonstrate that, despite the ease with which they lent themselves to "oral recitation," his poems were the product of extraordinary work and craftsmanship.[63]

Dimitris Garoufalias too discovered how fragile Constantine appeared to the opinions of others and how eager he was to hear news about his work and to boast. When Garoufalias arrived in Alexandria from Volos in 1931 at the age of eighteen, he met the poet at the apartment of Alekos Sengopoulos, his uncle's brother-in-law.[64] During the initial conversation, someone asked if Constantine's poetry was widely known in Greece. Garoufalias responded that a newspaper in Volos recently had published one of his poems. Immediately Constantine pressed Garoufalias for details about the date and place of publication, something that stunned the young visitor, who had not expected the eminent poet to bother with provincial newspapers. Anticipating courtesy but also indifference, Garoufalias was further surprised by the warmth Constantine showed him during dinner, clearly feeling that the poet "tried to capture my attention, to impress me."[65] One Sunday evening, upon returning from the Rialto Cinema on Rue Fuad, Garoufalias passed by a café and heard Constantine calling his name from inside in a raspy voice, signs perhaps of the cancer that would afflict his throat. Constantine then invited him home. The poet sat down across from his visitor, took a cigarette, cut it in half as was his habit, and began to smoke. And then, as if sensing Garoufalias's discomfort, he whispered: "I believe that sometimes a person has much to say but is not able." But he never finished his sentence.[66] After a few moments, Constantine stood up, shuffled to his study, and brought back two of his collections, one with the title "C. P. Cavafy. Poems. 1905–1915" and the other "C. P. Cavafy. Poems. 1916–1918," which he inscribed "to my friend Mitsos Garoufalias, C. P. Cavafy."[67]

Many young men witnessed the discreet, if not peremptory,

way the poet slipped copies of poems into their pockets with the expectation that they spread the message.[68] Some, such as Komis and Garoufalias, wrote books about him. Others, like Yiorgos Vrisimitzakis,[69] became advocates with a religious zeal. He joined the editorial staff of *Alexandrini Techni* and wrote an influential article about the poet in 1917. In the following two years, he published a number of essays on Constantine's work in Athens, which provoked responses and counterattacks and which contributed significantly to the spread of the poet's fame.[70] Along with Vasilis Athanasopoulos, P. Alites, Nikos Santorinios, and a few others, Vrisimitzakis also formed in 1917 the literary society Apuani to promote Constantine's poetry. When Vrisimitzakis moved to Annecy, France, in 1926, he carried on his apostolic mission. "I am so much in touch with myself," he wrote to his idol, "when I support you that I don't have to think about it. Have faith in me. I have so much to say."[71] And in a letter dated January 14, 1933, just months before the poet's death, Vrisimitzakis wrote: "Please don't cease your valuable work, Mr. Cavafy. Continue to give us the diamonds that you have been offering us until now . . . In time we will speak, and we will say and resay what we owe you."[72]

Vrisimitzakis constituted an ardent member of a diasporic network of Cavafy acolytes scattered throughout Greece and Europe. Even though Constantine preferred to deal face-to-face, he realized that his rising fame necessitated that he maintain contacts increasingly with supporters beyond Alexandria. Marios Vaianos was such an individual, a zealot most poets could only dream of. Although he only met Constantine in person when the poet arrived in Athens for cancer surgery, for ten years he had been spreading Constantine's fame by talking to journalists, placing articles and reviews in newspapers, and passing out copies of poems. He also devoted an entire issue of his journal

Nea Techni (1924)[73] to his work, the first such special issue of a Greek journal in Constantine's lifetime and a catalyst in the spread of his fame. Vaianos's promotion of Cavafy was so fervent and forceful that it provoked resistance on the part of those who disliked Cavafy's poetry.[74]

Born in Cairo, Vaianos moved to Athens in 1922 after a stay on Chios, a time when he began to hear about Constantine. Having read the seminal essay by Xenopoulos and a more recent article (1923) by the poet and critic Tellos Agras (1899–1944), Vaianos summoned the nerve on November 15, 1923, to write to the great Cavafy, who responded immediately with copies of his poems.[75] Vaianos described this initial letter as an "apocalyptic" moment, just as Tsirkas had, and from "then on Cavafy became a daily concern and intention."[76] After this initial letter, Vaianos began to receive large envelopes from Alexandria containing either the collections or, more often, individual poems, which he then tried to place in Athenian publications or pass on to influential Greek poets and critics.[77] Vaianos quickly developed not only an unflinching dedication to the advancement of Constantine's poetry but also something of a crush on the poet, sending him packages of figs, ouzo, and sweets from Chios. And he wrote a poem in the manner of Cavafy, "Tragoudi Akolasias" ("Song of Debauchery"), in 1931 about a friend who "admired absolutely / the poems of the Alexandrian poet Cavafy." The friend, a typical young man in the Cavafy world, lives in a "small society" unnoticed, wasting his life. But the speaker says: "And I with unease stared into his dark eyes, / dark like the abyss of my desires." Then in the penultimate stanza, the speaker says: "I wrote one song about you, my Dear, / but perhaps even this will pass unnoticed." He then implies that there was another "perhaps better man before you," who tore him from his "obsession."[78]

It gave Vaianos great pleasure to hear from visitors in Alexandria that the poet had identified the delicacies he was serving as having been sent by his "friend" Marios Vaianos. And Constantine always referred to him as a friend in his many letters to Rika and Alekos, who were in Athens in the early summer of 1928. He often asked them to extend Vaianos his greetings and his appreciation of their "friendship" and he anxiously inquired whether they had passed on copies of poems to him as well (June 16, 1928).[79] With almost every letter to Vaianos himself, he attached copies of recent poems. And he inevitably thanked him in a cursory manner for sending him articles or interviews about him or any sympathetic remarks someone had made about his work.[80]

Reading these letters, a person might rightly think that Constantine had been corresponding with a publicist or an agent rather than a "friend." For rarely did he inquire about Vaianos, a person much younger than him who might have needed some mentoring or a confirmation of friendship. Once, he sent an anxious letter to Vaianos's journal *Nea Techni*, asking about his whereabouts, not having heard from him for some time. But Constantine's anxiety revealed worry about his own poetry rather than concern for Vaianos. Even his expressions of gratitude seemed constrained: "Rika and Alekos [who had just returned from Athens] have told me much about you. How kind you are, and what a true friend you have appeared to me. They love you very much. They also told me about your warm feelings towards me—something that I have long recognized and I have often expressed my gratitude for all your efforts on my behalf."[81]

During his entire correspondence with Vaianos, Constantine never mentioned his health, not even in his last letter of March 17, 1931, even though he had begun to suffer worrisome pain in his throat a year earlier. For this reason, Vaianos was struck, as if by a "whip," to learn from reports in the press of

Constantine's sudden arrival in Athens in July 1932. Even under normal circumstances, the young Vaianos would have been apprehensive about confronting his idol face-to-face. These understandable misgivings were inflamed by the betrayal Vaianos felt at having learned from others about the poet's illness and appearance in the Greek capital. His pain was so deep that for days he avoided the Hotel Cosmopolite in Omonoia Square, where the poet was lodging.

Staying at home to nurse his wounds, Vaianos could not understand Constantine's silence about his illness. At the same time, he could no longer forestall the visit, especially as he had been hearing about Constantine's sad state, his hoarse voice, and the anguish in the faces of Rika and Alekos. So he decided to see Constantine in his hotel prior to his admittance to the hospital. But he was so "shaky" about their first meeting that, as he approached the room and then knocked, he prayed that no one would answer. When Constantine opened the door, Vaianos felt crushed. Expecting "an embrace, a kiss, some warmth," he received only formal courtesy and a firm handshake. When he later reflected on this encounter, he blamed himself for not being "a striking adolescent, nor an athletic young man" but a student "past his prime."[82]

Constantine only added to his visitor's consternation by addressing him in the third person: "My friend Marios Vaianos, whom I thought I would meet in Alexandria . . . He was so good to me, supporting my poetry all these years."[83] The poet was ill at ease himself, perhaps feeling awkward for not having informed his loyal "friend" of his trip. In the course of the visit, Constantine became more comfortable, pulling the chair closer to his guest, allowing their knees to touch, talking constantly, and with his right hand patting Vaianos's back, later his shoulder and thigh. And Vaianos, "finding himself in a dream that had become reality," listened and answered, his arms dangling "without purpose" down his sides.[84]

After that afternoon, Vaianos began to call on the poet more frequently. But one day at the hospital, he witnessed his cold, uncaring side. As he was about to leave the room, he bumped into Constantine's surgeon, who remembered Vaianos from an earlier visit and who asked why he had never returned for an operation to save the function of one ear. When one of the surgeon's assistants said that he could not afford it, the doctor insisted on the necessity of the operation.[85] At that point, Vaianos directed his eyes forward to see the effect this revelation might have on Constantine and on Rika and Alekos. Constantine just turned around in his bed, as Rika and Alekos stood motionless, staring at the poet's back, searching for some guidance from him. Though he said nothing, Vaianos took the poet's indifference to his own medical condition very hard. On the way home, he could not help but feel abandoned by Constantine: "I was a person who had helped him in every way . . . he knew that I needed a small operation to save the hearing of one ear . . . he was witness to an insistent conversation among specialists, but he did not show the slightest interest, and did not say a single word."[86] He accepted finally what he had always known, that Constantine was "self-interested and individualist and only thought of himself."[87] By the time of the hospital visit, however, Vaianos had identified his life with that of the poet so much that abandoning him would have meant jettisoning his life's purpose.[88]

But he also paid a price for his unstinting support of Constantine's work. As he confessed in 1973, because of his uncritical promotion of Constantine's poetry, he was shut out from the institute where he studied; many critics refused to speak to him and even Palamas himself sent back the latest issue of *Nea Techni* as "unacceptable." In his letter to Vaianos, written without a salutation, Palamas, still the reigning poet in Greece, demanded that his name be removed from the journal's list of "regular contributors."[89] Ultimately, Vaianos had much to gain in linking his fate with that of Constantine's, for as Constantine's fame spread, so did his own.

Many of Constantine's early disciples are known today because of their association with the poet. Although they serve as footnotes to a longer and more widely celebrated story, they have "become a name," to cite Tennyson's "Ulysses." In the give-and-take between the star and his fans, this was no small victory. By advancing his career, Constantine's acolytes received enormous recompense—a poem, a handshake, an afternoon with their idol, and a measure of immortality.

12

CONSTANTINE'S LITERARY RADIUS

For all the self-promotion they witnessed around them, the early proponents of Constantine's work did not fully understand how profoundly insecure the poet was about the reception of his verses, even in his hometown. They may have mistaken his bravado and charm for self-assurance. For Constantine was worried about the fate of his poetry in the Greek community of Alexandria, a society not favorably disposed toward his pathbreaking poetry. Although the city was lauded for its cultural cosmopolitanism and thriving literary culture, in reality the number of readers for poetry was limited, especially for experimental modernist verse laced with erotically provocative themes.[1] Constantine was grateful, therefore, for every bit of support he got and built his reputation one reader at a time, as can be gleaned from a draft of a letter he wrote (April 9, 1915) to a young devotee named Gregory to whom he offers his gratitude: "The appreciation you express for my work gives me great pleasure. When somebody from the new generation, I mean someone sophisticated like you, appreciates my verses, it pleases me especially . . . It makes me hope that the small edifice I have built is somehow solid. My efforts then were not in vain when with complete devotion and—sometimes if I may say, with much anguish—I tended to its stones."[2] At the age of fifty-two, he took care to respond to these "fan" letters and to write with candor about the toil he put into his work and its promotion.

Constantine, of course, had known all his life how precarious it was to publish poetry in Alexandria. In a draft letter (January 1908) to Grigorios Xenopoulos, he confessed his unease: "I am very disappointed with the little interest that the Greek public—here at least—shows in Greek writing. It is indeed a difficult thing for a person to sell Greek books."[3] Rika remembers that Constantine's chief fear was the indifference of the reading public to his type of poetry.[4] Antonis Komis similarly believed that the poet had become "a fanatical propagandizer of his own work" because of the apathy he sensed around him for his brand of writing.[5]

At the start of his career, many Alexandrians had been either unaware of or hostile to his work. When students, for example, founded the journal *Nea Zoï* in 1904, they never considered publishing him. Just by chance, Pavlos Petridis, a member of the magazine's editorial board and a doctor, heard from a bookseller that a "certain Cavafy lived here" and decided to visit him at his house on Rue Rosette.[6] Through Petridis, Constantine got to know the other collaborators of the magazine, and in 1909, he published a short critical piece in this venue and, in future issues, a few poems. But in that very year, at the age of forty-six, Constantine was not widely read outside his small coterie of admirers in Alexandria, a situation that caused him extraordinary anxiety. This all changed on April 23, 1909, when Petridis gave his talk "An Alexandrian Poet: Constantine P. Cavafy" in the meeting room of the magazine, the first ever on the poet in any venue.[7]

Even as he was gaining more adherents in Alexandria and

Athens, Constantine came to understand that he could not make a living through literature and that publication involved a financial loss. This might have been one of the reasons why he refrained from putting out a conventional collection of his poems. In fact, he never published his poems in book form.[8] Owing to the pressures of the market and his own tendencies to exercise supervision over the creative process, he chose to build his own reputation reader by reader. The initial hostility he faced in Alexandria for his progressive poetry pushed him to develop his own idiosyncratic but astute method of distributing his poems.[9]

In his early years, roughly up to 1904, apart from publishing poems in periodicals, he would often print them individually on broadsheets, which he would distribute among friends and relatives.[10] First publication then for him meant either the appearance of a poem in a periodical or in broadsheet form. In 1904, Constantine gathered fourteen of these broadsheets into a bound edition ("*tefchos*"), which he printed privately in one hundred copies. And in 1910, he had another bound edition made, now containing twenty-one texts, and printed in two hundred copies. Most of the recipients of these bound booklets were friends and relatives first in Alexandria and then beyond. With these booklets Constantine was creating a small but appreciative audience, gradually offering members a limited supply of a desirable good. Like an entrepreneur, he was playing with the market and tilting it toward his favor, so to speak. And by sending people individual broadsheets with new poems, he reminded them constantly of his existence.[11]

But around 1911, the year he himself considered a turning point in his career, he stopped circulating the bound booklets of 1904 and 1910 and even tried to retrieve some of them. Because he so regretted these early editions, he returned to his previous method of free circulation of broadsheets. He could remove a poem from circulation, make changes, and then recirculate it.[12] By 1916, he preferred to disseminate his work privately.[13] Constantine printed poems and then also circulated single copies of these texts. Or he often distributed copies before publication. But then he included these offprints in folders ("*sylloges*"), loosely held together by a clip, with a catalogue of titles written by hand. These folders then became an open work, always expanding and being revised.[14] The archives contain copies of poems already published and included in a folder but that show the poet's corrections. In time, Constantine created booklets of the poems that circulated along with the folders. Upon his death, there existed two sewn booklets of sixty-eight poems in thematic order and a folder of sixty-nine poems of more recently published poems arranged in order of their first publication.[15] What contemporary readers identified as Cavafy's work were these loose collections he had bound at home and circulated privately, each one seemingly unique though drawing on the same number of poems. The Cavafy oeuvre was material and immaterial at the same time, dispersed throughout Egypt, Greece, and Europe, held together by interpersonal relations, friendships, and alliances.

Many readers were aware that Constantine divided his poems into three broad thematic categories: philosophical, historical, and hedonistic.[16] When he first distributed his bound editions of 1904 and 1910, he arranged the poems thematically. Later folders were organized both thematically and chronologically, indicating that the poet was experimenting with both options.[17] Constantine spent much time assembling and producing his bound editions and folders for two reasons.[18] In addition to avoiding the permanence of the book, he strived to influence the public reception of his work. A bold author and a shrewd marketer, he saw poetry as both a commodity and an art. And he attempted to manage this dissemination of his work from an improvised "bindery" at home without the benefit of modern technology.

This "bindery" constituted a bare room, laid out with simple tables or trestles containing piles of paper, each pile constituting its own poem. When he was ready to send someone a new collection, the night beforehand he would note by hand the titles of poems in the table of contents. The next day, after placing the poems in the desired order, he would go to the study in order to record the changes. Sareyiannis, who personally witnessed this procedure, regrets having put Constantine to so much trouble when he asked for collections to take to Paris. He never knew how laborious the practice was.[19] Once the poems were ready, Constantine then began to worry about how to send his prized possessions. Distrusting the postal service, he preferred forwarding them via a reliable friend, such as Nikos Zelitas. If such a person could not be found, and only after considerable consternation, he would consider mailing the package. Interestingly, he avoided sending his poems to unknown readers, preferring that people solicit him through intermediaries.[20] Thus, he secured for himself a sympathetic and controlled readership. Although he lived in a globalized system made possible by the telephone, telegraph, and mass-produced books, he preferred the face-to-face intimacy of private communication. In a way, he both heralded and resisted the modern world.

It is no coincidence that the first complete edition of his poems in Greek was published in 1935, two years after his death, by Alekos and Rika Sengopoulos, in a deluxe, expensive, illustrated volume. Rika undertook the editorial work and Takis Kalmouchos, an artist whose work Constantine had known, created the typographic illustrations. The publisher was listed as "Alexandrini Techni, 10 Rue Lepsius, Alexandrie" even though the periodical had ceased to exist. The book was actually published in Athens.

All 2,030 copies were sold with the profits going to Rika and Alekos.[21]

This posthumous edition, which came to define the Cavafy poetic canon, also made possible the first translations of his collected work. In his lifetime, Constantine actively thwarted most requests for translations, a defiant position that dismayed friends and colleagues alike. Given the international reach of his ambitions, he should have been delighted by the repeated appeals he received from renowned authors abroad. Yet he equivocated and dissembled at these entreaties. Memas Kolaitis said that the poet loved to discuss Kolaitis's translations of English poetry but not translations of his own work. As a result, Kolaitis was surprised to learn that John had already rendered many of his brother's poetry into English. Furthermore, Constantine referred to the translations by George Valassopoulo only parenthetically. When Kolaitis mentioned that he had finally been able to secure a copy of Forster's *Alexandria: A History and a Guide*, which was published in 1922 and, to his delight, contained a translation of "The God Abandons Antony," Constantine did not wish to talk about it. When someone once questioned Constantine about his opinion of Atanasio Catraro's Italian translation of "The City," he responded that "Catraro is a very dear friend."[22] Perhaps he had hardened his position after receiving a cautionary letter from John, who was working in Helwan at the time: "Catraro's translations are not without value but I find that they are not good reproductions of the originals, and I know Italian sufficiently to perceive that the work was done without long and careful research" (January 24, 1920).[23]

His contemporaries, like Polys Modinos, wondered why Constantine was so skittish about translations of his poetry. While in Paris studying law, Modinos had met the renowned critic, Hellenist, and translator Hubert Pernot (1870–1946), who spoke favorably of Constantine's poetry and expressed a strong interest in translating it. Thinking this would please his idol, Modinos wrote to him in June 1920. But rather than receiving an enthusiastic and immediate response, he heard nothing. So Modinos sent another letter, only to get a short note (September 1, 1920) with a terse reference to Pernot's request: "I was very pleased with Pernot's favorable view of my poems. The view of this wise author is very valuable. His evaluation gratifies me very much."[24] But he did not express any interest in making this project possible.

In a letter dated September 15, 1920, Constantine wrote once again to Modinos, informing him that he had indeed received a letter from Pernot himself. Incredibly, he told Modinos that he could not respond because he had lost Pernot's address. Thus, he asked Modinos to tell Pernot that "I thank him warmly for his letter, that his favorable view of my poetry is especially valued, and that I am pleased that he translated a few of my poems which he hopes to publish."[25] In his reply of January 23, 1921, he made a passing reference to Pernot, saying that he assumed Modinos had expressed to the French scholar his gratitude for his interest in his poetry.[26] Modinos was completely mystified at the poet's continued resistance to what seemed like an obvious blessing.

E. M. Forster was equally frustrated by Constantine's evasiveness about foreign translation. Forster had been so awestruck by Constantine's poetry that, when he returned to England, he sought the poet's permission to publish an edition of his poems translated by George Valassopoulo, the only translator into English the poet had approved of, apart from John.[27] Forster repeatedly wrote to Constantine, imploring him for more poems, only to meet with relative silence. In one letter (September 16, 1919), he expressed his desire to publish poems in *The Athenaeum*:

"Let's try my dear Cavafy, let us try," and ended with a complaint: "I wish you ever wrote a letter!"[28] Constantine responded in his usual bureaucratese, cool and unmoved. Forster, for his part, emphasized that it was not easy to place translations with an English press and urged his friend to act quickly, given the favorable reception he had received in England.

Undaunted, Forster wrote to Valassopoulo that the poems had caught the attention of reviewers and pressed him to translate more: "I feel you owe this not only to Cavafy and yourself, but to Literature. If you don't do it, the (English-speaking) world will be definitely poorer."[29] But Constantine continued to vacillate. On May 7, 1923, Forster responded with excitement that Chatto & Windus, "one of our leading publishers," had expressed great interest in publishing his work. He again exhorted his friend to send more poems to Valassopoulo, ending his letter with much frustration: "I hate it when beautiful things are kept from places where they are needed. It makes me angry."[30]

In the meantime, Forster had been placing poems in periodicals like *The Nation* and making inquiries with the Hogarth Press.[31] In fact, he got Leonard Woolf to send Constantine an offer of publication on September 17, 1923, something extraordinary for a poet living in Alexandria and writing in Greek: "Our books find their way to a small public who would, I think, appreciate your poetry."[32] What an astonishing proposal this must have been from one of the avant-garde literary presses in the English-speaking world. Most poets would have been flattered by such a prospect. Yet implausibly there was only silence from Alexandria.

Rather than giving up, Forster sent more anxious inquiries, begging his friend permission to publish. He even wrote to T. S. Eliot, editor of *The Criterion*, for assistance. And in addition to Leonard and Virginia Woolf, Forster dispatched translated poems to Arnold Toynbee,[33] Robert Graves, and T. E. Lawrence. No writer could have asked for access to greater luminaries of English culture than these. Forster continued tirelessly and selflessly, even polishing some of the translations as requested by *The Nation*. And the only payment he wanted for his efforts was more poems: "For each poem I succeed in placing, will you please send me translations of two more," he wrote to Valassopoulo. As usual, Constantine responded in curt, unemotional sentences. "I am very, very thankful for the interest you take in my poetry; and the pains you take for making it known."[34] Forster, however, wrote effusively that it would make him very happy "to think I may have been able to introduce you to a few new readers. I am sure that your work will have a European reputation in the end, but it will take time."[35] But Constantine again brushed aside his pleas, prompting Forster to write to Valassopoulo that the poet's stonewalling "makes me think that he is against any publications in book form."[36]

Why did Constantine obstruct Forster's extraordinary support? Why would he not seek a European reputation, the type Forster had attained after the publication of *A Passage to India* (1924)? Modinos thought that his insecurity about his poems, especially the erotic ones, got the better of him, turning him into an obsessive overseer of his work.[37] The more his fame grew beyond the circle of friends and associates in Alexandria to whom he personally sent poems, the more he worried about the wider reception of his work. He feared that with more people reading him, his poetry would be "judged harshly and seem ridiculous."[38] Given his need to oversee each stage of a poem's circulation in Alexandria, it is understandable that a process he could not control would cause him much anxiety.

Supreme self-confidence went hand in hand with crippling self-doubt, not an unusual combination in creative people. On the one hand, Constantine was so persuaded of his brilliance that he battled for fame with Tennyson, Dante, and Homer.[39] But on the other hand, contemporaries, like Antonis Komis, also pointed to his insecurity as "a terrible fault that provoked in you a sadness for the poet because at that moment, Cavafy lost all his gravity and became a small child, a simple child who wants praise."[40] Alithersis said that Cavafy was terrified of how "objective readers"—that is, readers with no relationship to him—might interpret his work as "a totality."[41] While he tried to overcome his vulnerabilities about his poetry's possible reception through his idiosyncratic method of "publication," translation necessitated that he abandon the authority he coveted over the entire creative process to people in distant cities. Translation seemed many degrees removed from his circle of informal meetings, literary societies, and conversations. He understood, after all, that a translation resulted in the creation of a different poem, the original meaning and order of words taken apart and recast in another language.

At the same time, he was not only obsessive about his poetry's reception but also a perfectionist, a stickler for the minutiae of language. He could blow up in fury when discovering a missing accent or an omitted breathing mark on the printed page. One day Giangos Pieridis saw him hurrying toward the office of the periodical *Embros* to ask about a certain Mr. "Cavaris" who had appropriated his poems. Pieridis also remembers his outrage at the discovery of Jean Michel's French mistranslation of a line in "Waiting for the Barbarians." Michel conveyed the phrase "*me kentimenes toges*" (with embroidered togas) as "*coiffes en toques*" (wearing caps). Cavafy added to Pieridis ironically that it was difficult to imagine people wearing caps at that time, especially men.[42]

In those few instances when he approved of the translation,

he preferred to work closely with the translator, as he did with the poet Emmanouil Kaisara or John himself.[43] Constantine was a demanding reader of the sixty-three poems John had rendered into English. But he never encouraged him to publish them, fearing perhaps that readers would confuse the names of the poet and translator or might think it demeaning to have a brother translating his work.[44] On John's translation of "The Windows," a poem completed in 1897 and published six years later, he said that the words "*epano kato*" (up and down) "don't need to be translated literally as they don't fit with their surroundings." For this reason, he suggested that John convey them as "from here and from there." He was emphatic about the faithful rendering, however, of the final line: "You should write 'what new things' without any adjective." The absence of the adjective only strengthens the power of the expression: "For it is a high degree of 'pessimisme' for 'things' to be perceived as frightening simply for being 'new.'"[45]

We don't know whether the initial idea for these translations originated with Constantine or John. Hariclia Valieri insists that Constantine had asked his brother to do it. Constantine also suggested that she herself render some of his poems into French: "When you grow up, you will translate me into French," she remembers him telling her. "He wanted to become all-famous."[46] She also claims that John's translations "did not really excite" Constantine, which might explain why he did not encourage his brother's efforts any further. John, however, seemed troubled by the erotic poems and never discussed them with his brother or with anyone else.[47]

In other letters, Constantine praised his brother's efforts in creating a "gem," as in the translation of "Addition," but took exception with John's use of the phrase "smallest care." He insisted that he never meant nor could ever mean such an expression.

What he said was that "I don't examine if I'm happy or unhappy" and, therefore, suggested the following version: "It will not now be my care to examine whether I am happy or unhappy."[48] On the poem "Absence," he wrote, "The word 'sage' seems to me a bit 'clumsy.' Take a look at it. Perhaps it's just me. (Probably it's just me.) Does it sound pleasing to the ear? Wouldn't a pronoun—'him'—be better, as in the text? Wouldn't it have a greater 'cachet'?"[49] In all these notes, Constantine remained actively engaged, deleting words, commenting on syntax, grammar, and sound, and offering alternatives.

Their lively communication shows that Constantine was not opposed to translation that he could oversee but felt anxious about a process taking place abroad with publishing houses he could not supervise. It is therefore no surprise that the first English translation of his complete oeuvre would not appear until 1951, nearly two decades after his death, published by the Hogarth Press as *The Poems of C. P. Cavafy* and translated by John Mavrogordato.[50] Indeed, six years earlier, Leonard Woolf had written to Forster with the news: "I have just had one of the great triumphs of my life. I have received from Singopoulo a signed agreement giving me the right to publish Cavafy in Mavro's translation. I shall do it complete. The triumph would be complete if you would write an introduction to it."[51] It was not by chance that Forster too used this very word, "triumph," to describe his own part in the spread of Cavafy's fame. In a letter to George Savidis, he wrote, "How very proud I am, George, that I ever got to know him; it is certainly one of my 'triumphs.'"[52]

In his unstinting support of Constantine's poetry, Forster was not fully aware of the animosity that his friend's work had provoked first in Alexandria and then in Greece. Even Xenopoulos could not come to endorse the strongly erotic poems, having told Malanos in 1927 that he could not publish such material in

Nea Estia.[53] Like other Athenian intellectuals, he favored poems such as "Walls," "The City," "Candles," "The God Abandons Antony," "Voices," and "Caesarion," which treated cultural decline, social isolation, disappointment, metaphysical impasse, vanity, and futility.[54] As noted, many readers found his work unpoetic. Writing in the Athenian newspaper *Ethnos* on April 8, 1924, D. P. Tangopoulos summed up the hostility felt by many Greek critics: "If this is poetry," he complained, then the millions of poems he had read until then were in fact "prose" and he, "an idiot," had mistaken them for poetry. "Cavafianism," he said sardonically, "has a few proponents in our city. This does not impress me since so many epidemics come to us directly from Egypt."[55] Constantine's growing popularity itself provoked extreme reactions from influential Athenian intellectuals, most notably from Ioannis Psycharis, the foremost champion of the demotic language. He denounced the young men of *Nea Techni*, whose editor was Vaianos, for their special issue on Cavafy in 1924. Saying that they lacked critical judgment, he dismissed them as "youngsters" and referred to the special issue as "boisterous." But he saved his last insult for Constantine himself, casting him as the "*karagiozis*" of the Greek language—that is, the clownish protagonist of Greek shadow puppetry, a beloved form of popular folk culture.[56]

Closer to home, Constantine had to deal with rejection from his erstwhile friends. Fed up with the poet's egocentricity, Alithersis ended up denouncing his poetry as well, finding it so poor that it improved with translation. He even predicted that his fame would diminish considerably after his death.[57] Malanos, as shown in chapter eight, assumed his life's mission as tarnishing the hagiography promoted by Constantine's followers.[58] Their relationship took a negative turn in 1924 when Malanos gave a critical lecture on Cavafy's historical poems in the public library and dissolved two years later with the inauguration of *Alexandrini Techni*.[59] Constantine pushed back against Malanos indirectly. Under his supervision, an attack on Malanos appeared in *Alexandrini Techni*: "Malanos's enmity towards Cavafy is widely known in Alexandria." The article accused Malanos's writing of containing many inaccuracies. More important, it maintained that Malanos was no longer in prolonged contact with him: "Cavafy and Malanos neither talk nor greet each other . . . He acts as if he knew Cavafy very well . . . He no longer goes to his house and in the past only infrequently."[60]

Constantine thus experienced his share of personal betrayals by once-close friends and acquaintances that must have made him anxious and on guard about the acceptance of his poetry. He also endured stinging criticism of his work and person, starting with a negative article in the pro-demoticist periodical *Noumas* in 1906. The first scurrilous anti-Cavafy tract appeared in 1912, written by Roberto Kambos, the pseudonym of the poet Petros Magnis.[61] "Cavafy wants us to admire him even if our admiration of his works is bought with the murder of poetry," he wrote. Cavafy killed poetry, he proclaimed. Kambos was one of the first critics to write about the prosaic nature of Cavafy's poetry, arguing that he engaged in reportage about history rather than composing lyrics.[62] His words found a sympathetic audience in Alexandria and later Athens, among readers who, not appreciating the formal virtuosity of his poetry, characterized it as linguistically deficient.

Kambos's diatribe was followed by a regular barrage of hostile criticism in Alexandria and Athens, especially after 1924. As Cavafy's fame grew, many writers and critics began to feel that his brand of poetry threatened their own conception of lyricism. Most disappointing to Constantine was the decision of *Grammata*, which until then promoted his work, to publish an attack by Michalis Peridis in 1915. Peridis too wondered whether Cavafian verse could be considered poetry.[63] Particularly disturbing to Constantine were the ad hominem attacks launched against him in his home city. Among the most notorious were the defamatory articles the physician and journalist Socrates Lagoudakis (1864–?) wrote about him, calling him, in one instance, the "new Wilde." Lagoudakis was renowned in Alexandria for his exploits as a volunteer in the Cretan War of Independence against the Ottoman Empire in 1899, his war correspondence for a Parisian newspaper, and his participation as an athlete in the first modern Olympics in Athens (1896). He tended to circulate alone in the streets of Alexandria, dressed in black as if returning from a funeral.[64] Malanos writes that the conflict between them originated trivially over Constantine's decision to accentuate the Greek translation of the word "York" (from New York) with a smooth breathing mark rather than the rough mark preferred by Lagoudakis.[65] In April 1924, Lagoudakis gave a slanderous lecture about the poet. Aware of his malicious columns, Constantine's friends and supporters went to the lecture expecting trouble. But they were shocked to hear this Greek hero make insulting insinuations about the poet's personal life with references to "secret bedrooms" and "unnatural and unlawful loves."[66] Horrified by what they were hearing, some asked Lagoudakis to stop, interrupting his talk with shouts of "down with the libeler." When he refused, "supporters and friends of the poet, amongst the first of whom was Malanos, . . . moved threateningly towards the podium, stopped him, led him down, and escorted him out of the hall."[67] In the words of Vaianos, Constantine understood at this moment the affection and support he had from his followers and friends.[68] And Vaianos, ever the loyal acolyte, spearheaded his own protest in Athens by writing a letter, cosigned by leading intellectuals and authors of the time, which was published in four Athenian dailies: *Elefthero Vima*, *Politia*, *Eleftheros Typos*, and *Eleftheros Logos*.[69]

Constantine himself never responded to Lagoudakis's attack or any libelous allegations, especially those about his homosexuality. He expressed his annoyance certainly at the betrayal of his supposed friends. With irony he would claim not to know Alithersis, or how to spell his name: "Which Alithersis do you mean?"[70] Averse to conflict, he preferred to let his friends and associates intervene on his behalf.[71] Like a Phanariot dragoman (translator) in the Ottoman court, he tried to maintain good diplomatic relations with all sides.[72] But despite the many fan letters he received from Greece and Europe, he continued to be the object of vicious attacks.[73] The only way he survived these skirmishes around him, the personal betrayals and public assaults, was by keeping his dedication sharply focused on his compositions. He was primarily a poet, after all, a craftsman of words, that side of himself that he kept hidden in his apartment. His very visible and ongoing promotion of his work, which had provoked so much malice, belied what was for him a daily, almost metaphysical activity—writing, revising, rejecting, starting anew. When the final guests said their goodbyes or when he returned from a promenade or a dinner, he would sit in the hall by the bookcase, his bindery, or his salon, take out his writing pad, or more likely the back of a letterhead, and begin the magic process of recalling the past, of asking words to create a mood, of linking phrases to capture a particular scene. Constantine's public persona, his showmanship, his exploitation of those around him to further his own fame, disguised the fact that for him poetic composition was an operation of craftsmanship and some enchantment. Not given to romantic notions of inspiration, he nevertheless begged the muses to work through him and create a poem, as captured in his "Birth of a Poem," which he composed in 1922 but never finished. This poem is typical of the Cavafy oeuvre in being self-conscious, speaking of itself as art, and describing the activity of its own creation:

A night when the lovely light of the moon
poured into my room . . . Imagination,
taking something from life, though little—
a remote scene, a far-off pleasure—
brings its own vision of flesh,
its own vision of a sensual bed . . .
One night when the lovely light of the moon
poured into my room.

This is Constantine in his willed isolation, invoking imagination to carry images of a lost fullness, to bear episodes, lines, glimpses of a youth long gone, and pour them into his mind, like the moon that floods his room so that he can finish his revisions. "Birth of a Poem," insofar as it is incomplete, comes to stand for his entire oeuvre being a work in progress.

Constantine must have sensed that the attacks on him were skirmishes of a greater struggle over the future direction of Greek poetry. The language conflict between katharevousa and demotic continued to divide people for nearly a century. Demoticism was clearly on the upswing by the time Constantine began to write poetry, having won the ideological war for the hearts of the people. Its adherents crowned Kostis Palamas as the new national poet, a position that enabled him to dominate and define the

Greek lyric in the early twentieth century. Constantine understood that his poetry put him at odds with the dominant Greek literary trends of the time.

Yet a growing number of critics, especially those conversant with European modernist poetry, began to recognize in him an instrument to modernize Greek poetry. Kleon Paraschos (1894–1964) wrote in 1924 in the newspaper *Elefthero Vima* about Cavafy's "fanatical followers" in Athens who were yearning for novelty in poetic form and content.[74] Like Paraschos, critics from all over the Greek-speaking world were beginning to discover that Constantine was creating a revolutionary poetics. They realized that young readers found contemporaneous demotic poetry a worn-out orthodoxy, irrelevant to modern sensibilities and ways of living.[75] So they embraced his poetry, discovering in Cavafy an urban, restrained, and international writer who had reformed Greek poetry. Alkis Thrylos openly announced in 1932 what many writers had been saying for a decade: that Cavafy stood among the rank of world poets like Rimbaud, Mallarmé, Heine, and Shelley.[76]

Those promoting the traditional poetry of Kostis Palamas, however, were threatened by the campaign to declare Cavafy a world poet. They resented Cavafian characterizations of Palamas's poetry as flamboyant, rhetorical, rural, and folkloric. So they attacked both Cavafy and his supporters. Even Palamas himself joined the fray, disgusted as he was by the special Cavafy issue of *Nea Techni* (1924). The publication of this special issue further incited many hostile and satirical articles by traditional critics who tried to minimize the further reception of Cavafy's poetry. But they could not stem the stream of Cavafian enthusiasm in the form of glowing articles and special issues of magazines devoted to the poet's work.[77]

In Greece the conflict between supporters of Cavafy and Palamas continued at a furious pace, a quarrel that pitted the two poets against each other and forced readers to take sides.[78] The struggle came to symbolize the two divergent ways of conceiving poetry and language that dominated poetic discussions for years and constituted one of the most dynamic Greek cultural rivalries of the early twentieth century. To be sure, the two poets could not have been more different from each other. For his part, Palamas wrote about Greece as a synthesis of previous cultural periods. His two most popular poems, *The Dodecalogue of the Gypsy* (1907) and *The King's Flute* (1910) are epic in scale. The speaker of *The Dodecalogue* is a Roma figure who delivers his prophecy about the downfall of Constantinople and the rise of the Greek nation. "The Eighth Lay" begins in this way: "The Prophet who watches with second sight and preaches with the mouth of the morrow, / Moved by what spirit I do not know, being himself a spirit, / Forsakes his brethren, the lion and the eagle, and his secret books."[79] The prophet here comes to represent the vibrant spirit of Hellenism and looks hopefully into the future. He bears no relationship to the ironical figures in Cavafy's poetry. Rather than write about seers, Constantine focused on the forgotten or marginalized personages in Greek history—the pompous officials in the Roman provinces who vainly try to hang on to Greek identity or Byzantine emperors who are crowned with fake jewels because they can't afford real ones.

For this reason, few Athenian critics apart from Constantine's fanatical followers could have imagined that an obscure poet writing from Alexandria in a mixture of the vernacular and purist registers about homoerotic desire would one day become a global poet. Nor could anyone have predicted that Palamas would in the future hardly be known outside of Greece. Unlike Constantine, Palamas was promoted by the institutions of the state. His funeral in Nazi-occupied Athens in February 1943 turned into a major manifestation of Greek resistance, attended by more than one hundred thousand people, with the poet Angelos Sikelianos reciting a poem he had composed for the occasion. Despite Palamas's position in the national psyche, Constantine acquired more adherents with each year. Between the date of Xenopoulos's articles in 1903 and 1917, there were only nineteen references by Athenian critics to his work. But as of 1915, more recipients of his poems began to appear in the poet's catalogues and by 1918, his stock in Athens began to rise appreciably.[80] Typical was the pattern of I. M. Panayiotopoulos, the editor of the journal *Mousa*, who wrote to Constantine asking for copies of poems to publish in his magazine.[81] A fan of Palamas, Panayiotopoulos was unprepared to appreciate Cavafy but was ultimately won over. With each day, Palamas became less relevant and Cavafy's star rose even more. The coinage of new words, such as *kavafolatreia* (the worship of Cavafy) and *kavafizo* (to write/act like Cavafy), the many parodies of Cavafian poems, as well as political cartoons in newspapers all bear testament to his spreading popularity.[82]

For this growing number of fans, the lack of an available published corpus was frustrating. With no accessible book, readers had to ask the poet himself for the pamphlets and booklets. Tellos Agras, for instance, wrote on December 21, 1927, to thank Constantine for mailing copies of his work via Myrtiotissa.[83] One Timothée Glückmann sent a second letter from France on December 21, 1931, reminding Constantine that he wanted copies of his poems.[84] Constantine's own cousin in Germany, Jean Coulmas, wrote on May 12, 1932, that, after hearing a lecture on Cavafy by the German translator of his work, Karl Dieterich, he wanted his own copies.[85] And John Mavrogordato sent the poet a copy of his short history of Greece on

February 24, 1932, and asked in exchange for his most recent poems. He was "anxious to complete my collection" but recognized that the poems could not be "bought from a bookseller in the ordinary way."[86]

Just as important, other Greek poets began writing poems in Cavafian style, referred to his name in the text itself or title, or cited lines from his oeuvre.[87] To be sure, many of Constantine's supporters and friends either dedicated poems to him or actually wrote in his manner—a process that continued with augmented pace after his lifetime.[88] Given his growing popularity, in 1926 Constantine was awarded the Order of the Phoenix by Theodoros Pangalos, the Greek dictator who ruled as prime minister from June 1925 to July 1926 and as president for one month in 1926. In a handwritten letter dated September 8, 1926, the Greek consul general of Alexandria informed the poet of this distinction bestowed upon him "in recognition of your poetic work."[89] Many of his friends suggested that he decline this award from a dictator. But Constantine, thirsting as ever for public applause, refused to do so, saying that it had been granted to him by the Greek state and thus he could not insult the government by rejecting it.[90]

What was perhaps predictable is that foreigners came to value Constantine's poetry so early on. Not beholden to Greek aesthetic tastes nor entangled in the country's ideological and linguistic tensions, they could appreciate his stylistic and thematic innovations. Rika was among the first to realize this. From her own perch in Alexandria, she understood that Constantine posed a threat to traditional poets and critics in Greece who, in reaction, tried actively to marginalize his work.[91] She was one of the first people to proclaim Cavafy a "great poet" in the 1927 dedication of her poem "Dejection."[92] It's doubtful, however, that this loyal and indefatigable friend could have foreseen Cavafy's current international stardom. Not even Constantine Cavafy himself, the man who always believed in the majesty of his own talents, could have imagined, as he shuffled through the streets of Alexandria, that one day he would conquer the globe as few other modern poets have done.

EPILOGUE

> Nor can we name the biographer whose art is subtle and bold enough to present that queer amalgamation of dream and reality, that perpetual marriage of granite and rainbow.
>
> —VIRGINIA WOOLF, "THE NEW BIOGRAPHY"

Constantine took care to archive his adult life, saving almost every document, great or small, from his entry card to the Alexandria stock exchange, to theater tickets, drafts of letters, lists of things to do, and, of course, various versions of his poems. It was as if, from middle age on, he had expected someone to write his life story. And it is not unreasonable to assume that he had suggested this to Rika. In fact, his first biographer should have been Rika. That at least had been her intention immediately after Constantine's death. If there was anyone who might have come close to understanding the poet's own "queer amalgamation," what Virginia Woolf identified as the very essence of biography with its ingenious division of dream and reality into rainbow and granite, it was the subtle and sensitive Rika. She remained a steadfast supporter who attended to Constantine's needs to the very end. Although married to Alekos, Rika was in reality Mrs. Cavafy, the poet's de facto spouse—his editor, critic, secretary, nurse, and errand-runner—the sole woman in his life. She had made his world and his art her own. In his final days, many people came to ask about the type of person he was. So did she. Was he the egocentric, self-involved poet who could not see past his own fame, as so many in Alexandria insisted? Or was the real Constantine the man with the tender heart who had revealed himself to her in his final weeks?

She came to admire his "bravery" in his last days, noting that he had not once complained of pain or discomfort. For this reason, she could not help but recall lines from "The God Abandons Antony"—" 'as if prepared for a long time, as if brave,' he bid farewell to life." But during these difficult weeks, she also had a rare glimpse into his inner turmoil. She wrote about one special moment when, hours before his last breath, unable to speak or even scribble a note, he looked her in the eye, as if to ask "why the tears," and then, touching his head and heart, he tried to reassure her. Did he mean to convey that all was well and things would turn out fine, or that he was ready to go? The stoicism and empathy he then showed is why he would remain for her "a great poet and a great man. An extraordinary person and extraordinary personality."[1]

Rika was probably the only person who knew that in his final months the poet felt terrified of being alone, that he feared loneliness more than death. While in the hospital, he insisted on the company of Alekos and Rika, his niece Eleni Coletti, and Giorgos Papoutsakis. Over the years, Rika had come to understand how the anxiety of isolation haunted him. She remembered how, when walking along the street to their building, he would point up to his apartment and say of himself—"alone up there, hero and victim."[2] Knowing his dread of being abandoned, Rika took comfort that at the end he felt himself closer to her than to anyone else, finding in her much understanding and love. This explains the astonishing confessional note he scribbled down for her in his final hours, seeking her pardon for mistreating her. She saved it along with the other notes despite their having been composed in squiggly lines and with broken syntax: "Rika, like the brave and better* woman that you are"—after the adjective the signature Cavafian asterisk signaled the addition of the word "artist" that he added at the top of the note—"pity your friend with all your good spirit, and with my blessings, pity the old man who is suffering, the artist, and try to forget the agitation I have caused you. My tears, proof of my sincerity."[3] Was he implying with the inserted word "artist" that she was a good poet? He had never recognized her poems before, even "Dejection," which she published in *Alexandrini Techni* in February 1927 and dedicated "to the great poet, C. P. Cavafy." It was in his shadow and in imitation of "The City," one of his most famous poems: "You said: my current life is a dejection / with its implausible hopes and futile joys . . ."[4]

The note raises questions about whether he was agonizing in some way over his past treatment of her. How might she have interpreted it, given that he had never written anything so confidential to her or anyone? In the letters he had sent to her and Alekos when they were visiting Athens five years earlier, he rarely expressed much cordiality, let alone anything admitting to fragility. Although he dispatched them almost daily, each letter followed the same pattern: Had they seen so and so about his work? Had they looked at the latest issue of *Tachydromos*, which had an article on him? He informed them about the progress of *Alexandrini Techni*. Only once did he suggest that Alekos take the rest "he deserved."[5] Yet here in his final hours or days,

Constantine expressed his vulnerability and seemed to ask for forgiveness. This was a Constantine that no one knew.

Rika had access to many other notes he had composed ever since his tracheotomy. With the exception of the one written to her, most are jottings, scribbled here and there, expressing thoughts, desire for something, or directives for chores. One slip stands out almost in an abject vacuum: "I am a victim." In many he simply asks for things or would answer, "I will wait for him," or, "If Mrs. Sengopoulos is sleeping, he should wake her up." To save paper, he would often cross out his previous request and write over it. Some were recorded on blank paper, others on the hospital's letterhead in Greek and French. In one, jotted down in the "Hotel Cosmopolite, Athenes, Place Omonia" (October 12, 1932), he complains of not being able to sleep but then adds, "I am fine now." Going over them is like reading a modernist, experimental novel with disconnected expressions floating in space: "You take care of me day and night," one reads. They also resemble his dramatic monologues, like "Philhellene," where the reader listens to one side of a conversation.[6]

Unaffected by the arguments made by Malanos and Alithersis that Constantine coerced his supporters to submerge their personalities into his and dedicate themselves to his glory, Rika remained steadfast in her mission. The task of ordering the remnants of his legacy and overseeing the first edition of his poems fell to her. Most pressing was the matter of his personal effects, notably the contents of his study. Where should she file the scribbled hospital notes along with all the poet's material hoardings? In addition to the slips and scraps, she had to intervene in major textual matters: What, for instance, was the status of the final draft of "On the Outskirts of Antioch," the poem he was revising up through his final days? Of course, it had not surprised her or anyone who knew him that he was working on corrections of this poem, hoping to get the finished text to the printers before he died. He had brought his poems with him to the hospital, keeping them on his bedside table, next to his medications. It comforted him to have them there, like a cup of tea. He felt that he still had many more poems to write and was thrilled to see the publication of "Days of 1908" on November 17, 1932. Writing after all was what he lived for. While in Athens for the operation, he kept on saying that he still had twenty-five poems to write,[7] a considerable number given his exactitude, perfectionism, and pace of composition. For this, surely, he would have needed another ten years, if not more. And in his final days, he maintained that he still had fifteen more poems to complete.[8] Even at the very end, he never ceased thinking of his work; "the poetic idea continued to come and go," as he wrote in his great poem "Darius."

Rika had much to ponder, as the task of editing and producing the first volume of Cavafy's poems loomed before her as well as his biography. She was well placed to meet this challenge. As his caregiver and intimate friend, she alone was in a position to understand the contradictions in his personality, the flux between his "réservé,"[9] as she called it, the English "training" in self-control, as his niece Eleni Coletti referred to it, and his effusive charm and theatrical manner. Rika alone could identify the most defining tension in his life: the contrast between the warm, loving, affectionate young man and the self-interested, self-involved poet of middle and old age. More than anyone else in Alexandria, she was poised to untangle this paradox and offer a compelling portrait of the poet.

But before setting herself to address any of this, there was much to be done. There were the many telegrams she and Alekos were receiving, notable among which was one from Antonis Benaki in Athens: "Condoléances sincères."[10] She and Alekos had to plan the funeral and then face the complex and overwhelming reality of how to handle and manage the tributes and testimonials that would be forthcoming. Much of this had to be approached with an eye toward editing the poems and launching the first published collection, the centerpiece of their promotional strategy. All would come to hinge on this mighty endeavor, and in the process, Rika's marriage would undergo tremendous strain, buckling and ultimately dissolving under the weight of her having to manage Cavafy's growing reputation.[11]

The funeral was solemn enough and predictable, as were the accompanying tributes. At the conclusion of the religious ceremony, Pericles Skeferis, the consul general of Greece in Alexandria, offered a eulogy. "As a representative of Hellenism" in Alexandria, he declaimed, he had come to honor "the extraordinary poet and rare artist" who, expressing the spirit of Alexandria, was proud "to have deserved such a city," referring here to Constantine's popular poem "The City." With his illustrious poetry, Skeferis continued, Cavafy "created a poetic school and brought about a new blossoming of the Hellenic spirit in Alexandria." And he concluded with these words: "Poet, the nation bids you farewell with sorrow as does Alexandria which loses you."[12] The casket, covered by a cross of laurel, an offering from Alexandria's poets and intellectuals, was transported along the customary path to the Chatby cemetery for burial at the family grave site.[13] The procession was led by Metropolitan Theofanis and priests from Saint Savvas. Present were many of the prominent culturati of Alexandria.[14] Once through the gates of the cemetery, the casket and mourners passed into what amounted to a little city in itself, a Greek necropolis characterized by many grand monuments, some resembling small temples in their own right. Similar to other famous Greek cemeteries of the diaspora cities of Vienna, Trieste, London, and Istanbul, Chatby contained impressive tombs, notably the opulent monuments of the

Salvago, Benaki, Ralli, Rodocanachi, Zervoudaki, and Averoff families. By comparison, the Cavafy grave site was modest. Surrounded by an iron rail a few feet in height, the plot contained one tall rectangular monument that was more imposing than its other two and on top of which rested a marble cross. On the sides of this monument were listed the names of Haricleia, Peter John, and the brothers Peter, George, Aristides, and John. The gravestone for Constantine was separate, and on it Rika and Alekos would have the word "poet"[15] inscribed, lest there be any doubt in the minds of future mourners:

CONSTANTINE P. CAVAFY
POET
DIED IN ALEXANDRIA
29 APRIL 1933

Before the casket was interred, Constantine's friend Apostolos Leontis delivered the final eulogy. Like the consul general, he too alluded to the poetry, specifically to "The God Abandons Antony." Addressing Constantine in the second person, Leontis said that, as the footsteps of death became louder, "you, peaceful and collected, prepared yourself to receive death . . . and faithful to your immortal verses you did not deceive yourself, saying that this was all a dream, that your ears had fooled you."[16] It seemed appropriate, somehow, that everyone would cite this same poem at the end. The funeral was covered by the press in Alexandria and also in Athens.[17] The tributes and planned commemorations would now begin in earnest. Just a few weeks after the funeral, the journal *Panaigyptia* devoted a special issue to Cavafy's work. Gaston Zananiri suggested that the city of Alexandria erect a bust of Cavafy in a public space, an idea seconded by Papoutsakis.[18]

In the meantime, Papoutsakis and Zananiri organized a "literary memorial" service in the American Mission Hall on June 22, 1933, where they both delivered speeches along with other leading intellectuals, with the noted exception of Malanos. Already by 7:00 p.m. the hall was filled with friends, colleagues, and lovers of poetry. Among the distinguished guests were the Greek consul general accompanied by two colleagues, jurists, the famous painter Mahmoud Bey Said, directors of the foreign schools, scholars, and many journalists. Overall, 450 people were in attendance, a record for such an event, which consisted of a series of speeches and readings from the Cavafy corpus.[19] In his tribute, Constantine's friend Christophoros Nomikos[20] remembered how Alexandrians met the great poet on the street, finding him eager to see old acquaintances but guarded when introduced to new people. At home, always the consummate host, he regaled guests with his prodigious knowledge of Greek history and his irony: "He lived for his work which was for him . . . the ideal and to which he devoted all his energies and talents . . . For his friends and admirers, he lived a solitary life, psychically locked up within his 'walls,' as if forgotten by previous ages."[21] Nomikos asked what type of person would close himself up in his house in the name of his "own ideals and his own work." These were unkind and perhaps inappropriate words to utter at a memorial service, condemnatory praise in the form of a eulogy. But they captured, to the uncomfortable recognition of those in attendance, the truths in Constantine's life—gargantuan aspirations, a monastic focus on his craft, and a loveless existence.

Michalis Peridis emphasized the centrality of Alexandria as Constantine's place and organizing metaphor. He finished by declaring Cavafy's complete originality—a poet without precursors who represented not only the flowering of Greek Egyptians but also of modern Hellenism in general.[22] Papoutsakis then offered his own remembrance of the "beloved teacher" and gave the most literary talk, analyzing Constantine's poems. "In all of Neohellenic creation, Cavafy's work alone stands as a self-sufficient and self-begetting world."[23] Zananiri, speaking in French, struck a more personal note, portraying the poet's idiosyncrasies to the hundreds of people who had never met him. Unable to take part, Christopher Scaife wrote from London that his friendship with Constantine was one of the greatest gifts bestowed upon him in Egypt.[24] He would write a memorial poem titled "Epitaph" (1934) that contained the following: "Do not bring laurel here, or tears, / But, if you have some beauty turn / And greet your lover— / This is Cavafy's urn."[25]

Rika in turn would commemorate Constantine's death by recording a series of observations in preparation for her projected biography. In the introduction to this project, she admitted that "I am the only person who could do this [write the biography]. I lived next to him for ten whole years. In his final years he had no family near him." And she pointed to the fact that she possessed all his papers, his correspondence, his private notes, his autobiographical remarks, in short, a full archive. She felt quite confident that "having lived in the same house with him" and having spent so many hours on his papers, she had formed a clear picture of the poet in her mind. At the same time, however, she was uncertain about the project, feeling perhaps that she should let time pass so that she could avoid being influenced by his "charm." She also recognized how "difficult is the task that I am assuming." But in the end "it is my duty to present Cavafy." She composed many pages of notes, with comments on the poet's life and work, all evidence that she had carefully studied the material in her possession. She resolved to create an "honest" portrait, to capture the complexity of the man, even if this was "beautiful or ugly." Curiously enough, her proposed title for the book was in French,

"Cavafes en pantoufles" (Cavafy in slippers), an intimate portrait of a man few people, if any, had actually known.[26]

In the process of her research, Rika had recourse to two diaries Constantine had written as a young man, the one describing the final days of his dear friend Mikès Ralli in 1889 and the second relating to his mother's illness and death in 1899. The image of an affectionate son and loving friend that emerged in these texts was clearly that of a man she could not recognize, nor could anyone else, for that matter. Most of his friends and supporters would have been surprised with the outpouring of tenderness in these pages. Now she could better understand the confessional note he had scribbled down for her days before his death, an expression of atonement and defenselessness. Here in the diaries was a Constantine unguarded and exposed. But Rika, like the speaker in the poem "Myris," did remember rare moments when Constantine had allowed his tenderness to appear. During the funeral of the scholar Yiorgos Petridis, his brother Pavlos, a well-known doctor and intellectual, sobbed uncontrollably.[27] Rika observed how Constantine sat next to the inconsolable brother silently, and when the others had left, he approached Pavlos, saying: "I commiserate with you, my dear Pavlos. Trust me, no one here can feel your anguish more than me. Remember that I have lost five brothers."[28]

If people had little sense of the man behind the disarming allure, it was because this public person gave off a much different aura. Alexandrians knew the man capable of delivering the right word at the right time and in the right social context, as in that famous encounter with the Italian futurist poet Filippo Tommaso Marinetti in January 1930:

> "Bonsoir, Excellence! Je suis trés honoré."
>
> "Entre poètes le mot 'Excellence' n'a pas de place, cher Kavafis."[29]

This was Constantine the flatterer, whom most people knew or had heard about. It is not surprising, then, that no complete image of the poet emerged after his death. What began to circulate were bits and pieces of a fragmented portrait as people tried to supply the missing parts from memory. On the basis of her notes, not even Rika, it seems, had such a full picture. Did she know, for instance, that Constantine could be tenderhearted with children? Yet this is the image that Maria Alkaiou drew from her childhood memories of visits to Alexandria with her parents from Athens. She saw the poet so frequently that she came to associate the city "with Cavafy." They often went to the theater together and Alkaiou remembers that he smelled of cedar. Was she breathing the odor of the clothes Constantine kept in a cedar chest? This innocent observation is the only time that someone evokes the scent he exuded: like an old chest, soft, smooth, and protective. And when they left the theater, they sometimes returned to his apartment, where, sitting on his sofa, he would sit her on his knees and, pointing to his legendary candles, say, "Look at how we can see them but they can't see us." And then, astonishingly, they would recite "Ithaca," he starting with the first line and she the second until they came to the end.[30]

We don't know if Rika ever met Alkaiou. But her notes, along with the text of her sole Cavafy lecture, remain a unique source of information about the poet's less public persona. When Rika jotted down her notes for the biography one year after Constantine's passing, she was no longer dealing with a private individual but with a public personality. This process, the conversion of a man into an author, had, of course, already started to a lesser degree with the first appearance of his poems in print. Now with the poet's death, it became inexorable, and what came to dominate readers' attention was less the man in his slippers than the poetic phenomenon. Rika continued with her plans to compose a biography, a project she was uniquely placed to execute. Sadly, for reasons we will never know, she never went beyond this initial stage. In fact, nothing more of this project remains in the Cavafy archive than these preliminary remarks. And she failed to publish anything on Cavafy beyond the few essays after his death and the deluxe edition of his collected work.[31] But after decades of silence, she finally gave a lecture on Cavafy in Alexandria on March 20, 1956. She intended to offer the same presentation in Athens a couple of months later at the invitation of an Athenian cultural organization, having arrived with her second husband, Vangelis Karagiannis, with plans of traveling farther to Spain. But she died of complications arising from an acute pulmonary edema on May 20, 1956, in the Athenian suburb of Nea Smyrni.[32] The Athenian public never got a chance to hear this lecture, which was published only in 1970 in *Orizontes*, an obscure journal. Her talk, written with intelligence and sensitivity that demonstrated her talents as a literary critic, did try to explain the sphinx of Alexandria. Unlike the hagiographic portrayals she offered immediately after his death, this is fuller and more balanced, a text that attempts to disentangle the poet's many contradictions. It serves as a taste of what her biography might have been like.

Rika begins her talk by claiming the authority of testimony, for no one lived and worked in such proximity to Constantine as she had.[33] She then explains why it took her so long to write anything about him, confessing that she needed time to free herself from his domination. The "radiance" of this influence was so powerful that it was impossible for anyone approaching him not to be affected by it. This force, she argued, which she otherwise saw only in the poet Angelos Sikelianos and the novelist Nikos Kazantzakis, was "awesome" and "tyrannical" at the same time. Clearly, no one near him was unaffected and Rika needed to let almost a quarter of a century pass before she could return to him and examine more disinterestedly his impact on her and the world. It is hard not to believe that she felt both uplifted and crushed by him at the same time.

And she finally came to express what some of Constantine's critics had sensed all along: that only a dictatorial and overbearing personality, a poet hubristically assured of his own outsize talents, could create such an original oeuvre and provide an unprecedented perspective into the human psyche and onto the world. As she explained, even the critics who emerged from his salon were in some way products of his circle, his readings, his style. Deep down, they were trying to overthrow the Cavafian "yoke" that had been cast upon them. And Constantine had somehow foreseen this. In "Very Rarely," which he wrote in the crucial year of 1911 and published two years later, he describes an old man, exhausted and spent after a lifetime of abusive behavior. But when he returns home to hide the wreck of old age, he finds solace in that he still takes part in the life around him:

He is an old man. Exhausted and hunched,
broken by time and debauchery,
he crosses the alley with a sluggish gait.
But when he enters his house to conceal
his disheveled age, he reflects
on what he still keeps of his youth.

Young men now recite his lines.
His visions appear before their lit-up eyes.
Their healthy, sensual minds,
their firm flesh
are stirred by his notion of beauty.

If Constantine had this understanding of his own magnetism and genius in his late forties, he must have been fully persuaded two decades later of the impact he would have on the world. It is not surprising then that, according to Rika, in each attack against him, he found new "youthful vigor." Against these regular assaults, "the Alexandrian poet with his slow ruminative gait, his giant inquisitive eyes, behind his eyeglasses, would begin to move methodically, with a truly extraordinary strategy in the defense of his work."[34] He summoned friends and admirers, organized counterattacks, threw his enemies off-balance, and never allowed them to strike again. Rather than withdrawing into the limelight and resting on his laurels, Constantine found new vigor in his final years. Instead of seeking silence and repose, he wanted "noise and motion" to motivate him.[35]

He remembered in his declining years the lessons about poetry he had acquired in middle age and that he described in his poem "Of the Shop." In order to triumph, he had to fight in the public arena, having understood that his poetry could exist only to the extent that it was read, commented on, analyzed, and even despised. The more "noise" the better. And nothing succeeded more than commotion. Imagining him in his slippers, therefore, tells us only part of his story. Yes, he shuffled in and out of the special room he had set aside in his flat as his "scriptorium," the bindery where he spent countless hours assembling, arranging, and emending printed pages and self-bound volumes of his poems. At the same time, he managed to distribute some 2,200 handmade collections in one form or other,[36] a staggering amount and an almost unprecedented publishing procedure for a twentieth-century poet. This maniacal enterprise set the groundwork for a poetic reputation that was definitively launched with the 1935 Sengopoulos edition. As he predicted in his cryptic auto-encomium, the "future generations who are propelled by the progress of discoveries and the subtleness of their intellectual capacities" would come to appreciate him. And for someone who remained skeptical of translations, who thwarted the efforts of his brother John and of E. M. Forster to bring out a volume of his verse in English, we can only wonder what he would have thought about the current number of translations of his work (in English alone they number over thirty editions of either the select or complete poems, augmented by another sixteen translations of selections, by major literary figures). His strategy of withholding both a volume of his poems in Greek and a volume of translations in English paid off spectacularly.

Readers around the world today are indeed moved by his "notions of beauty," exactly as he predicted in "Very Rarely." Only someone loftily convinced of his own genius and powers of persuasion could have composed these lines. Constantine was the man who recklessly risked it all and won. In terse, disciplined verse, he provided readers beyond Alexandria and his own time with situations, characters, and vignettes they would find applicable in their own lives. From the confines of his whimsical apartment, stuffed with memories of loss, trauma, and deprivation, he foresaw the modern world as an interconnected expanse of ethnic, racial, and national groups. And though he did not live long enough to experience the "more perfect society" where people "made like him" would act and move freely, he fashioned for generations of marginalized queer people images, words, and ideas of self-representation. Moreover, by looking unsparingly into his family's experience with dispossession and into Hellenism's own history of decline and survival, he created poetry that transcended the limits of the Greek language and the Hellenic world. At the same time, he made this language into the subject of his poems. By writing in a mix of the vernacular and the purist registers and by incorporating words and phrases from other historical periods into his poems, he made the Greek tongue seem strange to Greek readers, giving them the impression that they were translating from their own language. Cavafy the poet lives on through the energy and aesthetic pleasure that others bring to and take from his poetry. Translation, that practice he so dreaded in an almost superstitious way, paradoxically has given him a tenacious afterlife. The man in his slippers ventured out of his house a luminary.

IMPORTANT PEOPLE IN C. P. CAVAFY'S LIFE

(Prepared in collaboration with Angeliki Mousiou)

ALITHERSIS, GLAFKOS (1897–1965) was the pen name of Michalis Chatzidimitriou, a poet and critic of Cypriot descent who lived most of his life in Alexandria. He was an early friend of the poet who later turned into a hostile critic of his work.

ANASTASIADES, PERICLES (1870–1950) was born in Alexandria, the son of Aristides Anastasiades, director of the Bourse. He studied in England and worked as a cotton broker, spending extended periods of time in Paris and London. He was a gifted painter and remained an intimate friend of Constantine, with whom he shared thoughts on art, society, and culture.

BENAKI, ANTONIS (1873–1954) was born in Alexandria. The son of Emanuel Benaki and brother of Penelope Delta, he was a member of one of the city's most affluent families. A close friend of Constantine and an ardent supporter of his work, he was also a passionate art collector whose holdings would be housed in the Benaki Museum that he established in Athens.

CAVAFY, ALEXANDER (1856–1905) was Constantine's brother and the fifth son of the Cavafy family. He was born in Alexandria and died in Athens of typhoid fever. He worked at the Thomas Cook & Son company in Port Said and in Alexandria. He was married to Thelxiopi Theodorou and had a daughter, Eleni Angeliki Loukia (Coletti), in 1902. Constantine traveled to Athens with Alexander in 1901 and later visited his dying brother there in 1905, keeping a brief journal of Alexander's illness and last days.

CAVAFY, ARISTIDES (1853–1902) was Constantine's older brother and the third son of the Cavafy family. He was born in Liverpool and died in Cairo. He worked at the Alexandrian stock exchange and later at the Laurens Tobacco Company. In 1889, he married Marie Vouros, with whom he had a daughter, Hariclia (Valieri), in 1896.

CAVAFY, GEORGE (1806–1891) was the poet's paternal uncle. He moved to England in 1827 and worked there before establishing the Cavafy trading company along with his brother Peter John. He married Mariora Thomas in 1834 and had a son, the physician John Cavafy. A successful businessman, philanthropist, and art patron and collector, he died in London.

CAVAFY, GEORGE (1850–1900), the eldest of the Cavafy brothers, was born in Istanbul and died in Alexandria. Following his father's death, he and his brother Peter worked for the family business and managed the family's financial assets. Following the dissolution of the business, he remained in England, where he worked in various trading houses, settling in Alexandria in 1897.

CAVAFY, HARICLEIA (1834–1899), née Photiades, was the poet's mother. Born in Istanbul, she was the eldest of her seven siblings (six sisters and a brother). She married Peter John Cavafy in 1849 at the age of fourteen and had nine children, two of whom died as infants. She died in Alexandria.

CAVAFY, JOHN (1838–1901) was the poet's cousin and the son of George and Mariora Cavafy. He was an eminent London doctor in charge of the Saint George Hospital's dermatology department and held various other positions both as physician and lecturer. An amateur artist, he illustrated many of his own medical publications. He married Marigo Ralli, with whom he had a daughter, Kitty.

CAVAFY, JOHN (1861–1923) was Constantine's older brother, the second youngest of the Cavafy siblings and the one closest to the poet. Born in Istanbul, he worked as an employee and later as a partner of the Alexandrian R. J. Moss & Co., retiring in 1919. Himself a poet, he wrote and published in English and translated many of his brother's poems into English.

CAVAFY, PAUL (1860–1920) was the third youngest of the Cavafy brothers. He was born in Alexandria and worked for the Municipality of Alexandria, leading an active social life. Between 1904 and 1908, he lived with his brother Constantine. Upon retiring in 1908, Paul moved to Hyères, France, where he died, after living a life of extreme hardship and poverty.

CAVAFY, PETER (1851–1891) was the second of the Cavafy brothers. He was born in London and was a British citizen. Following the death of his father, he worked for the family business and managed the family's finances with his brother George. He settled in Alexandria, where he worked at the Health and Sanitation Board of the municipality. He was awarded the medal of the Order of Osmanieh by the Ottoman government.

CAVAFY, PETER JOHN (1814–1870), the poet's father, was born in Thessaloniki. Along with his older brother George, he managed the Cavafy trading company. He married Haricleia Photiades in 1849 and lived and worked in England before settling in Alexandria with the family in 1855. There he helped establish the Greek community and oversaw the Egyptian branch of the flourishing family business. A naturalized British citizen, he was awarded the Metjidie medal by the Ottoman government.

COLETTI, ELENI (1902–1970), née Cavafy, was the poet's niece, daughter of his brother Alexander. She was born in Alexandria and married Massimo Coletti in 1923.

DELTA, PENELOPE (1874–1941), née Benaki, was a Greek author known for her historical novels and contribution to children's literature. She was born in Alexandria, the daughter of Emmanuel Benaki and the sister of Antonis Benaki. She was married to Stephanos Delta and maintained a long romantic relationship with Ion Dragoumis. She was a supporter of Cavafy's work.

DRAGOUMIS, ION (1878–1920) was a Greek politician, diplomat, writer, and revolutionary. During his service, he contributed to the organization of the Greek Struggle in Macedonia. An ardent supporter of the demotic language, he was one of the founders of the Greek Educational Association. He was an acquaintance of the poet and a recipient of collections of his poems.

GAROUFALIAS, DIMITRIS (1913–?) was an acquaintance of the poet and supporter of his work. He got to know Constantine through Alekos Sengopoulos, to whom he was related by marriage. He authored articles and published testimonies on Cavafy's life and work.

KAZANTZAKIS, NIKOS (1883–1957) was a Greek novelist, poet, travel writer, and essayist. He met Constantine in Alexandria in 1927 and wrote about his encounter with the poet.

KOLAITIS, MEMAS (unknown dates), also known by his pen name, Makis Antaios, was a translator, critic, and supporter of Constantine's work. His *Cavafy as I Knew Him* (1980) offers an invaluable and intimate portrait of the poet.

LAPATHIOTIS, NAPOLEON (1888–1944) was a poet, critic, and novelist, and an early supporter of Constantine's work in Athens. Lapathiotis, who was openly gay, visited Cavafy in Alexandria (1917) and met the poet again during his final stay in Athens.

MALANOS, TIMOS (1897–1984) was born in Piraeus and moved to Alexandria with his family at a young age. A poet, prose writer, and literary critic, he was an early friend and supporter of Constantine but later turned into a harsh critic. Following the poet's death, he authored a series of seminal studies, chief among which is his biocritical *The Poet C. P. Cavafy: The Man and His Work* (1933). In 1966, he relocated to Lausanne, where he spent the rest of his life, tirelessly pronouncing on all matters "Cavafy" right up until his final days.

MITROPOULOS, DIMITRI (1896–1960) was a conductor, pianist, and composer. Having begun his musical career in Athens, he subsequently worked in Europe (Germany, France, Italy) and in the Soviet Union. He was the director of the Minneapolis Symphonic Orchestra (1938–49) and the New York Philharmonic (1951–57). In 1926, he composed *10 Inventions*, setting Constantine's poems to music.

MODINOS, POLYS (1899–1988) was an Alexandrian of Cypriot origin. Educated in Paris, he served as a diplomat and was a scholar and the first rector of the University of Cyprus. In his youth, he practiced law in Alexandria and later served as a Cypriot ambassador in France, Spain, and the Vatican. A published poet himself, in 1918, along with Alekos Sengopoulos, he gave a well-known lecture on Cavafy's poetry in Alexandria.

OURANIS, KOSTAS (1890–1953) was a Greek poet, essayist, literary critic, and journalist. He was married to Eleni Ourani (whose pen name was Alkis Thrylos). He and his wife hosted a reception in honor of Cavafy in Athens in 1932 while the poet was undergoing medical treatment.

PALAMAS, KOSTIS (1859–1943) was celebrated in his lifetime as Greece's national poet. A central figure of the Greek literary generation of the 1880s, he was often seen as Constantine's chief rival for preeminence in Greek poetry.

PAPOUTSAKIS, GIORGOS (?–1967), a friend of the poet, was a supporter of Constantine's work and translator of his poems into French (his translations were published in Paris in 1958). He was born in Egypt and spent most of his life in Alexandria. He published essays on modern Greek and French literature and edited the first volume of Constantine's prose writings in 1963.

PERIDIS, MICHALIS (1894–1968) was born in Greece and settled in Alexandria at a young age. He was a friend of the poet and was one of the first scholars to study his archive. He authored the first biography of Cavafy in 1948.

POLITIS, ATHANASIOS (1893–1967) was a diplomat who served as the Greek consul general in Alexandria (as of 1923) as well as in Cairo. He wrote an important historical study on the Greek community in Egypt.

RALLI, MIKÈS (1866–1889) was a close friend and a classmate of the poet's at the Hermes Lyceum. He was born in Alexandria, the son of Theodore Ralli, who served as president of the Greek community of Alexandria. He died of typhoid fever at the age of twenty-three. Constantine kept a diary of Mikès's final days in Alexandria.

RODOCANACHI, JOHN (1866–?) was a close friend of Constantine. He moved to England at an early age, where he finished his studies and started working for the Ralli firm in Liverpool.

SAREYIANNIS, I. A. (1898–1962) was a friend and supporter of the poet. He was born in Alexandria and studied in France, eventually settling in Greece. He wrote critical essays on Constantine's work and published academic papers as a botanist.

SCAIFE, CHRISTOPHER (1900–1988) was a friend of the poet and a supporter of his work. A professor of English literature in the Department of English Language and Literature at the University of Cairo (Fuad I University of Cairo) and at the American University of Beirut, he also served as advisor on educational matters to the government of Iraq. He met Constantine through E. M. Forster and translated some of his poetry.

SCHILIZZI, STEPHEN (1867–1886) was born in Alexandria, the son of Zannis Schilizzi, a tradesman from Chios, and Marietta Frangopoulou. He was Constantine's classmate at the Hermes Lyceum and a close friend of the poet. Upon his death, Constantine dedicated a poem to him.

SENGOPOULOS, ALEKOS (1898–1966) was born in Halkida on February 2, 1898, the eldest of four brothers. He was a graduate of the Salvageios School of Commerce in Alexandria and worked for Greek companies in Egypt and also as a cotton broker. He first met Constantine in 1917 and became the poet's most intimate friend. He married Rika Agallianou in 1927 and lived in the same building as the poet at 10 Rue Lepsius. Upon the poet's death, he became his literary executor. He separated from Rika in 1939 and later married Kyveli Trechantzaki.

SENGOPOULOS, RIKA (?–1956), née Agallianou, was a close friend of the poet and the first wife of Alekos Sengopoulos. A gifted poet and intellectual, she studied law and worked at a law firm in Alexandria. Along with A. G. Simeonidis, she directed, edited, and wrote for the journal *Alexandrini Techni*. She also worked as a columnist for the newspaper *Tachydromos* and as a member of the press office of the Greek consulate in Alexandria. Along with her husband, she brought out the first edition of Cavafy's poetry in 1935. She separated from Alekos in 1939 and later married N. Karayannis. She died in Athens.

THEOTOKAS, YIORGOS (1905–1966) was a major novelist and essayist. Born in Istanbul, he lived in Athens and wrote critical articles on C. P. Cavafy's poetry.

THRYLOS, ALKIS (1896–1971) was the pen name of Eleni Ourani (née Negroponte). Thrylos was a prominent literary and theater critic and a strong supporter of Constantine's work in Greece. She was married to the poet Kostas Ouranis.

TSIRKAS, STRATIS (1911–1980) was the pen name of Ioannis Chatziandreas. A renowned novelist and critic, he was the author of two influential studies on Cavafy's life and poetry: *Cavafy and His Era* and *The Political Cavafy*.

VAIANOS, MARIOS (1905?–1975) was a Greek literary critic and journalist. He was an admirer and a friend of the poet and a strong supporter of his work in Athens. He was also the publisher of the literary journal *Nea Techni*, which became the first Athenian journal to feature an issue exclusively dedicated to the poet's work in 1924.

VALIERI, HARICLIA (1896–1983) was the poet's niece and daughter of his brother Aristides. She was born in Alexandria and married Geronimo Valieri in 1923. She died penniless on the Greek island of Mytilini, the last member of the immediate Cavafy family.

VENIZELOS, ELEFTHERIOS (1864–1936), Greek statesman, was the leader of the Liberal Party who held office as the prime minister of Greece for more than twelve years, spanning eight terms between 1910 and 1933. He enjoyed the strong support of many Alexandrian Greeks, the Benaki family in particular.

VOUTIERIDIS, ILIAS (1874–1941) was a literary critic and supporter of Cavafy's work.

VRISIMITZAKIS, YIORGOS (1890–1947) was a literary critic and poet. Born in Alexandria, he was a friend of the poet and a supporter of his work. He was a frequent collaborator of the journal *Grammata*. He moved to France in 1926 and lived there until his death.

XENOPOULOS, GRIGORIOS (1867–1951) was a renowned novelist, short-story writer, and critic. He was the editor of the youth journal *Diaplasis ton Paidon* (1896–1948) and the founder and director of the journal *Nea Estia* (1927–34). In 1903, he published an article that helped introduce Constantine's work to the Greek Athenian audience.

ZELITAS, EFTYCHIA (no dates), née Boiou, was the wife of Nikos Zelitas and had an active role in her husband's publishing activities, with the journals *Grammata* and *Panaigyptia*. She was a member of the intellectual circle of Alexandria and supporter of the poet's work. She kept a record of episodes from Constantine's life, covering events of the period 1926 to 1930.

ZELITAS, NIKOS (1888–1938), also known by his pen name, Stephanos Pargas, was born and lived in Alexandria. He was the cofounder and editor of the journal *Grammata* and owner of the Alexandrian bookstore and publishing house Grammata. In 1926, he founded the journal *Panaigyptia*. A close friend of the poet and ardent supporter of his work, he also published many Cavafy poems in the journals he edited.

NOTES

PREFACE: WRITING *ALEXANDRIAN SPHINX*

1. Archival material exists in three venues, all located in Athens: the Onassis Foundation (the bulk of this is digitally available), the Hellenic Literary and Historical Archive (ELIA-MIET), and the Benaki Museum Historical Archives.
2. In 1995, a Polish biography appeared by Zygmunt Kubiak, and in 2014, the Chilean Hellenist Miguel Castillo Didier published one in Spanish.
3. Sengopoulos 1970, 4.
4. Savidis 1985, 52.
5. This portion of the archive is now in possession of ELIA-MIET.
6. Savidis 1963, 1543.
7. Savidis 1985, 49–51.
8. Unpublished letters from Robert Liddell to Timos Malanos written in the 1970s and 1980s reveal the extraordinary extent to which Liddell was both indebted (and in thrall) to Malanos when writing his 1974 biography. Chapters were sent to Malanos for corrections and comments, with Malanos having the final say on numerous matters. In a letter to Madame Malanos following the critic's death, Liddell refers to him as "my friend for more than forty years—and I may also claim to be his pupil" (letter dated October 24, 1984, in possession of ELIA-MIET—Malanos File).
9. We do not engage with philological and editorial matters such as the poetic distribution of his poems during his lifetime and the posthumous arrangement of them by either date or theme. These topics have preoccupied Greek critics for decades and have been exhaustively treated in critical studies, namely by George Savidis.

PROLOGUE

1. All translations, unless otherwise stated, are our own. As Cavafy is the most frequently translated Greek poet into English, readers may turn to any one of these editions for alternative translations.
2. He is reported to have asked Rika Sengopoulos to find him a scholarly reference so he could complete this poem while in the hospital (Sareyiannis 1964, 50).

3. Forster 2004, 245.
4. *L&W*, 157.
5. Cavafy 2010, 143. This narrative was allegedly dictated in French for publication in a French newspaper and overheard by Eftychia Zelitas (Parga). Michaela Karampini-Iatrou notes the unacknowledged role of Apostolos Leontis in its transmission and composition (Karampini-Iatrou 2020, 47).
6. The conservative Athenian audience was bewildered by the atonal compositions and their cerebral and "degenerate aesthetics," as one review put it (Trotter, 63, 79), criticisms that were commonly leveled at Cavafy's poems by hostile Athenian critics.
7. Eleni Ouranis published criticism and prose under the male nom de plume Alkis Thrylos. Her parents, Miltiades and Maria Negroponte, were staunch financial supporters of Mitropoulos and powerful cultural benefactors. See Trotter, 53–55 and passim.
8. These very luminaries, writers like Tellos Agras, Kostas Ouranis, Napoleon Lapathiotis, and Marios Vaianos, accompanied the poet to the port of Piraeus to bid him farewell as he boarded the Turkish steamship *Aigaion* for his return journey to Alexandria.
9. Mitropoulos sent the poet an inscribed copy of the score, and Constantine requested that Alekos and Rika find him two additional copies in Athens (letters dated June 18, 1928, and July 8, 1928). A compendium of subsequent musical adaptations of Cavafy's poetry is available at the Cavafy Forum (University of Michigan): https://lsa.umich.edu/content/dam/modgreek-assets/modgreek-docs/CAVAFY/Cavafy%20Song%20Bibliography_Version3_3-3-22.pdf.
10. The *Inventions* used the original Greek text but Mitropoulos wished to include translations of the poems he scored in order to entice European audiences to perform them. Originally Mitropoulos had selected fourteen poems, most of which were chosen for their sensual and controversial content (Sakallieros, 178).
11. Letter dated July 15, 1926 (Merakou, 2010). Antonis Benaki was a family friend, an art collector, and the founder of the Benaki Museum in Athens.
12. The 1932 recital in Athens received a positive review in the Greek journal *Nea Estia*: "The impression was wonderful and so was the artistry of this original composer" (Sakallieros, 180). For a comprehensive list of musical renditions of Cavafy poems, see Lambropoulos, *C. P. Cavafy Music Resource Guide: Song and Music Settings of Cavafy's Poetry* (2022).
13. *L&W*, 166.
14. *L&W*, 167. For Rika's note, see GR-OF CA SING-S01-F01–0005 (1634).
15. This is how Rika Sengopoulos explains the presence of Metaxakis at Cavafy's deathbed (Karapanagopoulos, 72).
16. Meletios served as Archbishop of Athens (1918–20), Ecumenical Patriarch of Constantinople (1921–23), and Patriarch of Alexandria (1926–35). He was politically aligned with the Greek prime minister Eleftherios Venizelos, whose rise and fall from power directly affected the elevation and deposition of Meletios to and from various episcopal sees.
17. See Bryn Geffert, "Anglican Orders and Orthodox Politics" (2006), where she offers an interesting portrait of Metaxakis and outlines his political reasons for courting the Anglican Church and British politicians in the wake of the dissolution of the Ottoman Empire.
18. Meletios was an ethnarch who well understood the Greek diaspora, which he

manipulated adeptly to serve his own ends. When elected Ecumenical Patriarch in December 1921 in the months leading up to the Asia Minor Catastrophe—the defeat of the Greek army during the Greco-Turkish War—Meletios was barred from entering Istanbul to assume his ecclesiastical duties, so he managed to defy his enemies and gain entry to the patriarchal headquarters in the Phanar by accepting a lift from a French gunboat, thus sneaking into the city (Geffert, 286).

19. See Daskalopoulos (*L&W*, 167–71) for the various eyewitness accounts of the deathbed scene.
20. This according to Apostolos Leontis (*L&W*, 167).
21. Recounted in Manolis Halvatzakis's interview with Constantine's former colleague at the Office of the Irrigation Service, Ibrahim el Kayar (Liddell, 128).
22. That a hierarch as imposing and savvy as Meletios visited him on his deathbed was highly fitting for a connoisseur of ecclesiastical history and political drama. The presence of a patriarch in black hieratic regalia holding a chalice would have served as a poetic trigger, reminding Constantine of his lifelong fascination with all things Byzantine. There was an actual patriarch in his own family lineage—one coincidentally named Meletios—who served as Patriarch of Alexandria during the 1790s, a detail he proudly documented in his family genealogy (GN, 33). Constantine had even begun a poem titled "The Patriarch" in 1925 that he never quite finished but that chronicles the political intrigue surrounding the rise to power of Patriarch John XIV Kalekas, Patriarch of Constantinople (1334–47) during the tempestuous reign of the Byzantine emperor John Kantakouzinos.
23. *L&W*, 141. Theotokas knew that Cavafy was well aware of these comments (*L&W*, 157) and he seems to have felt some compunction about making them after visiting the ailing poet in Athens in 1932.

1. THE FAMILY COUNCIL

1. See the corrected dating of the actual printing of this poem to 1892 by Daskalopoulos (*L&W*, 33).
2. Letter dated October 8, 1882: GR-OF CA CA-SF02-S01-SS02-F20-SF001–0007 (382).
3. *GN*, 106, translated from the Greek of Constantine's *Genealogy* (1909–1911).
4. For the original Greek letter, see GR-OF CA SING-S01-F02-SF001–0005 (1406).
5. Cited in a letter from Forster to Isherwood, dated July 16, 1933 (Forster and Isherwood 2008, 23).
6. *CE*, 145; *TPC*, 33.
7. Malanos 1986, 16.
8. Made by the general manager of the National Bank of Greece, A. Zaimes, to the Greek Press in 1920 (Psyroukis 2000, 86).
9. *CE*, 20.
10. *TPC*, 63.
11. The Greek title of the book is *Ο Ελληνισμός και η Νεωτέρα Αίγυπτος.*
12. Gialourakis 2007, 232.
13. Politis vol. 2, 5.
14. Kitroeff 1989, 27, 171, 40.
15. Politis vol. 1, 327.
16. Owen, 81.
17. Metaxas, 10–11.
18. *CE*, 55.

19. He began compiling genealogical notes and constructing family trees with his brother John in 1883 and continued up through 1909–1911, when he undertook a final revision of what would remain an unfinished but invaluable family history. *Genealogical Gossip* (in English: GR-OF CA CA-SF02-S02-F25-SF002–0002 [1136]), *Memorandum About the Cavafy Family* (in English: GR-OF CA CA-SF02-S02-F25-SF002–0006 [1092]), and *Prose Notes* (in English: GR-OF CA CA-SF02-S02-F25-SF002–0003 [1091]) are part of the Onassis Foundation Archive. *Genealogy* (in Greek) is in possession of the Benaki Museum archive and was published, transcribed, and edited by Vangelis Karayiannis in his *Σημειώσεις από την Γενεαλογία του Καβάφη* (1983).
20. The Phanar is the neighborhood of Istanbul where the Greek Orthodox Patriarchate is located and where affluent Greeks resided. For centuries it remained the elite enclave of Greek intellectual, economic, and political power within the Ottoman Empire.
21. "The Cavafy's pedigree, tracing back the family's origins to the emperors of the house of Doucas, I have left out, it belonging rather to the region of tradition than of fact" (*Genealogical Gossip*: GR-OF CA CA-SF02-S02-F25-SF002–0002 [1136]). The Cavafy family had a family crest with a Byzantine helmet and two different Greek mottos: "ΥΠΕΡ ΧΡΙΣΤΟΥ ΚΑΙ ΚΑΙΣΑΡΟΣ / For Christ and Caesar" and "ΥΠΕΡ ΧΡΙΣΤΟΥ ΚΑΙ ΡΩΜΑΙΩΝ ΓΗΣ / For Christ and the Land of the Romans"; the crests were created by the Cavafy brothers and embossed on family stationery and used on select occasions (Ghika, 27, 31). According to his niece Hariclia Valieri, the name "Cavafy" likely derives from the Turkish word for "shoemaker" (*GN*, 110).
22. *GN*, 49.
23. Translated from the Greek (*CE*, 64).
24. *Prose Notes*, GR-OF CA CA-SF02-S02-F25-SF002–0003 (1091).
25. George Cavafy offered some rather interesting comments by way of advice to his brother Peter in this letter: "You are forgetting that in this world no state of man is absolutely good, or absolutely bad, and that everything is relative, and that the shortcomings and the advantages of every position are mixed and inseparable. Also, such setbacks are most useful for trying and taming any man, and for increasing his sense of happiness and pleasure when they stop existing" (M. Savidis, 2008, 27). See also GR-OF CA CA-SF02-S01-SS02-F21–0002 (1652).
26. *GN*, 104.
27. Anderson, 13–14.
28. Hullah, 4.
29. "The existence of rich young men such as Cavafy, with other sources of financial support, helped to depress the wages all apprentices received" (Anderson, 14).
30. George's son John would become a leading surgeon at Saint George's Hospital, London. See Victoria Solomonidis-Hunter 2020.
31. Macilwee, 1.
32. *LC*, 26.
33. Sharples and Pollard, 3.
34. These are docks in which water is maintained at a level that allows vessels to remain afloat.
35. Tibbles, 102.
36. In the words of David Fleming, director of Liverpool's National Museums (Tibbles, vi).

37. Sharples and Pollard, 10.
38. "Spirit of Liverpool," National Museums Liverpool, https://www.liverpoolmuseums.org.uk/spirit-of-liverpool.
39. This would have been the final month of the Cavafy family's second residency in Liverpool from 1876 to 1877, following their stay in London from 1874 to 1876, and Constantine and his siblings would have seen the statue, no doubt feeling proud that the city had erected a statue of a Greek goddess to represent itself. Like Liverpool herself, they were sitting—albeit precariously—on a bale of cotton, dependent as their family business had been on the trading value of this commodity.
40. The earliest church established in Liverpool in the thirteenth century was in fact dedicated to Saint Nicholas for this very reason (Hollinghurst, 75). As for the Greek church, two wealthy Greek shipping magnates, George Michael Papayiannis and Demetrios Theodore Rallis, spearheaded and financed the efforts to purchase land and commission an architect for the project. They ultimately chose the local architect Henry Sumners, who designed a striking building based on W & J Hay's idea of adopting a Byzantine model (Sharples and Pollard, 245).
41. It bears noting that this church, like the Saint Sophia church built by the Greeks in London later that decade, coincides with the Gothic Revival movement sweeping the country, which extended, on occasion, to the Byzantine style or some version of it. Not even in Greece or the great cities of the Greek diaspora were churches being designed with this level of authenticity or precise historical replication. The Byzantine spirit is more manifest in this church than in Alexandria's neo-Gothic Cathedral of the Annunciation, an eclectic structure built in 1856 that is rather devoid of anything approaching a Byzantine aesthetic.
42. Since Peter John attended evening classes in Liverpool as an adult, it is highly probable that his sons would also have taken classes, quite likely at the Mechanics' Institute.
43. Tosh, 92.
44. "The R. J. Moss & Co. was established in 1861 by a British businessman, Robert Johnson Moss. Initially, the company's business was in cotton and coal trading, later extending to antiquities and their transportation, through the purchase of important collections on behalf of the British Museum, in the 1890s." "R. J. Moss & Co.," Onassis Cavafy Archive, https://cavafy.onassis.org/creator/r-j-moss-co/.
45. We are indebted to Victoria Solomonidis-Hunter for these facts and many others relating to the Anglo-Greek community, which were presented at her lecture "Cavafy and England" (British Library, November 24, 2014). Solomonidis-Hunter is of the opinion that the three youngest Cavafy brothers must have studied at Hellenic College. Dimitrios Vikelas—author, journalist, and poet—was a member of the college's board of governors and was related through marriage to the Ionides and Cavafy families.
46. Solomonidis-Hunter has kindly shared her archival research documenting this detail.
47. Solomonidis-Hunter 2014.
48. A note in the family genealogy records a very early business alliance—"Cassavetti, Cavafy and Co."—dating back to 1847: GR-OF CA CA-SF02-S02-F25-SF002–0002 (1136). In addition to being business partners with the Ionides family, the Cavafy family was "doubly" related, both as in-laws and god-siblings. Cavafy's uncle George married Mariora Thomas, whose mother was the sister-in-law of Constantine Ionides. George's son John was baptized by Alexander Constantine Ionides and

married Marigo Ralli; their daughter Kitty in turn married an Ionides cousin, thus joining together three generations of Cavafy and Ionides descendants (Jeffreys 2015, 3).

49. These complex relations are all amply documented by Christopher Long at his website: http://www.christopherlong.co.uk/gen/index.html.
50. See Jeffreys 2015, chapter one.
51. See Macleod, *Art and the Victorian Middle Class* on the Ionides family and their relations to the arts.
52. Jeffreys 2015, 4–5.
53. Mancoff, 50.
54. Marie was the daughter of Euphrosyne Varsami and Michael D. Spartali, Honorary Greek Consul General to the UK from 1866 to 1879. Upon marrying the American journalist William Stillman, Marie's intellectual network widened to include her husband's American intellectual friends Charles Eliot Norton, James Russell Lowell, and Ralph Waldo Emerson. Later, while residing and painting in Florence, she became close with the novelist Vernon Lee (Violet Paget), acquainted with John Addington Symonds (the first modern historian of male homosexuality), and connected to Henry James (Frederick and Marsh, 19).
55. Frederick and Marsh, 82.
56. It is a curious coincidence that both the former dwelling of George Cavafy in Pembridge Gardens and the town house at Queensborough Terrace are currently low-budget hotels owned by the same Cypriot landlord. Although a plaque exists at the Queensborough Terrace site noting the poet's residency there, the landlord had no idea of the history of his other property in Pembridge Gardens or its connection to the Cavafy family.
57. Haricleia Ionides-Dannreuther's husband, Edward, was the founder of the London Wagner Society and lived nearby. In May 1877, the first reading of Wagner's *Parsifal* took place in her home and was attended by George Eliot. That same year, the Dannreuthers hosted Wagner and his wife and introduced them to their Anglo-Greek relations. Quite possibly Haricleia and her sons were in attendance (Solomonidis-Hunter 2014).
58. Uncle George's son John Cavafy married Marigo Ralli in August 1873 and their daughter Kitty (b. 1873) was baptized in February 1875, two family events that Haricleia and her boys would have attended (Solomonidis-Hunter 2014).
59. Pomian, 41.
60. The South Kensington Museum, it should be noted, evolved from the Great Crystal Palace Exhibition of 1851. In fact, Alexander C. Ionides, in his capacity as merchant banker and art collector, became one of the directors of the Crystal Palace in 1855, after it was permanently relocated to South London. Two other Anglo-Greeks are worthy of mention in this regard, as they also helped inaugurate the practice of connoisseurship and benefaction. George Eumorfopoulos, an eminent member of the community and vice president of Ralli Brothers, was an avid collector of Asian antiquities who left his extensive collection of Chinese ceramics divided between the Victoria and Albert Museum, the British Museum, and the Benaki Museum in Athens. And Stavros Dilberoglue, a partner of Cavafy and Co., was also a major art collector and philanthropist. He was also a close friend of Thomas Carlyle, George Eliot, Rossetti, and Whistler. See George Manginis's lecture on Eumorfopoulos (June 4, 2020), "'For the Benefit of the Nation': A Collection of Chinese Art for Greece," where he notes that Eumorfopoulos and Cavafy

were in London at the same time, lived in close proximity, were the same age, and likely met and played in the church garden. According to the school's records, Eumorfopoulos attended Hellenic College in 1873.

61. Constantine was writing under the sway of Baudelaire during this decade and composed a number of prose poems that are highly indebted to the French decadent poet.
62. Cavafy 2010, 84.
63. Ibid., 84.
64. Ibid., 85.
65. Ibid., 85.

2. TRAUMA, EXILE, AND LOSS

1. In her study *Return to Alexandria: An Ethnography of Cultural Heritage, Revivalism, and Museum Memory*, Beverley Butler explores the project of retrievalism in that city in light of the history and legendary status of the famous Mouseion, which she approaches through the discourse of museology. Alexandria, she notes, was from its inception preoccupied with origins and the need to rehouse memory in exile, leading to the creation of a new object: Greek Culture. It was also a city where the Greek diaspora could return to its cultural roots as perceived through books and knowledge (36), a place underpinned by both a "trauma of origin" and a "myth of redemption" (17). This applies to Constantine and the early life traumas he suffered, which he converts into a poetic formula for retrieval and redemption.
2. See chapters four and five for an account of this turmoil.
3. Quite possibly the poem "More Happy Thou, Performing Member" predates this.
4. *LC*, 45. For the manuscript of the "Constantinopoliad," see GR-OF CA CA-SF02-S02-F24–0003 (262).
5. *LC*, 49.
6. *LC*, 49.
7. For the letter, dated June 17, 1882, see GR-OF CA CA-SF02-S01-SS01-F18-SF002–0002 (1667).
8. *LC*, 45.
9. *LC*, 45–47.
10. *LC*, 47.
11. *LC*, 49.
12. *LC*, 49.
13. Cavafy 2015, 639.
14. Some sources speak of the house as a "*yali*," the Ottoman word for a villa on the sea. But on a visit in May 2019, Gregory Jusdanis interviewed current residents of Yeniköy and determined that it was not a yali but a house built along the main road snaking along the Bosporus. Ilias Koulouridis, a man in his eighties who was born in Yeniköy, remembers the Photiades house as standing slightly to the left of the Church of the Panagia Koumariotissa until the 1950s, when it was torn down to expand the road. Mr. Koulouridis said the house was not a yali but an "*epavli*" (in Greek, a manor house or villa). The Photiades family grave still stands in the Greek cemetery of Yeniköy, a ten-minute jaunt up the hill from the house.
15. *LC*, 47.
16. *LC*, 47.
17. Haas 1994, 302.

18. This is Meletios Mitrou's Greek book *Γεωγραφία Παλαιά και Νέα / Geography Old and New* (Venice, 1807).
19. Haas 1994, 302.
20. The current Greek community of Yeniköy has erected a bust of Cavafy in the courtyard of the Church of the Panagia Koumariotissa with verses from the poem "Nichori" engraved in Greek and Turkish translations.
21. We do not know if in Istanbul Constantine knew of the "gazel" tradition of Ottoman poetry, sung for beautiful women. He may, however, have heard about the tradition of the dancing boys and the music and songs associated with them—the transvestite köçek dancers, which had a long-standing cultural presence in Istanbul connected to both the imperial court and the urban underworld. Massavetas (2014, 422) notes that this subculture was written about by Greek intellectuals of the nineteenth century, in particular by Skarlatos Byzantios in his multivolume study *Constantinople* (1862), where he singles out the Greek neighborhood of Tatavla for the "disgraceful" presence of the köçek dancers amid the upstanding Greek residents. See also Kuru 2006, 163.
22. On the Phanariot poets and their influence, see the "Interlude" chapter.
23. Constantine's maternal grandfather was heavily involved in church matters, being a benefactor of the Patriarchate of Jerusalem, which had a great presence in Constantinople. See Massavetas (2013, 171), who notes that the Phanar was known as the place of the "patriarchates" owing to the presence of the Patriarch of Jerusalem, who spent prolonged periods in the Phanar and owned numerous properties there and many churches in the city (*metochia*) that were directly under his jurisdiction. The Nichori Church of Saint George was one of these, the land having been given by Photios Photiades, the poet's great-grandfather (*GN*, 89). Yiorgos Photiades was also a benefactor of local church institutions—the Baloukli hospital in particular (ibid.). On the Cavafy side, a handwritten promissory note of the Patriarchate of Jerusalem survives in the Onassis Foundation Cavafy Archive, recording that the Patriarchate borrowed a significant amount of money from John Cavafy (the poet's grandfather) in 1811 in order to restore the Holy Sepulchre. For the archival document, see GR-OF CA CA-SF03-F27–0001(2108). This deep involvement in church matters is fully documented in the notes Constantine was amassing while in Istanbul and lends support to his prolonged interest in ecclesiastical history, which has always been tragically intertwined with the political history of medieval and modern Greece.
24. Massavetas 2007, 85.
25. See Svolopoulos (64) on the connection between the Tanzimat reforms and the burgeoning effect the toleration of a relatively free press had on the Greek community.
26. Svolopoulos, 86.
27. The Greek Philological Society of Constantinople was arguably the most important Greek cultural institution in the city outside of the Patriarchate in the nineteenth century. In addition to supervising and overseeing education in the capital and major cities of the Ottoman Empire, it kept the focus of the Greek community on education and reform and encouraged progressive intellectual activity by means of its public lectures, classes, library, and publications whereby it promoted the idea of Ottoman Hellenism's legitimate and assured cultural presence in the city. It encouraged Ottoman Greeks to take a leading role in the cultural, bureaucratic, and commercial administration of the failing empire, which they planned

to "reform" into a multicultural nation that they would be positioned to dominate (Panakopoulos, 1998). All of these ambitions were thwarted by the rise of the Revolution of the Young Turks in 1908 and were terminated with the 1922 defeat of the Greek armies in Asia Minor. See also Sümertas.

28. De Amicis, 24.
29. De Amicis, 49–50.
30. For a detailed overview of the Greek presence in Galata and Pera, see Massavetas (2007), who notes that following the Greek Revolution of 1821, "Pera became the new force, and its markedly secular and westernizing elite took over from the Phanari theocracy the leadership of Constantinopolitan Hellenism" (89). In a similar vein, Galata, he argues, "became the dying empire's window to modernization" (141).
31. The Greeks of the city (the Rum Millet / Roman Nation as they were called by the Ottomans) had resided there since Byzantine times, spoke Turkish, and were integrated into the life of the empire. Unlike the Greeks of Alexandria, who spoke little to no Arabic, they were not commercial interlopers but heirs to an unbroken historical and cultural presence in a city they felt to be their own.
32. Kirli, 177.
33. Sagaster, 101.
34. Sagaster, 102.
35. De Amicis, 20.
36. De Amicis, 32.
37. Massavetas 2007, 165.
38. De Amicis, 53, 155–56.
39. Ash, 19.
40. Constantine likely knew about two significant publications related to the Byzantine monuments of Istanbul (his grandfather's allegedly rich library might even have possessed them): Skarlatos Byzantios's three-volume *Η Κωνσταντινούπολις: Η Περιγραφή Τοπογραφηκή, Αρχαιολογική και Ιστορική της Περιωνύμου Ταύτης Μεγαλοπόλεως . . . / Constantinople: A Topographical, Archeological, and Historical Description of this Illustrious Great City . . .* (Athens: 1851, 1862, 1869)—the historical description of the neighborhoods in volume two (including Neochorion, Therapia, and Kalinderi) may have served as an inspiration for the poet's own ethnographic composition on the town; and a less expansive but significant publication published by the Greek Philological Society, A. G. Paspatis's *Βυζαντιναί Μελέται: Τοπογραφικαί και Ιστορικαί / Byzantine Studies: Topographical and Historical* (1877). Paspatis's book contains elegant engravings of the city's walls and other monuments as well as plates of all the converted churches (these by Demetrios Galanakis). Paspatis and Byzantios both provide detailed descriptions of the surviving churches, offering Greek residents of the city the opportunity to learn about the buildings' history and conversion into mosques as well as encouraging their exploration.
41. Recorded in a letter to his mother (Freely, 262).
42. The Cavafy family church became iconic in 1955 when it was featured in the world press following the pogrom against the Greeks of Istanbul, with the Ecumenical Patriarch Athenagoras photographed amid its burned ruins, praying with his head uncovered before the decimated altar and apse (Massavetas 2007, 110).
43. Samatya (Turkish)/Psomathea, from the Greek "Υψωμα Θείον" (Divine Elevation). In his *Genealogical Gossip*, Constantine notes the connections of both the

Photiades and Cavafy families to this church. The Photiades family also had early roots in Psomathea (*GN*, 92). His paternal great-grandfather and grandfather were allegedly wardens of this church (*GN*, 20). Massavetas also notes the name of the parish's abutting elementary school, "The Photiadeios School," founded by Alexander and Nicholas Photiades, Constantine's uncles (2007, 113).

44. Namely the Monastery of Christ Pantocrator / Zeyrek Camii; the Church of the Chora / Karye Camii; the Church of the Virgin of the Mongols; the Church of the Virgin Kyriotissa / Kalenderhane Camii; the Church of the Virgin Pammakaristos / Fethiye Camii; the Church of Christ Pantepoptis / Eski Imaret Camii; the Myrelaion / Budrum Camii; the Monastery of the Theotokos of Lips / Fenari Isa Camii; the Vlachernai Palace of the Porphyrogenitus / Tekfursarayi.
45. Karapanagopoulos, 14. Rika does not use the word "homosexuality," but rather refers to Constantine's "anomalia" (abnormality), the term frequently employed at the time. She goes so far as to deny that he had any homosexual relations after 1903, much to the astonishment of her interviewer, Alekos Karapanagopoulos, who asks her to explain why he had gone on to write so many homoerotic poems.
46. Delice, 151.
47. Semerdjian, 254.
48. Ergin, 143.
49. Ze'evi, 87.
50. GR-OF CA CA-SF02-S01-SS01-F18-SF002–0063 (1699).
51. GR-OF CA CA-SF02-S01-SS01-F18-SF002–0025 (1673).
52. GR-OF CA CA-SF02-S01-SS01-F18-SF002–0025 (1673).
53. Cavafy 2010, 155.
54. Cavafy 2010, 74.
55. Written in the style of the ancient Greek poet Anacreon, who was renowned for celebrating love and wine.

3. FAMILY AFFAIRS

1. *GN*, 144, 149.
2. GR-OF CA CA-SF02-S01-SS02-F20-SF001–0001 (376). The transcriptions of John's letters excerpted below and elsewhere are those edited by Katerina Ghika, which are accessible electronically through the Onassis Foundation Cavafy Archive. John's letters have been translated into Spanish by the Chilean Hellenist Miguel Castillo Didier (2020).
3. GR-OF CA CA-SF02-S01-SS02-F20-SF001–0002 (377).
4. GR-OF CA CA-SF02-S01-SS02-F20-SF001–0003 (378).
5. GR-OF CA CA-SF02-S01-SS02-F20-SF001–0009 (384).
6. The title of a poem that translates to "Eros, the bearer of pain."
7. GR-OF CA CA-SF02-S01-SS02-F20-SF001–0011 (386).
8. GR-OF CA CA-SF02-S01-SS02-F20-SF001–0012 (387).
9. These are titles of poems written by John.
10. GR-OF CA CA-SF02-S01-SS02-F20-SF001–0015 (390).
11. GR-OF CA CA-SF02-S01-SS02-F20-SF001–0016 (391).
12. GR-OF CA CA-SF02-S01-SS02-F20-SF001–0026 (401).
13. GR-OF CA CA-SF02-S01-SS02-F20-SF001–0029 (404).
14. John died in 1923, leaving the bulk of his estate to his niece Hariclia and to his mistress—Madame Deker—with only a small portion (one thousand Egyptian pounds) to his younger brother (*GN*, 150). At John's funeral, according to

Malanos, Constantine leaned into the coffin and with "spasmodic, almost comical gestures" whispered into the dead man's ear, "John, John." When pressed, Constantine said that he merely wanted to make sure that John was not still alive (*TPC*, 198).

15. GR-OF CA CA-SF02-S01-SS02-F20-SF001–0049 (424).
16. GR-OF CA CA-SF02-S01-SS02-F20-SF001–0050 (425).
17. GR-OF CA CA-SF02-S01-SS02-F20-SF001–0066 (441).
18. GR-OF CA CA-SF02-S01-SS02-F20-SF001–0067 (1149).
19. There is also the curiously collaborative poem "Darkness and Shadows" (1882?), which is allegedly "a transcription from the French of C.F.C." (*LC*, 76–77), but John presents it (in a slightly different version) as his own composition in his *Early Verses*.
20. We know from the genealogical notes that upon marrying, Haricleia had tutors in Liverpool for instruction in languages and drawing. She surely had achieved an advanced level of literacy in Greek prior to her marriage.
21. The first of these was recorded while she was staying in Istanbul following the bombardment.
22. GR-OF CA CA-SF02-S01-SS02-F20-SF003–0004 (1103).
23. GR-OF CA CA-SF02-S01-SS02-F20-SF003–0009 (1109).
24. GR-OF CA CA-SF02-S01-SS02-F20-SF003–0010 (1110).
25. GR-OF CA CA-SF02-S01-SS02-F20-SF003–0012 (1112).
26. GR-OF CA CA-SF02-S01-SS02-F20-SF003–0013 (1113).
27. We will see echoes of these solicitous sentiments in Constantine's letters to Alekos Sengopoulos in 1918–19, who is working as an intern in a business in Benha (discussed in chapter eight).
28. The notes on Haricleia's last days are, with a few exceptions, written in Greek. Many are undated and all are composed in Constantine's abbreviated shorthand. The 1903 genealogical comments are in English and also recorded in shorthand. For the manuscript of the notes on Haricleia's death, see GR-OF CA CA-SF02-S02-F24–0006 (473), which were transcribed and edited by Pieris (1991). Our translated citations from this source are taken from Pieris and include his editorial renderings of Constantine's shorthand.
29. Pat Jalland, in her study *Death in the Victorian Family*, notes the prevalence of diarized deathbed memorials in the nineteenth century. These involve intimate accounts of deathbed scenes and daily, even hourly, events, including symptoms, medical treatment, visitors, and conversations (Jalland, 10).
30. GR-OF CA CA-SF02-S02-F25-SF002–0003 (1091), p. 20, p. 27.
31. GR-OF CA CA-SF02-S02-F25-SF002–0003 (1091), p. 28.
32. George, it appears, visited and stayed with the family for intermittent periods when passing through Alexandria.
33. *CE*, 300.
34. A cousin of his deceased friend Mikès Ralli.
35. Cavafy 1991, 181–82.
36. Cavafy 1991, 184.
37. Cavafy 1991, 205–206.
38. Cavafy 1991, 184.
39. The story involves a marriage plot between commercial traders and fallen aristocrats, a plotline sure to have engaged Haricleia.
40. Cavafy 1991, 199.

41. Cavafy 1991, 197.
42. Cavafy 1991, 183.
43. Cavafy 1991, 192.
44. Cavafy 1991, 191.
45. Cavafy 1991, 190.
46. Cavafy 1991, 182.
47. Cavafy 1991, 198.
48. Cavafy 1991, 197. We have not been able to determine the exact meaning of this Italian phrase.
49. Cavafy 1991, 187.
50. Of himself he writes: "Has achieved very little in practical life; less than what he might have done, perhaps, had he directed his energies better": GR-OF CA CA-SF02-S02-F25-SF002–0003 (1091), 37–38.
51. Ibid., 31.
52. Ibid., 32.
53. Ibid., 35.
54. *GN*, 136–37.
55. GR-OF CA CA-SF02-S01-SS02-F19–0004 (448)
56. GR-OF CA CA-SF02-S01-SS02-F21–0010 (1156).
57. GR-OF CA CA-SF02-S01-SS02-F19–0005 (449).
58. The source for this is based on rumor and innuendo propagated by Dimitris Garoufalias (Papanikolaou, 183).
59. A local newspaper.
60. GR-OF CA CA-SF02-S01-SS02-F21–0018 (1160).
61. See his letter dated July 12, 1908, cited below.
62. GR-OF CA CA-SF02-S01-SS02-F21–0019 (1161).
63. GR-OF CA CA-SF02-S01-SS02-F21–0020 (1162).
64. GR-OF CA CA-SF02-S01-SS02-F21–0019 (1161).
65. In later letters from Paul to John and Constantine written from France, the guilt of how shabbily he treated his mother consumes him. He dreams of her and requests that they send him her photo.
66. Paul's dire situation forced him to consider an arranged marriage in 1903 to a wealthy Anglo-Greek with a £10,000 dowry through the agency of his cousin John's wife, Marigo Cavafy. See GR-OF CA CA-SF02-S01-SS02-F21–0028 (1168), letter dated May 16, 1903. The intended bride, Babette Valieri, Marigo informs him in a subsequent letter, declines, wishing to marry "for love." GR-OF CA CA-SF02-S01-SS02-F21–0030 (1170), letter dated June 5, 1903.
67. Paul was fond of soldiers and has in his scrapbook a collection of photos from handsome English military men, including one with the curious name of Enrico Spy. His letters to Constantine from Hyères describe social encounters with soldiers during the war that strongly hint at a sexual flirtation. For Paul's scrapbook, see GR-OF CA CA-SF02-S02-F25-SF005–0005 (1901).
68. Letter dated December 7, 1908: GR-OF CA CA-SF02-S01-SS02-F20-SF002–0007 (525).
69. Letter dated January 5, 1909: GR-OF CA CA-SF02-S01-SS02-F20-SF002–0009 (527).
70. Letter dated March 1, 1909: GR-OF CA CA-SF02-S01-SS02-F20-SF002–0011 (529).
71. Letter dated April 28, 1909: GR-OF CA CA-SF02-S01-SS02-F20-SF002–0021 (539).

72. Letters dated June 6, 1909 [GR-OF CA CA-SF02-S01-SS02-F20-SF002–0025 (543)], and June 19, 1909 [GR-OF CA CA-SF02-S01-SS02-F20-SF002–0026 (544)].
73. Letter dated May 17, 1910: GR-OF CA CA-SF02-S01-SS02-F20-SF002–0028 (545).
74. In her biographical notes, Rika Sengopoulos records a detail from a letter from Paul where he references a one-act "farce" he wrote to be staged at the Avenue Theatre in London [GR-OF CA SING-S01-F01–0014 (1630)]. To date, no traces of Paul's dramatic compositions have been found.
75. The name Prince Paul, curiously enough, appears in an early Oscar Wilde play—his first—*Vera; or, the Nihilists* (1880), which was staged in New York in 1883 but bombed miserably. Aside from the obvious interest Paul would have had in Wilde as a dandy, playwright, wit, and gay martyr, he may have even met him through the social network of London aesthetes associated with his relatives there. Wilde was well acquainted with Paul's Anglo-Greek relation Maria Zambaco, having dined on numerous occasions with her in Paris in the company of John Singer Sargent and Paul Bourget (Sturgis, 277). Bourget will eventually settle in Hyères in the social orbit of Edith Wharton, who begins building her final architectural masterwork Château Sainte-Claire while living at the Pavillon Colombe in nearby Saint-Brice-sous-Forêt in 1919, during the final year of Paul's life (Lesage, 186 and passim).
76. GR-OF CA CA-SF02-S02-F25-SF007–0040 (619).
77. Mentioned in a letter dated August 8, 1913: GR-OF CA CA-SF02-S01-SS02-F20-SF002–0067 (584).
78. Letter dated May 30, 1914: GR-OF CA CA-SF02-S01-SS02-F20-SF002–0074 (590).
79. Letter dated October 3, 1919: GR-OF CA CA-SF02-S01-SS02-F21–0034 (1177).
80. GR-OF CA CA-SF02-S01-SS02-F20-SF001–0071 (1176).
81. GR-OF CA CA-SF02-S01-SS02-F20-SF001–0072 (1183).
82. GR-OF CA CA-SF02-S01-SS02-F20-SF003–0033 (1187).
83. Cited in Manolis Savidis's introduction to *C. P. Cavafy: Sixty-Three Poems Translated by J. C. Cavafy* (ix).
84. Sarah Ekdawi notes the irony of the use of the word "council" by Constantine given that his brother Peter worked for the "Sanitary Council": "Cavafy may not have belonged to any Sanitary Council . . . It is easy to imagine the two titles becoming interchangeable, in a kind of family joke: Family Council, Sanitary Council" (1997, 226).
85. Catraro 1970, 31–32.
86. Gialourakis 1974, 205.
87. This unpublished letter was provided by Nicolas Sarafis, to whom we are grateful for permission to cite it, and according to whom the intended recipient was likely Costas Rodocanachi of Alexandria. Maria Vouros, Hariclia's mother, was the daughter of Julia Rodocanachi.
88. Paul experienced complications in receiving his pension payments from the municipality. It's not evident how Hariclia expected to receive a pension, as there is no record of her having worked for the Department of Public Works. It should be recalled that Paul attempted to arrange a marriage with a Babette Valieri (see note 66 above) of London, who may well have been a distant relative of Hariclia's future husband.
89. She also inherited jewelry from her grandmother Haricleia Cavafy (*GN*, 152).

90. *GN*, 152.
91. We are grateful to Marjorie Salvodon for providing this English translation from the French original.
92. From an unsigned article published in the Greek newspaper *Ακρόπολις* (March 11(?), 1983).

4. CONSTANTINE'S WORLD

1. These are the modern street names. The Metropole Hotel was established in 1932; beforehand it was known as the Iorio Palace Hotel and originally as the Anglo-American Hotel, constructed in 1890.
2. Chatzifotis, 75.
3. Liddell, 129.
4. Ibid., 130.
5. Tsirkas 1963, 687. Between 1889 and 1892, he worked as an unpaid apprentice. He would stay in this department for thirty years, starting with a monthly salary of £7 and ending in 1922 with the monthly intake of £33.6 (*CE*, 225).
6. GR-OF CA CA-SF02-S01-SS03-F22-SF002–0001 (987).
7. Gialourakis 1959, 143.
8. Forster 1980, 91.
9. Haag 2004a, 60.
10. The apartment has recently been renovated by the Onassis Foundation and re-conceptualized as a cultural space that illustrates the poet's life and reflects his twenty-first-century status as a global literary figure.
11. Gialourakis 2007, 225.
12. Zananiri, 14.
13. Pieridis, 18.
14. Malanos 1978, 78–80.
15. Malanos 1978, 85.
16. Boddy, 60.
17. The Zizinia Theatre, designed by Pietro Avoscani and inspired by La Scala of Milan, stood on Rue Rosette. See chapter seven for a discussion of "In Broad Daylight."
18. Cavafy 2010, 87, 90.
19. Hanley, 43.
20. Boddy, 55–56.
21. The English traveler and writer Amelia B. Edwards (1831–92) provides a vivid description of Cairo during her trip to Egypt of 1873, which gives us a glimpse of what Alexandria might have been like twenty-five years before Boddy's visit. "The houses are high and narrow. The upper stories project; and from these again jut windows of delicate turned lattice work in old brown wood, like bird cages. The street is roofed in overhead with long rafters and pieces of matting through which a dusty sunbeam struggles here and there, casting patches of light upon the moving crowd" (Edwards, 2).
22. Briggs, 17–18. Like many travelers to Alexandria before and after, Briggs dismisses as "Oriental" this part of the city for not living up to the cosmopolitan promise of the European side of town.
23. Forster 1982, 111.
24. GR-OF CA CA-SF02-S02-F25-SF006–0003 (1141).
25. Malanos 1971, 56–58.

26. For a fascinating history of this important institution of Alexandrian social life, see Liapi.
27. Hanley, 34, 44.
28. GR-OF CA CA-SF0-S02-F25-SF0006–0002 (979).
29. Malanos 1971, 116.
30. Forster 1982, 111.
31. Boddy, 63. In true Orientalist manner, Boddy, preferring the European side of Alexandria, was bothered by "the swarthy faces, the turbans and *galabíyehs* of the many Fellaheen passing by and the veiled women with tinkling silver anklets."
32. Briggs, 17.
33. Constantine kept the announcement of Stephen's death that appeared in the newspaper *Telegrafos*, April 9, 1886.
34. Boddy, 256.
35. Haag 2004a, 67.
36. The café changed its name in 1905 and became the Grand Trianon (Malanos 1971, 50). It exists today in all its glory as one of the few reminders of the refined elegance Constantine experienced in the city.
37. Malanos 1971, 50.
38. Haag 2004a, 55; Issa, 1.
39. In 1902, he admitted in a personal note that "I have never lived in the countryside. I have never visited the countryside even for brief periods." He then added that he wrote a poem about nature (which does not survive), which "is the most insincere thing there is; a proper lie." Yet, "art lies the most when it creates the most" (Cavafy 2010, 129). See GR-OF CA CA-SF01-S03-F09–0001 (196).
40. Cavafy 1963b, 283, 279. For the manuscript of Constantine's 1901 travel journal, see GR-OF CA CA-SF02-S02-F24–0001 (1650).
41. Malanos 1971, 49. "Salade cresson" is French for "watercress salad."
42. Malanos 1971, 54.
43. Before his departure for Paris in 1920, Kephalinos drew a portrait of Constantine, which he later used for his famous engraving of the poet (Malanos 1971, 73). This was reproduced on the cover of the Ikaros edition of the poet's collected works (Papargyriou, 256).
44. Malanos 1971, 61.
45. Pieridis, 10.
46. Gialourakis 1959, 68.
47. It remained open until the 1980s and was demolished in 1995. The Café Al Salam, another favorite meeting place, is now gone. Athineos still functions as a family restaurant today. The current owner, Mr. Yagcoub Nassar, says that his father bought it in 1970 from the Greek owners during the period of nationalization. (Message conveyed to Gregory Jusdanis via Zahraa Adel Awad, November 12, 2019.)
48. Sareyiannis 1964, 41.
49. Pieridis, 40.
50. Zananiri, 14.
51. Malanos declines to cite the verb and substitutes a series of dots from which we can infer that sexual activity is implied.
52. Malanos 1971, 295–98.
53. Haas 1983, 91.
54. This "self-comment" also includes the following revealing words: "A youth in bed

with another youth, lovely, but with an old man, disgusting" (Haas 1983, 92). See GR-OF CA CA-SF01-S03-F11–0007 (232).

55. Haas 1983, 93.
56. Malanos 1971, 145–50.
57. Ibid., 145.
58. Ibid., 147.
59. Ibid., 148.
60. The Onassis Foundation Cavafy Archive contains many such short letters requesting that Nikos Zelitas do some type of favor or task. Although most of these notes are undated, the few dates suggest that they were written in the 1920s at the height of Constantine's popularity, a time when he would have needed practical assistance to promote his career. See item GR-OF CA CA-SF03-F29–0003 (1884).
61. Rota, 100.
62. Constantine was so irate with Peridis that he stopped speaking to him until 1919 (Peridis, 98–100). Peridis later recanted these views and came to support the poet, becoming another acolyte and writing a study of his life and work in 1947. Seen by Malanos as a hagiographic treatment of Constantine, it remained the only biography until the publication of Liddell's study.
63. Forster 1982, 155.
64. Malanos notes that Constantine often went to this library for research (1971, 95). He also borrowed from the municipal library as well as from the libraries of his friends (Peridis, 64; Karapanagopoulos, 55).
65. Forster 1982, 114.
66. Cavafy 1963b, 268.
67. Ibid., 269.
68. Kolaitis does not remember if it was 1928 or 1929.
69. Kolaitis, 82.
70. Gialourakis 1959, 124–25.
71. Forster 1982, 161. The Temple of Serapis stood near this pillar.
72. Ibid., 163. See also Issa, 187.
73. Haag 2004a, 8.
74. Cavafy 1963b, 265.
75. Ibid., 264,
76. Ibid., 285.
77. See Maria Boletsi's *Specters of Cavafy* (2024) for more on the spectral aspect of Cavafy's poetry.
78. Cavafy 1963b, 161.
79. The collection was formed in 1892 and displayed in a house. Constantine published an article about its opening in the Alexandrian paper *Telegraphos* (July 12, 1892). Speaking with pride, he called the museum a "treasure" that charts "our glorious Hellenism of Alexandria." The article prompted a note of appreciation in Italian from the director, Dr. Giuseppe Botti, thanking Constantine for his interest in the "newly built museum" (Cavafy 1963b, 161). It was then moved to the new building in 1895.
80. Forster 1982, 115.
81. Although he drew attention to the Hellenistic period before others, his Hellenocentrism kept Constantine from being swept up by the Egyptomania that had taken over Europe and North America in the first two decades of the twentieth century, particularly after the sensational discoveries of the bust of Queen

Nefertiti in 1913 and the tomb of Tutankhamen in 1922. We don't have any references in his work or correspondence to these momentous events in Egypt. Of course, this Egyptomania was a European and American phenomenon and most of the archaeological excavations until Egyptian independence in 1922 remained in the hands of British, German, French, Italian, and American archaeologists, which explains why a majority of the finds until 1922 ended up in foreign museums. Moreover, the discovery of Tutankhamen's tomb coincided with the growing Egyptian nationalism and interest in pre-Islamic history. Like other nations, Egypt wanted to establish a sense of historical continuity, and the excavation of this tomb constituted a moment of national pride and opportunity to assert control over the past. Stung by the transferral of Nefertiti to Berlin, Egyptian officials ensured that the more than five thousand artifacts in Tutankhamen's tomb remained in the Museum of Egyptian Antiquities in Cairo. As an Egyptian-Greek, Constantine did not feel himself part of this national story and preferred to set his poetic characters in the Hellenistic, Roman, and Byzantine periods. He is on record as saying, "I don't understand those big immobile things" (Sareyiannis 1964, 45). On Egyptomania, see Wilkinson, 414–18.

82. Zananiri, 14.
83. The word she used was "*arapis*" (singular) and "*arapides*" (plural). *Arapis* was a highly derogatory term denoting someone who was seen as black or belonging to a black race. It was frequently used to indicate Arabs/Muslims in Egypt. Its etymology is Turkish but ultimately seems to go back to Arabic: https://www.greek-language.gr/greekLang/modern_greek/tools/lexica/triantafyllides/search.html?lq=%CE%B1%CF%81%CE%AC%CF%80%CE%B7%CF%82&dq=). We thank Brian Joseph, professor of linguistics at the Ohio State University, for his explanation of the etymology of this word.
84. Ouranis, 1468.
85. Kampanis [1933] 1963b, 1488.
86. Ibid., 1488.
87. We don't have a list of all his servants, but Constantine kept a copy of a letter of reference he wrote in English and French for one of them: "May 1918. Morgani Osman has been in my service since 1909. He left me about two months ago, as he wanted to seek some employment other than household work. All the time, he was in my service I found him capable, very honest, and active; indeed, a very good servant." GR-OF CA CA-SF02-S02-F25-SF004–0019 (976).
88. On Cavafy's library, see Karampini-Iatrou (2003). On the opposite wall, there was a mirror, a stool, and various other pieces of small furniture. Dark-colored oriental rugs covered the floor.
89. Zananiri, 14.
90. Karampini-Iatrou 2003, 160.
91. Zananiri, 14.
92. Sareyiannis 1964, 37–38.
93. Cavafy 2015, 575–76.
94. Constantine himself stopped in Marseilles with John on their European trip in May–June of 1897.
95. Catraro 1970, 30–32.
96. Gialourakis 1959, 124.
97. Zananiri, 14.
98. Catraro 1970, 32.

99. Ibid., 30, 32.
100. When Haricleia moved the family to England, she left most of this furniture in a rented apartment on Boulevard de Ramleh (*CE*, 127).
101. Sareyiannis 1964, 32.
102. Sareyiannis met Constantine in 1915 just before leaving for studies in Paris. Eventually he settled in Greece, where he distinguished himself as a botanist and as one of the most sensitive readers of Cavafy.
103. Pieridis, 18.
104. Pieridis, 20. He had in fact moved to Rue Lepsius in 1907 with Paul.
105. *TPC*, 21–23.
106. Pieridis, 20–21.
107. Kampanis 1963a, 1421.
108. Ouranis, 1468.
109. *TPC*, 22. Kampanis too was taken by the round glasses that framed the poet's large eyes, with their dark eyelids and thick eyelashes (Kampanis 1963a, 1421).
110. Lechonitis, 19. The critic G. Lechonitis, who had distanced himself from Constantine after the publication of his more explicitly erotic verses, had asked the poet in 1930 for a series of interviews on his poems. Unfortunately, he never published these verbatim comments and offered them to Malanos, who issued them in 1942.
111. *TPC*, 21–23.
112. Kazantzakis, 74–75.
113. Myrtiotissa, 84.
114. His mother's younger sister, Sevaste, was married to the Belgian diplomat Leon Verhaeghe de Naeyer; she stopped in Istanbul in 1884 on the way from Shanghai and met Constantine (Kourelis, 239). Photography as technology rarely appeared in Constantine's poetry. The Greek modernist sought to portray himself as a nineteenth-century dandy even in 1929—that is, three decades after the establishment of the first cinema in Alexandria in 1897 on the Rue de la Gare du Caire. The Lumière brothers visited Alexandria in 1896 and showed short films in the Café Zawani, less than a year after screening their first film in Paris (Issa, 371). We have no evidence that Constantine attended this event.

5. A TALE OF TWO CITIES

1. Pieridis, 22.
2. Cavafy 1991, 209.
3. Liddell, 129. Manolis Halvatzakis, an Alexandrian Greek, who interviewed el Kayar himself, admitted that his visit to el Kayar's home in 1967 was only the second time he had been in an Egyptian house (Liddell, 127).
4. The obliviousness of foreigners to Muslim Alexandria is reflected in how later readers came to see Cavafy himself. Enamored of the city's cosmopolitanism, lovers of Cavafy's poetry looked past contemporary Alexandria to Cavafy's city, which itself was built on the exclusion of the Arabs. For Europeans, Alexandria has been a city of nostalgia, of homecoming, a return to the Hellenistic past, a time before nationalism and ethnic hatred. Critics have depicted the post-Nasser city as having fallen from grace (Halim 2013, 45). On how the modern library of Alexandria, the Bibliotheca Alexandrina, exploits this Western fascination with the Hellenistic past, see Butler.

5. In the fall of 1932, when Constantine was in Athens for his surgery, he asked Sareyiannis to arrange a rendezvous with Delta, whom Constantine had not seen since her departure from Alexandria seventeen years earlier. After so many years, however, they rekindled their long friendship and began to reminisce about the "atmosphere of the salons of Alexandria," which they both missed (Yialourakis 1959, 36). Her house represented the height of Alexandrian sophistication and wealth.
6. Delta 1980, 217.
7. Delta 1980, 146.
8. Mademoiselle Dufay, like Penelope's English teacher, did not acquire other languages, ensconced as she was within the monolingual islands of their French and English communities. The linguistic limitations of the Benaki teachers reveal the prejudice of the English and the French toward other cultures. Dufay openly displayed her contempt for the Greek language while the English teacher herself expressed disdain for French by referring to Dufay as a "frog-eater" (Delta 1980, 118).
9. Carswell, 141. Of the forty-four pieces, seventeen belonged to Alexandre Benaki, fifteen to Nomikos, and five to Lagonikos. Only the Antonis Benaki collection is intact today (Carswell, 141). See also the lecture by Nina Moraitou, curator of the Benaki Museum of Islamic Art.
10. In the nineteenth century, neither did the Turkish rulers mix with the Arabs (Mansel, 67). Mohammed Ali considered himself primarily an Ottoman administrator, as did his entire officer class; Egyptians were not allowed to rise beyond the rank of captain. The racial attitudes of the Ottoman Turks coincided with those of the Europeans (Mansel, 80). Arabs were exploited and marginalized by both sides.
11. See the earlier discussion of this derogatory term in chapter four.
12. Delta 1980, 102.
13. The British did not refrain from imposing their own cruelty upon the local population. Penelope describes an episode when a "handsome and polite" British officer ordered a fellahin at the train station to move and create a free path. When the latter responded with an "I don't care," the officer charged upon the man with his horse (ibid., 78).
14. Constantine is often credited with coining the term "Αιγυπτιώτες" to refer to the Greeks of Egypt.
15. Antaios is using here another version of the derogatory term "*arapides*," the plural of "*arapis*," to indicate "black people." Makis Antaios is the pen name of Memas Kolaitis.
16. GR-OF CA CA-SF03-F29–0002 (1883). This episode took place in 1928. Although the note comes from Eftychia Zelitas's notebook, it seems that Antaios himself was also involved in recording the anecdote.
17. Officials registered non-European residents of the city as *fellahin* (peasants), *ibn al-balad* (city dwellers), *ibn 'Arab* (nomads or Bedouins), *barbari* (those stemming from the south of Egypt), or *raya* (protected minorities). For much of Constantine's life, few of his fellow Muslim residents of the city would have seen themselves as Egyptian, though they would have differentiated themselves from Europeans and from the Christian Copts. By World War I, however, these locals began to adopt a national identity (Hanley, 259, 275). Although the Ottoman Empire established an Ottoman nationality law in 1869, Egypt did not pass its own nationality law until 1926 (Hanley, 245). Until then, Egyptians traveling abroad represented themselves as Ottoman subjects.

18. Moreover, they saw Egyptians as a separate racial group, since the national category of Egyptian did not really emerge until the 1920s (Hanley, 259). Their extensive trade networks in the Mediterranean stood in stark contrast to the inward pull of their ethnic identities (Mabro, 260).
19. In Greek, there exist two terms to convey the sense of foreign community: "*apoikia*," which suggests an overseas colony; and "*paroikia*," which conveys the meaning of a settler community abroad. In this sense, the Greeks of Alexandria constituted a *paroikia* (Psyroukis 1974, 129).
20. Kitroeff 1989, 126; Karanasou, 37.
21. Mansel, 107. Indeed, the Greeks showed the highest rate of endogamy (Karanasou, 34).
22. Dragoumis also met Constantine in 1905 and stayed in communication with the poet. On September 10, 1910, he sent a letter to Constantine informing him that he had received his poems. Unlike his other correspondents, who disappeared in Constantine's shadow, Dragoumis wanted to shine himself. He did not spend time on Constantine's poems, preferring to discuss his own projects, like the formation of an education association (*ekpaideftikos omilos*). See item GR-OF CA CA-SF02-S01-SS01-F18-SF003–0030 (1656). Constantine referred to this association in a letter to Alekos Sengopoulos on November 22, 1918, and January 22, 1919—items GR-OF CA SING-S01-F02 SF001–0021 [1422] and GR-OF CA SING-S01-F02 SF001–0043 [1444]. On Dragoumis's involvement in this project along with that of the socialist thinker Yeorgios Skliros, see Rena Stavridi-Patrikiou (1988).
23. The Benakis were ardent supporters of the anti-royalist Greek politician Eleftherios Venizelos and thus politically at odds with Dragoumis. Critics have tried without much success to place Constantine in this political controversy. But his name was not on the first list of Venizelos supporters that was published between March 16 and 20, 1917, in the Alexandrian newspaper *Tachydromos*, which was edited by Sotiris Liatsis, a Venizelos supporter and friend of Constantine. It did appear in the second list printed in the paper *Omonoia* on March 23, 1917 (Haas 2014, 98).
24. Delta 2007, 343. Penelope fell in love with Ion even though she had been married for ten years to Stephanos Delta. Finding Dragoumis interesting but not charming (Delta 1996, 4), she nevertheless succumbed to the daring politician. Dragoumis was assassinated on the streets of Athens in July 1920. Years later, his brother Phillipos sent Penelope Ion's archives. She, having worn black since his assassination, committed suicide in 1941.
25. Delta 1980, 77.
26. The Greeks used the term "Levantine" to refer primarily to Christian Arabs and Italians, but the British employed it more widely to cover all Christians and even Jews.
27. Delta 1980, 151.
28. Gialourakis 1959, 45.
29. The club brochure from 1902 contains the rules and privileges, and its list of members reads like a who's who of prominent Alexandrians.
30. This comes from Paul's "Scrapbook": GR-OF CA CA-SF02-S02-F25-SF005–0005 (1901).
31. Cavafy 1963b, 260.
32. Ibid., 262–63.
33. Ibid., 284–85.
34. She relayed this to Malanos in 1955 (Malanos 1963, 74, 79).
35. Abdulhaq, 2.

36. Ilbert, 28.
37. Politis vol. 1, 357.
38. Trimi and Yannakakis, 67.
39. Boddy, 57,
40. Hanley, 100.
41. Kitroeff 1989, 37.
42. Ibid., 3.
43. Primarily identifying these Christians living in the Ottoman territories, the term "Levant" was another name for what in Britain defined the Near East and became increasingly known after World War I under American influence as the Middle East. It signified to Western Europeans the lands on the shores of the eastern Mediterranean (today's Greece, Turkey, Syria, Lebanon, Israel, and Egypt). But, as Mansel notes, it was "an area, a dialogue, and a quest," also "a dialogue between East and West" (Mansel, 1).
44. Chatziioannou, 163.
45. Greeks continued to flourish in Egypt after the abolition of the Capitulations in 1937 and until Gamal Abdel Nasser nationalized the Egyptian economy in 1952.
46. Mansel, 74.
47. Goldschmidt, 20.
48. Reid, 220.
49. Cole, 55.
50. Sayyid-Marsot, 72.
51. Cole, 65.
52. Reid, 231; Mansel, 118.
53. Annesley, 216.
54. Darwin, 17.
55. Annesley, 223.
56. GR-OF CA CA-SF02-S01-SS02-F20-SF001–0013 (388).
57. Goldschmidt, 44.
58. Mansel, 130; Darwin, 19.
59. When Peter John moved to Alexandria in 1855, he rented a house from the Zizinia family on Place des Consuls, later renamed Place Mohammed Ali, then the center of Alexandria high society. As was the manner of the time, he housed his offices on the ground floor and the family dwelling on the second. The apartment on el Faliki, with eight rooms and a kitchen, cost seventy pounds annually. They had one servant. GR-OF CA CA-SF02-S02-F25-SF002–0003 (1091).
60. *CE*, 127.
61. John feared that with the number of bureaucrats involved from Britain, Egypt, and Greece the matter would stretch into the future (letter dated October 8, 1882). See items GR-OF CA CA-SF02-S01-SS02-F20-SF001–0001 (376), GR-OF CA CA-SF02-S01-SS02-F20-SF001–0002 (377), and GR-OF CA CA-SF02-S01-SS02-F20-SF001–0007 (382).
62. GR-OF CA CA-SF02-S01-SS02-F21–0006 (1147).
63. GR-OF CA CA-SF02-S01-SS02-F20-SF001–0002 (377).
64. John reported that Arabi was going to be brought to Alexandria: "The scoundrel will put a long face on, when he is driven about in the streets as a rebel, where, if you remember, three months ago he passed with the bearing of a sovereign!" (letter dated September 17, 1882). GR-OF CA CA-SF02-S01-SS02-F20-SF001–0003 (378). Malanos, who knew John, claims he was "almost English" and the entire family was "pro-English to the bone and protected by the English" (Gialourakis

1959, 69). With each letter John relayed more information about the state of the city itself. GR-OF CA CA-SF02-S01-SS02-F20-SF001–0004 (379); GR-OF CA CA-SF02-S01-SS02-F20-SF001–0005 (380); GR-OF CA CA-SF02-S01-SS02-F20-SF001–0006 (381); GR-OF CA CA-SF02-S01-SS02-F20-SF001–0011 (386); GR-OF CA CA-SF02-S01-SS02-F20-SF001–0012 (387).

65. Reid, 237.
66. Mansel, 126.
67. GR-OF CA CA-SF02-S01-SS02-F20-SF001–0063 (438).
68. *LC*, 89.
69. In the journal dealing with his mother's death, Constantine referred to Ahmed, their cook, and Mohammed, their server, and other servants they had hired over the years (Cavafy 1991, 186).
70. *LC*, 38; *L&W*, 26.
71. The doctor, in other words, saw his brother as an Egyptian Greek, different from the territorial Greeks he was treating. Constantine had recorded this in a diary he kept during this difficult visit. GR OF CA CA-SF02-S02-F24–0002 (475).
72. Gialourakis 1959, 69.
73. Abdulhaq, 55. The Alexandria to which his father arrived had been primarily an Ottoman city, with many of the notables and merchants stemming from the different ethnic and religious groups of the Ottoman Empire. But when the Cavafy family returned to Alexandria in 1885, the city had become an outpost of the British Empire (Kazamias, 105).
74. Stratis Tsirkas writes that Selím's age is uncertain and that he was between twenty-two and twenty-five years old (*PC*, 81). Hala Halim notes that the youth's actual name in Arabic is Yusuf Husayn Silim (Halim 2013, 99).
75. See Halim's reading of this poem ("C. P. Cavafy as an Egyptiote," 2021) where she notes the folkloric dimensions of this lament, as well as Stamatia Laoumtzi (2021, ch. 3), who makes compelling connections between the poem and Greek demotic folk songs. Laoumtzi provides an extensive commentary on this poem as well as hitherto unpublished photographs from the trial and executions. For the definitive work on the Greek ritual lament, see Alexiou (1974).
76. Goldschmidt, 60–61.
77. The Denshawai incident only brought to the surface the economic grievances of the peasants. In 1907, for instance, 140,000 foreigners owned 15 percent of the land. Moreover, 75 percent of the land was in the hands of 147,000 large and median holders, while 21 percent of the population remained landless. Taxation was still relatively high, consuming much of any surplus the farmer might have had, and little of it was reinvested in agriculture (Toledano, 272).
78. Halim 2013, 103.
79. Ibid., 104.
80. GR-OF CA-SF01-S02-F05–0002 (939). We follow here Halim's reading of the passage and the words "*aneptigmeni merida* / greater part" (Halim 2013, 100).
81. *PC*, 92.
82. The clippings present us with a snapshot of what Constantine would have been reading at the time: along with the Wardani case, he would have learned of an anarchist attack at the Teatro Colón in Buenos Aires, of a gold discovery in British Columbia, and the fall of Zeppelin VII. There was also an advertisement for Martell Cognac, "walk-over shoes for children," and baby formula from Nestlé that was a "substitut du lait maternel." See item GR-OF CA-SF02-S02-F25-SF007–0038 (1364).

83. It was founded in 1921 by the Belgian professor of French literature at the University of Cairo Paul Vanderborght.
84. Cavafy 2010, 68–69.
85. Cavafy 1963b, 154.
86. Ibid., 150–51.
87. Rika Sengopoulos also provided details of this in notes for the biography she was preparing: GR-OF CA SING-S01-F01–0017 (1633).
88. This is in contrast to Pericles Anastasiades and Paul, who both enjoyed the company of British officers during the war.
89. Gialourakis 2007, 202.
90. Karapanogopoulos, 30.
91. Modinos 1980, 9.
92. Gialourakis 1959, 141.
93. Malanos 1986, 15.
94. *TPC*, 183.
95. Gialourakis 1959, 66.
96. *CE*, 363.
97. Peridis 1948, 94.
98. Gialourakis 1959, 74.
99. Malanos 1986, 17. Constantine followed the trial of Oscar Wilde and had a personal copy of *The Oscar Wilde Calendar*, which carried the subtitle "A Quotation from the Works of Oscar Wilde for Every Day in the Year" (Wilde 1910). He seemed to have read the book closely, as he marked relevant pages with his pencil.
100. Malanos 1957, 235.
101. In *La Semaine Égyptienne* 1929, 25.
102. Gershoni and Jankowski, 46.
103. Although this autonomy was subject to four conditions, Britain declared Egypt independent on February 22, 1922. These conditions were that Britain preserve its transportation links to India, that it maintain the security of Egypt from external threats, that it protect its financial interests and the safety of the minorities, and that it continue its administration of Sudan (Botman, 285).
104. Hanley, 170; Goldschmidt, 64.
105. Marsot, 93.
106. Gershoni and Jankowski, 143, 193.
107. Muslim Egyptians complained that nearly all public utilities, manufacturing firms, hotels, banks, and insurance companies were either owned or managed by foreigners (Goldschmidt, 72).
108. Zubaida, 26. Hassan al-Banna, a twenty-one-year-old teacher from Ismalia, proclaimed as much in his original statement and oath of allegiance: "We are sick of this life: a life of shame and shackles. Here you see that the Muslim Arabs have no chance of status and respect in this country" (Frampton, 11).
109. Al-Banna himself witnessed the degradations of colonialism and the gap separating him from secular Egyptians. When, as a devout Muslim, he arrived in Cairo for the first time in 1923, he was appalled at what he saw as the degeneracy of Islamic morals, with many Egyptians having adopted a secular way of life. Walking through the streets of Cairo, he felt his life was turned upside down, with so many traditional practices challenged or displaced (Frampton, 14). At the same time, he believed that the West sought to maintain Egypt in a state of dependency. He thus established the Muslim Brotherhood in order to call back Muslims to their true faith as well as overthrow Western colonialism. He out-

lined the goals in his proclamation that the "Islamic fatherland be free from all foreign domination" and that "a free Islamic state may arise in this free fatherland, acting according to the principles of Islam" (Frampton, 24).

110. Kazantzakis, 63.
111. Ibid., 71.
112. They were written by Takis Papatsonis and Y. Vrisimitzakis, Kleon Paraschos, E. P. Papanoutsos, I. A. Sareyiannis, and poets such as Miltiadis Malakasis.
113. Enright, 28.
114. Gialourakis 1959, 81; *CE*, 288.
115. Gialourakis 1959, 115. When Athanasopoulos took Malanos to the spot forty years later, they discovered that the building no longer existed (Malanos 1971, 343).
116. Cavafy 2015, 573.
117. Sareyannis 1964, 121.
118. Malanos 1971, 148.
119. Unpublished personal comment (Cavafy 2010, 135).

6. FRIENDSHIP AND INTIMACY

1. Cavafy 2015, 617.
2. Constantine was well-read in ancient Greek philosophy and his library contained a 1556 Latin translation of Aristotle's works, *De Republica, qui Politicorum dicuntur, Libri oct* (Karampini-Iatrou 2003, 54).
3. Barbara Caine notes that the Greek term "*philia*" (friendship) "covered a much wider range of relationships than we would usually characterize as friendship today" (Caine, x). Aristotle's theories may be found in his *Nicomachean Ethics.*
4. Malanos 1986, 16.
5. Long, 6.
6. Only the Rothschilds were substantially richer (Harlaftis, 53).
7. See Martin McKinsey, *Hellenism and the Postcolonial Imagination: Yeats, Cavafy and Walcott* (2010), where he offers a postcolonial critique of Cavafy's poetic mimicry and what he reads as an ensuing ambivalence and even mockery in certain poems; and Hala Halim's critique of the Alexandrian Eurocentrism, *Alexandrian Cosmopolitanism: An Archive* (2013).
8. Letter dated October 30, 1883: GR-OF CA CA-SF02-S01-SS01-F18-SF002–0019 (1749).
9. Although technically not letters about friendship in the strict tradition of collections such as Cicero's *Letters to Friends* (*Epistulae ad familares*), on which the high Renaissance humanists based their cult of friendship, these exchanges function in much the same way. Petrarch's discovery of Cicero's letters in 1345 inaugurated a tradition of collections of letters to friends about friendship. See Carolyn James and Bill Kent, "Renaissance Friendships: Traditional Truths, New and Dissenting Voices," where they note that around 1600 "a new literary genre appeared. Some 1500 examples of *liber amicorum*—the 'book of friends'—survive" (James and Kent, 136).
10. GR-OF CA CA-SF02-S01-SS01-F18-SF002–0019 (1749).
11. As John Tosh writes, bourgeois masculinity was very much "attuned to the market . . . [The] social practice of unmarried young men—the homosocial networks, the appropriated public spaces, the drinking and whoring, the balance between comradeship and competition" created a new type of gendered behavior unique to the period (Tosh, 63, 77–78).

12. Mikès's father, Theodore Ralli, was president of the Greek community in Alexandria (Politis vol. 1, 256).
13. Constantine Papazis was the ill-respected and despised teacher under whom the boys studied in Alexandria.
14. GR-OF CA CA-SF02-S01-SS01-F18-SF002–0002 (1667).
15. GR-OF CA CA-SF02-S01-SS01-F18-SF002–0004 (1668).
16. Letter dated October 18–19, 1882: GR-OF CA CA-SF02-S01-SS01-F18-SF002–0005 (1741).
17. GR-OF CA CA-SF02-S01-SS01-F18-SF002–0010 (1666).
18. These sensationalist Victorian bestsellers—*The Channings*, *East Lynne*, and *Roland York*—are by the author Mrs. Henry Wood (Ellen Price, 1814–87).
19. Letter dated February 28, 1883: GR-OF CA CA-SF02-S01-SS01-F18-SF002–0010 (1666).
20. GR-OF CA CA-SF02-S01-SS01-F18-SF002–0009 (1744).
21. This was likely needed for the essay "Fragment on Lycanthropy," where he quotes from Tennyson's "The Coming of Arthur" in *Idylls of the King* (Cavafy 2003, 189).
22. GR-OF CA CA-SF02-S01-SS01-F18-SF002–0025 (1673).
23. GR-OF CA CA-SF02-S01-SS01-F18-SF002–0027 (1675).
24. GR-OF CA CA-SF02-S01-SS01-F18-SF002–0029 (1677).
25. GR-OF CA CA-SF02-S01-SS01-F18-SF002–0033 (1681).
26. GR-OF CA CA-SF02-S01-SS01-F18-SF002–0037 (1684).
27. GR-OF CA CA-SF02-S01-SS01-F18-SF002–0040 (1686).
28. GR-OF CA CA-SF02-S01-SS01-F18-SF002–0085 (1716).
29. GR-OF CA CA-SF02-S01-SS01-F18-SF002–0044 (1689).
30. GR-OF CA CA-SF02-S01-SS01-F18-SF002–0064 (1700).
31. This letter includes an analytical appreciation of *Le Maître de Forges* of Georges Ohnet, "a man whose genius is not inferior to that of Dickens or Thackeray," and reveals the unique nature of their bond, and how literature served as an instrument for communication: GR-OF CA CA-SF02-S01-SS01-F18-SF002–0054 (1694).
32. He takes in theatrical performances (Marlowe's *Doctor Faustus*) and visits the Royal Academy, which, he writes, "pleased me immensely, especially as I have begun taking an interest in painting" (June 24, 1886): GR-OF CA CA-SF02-S01-SS01-F18-SF002–0077 (1708).
33. "[John] is £120 in debt. [. . .] Your humble servant about £40. The matter stands thus. We spend all we get and never pay clothing, etc. I fell into the trap by drawing £25 to pay for my clothing and not paying a simple thing. In the meanwhile I have ordered shirts, clothes, boots, dress suit etc., which amount somewhere near £40. You may be certain that they will learn nothing of the matter at home" (July 27, 1886): GR-OF CA CA-SF02-S01-SS01-F18-SF002–0082 (1713).
34. GR-OF CA CA-SF02-S01-SS01-F18-SF002–0076 (1707).
35. Cavafy 1963b, 253. For the manuscript of the journal, see GR-OF CA CA-SF02-S02-F24–0007 (1649).
36. Cavafy 1963b, 254.
37. Cavafy 1963b, 255.
38. Cavafy 1963b, 256.
39. Cavafy 1963b, 258.
40. John Skylitzes famously wrote the *Synopsis historiarum* that chronicled the years

811–1057, serving as a civil servant in the judiciary under the Emperor Alexios Komnenos (Wortley, x).

41. On Byzantine historians, Cavafy reputedly stated: "They are not appreciated as they should be. One day they will be discovered and will be admired for their originality . . . They wrote history dramatically" (Sareyiannis 1983, 113). The Comnenian court would become the subject of numerous poems in his later work.
42. Although no evidence exists documenting any discussion between Constantine and Stephen regarding this Byzantine genealogy, the Anglo-Greeks from Chios were very conscious of their Byzantine roots and document lineages linking them back to imperial aristocratic families. See George Kakavas, *Ελλήνων Κειμήλια*, 83–103, for examples of the various heraldic crests of the Anglo-Greek families who were benefactors of the Cathedral of Saint Sophia in London. Christopher Long also provides a useful webpage on this heraldry: http://www.christopherlong.co.uk/per/vlasto.byzantium.html.
43. See Jeffreys (2009), "Introduction," for the history of this controversy. According to Richard Clogg, Cavafy was put forward as a candidate for this position. See the fuller discussion of Constantine's view of translation in chapter twelve.
44. "The Houses of Parliament which we saw all through, admiring the splendour of the internal decoration and wondering at the simplicity of the House of Commons, which contrasts very much with the rest of the building. Westminster Abbey, where we [***] around and saw nearly all the monuments. Nothing but a simple slab covers the remains of the celebrated naturalist Charles Darwin. The National Gallery and the British Museum in which we passed whole days looking over the pictures at the first and over the sculptures and mummies at the second. The Obelisk or Cleopatra's Needle which is situated in a position where it does not show at all but is nevertheless very well mounted." GR-OF CA CA-SF02-S01-SS01-F18-SF002–0019 (1749).
45. Donkey boy—a pejorative term for a native Egyptian fellahin who handles donkeys.
46. GR-OF CA CA-SF02-S01-SS01-F18-SF002–0075 (1706).
47. GR-OF CA CA-SF02-S01-SS01-F18-SF002–0013 (1739).
48. GR-OF CA CA-SF02-S01-SS01-F18-SF002–0015 (1746).
49. GR-OF CA CA-SF02-S01-SS01-F18-SF002–0035 (1760).
50. Constantine was likely channeling a line of emotional interaction he had gleaned from the reading material he was sharing with his friends. Scholars and historians of the long nineteenth century have amply documented the phenomenon of how the reading populace increasingly took their models of friendship from novels—men in particular. Much of this had to do with the influence of merchant capitalism and the need for men to forge business alliances—political friendships as it were, as David Garrioch notes (Garrioch, 166–68). At the forefront of this reading material was Tennyson's *In Memoriam* and Dickens's *David Copperfield* and *Great Expectations*, where, for the first time, intense male friendship received an emotional emphasis, becoming "one of the most prominent literary themes of the century," as argued by Carolyn Oulton (46). On the powerful link between our need for friends and our desire for fiction, see Jusdanis (2014), who writes: "In friendship, as in literature, we enter into the zone of fantasy and possibility" (15).
51. GR-OF CA CA-SF02-S01-SS01-F18-SF002–0001 (1730).
52. GR-OF CA CA-SF02-S01-SS01-F18-SF002–0059 (1735).
53. GR-OF CA CA-SF02-S01-SS01-F18-SF002–0073 (1737).

54. These early essays, begun in Istanbul, include the following: "Fragment on Lycanthropy," "Coral from a Mythological Perspective," "The Inhumane Friends of Animals," "Misplaced Tenderness," "Masks," "Romaic Folk-lore of Enchanted Animals," "Woman and the Ancients," and "Persian Manners."
55. Letter dated March 9 [no year]: GR-OF CA CA-SF02-S01-SS01-F18-SF002–0073 (1737).
56. Letter dated July 30, 1884: GR-OF CA CA-SF02-S01-SS01-F18-SF002–0046 (1732).
57. Ibid.
58. Letter dated September 19, 1884: GR-OF CA CA-SF02-S01-SS01-F18-SF002–0047 (1733).
59. Merrill numbers among the many twentieth-century poets who were significantly influenced by the Alexandrian. He composed a number of "Days of . . ." poems "à la manière de Cavafy," some verses patterned on Cavafian prototypes, and a few direct translations. In his review of Liddell's biography and Sherrard/Keeley's translations, Merrill pays insightful tribute to Cavafy: "The unity of divine and human, of past and present, is as real to him as their disparity. Between the poor, unlettered, present-day young men and the well-to-do, educated ones in his historical poems . . . there is an unbroken bond of type and disposition: what [Luis de] Gongora called 'centuries of beauty in a few years of age.' This bond is at the marrow of Cavafy's feeling" (Merrill 1975, 14).
60. On Cavafy's debt to Poe, see Lavagnini (2003, 2020), Athanasopoulou (2003), and Jeffreys (2015). Poe's short story "The Gold Bug" involves a treasure hunt and the discovery of an iron-banded treasure chest containing gold and jewels.
61. Lavagnini notes that the narration of the story dates between 1891 and 1897, although the events of the story occur a decade earlier (2020, 81).
62. Cavafy 2010, 86.
63. As Michael Haag notes, it was built "as a summer hotel by the sea in 1886, and possessing a theater, a concert hall, tennis courts and a private beach, it was modeled after the fashionable casinos at such places as Deauville, Trouville, and Ostende along the French and Belgian coasts. As many as five thousand people might show up on a Sunday during the high season" (Haag 2008, 92).
64. Cavafy 2010, 86.
65. Cavafy 2010, 87.
66. Cavafy 2010, 87.
67. Cavafy 2010, 91.
68. Cavafy 2010, 91–92.
69. Cavafy 2010, 92.
70. Cavafy 2010, 92.
71. A number of details bear this out: Alexander lives on Rue Chérif Pasha, where the Cavafy family once resided in grand style; at one point, he reads the journal *Hesperus*, the Leipzig-based Greek periodical where Constantine had published his very first poems in 1886: "Vain, Vain Love" and "The Poet and the Muse." Many of the story's autobiographical details have been amply documented by Renata Lavagnini (2020, 80).
72. Cavafy 2010, 86.
73. In his study *Queer Friendship*, George Haggerty aptly writes: "All elegies have an urgent desire to speak of the emotional attachment to the figure who is lost and who represents loss. The project of the elegy is perhaps to find some mode of

sublimation that can lead one from the paralysis of grief to the kind of transformation that poetry makes possible" (42).

74. Cavafy 2015, 461. The word "diaphanous"—an extraordinary lexical choice—remarkably echoes Walter Pater's concept of "diaphaneité" that was defined at length in an essay by that very title delivered in 1864 and thereafter distilled into much of his writing: the idea of a transparent desire, a crystal nature, a quality of a certain moral type: of the artist. To quote from the essay: "As he comes nearer and nearer to perfection, the veil of an outer life not simply expressive of the inward becomes thinner and thinner." This is not to suggest that Constantine had access to this essay when he wrote this early poem, well-read though he was. What's so astonishing here is that, in this early poem, he anticipates Pater so profoundly. With just one word he pivots in the direction of the master of Victorian prose and aesthetic writing. And this moment comes out of the death of one of his closest comrades. The word "diaphaneité" will eventually constitute a "homosexual code of sorts," inaugurating a strain of thought in Pater's mature writing that critics today acknowledge as defining a "queer subjectivity" (Donoghue, 112). On Cavafy and Pater, see Jeffreys (2015), ch. 5.
75. Saint Stephen's Chapel was built by James Thomas Knowles Sr., who designed the Grosvenor Hotel at Victoria Station (his son Sir James Thomas Knowles was the founding editor of *The Nineteenth Century*, a periodical that Constantine read most faithfully). The Ralli Mausoleum was built by E. M. Barry, who later designed the Royal Opera House / Covent Garden. Another Ralli Mausoleum was designed by George Edmund Street, architect of the Royal Courts of Justice in London.
76. On Constantine's first cousin John's remarkable career as a doctor and philanthropist, see Victoria Solomonidis-Hunter, "John Cavafy, MD FRCP (1838–1901): A Victorian Greek, a Doctor's Doctor" (2020).
77. Noteworthy in this regard is the magnificent stele grave of Constantine Gennadius (1846–1866)—brother of John Gennadius—which replicates the classical stelae of the Keramaikos Cemetery in Athens and is engraved with a lengthy poetic epitaph—something that would certainly have stood out to the young Constantine when visiting the Greek Necropolis (Solomonidis-Hunter, 2021).
78. It was also becoming fashionable to plan outings at these new rural garden cemeteries, which were designed to offer an Edenic escape from the noise and pollution of the city.
79. The chapel was a mini replica of the Parthenon, with scenes from the Hebrew and Christian bibles standing in for Phidias's pagan sculptures.
80. George Cavafy and his son John were quite wealthy by Victorian standards. When John died in 1901, his estate was worth £38,641—approximately four million pounds in today's currency (Solomonidis-Hunter 2020, 9).

7. PERI

1. "And in loving a friend, men love what is good for themselves; for the good man in becoming a friend becomes good to his friend. Each, then, both loves what is good for himself, and makes an equal return in goodwill and pleasantness; for friendship is said to be equality, and both these are found most in the friendship of the good" (Aristotle, *Nicomachean Ethics*, 1157b31–1158a2 [Baltzly and Eliopoulos, 23–24]).
2. Nehamas, 137, 205, 210.

3. *CE*, 233–34.
4. Tsirkas dates their friendship to 1895, but Constantine mentions Peri in his account of Mikès's illness in 1889, so they were acquainted well before that date.
5. Peridis, 311. This letter is written in English.
6. Greek for "overdone it."
7. Peridis, 311.
8. Gabriele D'Annunzio (1863–1938) was an Italian author and poet who was prominent in the European decadent movement.
9. Indicative of this shift is Constantine's poem "Correspondence According to Baudelaire" (1891), where he translates and comments on the French sonnet. See the relevant discussion in the "Interlude" chapter.
10. Nehamas, 138.
11. Many of these letters from Constantine survive only in draft form, as it was the poet's habit to write drafts of letters, which he would later copy and send in finished form.
12. From his letters it appears that Peri worked remotely, conducting business for his father's company that involved speculating on cotton shares.
13. The unpublished letters in this chapter to and from Peri, unless otherwise indicated, are in possession of ELIA-MIET (The Papoutsakis Archive 4.3) and are reproduced with grateful acknowledgment.
14. Letter belonging to the Charitatou Archive.
15. Letter belonging to the Charitatou Archive.
16. Letter belonging to the Charitatou Archive.
17. GR-OF CA CA-SF02-S02-F25-SF009.
18. The staged performances they likely attended in Paris include the following: *La Carriére* (Abel Hermant); *Les Deux Gosses* (Pierre Decourcelle); *La Douloureuse* (Maurice Donnay); *Le Dindon. Piece en trois actes* (Georges Feydeau); *Le Chemineau* (Jean Richepin); *Porquoi? Comedie en un acte* (Leneka); *L'Autographe* (Henri Meilhac); *Oedipe Roi* (Musique d' Edmond Membreé); *La Joie Fait Peur* (Mme. De Girardin); *Le Barbier de Séville* (Pierre-Augustin Beaumarchais); *Faust* (J. Barbier et M. Carré); *Dépit Amoureux de Moliere / Le Monde ou L'on s'ennuie* (Edouard Pailleron); *Mithridate* (Jean Racine); *Tartuffe* (Molière); *Cinna ou la Clémence d'Auguste* (Pierre Corneille); *La Femme de Tabarin* (Catulle Mendès).
19. See Venita Datta, "A Bohemian Festival," where she notes that "in conjunction with the festival, they published *Le Journal de la Vache Enragée*, a compilation of poems and drawings dedicated to the mythic beast" (Datta, 195).
20. Rallis exhibited widely in Europe, England, and Egypt, attaining international fame as a successful and popular painter. In his earlier years, he spent time studying and working in England among the Anglo-Greeks in Manchester and London, opting out of a secure career in the Ralli family firm and preferring a life in art—a path Constantine will replicate. See Maria Katzanaki, *Θεόδωρος Ράλλης* (2018).
21. Palioura, 40–41.
22. To date, we have been able to locate only one of Pericles's paintings, which is in the possession of Nadine Lane. We are grateful to Alix MacSweeney for bringing it to our attention.
23. This unsigned sketch was attributed to Pericles by George Savidis.
24. We are indebted to Nicolas Sarafis for sharing these sketches by Peri, who lived in the same building in Alexandria as the Sarafis family.

25. In a draft of an undated letter discussing Zola, Cavafy comments on finishing the novel *Paris* (the final book of the Trilogy *Les Trois Villes*) and notes the novel's marvelous power. But he is critical of Zola's naturalist attempt to "refute or rid[icule] the neo-mysticism which pervades modern theology" and finds the positivist irreligious characters "cold" and "ugly" and is "shocked at having their righteousness thrust on me."
26. From an undated draft of a letter in the ELIA-MIET archive.
27. Written to Constantine during his visit to Greece in 1905 when he attends to his ailing brother Alexander. The conflict referred to is between the Greek and Bulgarian populations of Ottoman Macedonia who were engaged in guerrilla warfare in their attempts to claim the area for their respective nations. Ion Dragoumis, with whom Constantine was connected, was a central player in this struggle.
28. Cavafy 2010, 133. See Dimitris Papanikolaou's reading of this comment as reflective of Constantine's familiarity with the burgeoning discourse of sexology (2014, 109–38).
29. For a discussion of French authors who exerted an influence on Cavafy, see the "Interlude" chapter.
30. Moffat, 128–29.
31. Haag 2004a, 27.
32. Wendy Moffat notes that from the "verbatim snippets of men in their most extreme trials he gleaned a hidden story" of male bonding and love, something he named "Friendship" in his small notebook of collated fragments: "By honoring how hard it was for these men to relive these horrors, by recognizing the intimacy of both telling and witnessing, Forster became a gay historian" (Moffat, 133, 134).
33. It is quite possible Forster saw or had read about the famous twelfth-century icon of the Ladder of Divine Ascent possessed by the Saint Catherine's Monastery at Mt. Sinai. Foteini Dimirouli, in her edited and published annotations on the piece, notes that "through stylistic experimentation with the humorous and absurdist tropes of British pantomime, as well as its convention, dating to the Middle Ages, of placing 'heaven' and 'hell' on either side of the stage, in the sketch Forster draws attention to the incongruous coexistence of artists, the military, and the colonial administration in the city" (Dimirouli 2019, 359).
34. Bartle Edward Frere (1815–1933) was a British colonial administrator (Dimirouli 2019, 364).
35. Dimirouli 2019, 363.
36. Forster receives a similar parodic treatment in the play *The Inheritance* by Matthew Lopez (2018), a queer rendition of *Howards End* set in 2016 where the novelist appears as a character amid a group of gay millennial friends who accuse him of being less than courageous by not publishing *Maurice* or fully coming out during his lifetime.
37. Cited in Beauman, 297.
38. As Barbara Caine and Marc Brodie note, "The Apostles had always stressed the importance of frank and honest discussion of any and every subject, extended within Bloomsbury to include emotional and sexual questions as well as aesthetic, political and more strictly philosophical ones" (Caine and Brodie, 269).
39. Jeffreys 2009, 35.
40. Cavafy 2010, 131.
41. GR-OF CA CA-SF02-S01-SS01-F18-SF003–0092 (763). On this translation venture, see the discussion in chapter twelve.

42. Letter to George Savidis, dated January 6, 1964 (Jeffreys 2009, 17).
43. Jeffreys 2009, 101–102.
44. *CE*, 236.
45. Malanos 1963, 37.
46. Savidis 1982, np.
47. Nehamas, 206.

8. "IT WOULD HAVE BEEN YOU"

1. Malanos 1971, 357. Although Malanos does not name Sengopoulos here, there can be no doubt as to the identity of the person involved in this exchange. And while Malanos takes offense at the erotic/sexual implications of the hypothetical scenario of being the chosen one, he clearly relishes the emotional truth behind it, titling this chapter "A Scene That Says It All."
2. See the entries on Malanos and Sengopoulos in "Important People in C. P. Cavafy's Life" for biographical details.
3. Greeks use this term as a token of respect for older people.
4. Malanos 1971, 38.
5. Kolaitis, 48. Malanos concludes this account with the following sentence: "My own lack of interest, however, was enough to disabuse him for good of any false notions" (1971, 39). Kolaitis doubts such a brazen move on Constantine's part ever occurred and writes that the poet would never have compromised himself in such a manner (Kolaitis, 48).
6. According to Plutarch, "'The flatterer is nowhere constant' . . . By contrast, 'the true friend is neither an imitator of everything nor ready to commend everything, but only the best things'" (Baltzly, 44).
7. Wilde, 54.
8. On Malanos's psychoanalytic homophobia and its influence on subsequent Greek critics, see Papanikolaou (2014), 49–68 and passim.
9. Kolaitis, 26.
10. The poem's title is from line 60, Canto III of Dante's *Inferno*.
11. Dalven, Cavafy 1989, 295.
12. GR-OF CA CA-SF01-S03-F11–0030 (226).
13. Malanos 1963, 25.
14. The Apuani were a group of Alexandrian poets who modeled their group after the anarchist/fascist artists established by Enrico Pea and fellow Italian Alexandrians (Liddell, 162). See Lavagnini, "Μια Ιταλική Μαρτυρία για τον Γιώργο Βρισιμιτζάκη" (2020), for a discussion of the Apuani and Constantine's connection to Filippo Marinetti and Giuseppe Ungaretti.
15. Kolaitis, 49.
16. GR-OF CA CA-SF02-S01-SS01-F18-SF003–0167 (1191).
17. Kolaitis, 55.
18. *Isis*, October 30, 1926. Malanos will later praise Rika for being a most worthy intellectual companion to the poet (Malanos 1978, 48) and noting their particular "literary friendship" (Malanos 2003, 41).
19. GR-OF CA CA-SF02-S01-SS01-F18-SF003–0101 (1228).
20. A critical skirmish broke out between the supporters (and detractors) of Kostis Palamas and Cavafy, with interviews, articles, and letters published throughout 1926 in the literary venues *Isis* and *Othoni* (Cavafy 1979 / Mosxou, 162–64; Kolaitis, 51–55).

21. Karapanagopoulos, 63.
22. Kolaitis, 51.
23. Malanos died in 1984. That year, he agreed to include an article in a special edition of the gay magazine *AMPHI* dedicated to Cavafy. Although the piece was basically a pastiche of previously published comments, it is significant that he even appears in such a venue. From his personal exchanges with the editor (the poet Andreas Angelakis), Malanos had softened somewhat in his negative view of homosexuality. We are grateful to Dimitris Papanikolaou for sharing this information.
24. Malanos 2003, 10.
25. *TPC*, 21, 22, 28, 47, 54, 122, 156, 179.
26. *TPC*, 179.
27. Richard MacGillivray Dawkins (1871–1955) was a British archaeologist and a linguist, the Bywater and Sotheby Professor of Byzantine and Modern Greek Language and Literature at the University of Oxford (1920–39), and a fellow of Exeter College. In a letter he sent to Cavafy (March 13, 1933), he asks for copies of the poems and writes, "Your poems seem to me to carry on the whole Greek inheritance of beauty." GR-OF CA CA-SF02-S01-SS01-F18-SF003–0158 (1659).
28. Dawkins, 108.
29. Garoufalias 2013, 25.
30. During the years Constantine was fussing infatuatedly over Alekos, Forster was engaged in a similar pursuit of a young man (in Forster's case, the relationship with Mohamed el Adl was unabashedly sexual). In her biography of the British novelist, Wendy Moffat comments on the parallel homosexual lives of these two great figures of twentieth-century literature: "Up until now, Morgan [Forster] had not imagined any way to be a writer but to partake in a public world of letters. Inability to find an audience had always led him to what he called 'sterility.' But Cavafy proved there was a different path: by exercising authorial control he forged a homosexual culture . . . Glimpsing Cavafy's world had convinced him that, far from some sort of heroic sacrifice, celibacy was the embodiment of moral cowardice" (Moffat, 144, 147).
31. Malanos 1971, 265–69.
32. Malanos was the first to point out the value of this lecture. He published two versions of it in his book *Καβάφης 3* (1978, 92–117): the preliminary text, which he argues has all the intonations and inflections of Cavafy (an 1890s prose style and elements of the poet's unique idiom), parallel to the actual text delivered by Sengopoulos, which was altered to be more demotic. See also George Savidis's presentation of supplementary material to this lecture (Savidis 1987, 247–72) meant to be part of a book on Cavafy that never materialized. Savidis also notes the occurrence of a second lecture by Sengopoulos given on June 10, 1920, on Greek poets (Palamas, Cavafy, Gryparis, Papantoniou, Porphyra, Malakasis, and Mavilis) (1987, 255).
33. Malanos points out that Vrisimitzakis—whom he called a snake—hated Sengopoulos and maintained somewhat slanderously that Cavafy had appropriated him from another elderly man (Malanos 2003, 35–37).
34. Malanos 1971, 269. The last name is farcical in the extreme, serving as Greek slang for oral sex.
35. Malanos 1971, 269.
36. Papanikolaou 2014, 186–93.

37. Malanos's own critical analysis of the talk is purely biographical; he sees in "Dangerous Thoughts" echoes of the poet's sensual exploits as a youth in Istanbul.
38. Malanos 1978, 107–108.
39. Malanos 1978, 117.
40. Malanos also suffered from a health scare at this time, believing he had contracted the Spanish flu (Malanos 1971, 93).
41. Alekos will in fact wind up acting in a theatrical production in July 1919, as attested to by playbills in possession of ELIA-MIET.
42. GR-OF CA SING-S01-F02-SF001–0002 (1403). These excerpts from Cavafy's letters to Alekos (translated from the Greek) are from Katerina Ghika's transcriptions, published in the Onassis Foundation Cavafy Archive Digital Collection.
43. GR-OF CA SING-S01-F02-SF001–0003 (1404).
44. GR-OF CA SING-S01-F02-SF001–0005 (1406).
45. GR-OF CA SING-S01-F02-SF001–0006 (1407).
46. GR-OF CA SING-S01-F02-SF001–0013 (1414).
47. GR-OF CA SING-S01-F02-SF001–0014 (1415).
48. GR-OF CA SING-S01-F02-SF001–0018 (1419).
49. GR-OF CA SING-S01-F02-SF001–0006 (1407).
50. GR-OF CA SING-S01-F02-SF001–0011 (1412).
51. GR-OF CA SING-S01-F02-SF001–0046 (1447).
52. GR-OF CA SING-S01-F02-SF001–0018 (1419).
53. Malanos 1978, 91.
54. Malanos 1986, 21.
55. It was rumored that Rika was conducting an affair with the Greek poet Angelos Sikelianos (Karampini-Iatrou 2016, 110).
56. Malanos 2003, 33.
57. This was the view of Atanazio Catraro, one that outraged Malanos for attempting to deny the sexual element of the relationship: As Malanos wrote, "I who knew him [Alekos] well both as an individual and a character, am quite sure that if he had to select from among the professions [gigolo or nurse], surely he would have found the use of his phallus more poetic than that of a prosaic enema" (Malanos 2003, 29).
58. GR-OF CA CA-SF02-S01-SS01-F18-SF003–0108 (1558).
59. Nikos Hager-Boufides (1899–1950), an avid enthusiast of Cavafy's work, was a poet, writer, and dramatist of the interwar period (Karampini-Iatrou 2019, 32).
60. Gialourakis 1959, 28.
61. Malanos 2003, 11.
62. Cavafy 2010, 138–39.
63. GR-OF CA CA-SF02-S02-F25-SF004–0023 (972).

INTERLUDE: CONSTANTINE'S READING

1. See Karampini-Iatrou 2003 and 2012.
2. Karampini-Iatrou 2012, 294.
3. This was given to him by J. Sareyiannis (Karampini-Iatrou 2012, 292).
4. These reveal the Anglo-French orientation of his reading choices. As his earliest critics were quick to point out, Constantine belongs more to English than Greek literature (Malanos, *TPC*, 221) and in the 1890s and early 1900s, he was fully in thrall to French literary currents, a point made by Glafkos Alithersis (*TPC*, 218). As David Ricks aptly notes, "Cavafy . . . *translates* so much of English literature

into Greek poetry . . . So the special esteem Cavafy enjoys in the English-speaking world is not the mere product of chance or puffing by E. M. Forster and a mafia of Kingsmen: it is, in part, because when English-speakers read Cavafy, they respond to something which is not entirely unfamiliar" (Ricks 1993, 86).

5. See the relevant discussion in chapter nine.
6. *CE*, 59.
7. *TPC*, 175–78.
8. As Kimon Friar writes, "Around 1880 a group of young poets in Greece formed the New School of Athens, in revolt against the Old School, in imitation of the Parnassians, and in an attempt to bring back objectivity and restraint to their art. Their influence was to last until about 1895 and prepare the way for the even greater influence of symbolism" (Friar, 18). Friar was an important translator and promoter of the poet and included him prominently in his 1973 edition of *Modern Greek Poetry*.
9. Beaton, 69.
10. Dascalopoulos 2013, 20.
11. See Roderick Beaton, who writes apropos of European Romanticism: "They [Solomos, Kalvos, and Palamas] neither imitated nor rejected what they found: they transformed it . . . What all these Greek writers did with the European literature before them was to read it, select from it, and make something of their own with what they read" (Beaton, 21). His "Introduction" offers a useful overview on how Greek writers interpreted European literary trends.
12. Regarding Romanticism of the Old School of Athens, Kimon Friar writes: "On the whole, their poetry was an exaggerated distortion of European romanticism expressed in a nostalgic revamping of classical myths, in a rhetorical eulogizing of heroes, in a preoccupation with death and disease, in an unrelieved patriotism, in sentimental love poems and heart-rending threnodies, and in some political satires of power" (Friar, 14).
13. A comment made to Yiorgos Theotokas in 1932 (*L&W*, 157).
14. Potolsky, 5. As Potolsky argues in his reappraisal of decadence in *The Decadent Republic of Letters*, the key figures in the decadent movement "conceived of their work as part of a larger project . . . it is made up of knowing readers and the privileged texts they produce, admire, and circulate, its bonds fashioned through a shared taste for the perverse and a common sense of alienation from the political, artistic and erotic world engendered by bourgeois liberalism and nationalism" (Potolsky, 172).
15. Although Walter Pater is not on this list, his work was known to the poet (see Jeffreys 2015, ch. 4).
16. Interestingly, a Cavafy cousin named Pantelis Demetrios Cavafy published three translations of Shakespeare into Greek prose: *Two Gentlemen of Verona* (1874); *The Tempest* (1874); and *Twelfth Night* (1881). It is possible that Constantine was aware of these translations, published as they were in Istanbul (Cavafy 1993, 191).
17. These excerpts are from Act III, i, 1–44, and Act III, i, 116–32.
18. The titles of two other Shakespearean poems survive: "Lights, Lights, Lights" (1893) and "The State of Denmark" (1899) (Cavafy 1993, 170).
19. GR-OF CA CA-SF02-S01-SS02-F20-SF001–0018 (393).
20. The first chapter of *Self-Culture* includes a very solid religious premise that equates God with reason "whose offspring, as the pious old Greek poets sung, we all are, and in whom, as the great apostle preached, we live, and move, and have

our being" (Blackie, 12). Blackie pedantically intersperses his moral counsel with quotes from Plato and Aristotle and advises his readers to cultivate "a familiarity with the great writers—especially poets and historians—whose purely human thoughts 'make rich the blood of the world,' and enlarge the platform of sympathetic intelligence" (Blackie, 32).

21. Cavafy 2010, 34. On the struggle between those critics, poets, and novelists supporting demoticism and katharevousa, see Tziovas 1986.
22. Cavafy 2010, 35.
23. In his essay "The Poetic Principle," Poe famously inveighed against any didactic tendency in poetry.
24. Cavafy 2010, 27.
25. Cavafy 2010, 27. On Pater as a source for this essay, see Jeffreys (2015), 101–102.
26. Cavafy 2010, 59.
27. Cavafy 2010, 59.
28. This type of journalism was precisely what the targeted Greek readership expected: a synopsis with translations capped by general observations.
29. See Jeffreys (2015), ch. 2, for the relevant discussion.
30. "Philostratus' *The Life of Apollonius* is a book that all recognize by name but that few have read, even though it is a most curious work and a rewarding read . . . Nevertheless, I know of only one poem indebted to this lore. It is true that this poet, the English Keats, is a worthy adaptor of Philostratus, from whose beautiful work he fashioned a most worthy poem" (Cavafy 2010, 43).
31. Cavafy 2010, 49.
32. Cavafy 2010, 53.
33. Cavafy 2010, 53. See the relevant discussion on Tennyson in chapter ten.
34. On the influence of Browning on Cavafy, see David Ricks, "How It Strikes a Contemporary" (2003). On Tennyson's significance, see the relevant discussion in chapter eleven.
35. Cavafy 2010, 109–10.
36. Cavafy 2010, 111.
37. Cavafy 2010, 102.
38. GR-OF CA CA-SF02-S01-SS02-F20-SF001–0019 (394).
39. Marginal marks made to Richard Henry Stoddard's prefatory essay-memoir to Poe's *Poems* reveal an interest in Poe's drinking habits and the vagaries of his poetic reputation.
40. The book was borrowed from Clio Anastasiades, the sister of his friend Pericles.
41. Tsirkas first published these Greek comments with Greek translations of the relevant passages from Ruskin (*PC*, 223–65). Lavagnini/Luciani's Italian translations present these comments along with Ruskin's original English text (2021, 1796–1865). Liddell offers English translations of select comments in his biography (Liddell, 116–18).
42. Cavafy 2021, 1842. One wonders whether Constantine's overall hostility is partly owing to the Ruskin-Whistler trial of 1878, when the American painter sued Ruskin for libel and won. He was awarded a farthing in damages and ultimately bankrupted himself in the process. The Cavafy family, as noted in chapter one, were patrons of Whistler, so surely the high-profile trial that called into question the integrity of their taste in painting did little to endear its members to Ruskin. Tsirkas recalls the association in Constantine's mind between Palamas and Ruskin: "I remember Cavafy connecting in one sentence Palamas, Whitman

and Ruskin. He spoke of the members of the old school in contradistinction to his own art: 'the romantics, the rhetoricians, with their emotional exuberance, and their prophetic beards . . . I always imagine Palamas with a beard'" (*PC*, 227).

43. Liddell, 118.
44. N'as-tu pas, en fouillant les recoins de ton âme, / Un beau vice à tirer comme un sabre au soleil, / Quelque vice joyeux, effronté, qui s'enflamme / Et vibre, et darde rouge au front du ciel vermeil? *Sagesse* (I, iii, II, 41–42). ["Have you not, in rummaging through the corners of your soul, / A beautiful vice to draw like a sword in the sun, / Some joyful vice, brazen, which inflames / And vibrates, and darts red at the front of the vermeil sky?"]
45. Liddell, 117.
46. Karampini-Iatrou 2012, 291. His "Ideal Library" (that which includes books currently missing from the surviving library) would have featured a much more extensive list of French books—some 870. See the following website, edited by Katerina Ghika: https://cavafy.onassis.org/el/ideal-library/.
47. Denommé, 22.
48. See Eleni Politou-Marmarinou, "Ο Καβάφης και ο Γαλλικός Παρνασσισμός" (1983) for a full exploration of Constantine's debt to the Parnassians.
49. As noted by Bowersock, who adds: "The poet sees in the midst of apparent confusion the signs which nature makes intelligible to the knowing" (Bowersock, 155).
50. Cavafy 2010, 136.
51. Bowersock, 5.
52. As noted by Haas 1982, 90.
53. Haas 1982, 59.
54. Mahmud of Ghazni (971–1030), the first ruler in history to assume the title of "sultan," founded the Ghaznavid Empire (https://www.thoughtco.com/mahmud-of-ghazni-195105).
55. Haas 1982, 81.
56. As noted by Haas 1982, 89.
57. Haas 1982, 89. Here the comment includes an excerpt from Longfellow's poem *Tales of a Wayside Inn—Part Third*, "The Spanish Jew's Second Tale." Scanderbeg's fame, as noted by Samuel Chew, was "immense in Renaissance Europe. Spenser calls him the 'scourge of Turks and plague of infidels,' 'great both in name and great in power and might.' There was an Elizabethan tragedy, now lost, on his career" (Chew, 60).
58. Haas 1982, 79.
59. The common enemy of Papparigopoulos and Greek folklorists of this period was Jakob Philipp Fallmerayer (1790–1861), who argued that modern Greeks were descended from Hellenized Slavs and Albanians. See Michael Herzfeld, *Ours Once More* (2020), ch. 4, for a full discussion of this debate and its centrality in the formation of the modern Greek identity.
60. Krumbacher's *Geschichte der byzantinischen Litteratur, von Justinian bis zum Ende des oströmischen Reiches (527–1453)* was published in 1891.
61. Cavafy 2010, 40. The unpublished "On *The Chronicle of Morea*" (1906) is another important text that documents his interest in medieval Hellenism and the Frankish occupation of Greece in particular.
62. For the titles of the books written by these authors, see Karampini-Iatrou (2003), sections 7 and 8.

63. Cavafy 2010, 112–13. See also his unfinished "Fragment on the Sophists" (1892–97) (Cavafy 2003, 227–37).
64. Cavafy 2010, 60.
65. Cavafy 2010, 64–65.
66. Cavafy 2010, 65.
67. See the links for ancient Greek and Latin texts in "The Ideal Library": https://cavafy.onassis.org/el/ideal-library/.
68. Among these is William Smith's *A Dictionary of Greek and Roman Biography and Mythology* (London, John Murray, 1902). See the discussion in chapter ten on Constantine's self-comments on historical research.
69. On Cavafy and Callimachus, see Benjamin Acosta-Hughes (2003).
70. See also the related poem "The Displeasure of Selefkidis" (1910/1916).
71. Haas 2018, 101–102 (translated from the Greek).
72. On this classification of how folktales and songs preserve and document culture, see Herzfeld, 114 and passim.
73. On the folkloric analogues for this motif, see Jeffreys (2005), 59–66.
74. See Laoumtzis (79–125) for an extensive analysis of this poem and its analogues.
75. "The collection of demotic songs which Mr. Politis offers I believe will please those interested in our folk poetry—it was made with great care, has explanatory notes for each song, and other notes that gloss uncommon words and forms, has a very good index that documents sources with accuracy and clarity, and is successfully arranged into 14 sections with two addenda" (Cavafy 1963b, 107).
76. Cavafy 1963b, 121.
77. His maternal great-grandmother (Kokona Balasi Soumeliotissa-Trapezountissa)—Yiorgos Photiades's mother—was of Pontian extraction (*GN*, 88).
78. This is also the year Nikolaos Politis died (January 12, 1921), which may have spurred Constantine to compose the poem (March 1921) as a tribute to the passing of such an important figure.
79. This was first noted by the Greek critic Z. Carelli (cited in Kokolis, 70).
80. The klephts were the freedom fighters of the Greek Revolution of 1821 who often waged guerrilla warfare against the Ottoman Turks.
81. The song that opens Politis's book is titled "Της Αγιάς Σοφιάς / Of Haghia Sophia," but the text he quotes in the poem is a variation of this song he drew from Arnold Passow's *Carmina popularia Graeciae recentioris* (Lipsiae 1861) along with the Pontian song. Politis also includes a version of the Trebizond lament in his addendum (263–64) although the name of the youth is not given in this version.
82. Trebizond was located on the Black Sea and at one point served as the capital of the Byzantine Trapazuntine Empire (1204–1461).
83. See Margaret Alexiou, *After Antiquity: Greek Language, Myth, and Metaphor* (2002), ch. 10 and passim.
84. See Laoumtzi's analysis of this poem (299–340), in which she cleverly connects the poem to Forster's comment on Cavafy's wide-ranging sentences that include "the dialects of the interior of Asia Minor" (305).
85. Savidis notes that 54–56 of the songs selected by Cavafy were included in the final list published by the Egyptian Educational Association in 1921 (Savidis 1987, 226).
86. Savidis 1987, 233–34 (translated from the Greek).
87. See the relevant discussion in chapter eleven.

88. These include Vitzentzos Kornaros, Dionysios Solomos, Athanasios Christopoulos, Emmanuel Roidis, Aristotle Valaoritis, Kostis Palamas, Yiorgos Stratigis, Alexandros Papadiamantis, Miltiadis Malakasis, Jean Moréas, Pavlos Nirvanas, Grigoris Xenopoulos, Angelos Sikelianos, Sotiris Skipis, Ioannis Psycharis, Glafkos Alithersis, Giorgos Drosinis, Kostas Karyotakis, and Achileas Paraschos.
89. Cavafy 1963b, 105–106.
90. Cavafy 2003, 307. Constantine possessed volumes of Valaoritis's poems that show signs of careful reading.
91. To this list may be added the essay on the "Mimes of Herodas" by C. Whibley that appeared that same year in *The Nineteenth Century* and inspired a poem on the subject titled "The Mimes of Herodas" (1892).
92. James Rennell Rodd (1858–1941) was a British diplomat, poet, classicist, and politician who served as British ambassador to Italy during the First World War.
93. Rodd, 130.
94. Cavafy 2003, 307.
95. Beaton, 60.
96. Beaton, 310.
97. Cavafy 2003, 204.
98. Cavafy 1963b, 70.
99. Papoutsakis's prose volume reproduces the article as it appeared in *The Telegraph* on January 14, 1893 (70). Pieris, following Savidis (Savidis 1987, 292), inserts a [δεν/not] into the sentence (Cavafy 2003a, 83), upending decades of commentary based on this single sentence.
100. The matter of Cavafy's formal place in the language question is beyond the scope of this biography, as, to date, Greek philologists and critics continue endlessly to debate the matter and find corroborating arguments that bolster his affinity to both linguistic registers. A definitive study of this subject will only be possible once full scholarly editions of the poems are produced.
101. *LC*, 317. The letter is dated September 9, 1906, and written in Greek: GR-OF CA CA-SF02-S01-SS02-F19–0028 (474).
102. Karampini-Iatrou 2012, 284.
103. These lesser-known decadent French writers include Adolphe Belot, Camille Lemonnier, Gustave Toudouze, Jean Lorrain, Joséphin Péladan, and Félicien Champsaur (Papanikolaou 2013, 121).
104. Papanikolaou 2013, 120–28.
105. *TPC*, 45.
106. A point made by the Greek critic Dimitris Maronitis: "Reading constitutes perhaps the continuous and evolving poetic method of Cavafy from his first to his final hour . . . The Cavafian poem depends entirely on reading as its pretext, often transforming itself into a reading, and sometimes even the poem itself contains someone reading, so that the poetic act itself is identified with a fixation on reading" (Maronitis, 39, 42). See also Jusdanis 1987.

9. ART ABOVE EVERYTHING

1. Malanos 1971, 148.
2. Cavafy 1983, 64. For the manuscript in the archive see GR-OF CA CA-SF01-S03-F09–0017 (869). There remains another, perhaps earlier poem in English, "More Happy Thou Performing Member," written sometime between 1877 and 1882, without a formal title.

3. Cavafy 2010, 140.
4. Cavafy 1963b, 240.
5. Papoutsakis had acquired a certain portion of Cavafy's papers, the main part of which is now housed in ELIA. He edited Constantine's prose works in 1963 and translated his poetry into French.
6. Cavafy 1963b, 248.
7. GR-OF CA CA-SF02-S01-SS02-F20-SF001–0014 (389).
8. GR-OF CA CA-SF02-S01-SS02-F20-SF001–0010 (385).
9. GR-OF CA CA-SF02-S01-SS02-F20-SF001–0014 (389).
10. GR-OF CA CA-SF02-S01-SS02-F20-SF001–0015 (390).
11. GR-OF CA CA-SF02-S01-SS02-F20-SF001–0026 (401).
12. *LC*, 122.
13. John's niece Hariclia Valieri found him regal in his personality, a man who "kept his distance" (*GN*, 147). According to her account, even within the family, the brothers were very cold to one another. Valieri remembers as a child visiting the Cavafy household and finding the brothers each "locked in his own room" like monks (*GN*, 148).
14. Yet he remained bighearted to his sibling, supporting him emotionally and financially for years. The monthly remittances stopped, however, when John learned that Constantine had borrowed money from the Benaki family, something he took as a slight (*GN*, 147).
15. *LC*, 122.
16. GR-OF-CA-SF02-S01-SS02-F20-SF003–0001 (1148).
17. Constantine had written a poem about this poet that does not survive (*L&W*, 26). See Lavagnini (2020), "Καβάφης και Χρηστόπουλος," for a full exploration of his engagement with Christopoulos.
18. "Builders," published in the journal *Attikon Mouseion* in 1891, was his first poem to appear in Athens. That very year, he also printed his first essay, "An Update on the Elgin Marbles," in the Greek newspaper *Ethniki*. "Give Back the Elgin Marbles" appeared in English in *Rivista Quindicinale* (1891), which was published in Egypt.
19. Cavafy 2015b, 47–48. All of the original notes and introductory texts of the dictionary can be located at the Onassis Foundation Cavafy Archive, as part of folder GR-OF CA CA-SF01-S02-F06.
20. Cavafy 2015b, 96, 196, 257.
21. Karaoglou 1990, 92.
22. Savidis 1966, 143. He changed "Sweet Voices" to "Voices," "Memory" to "Ionic," and "The Footsteps of the Eumenides" to "The Footsteps," and revised "The Funeral of Sarpedon." The very high standards Constantine held for his poems meant that he only published a small number of the texts he ever wrote. At the end of his life, he left behind four group of poems: 154 poems that he circulated and published and recognized as his canon; 27 published poems that he rejected, though he rewrote four; 74 finished but unpublished poems; and 30 unfinished poems.
23. Looking back at his poems about old age in a note of 1906, Constantine wrote, "Advancing towards old (or middle) age, I realise that the last poem of mine ['An Old Man'] does not contain an accurate appreciation. 'The Souls of Old Men' I still consider to be accurate. But when I turn seventy perhaps I will find it inaccurate. 'Candles' I believe is safe" (Cavafy 2010, 134). For the archival item and original note in Greek, see GR-OF CA CA-SF01-S03-F09–0009 (201).

24. The date of this letter is uncertain, as it could have been written in 1897, '98, or '99 (Benaki Archive). The full letter is cited in chapter seven.
25. Savidis 1987, 163–65.
26. Rika also asserted that, being the youngest, he was spoiled by the other family members, especially his mother. GR-OF-CA SING-S01-F01–0016 (1632).
27. Hariclia Valieri, the daughter of Aristides, claims that her mother, Maria, neither liked him nor his poetry (*GN*, 135).
28. Various people through the years, most recently Martin McKinsey (2015), believe that Constantine was referring here to masturbation.
29. Peridis, 46–47.
30. Cavafy 2010, 134.
31. Peridis, 47.
32. As noted earlier, Constantine often visited this house surreptitiously in his youth at one or two in the morning.
33. Martin McKinsey makes this point in Cavafy 2015c, 125.
34. To the extent that Constantine rendered the sexual self as constructed rather than inherited, he was a forerunner of a broader European phenomenon, ahead of similar efforts made by James Joyce in *Ulysses* (1922), Virginia Woolf in *Mrs. Dalloway* (1925), and Robert Musil in *The Man Without Qualities* (1930–43). Traditionally World War I stands as the historical point by which artists and philosophers began to rethink human identity. But Constantine had undertaken his revision of sexual subjectivity many years before the war.
35. Papanikolaou 2014, 129, 244.
36. This is a draft of a letter to Marigo Cavafy, the wife of his cousin John in London, dated February 24, 1902: GR-OF-CA CA-SF02-S01-SS02-F19–0024 (950).
37. Cavafy 1963b, 263. For the manuscript of the diary, see GR-OF CA CA-SF02-S02-F24–0001 (1650).
38. Cavafy 1963b, 259.
39. Cavafy 1963b, 263.
40. Cavafy 1963b, 265, 282, 281–82. He did keep the program of a comic opera, *Les mousquetaires au couvent*, that he attended at the Theatre of Phaleron in July: GR-OF-CA-SF02-S02-F25-SF006–0006 (1197).
41. *LC*, 260.
42. Bastea, 126.
43. For instance: "This morning was in town at 10.30. Followed the Rue d'Athéna, entered the Rue d'Eole, thence the Rue de Sophocle, thence the Rue du Parthénagogée, and from the latter street got to the Rue du Stade. I ate a 'pasta' [pastry] at a confectioner's, and then crossing the Rue de Coray I went to the Catholic Cathedral of St. Denis in the Rue de l'Université . . . It is a fine cathedral, but smaller than St. Catherine's at Alexandria." Cavafy 1963b, 281–82.
44. Cavafy 1963b, 289.
45. However, he had to borrow £100 from Pericles Anastasiades to make the trip (*CE*, 236).
46. A surprising number of journals had sprung up in Alexandria in the first half of the twentieth century: *Nea Zoï*, the most long-lived (1904–27); *Serapion* (1909–1910); *Grammata* (1911–21); *Argo* (1923–27); *Alexandrini Techni* (1926–30); *Panaigyptia* (1926–38); and *Alexandrini Logotechnia* (1947–53). Of these, *Grammata* was considered the most prestigious, its influence extending to Greece itself. *Alexandrini Techni*, as noted, was founded and supported by Constantine himself and was known as a platform for his work. These journals provided

important venues for Constantine's poetry as well as for lively criticism to develop around his work, both positive and negative.

47. Daskalopoulos 1990, 37.
48. Cavafy 1963b, 271.
49. Cavafy 1963b, 280.
50. Cavafy 1963b, 284.
51. Cavafy 1963b, 287.
52. It is notable that he referred to Constantine as a merchant, since by this time the poet had abandoned all interests in markets and business. Writing about this meeting twenty years afterward to Malanos and thus relying on his memory, Xenopoulos said that Constantine told him he was a merchant. Had he allowed Xenopoulos to assume this because he was embarrassed to admit he worked in a municipal office? Xenopoulos said that Constantine did not spend much time talking about his own poetry, preferring to discuss Xenopoulos's own work. If this is indeed true, then we could say that this image does not correspond to one we gain from his own private notes of the period. Perhaps he was being very cautious, not wishing to appear overconfident in front of such a luminary.
53. Xenopoulos, 23–24.
54. Cavafy 1963a, 50.
55. Immediately there followed a short critique of the poem in the newspaper *Athena* accusing the author of "simplifying poetry" (*LC*, 293), a criticism that marked a growing dissatisfaction within certain poetic circles in Athens with the seeming prosaic and plain style of Constantine's verse.
56. Haas 2015, 103. For the sake of clarity, we present all abbreviated notes and diary entries in their final edited form.
57. As noted in Haas (2015, 114): GR-OF CA-SF02–501-SS02-F19–0027 (505).
58. For a long time, critics believed that the "F" represented his mother's maiden name, Fotiades/Photiades, and in using it, Constantine was honoring his maternal grandfather. Hariclia Valieri claimed that the "F" stood for Constantine's second name, Fotis, given to him during his baptism. His baptismal certificate, however, only lists the name "Konstantinos" (*GN*, 96–97, 99).
59. Malanos 1986, 17.
60. Sareyiannis 1964, 128.
61. Savidis 1966, 192.
62. Martin McKinsey (Cavafy 2015c) translates Constantine's personal notes and poems from this period and, in so doing, provides an excellent account of this transition. The magical importance Constantine attached to 1911 reminds us of the provocative remark made by Virginia Woolf in her essay of 1924, "Mr. Bennet and Mrs. Brown," that "on or about December 1924, human character changed" (Woolf 1950, 96).
63. Politis 1930, 448. As noted earlier, this entry is based on material Constantine had supplied to Politis.
64. We have no record of their conversation because Constantine did not keep a journal as he had done two years earlier. It is quite probable that they discussed the article Xenopoulos was to publish in November, which provoked both praise and criticism among Athenian critics (*L&W*, 56).
65. Although the editor Michalis Peridis named it "Ars Poetica," the text does not offer a theory of poetry, as the title implies, but discusses the practical aspects of writing, especially Constantine's own attempt at "Emendatory Work." It has also been titled "Philosophical Self-Scrutiny."

66. Cavafy 2010, 116.
67. Cavafy 1983, 64.
68. We know it only through his posthumously published notes and others still unpublished in the archive.
69. Cavafy 2010, 119. The original editor of this text transcribed this phrase as "crapulence of libations," which does not make sense. George Savidis has suggested the more probable "crisis of liberation" (1966, 144).
70. Constantine refers here to Alexander Mavroudis, a critic and poet who later moved to Paris, writing under the name of Alex Madis, to whom Constantine sent one of his first pamphlets. He seems to have had a crush on Mavroudis, though we have no evidence of an actual love affair. Sul. and Bra. may also be abbreviated names of men he fell in love with.
71. Robinson 1988, 31.
72. Robinson 1988, 31.
73. Dimiroulis 2015, 89–95.
74. Alithersis, 36.
75. Cavafy 2009, xviii. On Cavafy's language, diction, and grammar, see Menas (1985).
76. Cavafy 2010, 139: GR-OF CA CA-SF01-S03-F09–0022 (213).
77. Michalis Pieris notes that the essay is significant for its references to Solomos, Hugo, Racine, Byron, Banville, and Leigh Hunt (Cavafy 2003, 347).
78. Cavafy 1963b, 27–29.
79. Georgios Stratigis (1860–1938) was a lawyer, poet, and playwright. He was a translator of Goethe, Shakespeare, and Dante and practiced law in Athens and Alexandria. His collection of poems, *Νέα Ποιήματα / New Poems*, was published in Athens in 1892. Constantine's review essay also references numerous other poets that he would have been reading at the time: Keats, Browning, Thomas Hood, A. Rangavi, and A. Valaoritis (noted by Pieris, Cavafy 2003, 353).
80. Politis 1930, 455.
81. Mackridge, 127.
82. "A metrical foot consisting of a long syllable between two short syllables in quantitative verse or of a stressed syllable between two unstressed syllables in accentual verse." https://www.merriam-webster.com/dictionary/amphibrach.
83. Mackridge, 129.
84. Mackridge, 129. Synizesis is when a poet contracts two syllables into one by uniting in pronunciation two adjacent vowels. See Rae Dalven's illuminating discussion of Cavafy's craft where she notes: "Cavafy's stanzas vary greatly in length and arrangement as the thought and feeling of the poem dictate. The stanza is in itself a poetic device . . . Cavafy gave much thought to phonic values . . . makes effective use of repetition . . . is a master of the run-on line . . . uses feminine and masculine endings in all possible combinations" (Dalven 292–93).
85. Robinson, 36.
86. Dalven, 294–95.
87. Menas notes that Cavafy makes use of only 610 adjectives, 18.1 percent of his word count (Menas, 118).
88. Ion Dragoumis served as vice-consul of Greece in Alexandria in 1905. He and the poet corresponded a few times, during which Constantine showed his usual terse self. On the poem "Samothrace" that Ion had sent him, Constantine remarked: "I read 'Samothrace.' It's a beautiful work" (Ioannou, 540). See the relevant discussion in chapter five.

89. Dragoumis, 62–63.
90. Dragoumis, 98.
91. It seems that he was cared for by women friends and acquaintances while at the hotel but could not get any rest. GR-OF CA CA-SF02-S02-F24–0002 (475).
92. One cannot discount the Victorian influence of the cult of death here that heavily colored the Cavafy family's approach to dying and bereavement.
93. It is probable that Constantine wrote the death announcement in the newspaper *Telegraphos*, March 7, 1891 (*CE*, 194–95).
94. Dimitris Dimiroulis rightly claims that in Cavafy's life there were only losses and no additions (Cavafy 2015a, 19).
95. Critics often point to these changes as signs of internal transformation (Savidis 1966, 143–44). This is hard to determine, as many people modify their patterns of living in middle age.
96. Malanos 1971, 257. And she wrote about her encounter a year later in a special issue of the periodical *Nea Techni*, devoted to Cavafy. In the days after her visit with Constantine, she gave a reading of her own work in a program organized by Nikos Zelitas (Malanos 1971, 256).
97. Myrtiotissa [1924] 1983, 84.
98. *LC*, 154.
99. *L&W*, 38. In March 1897, he published his essay "A Page of Trojan History," the last he would sign with the name C. F. Cavafy (*L&W*, 42).
100. GR-OF CA CA-SF02-S02-F25-SF006–0003 (1141).
101. Pieridis, 12.
102. Sareyiannis 1964, 80–81.
103. Pieridis, 13.
104. Sareyiannis 1964, 38.
105. GR-OF CA SING-S01-F02-SF001–0038 (1439).
106. GR-OF CA SING-S01-F02-SF001–0039 (1440).
107. GR-OF CA SING-S01-F02-SF001–0040 (1441). On January 20, he ate again at the Benaki household and wrote to Alekos that he had been invited to a wedding the following Sunday (January 20, 1919). The next day, Atanasio Catraro dropped by in the afternoon along with Zelitas and Andreas Zotos, whose wedding Constantine would attend on Sunday (January 21, 1919). GR-OF CA SING-S01-F02-SF001–0041 (1442); R-OF CA SING-S01-F02-SF001–0042 (1443).
108. Even late in his life, he rarely declined invitations to formal events. On March 13, 1930, he took part in a reception in the Greek Club honoring the visiting minister of external affairs for Greece. Constantine insisted that *Alexandrini Techni* cover the event, especially after the minister's recognition of the poet as a "distinguished representative of Greek literature." The minister's warm words were followed by a poetry reading, with Giakos Pieridis reciting "Voices" and "Desires," and Polys Modinos reciting "Candles" (*Alexandrini Techni*, April 3, 1930, 125).

10. THE BIG POETIC CHANGE

1. Auden echoed Myrtiotissa's sentiments when he claimed that his poetry is so original that it's impossible to misrecognize a poem by Cavafy (Auden, viii).
2. Myrtiotissa, 84.
3. *LC*, 260.
4. Dragoumis, 63.
5. Cavafy 2010, 135. For the original note in the Cavafy Archive, see GR-OF CA CA-SF01-S03-F09–0012 (204).

6. Cavafy 2010, 129.
7. Constantine offered here an insight about art that Herman Melville expressed in his novella *Billy Budd, Sailor* (posthumously published in 1924), namely that unpolished reality in itself is neither interesting nor does it move us: "Truth uncompromisingly told will always have its ragged edges" (Melville, 128).
8. For a full analysis of this poem, see Jusdanis, "Cavafy, Tennyson and the Overcoming of Influence" (1982–83).
9. Cavafy 2010, 127. This note was composed in English.
10. Modinos introduced the lecture Alekos Sengopoulos gave on Constantine's poetry on February 23, 1918 (see chapter eight, pp. 241–43).
11. Modinos 1963, 615.
12. Haas 1982, 38.
13. *TPC*, 77.
14. *TPC*, 77.
15. Sareyiannis 1964, 35.
16. Pieridis, 25.
17. Mary Beard, writing on the memoirs of Peter Brown, the celebrated historian of late antiquity, notes that Brown is credited with overturning the reigning assumptions about this period. Yet Constantine criticized Gibbon and brought attention to figures like Julian and Simeon Stylites eighty years before Brown (Beard 2023, 3).
18. Haag 2004a, 22. The British vice-consul of Alexandria at the time, Laurence Grafftey-Smith, describes Furness's "exquisite literary tastes" and his fascination with the "obscure 'curiosa' of the Greek Anthology" (Grafftey-Smith, 70) and expresses his gratitude to Furness for having introduced Constantine to him.
19. Forster 1980, 94.
20. See Edmund Keeley's *Cavafy's Alexandria* (1996).
21. Haas 1983, 98.
22. Haas 2019, 68–69.
23. Haas 2012, 202. Ecbatana and Susa were major cities in Persia.
24. Haas points out that neither Ctesias nor Plutarch referred to Persepolis in this context (Haas 2012, 207).
25. Haas 2012, 202–203.
26. Haas believes Constantine probably wrote this note around 1903–1904—that is, during the period of his "philosophical scrutiny" when he was taking stock of his work (Haas 2012, 208). This means he worked on the poem for about four to five years before deciding against publication.
27. For some of Cavafy's personal notes, including the aforementioned lists, see folder GR-OF CA CA-SF02-S02-F25-SF004.
28. For his mother's recipes, see GR-OF CA CA-SFO2-S02-F25-SF005–0008 (1208).
29. He also wrote down notes like this: "Now I remember it—after a 'déboire' [disappointment] with Pal. I played with Cos Kap. And lost 10 fr. Happily, he was in a hurry to get the midday train or else through inattentiveness I would have lost more": GR-CA CA-SF02-S02-F25-SF004–0001 (974).
30. For the receipts and tickets, see GR-OF CA CA-SF02-S02-F25-SF003–0006 (983) and GR-OF CA CA-SF02-S02-F25-SF003–0010 (984).
31. GR-OF CA CA-SF02-S02-F25-SF004–0014 (991) and GR-OF CA CA-SF02-S02-F25-SF004–0010 (992).
32. GR-0F CA CA-SFO2-S02-F25-SF004–0036 (881).

33. GR-OF CA CA-SF02-S02-F25-SF004–0003 (994).
34. GR-OF CA CA-SF02-S02-F25-SF003–0020 (1000).
35. GR-OF CA CA-SF02-S02-F25-SF003–0002 (1076).
36. GR-OF CA CA-SF02-S02-F25-SF003–0024 (1085).
37. GR-OF CA CA-SF02-S02-F25-SF004–0009 (1200). He also kept a list of his mother's jewelry he inherited and a note signed by Alexander (2.2.1900) in which he relinquished his share of his mother's jewelry to Constantine: GR-OF CA CA-SF02-S02-F25-SF004–0004 (1195).
38. GR-OF-CA CA-SF02–502-F25-SF004–0033 (865). For a reconstruction of the text, see *LC*, 252–54.
39. Lechonitis, 22; Malanos 1971, 148.
40. Cavafy 2010, 111.
41. Cavafy 2010, 111.
42. Constantine characterized this essay as a "curiosity of literature" in a letter to Pericles Anastasiades (Peridis, 311)—for which, see chapter seven.
43. Cavafy 2010, 109.
44. Cavafy 2010, 82–83.
45. Writing from Cairo in January 1906, John apologized to Constantine for neglecting the translations for some time. "But I do not abandon the cherished project." He asked Constantine to send a copy of the journal *Panathenaia* "that I may enjoy [the poem] 'Trojans' in print": GR-OF CA CA—SF02-S01-SS02-F20-SF001–0069 (1174).
46. Xenopoulos, 30–31.
47. Cavafy 2010, 132–33. For the original note, see GR-OF CA CA-SF01-S03-F09–0005 (211).
48. Cavafy 2010, 123.
49. Cavafy 2010, 134. For the original note, see GR-OF CA CA-SF01-S03-F09–0008 (200).
50. Vaianos 155, 157.
51. Sareyiannis 1964, 121.
52. Gialourakis 1959, 85.
53. Alithersis, 34.
54. Cavafy 2010, 130. For the original note, see GR-OF CA CA-SF01-S03-F09–0002 (193). Yet, as he wrote about himself in the "Memorandum About the Cavafy Family," he had "achieved very little in practical life." And then he added the following comments, which he tellingly crossed out: "He might have done [so] perhaps [attained a practical life] had he directed his energies better": GR-OF CA CA-SF02-S02-F25-SF002–0003 (1091).
55. His colleague Ibrahim el Kayar remembers that he would spread files all over the desk, complaining of excessive work, and then he would clear them up at the end of the day. Often, he would close the door to keep his assistants out in order to work on his poetry. When el Kayar looked through the keyhole, he found Constantine writing down something "as if in a moment of inspiration." Kayar adds that he was a pedant, reading a letter many times and insisting on correct punctuation. He would call an employee to his office to correct a misplaced comma (Liddell, 127).
56. Even in retirement he did not seek personal wealth, despite his fears about economic insecurity. When in 1927 Christophoros Nomikos asked him why he had not written history, Constantine answered, "To write history you need sources and

a personal library and my finances don't allow me to have these things." Nomikos suggested that he take out an insurance policy so that "instead of having a yearly income of say 300–400 pounds, you would double that amount, provided that after your death your estate would become property of the insurance company." Constantine, being a superstitious man, rebuffed the idea, adding that "if I decide today to make this investment in a company, I can assure you, Christopher, that tomorrow I will die and the insurance company will win" (Malanos 1957, 251).

57. Gialourakis 1959, 34, 35.
58. Gialourakis 1959, 34.
59. "At the Benaki household I met John Synadinos, who is both a friend of mine and a close friend of Antonis Benaki" (December 27, 1918). He liked to repeat to Alekos how much courtesy and hospitality the Benaki family showed him (January 30, 1919). At the end of a public lecture, he ran into Mr. and Mrs. Benaki, who had invited him to dinner that evening as the only guest, and he stayed there until 11:30 p.m. (February 16, 1919). GR-OF CA SING-S01-F02-SF001–0033 (1434); GR-OF CA SING-S01-F02-SF001–0048 (1449); GR-OF CA SING-S01-F02-SF001–0059 (1460).
60. Cavafy 2010, 89.
61. Sareyiannis 1964, 49. Wilde's trial began in 1895 and Constantine often referred to it in conversation (Alithersis, 31). By a little-known coincidence, Lord Alfred Douglas, Wilde's lover, came to Egypt in 1893 to stay with Lady and Lord Cromer, having been sent there by his mother to escape Wilde (Ellman, 414). See Ekdawi (1993) on the impact of the Wilde trial on Cavafy's "Days of" poems.
62. Sareyiannis 1964, 49. Unfortunately, Sareyiannis does not provide any details about these incidents.
63. Gialourakis 1959, 121.
64. It should be said that his friends maintained this same silence as well. During his lifetime, no one wrote overtly about his sexuality even though each one of them must have had information. Speaking about the climate of "corruption" in Alexandria, Stratis Tsirkas, who knew many people of Constantine's circle, characteristically said: "It is not right nor do I wish to refer to names; apart from his brother Paul, I was told of others—perhaps three out of ten in his circle—who had the same tendency [i.e., homosexuality]" (*CE*, 290). This reticence of Alexandrians to refer explicitly to what they all knew explains in part the paucity of details regarding Constantine's sexual life. Apart from occasional and brief references, there reigns a tacit silence that has prevented later critics from fully understanding his relations with men.
65. Cavafy 2015, 108. For the original note, see GR-OF CA CA-SF01-S03-F09–0019 (210).
66. Cavafy 2015, 100.
67. Haas 1983, 105.
68. See Papanikolaou (2014) on the centrality of this poem for Cavafy's queer poetics.
69. Cavafy 1983, 38. He wrote it on January 3, 1907. For the original note, see GR-OF CA CA-SF01-S03-F09–0010 (202).
70. Ftyaras, 545.
71. Catraro 1970, 42. Catraro introduced Constantine to the Italian futurist poet Filippo Tommaso Marinetti in December 1929. During a subsequent meeting in 1930 during which Marinetti claimed Cavafy as a futurist for "having broken with the rotten poetic world of the tearful romanticism of the nineteenth century,"

Constantine replied: "Your idea is really wonderful, dear Marinetti. But it seems to me that I am far from futurism." To which Marinetti retorted: "Whoever is in advance of his time and art or in life is a futurist" (Liddell, 203–204).

72. Peridis, 261.
73. Sareyiannis 1964, 45.
74. *TPC*, 54.
75. Cavafy 1983, 59. Constantine wrote this note in his personal shorthand. George Savidis and his editors deciphered the full text.
76. Gialourakis 1959, 28–29.
77. GR-OF CA CA-SF02-S01-SS02-F20-SF001–0018 (393).
78. See the epilogue for a discussion of this note.
79. Personal communication to Gregory Jusdanis by Georges Kypreos, who was born in Alexandria and whose grandmother knew Constantine. Interview conducted in Alexandria, May 28, 2017. In fact, Kypreos's grandmother was scandalized that her "petit adorable Georges" was studying the poetry of the "hideous" Cavafy at school in 1963. In his memoir, Kypreos adds that Alexandrian high society saw Constantine as a "scapegoat" when he was still alive and did not wish to be associated with him. Only Penelope Delta had accepted him (2010, 13–15). That Kypreos's grandmother could express such contempt for Constantine's poetry one hundred years after the poet's birth points to the difficulties he must have faced in Alexandria. See also Polys Modinos's comments to this effect in his interview: https://www.youtube.com/watch?v=tkksWnnHxZ0&t=2264s.
80. "In the Same City" (1894), an early version of "The City," was, as Constantine wrote to Pericles, "from one point of view perfect." The "versification and chiefly the rhymes are faultless." But he was less satisfied with the second stanza, fearing that he had "overdone the effect and strained the sentiment, both fatal accidents in art." Yet, despite his satisfaction with the poem, he continued to work on it, even changing its title and eventually publishing it in 1910.
81. Alithersis, 15.
82. This idea was first expressed by Polys Modinos, who was citing Henrik Ibsen's remark on a fellow Norwegian writer (Modinos [1963] 1983, 614).
83. Pieridis, 28.
84. This material comes from the notes Rika was keeping for her biography. GR-OF CA SING-S01-F01–0016 (1632).

11. THE QUEST FOR GLORY

1. Constantine enhanced the actual beauty of the poem by ending each line in strong rhymes of *aa*, *bb*, *cc*, *dd*, *ee* whereby rhyming couplets are homonyms: "taxi" (order) "metaxi" (silk); "krini" (lilies) "krini" (he judges); "physi" (nature) "aphysi" (he lets).
2. Simeonidis, 21.
3. Petridis, 36.
4. *TPC*, 33.
5. Mendelsohn (2009, 391–92) offers an extensive and insightful commentary on this poem. See the "Interlude" for a discussion of Cavafy's essay on Lucian.
6. Katsimbalis, 3.
7. Kampanis 1963a, 1421.
8. Politis 1930, 448.
9. Politis 1930, 453.

10. Politis 1930, 447.
11. It was Constantine's idea to name the journal "Alexandrian Art" so as to emphasize the continuity of Greek poetry in his city from the Hellenistic period to his day (Garoufalias, 54–55).
12. June–July 1929, 248.
13. One unsigned article brought attention to the prediction by Alkis Thrylos that Cavafy was destined to achieve a European reputation. See Thrylos, 27.
14. In time, Cavafy would unofficially become the national poet of Greece (Foteini Dimirouli, 2021).
15. An early and astute critic, he was the first to speak of the political Cavafy. He also wrote for the inaugural issue of *Alexandrini Techni*, which appeared in December 1926.
16. Vrisimitzakis, 87–88.
17. Catraro 1970, 17, 29, 34.
18. Malanos, *TPC*, 193.
19. *TPC*, 239.
20. Malanos 1971, 179. But we cannot exclude the possibility that he might have felt rejected by the poet, as was the case with Malanos (Alithersis, 12–13, 34). See also Pieridis, 58.
21. Ftyaras does not remember if it was 1928 or 1929 (Ftyaras, 545–47).
22. What these boys did not know was that by that time he felt isolated and needed their company (Sengopoulos, 2). See the epilogue for a fuller discussion.
23. Liddell, 130.
24. Karapanogopoulos, 26, 28.
25. Sareyiannis 1964, 39.
26. Malanos 1971, 81.
27. Eftychia Zelitas provided a description of the scene in a letter to Timos Malanos many years later (*L&W*, 100). Although there exists a recording of Tennyson, there are no tapes of Cavafy's voice nor any video footage of him, a poet much younger than his English predecessor.
28. Sareyiannis 1964, 41.
29. Malanos 1971, 152.
30. Kolaitis, 34.
31. Sareyiannis 1964, 31. In the introduction to the *Self-Comments* by G. Lechonitis, Malanos says that in 1925 he actually aspired to being Constantine's Eckermann—that is, Goethe's disciple who recorded and published his conversation with the poet in three volumes (Malanos 1942, 9). Malanos remarks disparagingly that, not possessing a theoretical mind, Constantine would have been incapable of carrying a conversation about art and poetry for long (Gialourakis 1979, 152). Malanos could make this claim because he had no access to the many unpublished texts Constantine had written about art. And a large part of his poetry, as Gregory Jusdanis has shown, is self-conscious, dealing exactly with the theoretical dimension of poetic creation. When his poetry is examined in conjunction with these published and unpublished comments, it shows a fully developed poetic theory (Jusdanis, 1987).
32. Both anecdotes are in *TPC*, 258–60. Constantine also hated being wrong. One evening, he was involved in a heated debate with the art historian Christophoros Nomikos, to whom he seemed to be losing the argument. When Nomikos appeared the next day with the necessary books to prove his point, Constantine did not ar-

rive as he'd promised. And indeed, he would not agree to meet until Nomikos had returned the volumes to the library (Malanos 1971, 186).

33. The famous Egyptologist Dionysios Kyttikas was impressed by Constantine's grasp of Egyptian history. After leaving the poet's apartment one day, he confessed to a friend that before the visit he "did not imagine that Cavafy knew so much about ancient Egypt" (Pieridis, 24).
34. Pieridis, 22.
35. "We listened with our mouths open . . . I had later listened to Charles Diehl [a renowned Byzantinist] at the Sorbonne but I could not compare him as teacher to Cavafy. He conveyed the entire atmosphere of an epoch in each detail . . . The passion with which he picked up a book to make a point was very impressive . . . He wanted to teach, he wanted to speak, this was the reason, I think, he offered us the lessons" (Ftyaras, 547).
36. "This is inaccurate," he says about Gibbon's reference to the city of Thebes. At another point, he disputes the historical reality of a particular ruler: "Ninus never existed." Elsewhere he writes: "no such martyr figures on the Greek ecclesiastical calendar." He often expresses his enthusiasm for historical details. In a reference to Cleopatra as a "Barbarian queen," he says, "I should much like to know in which Greek or Latin author this extraordinary expression occurs" (Haas 1982, 31, 32, 36, 42).
37. Sareyiannis 1964, 43.
38. Karapanagopoulos, 22.
39. *TPC*, 22.
40. *TPC*, 196.
41. Malanos 1971, 330; *TPC*, 37.
42. Alithersis, 19.
43. For this reason, Constantine cited in the inaugural issue of his *Alexandrini Techni* a laudatory article on his work that had appeared in the newspaper *Eleftheria* of Larissa, a small, provincial city in central Greece: Among the "merchants of poetry today" it is rare to find an artist who in thirty years has written only 123 poems. "It is even more rare to find a poet who has managed to pour into these 123 poems a whole life, a whole theory of life" (Frangos, 24).
44. *CE*, 13–14.
45. *CE*, 13. Tsirkas writes that Constantine took the "initiative" to introduce himself in the office of *Alexandrini Techni*. He also made sure to attend their last meeting in the Billiards Palace, where Tsirkas and his friends were discussing the formation of a new literary society (*CE*, 14).
46. Pieridis, 13; Catraro 1970, 29.
47. Lapathiotis, 261. Malanos met Lapathiotis in Athens ten years later. He also sent him a copy of François Porché's book, which had just appeared in 1927 with the daring Wildean title *L'amour qui n'ose pas dire son nom* (*The Love That Dare Not Speak Its Name*). In his thank-you letter, Lapathiotis wrote that had Porché known of Cavafy, he would have called his book "L'amour qui ne fait autre chose que dire son nom" / "The love that does nothing else but call itself by its name" (Malanos 1971, 237).
48. Vaianos, 152.
49. Vaianos, 156.
50. In an interview with the journalist Stephanos Charmidis in *To Elefthero Vima* (July 9, 1923), Napoleon described Cavafy's poetry as manifesting the third

level in the evolution of Greek letters after the poet Dionysios Solomos and the short-story writer Alexandros Papadiamantis. GR-OF CA CA-SF02-S02-F25-SF007–0043 (1344).

51. All letters from Scaife, unless otherwise noted, are in possession of ELIA-MIET (Papoutsakis File 4.4).
52. This letter is part of the Charitatou Archive. Many young men developed this passionate, almost physical admiration for the poet. Christos Zervos, one of the collaborators of the journal *Grammata*, wrote to Nikos Zelitas from Paris asking him to pass on to Constantine his "cordial" greetings: "Tell him that I miss his affable company, his house" and the treats he served. "I miss his company excessively. I doubt that I can find such a person here." Undated note by Zervos to Zelitas from Paris. GR-OF CA CA-SF02-S02-F25-SF007–0043 (1344).
53. Scaife would publish a translation of "The Hall Mirror" in *The Spectator* (1935). The Onassis Archive has an undated draft letter by Constantine to Scaife in which Constantine refers to this poem. He also mentions a lecture on *Hamlet* that Scaife was preparing: GR-OF CA CA-SF02-S01-SS01-F17-SF003–0037 (959). Another document contains Scaife's translation of Constantine's poem "Myris: Alexandria. 340 A.D." with notes and cancellations possibly by Constantine himself: GR-OF CA CA-SF01-S04-F12-SF003–0008 (1262). Scaife praised Constantine's English, saying that "the Greek spirit had been transformed through his mouth into a Teutonic language" (Scaife [1933] 1983, 18).
54. Sareyiannis 1964, 121.
55. Ouranis, 1469, 1470.
56. Although Minotis does not provide the exact date, the year 1926 is when his name appears for the first time in Constantine's catalogue of people receiving his work.
57. It was built by B. Konelianos, a Greek-Jewish businessman (Gialourakis 2006, 40). Constantine found it superior to the "Variété" theater in Athens where he and Alexander saw Puccini's *La Bohème* on July 13, 1901: "Quite a third rate company. The theater itself is as large as the 'Theatron tis Omonoias' but less clean and neat and its café is simply an oven. Still it is better than Tsocha's. But they are all three inferior to the 'Edem' or the 'Alhambra' of Alexandria" (Cavafy 1963b, 281).
58. Minotis, 316.
59. Minotis, 316. To Minotis's surprise, Constantine came to the performance of *Macbeth* and sought him out even though he had a minor role—that of the nobleman Ross. "You were brilliant, Minoti."
60. Minotis, 320. Before parting, Minotis informed Constantine that he had received a telegram that his girlfriend, the future actress Katina Paxinou, would be arriving in Alexandria. He would later marry Paxinou, who became renowned in Greece and the United States, having won an Academy Award and a Golden Globe Award for Best Supporting Actress for her role in *For Whom the Bell Tolls* (1943). When Minotis went to the port to receive Paxinou, whom did he see descending the plank of the liner *Arcadia*? Constantine himself, holding the actress's hand. He had apparently received permission to enter the ship after it docked, to welcome Paxinou with flowers and to make the dramatic descent into the city. And eight years later, when Constantine was at the hospital in Athens, convalescing after his tracheotomy, he visited Paxinou, who, by coincidence, had been admitted for typhus.
61. Minotis, 319, 321. Constantine sent copies again in 1927 and 1928. On the collections Minotis received from Constantine, see Savidis (1966), 249, 256, 262, 268, 269, 270.

62. Komis was the publisher of the Alexandrian journal *Skepsi* (Thought). His memoir of his encounter with Constantine, which appeared in 1935, is one of the most vivid firsthand accounts we have of the poet.
63. Komis, 15.
64. Garoufalias was born in Volos in 1913 and in 1931 went to Alexandria, where his brother Yiorgos and uncle Yiannis had settled. The latter was married to Alekos Sengopoulos's sister.
65. Garoufalias, 26.
66. Garoufalias, 42.
67. Both folders contained a page with the year of each poem's composition. In some instances, page numbers bore the corrections by the poet's hand. Constantine kept a record of those who received his collections, noting in the catalogue of 1932 "Dimitris Garoufalias" and in that of 1929 his uncle "Yiannis Garoufalias" (Dimiroulis 2014, 35).
68. Konstantinos Ftyaras remembers this. Then a student and ardent reader of poetry, Ftyaras was in his late teens when around 1920, he, along with like-minded Greek youths in Alexandria, formed a literary group that published a journal, *Argo*. Constantine often stopped by their gatherings to speak about poetry. In his meticulous catalogue, Constantine noted that he had given Ftyaras his poems (Savidis 1992, 273).
69. Born in Cairo in 1890, he died in Greece in a car accident in 1947. On the allure of intellectual currents in Italy and the cultural bridges connecting Alexandria, Paris, and Italy, see Lavagnini (2020, 135–45).
70. Karaoglou, 24.
71. Vrisimitzakis, 97 (letter dated January 5, 1927).
72. Vrisimitzakis, 99. For the original, see GR-OF CA CA-SF02-S01-SS01-F18-SF003–0156 (745).
73. Vaianos, 39–40; Mavrogiannis, 148. Vaianos began publishing *Nea Techni* in 1924. He founded it in the café Themis, along with fellow students from Chios. It should not be confused with *Nea Zoï*, the literary journal appearing in Alexandria between 1904 and 1927.
74. Katsimbalis, 6.
75. Interview with Marios Vaianos by Giannis Mavrogiannis in Athens in 1973.
76. Vaianos, 42.
77. Mavrogiannis, 152.
78. Daskalopoulos 2003, 47.
79. GR-OF CA SING-S01-F02-SF001–0072 (1544). Writing to Rika on July 10, he inquired anxiously whether Vaianos had received the collections destined for certain Athenian critics. Four days later, he asked her to relay to Vaianos that along with the *tefchi* (bound editions), he was sending him a collection, which he should give to the iconoclastic poet Kostas Karyotakis. Letters dated July 10, 1928: GR-OF CA SING-S01-F02-SF001–0082 (1554); and July 14, 1928: GR-OF CA SING-S01-F02-SF001–0083 (1555).
80. On March 31, 1924, he wrote: "I was pleased with Malakasis' favorable opinion [of my work]" (Cavafy 1979, 38). The poet Miltiadis Malakasis (1869–1943) gave an interview on Cavafy to Vaianos that was published in the newspaper *Eleftheros Typos* on March 19, 1924. In another, he cited an article on Cavafy's poetic technique by Palamas. (Palamas referred for the first time to Cavafy's poetry in 1921 [Karaoglou, 29]). And he mentioned an article in the newspaper *Athina* on June 15, 1925, by the journalist Yiorgios D. Koromilas, who had met Constantine

in Alexandria in 1925. This article was reprinted in *Tachydromos* (Alexandria) on April 20, 1925. Cavafy 1979, 39, 40.

81. Cavafy 1979, 67.
82. Vaianos, 141. The poet Thanasis Papathanasopoulos captured the disappointment of Vaianos in the poem "Kavafi acharistia" (Cavafy's Ingratitude), where he cites a few lines from the former's memoir after the title. He then relates the whole scene previously described by Vaianos: "And Marios descends the stairs in bitterness / certain that this is how kindness is rewarded" (Daskalopoulos 2003, 183–85).
83. Vaianos, 141.
84. Vaianos, 142.
85. Vaianos did in fact lose his hearing in that ear.
86. Vaianos, 164.
87. Vaianos, 164.
88. Cavafy 2015a, 34.
89. Mavrogiannis, 150.

12. CONSTANTINE'S LITERARY RADIUS

1. Many contemporaries agreed. See Ftyaras, 546; Catraro 1970, 44; *TPC*, 67.
2. GR-OF CA CA-SF02-S01-SS01-F17-SF003–0015 (496). Diana Haas believes that the addressee of the letter was Gregory Sarris, a recipient of Constantine's poetry and member of the literary society Nea Zoï (Haas 2019, 80).
3. GR-OF CA CA-SF02-S01-F17-SF003–0012 (494). This was true also in Greece, as Constantine discovered during his visit of 1901. In his diary, he recorded his meeting with Georgios Tsokopoulos (1871–1923), dramatist, journalist, and editor of *Estia* (1920–22). He noted that they "talked mostly about literature and the enormous difficulty met by authors to get an edition to sell" (Cavafy 1963b, 267–68). Tsokopoulos wrote what is regarded as the first critical work on Cavafy. In his book on Greek Alexandria (1898), he spoke glowingly of Constantine's early verses. Tsokopoulos stayed in Alexandria for three years, got to know the poet, and published four of his poems (Malanos 1978, 81).
4. Karapanagopoulos, 22.
5. Komis, 9–11.
6. When learning of his profession, Constantine uttered one of his ambiguous phrases that people did not know how to interpret, seriously or ironically: "Medicine is a distinguished profession. The other professions are fine but medicine is a distinguished profession" (Peridis, 92).
7. Constantine most likely had initiated this presentation if not writing the paper himself (Tsirkas 1963, 691). Petridis placed Constantine's work on the same level as Palamas and Alexandros Papadiamantis, a founder of the Greek short story (Petridis, 36).
8. He may have decided to abandon the book form in 1903 (Ekdawi 2001, 84).
9. Savidis's *I Kavafikes Ekdoseis / Cavafian Editions* (1966/1992) remains the standard analysis of Cavafy's method of publication. Our discussion here is indebted to Savidis.
10. This method of dissemination was not that unusual in Greece or elsewhere in Europe (Savidis 1992, 118).
11. Alithersis, 19.
12. Savidis 1992, 186.

13. Ekdawi 2001, 70.
14. Recent scholarly work has pointed to the "fundamental instability" of Cavafy's texts (Emmerich 2017, 158) and the existence of new ways by which readers may experience and "assemble" them (Stroebel 2018, 305). Stroebel argues that a Cavafy poem "evolved while it was being shared and read." The future editing of Cavafy's work will depend on how the archival material will be approached digitally and on how new editing strategies will be applied to archival material. Early critics, such as Seferis, saw Cavafy's oeuvre as a work in progress rather than a finished product.
15. Keeley and Savidis 1963, x. The archive contains copies of poems already published and included in a folder but which show the poet's corrections. In the Benaki Archive, there is such a copy of the rejected poem "Builders," published in 1891, which shows Constantine's handwritten corrections upon an already-printed text. This is the first poem he had ever printed privately.
16. This final category may be nuanced to include erotic and sensual. See Hirst (1995).
17. When the Sengopoulos couple published the first edition of the poems, they followed a chronological pattern. Savidis used a mixed template for his 1963 two-volume issue of the canon, with the first volume following a thematic order and the second a chronological one. For this reason, the publication history of Constantine's work is plagued by editorial disagreements. One point of contention involves the actual arrangement of the 154 canonical poems. Compelling arguments have been made by Hirst regarding intended meaning generated by the actual juxtaposition of poems arranged thematically and the "mutually disruptive way poems seem to comment on each other" (Hirst 1995, 50).
18. One case in point is the so-called Sengopoulos notebook that dates from roughly 1927 (George Savidis estimates the date; Savidis 2002, 8). Sewn together and handwritten in Constantine's beautiful penmanship, it contains twenty-one of his most famous poems from 1896 to 1910. It is now available in the Digital Collection of the Onassis Foundation Cavafy Archive via the microfilm shots made by G. P. Savidis in 1963: GR-OF CA CA-SF01-SO1-F01-SF001–0196 (1896). Savidis (1966) discusses other examples of similar booklets of what he calls "aftografa tetradia" (91–95).
19. Sareyiannis 1964, 33–34.
20. His favorite method of circulating his work was to hand out copies to people in person (Malanos 1978, 46).
21. See Karampini-Iatrou (2016) and Daskalopoulos (1988).
22. Kolaitis, 79.
23. John wrote the letter in Greek with a few phrases in English. GR-OF CA CA-SF02-S01-SS02-F20-SF001–0072 (1183).
24. Modinos 1980, np.
25. Modinos 1980, np.
26. Pernot's *La Gréce actuelle dans ses poètes* (1921) included six of Constantine's poems. Constantine wrote an unpublished review of Pernot's *Grammaire du Grec Moderne* in 1918.
27. Gradually Constantine's reputation began to grow overseas, with translations in key European languages: Karl Dieterich translated some poems into German and also wrote an article about him in Berlin in 1923. Favorable articles appeared in French publications in 1919 and 1925. Catraro published a positive piece in

Popolo Romano in 1921. G. H. Blanken translated a booklet of twenty-five poems into Dutch a year after the poet's death in a limited edition of one hundred copies.

28. Jeffreys 2009, 43.
29. Jeffreys 2009, 51.
30. Jeffreys 2009, 52.
31. Forster's role in securing Cavafy's fame in the Anglophone world is immeasurable. His essay "The Poetry of C. P. Cavafy" was published in *The Nation* and *The Athenaeum* (April 25, 1919) and reprinted in *Pharos and Pharillon* (1923). He gave an interview on Cavafy for the Alexandrian newspaper *Tachydromos* (September 26, 1929). He dedicated the second edition of *Alexandria. A History and Guide* to C. P. C. (1938). Finally, he reviewed the translation by John Mavrogordato in *The Listener* (July 5, 1951).
32. Jeffreys 2009, 60.
33. Forster included Toynbee in his translation project, but at that time, the historian was embroiled in controversy over his publication about the Asia Minor Catastrophe; he was the first holder of the Koraes Chair at King's College London, which had been endowed by leading Anglo-Greeks like Dimitris Cassavetti, Alexander C. Ionides, and Helen and Stephen Schilizzi (Solomonidis-Hunter, 2014). He resigned his position in 1924. Constantine, who followed the controversy from Alexandria, would have been loath to offend the Anglo-Greek community. See Jeffreys (2009), "Introduction," for the details of this imbroglio.
34. Jeffreys 2009, 71.
35. Jeffreys 2009, 75.
36. Jeffreys 2009, 65.
37. Constantine remained guarded with respect to the erotic poems, fearing with some justification the hostile reactions of readers. When nonfriends asked for his work, he sent them the *tefchos* (bound edition) of 1908–1914, which did not contain explicitly erotic poems (Alithersis, 21).
38. Alithersis, 19.
39. See chapter ten for a discussion of this poetic struggle.
40. Komis, 59.
41. Alithersis, 19.
42. Pieridis, 57, 47.
43. In a letter to Kaisara (December 4, 1932) on the French translation of "Far Away," he provided detailed comments and alternative phrasing of the translation (Gialourakis 1963, 1575).
44. *TPC*, 246. Malanos does not remember the date Cavafy showed him John's translations but thinks it was before 1920.
45. Cavafy 1963b, 237.
46. *GN*, 149.
47. Hariclia called him a "Victorian prude" (*GN*, 147).
48. Cavafy 1963b, 239–40. Constantine wrote this poem in 1897 but left it unpublished in his files; the note to John is dated September 21, 1898. See GR-OF CA CA-SF01-S03-F11–0002 (1640).
49. Cavafy 1963b, 242. This original Greek poem does not appear to have survived. In their correspondence between 1882 and 1883, when Constantine was in Istanbul and John in Alexandria, John showed himself to be fanatical about writing and exact expression. In answer to a query from Constantine, John wrote that "some phrases cannot be translated literally from one language to another." GR-OF CA CASF02-SO1-SS02-F20-SF001–0009 (384).

50. Apparently, Mavrogordato experienced difficulties in finding a publisher who did not demand some form of financial assistance. In despair, he sent Malanos a telegram, saying "regret no prospect of publication of my Cavafy translation without subvention" (Malanos 1986, 21). When Malanos showed the telegram to Alekos Sengopoulos, the latter returned it without any comment.
51. Jeffreys 2009, 115. Forster never managed to write the introduction to this volume, which was ultimately written by Rex Warner. Forster was not a fan of Mavrogordato's translations.
52. Jeffreys 2009, 120.
53. Malanos 1963, 13.
54. Karaoglou, 42.
55. Tangopoulos, 1403.
56. Psycharis 1963, 1404.
57. Pieridis, 40; Alithersis, 21, 56.
58. Malanos saved his most salacious observations for his later writings. In one memorable incident, he described the day he accompanied Constantine (in 1921 or 1922) to the bar Sereli. As they sat down, Cavafy motioned to a cat. Seeing the animal approaching them, Malanos bent down to pet it and with his head under the table, he spotted the strings of the poet's long underwear hanging over his shoe. This sight apparently provoked such repugnance that he saw fit to record it many decades after, while also mentioning that the poet had by then lost most of his teeth (Malanos 2003, 18).
59. Tsirkas 1963, 697. According to Rika and Memas Kolaitis, Malanos's animosity manifested itself as early as 1917 (Karapanogopoulos, 62–65; Kolaitis, 49).
60. *Alexandrini Techni* (May 1927, issue 6), 37–40.
61. Tsirkas 1963, 691.
62. Kambos, 641, 644.
63. This question continued to haunt Cavafian criticism for many decades (Georgiou, 655).
64. Malanos 1971, 206.
65. Malanos 1971, 206–207.
66. Garoufalias 2013, 52. Given the tacit silence in Alexandria about the poet's homosexuality, these blunt statements must have seemed outrageous. Konstantinos Ftyaras reports that he and fellow students had known about his "peculiarity," meaning here his homosexuality, but had not heard of any specific incidents (Ftyaras, 546).
67. Vaianos, 47–48.
68. Malanos 1971, 209. Even though his relationship with Malanos had cooled by then, Constantine appreciated his stance (Kolaitis, 49).
69. On April 23, 1924, Constantine thanked Vaianos for spearheading the entire campaign (Cavafy 1979, 37). He also expressed his gratitude to Lapathiotis (Vaianos, 52).
70. Pieridis, 51.
71. Sareyiannis 1964, 48.
72. Gialourakis 2007, 306.
73. Ilias Gkanoulis sent a hostile and undated letter via Nikos Zelitas in which he accused Constantine of being "self-interested": "Unless you cease being hypocritical and foolish [both underlined], we will put you in your place. I don't want to have a relationship with you." But on July 1, 1926, he wrote a typed letter where he renounced the previous one and apologized for its contents. GR-OF CA CA-SF02-S01-SS03-F23–0003 (1227).

74. Paraschos, 109, 113.
75. Vaianos, 49–50.
76. Thrylos, 1418.
77. In 1932, Constantine celebrated another triumph with the appearance in *O Kyklos* of many laudatory articles. In Egypt, the Francophone magazine *Semaine Égyptienne* published another issue on the poet on April 25, 1929, with contributions from major poets and thinkers in Egypt and Greece. The publication declared that "Cavafy est grand" (17). Interestingly, Rika referred to Cavafy as a "vrai grec d'Egypte" (a true Egyptian Greek) (25).
78. Although he never participated publicly in this rivalry, Constantine once told a visiting professor that "I want Palamas to get the Nobel Prize, not for Palamas—I am indifferent here—but for Greece" (Peridis, 119). This was recorded by Eftychia Zelitas in her notes: GR-OF CA CA-SF03-F29–0002 (1883). In an interview with Gregory Jusdanis on May 3, 2022, Pantelis Voutouris, a specialist in the work of Palamas, suggested that the conflict between Cavafy and Palamas was less a personal struggle between two poets than a public phenomenon.
79. Palamas, 1969, 103.
80. Karaoglou, 17.
81. Letter dated July 27, 1921 (ELIA-MIET Archive).
82. Karaoglou, 24.
83. GR-OF CA CA-SF02-S01-SS01-F18-SF003–0105 (1230).
84. GR-OF CA CA-SF02-S01-SS01-F18-SF003–0144 (1234).
85. GR-OF CA CA-SF02-S01-SS02-F20-SF003–0035 (1236). Constantine responded on May 30, 1932, thanking him for his interest in his work. At the same time, he expressed his surprise that Coulmas knew Karl Dieterich. So he asked Coulmas to thank Dieterich for his translations and especially for the lecture the latter had given on his work. As part of his appreciation, he sent Coulmas the collections of 1905, 1915, and 1916–18. For Constantine's reply, see GR-OF CA CA-SF02-S01 SS02-F19–0034 (962).
86. GR-OF CA CA-SF02-S01-SS01-F18-SF003–0149 (1235).
87. The first such poem, "Epikouros," by Takis Sarakinos, appeared in 1909. That very year, K. N. Konstantinidis printed "Balsama" and dedicated it "to the poet C. P. Cavafy." Two years later, Petros Magnis published the first of many Cavafian parodies—"Adrianos"—with the subtitle "Of C. P. Cavafy."
88. For instance: Malanos, Nikos Santorinios, Lapathiotis, Kleon Paraschos, Rika Sengopoulos, Giorgos Papoutsakis, Miltiadis Malasakis, and Vaianos. See Dimitris Daskalopoulos (2003).
89. For the item in the archive, see GR-OF CA CA-SF02-S02-F25-SF001–0012 (468).
90. Tsirkas 1963, 699.
91. Karapanagopoulos, 60–61.
92. *Alexandrini Techni* (February 1927, 4).

EPILOGUE

1. GR-OF CA SING-S01-F01–0005 (1634).
2. Sengopoulos, 4.
3. GR-OF CA CA-SF02-S02-F25-SF004–0023 (972). These notes were never bound together and this particular one runs over a number of pages. We have interpreted these pages as they exist and are ordered in the Onassis Foundation Cavafy Archive.

4. *Alexandrini Techni* 3 (Feb. 1927): https://lekythos.library.ucy.ac.cy/bitstream/handle/10797/12967/ale_tech_feb1927.pdf?sequence=41&isAllowed=y.
5. For Cavafy's letters to Aleko and Rika, during the summer of 1928 when they were in Athens, see Folder GR-OF CA SING-S01-F02-SF001, Items 0072 (1544) to 0085 (1557).
6. Over the years, Rika had resigned herself to editing *Alexandrini Techni*, organizing appointments, checking facts, and sending out endless envelopes containing his poems. She had her own life, of course. After her studies in Paris, she worked in a law office, while also serving as a correspondent for two newspapers and as press attaché in the Greek consulate of Alexandria. She also wrote poetry herself. But none of her other ambitions rose to the same heights as what would become the great goal of her life: to turn Constantine the man into Cavafy the poet.
7. Agras, 1450.
8. Savidis 1985, 54, fn 42.
9. GR-OF-CA SING-SO1-F01–0005 (1634).
10. GR-OF CA SING-S01-F02-SF002–0008 (1793).
11. See Karampine-Iatrou (2016, 111), where she reiterates the view first put forth by A. Karapanagopoulos that Alekos became jealous of the credit she received for the high literary quality of the edition.
12. Skeferis, 707–708. The Greek Alexandrian newspaper, *Tachydromos*, announced that Constantine died at 2:00 a.m. and that his funeral would take place at 4:00 p.m. The next day, it printed the eulogy given by Skeferis, which reappeared in a special issue of the journal *Epitheorisi Technis* 108 (1963): 707–708.
13. Catraro 1970, 78–81.
14. Papoutsakis, 11.
15. The word "poet" also appeared on Constantine's final passport to indicate his profession.
16. Leontis, 708.
17. Katsimbalis provides a list of all the newspapers in his *Bibliography* (1943).
18. Catraro reports that a Venetian sculptor living in Alexandria was commissioned to create the bust. But it seems to have gotten lost (Catraro 1970, 81). In 1948, the city of Alexandria attached a plaque outside the wall of Constantine's house marking his residence in English, Arabic, and Greek.
19. These speeches and poems appeared in a special issue of *Panaigyptia* on July 8, 1933, which was reissued in 1983 by ELIA.
20. Nomikos had written a touching letter of condolence to Constantine upon John's death: GR-OF CA CA-SF02-S01-SS01-F18-SF003–0075 (686).
21. Nomikos 1933, 2.
22. Peridis, 4. In so doing, Peridis offered a picture of Constantine that Constantine had long created about himself as having no precursors.
23. Papoutsakis, 11.
24. Scaife, 18.
25. Jeffreys 2009, 94.
26. GR-OF-SING-SO1-F01–0017 (1633).
27. Yiorgos had received copies of Constantine's poetry (Savidis 1966, 97, fn 16).
28. Sengopoulos, 6. Pavlos recognized Constantine's originality very early and gave the first ever talk on his work, on April 22, 1909, which he published that year in the journal *Nea Zoï*. They shared many intellectual interests, having attended together the inauguration of the periodical *Grammata* in December 1913 (Stavridi-Patrikiou, 157).

29. "Good evening, your Excellency! I am truly honored." "Between poets, dear Cavafy, the word 'Excellency' has no place" (Catraro 1970, 74).
30. Alkaiou, 331–32.
31. Savidis claims that Rika never published anything on Cavafy after her divorce from Alekos. Citing Rika's brother, Yiorgos Agallianos, Savidis writes that no Cavafy manuscripts were found among Rika's papers after her death (Savidis 1985, 49).
32. In his obituary, Evangelos Papanoutsos recognized her contributions to modern Greek letters as an editor and author. But he especially praised her promotion of Cavafy's work and her publication of the first full collection of the poet's works (Papanoutsos, 787).
33. Sengopoulos, 1.
34. Sengopoulos, 2.
35. Why did Rika give up the battle over Cavafy? Why had she not completed the biography? Perhaps she was overwhelmed by the task of culling the information and shaping it into a story. Possibly she felt pushed out by the men around her who claimed to own Cavafy—Malanos, Peridis, Sareyiannis, Papoutsakis, Vaianos, Vrisimitzakis. Of course, after her divorce from Alekos, she lost access to the poet's papers. But had she been able to, she would have finished the biography long before 1956. The only woman in Constantine's life, the one who knew him most intimately, withdrew to the margins of Cavafy criticism.
36. Emmerich, 136.

WORKS CITED

Abdulhaq, Najat. 2016. *Jewish and Greek Communities in Egypt: Entrepreneurship and Business Before Nasser.* London: I. B. Tauris.

Acosta-Hughes, Benjamin. 2003. "The Poem Remembers: Conceptualization of Memory in the Poetry of Callimachus and Cavafy." *Classical and Modern Literature* 23, no. 2: 19–36.

Agras, Tellos. 1963. "Γραμματολογικά και άλλα." *Νέα Εστία*, no. 872: 1450–57.

Alexiou, Margaret. 1974. *The Ritual Lament in Greek Tradition.* Cambridge: Cambridge University Press.

———. 2002. *After Antiquity: Greek Language, Myth, and Metaphor.* Ithaca, NY: Cornell University Press.

Alithersis, Glafkos. 1934. *Το πρόβλημα του Καβάφη.* Alexandria: Spyros N. Grivas.

Alkaiou, Maria. 1983. "Ο Καβάφης όπως τον γνώρισα." *Η Λέξη*, no. 23: 331–32.

Anderson, Gregory. 1976. *Victorian Clerks.* Manchester: Manchester University Press.

Annesley, George. 1994. *The Rise of Modern Egypt: A Century and a Half of Egyptian History, 1798–1957.* Edinburgh: The Pentland Press.

Anonymous. 1927. "Σημειώματα." *Αλεξανδρινή Τέχνη*, no. 5: 25–30. https://kosmopolis.library.upatras.gr/index.php/alexandrini_texni/article/view/65245/64121.

Anonymous. 1929. "Σημειώματα." *Αλεξανδρινή Τέχνη*, nos. 6–7: 245–48. https://kosmopolis.library.upatras.gr/index.php/alexandrini_texni/article/view/65547/64423.

Anonymous. 1929. "Σημειώματα." *Αλεξανδρινή Τέχνη*, no. 4: 157–60.

Ash, John. 1995. *A Byzantine Journey.* New York: Random House.

Athanasopoulou, Maria. 2003. "Κ. Π. Καβάφη, 'Εις το Φως της Ημέρας' (1896): το υπερφυσικό ως εκδήλωση του νεωτερικού." *Νέα Εστία*, no. 1761: 652–65.

Auden, W. H. 1976. "Introduction." *The Complete Poems of Cavafy.* Translated by Rae Dalven. New York: Harcourt Brace Jovanovich.

Baltzly, Dirk, and Nick Eliopoulos. 2009. "The Classical Ideals of Friendship." In *Friendship: A History*, edited by Barbara Caine. London: Equinox, 1–64.

Bastea, Eleni. 2000. *The Creation of Modern Athens: Planning the Myth.* Cambridge: Cambridge University Press.

Beard, Mary. 2023. "Travels with His Aunts." *The Times Literary Supplement*, September 22, 2023: 3.

Beaton, Roderick. 1994. *An Introduction to Modern Greek Literature*. Oxford: Clarendon Press.

Beauman, Nicola. 1994. *E. M. Forster: A Biography*. New York: Alfred A. Knopf.

Blackie, John Stuart. 1879. *Self-Culture: Intellectual, Physical, and Moral: A Vade Mecum for Young Men and Students*. Edinburgh: David Douglas.

———. 1891. "Shakespeare and Modern Greek." *The Nineteenth Century* 30 (July–December): 1006–17.

Boddy, Alexander A. 1900. *From the Egyptian Ramleh: Sketches of Delta Life and Scenes in Lower Egypt*. London: Gay and Bird.

Boletsi, Maria. 2024. *Specters of Cavafy*. Ann Arbor: University of Michigan Press.

Botman, Selma. 1998. "The Liberal Age." In *Modern Egypt from 1517 to the End of the Twentieth Century*, vol. 2 of *The Cambridge History of Egypt*, edited by M. W. Daly. Cambridge: Cambridge University Press, 285–308.

Bowersock, G. W. 2009. "Cavafy and Apollonios." In *From Gibbon to Auden*. Oxford: Oxford University Press, 151–59.

———. 2009. "Gibbon's Historical Imagination." In *From Gibbon to Auden*. Oxford: Oxford University Press, 3–19.

Briggs, Martin S. 1918. *Through Egypt in War-Time*. London: T. F. Unwin.

Butler, Beverley. 2007. *Return to Alexandria: An Ethnography of Cultural Heritage, Revivalism, and Museum Memory*. Walnut Creek, CA: Left Coast Press.

Byzantios, Skarlatos. 1851–69. *Η Κωνσταντινούπολις: Η περιγραφή τοπογραφική, αρχαιολογική και ιστορική της περιωνύμου ταύτης μεγαλοπόλεως*. 3 vols. Athens.

Caine, Barbara, ed. 2009. *Friendship: A History*. London: Equinox.

Caine, Barbara, and Marc Brodie. 2009. "Class, Sex and Friendship: The Long Nineteenth Century." In *Friendship: A History*, edited by Barbara Caine. London: Equinox, 223–77.

Calvocoressi, Peter. 1986. *From Byzantium to Eton: A Memoir of a Millennium*. London: King's College Center of Contemporary Greek Studies.

Carswell, John. 2000. "The Greeks in the East: Alexandria and Islam." *Discovering Islamic Art: Scholàrs, Collectors, and Collections, 1850–1950*. Edited by Stephen Vernoit. London: I. B. Tauris, 138–46.

Castillo Didier, Miguel. 2014. *Vida De Kavafis*. Santiago, Chile: Ediciones Universidad Diego Portales.

———. 2020. *Cartas al Joven Kavafis. Las Cartas de John*. Santiago de Chile: Centro de Estudios Griegos, Byzantinos, y Neohelénicos.

Catraro, Atanasio. 1929. "Constantin Cavafy et la renaissance de la poesie neogreque." *La Semaine Égyptienne*, no. 22.

———. 1970. *Ο φίλος μου ο Καβάφης*. Translated by Aristeas Rallis. Athens: Ikaros.

Catsiyannis, Timotheos. 1986. *Pandias Stephen Rallis 1793–1865*. London.

Cavafy, C. P. 1963a. *Ανέκδοτα πεζά κείμενα*. Edited by Michalis Peridis. Athens: Fexi.

———. 1963b. *Πεζά*. Edited by G. A. Papoutsakis. Athens: Fexis.

———. 1979. *Επιστολές στον Μάριο Βαϊάνο*. Edited by E. N. Moschos. Athens: Estia.

———. 1983. *Ανέκδοτα σημειώματα ποιητικής και ηθικής*. Edited by George P. Savidis. Athens: Ermis.

———. 1991. "Σημειώματα για τα τελευταία χρόνια και την αρρώστια της Χαρίκλειας Καβάφη (1899)." Edited by Michalis Pieris. *Μολυβδο-κονδυλο-πελεκητής* 3: 171–210.

———. 1993. *Κ. Π. Καβάφης: Κρυμμένα ποιήματα, 1877–1923*. Athens: Ikaros.

———. (1994) 2006. *Ατελή Ποιήματα, 1918–1932.* 2nd ed. Edited by Renata Lavagnini. Athens: Ikaros.

———. 2003a. *Κ. Π. Καβάφη: Τα Πεζά (1882–1931).* Edited by Michalis Pieris. Athens: Ikaros.

———. 2003b. *C. P. Cavafy: Sixty-Three Poems Translated by J. C. Cavafy.* Athens: Ikaros.

———. 2010. *Selected Prose Works.* Translated by Peter Jeffreys. Ann Arbor: University of Michigan Press.

———. 2015a. *Clearing the Ground: C. P. Cavafy, Poetry and Prose, 1902–1911.* Translated by Martin McKinsey. Chapel Hill, NC: Laertes Press.

———. 2015b. *Τα ποιήματα: Δημοσιευμένα και αδημοσίευτα.* Edited by Dimitris Dimiroulis. Athens: Gutenberg.

———. 2015c. *Το λεξικό παραθεμάτων.* Edited by Michalis Pieris. Athens: Ikaros.

———. 2015d. *Unfinished and Uncollected: Finishing the Unfinished Poems of C. P. Cavafy and the Uncollected Poems & Translations.* Translated by George Economou. Emersons Green, UK: Shearsman Books.

———. 2021. *Poesie E Prose di Konstantinos Kavafis.* Edited by Renata Lavagnini and Christiano Luciani. Bilingual Greek/Italian edition. Milan, Italy: Bompiani.

Çelik, Zeynep. 1993. *The Remaking of Istanbul: Portrait of an Ottoman City in the Nineteenth Century.* Berkeley: University of California Press.

Chandler, George. 1960. *Liverpool Shipping: A Short History.* London: Phoenix House.

Charis, Petros. 1963. "Μία ώρα με τον αλεξανδρινό ποιητή Κ. Π. Καβάφη." *Νέα Εστία*, no. 872: 1420–21.

Charmidis, Stephanos. (1923) 1933. "Ομιλούν οι νέοι." *Το Ελεύθερο Βήμα.* Reprint edition.

Chatzifotis, I. M. 1973. *Η Αλεξάνδρεια και ο Καβάφης.* Athens: Alkaios.

Chatziioannou, Maria Christina. 2016. "Merchants-Consuls, and Intermediary Service in the Nineteenth-Century Eastern Mediterranean." In *The Greeks and the British in the Levant, 1800–1960s: Between Empires and Nations*, edited by Anastasia Yiangou, George Kazamias, and Robert Holland. London: Routledge, 159–78.

Chew, Samuel C., ed. 1936. *Lord Byron's Childe Harold's Pilgrimage and Other Romantic Poems.* New York: Doubleday, Doran and Company, Inc.

Cole, R. I. Juan. 1993. *Colonization and Revolution in the Middle East: Social and Cultural Origins of Egypt's Urabi Movement.* Princeton, NJ: Princeton University Press.

Dalven, Rae. 1989. "Biographical Note" and "Notes." *The Complete Poems of Cavafy.* Translated by Rae Dalven. New York: Harvest, 283–309.

Darwin, John. 2016. "The Levant as Middle Ground." In *The Greeks and the British in the Levant, 1800–1960s: Between Empires and Nations*, edited by Anastasia Yiangou, George Kazamias, and Robert Holland. London: Routledge, 11–24.

Daskalopoulos, Dimitris. 1988. *Κ. Π. Καβάφης. Σχέδια στο περιθώριο.* Athens: Diatton.

———. 1990. *Λογοτεχνικά περιοδικά της Αλεξάνδρειας, 1904–1953.* Athens: Diatton.

———, ed. 2003. *Ελληνικά καβαφογενή ποιήματα (1909–2001).* Patras, Greece: Ekdoseis Panepistimiou Patron.

———. 2003. *Βιβλιογραφία Κ. Π. Καβάφη: 1886–2000.* Thessaloniki: Center for the Greek Language.

———. 2013. *Κ. Π. Καβάφης: Η ποίηση και η ποιητική του.* Athens: Kichli.

Daskalopoulos, Dimitris, and Maria Stassinopoulou. (2002) 2013. *Ο Βίος και το έργο του Κ. Π. Καβάφη*. Rev. ed. Athens: Metaixmio.
Datta, Venita. 1993. "A Bohemian Festival: La Fête de la Vache Enragée." *Journal of Contemporary History* 28 (1993): 195–213.
Dawkins, R. M. 1934. "Review of T. Malanos's *Ο Ποιητής Κ. Π. Καβάφης*." *The Journal of Hellenic Studies* 54: 107–108.
De Amicis, Edmondo. 1896. *Constantinople*. Translated by Caroline Tilton. New York: Putnam's Sons.
Delice, Serkan. 2015. "The Janissaries and Their Bedfellows: Masculinity and Male Friendship in Eighteenth-Century Ottoman Istanbul." In *Gender, Sexuality in Muslim Cultures*, edited by Gul Ozyegin. Burlington, VT: Ashgate, 115–38.
Delta, Penelope. 1980. *Πρώτες ενθυμήσεις*. Edited by Al. P. Zannas. Athens: Ermis.
———. 1991. *Αναμνήσεις 1899*. Edited by Al. P. Zannas. Athens: Ermis.
———. 1996. *Αναμνήσεις 1921*. Edited by Al. P. Zannas. Athens: Ermis.
———. 2007. *Αναμνήσεις 1940*. Edited by Al. P. Zannas. Athens: Ermis.
Denommé, Robert. 1972. *The French Parnassian Poets*. London: Feffer and Simons.
Desmarais, Jane, and Chris Baldick. 2012. *Decadence: An Annotated Anthology*. Manchester: Manchester University Press.
Dimirouli, Foteini. 2019. "Introduction to 'Pericles in Paradise.'" *PMLA* 134, no. 2: 359–65.
———. 2021. "C. P. Cavafy in the World: Origins, Trajectories and the Diasporic Poet." British School at Athens Virtual Upper House Seminar, February 1. www.bsa.ac.uk/videos/foteini-dimirouli-cp-cavafy-in-the-world/.
Dimiroulis, Dimitris. 2014. "Ένας Θεσσαλός στην Αλεξάνδρεια του Καβάφη. Η περίπτωση του Δημήτρη Κ. Γαρουφαλιά." *The Athens Review of Books*, no. 57: 35–37.
———, ed. 2015. "Εισαγωγή." *Κ. Π. Καβάφης. Τα ποιήματα. δημοσιευμένα και αδημοσίευτα*. Athens: Gutenberg, 13–156.
Donoghue, Denis. 1995. *Walter Pater: Lover of Strange Souls*. New York: Alfred A. Knopf.
Dragoumis, Philippos Stefanos. 1984. *Ημερολόγιο 1916*. Athens: Dodoni.
Duhamel, G. 1929. "Cavafy est grand." *Semaine Égyptienne*: 17. Reissued by ELIA, Athens, 1983.
Edwards, Amelia B. 1888. *A Thousand Miles up the Nile*. London: Darf Publishers.
Ekdawi, Sarah. 1993. "Days of 1895, '96, and '97: The Parallel Prisons of C. P. Cavafy and Oscar Wilde." *Modern Greek Studies Yearbook* 9: 297–305.
———. 1997. "Cavafy's English Poems." *Byzantine and Modern Greek Studies*, no. 21: 223–30.
———. 2001. "Missing Dates: The Meres Poems of C. P. Cavafy." *Byzantine and Modern Greek Studies* 35, no. 1: 70–91.
Emmerich, Karen. 2011. "The Afterlife of C. P. Cavafy's Unfinished Poems." *Translation Studies* 4, no. 2: 197–212.
———. 2017. *Literary Translation and the Making of Originals*. New York: Bloomsbury Publishing.
Enright, D. J. 1953. *The Laughing Hyena and Other Poems*. London: Routledge and Kegan Paul.
Ergin, Nina. 2011. "Bathing Business in Istanbul: A Case Study of the Çemberlitas Hamani in the Seventeenth and Eighteenth Centuries." In *Bathing Culture of Anatolian Civilizations: Architecture, History, and Imagination*, edited by Nina Ergin. Leuven, Belgium: Peeters, 142–68.

Fahmy, Khaled. 2004. "For Cavafy, with Love and Squalor: Some Critical Notes on the History and Historiography of Modern Alexandria." In *Alexandria, Real and Imagined*, edited by Anthony Hirst and Michael Silk. Aldershot, UK: Ashgate, 263–79.

Fletcher, Edwin W. 1915. *Hellenism in England*. London: Faith Press.

Forster, E. M. 1980. "The Poetry of C. P. Cavafy." *Pharos and Pharillon*. Berkeley, CA: Creative Arts.

———. 1982. *Alexandria: A History and a Guide*. London: Michael Haag Ltd.

———. 2004. *Alexandria: A History and a Guide and Pharos and Pharillon*. Abinger Edition vol. 16. Edited by Miriam Allott. London: Andre Deutsch.

———. 2019. "Pericles in Paradise." Edited by Foteini Dimirouli. *PMLA* 134, no. 2: 359–65.

Forster, E. M., and Christopher Isherwood. 2008. *Letters Between Forster and Isherwood on Homosexuality and Literature*. Edited by Richard E. Zeikowitz. New York: Palgrave Macmillan.

Frampton, Martyn. 2018. *The Muslim Brotherhood and the West: A History of Enmity and Engagement*. Cambridge, MA: Harvard University Press.

Frangos, T. N. 1926. [No Title]. *Αλεξανδρινή Τέχνη*, no. 1: 23–24; https://kosmopolis.library.upatras.gr/index.php/alexandrini_texni/article/view/65200/64076.

Frederick, Margaretta, and Jan Marsh. 2015. *Poetry in Beauty: The Pre-Raphaelite Art of Marie Spartali Stillman*. Wilmington: Delaware Art Museum.

Freely, John. 1996. *Istanbul: The Imperial City*. New York: Viking Press.

Friar, Kimon, ed. 1973. *Modern Greek Poetry: From Cavafis to Elytis*. Translation, introduction, and notes by Kimon Friar. New York: Simon and Schuster.

Ftyaras, Constantinos. 1983. "Το 1928 ή '29 μ.Χ. στην Αλεξάνδρεια." *Χάρτης*. Special issue on Cavafy, nos. 5–6: 545–47.

Furbank, P. N. 1977–78. *E. M. Forster: A Life*. New York: Harcourt Brace Jovanovich.

Garrioch, David. 2009. "From Christian Friendship to Secular Sentimentality: Enlightenment Re-evaluations." In *Friendship: A History*, edited by Barbara Caine. London: Equinox, 165–214.

Garoufalias, Dimitris K. 1945. *Συμβολή στη μελέτη του Καβάφη*. Athens: Arist N. Mavridis.

———. 2013. *Αλήθειες & ψέματα για τον Κ. Π. Καβάφη*. Athens: Odos Panos.

Geffert, Bryn. 2006. "Anglican Orders and Orthodox Politics." *The Journal of Ecclesiastical History* 57, no. 2: 270–300.

Georgiou, M. H. 1933. "Ο Καβάφης και η άρνηση." *Επιθεώρηση Τέχνης*, no. 108: 652–69, reprinted by ELIA, Athens.

Gershoni, Israel, and James P. Jankowski. 1986. *Egypt, Islam, and the Arabs: The Search for Egyptian Nationhood*. New York: Oxford University Press.

Ghika, Katerina. 2009. "'Τοις Ρωμαίων έμμενε': εμβλήματα του Κωνσταντίνου Καβάφη." *Νέα Εστία* 165, no. 1818 (January): 18–53.

Gialourakis, Manolis. 1959. *Ο Καβάφης του κεφαλαίου Τ. Συνομιλίες με τον Τίμο Μαλάνο*. Alexandria.

———. 1963. "Ο Καβάφης για τις μεταφράσεις." *Νέα Εστία*, no. 872: 1575.

———. 1963. "Πώς έβλεπε ο Καβάφης το ποιητικό του έργο." *Νέα Εστία*, no. 872: 1624–26.

———. 1974. *Στην Αλεξάνδρεια του Καβάφη*. Athens: Olkos.

———. 2006. *Η Αίγυπτος των Ελλήνων. Συνοπτική ιστορία του ελληνισμού της Αιγύπτου*. 2nd ed. Athens: Kastaniotis.

———. 2007. *Στην Αλεξάνδρεια του Καβάφη*. 2nd ed. Athens: Panepistimiakos Typos.

Giannakopoulos, George. 1998. "Ο ελληνικός φιλολογικός σύλλογος Κωνσταντινουπόλεως (1861–1922): Η ελληνική παιδεία και επιστήμη ως εθνική πολιτική στην Οθωμανική Αυτοκρατορία." PhD diss., www.didaktorika.gr/eadd/handle/10442/11026.

Goldschmidt, Arthur. 2004. *Modern Egypt: The Formation of a Nation-State*. Cambridge, MA: Westview Press.

Grafftey-Smith, Laurence. 1970. *Bright Levant*. London: J. Murray.

Haag, Michael. 1982. "A City of Words." In *Alexandria: A History and a Guide*, by E. M. Forster. London: Michael Haag Ltd, 237–70.

———. 2004a. *Alexandria: City of Memory*. New Haven, CT: Yale University Press.

———. 2004b. *Alexandria Illustrated*. Cairo: American University in Cairo Press.

———. 2008. *Vintage Alexandria: Photographs of the City 1860–1960*. New York: American University in Cairo Press.

Haas, Diana, ed. 1982. "Cavafy's Reading Notes on Gibbon's 'Decline and Fall.'" *Folia Neohellenica* 4: 25–96.

———. 1983. "Σχόλια του Καβάφη στα ποιήματά του." In *Κύκλος Καβάφη*. Athens: Society of Neohellenic Culture and General Education, 83–109.

———. 1994. "Κωνσταντίνου Καβάφη: Constantinopoliad, an Epic." *Ζητήματα ιστορίας των νεοελληνικών γραμμάτων*. Thessaloniki, Greece: 281–304.

———. 2012. "Ανέκδοτο αυτοσχόλιο στο ποιήμα 'Η Ναυμαχία.'" *Logeion: A Journal of Ancient Theatre*, no. 2: 200–215. logeion.upatras.gr/sites/logeion.upatras.gr/files/pdffiles/HAAS_Logeion_2_0.pdf.

———. 2013. "Ανέκδοτο αυτοσχόλιο στο ποιήμα 'Τα δ'άλλα εν 'Αδου τοις κάτω μυθήσομαι.'" *Logeion: A Journal of Ancient Theatre* 3: 132–45. logeion.upatras.gr/sites/logeion.upatras.gr/files/pdffiles/HAAS_2013Final_0.pdf.

———. 2014. "Cavafy, Venizelos, and the National Schism: Revisiting a Debate." Edited by Stamatia Dova. Special issue, *Classics@* 10. classics-at.chs.harvard.edu/classics10-diana-haas-cavafy-venizelos-and-the-national-schism-revisiting-a-debate/.

———. 2015. "Κ. Π. Καβάφης: Ανέκδοτο αυτοσχόλιο στο ποιήμα 'Φωνές.'" *Κονδυλοφόρος*, no. 14: 101–30.

———. 2018. "Κ. Π. Καβάφης: Αυτοσχόλια στα ποιήματα 'Δημητρίου Σωτήρος (162–150 π.Χ.)' και 'Η Δυσαρέσκεια του Σελευκίδου.'" *Κονδυλοφόρος*, no. 16: 97–140.

———. 2019. "Κ. Π. Καβάφης: Αυτοσχόλια στα ποιήματα 'Η Συνοδεία του Διονύσου' και 'Τυανεύς Γλύπτυς.'" *Κονδυλοφόρος*, no. 17: 63–121.

Haggerty, George. 2018. *Queer Friendship: Male Intimacy in the English Literary Tradition*. Cambridge: Cambridge University Press.

Halim, Hala. 2013. *Alexandrian Cosmopolitanism: An Archive*. New York: Fordham University Press.

———. 2021. "C. P. Cavafy as an Egyptiote." *boundary 2* 45, no. 2 (May): 123–60.

Hanley, Will. 2017. *Identifying with Nationality: Europeans, Ottomans and Egyptians in Alexandria*. New York: Columbia University Press.

Harlaftis, Gelina. 1996. *A History of Greek-Owned Shipping*. London: Routledge.

Herzfeld, Michael. (1986) 2020. *Ours Once More: Folklore, Ideology, and the Making of Modern Greece*. Rev. ed. New York: Pella Publishing Company, Inc.

Hibberd, Dominic. 2002. *Wilfred Owen: A New Biography*. London: Weidenfeld & Nicolson.

Hirst, Anthony. 1995. "Philosophical, Historical and Sensual: An Examination of

Cavafy's Thematic Collections." *Byzantine and Modern Greek Studies*, no. 19: 33–93.

Hirst, Anthony, and Sarah Ekdawi. 1996. "Hidden Things: Cavafy's Thematic Catalogues." *Modern Greek Studies*, no. 4: 1–34.

Hollinghurst, Hugh. 2018. *Historic England: Liverpool*. Gloucestershire, UK: Amberly Books.

Hullah, Frances. 1886. *The Life of John Hullah*. London: Longman, Green and Co.

Ilbert, Robert. 1997. "A Certain Sense of Citizenship." In *Alexandria 1860–1960: The Brief Life of a Cosmopolitan community*, edited by Robert Ilbert and Ilios Yannakakis. Alexandria: Harpocrates Publishing, 18–34.

Ioannou, Giorgos. 1983. "Δύο επιστολές του Κ. Π. Καβάφη προς τον Ίωνα Δραγούμη και ένα σημείωμά του προς τον Φίλιππο Δραγούμη." *Χάρτης*, nos. 5–6: 534–47.

Issa, Islam. 2024. *Alexandria. The City That Changed the World*. New York: Pegasus.

Izenberg, Gerald. 2016. *Identity: The Necessity of a Modern Idea*. Philadelphia: University of Pennsylvania Press.

Jalland, Pat. 1996. *Death in the Victorian Family*. New York: Oxford University Press.

James, Carolyn, and Bill Kent. 2009. "Renaissance Friendships: Traditional Truths, New and Dissenting Voices." In *Friendship: A History*, edited by Barbara Caine. London: Equinox, 111–64.

Jeffreys, Peter, 2005. *Eastern Questions: Hellenism and Orientalism in the Writings of E. M. Forster and C. P. Cavafy*. Greensboro, NC: ELT Press.

———, ed. 2009. *The Forster-Cavafy Letters: Friends at a Slight Angle*. Cairo: American University in Cairo Press.

———. 2015. *Reframing Decadence: C. P. Cavafy's Imaginary Portraits*. Ithaca, NY: Cornell University Press.

Jusdanis, Gregory. 1982–83. "Cavafy, Tennyson and the Overcoming of Influence." *Byzantine and Modern Greek Studies* 8, 123–36.

———. 2014. *A Tremendous Thing: Friendship from the Iliad to the Internet*. Ithaca, NY: Cornell University Press.

Kakavas, George. 2002. *Ελλήνων κειμήλια, δωρεές στον καθεδρικό ναό της Αγίας Σοφίας του Λονδίνου*. Athens: Byzantine and Christian Museum.

Kambos, Roberto. 1963. "Το ποιητικό έργο του Κ. Π. Καβάφη." *Επιθεώρηση Τέχνης*, no. 108: 640–44. Reprinted by ELIA Athens, 1983.

Kampanis, Aristos. 1963a. "Ένας Ποιητής." *Νέα Εστία*, no. 872: 1421–22.

———. 1963b. "Ο θάνατος του ποιητού." *Νέα Εστία*, no. 872: 1488–89.

Karampini-Iatrou, Michaela. 2003. *"Η Βιβλιοθήκη Κ. Π. Καβάφη."* Athens: Hermes.

———. 2012. "Relics of a Library: How C. P. Cavafy's Library Survived Through Auction, Sales, Book Loans, and Relocations." *Journal of Modern Greek Studies* 30, no. 20: 277–98.

———. 2016. "Η Ρίκα Σεγκοπούλου και η «πορνοειδής» έκδοση του Κ. Π. Καβάφη, Ποιήματα 1935." In *Η εκδοτική των κειμένων της ελληνικής γραμματείας*. Institute of Modern Greek Studies at the University of Thessaloniki, Greece, 109–25.

———. 2019. "Γέρο μου: Η μόνη διασωθείσα επιστολή του Αλέκου Σεγκόπουλος πρός τον Κ. Π. Καβάφη." *Μικρό Φιλολογικά*, no. 46: 30–33.

———. 2020. "Για το 'Αυτοεγκώμιο' του Καβάφη." *Μικρό Φιλολογικά*, no. 45: 45–48.

Karanasou, Floresca. 1999. "The Greeks in Egypt from Mohammed Ali to Nasser." In *The Greek Diaspora in the Twentieth Century*, edited by Richard Clogg. London: Macmillan Press, 24–57.

Karaoglou, Ch. L. 1985. *Η Αθηναϊκή κριτική και ο Καβάφης, 1918–1924*. Thessaloniki, Greece: University Studio Press.

———. 1990. "Ριμάριο." *Μολυβδο-κονδυλο-πελεκητής*, no. 2: 71–123.

Karapanagopoulos, Alekos. 1985. *Ο Κ. Π. Καβάφης. Συζητήσεις με τη Ρίκα Σεγκοπούλου*. Athens: Dodoni.

Karayiannis, Vangelis. 1977. *Στο σπίτι του Καβάφη*. Athens.

———. 1983. *Σημειώσεις από την Γενεαλογία του Καβάφη*. Athens: Hellenic Literary and Historical Archive.

Katsimbalis, G. B. 1943. *Βιβλιογραφία Κ. Π. Καβάφη*. Athens: Sergiadis.

Katzanaki, Maria. 2018. *Θεόδωρος Ράλλης*. Athens: Leventis Foundation.

Kazamias, Alexander. 2021. "Another Colonial History: How Cosmopolitan Was Cavafy's Contemporary Alexandria?" *boundary 2* 48, no. 2: 89–121.

Kazantzakis, Nikos. 1975. *Journeying: Travels in Italy, Egypt, Sinai, Jerusalem, and Cyprus*. Translated by Themi Vasils and Theodora Vasils. Boston: Little, Brown.

Keeley, Edmund. 1976. *Cavafy's Alexandria: A Study of a Myth in Progress*. Cambridge, MA: Harvard University Press.

Keeley, Edmund, and George Savidis. 1963. "Introduction." *Passions and Ancient Days*, New York: Dial Press.

Kirli, Cengiz. 2016. "Coffeehouses: Leisure and Sociability in Ottoman Istanbul." In *Leisure Cultures in Urban Europe, circa 1700–1870: A Transnational Perspective*, edited by Peter Borsay and Jan Hein Furnée. Manchester: Manchester University Press, 161–82.

Kitroeff, Alexander. 1989. *The Greeks in Egypt 1919–1937: Ethnicity and Class*. London: Ithaca Press.

———. 2019. *The Greeks and the Making of Modern Egypt*. New York: American University in Cairo Press.

Kokolis, X. A. 1983. "Γλωσσική ασυμβατότητα, ποιητική τεχνική και πολιτική εγρήγορση στο 'Πάρθεν' του Καβάφη." *Διαβάζω*, no. 78: 61–73.

Kolaitis, Memas. 1980. *Cavafy as I Knew Him: With 12 Annotated Translations of His Poems*. Santa Barbara, CA: Kolaitis Dictionaries.

Komis, Antonis. 1935. *Κ. Π. Καβάφης*. Kerkyra, Greece.

Koulourides, Ilias. 2019. Interview by Gregory Jusdanis, May 1, Istanbul.

Kourelis, Kostis. 2015. "Closing the Window on Cavafy: Foregrounding the Background in the Photographic Portraits." *Journal of Greek Media and Culture* 1, no. 2: 227–52.

Kubiak, Zygmunt. 1995. *Kawafis Aleksandryjczyk*, Warsaw: Wydawn. Tenten.

Kuru, Selim S. 2006. "Naming the Beloved in Ottoman Turkish Gazel: The Case of Ishak Çelebi. (D 1537/8)." In *Ghazal as World Literature II*, edited by Thomas Bauer and Angelika Neuwirth. Würzburg, Germany: Ergon Verlag, 163–74.

Kypreos, Georges. 2010. *Αλεξάνδρεια. Τέλος εποχής*. Athens: Ekdoseis Iambos.

———. 2017. Personal communication with Gregory Jusdanis, May 28, Alexandria.

Lambropoulos, Vassilis. 2022. "C. P. Cavafy Music Resource Guide: Song and Music Settings of Cavafy's Poetry." Modern Greek Program and C. P. Cavafy Professorship in Modern Greek, Department of Classical Studies and Comparative Literature, University of Michigan. https://lsa.umich.edu/content/dam/modgreek-assets/modgreek-docs/CAVAFY/Cavafy%20Song%20Bibliography_Version3_3-3-22.pdf.

Laoumtzi, Stamatia. 2021. *Κ. Π. Καβάφης και το δημοτικό τραγούδι*. Athens: Ikaros.

Lapathiotis, Napoleon. 2009. *Η ζωή μου.* Edited by Yiannis Papakostas. Athens: Kedros.
Lavagnini, Renata. 2003. "Ενα Διήγημα του Καβάφη." *Το Δέντρο,* nos. 125–26: 75–87.
———. 2020a. "'Εις το Φως της Ημέρας.' Ενα Ανέκδοτο Διήγημα του Καβάφη." *Γύρω στον Καβάφη.* Athens: MIET, 68–98.
———. 2020b. "Καβάφης και Χρηστόπουλος." *Γύρω στον Καβάφη.* Athens: MIET, 170–77.
———. 2020c. "Μια Ιταλική μαρτυρία για τον Γιώργο Βρισιμιτζάκη." *Γύρω στον Καβάφη.* Athens: MIET, 135–45.
Lechonitis, G. 1942. *Καβαφικά αυτοσχόλια.* Edited by Timos Malanos. Alexandria.
Leontis, Apostolos. (1933) 1963. "Η χθεσινή κηδεία του ποιητού Καβάφη." *Επιθεώρηση Τέχνης,* no. 108: 707–708.
Lesage, Claudine. 2018. *Edith Wharton in France.* Lenox, MA: The Mount Press.
Liapi, Evangelia H. 2018. "Το λημνιακό ζαχαροπλαστείο 'Παστρούδης' της Αλεξάνδρειας." Blog. July 30. http://kokkinovraxos.blogspot.com/2018/07/pastroudis.html?m=1.
Liddell, Robert. 1974. *Cavafy: A Critical Biography.* London: Duckworth. 2000.
Lilti, Antoine. 2017. *The Invention of Celebrity, 1750–1850.* Translated by Lynn Jeffress. Cambridge, UK: Polity Press.
Long, Christopher. 1998. "Heraldry in Byzantium & the Vlasto Family." www.christopherlong.co.uk/per/vlasto.byzantium.html.
———. "Family History Genealogy Index." https://www.christopherlong.co.uk/gen/index.html.
Long, Helen. 1992. *Greek Fire: The Massacres of Chios.* Bristol, UK: Abson Books.
Lopez, Matthew. 2018. *The Inheritance.* London: Faber and Faber.
Lounsbury, Carl R. 2010. "Architecture and Cultural History." In *The Oxford Handbook of Material Culture Studies,* edited by Dan Hicks and Mary C. Beaudry. Oxford: Oxford University Press, 484–501.
Mabro, Robert. 2004. "Alexandria 1860–1960." In *Alexandria, Real and Imagined,* edited by Anthony Hirst and Michael Silk. Aldershot, UK: Ashgate, 247–62.
Macilwee, Michael. 2011. *The Liverpool Underworld: Crime in the City, 1750–1900.* Liverpool: Liverpool University Press.
Mackridge, Peter. 1990. "Versification and Signification in Cavafy." *Μολυβδο-κονδυλο-Πελεκητής,* no. 2: 125–43.
Macleod, Dianne Sachko. 1996. *Art and the Victorian Middle Class: Money and the Making of Cultural Identity.* Cambridge: Cambridge University Press.
Malanos, Timos. 1942. "Εισαγωγή." *Καβαφικά αυτοσχόλια.* Edited by G. Lechonitis. Alexandria: n.p.
———. (1933) 1957. *Ο ποιητής Κ. Π. Καβάφης. Ο άνθρωπος και το έργο του.* Athens: Difros.
———. 1963. *Καβάφης 2.* Athens: Fexi.
———. 1971. *Αναμνήσεις ενός Αλεξανδρινού.* Athens: Boukoumani.
———. 1978. *Καβάφης 3.* Athens: Argo.
———. 1984. "Κ. Π. Καβάφης: Αναμνήσεις, βιώματα και παρατηρήσεις ενός Αλεξανδρινού κριτικού." *ΑΜΦΙ-Αφιέρωμα Κ. Π. Καβάφη,* no. 2: 16–17.
———. 1986. *Ο Καβάφης έλεγε.* Edited by Tasos Korfis. Athens: Prosperos.
———. 2003. *Σελίδες απόκρυφες. Ματιές στον καβαφικό περίγυρο.* Edited by Panagiotis Karmatzos. Athens: Ekati.
Mancoff, Debra N. 1998. *Burne-Jones.* San Francisco, CA: Pomegranate.
Manginis, George. 2020. "'For the Benefit of the Nation': A Collection of Chinese Art for Greece." Lecture on Eumorfopoulos, June 4. https://www.benaki.org/index

.php?option=com_multimedia&view=multimediaitem&lan_g=en&id=2445&Itemid=621&lang=el.

Mansel, Philip. 2011. *Levant: Splendor and Catastrophe on the Mediterranean*. New Haven, CT: Yale University Press.

Maronitis, Dimitris. 2007. *Κ. Π. Καβάφης. Μελετήματα*. Athens: Pataki.

Massavetas, Alexandros. 2007. *Going Back to Constantinople: A City of Absences*. Athens: Athens News.

———. 2013. *Διαδρομές στο Φανάρι τον Μπαλτά και τις Βλαχέρνες*. Istanbul: Istos.

———. 2014. *Κωνσταντινούπολη, η πόλη των απόντων*. 10th ed. Athens: Patakis.

Mavrogiannis, Giannis. 1978. "Η διαμάχη Παλαμά—Καβάφη." *Κριτικά Φύλλα*, no. 6: 145–55.

McKinsey, Martin. 2010. *Hellenism and the Postcolonial Imagination: Yeats, Cavafy, Walcott*. New York: Fairleigh Dickinson University Press.

Melville, Herman. 1962. *Billy Budd, Sailor*. Edited by Harrison Hayford and Merton M. Sealts Jr. Chicago: The University of Chicago Press.

Merakou, Stafania. 2011. "Αλληλογραφία του Δημήτρη Μητρόπουλου-Κωνσταντίνου Καβάφη." https://hellenic-music-lab.music.uoa.gr/dimitri-mitropoulos/2010–04–11–08–14–38/2010–10–25–13–53–18.html.

Menas, K. K. 1985. *Η γλώσσα του Καβάφη από γραμματική και λεξιλογική άποψη*. Ioannina, Greece: Dedoni.

Mendelsohn, Daniel, trans. 2009. *C. P. Cavafy: Collected Poems*. New York: Alfred A. Knopf.

Merriam-Webster. "Amphibrach." https://www.merriam-webster.com/dictionary/amphibrach.

Merrill, James. 1975. "Marvelous Poet." *New York Review of Books* 22, no. 12 (July): 12–17.

———. trans. 1983. "'In Broad Daylight' by C. P. Cavafy." *Grand Street* 2, no. 3 (Spring): 99–107.

Metaxas, K. Ch. 1974. *Κ. Καβάφης: Ανέκδοτα στοιχεία της οικογένειας του ποιητού*. London.

Minotis, Alexis. 1978. "Γνωριμία και ανάμνηση του Κ. Π. Καβάφη." *Κριτικά Φύλλα*, no. 6: 312–22.

Modinos, Polys. 1963. "Διάλεξις περί του ποιητικού έργου του Κ. Π. Καβάφη του κ. Αλ. Σεγκόπουλου: Ο πρόλογος του κ. Πόλυ Μοδινού." *Επιθεώρηση Τέχνης*, no. 108: 614–16.

———. 1980. *Τρείς επιστολές του Καβάφη*. Athens: ELIA.

———. 2011. "Κώστας Καβάφης-50 Χρόνια από τον θάνατό του." YouTube. https://www.youtube.com/watch?v=tkksWnnHxZ0&t=2264s.

Moffat, Wendy. 2010. *A Great Unrecorded History: A New Life of E. M. Forster*. New York: Farrar, Straus and Giroux.

Moraitou, Nina. 2020. "'Mr. Byzantoine et ses amis': Antonis Benakis and the Art Scene of Alexandria." Lecture by the curator of the Benaki Museum of Islamic Art, May 28. https://www.benaki.org/index.php?option=com_multimedia&view=multimediaitem&id=%202431:mr-byzantoine-et-ses-amis-antonis-benakis-and-the-art-scene-ofalexandria&Itemid=202&lang=el&Itemid=615&lang=en.

Moser, Benjamin. 2019. *Sontag: Her Life and Work*. New York: Ecco.

Museum of Liverpool. 2012. *Liverpool: The Story of a City*. Liverpool: Liverpool University Press.

Myrtiotissa. 1924. "Μια εντύπωση." *Νέα Τέχνη*, nos. 7–10: 84–85.

National Museums Liverpool. "Spirit of Liverpool." https://www.liverpoolmuseums.org.uk/spirit-of-liverpool.

Nehamas, Alexander. 2016. *On Friendship*. New York: Basic Books.

Nelson, Claudia. 2007. *Family Ties in Victorian England*. London: Praeger.

Onassis Foundation Cavafy Archive. "Ιδανική Βιβλιοθήκη," edited by Katerina Ghika. https://cavafy.onassis.org/el/ideal-library/.

———. "R. J. Moss & Co." https://cavafy.onassis.org/creator/r-j-moss-co/.

Oulton, Carolyn. 2007. *Romantic Friendship in Victorian Literature*. Aldershot, UK: Ashgate.

Ouranis, Kostas. 1963. "Ο σεξουαλισμός του Καβάφη." *Νέα Εστία*, no. 872: 1468–74.

Owen, Edward Roger John. 1969. *Cotton and the Egyptian Economy 1820–1914*. Oxford: Oxford University Press.

Palamas, Kostis. 1969. *The Twelve Lays of the Gypsy*. Translated by George Thomson. London: Lawrence & Wishart.

Palioura, Mirka. 2015. *Θεόδωρος Ράλλης: Με το βλέμμα στην Ανατολή*. Athens: Benaki Museum.

Panagiotopoulos, I. M. 1946. *Τα πρόσωπα και τα κείμενα*. Athens: Aetos.

Papanikolaou, Dimitris. 2014. *"Σαν κι εμένα καμωμένοι": ο ομοφυλόφιλος Καβάφης και η ποιητική της σεξουαλικότητας*. Athens: Pataki.

Papanoutsos, Evangelos. 1956. "Ρίκα Καραγιάννη." *Νέα Εστία*, no. 694: 787.

Papargyriou, Eleni. 2015. "Photographic Adaptions of Cavafy." *Journal of Greek Media and Culture* 1, no. 2: 253–76.

Papoutsakis, G. A. 1933. "Η ομιλία του κ. Γ.Α. Παπουτσάκη." *Παναιγύπτια*, no. 233 (July 8): 11–13.

Paraschos, Kleon. 1985. "Νεοέλληνες λογοτέχναι. Κωνσταντίνος Καβάφης." In *Η αθηναϊκή κριτική και ο Καβάφης (1918–1924)*, by H. L. Karaoglou. Thessaloniki, Greece: University Studio Press, 108–14.

Parini, Jay. 2004. *One Matchless Time: A Life of William Faulkner*. New York: Harper Collins.

Paspatis, Alexandros G. 1877. *Βυζαντιναί μελέται: Τοπογραφικαί και ιστορικαί*. Constantinople.

Peridis, Michalis. 1933. "Η ομιλία του κ. Μ. Περίδη." *Παναιγύπτια*, no. 233: 3–4.

———. 1948. *Ο βίος και το έργο του Κωνσταντίνου Καβάφη*. Athens: Ikaros.

Pessoa, Fernando. 1998. *The Book of Disquiet*. Translated by Richard Zenith. New York: Penguin.

Petridis, Pavlos. 2008. "Ένας Αλεξανδρινός ποιητής." In *Εισαγωγή στην ποίηση του Καβάφη*, edited by Michalis Pieris. 7th ed. Iraklio, Greece: University of Crete Press, 35–46.

Pieridis, Giangos. 1944. *Ο Καβάφης: συνομιλίες, χαρακτηρισμοί, ανέκδοτα*. Athens: Orion.

Pieris, Michalis, ed. 1994. *Εισαγωγή στην ποίηση του Καβάφη. Επιλογή κριτικών κειμένων*. Iraklio, Greece: University of Crete Press.

Pinchin, Jane Lagoudis. 1977. *Alexandria Still: Forster, Durrell, Cavafy*. Princeton, NJ: Princeton University Press.

Politis, Athanasios G. 1928, 1930. *Ο Ελληνισμός και η νεωτέρα Αίγυπτο*. 2 vols. Alexandria: Grammata.

Politou-Marmarinou, Eleni. 1983. "Ο Καβάφης και ο Γαλλικός Παρνασσισμός." In *Πρακτικά τρίτου συμποσίου ποίηση, αφιέρωμα Κ. Π. Καβάφη*, edited by S. Skartsis. Athens: Gnosi, 315–46.

Polyzoides, A. J. 2014. *Alexandria: City of Gifts and Sorrows: From Hellenistic Civilization to Multiethnic Metropolis*. Brighton, UK: Sussex Academic Press.
Pomian, Krzysztof. 2011. "The South Kensington Museum: A Turning Point." *Art and Design for All: The Victoria and Albert Museum*. Edited by Julius Bryant. London: V & A Publishing, 41–45.
Portal for the Greek language. "Αράπης." Centre for the Greek Language. https://www.greek-language.gr/greekLang/modern_greek/tools/lexica/triantafyllides/search.html?lq=%CE%B1%CF%81%CE%AC%CF%80%CE%B7%CF%82&dq=).
Potolsky, Matthew. 2013. *The Decadent Republic of Letters: Taste, Politics, and Cosmopolitan Community from Baudelaire to Beardsley*. Philadelphia: University of Pennsylvania Press.
Psycharis, Ioannis. 1963. "Ένας Καραγκιόζης." *Νέα Εστία*, no. 872: 1404.
Psyroukis, Nikos. 1974. *Το νεοελληνικό παροικιακό φαινόμενο*. Athens: Epikairotita.
———. 2000. *Μικρασιατική καταστροφή 1918–1923*. Lefkosia, Greece: Aigion.
Radopoulos, R. G. 1928. *Εισαγωγή εις την ιστορίαν της ελληνικής κοινότητος Αλεξάνδρειας 1830–1927*. Alexandria: Kasimatis & Ionia.
Reid, Donald Malcolm. 1998. "The Urabi Revolution and the British Conquest 1879–1882." In *Modern Egypt from 1517 to the End of the Twentieth Century*, vol. 2 of *The Cambridge History of Egypt*, edited by M. W. Daly. Cambridge: Cambridge University Press, 217–38.
Ricks, David. 1993. "Cavafy Translated." *Κάμπος: Cambridge Papers in Modern Greek*, no. 1: 85–119.
———. 2003. "How It Strikes a Contemporary: Cavafy as a Reviser of Browning." *Κάμπος: Cambridge Papers in Modern Greek*, no. 11: 131–52.
Robinson, Christopher. 1988. *C. P. Cavafy*. Bristol Studies in Modern Greek. Exeter, UK: Short Run Press.
Rodd, James Rennell. 1891. "The Poet of the Klephts: Aristoteles Valaoritis." *The Nineteenth Century* 173 (July): 130–44.
Rota, Maria S. 1994. "Το περιοδικό *Γράμματα* της Αλεξάνδρειας." PhD thesis, Athens.
Sagaster, Börte. 2011. "The Role of Turcophone Armenians as Literary Innovators and Mediators of Culture in the Early Days of Modern Turkish Literature." In *Between Religion and Language: Turkish-Speaking Christians, Jews, and Greek-Speaking Muslims and Catholics in the Ottoman Empire*, edited by Evangelia Balta and Mehmet Ölmez. Istanbul: Eren, 101–10.
Sakallieros, Giorgos. 2016. *Dimitri Mitropoulos and His Works in the 1920s: The Introduction of Musical Modernism in Greece*. Athens: The Hellenic Music Centre.
Sareyiannis, I. A. 1964. *Σχόλια στον Καβάφη*. Athens: Ikaros.
———. 1983. "What Was Most Precious—His Form." *Grand Street* 2, no. 3: 108–26.
Savidis, George. 1963. "Το αρχείο του Καβάφη." *Νέα Εστία*, no. 872: 1539–47.
———. 1966. *Οι καβαφικές εκδόσεις 1891–1932*. Athens: Ikaros. 1992.
———. 1982. *Κ. Π. Καβάφης. Πανομοιότυπα των πέντε πρώτων φυλλαδίων του (1891–1904)*. Athens: Hellenic Literary and Historical Archive, reprinted in 2003.
———. 1985. *Μικρά Καβαφικά*. Vol. 1. Athens: Ermis.
———. 1987. *Μικρά Καβαφικά*. Vol. 2. Athens: Ermis.
———. 2002. *Κ. Π. Καβάφης. Αυτόγραφα ποιήματα 1896–1910. Το Τετράδιο Σεγκόπουλου σε πανομοιότυπη έκδοση παρουσιασμένη από τον Γ.Π. Σαββίδη*. Athens: Hermes.
Savidis, Lena, ed. 1983. *Λεύκωμα Καβάφη*. Athens: Ermis.

Savidis, Manolis. 2003. "Introduction." In *C. P. Cavafy: Sixty-Three Poems Translated by J. C. Cavafy*, by C. P. Cavafy. Athens: Ikaros, ix–x.

———. 2008. *Κ. Π. Καβάφη: Κατάλογος Εκθεμάτων. / C. P. Cavafy. Exhibit Catalogue.* Athens: Center for Neo-Hellenic Studies.

Sayyid-Marsot, Alaf Lufti. 1985. *A Short History of Modern Egypt*. Cambridge: Cambridge University Press.

Scaife, Christopher. 1933. "Δύο γράμματα άγγλων." *Παναιγύπτια*, no. 233: 17–18.

Semerdjian, Elyse. 2015. "Sexing the Hammam: Gender Crossing in the Ottoman Bathhouse." In *Gender, Sexuality in Muslim Cultures*, edited by Gul Ozyegin. Burlington, VT: Ashgate, 115–38.

Sengopoulos, Alekos. 1994. "Διάλεξις περί του ποιητικού έργου του Κ. Π. Καβάφη." In *Εισαγωγή στην ποίηση του Καβάφη. Επιλογή κριτικών κειμένων*, edited by Michalis Pieris. Iraklion, Crete: University of Crete Press, 47–56.

Sengopoulos, Rika. 1929. [No Title]. *La Semaine Égyptienne* (April 25): 25–26.

———. 1970. "Ο Καβάφης, 37 χρόνια ύστερα από το θάνατό του." *Ορίζοντες* 2 (April–May): 1–9.

Sharples, Joseph, and Richard Pollard. 2004. *Liverpool: Pevsner Architectural Guides*. New Haven, CT: Yale University Press.

Simeonidis, A. G. 1927. "Πάνω σε μια ξένη γνώμη για τον Καβάφη." *Αλεξανδρινή Τέχνη*, no. 3: 20–22; https://kosmopolis.library.upatras.gr/index.php/alexandrini_texni/article/view/65220/64096.

Skeferis, Periklis. (1933) 1963. "Η χθεσινή κηδεία του ποιητού Καβάφη." *Επιθεώρηση Τέχνης*, no. 108: 707–708.

Solomonidis-Hunter, Victoria. 2014. "Cavafy and England." Lecture at the British Library, November 24.

———. 2020. "John Cavafy MD FRCP (1838–1901): A Victorian Greek, A Doctor's Doctor." *Friends of West Norwood Cemetery Newsletter*, no. 99 (September): 4–9.

———. 2021. "Constantine Gennadius: The 'Lost' Brother." *Friends of West Norwood Cemetery Newsletter*, no. 102 (September): 8–10.

Stavridi-Patrikiou, Rena. 1988. *Ο Γ. Σκληρός στην Αίγυπτο: Σοσιαλισμός, δημοτικισμός και μεταρρύθμιση*. Athens: Themelio.

Stroebel, William. 2018. "Some Assembly Required: Suspending and Extending the Book with Cavafy's Collections." *Book History* 21: 278–316.

Sturgis, Matthew. 2018. *Oscar: A Life*. London: Head of Zeus Ltd.

Sümertas, Firuzan Melike. 2023. "The Loss of the Literary Society of Constantinople. The Dismantling of an Institution, Displacement of a Library, and Dissolution of an Intellectual Hub." *Turkish Historical Review* 14: 224–51.

Svolopoulos, Constantine. 1994. *Κωνσταντινούπολη 1856–1908: Η ακμή του ελληνισμού*. Athens: Athenian Publishing.

Szczepanski, Kallie. "Biography of Mahmud of Ghanzi, First Sultan in History." ThoughtCo. https://www.thoughtco.com/mahmud-of-ghazni-195105.

Tangopoulos, D. P. 1963. "Καβαφισμός." *Νέα Εστία*, no. 872: 1403–1404.

Thrylos, Alkis. 1963. "Μερικές ακόμα εντυπώσεις από το έργο του Καβάφη." *Νέα Εστία*, no. 872: 1417–19.

Tibbles, Anthony. 2018. *Liverpool and the Slave Trade*. Liverpool: Liverpool University Press.

Tippins, Sherill. 2005. *February House*. Boston: Houghton Mifflin.

Toledano, Ehud R. 1998. "Social and Economic Change in the 'Long Nineteenth Century.'" In *Modern Egypt from 1517 to the End of the Twentieth Century*, vol. 2 of

The Cambridge History of Egypt, edited by M. W. Daly. Cambridge: Cambridge University Press, 252–84.

Tosh, John. 2005. *Manliness and Masculinities in Nineteenth-Century Britain*. Harlow, UK: Pearson Education Limited.

Trimi, Katerina, and Ilios Yannakakis. 1997. "The Greeks: The *parikia* of Alexandria." In *Alexandria 1860–1960: The Brief Life of a Cosmopolitan community*, edited by Robert Ilbert and Ilios Yannakakis. Translated by Colin Clement. Alexandria: Harpocrates, 65–71.

Trotter, William R. 1995. *Priest of Music: The Life of Dimitri Mitropoulos*. Portland, OR: Amadeus Press.

Tsimbidaros, Vasos. 1974. *Οι Έλληνες στην Αγγλία*. Athens: Alkaios.

Tsirkas, Stratis. 1958. *Ο Καβάφης και η εποχή του*. Athens: Kedros.

———. 1963. "Κ. Π. Καβάφης. Σχεδίασμα χρονογραφίας του βίου του." *Επιθεώρηση Τέχνης*, no. 108: 676–708.

———. 1971. *Ο πολιτικός Καβάφης*. Athens: Kedros.

Tziovas, Dimitris. 1986. *The Nationism of the Demoticists and Its Impact on Their Literary Theory (1888–1930)*. Amsterdam: Adolf M. Hakkert.

Vaianos, Marios. 2005. *Αναμνήσεις από τη λογοτεχνική του ζωή και τη γνωριμία του με τον Καβάφη*. Athens: Drimos.

———. 1973. Interview by Giannis Mavrogiannis, Athens.

Valieri, Hariclia. 1983. "Η τελευταία συνέντευξη της ανιψιάς του μεγάλου ποιητή." *Ακρόπολις*.

Vikelas, Dimitris. 1908. *Η ζωή μου*. Athens: Society for Useful Books.

Vrisimitzakis, Yiorgos. 1984. *Το έργο του Κ. Π. Καβάφη*. Edited by George P. Savidis. Athens: Ikaros.

Warner, Rex. 1951. "Introduction." *The Poems of C. P. Cavafy*. Translated by John Mavrogordato. London: Hogarth Press.

Wilde, Oscar. 1910. *The Oscar Wilde Calendar: A Quotation from the Works of Oscar Wilde for Every Day in the Year with Some Unrecorded Sayings Selected by Stuart Mason*. London: Frank Palmer.

———. 2008. *The Major Works*. Edited by Isobel Murray. New York: Oxford University Press.

Wilkinson, Toby. 2020. *A World Beneath the Sands: The Golden Age of Egyptology*. New York: Norton.

Woolf, Virginia. 1950. *The Captain's Death Bed and Other Essays*. New York: Harcourt, Brace and Company.

———. 1967. "The New Biography." In *Collected Essays by Virginia Woolf*. Vol. 4. London: The Hogarth Press, 229–35.

Wortley, John. 2010. *John Skylitzes: A Synopsis of Byzantine History, 811–1057*. Cambridge: Cambridge University Press.

Xenopoulos, Grigorios. 2008. "Ένας ποιητής." *Εισαγωγή στην ποίηση του Καβάφη*. 7th ed. Edited by Michalis Pieris. Iraklio, Greece: University of Crete Press, 23–34.

Zananiri, Gaston. 1933. "Η ομιλία του κ. Gaston Zananiri." *Παναιγύπτια*, no. 233: 14–15.

Ze'evi, Dror. 2006. *Producing Desire: Changing Sexual Discourses in the Ottoman Middle East, 1500–1900*. Berkeley: University of California Press.

Zubaida, Sami. 1999. "Cosmopolitanism and the Middle East." In *Cosmopolitanism, Identity, and Authenticity in the Middle East*, edited by Roel Meijer. Richmond, UK: Curzon Press, 15–34.

ACKNOWLEDGMENTS

This biography began many years ago when Peter invited Gregory to consider cowriting a new life of Cavafy. For both of us this project required not only much reading and many conversations, extensive field research, numerous archival visits, and endless Zoom and telephone calls but also a new way of writing.

In Alexandria, we would like to thank Zahraa Adel Awad, an experienced guide to Cavafy's city, and Mohammed el Said, who ran the Cavafy Museum and who provided warm hospitality along with invaluable help. Prof. Sahar Hamouda of the Library of Alexandria, Dr. Mohamed Awad, and George Kypreos shared their extensive knowledge of Alexandria and its history.

In Istanbul, Victoria Holbrook and Nejat Ege helped in identifying the house of Cavafy's maternal grandfather. We acknowledge the assistance of M. Asım Karaömerlioğlu, Ilias Koulouridis, and Mr. Vigas for information on Cavafy's early life in Istanbul.

In the UK, we would like to acknowledge Peter Baird and in Hyères, France, Jérôme Mattio of the Médiathèque Archival Library.

In Athens, we are grateful to the Onassis Foundation Cavafy Archive for their unstinting support of this project. Special thanks are due to Effie Tsiotsiou, Marianna Christofi, Angeliki Mousiou, and Theodoros Chiotis. The holdings of the Cavafy Archive of ELIA (Hellenic Literary and Historical Archive) were made accessible thanks to the generous assistance of Sophia Bora, and we are grateful to Aspasia Louve for granting permission to reproduce unpublished material held by ELIA. Archival permissions were generously granted by Alexandra Charitatou for material in her possession. We are grateful to Tassos Sakellaropoulos at the Cavafy Archive of the Benaki Museum for accommodating our research needs.

Nicolas Sarafis of Geneva shared personal archival material and artwork by Pericles Anastasiades, as did Alix MacSweeney and Daphni Kasdagli. We relied on Mary Bisbee-Beek for priceless advice on the publishing world.

People who read the manuscript in its entirety at various stages include Elsa Amanatidou, Byron MacDougall, Maria Boletsi, Peter Hawkins, Michaela Karampini-Iatrou, Sarah Ekdawi, Victoria Solomonidis-Hunter, Hilary Nanda, Angeliki Mousiou, and Celeste Kostopulos-Cooperman. People who read portions of the manuscript include Hala Youssef Halim, Ric Rader, and Michelle Zerba.

Yiorgos Anagnostou and Dimitris Tziovas answered our many questions and provided critical help in our translations of poems. Our conversations over the years with Artemis Leontis and Vassilis Lambropoulos helped shape our thinking about Cavafy.

We would like to thank Maria Georgopoulou, Irini Solonomidi, and Soula Panagopoulou of the Gennadios Library in Athens for help in locating documents and for sending material to us via email.

Rhea Karabelas Lesage, the Librarian for Hellenic Studies at

Harvard's Widener Library, offered support and assistance with Greek academic sources.

Mary Kidwell worked tirelessly to format the bibliography.

Angeliki Mousiou assisted with the documentation of archival sources and also contributed to the research of the addendum "Important People in C. P. Cavafy's Life." We owe her a tremendous debt of gratitude.

We wish to thank Duke University Press for permission to include previously published material from "Cavafy's Levant: Commerce, Culture, and Mimicry in the Early Life of the Poet," by Peter Jeffreys, in *boundary 2: an international journal of literature and culture* 48, no. 2: 7–39. (Copyright 2021, Duke University Press. All rights reserved. Republished by permission of the publisher. www.dukeupress.edu.)

We also wish to thank Dimitris Papanikolaou, Keith Hunter, and Marjorie Salvodon for their contributions and support of the process along the way.

The Department of Classics at the Ohio State University provided financial assistance in hiring an RA to help with the bibliography.

Michael Mungiello, our agent at Inkwell Management, picked up the biography when sixty other agents passed. We are profoundly grateful for his judgment, his sensitivity in reading the manuscript, and all his efforts in shepherding the project through its final stages.

We are grateful to Katie Liptak, Oona Holahan, and Sophie Albanis at Farrar, Straus and Giroux, and to Logan Hill, Jane Elias, and Judy Kiviat, for overseeing the production of the book and offering their invaluable editorial expertise along the way.

Jonathan Galassi, our editor at Farrar, Straus and Giroux,

told us that Cavafy was the quintessential FSG author. We thank him for believing in the book and for bringing out the best in the manuscript by reading it many times and by bringing his finely tuned skills as translator to the poems.

Peter Jeffreys wishes to thank Michael Tandoc, Irene Jeffreys, Angelica Jeffreys, Chip Savery, Maria Moschoni, Amy Monticello, Theresa Maronna, George Kalogeris, Demetres Tryphonopoulos, and Maria Koundoura for their intellectual and moral support. Suffolk University generously supported this project through travel grants and a sabbatical leave.

Gregory Jusdanis would like to thank the National Endowment of the Humanities for a generous fellowship at the American School of Classical Studies in 2016, which enabled him to undertake research at the Gennadius Library as well as visit the archives of the Onassis Foundation and ELIA. He is grateful to the Department of Classics at Ohio State for its financial support of the project.

Julian Anderson, his wife, read the manuscript, went over translations many times, and provided much support over the years he worked on the project. Without her assistance the biography would have been much harder to accomplish. His children, Adrian, Alexander, and Clare, brought much good cheer and helped him place the biography in a wider context of the world.

INDEX

Acropolis, 131, 295
Addison, Joseph, 45, 253
Adl, Mohammed el, xxi, 224, 460*n30*
Adolescents (Rhodes), 277
Adolphus and Placidia, 263
Adventures of Philip, The (Thackeray), 76
Aeschylus, 245, 267; *The Persians*, 327–28
Aesthetic movement, 35, 252
Agras, Tellos, 376, 400, 430*n8*
Aida (Verdi), 153
Alexander the Great, 131
Alexandria, xxii, xxiii, 48, 54, 57, 58, 61–63, 111–42, 143–51, 165, 185, 219, 222, 292, 311, 401, 408, 409, 442*n21*, 450*n73*; absence of classical antiquity in, 131, 132, 320; Alekos Sengopoulos's talk on Cavafy's poetry in, 241–43, 246; Billiards Palace in, 122, 123, 125, 127, 173, 315, 316; bookshops in, 117, 124, 127–29, 133, 316; Bourse in, 119, 208, 220, 286; Briggs on, 116–17, 119–20, 442*n22*; Britain and, 156, 159, 166; British bombardment of, xvi, 25, 43–46, 50, 54, 58, 63, 118, 155–57, 171, 283, 286; Cathedral of the Annunciation in, 433*n41*; Cavafy in, 62, 64, 65, 112–42, 143–44, 159, 174–75, 318–19, 323; Cavafy family in, 19, 27, 94, 115, 449*n59*, 450*n73*, 455*n71*; Cavafy family's escape from, to Istanbul (1882), xvii, 43–52, 64, 66, 155, 171, 183; Cavafy family's return to, from England (1877), xvii, 43, 55, 85–86, 153, 156, 181–82; Cavafy family's return to, from Istanbul (1885), 156, 158, 202, 208, 286, 450*n73*; Cavafy's apartment in, 12, 112, 114, 115, 132–42, 166, 370, 373, 417, 442*n10*; Cavafy's literary reputation in, 364, 381–83, 475*n79*; in Cavafy's poetry, 123, 132, 160, 172–75, 310, 320, 325, 410, 446*n4*; Chatby

Alexandria (*cont.*)
cemetery in, 12–13, 120, 408–409; churches in, 129–30; Corniche in, 112, 121, 123, 152; cultural life of, 296; Europeans in, 45, 58, 115, 117–21, 124, 143–46, 443*n31*; first cinema in, 446*n114*; Forster's writings on, 129, 132, 189, 223, 386; Greco-Roman Museum in, 132, 444*n79*; Greek community in, 23–24, 115, 144–52, 157, 208, 296, 317, 437*n31*, 448*n19*, 453*n12*; Hellenistic, 61, 114, 132, 320, 323–25, 408, 410, 446*n4*; Islamic art exhibition in, 145; journals in, 468*n46*; Lenten carnival in, 147–48; Mohammed Ali Club in, 117, 223; Mohammed Ali Square, 115, 118, 147, 173; monuments in, 131, 132, 143; moral climate of, 340, 343; Muslims in, 58, 143–46, 152, 446*n4*, 447*n17*; poverty in, 152; Ramleh suburb of, 120, 188, 190, 199; restaurants and cafés in, 112, 117–18, 120–21, 123, 125–27, 173, 316, 443*n47*; riot in, 154; Rue Chérif Pasha, 19, 115, 116, 119, 120, 138, 147, 156, 455*n71*; Rue Lepsius, 6, 12, 112, 114, 115, 132, 133, 142, 159, 166; Rue Rosette, 114, 116–18, 147, 300, 338; Sa'ad Zaghloul Square, 121; San Stefano Casino in, 86, 120, 199, 201, 292; Shari' Al-Sab', 118; Tositsas School in, 231; traffic in, 116, 118; trams in, 120

Alexandrini Logotechnia, 468*n46*

Alexandrini Techni, 8–9, 217, 237–38, 360, 363–64, 375, 385, 394, 405, 468*n46*, 471*n108*, 476*n15*, 477*nn43*, *45*, 485*n6*

Alhambra Theatre, 372

Ali Pasha, 273

Alites, P., 375

Alithersis, Glafkos, 305, 341, 365, 369–70, 393, 396, 406; biographical note on, 419

Alkaiou, Maria, 413

Allen, George, 259

American Civil War, 24, 153, 223

American Mission Hall, 410

Amis de l'Art, 171

Among My Books (Lowell), 255

AMPHI, 460*n23*

Anastasiades, Aristides, 208

Anastasiades, Pericles "Peri," 181, 206, 207–29, 245; as artist, 217; biographical note on, 419; Cavafy loaned money by, 227–28; Cavafy's correspondence with, 64, 208–22, 226, 289, 475*n80*; cooling of Cavafy's friendship with, 228; family background of, 207–208; Forster and, 222, 223, 227; Levon and, 218–19, 222

Anatolia, 166

Anglo-Greek community, 21–22, 27, 29–32, 36, 43, 92, 159, 184, 195, 203, 216, 256, 454*n42*, 482*n33*; art scene and, 35–40; Cavafy family in, 27–28, 30, 35, 39, 149, 182; Cavafy's Anglophilia and, 35–36, 39; Ionides family in, 27, 36–39; West Norwood Cemetery and, 203–205

Antaios, Makis, 146

Antiochos III the Great, 267–68

Antiquary, The (Scott), 250

Antony, Mark, 121, 131, 235

Apuani, 236, 375, 459*n14*

Arabi, Ahmed Bey, 154, 155, 157, 449*n64*

Arabi rebellion, 154–55, 157, 161, 171, 449*n64*

Arabs, 144, 146, 159, 160, 445*n83*, 447*n10*; *see also* Muslims
arapides, 145–46
Argo, 468*n46*, 479*n68*
Aristobulos, 162–63
Aristotle, 249–50, 253, 452*n2*; on friendships, 180, 181, 184, 207, 456*n1*; *Nicomachean Ethics*, 456*n1*
Armenia, 367
art, 219–20, 260, 266; Cavafy family and, 19, 35–40, 94; Cavafy's interest in, 215–16; in London, 35–40; Old Masters, 215–16, 219–20; Pre-Raphaelites, 37–38, 256; Ruskin's views on, 259–60
Arvers, Felix, 253
Ash, John, 59
Asia Minor, 22
Asia Minor Catastrophe, 166–69, 270–71, 431*n18*, 437*n27*, 482*n33*
Atatürk, Kemal, 166
Athanasopoulos, Vasilis, 173, 375
Athena, 469*n55*
Athenaeum, The, 189, 387–88
Athenagoras, Patriarch, 437*n42*
Athens, xvii, 8, 23, 54, 86, 116, 131, 150, 152, 172, 184, 320, 321, 324–25, 377, 385; Alexander Cavafy in, 122–23, 131, 148, 149, 158, 294–96, 478*n57*; Cavafy in, 122–23, 131, 148, 149, 158, 294–97, 301, 302, 311–12, 318, 361–62, 370–72, 375, 378–79, 407, 447*n5*, 478*n60*; Cavafy's literary reputation in, 296–97, 383, 393, 398, 400; center of, 295; Hotel Cosmopolite in, 6, 362, 378, 406; literary establishment in, 228; Olympics in, 149, 395; Palamas's funeral in, 400
Athina, 479*n80*
Athineos (café), 120–21, 443*n47*
Athineos, Constantine Jean, 121
Attalus, Priscus, 263
Attikon Mouseion, 18, 467*n18*
Augustus, 326
Austen, Jane, 168
Averoff, George, 120, 149–50
Averoff family, 409

Bal de Sceaux, Le (Balzac), 88
Balkan Wars, 166, 168, 169
Balzac, Honoré de, 88, 253, 261
Bank of Egypt, 25
Banna, Hassan al-, 170, 451*nn108*, *109*
Banville, Théodore de, 260
Barnard, Anne, 93
Barry, E. M., 456*n75*
bathhouses, 62–63
Baudelaire, Charles, 5, 79, 199, 209, 210, 261, 262, 277, 324, 435*n61*; "Correspondances," 261–62
Beard, Mary, 472*n17*
Beaton, Roderick, 275, 462*n11*
Beguiling of Merlin, The (Burne-Jones), 37
Beirut, 151
Bell, Vanessa, 38
Benaki, Alexandre, 145
Benaki, Antonis, 7, 144, 145, 246, 316, 342, 407; biographical note on, 419
Benaki, Argini, 144
Benaki, Emmanuel, 164, 169
Benaki family, 113, 147, 148, 409, 448*n23*, 467*n14*, 474*n59*
Benaki Museum, 83, 145, 434*n60*
Benha, 241, 243–44
Bernhardt, Sarah, 218
Bevan, Edwyn Robert, 266, 268–69
Billiards Palace, 122, 123, 125, 127, 173, 315, 316
Billy Budd, Sailor (Melville), 162, 472*n7*

biographies, xvi, xxii, xxiii; of Cavafy, xvi, xxii–xxiii, 403–404, 407, 411–14, 429*n8*, 444*n62*, 486*n35*; Woolf on, 403
Blackie, John Stuart, 254–55, 273, 462*n20*
Black Sea, 183, 270–71
Blanken, G. H., 482*n27*
Bloom, Harold, 325
Bloomsbury Group, 225, 369, 458*n38*
Boddy, Alexander A., 116, 150, 442*n21*, 443*n31*
Bohème, La (Puccini), 294, 478*n57*
Bosporus, 45, 50, 51, 64, 65, 68, 189
Bossuet, Jacques-Bénigne, 253
Botti, Giuseppe, 444*n79*
Bouché-Leclercq, Auguste, 266
Bourget, Paul, 441*n75*
Bourse, 119, 208, 220, 286
Bowersock, Glen, 262–63
Briggs, Martin S., 116–17, 119–20, 442*n22*
Britain, *see* England; Great Britain
British Ministry of Public Works, 11
British Museum, 40, 433*n44*, 434*n60*, 454*n44*
brothels and prostitutes, 62, 114–15, 118, 173, 174, 186, 214
Brown, Ford Madox, 38
Brown, Peter, 472*n17*
Browning, Robert, 245, 253, 256–59
Budapest, 219
Bulwer-Lytton, Edward, 189, 253
Burne-Jones, Edward, 37, 38, 324
Burns, Robert, 255
Bury, J. B., 266
Butler, Beverley, 435*n1*
Byron, Lord (George Gordon), 48, 49, 60, 253
Byzantine Empire, 22, 26, 52, 191, 265, 323, 431*n22*, 454*n42*; aesthetic of, 433*n41*; Cavafy on historians of, 454*n41*; in Cavafy's poetry, 31–32, 60–61, 67–68, 103, 265, 302, 310, 323–24, 399, 445*n81*; Istanbul monuments from, 59–61, 437*n40*; poets in, 264, 265
Byzantios, Skarlatos, 436*n21*, 437*n40*
Byzantium, 31–32, 52, 59, 68, 265

Caesar, Julius, 326
Caesareum, 121
Caesarion, 139, 168, 174, 235, 325–27, 331, 333
Café Al Salam, 125–27, 173, 443*n47*
Cairo, 45–46, 48, 86, 153, 166, 170, 171, 217, 442*n21*, 445*n81*, 451*n109*
Callimachus, 222, 267, 325
Callistratus, 266
Cambridge Apostles, 225, 458*n38*
Cameron, Julia Margaret, 38
Capitulations of the Ottoman Empire, 151, 449*n45*
Carlyle, Thomas, 189, 266, 434*n60*
Carpathian Demotic Songs (Michaelidou), 270
Cassavetti, Dimitris, 482*n33*
Cassavetti family, 24, 27, 36
Castore, SS, 44, 46–50, 250
Catacombs of Kom el Shoqafa, 131
Cathedral of the Annunciation, 433*n41*
Catraro, Atanasio, 103, 135, 348, 364, 386, 461*n57*, 471*n107*, 481*n27*
Cavafy, Alexander (brother), 26, 34, 45–47, 49, 85–88, 129, 157; in Athens, 122–23, 131, 148, 149, 158, 294–96, 478*n57*; biographical note on, 419–20; birth of, 34; daughter of, *see* Coletti, Eleni; death of, 311–12; marriage of, 86
Cavafy, Aristides (brother), 26, 28, 34, 36, 45, 46, 49, 80, 91–94, 103, 115, 156, 157, 193, 409; *Album de Dessins*, 93–94; biographical note on, 420; birth of, 34; Constantine's artistic

relationship with, 93–94; Constantine's correspondence with, 92–93; daughter of, *see* Valieri, Hariclia; death of, 312; education of, 34–35; financial difficulties of, 82; marriage of, 92–93

Cavafy, Constantine P.: aesthetic tastes and interests of, 39–40, 215–16; Anglophilia of, 35–36, 39, 221, 250; apartment of, 12, 112, 114, 115, 132–42, 166, 370, 373, 417, 442*n10*; archives and heirlooms kept by, xv–xxii, 91, 103, 106, 267, 328–29, 384, 403, 411, 414, 417; biographies of, xvi, xxii–xxiii, 403–404, 407, 411–14, 429*n8*, 444*n62*, 486*n35*; birth of, 34, 115; burial of, 12–13; charm and flattery of, 365–66, 373, 407, 412–13; chronology of events in life of, xi–xiv; civil servant position of, xv, 11, 25, 112–14, 120, 159, 164, 193, 202, 288–89, 328, 339, 341, 353, 469*n52*; commemorations of, 21, 264; death of, xvii, xviii, xxii, xxiv, 3–13, 130, 180, 230, 233, 238, 349, 403–408, 412, 413, 431*n22*; deaths of people close to, xxiii, 195, 202–204, 311–13, 315, 350, 412, 471*n94*; diaries and journals of, 44–52, 72, 86, 96, 99–100, 129, 131, 143, 172, 185, 190, 191, 291, 294–96, 311–12, 320, 341, 349–50, 412, 450*nn69, 71*; dictionary compiled by, 283, 287; early life of, xviii, 18–20, 26, 27, 31; education of, xvii, 28, 34, 43, 288, 320; electricity eschewed by, 133, 138–39; estate settlement of, 228; family genealogical history compiled by, 25–26, 33, 52, 60–61, 68, 71, 85, 91–92, 102, 270, 431*n22*, 432*n19*, 437*n43*, 439*n28*; finances and financial records of, 329–30, 339; funeral for, 12, 246, 407–409; gravestone for, 409; historical knowledge of, 52, 265–67, 367–68, 410, 477*nn33, 36*; important people in life of, 419–27; isolation of, 291, 292, 311, 313–15, 404–405, 410; languages spoken by, 19, 27–28, 44, 143–44; lexicon compiled by, 287–88; light as preoccupation of, 139–40; l ists made by, xv, xix, 328–31, 341; middle-age anxieties of, 330–31; middle initial changed by, 300, 314; national identity of, 158, 169; Order of the Phoenix awarded to, 401; as Orthodox Christian, 129–30; physical appearance of, 127, 140–42, 297, 311, 364, 365, 446*n109*; politics as viewed by, 168–72; portrait of, 142, 443*n43*; rhyming dictionary compiled by, 288–89; self-centeredness of, 368–69, 377, 379, 393, 404, 407; shorthand used by, xx, 193, 298, 330; smoking of, 4; social life of, 313–14, 316–17, 342, 351, 471*n108*; speaking voice and style of, xvi–xvii, 5, 27–28, 140, 141, 251, 297, 311, 367; theatrical manner of, 364–65, 367, 407; throat cancer and surgery of, xvii, 3, 5, 9, 130, 180, 222, 246, 248, 315–16, 340, 361–62, 370–72, 374, 375, 377–78, 406, 407, 478*n60*; translation work of, 253, 256–57, 261–62, 287; tributes to, 409–11

Cavafy, Constantine P. (*cont.*)
CORRESPONDENCE, xvi–xviii, 63, 167, 180, 183–95, 224, 249, 267, 285–86, 328; with Alekos Sengopoulos, xix, 21, 241, 243–48, 316, 342, 377, 405, 439*n27*; with Aristides Cavafy, 92–93; Cavafy's drafts of, 457*n11*; with Christopher Scaife, 371–72; with E. M. Forster, 225–27; with Haricleia Cavafy, 84–85; with John Cavafy, xvi, xvii, xix, 69–83, 100–102, 155–58, 253, 254, 258–59, 283, 284, 289, 290, 349, 482*n49*; with John Rodocanachi, 193–95; loss of, xix; with Marios Vaianos, 376–77; with Mikès Ralli, 183–90; with Paul Cavafy, 95, 97, 99–100, 440*nn65*, *67*; with Pericles Anastasiades, 64, 208–22, 226, 289, 475*n80*; with Stephen Schilizzi, 183, 191–93; with Timos Malanos, 236–38
FRIENDSHIPS, xxii–xxiv, 179–206, 210, 228–29, 231, 410; Cavafy's mentorship approach to, 233; Cavafy's work and, 348–49, 354; rejections of Cavafy by his friends, 393–94, 396; *see also* Anastasiades, Pericles "Peri"; Malanos, Timos; Ralli, Mikès; Rodocanachi, John; Schilizzi, Stephen; Sengopoulos, Alekos; Sengopoulos, Rika
LITERARY REPUTATION, xviii, xxiv, 3, 171, 235, 296, 347–48, 359–80, 381–402; in Alexandria, 364, 381–83, 475*n79*; *Alexandrini Techni* and, 8–9, 217, 237–38, 360, 363–64, 375, 385, 394; Anastasiades and, 227–28; in Athens, 296–97, 383, 393, 398, 400; bibliography and, 362; Cavafy family name and, 20–21, 26, 103; Cavafy's Athens trip and, 296–97; Cavafy's management of, xviii–xix, xxii, xxiv, 4, 18, 23, 103, 104, 285, 360–65, 369–70, 396; Cavafy's personal relationships and, 348–49; Cavafy's self-doubts and, 40, 292, 296, 300, 347–48, 363, 381, 382, 389–90, 394; Cavafy's sexual life and, 342–43; fame, xviii, xix, xxiii, xxiv, 3, 12, 100, 136, 180, 338, 355, 364, 369, 375–76, 389, 391, 394, 396, 404; foreigners and, 401; Forster and, 225, 226, 387–89, 392, 417, 482*n31*; global, xxiv, 3, 12, 13, 240, 359, 399, 401–402, 442*n10*; and lectures on Cavafy, 241, 382, 393–95, 400, 413–15; Palamas and, 397–400; Rika Sengopoulos's management of, 403–408; Vaianos and, 375–80; Xenopoulos and, 296–98, 338; young followers and, 369–75, 380, 381–82, 398
PROSE WRITING, 40, 55–56, 64, 67, 119, 256, 269, 285–87; on Browning, 257–59; on Byzantine poets, 265; "Constantinopoliad, an Epic," 44–52, 72, 96, 99–100, 250; on Elgin Marbles, 40, 256, 287, 467*n18*; on Greco-Roman Museum, 132; on Greek folklore, 269, 270; on Greeks in Egypt, 165–66; influences on, 269–70; on katharevousa, 276; on Keats, 256–57; on Lucian, 266–67; "The Musings of an Aging Artist," 336; on Odysseus, 257–58, 331–33; *Prose*, xx, 276; on prosody, 307–308; on Roidis, 275; on

Shakespeare, 253–56; on sophists, 266; on Tennyson, 257–58; "What I Remember of My Essay on Christopulus," 67, 251
READING AND LIBRARY, 135–36, 245, 249–78, 284, 452*n2*, 454*n50*; alternative sexuality, 277; French literature, 260–61, 277, 461*n4*; Greek literature, 250–52, 269–77; history, 250, 262–69
SEXUALITY, xx–xxiii, 7, 10, 44, 97, 103, 159, 165, 195, 214, 239, 242, 293, 294, 302–303, 319, 330–31, 337, 339–47, 417, 460*n30*, 474*n64*; anguish about, 291–92, 314–15; in denunciations of Cavafy, 237, 395–96; dread of scandal and, 149, 342–43; eroticism in poems, xv, 4, 10, 41, 120, 122, 123, 172–73, 195, 197, 224, 241–43, 293–94, 302–304, 314–15, 324, 326, 331, 340, 343–47, 381, 389, 391–93, 399, 438*n45*, 446*n110*, 482*n37*; experiences in youth, 53, 62–63, 125–27, 146, 184, 195, 340; Malanos and, 240; reading and, 277; thoughts on, 221–22, 293–94, 468*n34*

Cavafy, Constantine P., poetry of, xxii, xxiv, 4, 64, 281–317, 318–55; canon of 154 poems, 3, 13, 104, 467*n22*, 481*n17*; Cavafy family's attitudes towards, 290–91; Cavafy's change of signature and, 300, 314; Cavafy's readings of, 366; criticisms of, 306, 308, 309, 348, 363, 383, 392–93, 394–95, 397, 398, 415, 416, 430*n6*; first, 51, 282–83; Greek language in, 52, 64, 66, 172, 276, 282, 287, 299, 303, 305–306, 333, 393, 394, 417–18; imitations of, 310, 376, 401; influences on, xxiv, 53, 252, 260–62; inventory of, 328; modernity and innovation in, 6, 8, 138, 172, 283, 305, 310, 381, 383, 398, 401, 410, 417, 474*n71*; musical adaptations of, 7; and need to earn a living, 338–39, 341–42, 360–61, 383; 1911 as decisive year in, 301, 311, 350, 415, 469*n62*; parodies of, 171, 310, 400; reinvention period of, 282, 300–303, 311–13, 319, 331, 350; repudiation of earlier work, xxiii, 113, 282, 285, 292–93, 298–303, 309, 330, 341, 350, 467*n22*; "retrieval" process in, 43, 435*n1*; revisions of, 283, 298–99, 301–302, 304, 328, 339, 384, 396, 397, 406–407, 467*n22*, 475*n80*, 481*nn14*, *15*; traditional Greek poetry and, 53, 240, 252, 282, 292, 298, 318, 335, 337–38, 348, 398, 401, 410
FORMS AND STYLES, 283, 305; avoidance of adjectives, 305; commitment to writing in Greek, 64, 172; demotic, 172, 276, 299, 305, 335; ekphrasis, 346; katharevousa, 52, 66, 172, 276, 282, 287, 303, 333; metrics and rhythm, 209, 305–10; rhymes, 209, 289, 305–10; stanzas, 470*n84*
PRINTING, DISTRIBUTION, AND PUBLISHING, 3, 12, 171, 296, 301, 302, 330, 338, 360, 383–92, 400–401, 455*n71*, 481*nn17*, *18*; in Aristides Cavafy's book, 93–94; bound editions and bindery for, 18, 300, 383–85, 416; on broadsheets, 18, 83, 93, 383–84; Cavafy's perfectionism

Cavafy, Constantine P. (*cont.*)
and, 390–92, 467*n22*; first complete edition, xviii, 13, 94, 385–86, 406–408, 416; first English translation of complete poems, 247, 392; forwarding and mailing, 385; in John Cavafy's book, 83; in periodicals, 18, 128, 171, 400; translations, xvi, 38, 171, 192, 198, 226, 227, 247, 289, 360, 362, 371, 386–91, 417, 418, 481*n27*, 483*n50*; translations by John Cavafy, 83, 93, 228, 289, 291, 337, 386, 391–92, 417, 482*n49*
SUBJECTS AND THEMES, 310, 322; Alexandria, 123, 132, 160, 172–75, 310, 320, 325, 410, 446*n4*; Aristobulos, 162–63; Battle of Salamis, 327–28; Byzantine, 31–32, 60–61, 67–68, 103, 265, 302, 310, 323–24, 399, 445*n81*; Caesarion, 139, 168, 325–27, 331; death, 12, 202–205, 350–51; ethnicity, 159, 293; historical portraits, 368; homoeroticism, xv, 4, 10, 41, 120, 122, 123, 172–73, 195, 197, 224, 241–43, 293–94, 302–304, 314–15, 324, 326, 331, 340, 343–47, 381, 389, 391–93, 399, 438*n45*, 446*n110*, 482*n37*; Ionia, 167; Julian the Apostate, 4, 323; light, 139; nature, 66, 121–23, 443*n39*; Odysseus, 333–35; old age, 126–27, 134, 137–38, 140, 198, 289, 330, 415, 467*n23*; overlooked and unconventional historical figures and epochs, 174, 320, 322–24, 331, 399; poetry, 293, 321, 326, 341, 397; politics, 159–64, 168; Simeon the Stylite, 320–22; youth, 134, 160, 174, 180, 198, 243, 397
BY TITLE: "Absence," 392; "According to the Recipes of Ancient Helleno-Syrian Magicians," 134; "Addition," 291, 391; "The Afternoon Sun," 303–304; "Aristobulos," 162–63; "Ars Poetica," 301; "Artificial Flowers," 209; "At the Entrance of the Café," 173; "Bacchic," 287; "The Bank of the Future," 290, 291; "Beautiful, White Flowers That Matched So Well," 304; "Below the House," 173; "The Beyzades to His Beloved," 52–53, 269–70; "Birth of a Poem," 397; "The Blooms of May" ("The Elegy of the Flowers"), 93; "Body Remember," 346; "Builders," 17–18, 24, 103, 287, 481*n15*; "By the House," 111; "Byzantine Nobleman in Exile Composing Verses," 237; "Caesarion," 139, 325–27, 331, 333, 393; "Candles," 139, 209, 289, 297, 298, 330, 393, 467*n23*; "Che Fece . . . Il Gran Rifiuto," 234–35, 297; "The City," 347, 352, 386, 393, 405, 408; "A Company of Four," 179–80; "Confusion," 315; "Correspondence According to Baudelaire," 457*n9*; "Darius," 45, 407; "Days of 1896," 97, 314, 345; "Days of 1908," 4, 122, 217, 407; "December [of] 1903," 302; "Dünya Güzeli," 53, 83–84, 93, 270; "Emendatory Work," 301; "The Enemies," 335–36; "The First Step," 297–98; "Following the Recipe of Ancient Greco-Syrian Magicians," 180; "The Footsteps," 467*n22*; "From Nine

O'clock," 312–13; "From *The Secret History*," 67–68; "The Funeral of Sarpedon," 467*n22*; "The Glory of the Ptolemies," 327; "The God Abandons Antony," 175, 301, 373, 386, 393, 404, 409; "Gray," 366; "The Hall Mirror," 371–72; "He Came to Read," 186, 196, 249; "He Is the One," 361; "He Swears," 292; "He Was Asking About the Quality," 123; "Hidden," 346–47; "The House of the Soul," 260–61; "I Brought to Art," 134, 353–54; "In an Old Book," 117, 345–46; "In Broad Daylight," 116, 172, 198–202, 342; "In Church," 31–32; "In Despair," 344; "Inkwell," 296; "Interruption," 297; "In the Cemetery," 205; "In the Evening," 137–39, 174; "In the Month of Hathor," xviii, 8; "In the Same City," 209; "In the Street," 172–73, 345; "Invigorating," 341; "Ionic," 167, 467*n22*; "Ithaca," 258, 301, 333–35, 413; "It Had to Be the Alcohol," 136–37; "It Was Seized," 270–72; "I Went," 195–96, 242, 346; "La Jeunesse Blanche," 261; "Julian in the Mysteries," 323; "June 27, 1906, 2:00 p.m.," 159–64; "King Claudius," 253; "Leaving Therapia," 50, 64; "Long Ago," 242; "Longings," 345; "Memory," 467; "The Month of Hathor," 350–51; "Morning Sea," 121–23; "Myris: Alexandria of 340 AD," 351, 412; "The Naval Battle," 327–28; "News in the Paper," 173–74; "Nichori," 64, 66; "A Night Out in Kalinderi," 64–66; "Ode and Elegy of the Streets," 83, 314; "Of Colored Glass," 61, 106, 283; "Of Dimitrios Sotir (162–150 BC)," 267–69; "Of the Shop," 359–61, 416; "An Old Man," 126–27, 330, 467*n23*; "On Behalf of Those Who Fought in the Achaean League," 168; "One Night," 173; "On the Outskirts of Antioch," 4, 323, 406–407; "Orophernis," 283; "Passing," 133–34, 345; "The Patriarch," 431*n22*; "Ta Ploia / The Ships," 40–42; "The Poet and the Muse," 287, 455*n71*; "Prayer," 216, 297; "The Retinue of Dionysus," 327; "Return," 242; "Return from Greece," 159; "Second Odyssey," 332–33, 335; "September [of] 1903," 302; "Sham-el-Nessim," 172; "Simeon," 321–22; "So That They Come," 134; "The Souls of Old Men," 10, 467*n23*; "Sweet Voices," 296, 298–99, 467*n22*; "Their Beginning," 293; "Thermopylae," 297; "Things That Are Finished," 128; "Thinking Dangerously," 242–43; "Thus I Gazed," 134; "Tomb of Evrion," 202–203; "To Remain," 293, 346; "To Stephen Schilizzi," 203; "Two Young Men, Twenty-Three to Twenty-Four Years Old," 197–98, 346; "Understanding," 174; "Vain, Vain Love," 93, 270, 455*n71*; "Very Rarely," 415, 417; "Voice from the Sea," 287; "Voices," 11, 281, 298–300, 393, 467*n22*; "Vulnerant Omnes, Ultima Necat," 113, 261; "Waiting for the Barbarians," 194, 300, 390; "Walls," 83, 93, 228, 232, 289, 297, 298, 337–38, 347, 393;

Cavafy, Constantine P. (*cont.*) "When, My Friends, I Was in Love," 93; "When They Come Alive," 232; "Whoever Has Failed," 352–53; "The Window of the Tobacco Store," 345; "The Windows," 289, 297, 391; "You Didn't Understand," 171; "A Young Man, Versed in Literature, in His Twenty-Fourth Year," 196–97

Cavafy, Eleni (sister, died as infant), 20, 34

Cavafy, George (brother), 28, 35, 91, 115, 409; birth of, 33; death of, 312; education of, 34–35; letter to Peter from, 432*n25*

Cavafy, George (uncle), 27, 35–37, 39, 115, 204, 205, 433*n48*, 434*n58*, 456*n80*; biographical note on, 420; letter to Peter John from, 27

Cavafy, Haricleia (mother), xxiii, 19, 20, 33–34, 37, 43, 53, 66, 76, 81–82, 83–91, 103, 115, 143, 148, 156–58, 201, 204, 228, 244, 286, 291, 330, 368, 409, 441*n89*, 468*n26*; biographical note on, 420; birth of, 33; Constantine's change of middle initial and, 300; Constantine's correspondence with, 84–85; Constantine's relationship with, 85, 86, 88–91; funeral for, 91; Greek literacy of, 84; illness and death of, 84, 85, 89–91, 94, 95, 120, 311, 312, 329, 349, 412; John's correspondence with, 84–85; in Liverpool, 28–31; marriage of, 33; in move to England, xvii, 35, 39; in move to Istanbul, 44–47, 49; Paul's correspondence with, 95–96; Paul's relationship with, 85–87, 96, 440*n65*; strokes suffered by, 84, 91

Cavafy, John (brother), 19, 20, 29, 32, 34, 36, 45, 46, 49, 63, 69, 86, 89, 95, 98, 104, 156, 158, 187, 228, 244, 254, 284, 314, 330, 409, 432*n19*, 449*n64*, 467*n14*; Aristides's marriage and, 92–93; biographical note on, 421; birth of, 34; Constantine loaned money by, 228; Constantine's correspondence with, xvi, xvii, xix, 69–83, 100–102, 155–58, 253, 254, 258–59, 283, 284, 289, 290, 349, 482*n49*; Constantine's mentorship relationship with, 70, 72, 76, 79, 82; Constantine's poetry translated by, 83, 93, 228, 289, 291, 337, 386, 391–92, 417, 482*n49*; and Constantine's proposed marriage between Eleni Coletti and Alekos Sengopoulos, 78, 246; Constantine's view of, 102; cooling of Constantine's relationship with, 78, 228; death of, xix, 78, 103, 228, 438*n14*; funeral for, 438*n14*; Haricleia's correspondence with, 84–85; in London, 168, 213, 214, 291, 314; in Paris, 213–14, 216, 218, 219, 291, 314; Paul's correspondence with, 97, 100, 440*n65*; as poet, 18, 19, 74, 82–83, 93, 94, 221, 284–85, 290–92, 298, 300, 308, 354, 439*n19*; reading interests of, 253, 256

Cavafy, John (cousin), 420–21, 433*n48*, 434*n58*, 456*n80*

Cavafy, John (grandfather), 36, 436*n23*

Cavafy, Marie Vouros (sister-in-law), 92–93

Cavafy, Marigo Ralli (cousin), 295, 318, 434*nn48*, *58*, 440*n66*

Cavafy, Pantelis Demetrios (cousin), 462*n16*

Cavafy, Paul (brother), 19, 20, 29, 32, 34, 36, 44–47, 49, 89, 90, 94–100, 103, 104, 114, 218, 300, 330; biographical note on, 421; birth of, 34; Constantine's correspondence with, 95, 97, 99–100, 440*nn65, 67*; Constantine's poetry and, 100; death of, 100–102; financial difficulties of, 97, 100, 102, 440*n66*, 441*n88*; Haricleia's correspondence with, 95–96; Haricleia's relationship with, 85–87, 96, 440*n65*; John's correspondence with, 97, 100, 440*n65*; marriage considered by, 440*n66*, 441*n88*; newspaper writing of, 98–99; playwright ambitions of, 98; private secretary position of, 97–98; sexuality of, 86, 94, 97, 103, 440*n67*, 474*n64*; social life of, 148; soldiers and, 440*n67*; Wilde and, 441*n75*

Cavafy, Paul (brother, died as infant), 34

Cavafy, Peter (brother), 34, 35, 45, 49, 72, 91, 115, 156, 158, 409; biographical note on, 421; birth of, 33–34; death of, 312; education of, 34–35; letter from George to, 432*n25*; Sanitary Council position of, 441*n84*

Cavafy, Peter John (father), xvii, 23, 26–28, 32, 33, 39, 115, 156, 251, 409, 449*n59*; biographical note on, 421; birth of, 26; as businessman, 19, 22, 24–28, 32, 35, 36, 42, 84, 94, 159; Constantine's change of middle initial and, 300; death of, xvii, 18, 19, 26, 27, 34, 35, 55, 106, 153, 353; funeral for, 120; letter from brother George to, 27; lifestyle of, 19

Cavafy, Thelxiope Theodorou (wife of Alexander), 86

Cavafy family, xxii, xxiii, 17–42, 69–107, 153, 228–29, 411, 417; in Alexandria, 19, 27, 94, 115, 449*n59*, 450*n73*, 455*n71*; in Anglo-Greek community, 27–28, 30, 35, 39, 149, 182; arts and, 19, 35–40, 94; British character of, 27–28, 449*n64*; business of, 19, 22, 24–28, 34–36, 40–42, 91, 94, 433*n39*, 434*n60*; Church of Saint Constantine and, 60; Constantine's genealogical notes on, 25–26, 33, 52, 60–61, 68, 71, 85, 91–92, 102, 270, 431*n22*, 432*n19*, 437*n43*, 439*n28*; Constantine's literary reputation and, 20–21, 26, 103; "council" of, 44, 47, 83, 102, 103, 441*n84*; crest of, 432*n21*; financial collapse of, xvii, 18, 19–21, 23, 26, 36, 43, 47, 55, 69, 72, 73, 76–82, 84, 89–93, 97, 104–106, 115, 149, 156, 183, 189–90, 202, 210, 286, 353, 417; grave site of, 26, 409; house and possessions lost by, xvii, 70–71, 156, 171, 283; indemnity claims of, 71, 80, 82, 156–58; labor distribution in, 32–34; in Liverpool, 28–32, 34–36, 39, 433*n39*; in London, 28, 31, 33–35, 39, 264, 433*n39*, 434*n56*; maternal (Photiades) side of, 25, 33, 44, 52, 54, 60, 435*n14*, 438*n43*; move to England (1872), xvii, 35; move to Istanbul (1882), xvii, 43–52, 64, 66, 155, 171, 183; origin of name, 432*n21*; return to Alexandria from England (1877), xvii, 43, 55,

Cavafy family (*cont.*)
85–86, 153, 156, 181–82; return to Alexandria from Istanbul (1885), 156, 158, 202, 208, 286, 450*n73*; wealth and social position of, 19–21, 23, 24, 26, 84, 115, 148–49, 159, 183; Whistler and, 37, 463*n42*
Cavafy Museum, 114
Celestine, Pope, 234
Cemberlitas Hamami, 62
Chatby cemetery, 12–13, 120, 408–409
Chatto & Windus, 388
Chios, 182–85, 191, 376, 454*n42*
Choniatis, Nikitas, 265
Choremi-Benaki Company, 113
Christ, 130
Christianity, Christians, 4, 131, 151, 154, 162, 167, 263, 324; Greek Orthodox, 10, 11, 129, 147, 203–205, 266, 432*n20*
Christopoulos, Athanasios, 67, 251, 286, 287, 292
Church of Saint Constantine, 60
Church of Saint George, 436*n23*
Church of Saint Mark, 118, 119
Church of Saint Nicholas, 30–32, 60, 129, 433*n40*
Church of Saint Savvas, 114, 129, 137, 408
Church of Saint Theodore, 31, 60–61
Cicero, 452*n9*
Cinema Amir, 118
Civil War, American, 24, 153, 223
Cleopatra, 121, 131, 139, 168, 235, 326
Coletti, Eleni, 78, 104, 149, 246, 404, 407; biographical note on, 422
Colossus of Maroussi, The (Miller), 362
Constantinople (Byzantios), 436*n21*
Constantinople, *see* Istanbul
Copts, 146, 151
Corniche, 112, 121, 123, 152
Coronio, Aglaia, 37
Correggio, Antonio da, 216
Costantinopoli (De Amicis), 56–59
cotton, 24, 25, 29, 30, 92, 94, 106, 115, 119, 123, 153, 159, 164, 208, 243, 244, 286, 433*nn39, 44*; Bourse, 119, 208, 220, 286
Coulmas, Jean, 400
Cowper, William, 46, 47, 253
Crane, Walter, 37
Crete, 168, 395
Crimean War, 24
Criterion, The, 171, 388
Cromer, Lord (Evelyn Baring), 25, 161, 474*n61*
Crystal Palace Exhibition, 434*n60*
Ctesias, 328
Cyprus, 287

d'Agris, Henri, 277
Dalven, Rae, 234, 310
Dannreuther, Edward, 434*n57*
D'Annunzio, Gabriele, 208, 209, 245, 457*n8*
Dante Alighieri, 332–35, 360, 390
Darius the Great, 327
Darwin, Charles, 454*n44*
Daskalopoulos, Dimitris, xvi
Daudet, Alphonse, 277
David Copperfield (Dickens), 454*n50*
Dawkins, R. M., 240, 460*n27*
De Amicis, Edmondo, 56–59
Death in the Victorian Family (Jalland), 439*n29*
Decadent Republic of Letters, The (Potolsky), 462*n14*
decadent writers, 209, 222, 225–26, 252–53, 260, 263, 265, 277, 310, 324, 342, 462*n14*
Decline and Fall of the Roman Empire (Gibbon), 262–64, 320, 323
Delos, 148
Delta, Penelope, 144–47, 169, 342, 447*n13*, 448*n24*, 475*n79*; biographical note on, 422

Delta, Stephanos, 448*n24*
Demadis, Pericles, 54
Demosthenes, 267
Denshawai Affair, 160–66, 450*n77*
Déséquilibrés de l'amour, Les (Dubarry), 277
Diakos, Athanasios, 273
"diaphaneité" concept, 456*n74*
Dickens, Charles, 48–49, 72, 73, 75, 76, 189, 253, 453*n31*; *David Copperfield*, 454*n50*; *Great Expectations*, 454*n50*
Diehl, Charles, 266, 477*n35*
Dieterich, Karl, 171, 400, 481*n27*
Dilberoglue, Stavros, 434*n60*
Dimirouli, Foteini, 458*n33*
Dimiroulis, Dimitris, 471*n94*
Diocletian, Emperor, 131
Dionysus, 327
Disraeli, Benjamin, 189
Dodecalogue of the Gypsy, The (Palamas), 399
Douglas, Alfred, 474*n61*
Dragoumis, Ion, 147, 169, 311, 448*nn22, 23, 24*, 458*n27*, 470*n88*; biographical note on, 422
Dragoumis, Philippos, 311–14, 319
Drakopoulou, Theoni, *see* Myrtiotissa
Drosinis, Yiorgos, 252
Dubarry, Armand, 277
Ducas, House of, 26, 71
Dufay, Mademoiselle, 145, 447*n8*

Eckermann, Johann Peter, 233, 367, 476*n31*
Edwards, Amelia B., 442*n21*
Egypt: Arabi rebellion in, 154–55, 157, 161, 171, 449*n64*; army of, 153–54; bankruptcy of, 152–53; British control of, 153, 155–57, 159–61, 169–70, 451*n103*; building projects in, 153; Capitulations and, 151; Cavafy's articles on Greeks in, 165–66; Cavafy's national identity and, 158; Denshawai Affair in, 160–66, 450*n77*; "Egyptianism" national identity, 170; Egyptomania, 444*n81*; Europeans in, 146, 151–54, 170; fellahin (peasants) in, 145–46, 152–54, 159–61, 163, 165, 170, 217, 443*n31*, 447*nn13, 17*, 450*n77*; Greek community in, 21–25, 147, 149–52, 167, 169, 170; independence of, 445*n81*, 451*n103*; monasteries in, 367–68; Muslims in, xx, 58, 143–46, 151–52, 154, 169–70, 445*n83*, 451*n107*; nationalism in, 121, 152, 154, 159–61, 168–70, 445*n81*; nationality in, 447*n17*, 448*n18*; poverty in, 152, 161; rail networks in, 120; Tutankhamen's tomb in, 445*n81*; Wardani case in, 164, 450*n82*
Egyptian Gazette, 119
Ekdawi, Sarah, 441*n84*
Eleftheria, 477*n43*
Eleftheros Logos, 396
Eleftheros Typos, 396, 479*n80*
Elefthero Vima, 396, 398
Elgin Marbles (Parthenon Marbles), 40, 256, 273, 287, 467*n18*
Eliot, George, 434*nn57, 60*
Eliot, T. S., 226, 305, 388
Embros, 390
Emerson, Ralph Waldo, 434*n54*
Eminönü, 56
England, 85, 192; Aesthetic movement in, 35, 252; Cavafy family's move to (1872), xvii, 35; Cavafy family's return to Alexandria from (1877), xvii, 43, 55, 85–86, 153, 156,

England (*cont.*)
181–82; Forster's promotion of Cavafy's poetry in, 225, 226, 482*n31*; Greek communities in, *see* Anglo-Greek community; *see also* Great Britain; Liverpool; London
English literature, 221–22, 240, 256, 461*n4*; poetry, 257–59
English periodicals, 256
Enlightenment, 54, 141, 265
Enright, D. J., 173
Epitaphios, 130
L'Ersatz d'amour (Gauthier-Villars), 277
Essai sur Tite Live (Taine), 250
Estia, 480*n3*
Ethnos, 393
Eumorfopoulos, George, 434*n60*
Eunapius, 266
Euripides, 267

Fallmerayer, Jakob Philipp, 464*n59*
Familiar Studies in Men and Books (Stevenson), 250
Faulkner, William, 316–17
Faust (Goethe), 235, 236
fellahin (peasants), 145–46, 152–54, 159–61, 163, 165, 170, 217, 443*n31*, 447*nn13*, *17*, 450*n77*
Fête du Boeuf Gras, 214
films, 446*n114*
Finlay, George, 266
Fleurs du Mal, Les (Baudelaire), 262
Forster, E. M., xxi, 5, 21, 38, 114, 119, 131, 132, 166, 192, 222–27, 240, 324–25, 371; Alexandria writings of, 129, 132, 189, 223, 386; Anastasiades and, 222, 223, 227; Cavafy's correspondence with, 225–27; Cavafy's poetry promoted by, 225, 226, 387–89, 392, 417, 482*n31*; el Adl and, xxi, 224, 460*n30*; friendships of, 225; Furness and, 222; homosexuality of, xxi, 223–26, 460*n30*; *Howards End*, 225, 458*n36*; *Maurice*, xxi, 224, 347; *A Passage to India*, 227, 389; "Pericles in Paradise," 223; *Pharos and Pharillon*, 324–25; soldiers and, 222–23
Fortnightly Review, The, 256
Fort Qaitbay, 121
France, 151, 153, 155, 210, 218, 221, 222, 251; Revolution in, 168; *see also* Paris
France, Anatole, 245, 261, 282
French literature, 240; in Cavafy's library, 260–61, 277, 461*n4*; Parnassian, 251, 252, 260–61, 462*n8*
Friar, Kimon, 462*nn8*, *12*
friendships, 180, 452*n9*; Aristotle on, 180, 181, 184, 207, 456*n1*; of Cavafy, *see under* Cavafy, Constantine P.; of Forster, 225; Malanos on, 248; Nehamas on, 207, 228–29; novels and, 454*n50*
Friends of the Book, 117
Froude, James, 88
Ftyaras, Konstantinos, 365, 368, 479*n68*, 483*n66*
Furness, Robin, 222, 324

Galanakis, Demetrios, 437*n40*
Garoufalias, Dimitris, 375, 376; biographical note on, 422
Gauthier-Villars, Henry, 277
Gautier, Théophile, 260
gazel tradition, 436*n21*
Gennadius, Constantine, 456*n77*
Gennadius, John, 456*n77*
Gentlemen's Magazine, The, 77, 256
Germany, 369; Nazi, 400
Ghali, Butrus Pasha, 164
Giannopoulo, Nicola, 294

Gibbon, Edward, 262–64, 320, 323, 368, 472*n17*, 477*n36*
Gkanoulis, Ilias, 483*n73*
Glückmann, Timothée, 400
Goethe, Johann Wolfgang von, 235, 236, 253, 360; Eckermann and, 233, 367, 476*n31*
Golden Horn, 51, 58, 60
Goldsmith, Oliver, 189
Gothic Revival movement, 60, 129, 433*n41*
Grafftey-Smith, Laurence, 472*n18*
grain, 24, 94
Grammata, Ta, 128, 270, 367, 394–95, 468*n46*, 478*n52*, 485*n28*
Grammata Bookshop, 127–29, 133, 146, 316, 367
Grand Street, 198
Graves, Robert, 389
Great Britain: Alexandria and, 156, 159, 166; Alexandria bombarded by, xvi, 25, 43–46, 50, 54, 58, 63, 118, 155–57, 171, 283, 286; Cavafy's view of, 159, 165; Denshawai Affair and, 160–66; Egypt controlled by, 153, 155–57, 159–61, 169–70, 451*n103*; Egyptian independence from, 451*n103*; imperialism of, 159, 163, 165, 166, 226; trade and, 22, 24, 25, 152
Great Crystal Palace Exhibition, 434*n60*
Great Expectations (Dickens), 454*n50*
Great School of the Nation, 53–54
Greco-Roman Museum, 132, 444*n79*
Greece, 21, 151, 166, 321, 399; in Asia Minor Catastrophe, 166–69, 270–71, 431*n18*, 437*n27*, 482*n33*; Cavafy's visit to, 185, 227–28; in Greco-Turkish War, 22, 192, 431*n18*; independence from Ottoman Empire, 182, 273–74, 437*n30*; nationalism in, 300, 318
Greek Anthology, The, 245, 267
Greek Club, 471*n108*
Greek communities, 21, 32, 36, 151, 408, 430*n18*, 433*n41*, 435*n1*, 436*n27*; in Alexandria, 23–24, 115, 144–52, 157, 208, 296, 317, 437*n31*, 448*n19*, 453*n12*; cemeteries of, 408; churches of, 130; in Egypt, 21–25, 147, 149–52, 167, 169, 170; in England, *see* Anglo-Greek community; in Istanbul, 55, 159, 284, 437*nn31*, *42*; Megali Idea and, 22; terms used for, 448*n19*
Greek culture, 21, 22, 24, 54–56, 251–52, 265, 269, 435*n1*, 436*n27*
Greek diaspora, *see* Greek communities
Greek Educational Association, 272
Greek history: Cavafy's knowledge of, 52, 265–67, 367–68, 410; Hellenistic period, 52, 61, 114, 132, 139, 174, 226, 266–68, 293, 320, 323–25, 331, 333, 365, 367–68, 417, 444*n81*, 445*n81*, 446*n4*
Greek language, 55, 144–45, 224, 447*n8*; Blackie on, 254–55; Cavafy's dictionary of, 283, 287; Cavafy's lexicon of, 287–88; in Cavafy's poetry, 52, 64, 66, 172, 276, 282, 287, 299, 303, 305–306, 333, 393, 394, 417–18; Cavafy's rhyming dictionary of, 288–89; debate on, 275–77, 397, 401; demotic, 172, 254–55, 270, 272, 275, 276, 287–88, 299, 305, 335, 337, 393, 394, 397–98, 450*n75*; katharevousa, 52, 66, 172, 275–76, 282, 287, 303, 333, 337, 397

Greek literature, 250–52, 382, 461*n4*; in Cavafy's library, 250–52, 269–77; folklore, 53, 56, 65, 251, 252, 269–73; New and Old Athenian schools of, 250–51, 287, 462*nn8*, *12*; realism in, 251; Shakespeare and, 255–56; *see also* Greek poetry
Greek necropolises, 203–5, 408, 456*n77*
Greek Orthodoxy, 10, 11, 129, 147, 203–205, 266, 432*n20*
Greek Philological Society, 55–56, 65, 436*n27*, 437*n40*
Greek poetry, 6, 12, 264, 265, 269, 270, 272–74, 283, 288, 397; traditional, and Cavafy's work, 53, 240, 252, 282, 292, 298, 318, 335, 337–38, 348, 398, 401, 410; demoticist revolution in, 287
Gregoras, Nikephoros, 265
Gritsanis, Panagiotis, 307
Grivas, Spyros, 124
Grote, George, 266
Gryparis, Ioannis, 252

Haag, Michael, 131
Hager-Boufides, Nikos, 248
Haggerty, George, 455*n73*
Hagia Sophia, 56, 60, 270
Halley's Comet (store and bar), 124
hamams, 62–63
Hamlet (Shakespeare), 47, 218, 253
Haqqi, Mahmud Tahir, 164
Harrison, Frederick, 273
Headlam, Walter, 245
Heine, Heinrich, 398
Hellenism, modern, 21, 22, 33, 53, 56, 62, 265, 311, 399, 408, 410, 436*n27*, 437*n30*
Hellenism and Modern Egypt (Politis), 23, 308–309
Hellenistic period, 52, 61, 114, 132, 139, 174, 226, 266–68, 293, 320, 323–25, 331, 333, 365, 367–68, 417, 444*n81*, 445*n81*, 446*n4*
Henley Regatta, 95
Hérédia, José-Maria de, 260
Hermes Lyceum, 182
Herod I, King, 162–63
Herodotus, 253, 266, 327–28
Hesiod, 45
Hesperus, 287, 455*n71*
Hesseling, D. C., 266
Himerius, 266
Hirst, Anthony, 481*n17*
Histoire de la littérature romaine (Pierron), 250
Historical and Ethnological Museum, 296
History of Byzantine Literature, The (Krumbacher), 265
History of England, The (Hume), 250
History of England, The (Milner), 250
History of Scotland, The (McKenzie), 250
History of the Decline and Fall of the Roman Empire, The (Gibbon), *see Decline and Fall of the Roman Empire* (Gibbon)
History of the Greek Nation (Paparrigopoulos), 265
Hoche, Jules, 277
Hogarth Press, 38, 192, 388, 392
Holland Park, 37–39
Homer, 41–42, 160, 162, 257–58, 267, 321, 331–35, 390
homosexuality, xxi, 62–63, 146, 192–93, 233, 293–94, 340, 344, 346, 434*n54*; of Cavafy, *see under* Cavafy, Constantine P.; in Cavafy's poetry, xv, 4, 10, 41, 120, 122, 123, 172–73, 195, 197, 224, 241–43, 293–94, 302–304, 314–15, 324, 326, 331, 340, 343–47, 381, 389, 391–93, 399; and Cavafy's views on sexuality, 221–22, 293–94, 468*n34*;

"diaphaneité" and, 456*n74*; of Forster, xxi, 223–26, 460*n30*; Malanos's views on, 240, 460*n23*; of Paul Cavafy, 86, 94, 97, 103, 440*n67*, 474*n64*; in poetry, xx–xxi, 222
Horace, 253
Horsey, William de, 97–98
Hotel Cosmopolite, 6, 362, 378, 406
Howards End (Forster), 225, 458*n36*
Hugo, Victor, 74, 253, 261
Hume, David, 250
Hunt, Leigh, 258, 263
Hyères, 97, 98, 101, 102

Iliad, The (Homer), 41–42, 160, 162
Inferno (Dante), 332–35
Inheritance, The (Lopez), 458
In Memoriam (Tennyson), 454*n50*
Ioakeim, Patriarch, 54
Ioannidis, 123
Ionia, 167
Ionides, Aglaia, 39
Ionides, Alexander Constantine, 27, 36–37, 39, 433*n48*, 434*n60*, 482*n33*
Ionides, Constantine (Constantine Ipliktzis), 36
Ionides, Constantine (son of Alexander), 37, 39, 433*n48*
Ionides, Helen, 37
Ionides, Luke, 38
Ionides-Dannreuther, Haricleia, 39, 434*n57*
Ionides family, 27, 36–39, 433*n48*
Irrigation Service, 11, 25, 112–14, 120, 202, 288–89, 328, 341
Irving, Washington, 253
Isis, 238, 459*n20*
Islam, *see* Muslims
Ismail Pasha, 19, 153, 154
Istanbul (Constantinople), xvii, 23, 30–31, 33, 43–44, 51–66, 130, 151, 152; architectural styles in, 58; Byzantine monuments in, 59–61, 437*n40*; Cadiköy district, 50–51; Cavafy in, 51–57, 59–67, 69, 156, 283, 285–86; Cavafy family's escape from Alexandria to (1882), xvii, 43–52, 64, 66, 155, 171, 183; Cavafy family's return to Alexandria from (1885), 156, 158, 202, 208, 286, 450*n73*; De Amicis on, 56–59; fall of, 270–71, 310, 399; Galata district, 54, 56–57, 59, 437*n30*; Great School of the Nation in, 53–54; Greek community in, 55, 159, 284, 437*nn31*, *42*; hamams in, 62–63; literary culture in, 55–57, 67; Megali Idea and, 22; Pera district, xviii, 54, 56–59, 63, 437*n30*; Phanar district, 54, 432*n20*, 436*n23*; Stamboul (old city), 59–60; Stoudion in, 60; Tanzimat reform movement and, 57; walls of, 59–60

Jacovides, Georgios, 296
Jalland, Pat, 439*n29*
James, Henry, 317, 434*n54*
Jerusalem, Patriarchate of, 436*n23*
Jewish people, 147
John VI Kantakouzinos, 106, 265, 431*n22*
John XIV Kalekas, 431*n22*
Josephus, Flavius, 266, 268–69
Joyce, James, 172, 468*n34*
Judea, 162–63
Julian the Apostate, 4, 323, 472*n17*
Julius Caesar (Shakespeare), 48
Jusdanis, Gregory, 435*n14*, 475*n79*, 476*n31*
Justinian I, 68

Kahira, El, 148
Kaisara, Emmanouil, 391
Kallinous, Amalia, 56, 157

Kalmouchos, Takis, 94, 385
Kalvos, Andreas, 250
Kambas, Nikos, 252
Kambos, Roberto, 128, 394
Kampanis, Aristos, 135, 362–63, 446*n109*
Karagiannis, Vangelis, 414
Karapanagopoulos, Alekos, 438*n45*
Karyotakis, Kostas, 136
Katsimbalis, Giorgos, 362
Kayar, Ibrahim el, 112, 144, 365, 473*n55*
Kazantzakis, Nikos, 141, 170, 414; biographical note on, 422
Keats, John, 256–57, 463*n30*
Kephalinos, Yiannis, 124, 443*n43*
King's College London, 192
King's Flute, The (Palamas), 399
Kingsley, Mary, 253
klephts, 274
Knowles, James Thomas, Sir, 456*n75*
Knowles, James Thomas, Sr., 456*n75*
köçek dancers, 436*n21*
Kolaitis, Memas, 130, 233, 238, 367, 386; biographical note on, 422
Komis, Antonis, 373–75, 382, 390
Komnene, Anna, 265
Konelianos, B., 478*n57*
Konstantinidis, K. N., 484*n87*
Korais, Adamantios, 141
Koromilas, Yiorgios D., 479*n80*
Kosmos, 314
Koulouridis, Ilias, 435*n14*
Krumbacher, Karl, 265, 269
Kyklos, O, 362, 484*n77*
Kypreos, Georges, 475*n79*
Kyttikas, Dionysios, 477*n33*

ladder of divine ascent, 223, 458*n33*
Lagonikos, M. S., 145
Lagoudakis, Socrates, 237, 395–96
Lamia, 256–57
Lanterne Sourde, 165, 171
Laoumtzi, Stamatia, 450*n75*
Lapathiotis, Leonidas, 370
Lapathiotis, Napoleon, 222, 339–40, 342, 346, 370–71, 430*n8*, 477*nn47*, *50*; biographical note on, 422
Lawrence, T. E., 226, 389
Lechonitis, Georgios, 140, 446*n110*
Leconte de Lisle, 260
Lee, Vernon, 434*n54*
Lélia (Sand), 76
Lemaître, Jules, 245
Lenten carnival, 147–48
Leonardo da Vinci, 216
Leontis, Apostolos, 409
Leopardi, Giacomo, 245
Lepsius, Karl Richard, 114
Letters to Friends (Cicero), 452*n9*
Levant, 21, 22, 147, 151, 182; use of term, 448*n26*, 449*n43*
Liatsis, Sotiris, 125, 448*n23*
Libre, 171
Liddell, Robert, xvi, xxii, 327, 444*n62*; Malanos and, 429*n8*
Life and Work of Constantine Cavafy, The (Peridis), xix
Life of Apollonius, The (Philostratus), 257, 463*n30*
Liverpool, xviii, 22, 28, 43, 54, 63, 123, 130, 140, 182, 186, 188, 189, 192, 194, 204; Cavafy family in, 28–32, 34–36, 39, 433*n39*; Church of Saint Nicholas in, 30–32, 60, 129, 433*n40*; Newsham Park, 28–29; *Spirit of Liverpool* statue in, 30, 433*n39*
Liverpool Mechanics' Institute, 27
London, xviii, 22, 27, 30, 43, 54, 63, 91, 92, 115, 130, 140, 152, 168, 182, 183, 189, 192, 204, 211, 213, 218, 219, 222, 226, 256, 319, 346; art scene in, 35–40; Bloomsbury authors in, 225, 369, 458*n38*; Cavafy family in, 28, 31, 33–35, 39,

264, 433*n39*, 434*n56*; Cavafy plaque in, 264; cemeteries in, 203–205; Constantine and John Cavafy in, 168, 213, 214, 291, 314; Holland Park, 37–39; Houses of Parliament, 454*n44*; museums in, 37, 39–40; Schilizzi in, 192, 454*n44*
Longfellow, Henry Wadsworth, 264
Longus, 253
Lopez, Matthew, 458*n36*
Lowell, James Russell, 255, 434*n54*
Lucian of Samosata, 266–67, 361

Macaulay, Thomas Babington, 189
Macbeth (Shakespeare), 372, 478*n59*
Macedonia, 458*n27*
Mackridge, Peter, 309–10
Madame Sans-Gêne (Sardou and Moreau), 214
Madis, Alex, 470*n70*
Magnis, Petros, 128, 394, 484*n87*
Mahaffy, J. P., 266
Mahmoud the Gaznevide, 263, 464*n54*
Maître de Forges, Le (Ohnet), 453*n31*
Malakasis, Miltiadis, 252, 479*n80*
Malanos, Timos, xxii, 23, 125–26, 139, 159, 168, 169, 171, 181, 228, 230–40, 245, 251, 277, 300, 323, 342, 343, 364–66, 369, 392–93, 406, 410, 444*n62*, 446*n110*, 449*n64*, 469*n52*, 476*n31*, 483*n50*, 486*n35*; Alekos Sengopoulos and, 230–31, 234, 241–42, 246–48; and Alekos Sengopoulos's lecture on Cavafy, 241, 460*n32*; biographical note on, 423; Cavafy's correspondence with, 236–38; Cavafy's difficult relationship and break with, 181, 233, 236–39, 393–94; Dawkins's rebuttals of, 240; death of, 460*n23*; friendship as viewed by, 248; on friendship with Cavafy, 235–36; homosexuality as viewed by, 240, 460*n23*; lecture on Cavafy given by, 393–94; Liddell and, 429*n8*; "The Macedonian Alexander," 232–33; *The Poet C. P. Cavafy*, 239–40; *Propylaia* journal of, 232; Rika Sengopoulos and, 237–38; writings on Cavafy by, xvi, xxii, 233, 235–36, 239–40
Mallarmé, Stéphane, 284, 398
Manchester, 22, 25, 27, 30, 36, 149
Man Without Qualities, The (Musil), 468*n34*
Mardi Gras, 214
Marinetti, Filippo Tommaso, 412–13, 474*n71*
Marseilles, 152, 214, 314
Mary I of England, 250
Massavetas, Alexander, 54, 436*n21*
Maurice (Forster), xxi, 224, 347
Mavilis, Lorenzos, 252
Mavrogordato, John, 247, 392, 400–401
Mavroudis, Alexander, 222, 344, 470*n70*
McKenzie, James, 250
McKinsey, Martin, 469*n62*
Measure for Measure (Shakespeare), 253, 255
Megali Idea, 22
Meleager, 267
Melville, Herman, 162, 472*n7*
Mendelsohn, Daniel, 306
Merivale, Herman, 214
Merrill, James, 198, 455*n59*
Metaxakis, Meletios, 10–11, 430*nn16*, *18*, 431*n22*
Metropole Hotel, 442*n1*
M. Gallet décédé / The Late Monsieur Gallet (Simenon), 250
Michaelides, Cimon, 296–97
Michaelidou, M. G., 270
Michel, Jean, 390
Mill, The (Burne-Jones), 37
Miller, Henry, 362

Milner, Thomas, 250
Milton, John, 45, 257
Minotis, Alexis, 372–73, 478*n60*
Misérables, Les (Hugo), 74
Mitropoulos, Dimitri, 6–8, 430*n7*; biographical note on, 423
Mixed Law Courts, 119
Modinos, Polys, 167, 316, 323, 386–87, 389; biographical note on, 423
Moeurs d'exception (Hoche), 277
Moffat, Wendy, 458*n32*, 460*n30*
Mohammed Ali Club, 117, 223
Mohammed Ali of Egypt, 118, 153, 447*n10*
Mohammed Ali Square, 115, 118, 147, 173
Mommsen, Theodore, 266
Mona Lisa (*La Gioconda*) (Leonardo), 216
Moore, G. E., 225
Moreau, Emile, 214
Morris, William, 37
Moss, R. J., & Co., 34, 433*n44*
Mousa, 400
Mouseion, 435*n1*
Mrs. Dalloway (Woolf), 468*n34*
Much Ado About Nothing (Shakespeare), 253
Munich, 219, 220, 295
museums, 37, 39–40
Musil, Robert, 468*n34*
Muslims, xx, 57, 58, 62, 143–46, 151–52, 154, 167, 169–70, 445*n83*, 446*n4*, 447*n17*, 451*nn107*, *109*; Islamic art, 145; Muslim Brotherhood, 170–71, 451*n109*
Myrtiotissa, 134, 141–42, 313, 314, 318, 366, 400
Mytilene, 104–105

Nassar, Yagcoub, 443*n47*
Nasser, Gamal Abdel, 155, 446*n4*, 449*n45*
Nation, The, 388, 389
National Gallery, 454*n44*
National Theatre of Athens, 372
Nea Estia, 392–93, 430*n12*
Nea Techni, 375–77, 379–80, 393, 398, 479*n73*
Nea Zoï, 270, 382, 468*n46*, 479*n73*, 485*n28*
Nefertiti, Queen, 444*n81*
Negroponte, Miltiades and Maria, 430*n7*
Nehamas, Alexander, 207, 228–29
Neugriechische Lyriker (Dieterich, ed.), 171
Nichori, 64, 66–67; Church of Saint George in, 436*n23*
Nicolopoulos family, 24
Nineteenth Century, The, 254, 256, 273, 456*n75*
Nomikos, Christophoros A., 145, 410, 473*n56*, 476*n32*
Norton, Charles Eliot, 434*n54*
Noumas, 394
Nubia, 146

Odysseus, 257–58, 331–35
Office of the Irrigation Service, 11, 25, 112–14, 120, 202, 288–289, 328, 341
Ohnet, Georges, 261, 453*n31*
Olympics, 149, 395
Onassis Foundation, xx, 442*n10*
Order of the Phoenix, 401
O'Rell, Max, 253
Orizontes, 414
Ossian, 253
Othoni, 459*n20*
Ottoman Empire, 26, 44, 52–53, 55, 57–58, 159, 168, 264, 270, 436*n27*, 447*n10*, 450*n73*; Capitulations of, 151, 449*n45*; Cretan war of independence against, 395; demise of, 264; gazel poetic tradition in, 436*n21*; Greek independence from, 182, 273–74, 437*n30*;

hamams in, 62–63; nationality law in, 447*n17*; Scanderbeg and, 263; Sublime Porte of, 154; Tanzimat reform movement in, 57; Young Turk Revolution in, 437*n27*
Oulton, Carolyn, 454*n50*
Ouranis, Eleni, *see* Thrylos, Alkis
Ouranis, Kostas, 7, 134–35, 140–41, 372, 430*n8*; biographical note on, 423
Our Mutual Friend (Dickens), 48–49
Owen, Wilfred, 346

paganism, 4, 131, 167
Paget, Violet, 434*n54*
Palamas, Kostis, 252, 337, 379–80, 397–400, 459*n20*, 463*n42*, 479*n80*; biographical note on, 423
Palatine Anthology, The, 267
Palladas, 245
Panaigyptia, 409, 485*n18*, 468*n46*
Panathenaia, 296–98, 339
Panayiotopoulos, I. M., 400
Pangalos, Theodoros, 401
Papadiamantis, Alexandros, 273, 478*n50*
Papaioannou, M. M., 23
Papalambrinoudi, Evoulia, 56
Papanikolaou, Dimitris, 277
Paparrigopoulos, Constantine, 265
Papathanasopoulos, Thanasis, 480*n82*
Papayiannis, George Michael, 433*n40*
Papazis, Constantine, 43, 182, 185, 187, 269
Papoutsakis, Giorgos, xxi, 9, 283, 404, 409–11, 486*n35*; biographical note on, 423–24
Paraschos, Kleon, 398
Pargas, Stephanos, 124
Paris, 85, 144, 152, 171, 210, 211, 213, 217–20, 222, 319, 395; Cavafy in, 168, 213–16, 291, 314; John Cavafy in, 168, 213–14, 216, 218, 219, 291, 314; Salon in, 216; Vachalcade in, 213–14
Parliament, Houses of, 454*n44*
Parnassians, 251, 252, 260–61, 462*n8*
Parsifal (Wagner), 434*n57*
Parthenon Marbles (Elgin Marbles), 40, 256, 273, 287, 467*n18*
Paspatis, A. G., 437*n40*
Passage to India, A (Forster), 227, 389
Passow, Arnold, 465*n81*
Pastroudis (restaurant), 117–18
Pastroudis, Yiorgos, 118
Pater, Walter, 324, 456*n74*
Pausanias, 52
Paxinou, Katina, 478*n60*
Pea, Enrico, 459*n14*
peasants (fellahin), 145–46, 152–54, 159–61, 163, 165, 170, 217, 443*n31*, 447*nn13*, *17*, 450*n77*
Peridis, Michalis, xvi, xix, xxi, xxii, 128, 169, 277, 282, 395, 410, 444*n62*, 486*n35*; biographical note on, 424
Pernot, Hubert, 386–87
Persepolis, 328
Persians, The (Aeschylus), 327–28
Petit Trianon, 124
Petrarch, 452*n9*
Petridis, Pavlos, 360, 382, 412
Petridis, Yiorgos, 412
Phaleron, 123, 149
Phanariots, 26, 36, 52, 53, 250–51, 287, 437*n30*
Pharos, 121
Pharos and Pharillon (Forster), 324–25
Philological Society, 55–56, 65
Philostratus, 257, 266, 463*n30*
Photiades, Photios, 436*n23*
Photiades, Yiorgos (maternal grandfather), xvii, 33, 44–45, 51, 436*n23*; death of, 312, 314

Photiades family, 25, 33, 44, 52, 54, 60, 435*n14*, 438*n43*
photography, 446*n114*
Phrosini, Kyra, 273
Physis, I, 314
Picture of Dorian Gray, The (Wilde), 233
Pieridis, Giangos, 390
Pieris, Michalis, 276
Pierron, Pierre Alexis, 250
Pinero, Arthur W., 214
Piraeus, 131
Pitaridou-Papou, Amalia, 286
Placidia and Adolphus, 263
Plato, 253, 267
Plomer, William, 240
Plutarch, 266, 328, 365–66, 459*n6*
Pnoi, 363–64
Poe, Edgar Allan, 65, 199, 255, 259, 316, 463*n39*; "The Gold Bug," 455*n60*
Poet C. P. Cavafy, The (Malanos), 239–40
poètes maudits, 260
poetry, poets, 262, 272; Byzantine, 264, 265; English, 257–59; French Parnassian, 251, 252, 260–61, 462*n8*; Greek, *see* Greek poetry
Polemis, Ioannis, 252, 296
Politia, 396
Politis, Athanasios, 142, 150, 301, 363; biographical note on, 424; *Hellenism and Modern Egypt*, 23, 308–309
Politis, Nikolaos, 269, 270, 271, 465*n81*
Polylas, Iakovos, 254
Pompey's Pillar, 131, 143, 199
Pontian Greeks, 270–71
Pope Joan (Roidis), 275
Porché, François, 477*n47*
Potolsky, Matthew, 253, 462*n14*
poverty, 152, 161, 173
Pre-Raphaelites, 37–38, 256
Prince Narcisse, Le (Scheffer), 277
Princess and the Butterfly, The (Pinero), 214
Princess from the Land of Porcelain, The (Whistler), 37–38
Principia Ethica (Moore), 225
Prinsep, Sara and Thoby, 38
Printezis, F., 314
Prodromos, Theodore, 265
Prokopios, 67–68, 265
proparaxytonos, 308
Propylaia, 232
prosody, 307–310
prostitutes, 62, 114–15, 118, 173, 174, 186, 214
Prudhomme, Sully, 260
Psellos, Michael, 265
Psycharis, Ioannis, 393
Ptolemaic rulers, 326
Public Opinion, 82
Puccini, Giacomo, 294, 478*n57*

Queen Mary (Tennyson), 48
Queen's Proctor, The (Merivale), 214
Queer Friendship (Haggerty), 455*n73*

Ralli, Augustus, 205
Ralli, Micky, 86
Ralli, Mikès, 43, 45, 63, 120, 180–93, 195–97, 202, 204, 216, 245; biographical note on, 424; Cavafy's correspondence with, 183–90; illness and death of, 190–91, 195, 197, 202, 204, 205, 208, 312, 349, 412
Ralli, Stephen, 204–205
Ralli, Theodore, 453*n12*
Ralli, Thodoris, 182
Ralli family, 36, 183–85, 188, 194, 409, 434*n60*, 457*n20*; mausolea of, 204–205, 456*n75*
Rallis, Anthony Theodore, 120
Rallis, Demetrios Theodore, 433*n40*
Rallis, Theodore, 216–17, 457*n20*

Ramleh (suburb of Alexandria), 120, 188, 190, 199
Rangavis, Alexandros Rizos, 251, 253, 292
Raphael, 216
Rassin, Ahmed, 165–66
Red Cross, 222, 315
Réforme, La, 164
Rembrandt, 220
Renaissance, 216
Return to Alexandria (Butler), 435*n1*
Revue des Deux Mondes, 265
Rhodes, Jean, 277
Ricks, David, 461*n4*
Rimbaud, Arthur, 282, 398
Riviera News, The, 98–99
Rivista Quindicinale, 285
Rodd, James Rennell, 273–74
Rodenbach, Georges, 260–61
Rodocanachi, Costas, 441*n87*
Rodocanachi, John, 43, 45, 180–83, 186, 193–95; biographical note on, 424; Cavafy's correspondence with, 193–95
Rodocanachi, Julia, 105, 441*n87*
Rodocanachi, Pandelis, 182
Rodocanachi family, 183, 205, 409
Roidis, Emmanuel, 275
Romanticism, 53, 251, 252, 298, 300, 303, 462*nn11, 12*, 474*n71*
Rome, 131, 266–68, 324, 445*n81*
Rose and Silver: The Princess from the Land of Porcelain (Whistler), 37–38
Rossetti, Dante Gabriel, 37, 38, 434*n60*
Royal Academy, 453*n32*
Rubens, Peter Paul, 220
Ruskin, John, 256, 259–60, 320, 463*n42*; Whistler and, 463*n42*

Sa'ad Zaghloul Square, 121
Said, Mahmoud Bey, 410
Said Pasha, 85
Saint Catherine's Monastery, 458*n33*
Saint Stephen's Chapel, 204, 456*n75*
Salamis, Battle of, 327–28
Salvago family, 408
Salvagos, Mikes, 342
Sand, George, 75, 76, 253
San Stefano Casino, 86, 120, 199, 201, 292
Santorinios, Nikos, 366, 375
Sapho (Daudet), 277
Sarafis, Nicolas, 441*n87*
Sarakinos, Takis, 484*n87*
Sardou, Victorien, 214
Sareyiannis, I. A., 138, 174, 301, 316, 324, 340, 348, 365–68, 372, 385, 446*n102*, 447*n5*, 486*n35*; biographical note on, 424
Sargent, John Singer, 441*n75*
Savidis, George, xx, 276, 392
Savidis, Manolis, xx
Scaife, Christopher, 371–72, 411; biographical note on, 424; "Epitaph," 411
Scanavi, Leoni, 192
Scanderbeg, George Castriot, 263–64
Scheffer, Robert, 277
Schilizzi, Helena, 191–92, 482*n33*
Schilizzi, Michalis, 182
Schilizzi, Stephen, 43, 45, 180–83, 185, 191–93, 195, 202–204, 482*n33*; biographical note on, 425; Cavafy's correspondence with, 183, 191–93; death of, 120, 195, 202, 203, 312
Schilizzi family, 82, 183, 192, 205
Schiller, Friedrich, 258
Schliemann, Heinrich, 131–32
Scott, Walter, 189, 250, 327
Sea Depths, The (Rallis), 216
Sea of Marmara, 51
Secret History, The (Prokopios), 67–68
Sections from the Songs of the Greek People (Politis), 270, 271, 465*n81*
Seferis, George, 167–68, 282
Selefkidis, Dimitrios, 267–69

Seleucid Empire, 267
Self-Culture (Blackie), 254, 462*n20*
Semaine Égyptienne, La, 165–66, 171, 484*n77*
Sengopoulos, Alekos, xviii–xxi, 8–9, 135, 181, 230–32, 234–36, 240–48, 364, 374, 378, 379, 392, 404, 405, 407, 409, 430*n9*; in Benha, 241, 243–44; biographical note on, 425; Cavafy lecture of, 241–43, 246, 460*n32*; Cavafy's correspondence with, xix, 21, 241, 243–48, 316, 342, 377, 405, 439*n27*; as Cavafy's heir, xviii, xix, xxi, 8, 104, 228, 231, 237, 486*n35*; Cavafy's letters and, xix; as Cavafy's protégé, 241, 245–46; Cavafy's relationship with, 241, 247; character of, 240–41; death of, xx; Eleni Coletti and, 78, 104, 246; first complete edition of Cavafy's poems published by, xviii, 13, 94, 385–86, 406–408, 416; Malanos and, 230–31, 234, 241–42, 246–48; Rika's divorce from, 247, 486*n35*; Rika's marriage to, 246, 408
Sengopoulos, Kyveli, xx
Sengopoulos, Rika, xviii–xix, xxi, 8, 169, 217, 237, 246, 290–91, 315, 354, 368, 377, 382, 401, 403–409, 414–16, 430*n9*, 441*n74*, 485*n6*, 486*n35*; Alekos's divorce from, 247, 486*n35*; Alekos's marriage to, 246, 408; biographical note on, 425; Cavafy biography planned by, xvi, 403–404, 407, 411–14, 486*n35*; Cavafy's confessional note to, 349, 405–406, 412; as Cavafy's heir, xvi, xviii, xxi, 235, 411, 486*n35*; Cavafy's illness and death and, 9–11, 246, 247, 349, 378, 379; Cavafy's letters and, xix; Cavafy's sexuality and, xxi, 62, 438*n45*; death of, 414; "Dejection," 401, 405; first complete edition of Cavafy's poems published by, xviii, 13, 94, 385–86, 406–408, 416; lecture on Cavafy given by, 413–15; Malanos and, 237–38; *Propylaia* and, 232
Serapion, 468*n46*
Shakespeare, William, 33, 45, 188, 189, 253–54, 273, 462*n16*; Cavafy's articles on, 253–56; Greek literature and, 255–56; *Hamlet*, 47, 218, 253; *Julius Caesar*, 48; *Macbeth*, 372, 478*n59*; *Measure for Measure*, 253, 255; *Much Ado About Nothing*, 253
Sham-el-Nessim, 172
Shelley, Percy Bysshe, 77, 253, 398
Sikelianos, Angelos, 305, 400, 414
Simenon, Georges, 250
Simeonidis, A. G., 237, 360
Simeon the Stylite, Saint, 320–22, 332, 472*n17*
Sinanos, Victor, 316
Skeferis, Pericles, 408
Skepsi, 479*n62*
Skylitzes, John, 191, 453*n40*
slavery, 30
Smith, William, 268–69
Smyrna, 22, 23, 151, 166–67
Socrates, 323
Sodome (d'Agris), 277
Solomos, Dionysios, 250, 275, 478*n50*
sophists, 266
South Kensington Museum (Victoria and Albert Museum), 37, 39–40, 434*n60*
Soutsos, Alexander, 251, 292
Soutsos, Panayiotis, 251, 292
Sparta, 325
Spartali, Christina, 37–38
Spartali, Marie, 37, 38, 434*n54*

Spartali, Michael D., 434*n54*
Spirit of Liverpool (Wood), 30, 433*n39*
Sporting Club, 148
Stassinopoulou, Maria, xvi
Stavrinos, Stavros, 165
Stephen, Leslie, 38
Stevens, William Bagshaw, 30
Stevenson, Robert Louis, 250
Stillman, Lisa, 38
Stillman, Marie Spartali, 37, 38, 434*n54*
Stillman, William, 434*n54*
Stoudion, 60
Strabo, 52
Stratigis, Georgios, 276, 308, 470*n79*
Street, George Edmund, 456*n75*
Sudan, 153
Suetonius, 245
Suez Canal, 155
Sumners, Henry, 433*n40*
Swinburne, Algernon Charles, 253
Symonds, John Addington, 434*n54*
Synadino family, 147
synizesis, 309, 470*n84*
Syria, Syrians, 147, 268, 269
Syros, 184

Tachydromos, 125, 405, 448*n23*
Tagore, Rabindranath, 135–36
Taine, Hippolyte, 250
Tangopoulos, D. P., 393
Tanzimat, 57
Tawfiq Pasha, 154, 155, 157
taxation, 151, 153, 450*n77*
Telegraphos, 119, 286, 444*n79*
Temple Bar, The, 256
10 Inventions (Mitropoulos and Cavafy), 7
Tennyson, Lord (Alfred), xvi, 48, 253, 256, 333, 390; *In Memoriam*, 454*n50*; "St Simeon Stylites," 320–22, 332; "Ulysses," 332–35, 380
Thackeray, Harriet "Minnie" Marian, 38
Thackeray, William Makepeace, 38, 75, 76, 189, 253, 453*n31*
Thebes, 477*n36*
Theocritus, 245–46, 267
Theodora, Empress, 103
Theodore the Studite, 60
Theofanis, Metropolitan, 408
Theotokas, Yiorgos, 6, 12; biographical note on, 425
Therapia, 50, 51, 64
Thessaloniki, 151
Through Egypt in War-Time (Briggs), 117
Thrylos, Alkis (Eleni Ouranis), 7, 128, 398, 430*n7*, 476*n13*; biographical note on, 425
Thucydides, 266
Tinos, 185
Titian, 216
Topkapi Palace, 56
Tositsas School, 231
To the Lighthouse (Woolf), 38
Toynbee, Arnold, 192, 389, 482*n33*
trade, 152, 182, 183; Britain and, 22, 24, 25, 152; cotton, *see* cotton; grain, 24, 94
Treaty of Lausanne, 167
Trebizond, 271
Tsalikis, Marika, 276, 299
Tsirkas, Stratis, xvi, 86, 370, 376, 463*nn41*, *42*, 474*n64*; biographical note on, 425–26
Tsokopoulos, Georgios, 296, 298, 480*n3*
Turkey, 22; in Asia Minor Catastrophe, 166–69, 431*n18*, 437*n27*, 482*n33*; in Greco-Turkish War, 22, 192, 431*n18*
Tutankhamen, 445*n81*

Ulysses (Joyce), 468*n34*
University of Athens, 185

Vachalcade, 213–14
Vaianos, Marios, 339–40, 342, 370–71, 375–80, 393, 395–96, 430*n8*, 486*n35*; biographical note on, 426; health issue of, 379; "Tragoudi Akolasias," 376
Valaoritis, Aristotle, 273–75
Valas, Alexander, 268
Valassopoulo, George, 171, 225, 386–89
Valieri, Babette, 440*n66*, 441*n88*
Valieri, Geronymo-Georgio, 104
Valieri, Hariclia, xix, 69, 92, 104–107, 391, 441*n87*, 467*n13*, 468*n27*, 469*n58*; biographical note on, 426
Vandergorght, Paul, 451*n83*
Van Dyck, Anthony, 220
Varsami, Euphrosyne, 434*n54*
Venice, 151
Venizelism, 10
Venizelos, Eleftherios, 191, 430*n16*, 448*n23*; biographical note on, 426
Vera; or, the Nihilists (Wilde), 441*n75*
Verdi, Giuseppe, 153
Verhaeghe de Naeyer, Leon, 446*n114*
Verlaine, Paul, 260, 262, 263, 324
Veronese, Paolo, 216
Victoria, Queen, 214
Victoria and Albert Museum (South Kensington Museum), 37, 39–40, 434*n60*
Victorian era, 20, 22, 28, 32, 35, 69, 75, 85, 100, 138, 184, 190, 193, 214, 256, 285, 343, 456*n80*; death and mourning in, 439*n29*, 471*n92*; painters in, 37–38, 256
Vienna, 58, 219
Vikelas, Dimitrios, 265
Volos, 374
Voltaire, 80
Vouros, George, 105
Vouros, Maria, 105, 441*n87*
Vouros family, 104, 105
Voutieridis, Ilias, 426
Vrisimitzakis, Yiorgos, 9, 241, 364, 375, 486*n35*; biographical note on, 426
Vryonis, Omer, 273

Wagner, Richard, 220, 434*n57*
Walker Art Gallery, 30
Wardani, Ibrahim al-, 164, 450*n82*
Watts, George Frederic, 37, 324
Webb, Philip, 37
West Norwood Cemetery, 203–205
Wharton, Edith, 441*n75*
Whistler, James McNeill, 37–38, 434*n60*; Ruskin and, 463*n42*
Whistler, William, 37
Whitman, Walt, 222–23, 463*n42*
Wilde, Oscar, 149, 233, 324, 343, 395, 451*n99*, 474*n61*, 477*n47*; Paul Cavafy and, 441*n75*; *Vera; or, the Nihilists*, 441*n75*
Willy et Ménalkas, 277
Woolf, Leonard, 38, 226, 388, 392
Woolf, Virginia, 38, 226, 388, 469*n62*; *Mrs. Dalloway*, 468*n34*; "The New Biography," 403; *To the Lighthouse*, 38
World War I, 22, 166, 168, 326, 468*n34*

Xenophon, 266
Xenopoulos, Grigorios, 296–98, 301, 338, 376, 382, 392–93, 400, 469*n52*; biographical note on, 426
Xerxes, 327

Year of Cavafy, 21
Yeniköy, 45, 51, 52, 56, 64, 157, 435*n14*, 436*n20*
Yiannakakis, Sakellaris, 241, 367–68
York, Roland, 186
Young Turk Revolution, 437*n27*

Zaghloul, Sa'ad, 121
Zambaco, Maria, 37, 38, 441*n75*
Zananiri, Gaston, 114, 125, 135–37, 409–11
Zelitas, Eftychia, 23, 127, 128, 133, 166, 174, 363, 447*n16*; biographical note on, 426–27
Zelitas, Nikos, 124, 127–28, 133, 141, 363, 385, 444*n60*, 478*n52*, 483*n73*; biographical note on, 427
Zervos, Christos, 478*n52*
Zervos, Stamos, 241
Zervoudaki family, 147, 192, 409
Zizinia family, 449*n59*
Zizinia Theatre, 116, 188
Zola, Émile, 217, 261, 458*n25*
Zotos, Zelitas and Adreas, 471*n107*

ILLUSTRATION CREDITS

We are grateful to the Onassis Foundation Cavafy Archive, the Hellenic Literary and Historical Archive (ELIA-MIET), the Benaki Museum Historical Archives, and these individuals for permission to include the following photos and reproductions. All images credited to the Onassis Foundation are reproduced by kind permission of the Cavafy Archive, Onassis Foundation.

1. Paul, Constantine, and John: GR-OF CA CA-SF02-S03-F26-SF001-0001 (1934), reproduced by kind permission of the Cavafy Archive, Onassis Foundation © 2016/2018 Cavafy Archive, Onassis Foundation
2. Peter John Cavafy: GR-OF CA CA-SF02-S03-F26-SF002-0003 (1967), reproduced by kind permission of the Cavafy Archive, Onassis Foundation © 2016/2018 Cavafy Archive, Onassis Foundation
3. John, Paul, and Constantine: GR-OF CA CA-SF02-S03-F26-SF001-0002 (1935), reproduced by kind permission of the Cavafy Archive, Onassis Foundation © 2016/2018 Cavafy Archive, Onassis Foundation
4. Greek Orthodox Church of Saint Nicholas, Liverpool: Photo by Samwalton9 (Wikimedia Commons, https://upload.wikimedia.org/wikipedia/commons/e/ee/Greek_Orthodox_Church_of_St_Nicholas_in_Liverpool.jpg)
5. John Cavafy and Dimitrios Zalichi: GR-OF CA CA-SF02-S03-F26-SF002-0009 (1989), reproduced by kind permission of the Cavafy Archive, Onassis Foundation © 2016/2018 Cavafy Archive, Onassis Foundation
6. Haricleia Photiades Cavafy: GR-OF CA CA-SF02-S03-F26-SF002-0011 (1955), reproduced by kind permission of the Cavafy Archive, Onassis Foundation © 2016/2018 Cavafy Archive, Onassis Foundation
7. Aristides Cavafy: GR-OF CA CA-SF02-S03-F26-SF002-0013 (1984), reproduced by kind permission of the Cavafy Archive, Onassis Foundation © 2016/2018 Cavafy Archive, Onassis Foundation
8. Sketch by Aristides Cavafy: Benaki Museum Historical Archives

9. Paul Cavafy: GR-OF CA CA-SF02-S03-F26-SF002-0005 (1993), reproduced by kind permission of the Cavafy Archive, Onassis Foundation © 2016/2018 Cavafy Archive, Onassis Foundation
10. Staircase of the Metropole Hotel: Peter Jeffreys
11. Constantine's apartment at Rue Lepsius: ELIA-MIET Photographic Archive
12. Hall of Constantine's apartment: GR-OF CA SING-S01-F04-0008 (2050), reproduced by kind permission of the Cavafy Archive, Onassis Foundation © 2016/2018 Cavafy Archive, Onassis Foundation
13. Constantine's bedroom: GR-OF CA SING-S01-F04-0009 (2051), reproduced by kind permission of the Cavafy Archive, Onassis Foundation © 2016/2018 Cavafy Archive, Onassis Foundation
14. Constantine's salon: GR-OF CA SING-S01-F04-0011 (2053), reproduced by kind permission of the Cavafy Archive, Onassis Foundation © 2016/2018 Cavafy Archive, Onassis Foundation
15. Constantine as a young man: GR-OF CA CA-SF02-S03-F26-SF001-0007 (1946), reproduced by kind permission of the Cavafy Archive, Onassis Foundation © 2016/2018 Cavafy Archive, Onassis Foundation
16. Constantine, 1932: GR-OF CA CA-SF02-S03-F26-SF001-0014 (1947), reproduced by kind permission of the Cavafy Archive, Onassis Foundation © 2016/2018 Cavafy Archive, Onassis Foundation
17. Constantine: GR-OF CA CA-SF02-S03-F26-SF001-0013 (2005), reproduced by kind permission of the Cavafy Archive, Onassis Foundation © 2016/2018 Cavafy Archive, Onassis Foundation
18–19. Menu from the San Stefano Casino: GR-OF CA CA-SF02-S02-F25-SF006-0003 (1141), reproduced by kind permission of the Cavafy Archive, Onassis Foundation © 2016/2018 Cavafy Archive, Onassis Foundation
20. Pericles Anastasiades: GR-OF CA CA-SF02-S03-F26-SF003-0033 (2001), reproduced by kind permission of the Cavafy Archive, Onassis Foundation © 2016/2018 Cavafy Archive, Onassis Foundation
21. Timos Malanos: ELIA-MIET Photographic Archive
22–25. Sketches by Pericles Anastasiades: Nicolas Sarafis
26. Alekos Sengopoulos: GR-OF CA CA-SF02-S03-F26-SF003-0041 (2024), reproduced by kind permission of the Cavafy Archive, Onassis Foundation © 2016/2018 Cavafy Archive, Onassis Foundation
27. Corrections to "Waiting for the Barbarians": GR-OF CA CA-SF01-S01-F02-SF001-0007 (1362), reproduced by kind permission of the Cavafy Archive, Onassis Foundation © 2016/2018 Cavafy Archive, Onassis Foundation
28. List of wins and losses: GR-OF CA CA-SF02-S02-F25-SF004-0001 (974), reproduced by kind permission of the Cavafy Archive, Onassis Foundation © 2016/2018 Cavafy Archive, Onassis Foundation
29. Wedding of Constantine M. Salvagos: GR-OF CA CA-SF02-S03-F26-SF001-0008 (2027), reproduced by kind permission of the Cavafy Archive, Onassis Foundation © 2016/2018 Cavafy Archive, Onassis Foundation
30. Rika Sengopoulos, Angelos Sikelianos, Alekos Sengopoulos, and unidentified fourth person: ELIA-MIET Department of Hellenism in Egypt
31. Note to Rika Sengopoulos: GR-OF CA CA-SF02-S02-F25-SF004-0023 (972), reproduced by kind permission of the Cavafy Archive, Onassis Foundation © 2016/2018 Cavafy Archive, Onassis Foundation